T0323690

The Global Financial Crisis
and Its Aftermath

The Global Financial Crisis and Its Aftermath

Hidden Factors in the Meltdown

EDITED BY A. G. MALLIARIS, LESLIE SHAW

AND

HERSH SHEFRIN

OXFORD
UNIVERSITY PRESS

OXFORD
UNIVERSITY PRESS

Oxford University Press is a department of the University of Oxford. It furthers
the University's objective of excellence in research, scholarship, and education
by publishing worldwide. Oxford is a registered trade mark of Oxford University
Press in the UK and certain other countries.

Published in the United States of America by Oxford University Press
198 Madison Avenue, New York, NY 10016, United States of America.

Library of Congress Cataloging-in-Publication Data
Names: Malliaris, A. G., editor.
Title: The global financial crisis and its aftermath : hidden factors in the
meltdown / edited by A. G. Malliaris, Loyola University Chicago, Leslie
Shaw, Chicago Psychoanalytic Society, Hersh Shefrin, Santa Clara University.
Description: New York : Oxford University Press, 2016. | Includes
bibliographical references and index.
Identifi ers: LCCN 2016008338| ISBN 9780199386222 (alk. paper)
Subjects: LCSH: Financial crises. | Global Financial Crisis, 2008–2009. |
Economic policy. | Social justice.
Classification: LCC HB3722 .G5856 2016 | DDC 330.9/0511–dc23 LC record available at
http://lccn.loc.gov/2016008338

CONTENTS

PREFACE AND ACKNOWLEDGMENTS

This book has its roots in a conference organized jointly by the Quinlan School of Business of Loyola University Chicago and the Leavey School of Business of Santa Clara University. The Chicago Mercantile Exchange Group through the Center for Risk Management at the Quinlan School of Business offered a generous grant to the three editors and charged them to organize a conference that examined the recent global financial crisis from the perspective of behavioral finance and ethical values.

The conference took place on April 11, 2013, and featured 11 speakers. A few months later, revised versions of these papers were submitted for possible publication to several publishers. Oxford University Press enthusiastically encouraged the editors to go significantly beyond the original 11 submissions and view the global financial crisis and its aftermath from various perspectives. To maintain cohesion, the editors were challenged to write both a lengthy introductory chapter and a concluding one.

This volume contains 21 chapters and offers a unique, innovative, and exciting exposition of the global financial crisis and its aftermath from three perspectives of hidden factors that intensified its meltdown. In particular, we explore hidden factors from economics, psychology, and values that help explain the intensity of the meltdown. Chapter 1 is ready to be read, so there is no need for duplication in this preface. It is our wish that readers begin with curiosity about the content of this book, and our hope that they find insight and instruction.

The editors are most thankful to the CME Group and the Center for Risk Management at the Quinlan School of Business for financing the original conference. Next, the editors are truly and profoundly grateful to Scott Paris, economics editor of Oxford University Press for his extensive advice to expand the volume and enrich its contents. We are also thankful to David McBride, Editor-in-chief for Social Sciences, Anne Dellinger, Associate Editor, Sasirekka Gopalakrishnan and Cathryn Vaulman for editorial expertise and generous encouragement. Finally, our sincerest thanks go to all of our valued fellow contributors.

CONTRIBUTORS

Antonio Argandona is emeritus professor of economics and business ethics and holds the "la Caixa" Chair of Corporate Social Responsibility and Corporate Governance at IESE Business School, University of Navarra. He is a member of the Royal Academy of Economics and Finance of Spain, president of the Standing Committee on Professional Ethics of the Economists' Association of Catalonia, and a member of the Commission on Anti-Corruption of the International Chamber of Commerce (Paris). He has published numerous books, book chapters, and articles in prestigious journals in economics and business ethics.

John Boatright is the Raymond C. Baumhart, SJ, Professor of Business Ethics in the Quinlan School of Business at Loyola University Chicago. He has served as the executive director of the Society for Business Ethics and is a past president of the Society. He was recognized by the Society in 2012 for a "career of outstanding service to the field of business ethics." He is the author of the books *Ethics and the Conduct of Business* and *Ethics in Finance,* and has edited *Finance Ethics: Critical Issues in Theory and Practice.* He serves on the editorial boards of *Business Ethics Quarterly, Journal of Business Ethics,* and *Business and Society Review.* He received his PhD in philosophy from the University of Chicago.

Graciela Chichilnisky is Visiting Professor of Economics and SIEPR at Stanford University and Professor of Economics and Statistics at Columbia University. She studied at MIT and UC Berkeley, has PhDs in Mathematics and in Economics and taught previously at Harvard and the University of Essex. Chichilnisky is the author of over 350 scientific publications in mathematics and in economics and of 13 books, some best sellers, which have been translated to nine languages. She created the concept of Basic Needs and the Formal Theory of Sustainable Development, was the US lead author of the UN IPCC, and designed and wrote the Carbon Market into the UN Kyoto Protocol. She has acted as Director of Research at UNITAR, held a UNESCO Chair, acts as a special adviser to the World Bank IMF and several UN organizations, and contributed to four articles of the Paris Agreement in December 2015, acting as an official adviser to Papua New Guinea and the 50 nations UN Rainforest Coalition. Chichilnisky is the CEO and co-founder of Global Thermostat, a company selected in 2015 as "World's Top Ten Most Innovative Company" in Energy by *Fast Company* Magazine, and was selected the "2015 CEO of the Year" by IAIR at the Yale Club. Chichilnisky is the creator of the concept of *carbon negative technology*™ and the co-inventor of an actual carbon negative technology that removes CO_2 directly from air, as the IPCC finds it necessary to avert climate change, which Global Thermostat uses for commercial purposes in water desalination, building materials, beverages, greenhouses, bio-fertilizers, and fuels. Chichilnisky was also the CEO and founder of FITEL, a financial telecommunications company that sold in Japan, and of Cross Border Exchange a financial telecommunications company that sold to JP Morgan. Chichilnisky was selected among the Top 10 most influential Latinos in the United States, named by *The Washington Post* as an "A-List Star", and by *Time Magazine* a Hero of the Environment. Chichilnisky has two children, was born in Argentina, is a US citizen, and lives currently in California.

Viktoria Dalko is a global professor of finance, a founding dean and founding discipline lead of finance at Hult International Business School, and an instructor at Harvard Extension School. She obtained a PhD in economics from the University of Pennsylvania. Dr. Dalko has focused on two research areas. One is on uncovering systemic risks to financial markets and preventing financial crisis. The other is on how financial crisis influences the well-being of people. In particular, she has studied worldwide financial crises and one of its causes, financial market manipulation. She and her co-authors summarized their research in the book *Regulating Competition in Stock Markets* (2012).

Werner De Bondt is professor of finance and founding director of the Richard H. Driehaus Center for Behavioral Finance at DePaul University in Chicago. He holds a PhD in business administration from Cornell University (1985). Werner De Bondt studies the rationality and irrationality of investors, markets, and organizations. In past years, he was a member of the faculty at universities in Belgium, Switzerland, and The Netherlands. Between 1992 and 2003, Werner De Bondt was the Frank Graner Professor of Investment Management at the University of Wisconsin–Madison.

John Dobson is a professor of finance in the Orfalea College of Business at Cal Poly, San Luis Obispo, California. Broadly, his publications have explored the connections between the theories of financial economics and moral philosophy. This exploration has centered primarily on the behavioral assumptions that underlie financial-economic theory. These assumptions traditionally depict human behavior in a relatively narrow conceptualization of opportunistic self-interest. Dobson explores the extent to which such assumptions are either descriptively accurate or prescriptively desirable. His research explores ways in which these behavioral assumptions—that form the foundation of much of financial-economic theory—can be enhanced in order to make them both more descriptively accurate and more prescriptively (i.e., ethically) desirable.

Raphael Douady is a French mathematician and economist specializing in financial mathematics and chaos theory. He holds the Robert Frey Endowed Chair of Quantitative Finance at Stony Brook University (SUNY), and is also the academic director of the Laboratory of Excellence on Financial Regulation (University of Paris–La Sorbonne and ESCP–Europe) and affiliated with the French National Centre for Scientific Research (CNRS). He co-founded fin-tech firms Riskdata (1999) and Datacore (2015). He has more than 20 years of experience in the banking industry (risk management, option models, trading strategies) and 35 years of research in pure and applied mathematics. His work in mathematical finance has focused on extreme risk, for which he developed the theory of polymodels. He also authored a generalization of the Heath–Jarrow–Morton interest rate model and a rating-based credit derivatives model that introduced the notion of "rating surface." His background in pure mathematics is in dynamical systems and chaos theory.

Paul Fitzgerald, SJ is professor of religious studies and president of the University of San Francisco. He holds doctoral degrees from the University of Paris–La Sorbonne and the Institut Catholique de Paris. He is the author of the book *L'Église comme lieu de formation d'une conscience de la concitoyenneté*, several scholarly articles, and popular essays. His work focuses on the crossroads of sociology and theology and treats such questions as ecclesial authority, environmental ethics, and public religious discernment. He has served as an adjunct lecturer at the Education College in Xiamen, China; as an assistant and associate professor at Santa Clara University; as a visiting lecturer at Hekima College, Nairobi, Kenya; and as a visiting chair at Seattle University. Prior to his current position he served as senior vice president for academic affairs at Fairfield University.

Brooke Harrington is a professor at the Copenhagen Business School in Denmark. Her new book on wealth management, offshore banking, and tax avoidance—titled *Capital without Borders*—will be published in July by Harvard University Press. Her previous books include *Pop Finance* (2008) and *Deception* (2009). She has received grants and awards from organizations including the National Science Foundation, the Academy of Management, and the American Sociological Association. Professor Harrington holds an MA and PhD in sociology from Harvard University, and a BA in English literature from Stanford University.

Steve Keen is a professor of economics and history at Kingston University, London. He was one of the handful of economists to realize that a serious economic crisis was imminent, and to publicly warn of it, as early as December 2005. This, and his pioneering work on complex systems modeling of debt-deflation, resulted in him winning the Revere Award from the *Real World Economics Review* for being the economist "who first and most clearly anticipated and gave public warning of the Global Financial Collapse and whose work is most likely to prevent another GFC in the future." The financial newspaper *City AM* ranks him as the third most influential economist in the United Kingdom.

Lawrence R. Klein Nobel Laureate in Economics (deceased.)

Robert W. Kolb holds two PhDs from the University of North Carolina at Chapel Hill (philosophy 1974, finance 1978) and has been a finance professor at five universities. He is currently a professor of finance at Loyola University Chicago, where he also holds the Considine Chair of Applied Ethics. Kolb's recent books are *The Financial Crisis of Our Time* (2011) and *Too Much Is Not Enough: Incentives in Executive Compensation* (2012), both published by Oxford University Press and both selected for the Financial Management Association's Survey and Synthesis Series. His most recent book project is *The Natural Gas Revolution: Markets, Society, and the World*, Pearson/Financial Times in Fall 2013.

Lola Lopes is professor emeritus of management and organizations at the Henry B. Tippie College of Business of the University of Iowa. Before retiring, she held the

Pomerantz Chair in Management and served for six years as associate provost for undergraduate education. In 2007–2008, she was appointed interim executive vice president and provost. Prior to coming to Iowa, she was chair of the Department of Psychology at the University of Wisconsin–Madison. Her research areas are decision making under risk, judgment processes, rational inference and choice, and the rhetoric of decision making.

A. G. Malliaris is currently professor of economics and finance and holds the Walter F. Mullady Sr. Chair at the Quinlan School of Business at Loyola University Chicago. He specializes in financial economics and has written numerous books and papers in the areas of derivatives markets, monetary policy, and asset price bubbles. His most recent co-edited book is *New Perspectives on Asset Price Bubbles*, published by Oxford University Press. Malliaris holds a BA in economics from the Athens University of Economics and Business, a PhD in economics from the University of Oklahoma, and a second PhD in mathematics from the University of Chicago.

John Riker has been a professor of philosophy at Colorado College for 48 years and chair of the department for about 20 of those years. He has received many awards at the college, including having been named professor of the year an unprecedented four times and advisor of the year an unprecedented three times. In 2003 he was appointed the Kohut Professor for that year at the University of Chicago. He has previously published three books intersecting psychoanalysis and philosophy: *Human Excellence and an Ecological Conception of the Psyche, Ethics and the Discovery of the Unconscious*, and *Why It Is Good to Be Good: Ethics, Kohut's Self Psychology, and Modern Society*.

S. Prakash Sethi, University Distinguished Professor of Management in the Zicklin School of Business, City University of New York, is a seasoned expert in the field of international business. He has authored, co-authored, and edited 25 books and more than 130 articles in scholarly, professional, and practitioner journals. In addition, he has also written for and appeared in various national and international news media including the *New York Times*, the *Wall Street Journal, Bloomberg BusinessWeek*, CNN, NPR, BNN-Toronto, and CBC (Canada), among others. Dr. Sethi received both his MBA and PhD from Columbia University.

Leslie Shaw consults with companies on a variety of decision process issues and is an invited speaker at corporate events and conferences in psychology and management. She received her MBA and a PhD in behavioral decision making from the University of Chicago. After her PhD she completed five years of training at the Chicago Institute for Psychoanalysis with interest in integrating theoretical psychoanalysis and the cognitive approaches that are foundational to behavioral economics. Selected publications include *Greed: Sex, Money, Power, Politics* (2011), published by International Psychoanalytic Books; and "The Uncanny and Long Term Capital Management" (2005), published in the *International Journal of Applied Psychoanalysis*.

Hersh Shefrin is the Mario L. Belotti Professor of Finance at Santa Clara University. He has published widely on a wide range of topics in mathematics, finance, and economics, and is best known for his work in behavioral finance. A 2003 article in the *American Economic Review* includes him in the top 15 economic theorists to have influenced empirical work. He is known for his work on a variety of topics, which include an economic theory of self-control featuring a formal system 1/system 2 model, a behavioral explanation for the dividend puzzle, the disposition effect, behavioral portfolio theory, behavioral corporate finance, behavioral pricing kernel theory, and behavioral risk management.

John Silvia is a managing director and the chief economist for Wells Fargo. Based in Charlotte, North Carolina, he has held his position since he joined Wachovia, a Wells Fargo predecessor, in 2002 as the company's chief economist. Prior to his current position, John worked on Capitol Hill as senior economist for the US Senate Joint Economic Committee and chief economist for the US Senate Banking, Housing, and Urban Affairs Committee. Before that, he was chief economist of Kemper Funds and managing director of Scudder Kemper Investments, Inc. John served as the president of the National Association for Business Economics (NABE) in 2015 and was awarded a NABE Fellow Certificate of Recognition in 2011 for outstanding contributions to the business economics profession and leadership among business economists to the nation. For the second time in three years, he was awarded the best overall forecast by the Federal Reserve Bank of Chicago, as well as the best unemployment rate forecast for 2011. John is on the Bloomberg Best Forecast list for his forecasts of GDP, the ISM manufacturing index, housing starts, and the unemployment rate.

Meir Statman is the Glenn Klimek Professor of Finance at Santa Clara University. His research focuses on behavioral finance. He attempts to understand how investors and managers make financial decisions and how these decisions are reflected in financial markets. Meir's award-winning book, *What Investors Really Want,* has been published by McGraw-Hill, and his book *Finance for Normal People: Behavioral Finance and Investors, Managers, and Markets* is forthcoming from Oxford University Press. He received his PhD from Columbia University and his BA and MBA from the Hebrew University of Jerusalem.

Nassim Nicholas Taleb spent 21 years as a risk taker before becoming a researcher in practical and mathematical problems with probability. Taleb is the author of a multivolume essay, the *Incerto* (*The Black Swan, Fooled by Randomness,* and *Antifragile*) covering broad facets of uncertainty. It has been translated into 36 languages. In addition to his trader life, Taleb has also published, as a backup of the *Incerto,* more than 45 scholarly papers in statistical physics, statistics, philosophy, ethics, economics, international affairs, and quantitative finance—all around the notion of risk and probability. He spent time as a professional researcher (Distinguished Professor of Risk Engineering at NYU's School of Engineering and Dean's Professor at the University of Massachusetts Amherst). His current focus is on the properties of systems that can handle disorder ("*antifragile*"). Taleb refuses all honors and anything that "turns knowledge into a spectator sport."

Michael H. Wang is a senior researcher at the Research Institute of Comprehensive Economics, a think tank in Boston. He received a PhD in mechanical engineering from the University of Illinois at Urbana–Champaign. Dr. Wang is one of the co-authors of *Regulating Competition in Stock Markets* (2012) that proposed 40 regulatory measures. The recently enacted securities regulations in the United States,

United Kingdom, Germany, France, Italy, China, and India bear a close similarity to several of the proposed measures.

Janet Yellen is the chair (2014–) of the Board of Governors of the Federal Reserve System of the United States. She is the first woman to hold this post. Yellen graduated summa cum laude in economics from Brown University in 1967 and received a PhD in economics from Yale University in 1971. She has held academic positions at Harvard University and the Haas School of Business at the University of California, Berkeley. She has also served as an economist for the Federal Reserve Board of Governors, as president of the Federal Reserve Bank of San Francisco, and as vice chair of the Board of Governors of the Federal Reserve.

PART ONE

Introduction

The Global Financial Crisis and Its Aftermath

A.G. MALLIARIS, LESLIE SHAW, AND HERSH SHEFRIN ∎

We are ready to accept almost any explanation of the present crisis of our civilization except one: that the present state of the world may be the result of genuine error on our part and that the pursuit of some of our most cherished ideals has apparently produced results utterly different from those which we expected.

—FREDERICK HAYEK

Panics do not destroy capital; they merely reveal the extent to which it has been previously destroyed by its betrayal into hopelessly unproductive works.

—JOHN STUART MILL

INTRODUCTION

The Global Financial Crisis of 2007–2009 has been described as the most severe, unpredictable, complex, systemic, and international crisis since the Great Depression of the early 1930s. Its severity is characterized by the considerable loss of output and 15 million jobs in the United States alone and the ushering of the sovereign debt crisis in the European Union. Its unpredictability is demonstrated by the widespread disbelief it created among economists in the private and public sectors, politicians, executives, investors, and traders. Its complexity is attributed to a plethora of dramatic events such as the bursting of the US housing bubble, the subprime mortgage debacle, the Lehman Brothers bankruptcy, the liquidity crisis, and the fire-sale externalities, among numerous other happenings. Its description as systemic refers to the classic financial panic that engulfed the economy's entire financial sector. Finally, the international character of this crisis is displayed by the large number of countries impacted financially, economically, and in terms of global trade.

Furthermore, the economic recovery that has followed the Global Financial Crisis has been both in the United States and the European Union subpar compared to several other recoveries since the Second World War (WWII). Lower income groups were disproportionately impacted by high unemployment foreclosure rates on home mortgages. In addition, the free enterprise ideology that had been bolstered by the collapse of the Soviet Union in 1989 has been sharply contested because of the instabilities of financial markets and the regulatory failures witnessed during this crisis.

It is the goal of this chapter to articulate the purpose of this book and describe its contribution to the current literature on financial crises. It is our intention to argue that the complexity of the Global Financial Crisis challenges researchers to offer more comprehensive explanations by extending the scope and range of their traditional investigations. We think our volume is unique in viewing the financial crisis simultaneously through three different lenses—economic, psychological, and social values. In this respect, what sets our volume apart is our discussion of what has gotten overlooked in the debates about the crisis, and how narrow framing has impacted social discourse about financial instability.

In this book we decided to go beyond the initial criticisms of orthodox economic theories by offering a constructive methodology that is suitable for exploring financial crises. We recognize how current economic analysis did not prepare academic economists, business economists, traders, and regulators to anticipate economic and financial crises. So, we search more extensively within the broader discipline of economics for ideas related to crises but neglected perhaps because they were not mathematically rigorous. The contributions of Hyman Minsky serve as our featured example. However, we do not stop with Minsky.

We affirm that the complexity of financial crises necessitates complementary research. Thus, to put the focal purpose of this book differently, we proceed to explore the Global Financial Crisis from three interconnected frameworks. First we review how the crisis is viewed by the standards of orthodox economic analysis, despite its shortcomings. Second, we examine Minskyan economics, which we expand to introduce ideas from psychology that form the basis of behavioral economics. Third, we follow the leadership of Deirdre McClosky (2006), who has emphasized the role of ideas and values in economics, and view the crisis from this dimension.

Values are the subject of both philosophy and psychology and can contribute to a better understanding of the Global Financial Crisis. Values, in general, have been relatively neglected by economists. This is not because there is doubt about their significance, but rather because welfare economics and collective choice still operate within the neoclassical paradigm. In this volume, we argue that analyzing the value implications requires moving from the neoclassical framework to something that is broader and multidisciplinary.

For this reason, we do not propose for economists to undertake all these investigations. Such a suggestion would contradict the deep fundamental truth of professional specialization, brilliantly articulated by Adam Smith. Rather, we plan to demonstrate that experts in psychology and philosophy can collaborate with economists and employ the multidisciplinary approach to study the Global Financial Crisis. This idea is discussed next.

A MULTIDISCIPLINARY METHODOLOGY

The response to the Global Financial Crisis has been very vigorous. The US Congress created the Financial Crisis Inquiry Commission to "examine the causes, domestic and global, of the current financial and economic crisis in the United States." The Commission was established as part of the Fraud Enforcement and Recovery Act (Public Law 111-21) passed by Congress and signed by President Barack Obama in May 2009. The Commission produced a detailed report which was the result of extensive research and hundreds of interviews with public officials, business executives, financial professionals, and experts; there were also numerous public hearings.

Simultaneously, the US Congress passed the Dodd-Frank Wall Street Reform and Consumer Protection Act (Public Law 111-203), and President Obama signed it into law on July 21, 2010. It brought the most substantial changes to financial regulation in the United States since the regulatory reform that followed the Great Depression. The Dodd-Frank Act made changes in the American financial regulatory environment that influence all federal financial regulatory agencies and almost every part of the nation's financial services industry.

These two substantial initiatives by the US government were accompanied by an enormous amount of published research—business, economic, financial, academic, legal, political, and journalistic—on a wide list of topics related to the Global Financial Crisis. Because of this extensive research, much progress has been achieved toward our understanding of financial crises. Yet, no one can claim today that we have eradicated all ignorance surrounding financial crises. Because there is little reason to expect that future financial crises are preventable, it is all the more important to increase our understanding of the economic, psychological, and social dimensions associated with mitigating the pain and cost of these crises.

In this book we argue that much can be learned from applying a multidisciplinary methodology to financial crises. More specifically, we choose a multidisciplinary methodology between selected schools of thought and concepts from economics, psychology, and values. To understand what this means, suppose for purposes of elucidation that we wish to address three questions: What are financial crises? What causes them? How can we respond to them? How can a multidisciplinary methodology benefit our investigations?

We offer four reasons in favor of such an approach. First, using economic, psychological, and philosophical reasoning allows financial crises to be framed more widely, thereby removing unnecessary constraints imposed by the limitations of specific disciplines. Such enlargement of framing contributes to intellectual clarity. Second, because each discipline adds value to the analysis, it follows that our understanding of the financial crisis will be enhanced by utilizing more than just one discipline. Third, there is synergy in a multidisciplinary approach that derives from interactions among the various disciplines. Finally, it is more probable that robust dynamic relationships can be found within a multidisciplinary framework than in a highly focused specialized discipline.

We proceed as follows: the topics of our investigation are the particular causes of the Global Financial Crisis of 2007–2009 and to what extent such causes appear more general. The discipline of economics has examined this problem extensively, and many useful answers have been offered; yet, there is currently no clear consensus about the precise causes of the recent crisis or about the exact causes of earlier crises. Therefore we begin with an examination of the financial crisis from the perspective of economic analysis. This leads us to a number of economic views about financial crises. Next we connect the economic hypotheses about a crisis to the discipline of psychology by drawing on a specific set of psychological concepts.

ORTHODOX ECONOMICS AND FINANCIAL CRISES

Reinhart and Rogoff (2009) provide a quantitative history of financial crises during the past eight centuries. Their work unmistakably demonstrates that financial crises are an integral part of the economic landscape. The authors instruct us not to regard each financial crisis as distinctive from the preceding ones. A methodology that focuses on the uniqueness of each financial crisis precludes the identification of shared causes. Thus, they propose that economists investigate financial crises primarily for their similar characteristics without, of course, dismissing features that are dissimilar. Psychologically, Reinhart and Rogoff urge us to avoid overweighting singular information relative to base rate information.

The characteristics that appear to be common across crises include states of an economy that exhibit excessive debt accumulation, speculative manias, the bursting of asset bubbles, bank runs, bank failures, currency crises, and international contagion, just to mention few. Also, some financial crises produce considerable disruptions to the real economy, while others do not. Reinhart and Rogoff also describe how each crisis contains some rather unique events, facts, causes, and triggering scenarios.

Reinhart and Rogoff (2009) have received extensive praise and numerous outstanding awards. Niall Ferguson, author of *The Ascent of Money: A Financial History of the World*, writes in the inside flap of the book:

> This is quite simply the best empirical investigation of financial crises ever published. Covering hundreds of years and bringing together a dizzying array of data, Reinhart and Rogoff have made a truly heroic contribution to financial history. This single marvelous volume is worth a thousand mathematical models.

This enthusiastic endorsement of a truly great book also highlights the uncompromising orthogonality that exists between the methodologies of logical literary narratives and mathematical analysis. Reinhart and Rogoff offer valuable data about financial crises collected with great effort over a very long period along with their own narratives underscoring similarities and differences across countries and periods. However, the authors do not attempt to propose an economic theory of financial crises, nor is a mathematical model to be found in their book.

Niall Ferguson passionately celebrates their approach. In sharp contrast, Robert Lucas, the 1995 Nobel Laureate in Economics, is equally categorical on the appropriateness of economic methodology, but on the other side. In his April 2001 Trinity University lecture, Lucas said:

> I loved Samuelson's Foundations. Like so many others in my cohort, I internalized its view that if I couldn't formulate a problem in economic theory

mathematically, I didn't know what I was doing. I came to the position that mathematical analysis is not one of many ways of doing economic theory: it is the only way. Economic theory is mathematical analysis. Everything else is just pictures and talk.

Several cohorts of macroeconomists during the past forty years have treasured the Lucas methodology of using rigorous mathematical analysis in constructing economic models. The original Keynesian model of consumption function, the marginal efficiency of investment, the demand for money, fiscal and monetary policies, and other innovative ideas introduced in the General Theory were slowly replaced by dynamic, stochastic general equilibrium macroeconomic models where agents' expectations are rational, as described in Lucas and Sargent (1979). This methodology offered numerous valuable insights but was not appropriate for predicting or explaining financial crises because the financial sector played only a very limited role.

The former president of the Federal Reserve Bank of Minneapolis, Narayana Kocherlakota (2010), writes:

I believe that during the last financial crisis, macroeconomists (and I include myself among them) failed the country, and indeed the world. In September 2008, central bankers were in desperate need of a playbook that offered a systematic plan of attack to deal with fast-evolving circumstances. Macroeconomics should have been able to provide that playbook. It could not. Of course, from a longer view, macroeconomists let policymakers down much earlier, because they did not provide policymakers with rules to avoid the circumstances that led to the global financial meltdown.

Olivier Blanchard, former chief economist at the International Monetary Fund (IMF) writes that during his academic career at the Massachusetts Institute of Technology (MIT), macroeconomists relied excessively on linear models for their analysis; and those linear models produced stable equilibria. As the honored speaker at a 2015 joint luncheon meeting of the American Economic Association and the American Finance Association, Blanchard pointed out the importance of developing nonlinear macroeconomic models, which possess what he called "dark corners," namely, regions in the parameter space that give rise to instability (Blanchard 2015).

Blanchard (2014) noted that the late economist Frank Hahn had warned him about the dangers of focusing excessively on nonlinear models. During the 1960s, Hahn and others had developed nonlinear growth models featuring short-term equilibria and heterogeneous capital goods. Hahn demonstrated that those models are inherently unstable, which led him to ask what economic forces actually allow real-world economies to exhibit stability.

To be sure, Minsky maintained that financial instability was inherent to capitalism. However, Minsky provided no clear model, either linear or nonlinear, to underlie his contention. Nevertheless, some of his followers did, most notably Steve Keen (2013), who has contributed a chapter to this volume. Keen's models are nonlinear, and not surprisingly generated periods of tranquility punctuated by periods of considerable instability. At the same time, all models have their limitations.

Our position is to avoid throwing out the baby with the bathwater. Mathematical models have their place, but should not be relied upon as a panacea. Descriptive methods also have their place, as do "pictures and talk" along with concepts that lie outside traditional economic analysis. In this regard, we suggest that a multidisciplinary approach increases the likelihood of comprehension of a complex phenomenon. At the same time, we acknowledge that such an approach brings with it a potential lack of cohesiveness.

In what follows, we first sketch a narrow view of the Global Financial Crisis as a classic financial panic. Then we describe the contributions of the papers in each of the three parts of the book: economics, psychology, and values. Afterward we invite the reader to review all the individual contributions, and in the last chapter we present the comprehensive story of financial crises that has emerged in this book.

A CLASSIC FINANCIAL PANIC

Ben Bernanke (2013) argues that "the recent global crisis is best understood as a classic financial panic transposed into the novel institutional context of the 21st century financial system" (p. 1). He gives a brief historical account of what happened during the 1907 panic and relates these happenings to the 2007–2009 crisis. Specifically, Bernanke illustrates that financial panics occur while the entire economy is weakening and an identifiable triggering event takes place. For example, during the 1907 crisis, the economy had entered into a recession in May of that year. The triggering event occurred on October 16, 1907, when a group of speculators led by F. Augustus Heinze and Charles F. Morse failed to corner the stock of United Copper Company.

These financiers had extensive connections with a number of leading financial institutions in New York City. Their failed speculation sparked great financial concerns, which initiated runs on banks associated with Heinze, including a bank at which Heinze was president. On October 18, there was a run on the Knickerbocker Trust, apparently the result of rumored association with Charles Morse. Then on October 19, Charles Morse's banks were struck with runs. The New York Clearing House reviewed the books of the banks under pressure and offered support in order to restore confidence. Runs continued in troubled banks. At last, J. P. Morgan and the US Treasury agreed to offer cash support to the New York Clearing House and its member banks and trust companies. By early November these steps were successful in stopping additional runs.

As with the financial crisis of 1907, the Global Financial Crisis of 2007–09 also occurred in an environment of a weakening economy. The National Bureau of Economic Research (NBER) decided that the US economy had entered a recession in December 2007, most likely because of the housing market decline from its peak in mid-2006. Banks, insurance companies, investment banks, and other financial institutions had accumulated mortgage-backed securities that were financed with very short-term loans and high leverage. Early signs of financial difficulties appeared at Bear Stearns when it announced liquidation of two of its hedge funds invested in mortgage-backed securities.

However, the triggering event for the Global Financial Crisis was the declaration of bankruptcy by Lehman Brothers on September 15, 2008. To this day, it remains controversial whether psychologically induced errors led the Federal Reserve and the Treasury to refrain from rescuing Lehman, which they could have done. In any event, creditors at Lehman Brothers and other investment banks were faced with large and uncertain losses.

Unlike the 1907 crisis with its bank runs, the loss of confidence by the creditors of investment banks during September 2008 caused them to drastically withhold lending to the market for repurchase agreements. Uncertainty in asset valuations was amplified significantly, collateral valuations declined, bank loans were drastically reduced, margin calls were issued, fire sales increased rapidly, and financial markets stopped performing their central function of allocating capital efficiently. It took massive lending by both the Treasury and the Fed to put an end to the vicious financial cycle of fast deleveraging by early March 2009, when the S&P 500 hit bottom and started climbing. The S&P 500, from a pre-crisis high of 1561 on October 8, 2007, had dropped to 683 on March 2, 2009—a loss of about 56% during that period.

Gorton (2010) describes the role of money market funds during the recent crisis, and Lucas and Stokey (2011) review the recent literature on liquidity crises. Financial panics as we briefly described them here induce liquidity crises because the increased economic uncertainty during the panic increases the demand for liquid assets. Investors who have such liquid assets are reluctant to exchange them for an uncertain valuation of long-term illiquid assets, bringing the financial intermediation process to a complete freeze. In other words, financial panics transmute into liquidity crises and ultimately into a temporary failure of financial markets, since transactions stop. A detailed survey of all the interrelated concepts of financial panics, liquidity crises, freezes of financial markets, fire sales, collateral valuations, maturity mismatching, securitizations breakdowns, the economics of contagions and the role of regulation are masterfully analyzed in Tirole (2011).

CONTRIBUTIONS FROM ECONOMICS

Now that we have sketched the financial crisis of 2007–2009 as a classic financial panic, we augment this story by introducing supplementary economic ideas. There are six contributions that view the crisis from both orthodox and also unorthodox economic perspectives. We believe that an interdisciplinary approach can also benefit from intra-disciplinary perspectives, and economics itself is very rich with various schools of thought.

Chapter 2 begins with the idea of business cycles. This concept emphasizes that macroeconomic variables such as GDP, consumption, investment, government spending, imports and exports, unemployment, and many others fluctuate over time. There are several theories of business cycles stressing real cycles, financial cycles, and a mixture of these two aspects of any modern economy. The NBER has developed a methodology that allows it to define peaks and troughs of each business cycle. Chapter 2 argues that it is useful to divide the cyclical behavior of contemporary mixed capitalist economies into four phases: an expansion, an upper turning period, a recession, and a lower turning period. This characterization of the business cycle is scientifically more demanding than the one currently followed by the NBER, which considers only the peak and trough of the cycle. However, the analysis of four phases brings additional insights related to the upper and lower turning periods.

To illustrate the usefulness of this approach, the current Global Financial Crisis is examined by Malliaris in this chapter in great detail, by first reviewing the expansion with the development of the housing bubble. Then, the beginning of the crisis is viewed as the upper turning period. The initial financial instability evolved into a full crisis during the Great Recession with its impact on unemployment. We also offer in this volume an entire chapter on the behavior of unemployment during the period before, during, and after the crisis. More about this will be presented later in this section. Finally, the ending of the crisis during the challenging period of the liquidity trap as the lower turning period is also analyzed.

Orthodox economic analysis offers valuable insights for both the expansion and recession phases but can also benefit from behavioral finance and Minsky's analysis. The upper turning period is Minskyan, and the lower turning period is an updated version of the Keynesian-Minskyan liquidity trap. In addition, the concavity and convexity properties of the upper and lower turning periods, analyzed by Taleb (2012), offer useful insights. Thus, while the Bernanke (2013) paper begins the story of the financial crisis by saying that at the beginning there was a weakening of the economy, this chapter enriches the story by examining the crisis in the context of the four phases of the cycle. In this setting, the pre-crisis expansion is viewed in an unconventional way in terms of behavioral finance and financial bubbles.

Until now the NBER only identifies peaks and troughs of business cycles and does not refer to financial crises; however, it could be argued that a subset of business cycles have identifying characteristics that are clearly financial in nature. Just for the sake of illustration, both the Depression of the 1930s and the Financial Crisis of 2007–2009 are dramatically different than several recessions during the period 1950–2007. Thus we can think in terms of Minsky, who has developed a detailed theory focusing on financial cycles of instability rather than moderate business fluctuations.

In this book we give serious consideration to Minsky's analysis. Chapter 2 introduces some key ideas of Minsky associated with asset bubbles during the late expansion and upper turning period. Chapters 3, 4, and 5 develop Minsky's ideas in some detail. In Chapter 3, Federal Reserve chair Janet Yellen explores asset price bubbles and the part they play in Minsky's view of how financial meltdowns arise. In particular, Yellen revisits the ongoing debate over the appropriate response of central banks to asset price bubbles. But, what is an asset price bubble? The concept is introduced in Chapter 2 and revisited throughout this book.

The term "bubble" was first introduced to describe the famous price run-up and crash of the shares in the South Sea Company in 1720 in England. Since then, numerous financial episodes described as bubbles have occurred and are illustrated in the first edition of Kindleberger (1978). Kindleberger and Aliber (2005) offer an update with recent financial bubbles prior to the Global Financial Crisis. Kindleberger (1978) describes an asset price bubble as an upward price movement over an extended range that suddenly implodes. Kindleberger does not introduce the notion of fundamentals in the definition of an asset bubble. He argues that bubbles form because the purchase of an asset is made based not on the rate of return on the investment but in anticipation that the asset can be sold to a "greater fool" at an even higher price in the future.

In Chapter 3, Yellen evaluates several issues related to asset price bubbles and the role of monetary policy. First, she maintains, for central banks to deflate an asset bubble, they need to be certain that a bubble exists. Establishing the existence of an asset bubble is controversial. Suppose that prices of an asset appear to be forming a bubble. At what point in this bubble creation does the central bank choose to act? Thus, timing a bubble becomes an issue. What if the bubble does not translate into inflation or does not contribute to the overheating of an economy? Since central banks have a mandate for price stability, what would justify a central bank to deflate a bubble when inflation is not a problem? What if price stability holds but the forming of an asset bubble generates risks for bursting, with potentially heavy economic losses in the future? In such a case, the central bank has to estimate the risk and decide what action is appropriate. If a central bank chooses to address the risk of an asset bubble crashing, what tools can be used to moderate or deflate such a bubble?

These and several related issues about bubbles and monetary policy have been labelled as the debate between the decision "to lean against the bubble or clean after its bursting." During the chairmanship of both the Greenspan and Bernanke Fed, decisions were made not to lean against asset bubbles but to act swiftly and decisively to minimize the risks associated with the bubble bursting. This rule worked well with the bursting of the Internet bubble. Unfortunately, the collapse of the housing bubble enormously increased the economy's financial risks and the preference of cleaning after instead of leaning against it proved to be a very expensive mistake. So the debate between "leaning vs. cleaning" is now receiving a renewed analytical assessment. If the costs of a bubble bursting are significant, then Minsky's famous "instability hypothesis" needs to be taken seriously. Yellen contributes to this debate by reminding us that one of Minsky's major prescriptions for addressing financial instabilities is the design of supervisory and regulatory policies known as macroprudential policies. Their purpose is to ensure financial stability for the whole economy.

Keen in Chapter 4 focuses on the nature and character of financial instability. The role of the financial sector in causing the post-2007 economic crisis is not in dispute: the controversy instead is about the causal mechanisms between the financial sector and the real economy. Keen follows Fisher, Schumpeter, and Minsky in assigning key roles to the growth and contraction of aggregate private debt. This viewpoint is rejected by New Keynesian economists on the a priori basis that private debts are "pure redistributions" that "should have no significant macro-economic effects," and as a corollary to the oft-repeated truism that "one person's debt is another person's asset."

Chapter 4 also follows the Post-Keynesian tradition of endogenous money in seeing the banking sector as an essential component of the macroeconomy, yet this is also dismissed by New Keynesian economists on the grounds that banks are merely a specialized form of financial intermediary, all of which can be safely ignored in macroeconomic models. When banks are introduced in New Keynesian models, they function not as loan originators but effectively as brokers between savers and borrowers. In response, authors in the Post-Keynesian and endogenous money traditions express exasperation that New Keynesian authors ignore credit creation and the accounting mechanics of bank lending, as laid out in numerous central bank publications.

In Chapter 4, Keen conclusively demonstrates how aggregate private debt and banks matter in macroeconomics by putting the two rival models of lending— loanable funds and endogenous money—on a common footing and provides a theoretical justification for the key role given to the level and change in aggregate private debt in Minsky's financial instability hypothesis. Minsky provided a succinct summary of his financial instability hypothesis, which emphasized the criticality of private debt to his analysis:

> The natural starting place for analyzing the relation between debt and income is to take an economy with a cyclical past that is now doing well. The inherited debt reflects the history of the economy, which includes a period in the not too distant past in which the economy did not do well. Acceptable liability structures are based upon some margin of safety so that expected cash flows, even in periods when the economy is not doing well, will cover contractual debt payments. As the period over which the economy does well lengthens, two things become evident in board rooms. Existing debts are easily validated and units that were heavily in debt prospered; it paid to lever. After the event it becomes apparent that the margins of safety built into debt structures were too great. As a result, over a period in which the economy does well, views about acceptable debt structure change. In the deal-making that goes on between banks, investment bankers, and businessmen, the acceptable amount of debt to use in financing various types of activity and positions increases. This increase in the weight of debt financing raises the market price of capital assets and increases investment. As this continues the economy is transformed into a boom economy. Stable growth is inconsistent with the manner in which investment is determined in an economy in which debt-financed ownership of capital assets exists, and the extent to which such debt financing can be carried is market determined. It follows that the fundamental instability of a capitalist economy is upward. The tendency to transform doing well into a speculative investment boom is the basic instability in a capitalist economy. (Minsky 1982, 66–67)

Therefore, since bank lending creates money and repayment of debt destroys it, the change in debt plays an integral role in macroeconomics by dynamically varying the level of aggregate demand. The omission of this factor from mainstream economic models is the reason that these models failed to warn of the dangers of the dramatic build-up in private debt since WWII—and especially since 1993, when the debt-financed recovery from the 1990s recession took the aggregate private debt level past the peak caused by deflation in the 1930s. It is also the reason why they failed to anticipate the crisis that began in 2007, and instead predicted that, as the Organization for Economic Cooperation and Development (OECD) put it in June 2007, "the current economic situation is in many ways better than what we have experienced in years . . . Our central forecast remains indeed quite benign" (OECD 2007). Policymakers relying upon mainstream economists as experts on the functioning of the economy thus not only received no warning about the worst economic crisis since the Great Depression, but were falsely led to expect benign rather than malignant economic conditions.

The main ingredients of the Global Financial Crisis are delineated in the report of the Financial Crisis Inquiry Commission (FCIC). The combination includes a bubble in housing prices, loose lending practices in the mortgage market, innovation and rapid growth of mortgage-based derivatives, and lax regulation of financial markets. All of these, and more, comprise key elements of Minsky's instability framework. Although the FCIC report makes no explicit mention of Minsky, those who worked on the report were well aware of his work. Shefrin in Chapter 5 presents the main elements in Minsky's analysis, and juxtaposes direct quotations from Minsky with illustrative excerpts from the FCIC report. The quotations help to make clear the tone and emphasis in his writings. The excerpts help to make clear how relevant is Minsky's framework to understanding the Global Financial Crisis that unfolded more than ten years after his death. In effect, the Global Financial Crisis that erupted in 2008 was a major out-of-sample test for Minsky's ideas. The juxtaposition also provides an opportunity for readers to judge for themselves the claim that Minsky's writings were opaque.

In Chapter 5, Shefrin argues that what lies at the heart of the Minsky dynamic is a concept Minsky called "Ponzi finance." Ponzi finance features debt financing for assets where full repayment of the debt only occurs if there is sufficient growth in the price of the assets. Significantly, Ponzi finance is what Minsky believes sustains asset pricing bubbles, up to the point at which they burst. Minsky's discussion does not emphasize the degree to which decisions about Ponzi finance are impacted by psychological elements. Indeed, one of the purposes of this chapter is to do so, drawing on examples from the financial crisis.

One of the most important psychological elements of Minsky's perspective is the extent to which financial crises are unavoidable. The behavioral-decision literature is replete with studies demonstrating the extent to which emotions, heuristics, and biases are hardwired into human cognitive processes. This chapter discusses how this literature adds to Minsky's perspective, using examples from the financial crisis to illustrate the theoretical arguments.

Although Minsky suggests that economic stability is unattainable, he does offer policy recommendations that can help mitigate the extent of instability. In this regard, Ben Bernanke, during the time he chaired the Fed, identified as one of the main lessons from the financial crisis the importance of placing financial market regulation on an equal footing with monetary policy. Notably, this was one of Minsky's major policy recommendations. Another of Minsky's main stabilization policy goals was the attainment of full employment, an issue clearly related to values.

In Chapter 6, Silvia discusses in detail the US labor market prior, during and after the Global Financial Crisis. The unprecedented expansion of credit in the years leading up to the Great Recession altered the way in which many parts of the economy functioned, including the labor market. With policies pushing homeownership and an expectations bias that home prices would continue to increase, credit flowed easily to borrowers across the credit spectrum. Unfortunately, this expansion of credit was not balanced against potential risks, such as rising interest rates and adverse economic conditions. While the adverse effects of rising interest rates came to fruition as early as 2006, strains in the credit sector did not come to a head until late 2008. For many parts of the economy, particularly the labor market, the turmoil was just beginning.

The immediate feedback from the credit shock was a downshift in the expectations for growth and therefore a decline in the demand for labor. By most measures of labor market health, conditions deteriorated to their weakest state in the post–WWII era. The depth of the deterioration, however, varied greatly across subgroups including gender, education, and age. Disparities across regions were heightened by negative equity reducing worker mobility.

Underlying the sharp deterioration in the labor market and subsequently slow recovery in the most recent business cycle has been several secular shifts. Included was the globalization of production that reduced the competitiveness of low- and semi-skilled workers and challenged the transmission of monetary policy and countercyclical fiscal stimulus. Moreover, the expansion of credit in previous years overstated the potential rate of growth for the economy.

Amid slower growth and weaker policy transmission, the workout of supply and demand for labor remains protracted. The subtle secular shifts that went unnoticed in good times have now been brought to the forefront. A widening gap between the median and average length of unemployment, a Beveridge curve that has yet to shift in, and a stark drop in labor force participation across the working-age population all suggest a lack of cost adjustment that has kept many workers on the sideline, quite possibly permanently. This has left a significantly lower base to support taxes and entitlement spending, and will alter the rate at which the US economy can ultimately grow.

Finally, as emphasized throughout Chapter 6, beliefs and values provide an underlying stream of patterns of decision-making that certainly influenced the extent of the housing boom, the subsequent financial crisis, and the ongoing adjustments in the real economy, especially the labor market.

The last contribution within economics introduces the new idea of anti-fragility developed extensively in Taleb (2012). Chapters 2 through 6 examine the Global Financial Crisis as an atypical business cycle with a housing bubble during its late expansion and a liquidity trap during its trough. Minsky proposes a more detailed explanation of financial crises by proposing the hypothesis that capitalism suffers from financial instability. Taleb's (2012) intellectual lenses would characterize the Global Financial Crisis as a "black swan," described statistically as a highly improbable, exceedingly risky event. Usually, complexity, nonlinearities, interdependence, efficiency, competition, globalization, and regulatory limitations, among other factors, cause black swans to occur. The authors of Chapter 7, Taleb and Douady, do not mention the concept of financial instability. But much in the spirit of Minsky, who accepted the reality of recurring crises, Taleb and Douady argue that increased uncertainty and its partial expression as asset volatility produce black swan events.

Some Black Swans, like the Great Depression of the early 1930s and the latest Global Financial Crisis, also portray financial instabilities. In general however, the concept of a black swan as a statistical phenomenon is much broader than the idea of financial instability. In view of the actuality of black swans, whose probability of occurrence is so insignificantly small and essentially unpredictable, what can be done to deal with the excessive damages of a black swan? Taleb and Douady introduce the new concept of "anti-fragility" and contrast it to the idea of fragility. Fragility is the property of breakability, frailty, weakness, instability, or vulnerability. It describes the defining characteristic of an object or a system that collapses when shocked. Illustrations include a glass bottle hit by a hammer or the Titanic colliding with an iceberg. In both cases neither the bottle nor the Titanic can be recovered. In contrast, anti-fragility is the property of a system that allows it to not only tolerate but also benefit from shocks, black swans, stress, risks, uncertainty, and volatility. For example, the mythological Hydra generated two heads each time one was destroyed; similarly, a forest devastated by fire is more vigorous several years later than it ever was before. Is it possible to make an economic system anti-fragile to black swans? Taleb and Douady address this question in Chapter 7.

CONTRIBUTIONS FROM PSYCHOLOGY

The transition from economics to psychology is attained by a discussion on incentives. For some decades now, the idea of incentives has played a key role in economics as well as in public policy analyses and implementations. Nevertheless, our general understanding of how incentives impact behavior is far from being full. The implicit understanding in the economics of incentives has been that there are gains to be achieved by parties to an agreement, and while economists do not specify that the agreement has exactly two parties, the most typical context studied in financial economics, at least, has been the problem of incentive alignment between a principal and the principal's agent.

In contrast to this limited conceptualization of incentives as prevailing in an arrangement between two parties, the actual use of the term is much broader. For example, in psychology or even religion a very different conception of incentive is introduced in which an emotion, such as fear, acts as an incentive. In Chapter 8, Kolb explores some of these broader conceptualizations of incentives and shows how the characteristically economic understanding of this term constricts our comprehension of the full role that incentives play in our discourse and throughout our society. Kolb uses the financial crisis of 2007–2009 as a laboratory of incentives and concludes that in large part this crisis was the result of many incentives operating together that arose organically from a variety of opportunities and interactively contributed to economic ruin that was anticipated by very few.

Incentives involve risks and rewards, but the topic of risk-taking under uncertainty is a significant area of inquiry. In Chapter 9, Lopes gives both a scientific exposition and a personal account of the development of this area of quantitative psychology and microeconomic decision-making under uncertainty. Academic thought on how people choose among risks can be traced back at least to the 17th century. The critical development for risk theory was the idea of expected value. This is the idea that, given an uncertain prospect with two or more possible outcomes, the overall value of the prospect is a probability weighted average of its individual possible outcomes. The expectation principle had immediate useful application to the emerging field of actuarial science, but it seemed to fail when applied to certain extreme examples. The most famous of these is called the St. Petersburg Paradox and it goes like this: A fair coin is tossed until it lands tails, at which point the player is paid 2n monetary units, say dollars, where n is the toss on which tails occurs. Tails on the first toss pays $2. Tails on the second toss pays $4. Tails on the third toss pays $8, and so forth. The question of interest is how much should a person be willing to pay for a single play of the game? Looked at through the lens of expected value, the answer is simple. The expected value of the game is infinite; therefore, a person should be willing to exchange all he or she has for a single play.

It was obvious to scholars at the time that this was a ridiculous conclusion and there were several different proposals for how this difficulty with the expected value rule could be bypassed. The most famous of these, suggested by Daniel Bernoulli, continues to provide the structural basis for modern-day theories about valuing risks. Bernoulli's proposal kept the mathematical structure of the expected value rule but replaced the objective value of each outcome by its subjective counterpart or utility. He pointed out that richer men value given increments in wealth less than poorer men, suggesting that the utility of wealth is a negatively accelerated function of actual value. Thus, if people maximize expected utility rather than value, the worth of the game becomes quite small and the paradox disappears. Since Bernoulli, most researchers on risk have assumed that Bernoulli's idea is essentially right, although the details and rhetoric have changed, and the utility function itself is commonly taken to provide both the cause and the mathematical description of what we call risk aversion, that is, people's typical preference for sure things in favor of actuarially equivalent risks. But strangely, even though Bernoulli's notion of diminishing marginal utility predicts the behavior of risk aversion, there is nothing in his formulation that can be used to define what it means for a gamble to be risky or to relate perceived riskiness to risk aversion.

Lopes does not address issues of the Global Financial Crisis. She does, however, explain well that risk choices are a central aspect of human life, worthy of all our efforts to define it, measure it, control it, understand the feelings generated by it as well as the feelings driving it, and—at the end, one would hope—survive and even thrive in the face of it.

Chichilninsky in Chapter 10 follows Lopes to present a mathematical framework for studying greed and fear that are pervasive in financial markets. The emphasis on greed and fear has been given by behavioral finance and supported by many years of experimental psychological studies. Chichilninsky describes that the problem arises due to a narrow notion of rationality that is founded on expected utility theory, which goes back to the axioms for choice under uncertainty introduced by Von Neumann, built on Kolmogorov's axioms, and developed by Kenneth Arrow, John Milnor, and others. These axioms disregard rare events that cause fear and greed. This chapter extends the notion of rationality with new axioms of choice under uncertainty, and the decision criteria they imply. In the absence of extreme rare events, the old and the new axioms coincide, and both lead to standard expected utility. A sharp difference emerges when facing rare events with important consequences, such as catastrophes. The author formulates a theorem that allows extreme responses to extreme events, including fear and greed, and characterizes the implied decision criteria as a combination of expected utility with external responses, a type of choice criterion that was not formerly used in the theory of choice under uncertainty, yet it is shown to be similar to what Lopes documents empirically in this volume.

The most complete history of psychological research that was foundational to behavioral economics is presented in Daniel Kahneman's (2011) professional auto-biography. This work demonstrates how far our behavior differs from the behavior of the mythical "rational actor" who obeys the rules of classical economics. In Chapter 11, Shaw offers a detailed analysis of how economics and behavioral economics relate to psychology and psychoanalysis. She examines both philosophically and also in terms of Minsky's financial instability hypothesis the dual system theory of "thinking" "fast and slow" that is articulated by Kahneman. She then compares the theory, which is exclusively cognitive, to the conscious and unconscious mind as it evolved in psychoanalytic theory. Shaw utilizes recent writing from eminent philosopher Jonathan Lear to argue that the mental two-system schema is like a simultaneous equation system which philosophically leaves unanswered the fundamental issues of a unified human being. The two-system model is limited because it does not include an ongoing dynamic of mental energy that is endogenous to and flows through human *being*. Shaw leads us to conceptualize an additional yet integrated duality that is fueled by anxieties and defenses. Hence given the vicissitudes of endogenous pressures, human beings may fluctuate, throughout life, between internal psychological structures that feel integrated and whole, yet aware of an immanent fragmentation that is always possible. If we are able to better conceptualize human anxiety and defense, hence the duality of endogenous integration and fragmentation, with all of their vicissitudes, we may be productive with new work and insight into Minsky's instability hypothesis.

Next, the chapter by Dalko, Klein, Sethi, and Wang discusses the presence of monopoly power in financial markets, by which is meant the ability to influence price directly. They write that there is general agreement that prices are not strong-form efficient, noting that corporate insiders and specialists have monopolistic access to information. However, they make a stronger statement by pointing to evidence that corporate insiders and specialists are not the only groups with monopolistic access to information.

The key finding in the chapter is that monopoly power in the stock market can be created and exercised through information-based market manipulation by a strategic trader. Moreover, successful execution of manipulation can result in substantial profit to the strategic trader but unfair losses to other investors, as well as excess volatility to the manipulated stocks.

Dalko et al. link the monopoly power issue to the asset pricing bubbles that are part of the work of Minsky and others. In this regard, they suggest policy measures featuring appropriate surveillance and regulatory measures, which they suggest can prevent a crisis. In addition, their analysis identifies a potential mechanism through which wealth inequality can increase through stock-trading. The issue of wealth inequality came to the fore during the "Occupy Wall Street" protests which began in September 2011.

In Chapter 13, De Bondt documents the long-term decline of confidence of the public-at-large in societal institutions and leaders. His analysis is carefully documented with an extensive bibliography and useful data from different region and different time periods. The "confidence gap" and the "crisis of authority" is not a new topic. In fact, it may be thought of as a classic topic in the social sciences—especially, political economy and sociology—with contributions by Karl Marx, Gustave LeBon, Vilfredo Pareto, R. H. Tawney, J. M. Keynes and Joseph Schumpeter. De Bondt argues that the Global Financial Crisis that started in 2007 was preceded by a long period of slow economic growth in the industrialized nations and has revealed the fragility of market-based democracies. Their lackluster performance is linked to technological change, the global spread of production, social inequality, and other root causes. The belief that democratic capitalism is inherently unstable, inefficient, unfair, and corrupt is widespread. The lack of confidence is not only a psychological burden. Intense distrust undermines the political and economic leadership that is needed to implement fundamental reforms. The fear of stagnation may also become a self-fulfilling prophecy. If consumers around the world felt better about the state of their economies, chances are that aggregate demand would rise. It is unclear what can be done in the short run to improve voter, consumer, investor, and business confidence, especially now that monetary and fiscal policies are both "tapped out." Thus, De Bondt concludes that this neglected issue of the authority crisis needs to be addressed.

Harrington in Chapter 14 defines financialization as an economic system in which the underlying mechanism of growth is "making money out of money." Not only do financial markets come to dominate a nation's economy, but financial actors assume controlling influence over economic policy and outcomes. Ironically, historical analyses of the phenomenon suggest that it was an adaptive response to mitigate the impact of the recurrent crises in capitalism. It now seems, however, that financialization has come to produce new sources of instability. Harrington asserts that fraud of the kind observed in the financial crisis of 2008 is not an aberration of the system, but rather how power and domination are expressed in a financialized economy. In this analysis, the source of the crisis lies not in individuals' ethical failures but in the structures of incentives, sanctions, and networks in which their lines of action unfold. As financial capitalism has become dominant—shifting the basis of the world's key political economies from industry to finance—both the opportunities and rewards for cheating have increased. This chapter analyses the social, economic, and political structures that have created the contemporary "criminogenic" environment, and assesses the outlook for future crises.

VALUES

Gretchen Morgenson and Joshua Rosner (2011), among many economic analysts and reporters, examine the impact of ethical values on the Global Financial Crisis. Cheating, greed, lack of trust, corruption, excessive ambition, and many other concepts are presented to explain how the financial engine crashed.

A value is a belief or a principle that is meaningful to an individual. For example, the statement, "I believe it is important to tell the truth," or "It is wrong to cheat," or "Only my personal gain matters," convey personal values. Every individual in a society has a set or core of personal values whether such a person is explicitly conscious or not of what such a set contains in detail. Personal values are supplemented by professional values, as in the case of the Hippocratic Oath for physicians or the accountant's duty to detect and report fraud. Professional values are promoted both legally and by ethical principles. Moral philosophers, from Aristotle to Adam Smith and to our current thinkers, have investigated these issues in great detail.

Research in behavioral decision-making has identified critical psychological features associated with cheating. For example, Gino et al. (2011) study cheating as a self-control problem. Gino, Ayal, and Ariely study how group composition influences people's decision to cheat. Although the literature indicates that there are substantial individual differences in people's proclivity to cheat, the general results suggest that given the opportunity to cheat, many people do.

The first contribution to our last section on values is by John Riker. Riker offers a persuasive transition from psychology to values. He achieves this transition in several steps: First, one of the complex factors bringing about the economic downfall of 2007–2009 was the presence of cheating and playing fast and loose with sound banking practices. Values of personal gain were often put ahead of those of ethical principles when the two conflicted, leading to both unsound business practices and to outright fraud. The violation of ethical and legal principles did not occur by chance but is a natural tendency of the kind of human being produced by economic society. That is, there is a contradiction at the heart of a capitalist market society. It was not the one which Marx saw—an ever-increasing proletariat that would overthrow the bourgeoisie—but one in which the kind of human being who best thrives in a market economy is also someone who is likely to undermine the ethical substructures which are necessary to maintain the integrity of property and exchange. Understanding the kind of human being which a capitalist market economy tends to produce reveals both why they are inclined to cheat and why morality does not have a strong claim on them.

Second, the loss of trust in the market was not just due to the instability of the market but also to the loss of trust in the integrity of some of the key players in the economic world. If an economic society has a tendency to produce players who are internally pressured to cheat, then it needs to have significant structures of surveillance and regulation, such as those that might be found in the oligopolistic banking sector of Canada—which did not suffer the downturn Gino et al. (2009). While business ethics training might help somewhat, they cannot undo strong personal tendencies to cheat if that is the best way to get ahead.

Third, Riker provides an understanding of the theory of self, proposed by psychoanalyst Heinz Kohut, allows us to see why modern economic individuals are often narcissistically inclined, as they have suffered injuries to their core selves. Persons with injured selves tend to defend against their inner emptiness by seeking grandiose markers of greatness and will often cheat if those markers are endangered.

Finally, the long-term solution to the contradiction which destabilizes economic society is the construction of social and economic practices and values which support the generation of self-structure in early childhood and sustain it later in adult life. Persons with strong, vitalized selves are not the kind of persons who cheat or who need grandiose markers to shore up an inner sense of worthlessness.

Meir Statman in Chapter 16 analyzes why financial professionals often complain that they do not receive enough respect, especially in the wake of the financial crisis. Respect is the currency of status, and Statman relates the issues to the "market for status." The respect people confer reflects the amount of social value they attach to the conferee, above and beyond financial remuneration for goods and services provided. Certainly the "Occupy Wall Street" movement, with its emphasis on the top 1% of the wealth distribution, made clear that at the very least, the financial industry has an image problem. In this regard, the underlying issues Statman addresses surfaced very strongly in the 2016 primaries, and propelled the campaign of Bernie Sanders, who was challenging Hillary Clinton for the Democratic nomination.

Statman contrasts financial professionals with physicians, as both are well compensated for the services they provide. However, when it comes to status, physicians typically receive much more respect than financial professionals. Part of the reason for this differential might involve the value of physicians' services being more transparent than financial services. However, Statman suggests that the issue is much deeper, and he links the conferring of respect to perceptions of fairness. He discusses various interpretations for how people understand the concept of fairness, and relates the discussion to the different ways that people earn respect.

John Boatright in Chapter 17 examines modern risk management, with its rich array of sophisticated mathematical measures and models as a focus of technical finance, values, and psychology. Risk management is a cardinal achievement of the past two decades. The ability of finance and, indeed, all business to enrich our lives has expanded greatly due to this incredible development. However, risk management also has its weaknesses and shortcomings, which were all too evident in the recent financial crisis.

Although it was only one of many causes of this crisis, the failure of risk management must cause considerable soul-searching among its practitioners and ultimate users. Much of this soul-searching has been of a technical nature, conducted by those most deeply involved in the field. The ethical and behavioral aspects of the failure of risk management have been comparatively neglected, and yet this perspective provides a valuable addition to the ongoing investigation of the crisis.

Ultimately, risk management is a tool or instrument, and its contribution to human welfare depends critically on how it is used. Since risk management is employed by human decision makers, it is vulnerable to all the biases that psychological research has discovered in cognitive processes and to the creation of a dangerous false sense of confidence that risks are well managed. Some features of organizational decision-making also lead to errors, such as using risk management merely for implementing strategy and not for developing it as well, failing to draw the right conclusions or develop an effective response, and substituting mechanical models for sound judgment.

The organizational setting for the implementation of risk management systems also has far-reaching consequences. Managerial incentives may lead to a focus on risks that can be easily and effectively managed. These are often well-known, common risks rather than the low-probability, high-impact events that may pose the greatest danger. In addition, risk management by organizations has profound impacts on society, especially in the identification of the risks to be managed, the means chosen to manage these risks, the determination of an acceptable level of risk, and the creation of a possibly false sense of confidence that risks are being well managed.

Finally, risk management may be criticized for acting as a smokescreen to obscure reckless risk-taking in the pursuit of profit, to maintain a convenient myth of managerial control, and to demonstrate mere regulatory compliance rather than real risk management. Boatright concludes that none of these ethical and behavioral aspects are fatal to the enterprise of modern risk management, but they indicate concerns that need to be addressed in order to realize the full promise of this remarkable development.

In a free and just society with a trustworthy marketplace, people should be able to depend upon the honesty and the ethics of the professionals who would do business with them as they seek to realize their financial plans. Alas, the marketplace is far too frequently dishonest and the professionals who work in it are far too often untrue to the ethical ideals of their chosen professions.

In Chapter 18, Paul Fitzgerald investigates the Global Financial Crisis through the lens of Catholic social doctrine. Catholic scholars have long reflected upon personal virtue and social morality, based in turn on Sacred Scripture and religious practice. After reviewing the relevant theological principles to be found in Catholic social doctrine, Fitzgerald then explores the moral failures of individuals and groups who contributed to the crisis. He concludes by identifying new policies of oversight and regulation as well as renewed ethical practices and principles that business people and business organizations should adopt.

Dobson in Chapter 20 agrees with Fitzgerald that the recent financial crisis is typically viewed as morally problematic. Indeed, from the perspective of conventional business ethics, financial crises are viewed as evidence of moral failure either at the individual level or at the level of capitalism in general; hence the calls for more regulation, more ethics education, or even the reconsideration of capitalism itself.

Argandoña examines the ethical foundations of the financial crisis. He argues that the financial crisis in which the world economy has been immersed since mid-2007 is an ethical crisis. By studying the behavior of the agents who made the decisions that led to the crisis, we do find evidence of many unethical mistakes. But bad conduct was also present before the crisis and in countries not affected by it: the fact that the crisis has an ethical dimension does not mean that this is its only cause. In Chapter 19, Argandoña argues that this crisis is a crisis of leadership or governance in a wide range of institutions, and this, in turn, reflects the failure of an economic and social model grounded on certain anthropological and ethical assumptions, and it is these assumptions that have ultimately failed.

In Chapter 20, financial crises are cast in a different moral light. Dobson invokes the concept of the business organization as derived from recent developments in virtue ethics theory. Within this theory, morally justifiable business organizations are viewed as combinations of institutions and practices. Both institutions and practices pursue their own kind of moral good by cultivating a distinct balance of virtues. This practice–institution balance requires vigilance by members of business organizations. Too exclusive a focus on cultivating the virtues associated with either practices or institutions could threaten this balance.

The focus of Dobson's argument is on the potential of practices to corrupt institutions. He argues that financial crises actually serve the morally beneficial role of tempering the corruptive power of practices. Financial crises do this by focusing attention on the value, to the organization as a whole, of those virtues associated primarily with institutions. In short, by placing economic pressure on the institution, crises force institutions to morally evaluate practices from the perspective of the institutional virtues. Crises in essence reassert the power of institutional virtues as foundational to the moral worth of the organization.

EPILOGUE

No single author could offer such a wide-ranging and insightful examination of the Global Financial Crisis as the distinguished contributors of this volume have done together. This editorial introduction and overview is an invitation to the reader to critically explore the ideas presented. If this overview has raised your expectations about this book, we are certain that reading it will offer you many valuable ideas.

REFERENCES

Bernanke, Ben. 2013. "The Crisis as a Classic Financial Panic." The Fourteenth Jacques Polak Annual Research Conference. Washington, DC. November 8.

Blanchard, Olivier. 2014. "Where Danger Lurks." *Finance& Development* 51 (3): 28–31, http://www.imf.org/external/pubs/ft/fandd/2014/09/blanchard.htm.

Gino, Francesca, Shahar Ayal, and Dan Ariely. 2009. "Contagion and Differentiation in Unethical Behavior." *Psychological Science* 20 (3): 393–398.

Gino, Francesca, Maurice E. Schweitzer, Nicole L. Mead, and Dan Ariely. 2011. "Unable to Resist Temptation: How Self-Control Depletion Promotes Unethical Behavior." *Organizational Behavior and Human Decision Processes* 115 (2): 191–203.

Gorton, Gary. 2010. *Slapped by the Invisible Hand: The Panic of 2007.* New York: Oxford University Press.

Morgenson, Gretchen, and Joshua Rosner. 2011. *Reckless Endangerment: How Outsized Ambition, Greed, and Corruption Led to Economic Armageddon.* New York: Times Books.

Kahneman, Daniel. 2011. *Thinking, Fast and Slow.* New York: Farrar, Straus, and Giroux.

Keen, Steve. 2013. "Predicting the 'Global Financial Crisis': Post-Keynesian Macroeconomics." *Economic Record* 89: 1–27.

Kindleberger, C. P. 1978. *Manias, Panics, and Crashes: A History of Financial Crises.* Hoboken, NJ: John Wiley and Sons.

Kindleberger, Charles, and Robert Aliber. 2005. *Manias, Panics, and Crashes: A History of Financial Crises.* Fifth Edition. Hoboken, NJ: John Wiley and Sons.

Kocherlakota, Narayana. 2010. "Modern Macroeconomic Models as Tools for Economic Policy." *The 2009 Annual Report Essay.* The Federal Reserve Bank of Minneapolis, 5–21.

Lucas, E. Robert Jr., and Thomas J. Sargent. 1979. "After Keynesian Macroeconomics." *Quarterly Review of the Federal Reserve Bank of Minneapolis,* 1–16.

Lucas, E. Robert Jr., and Nancy L. Stokey. 2011. "Liquidity Crises. Understanding Sources and Limiting Consequences: A Theoretical Framework." *Economic Policy Papers.* The Federal Reserve Bank of Minneapolis, 1–15.

McClosky, Deidre. 2006. *The Bourgeois Virtues: Ethics for an Age of Commerce.* Chicago: University of Chicago Press.

Minsky, Hyman. 1982. *Can It Happen Again? Essays on Instability and Finance.* Translated by M. E. Sharpe. New York: Armonk.

Reinhart, Carmen, and Kenneth Rogoff. 2009. *This Time Is Different: Eight Centuries of Financial Folly.* Princeton, NJ: Princeton University Press.

Taleb, Nassim Nicholas. 2012. *Antifragility: Things That Gain from Disorder.* New York: Random House.

Tirole, Jean. 2011. "Illiquidity and All Its Friends." *Journal of Economic Literature* 49: 287–325.

PART TWO

The Global Financial Crisis of 2007–2009 and Economics

2

From Asset Price Bubbles
to Liquidity Traps

A.G. MALLIARIS ■

We can model the euphoria and the fear stages of the business cycle. Their parameters are quite different. We have never successfully modeled the transition from euphoria to fear.

—ALAN GREENSPAN

INTRODUCTION

Cyclicality has been an enduring characteristic of many aggregate measures of economic activity for many countries across time. Beginning with biblical times, during Pharaonic Egypt's Middle Kingdom (2000–1782 BC), seven years of fat cows were followed by seven years of thin cows; this cyclicality has persisted to today. For example, in the US economy, several years of exuberant housing construction activities from 2002 to 2006 have been followed by several years of very weak housing from 2008 to 2015. This cyclical behavior has impacted both the financial and real sectors of the US and global economies.

Gottfried Haberler (1960), in his classic book *Prosperity and Depression: A Theoretical Analysis of Cyclical Movements*, exposits in detail numerous hypotheses that compete to explain the causes of the four phases of cyclical patterns: the economic expansion or prosperity, the upper turning point or period from expansion to contraction, the economic recession or depression phase, and finally, the lower turning point from economic contraction to economic expansion. However, the majority of the theories he develops apply to the prosperity or the recession stages; there are no dependable hypotheses about an economy's transition from prosperity to recession and vice versa, as Greenspan's quote in the epigraph indicates.

The profession's inability to satisfactorily articulate hypotheses that explain major swings in aggregate economic activity is demonstrated by the intense disbelief one experiences following the utter unexpectedness of cyclical turning points. Such surprise has surrounded the recent global financial crisis and the Great Recession it has caused. Characteristically, when Queen Elizabeth II visited the London School of Economics in November 2008, she asked the assembled academics, "How come nobody could foresee the global financial crisis?" This question remains unanswerable several years after the occurrence of such a dramatic turning point.

Blanchard (2014, 28) writes, "Until the 2008 global financial crisis, mainstream U.S. macroeconomics had taken an increasingly benign view of economic fluctuations in output and employment. The crisis has made it clear that this view was wrong and that there is need for a deep reassessment." Haldane (2012) traces the methodological evolution of economics during the last two hundred years and argues that early classical determinism was replaced during the 1950s by econometric modeling, characterized by a dual emphasis on a propagation mechanism and random shocks distributed normally. Such a scientific framework for modern economics seriously constrains prediction, leaving economists with surprises produced by random shocks.

PURPOSE OF THIS CHAPTER

In this chapter, we discuss the characteristic of the proposed four phases of the most recent economic cycle. Before we suggest these four phases or periods, we begin with the NBER (2010) classification of the latest business cycle and its emphasis with exactly one point for the end of an expansion (the peak) and only one point for the end of a recession (the trough). In the latest full cycle, the expansion period started in December 2001 and lasted to the end of November 2007; the peak was in November 2007, and the recession lasted from December 2007 to June 2009 with the trough occurring in June 2009.

To enrich the NBER classification, we distinguish four time periods. The expansion period lasted from December 2001 to January 2007, and the upper turning period from February 2007 to September 2008; this upper period contains the NBER peak in November 2007. We choose the period from October 2008 to June 2009 as the contraction period, which is shorter than that of the NBER classification, and, finally, the lower turning period from July 2009 to November 2010. Uncharacteristically, with past lower turning periods, the US economy did not return to robust and sustained growth during 2010–2014. Instead it experienced a period of slow growth with low inflation and Fed funds rate close to zero. In other words, the US economy during 2010–2014 found itself in a Keynesian liquidity trap.

We immediately recognize that these four periods are approximate and, unlike the NBER's (2010) classification of recessions, we allow for upper and lower turning periods rather than points. This deviation from the official NBER dating of a recession allows us to focus on upper and lower turning periods in more detail. In this paper, we discuss the latest upper turning period, from early 2007 to September 2008, and the lower turning period, from July 2009 to November 2010. It is during this upper turning period that the housing bubble deflated, and it is also during this lower turning period that the economy got stuck in a liquidity trap, hence the title of the paper. Our contribution is not in terms of arguing the methodology of selecting the upper and lower transition periods. This is a very difficult task, which needs to be addressed by a group of economists similar to the Business Cycle Dating

Committee. Our goal is to address important economic developments during such periods in the methodological spirit of Haberler (1960). Haberler documents the extensive work of pre–World War II economists, who articulated the behavior of an economy during the four phases of the business cycle. Keynes (1936) marginalized most of these economists and their views about the upper turning period. However, before examining Keynesian economics, which addresses why aggregate demand may be deficient and what can be done about it, we need to understand what causes economic booms and busts. Such booms and busts do not occur in each business cycle, but have been observed in the past and reappeared with the global financial crisis. Kindleberger (1978) and Kindleberger and Aliber (2005) give an excellent analysis of financial crises. A few remarks are in order.

First, there are numerous real and financial economic variables that exhibit cyclical patterns. A short list of some of these variables includes real GDP, disposable income, consumption, investment, housing, unemployment, equities, bonds, total wealth, mortgages, securitization volume of mortgages, interest rates, Fed funds rates, lending, debt, bank assets, liquidity, and several others. Their significance varies from cycle to cycle. In its definition of a recession, the Business Cycle Dating Committee of the NBER (2010) emphasizes the cyclical behavior of certain real economic variables. Specifically, it defines a recession as "a period of falling economic activity spread across the economy, lasting more than a few months, normally visible in real GDP, real income, employment, industrial production, and wholesale-retail sales." If the profession ever decides to expand the decomposition of the business cycles into the four subperiods, discussed in Haberler (1960) and revisited in this paper, we envision a detailed evaluation of the four phases similar to that of the NBER. So, our proposed dates are very tentative and are presented as illustrations.

Second, the cyclical behavior of real GDP is important, but as the economy grows in complexity and as economists become more sophisticated, other monthly economic variables mentioned above are also considered in identifying cycles. The NBER (2010) keeps a detailed record of the cyclical behavior of real business activities and has officially identified all past recessions with dates of peaks and troughs that frame economic recessions and expansions. It is interesting to note that since 1854 the NBER has recognized 33 cycles for the US economy.

As noted earlier, there is no record of turning periods; if instead of identifying only peaks and troughs, one chooses to allow for turning periods (as we do in this paper), these turning periods may overlap partially with the expansion or the contraction phases. We do so in our attempt to address Greenspan's concern about the transition from expansion to recession and vice versa. If such periods are not identified, they cannot be the subject of investigation. Using the NBER methodology with only one month as the transition period restricts the duration and menu of possible developments.

Figure 2.1 illustrates the long-term logarithmic growth of real GDP with its cyclical behavior. It is important to note the severity of the most recent official recession, which started in December 2007 and ended in June 2009, and to also remark on the unusually slow recovery.

Third, financial variables such as Fed funds, other interest rates, various money supply measures, inflation, equities, bonds, wealth, bank lending, debt, and collateral play an important economic role, but their cyclical behavior is not tracked and is not always considered as critical. The NBER does not distinguish between business

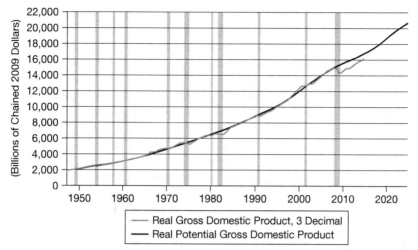

Figure 2.1 Long-term Logarithmic Growth of Real GDP.
SOURCE: St. Louis Fed.

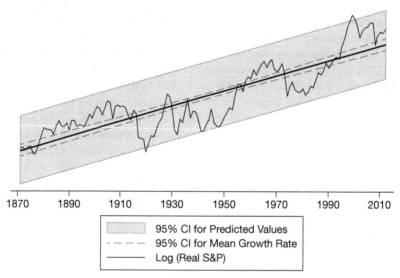

Figure 2.2 Real S&P: Confidence Interval for Trend (Log Scale) calculated by
author's assistant Ethan Alt.

cycles and financial panics. The two most recent major financial panics occurred
during the Great Depression of the early 1930s and the recent global financial
crisis of 2007–2009. During these two financial panics, a bursting of a financial
bubble occurred during the upper turning period, and the recession was followed
by a liquidity trap during the lower turning period. Figure 2.2 demonstrates the
cyclical behavior of equities as represented by the S&P 500 Index, and illustrates that
equities are more volatile than real variables. The S&P 500 Index peaked in October
2007 and, after dropping about 50%, bottomed out in March 2009 and then slowly
recovered and surpassed its former peak four years later in March 2013.

Fourth, the patterns of cyclical behavior of the mentioned economic and financial variables are complicated with unequal wavelengths, dissimilar amplitudes, and unsynchronized frequencies. Even if we choose to limit our search for only the mutually reinforcing propagation and amplification relationships between the S&P 500 Index and real GDP, such an undertaking cannot easily be accomplished. This is because equities exhibit many more cycles than real GDP. Also, while the range of growth for equities is wide and changing over longer periods, equity prices often drop rapidly during shorter periods. In contrast, real GDP grows and drops more slowly, and its cyclical waves evolve over several years, in contrast to equities that may exhibit corrections of up to 10% once or twice per year during certain periods. Thus, it is hard to list specific, stylized facts for the cyclical behavior of the S&P 500 Index, while it is much easier to do so for the real GDP as described by the NBER record of US recessions.

Fifth, in addition to the individual complex cyclical behavior of real GDP and the S&P 500 Index (in real or nominal prices), the relationships between these two variables are not clearly established, as indicated above. For example, it is reasonable to hypothesize that increases in the values of equities contribute to increases in wealth, and such wealth in turn increases stimulate consumption and GDP. Conversely, asset price theories explain the level and changes of the S&P 500 Index related to consumption and GDP. In particular, the canonical consumption capital asset pricing model hypothesizes that investors demand high expected returns when these returns co-vary strongly and positively with expected consumption growth which, in turn, is driven by expected real GDP growth. However, such a hypothesis connecting expected equity returns to the time-varying covariance between returns and consumption has not been confirmed, and remains an active area of both theoretical research and empirical testing. In other words, not only are the cyclical movements of several important economic and financial variables complicated, their interrelationships remain intractable.

Sixth, the presence of monetary and fiscal policies further challenges our investigation. Theoretically, the Fed is mandated to maintain both financial and economic stability. Financial stability means that the financial sector can withstand major random risks. Economic stability means that the economy grows at its potential without inflation. If we assume that the mixed, capitalist system is inherently unstable, then a prescient Fed can adhere to countercyclical policies to stabilize both the real and financial sectors. Not only is the Fed incapable of foreseeing turning points or periods, as Greenspan's quote clearly reminds us, but its doctrines and derived policies are often deficient. For example, prior to the 2007–2009 global financial crisis, the Fed postulated that price stability was sufficient for financial stability. This conjecture turned out to be false, since the price stability of the Great Moderation failed to prevent the 2007–2009 crisis. Therefore, as we trace the four phases of cyclical behavior, the force of the Fed's doctrines and policies need to be reexamined. In our discussion, we also address fiscal policy issues; however, it is clear that Fed policies are more critical, because monetary policy is less constrained than fiscal policy.

Finally, in contrast to the prosperity and recession periods that follow upward and downward movements with added noise, turning periods are more difficult to model statistically and to validate with a credible narrative. The typical patterns of turning periods are nonlinear but dissimilar; the upper turning period is concave, while the lower one is convex. Taleb (2013) has much to say about these two characteristics. The upper turning period has the unwelcome property of instability, sometimes financial or economic and often both. It is this instability characteristic of the capitalist system that is so damaging. It is during such turning periods that the "good times come to an end" without anyone knowing how bad the recession that follows will be or how long it will last. This is when "fear" replaces "greed" in the parlance of Wall Street, or euphoria turns to fear as Greenspan characterizes it. This neglected upper turning period receives much attention in this book. The lower turning period eventually ushers in better times for the economy with prospects for catching up in terms of pent-up demand, yet consumers and businesses do not easily shed the difficulties experienced during the recession.

Stated succinctly, we wish to give turning periods from prosperity to recession and from recession to prosperity special emphasis as integral components of the full business cycle. In particular, turning periods become significant objects of interest when business cycles evolve into financial crises. We propose that psychological ambivalence and the resulting excessive financial volatility are the driving forces during such switching periods. The top turning period unfolds when economic agents begin to doubt the endurance and prospects of the expansion but remain unsure about the actual probability of a recession. Similarly, during the lower turning period, economic agents fluctuate emotionally between the negative experiences of the most recent recession and the strength of certain indicators that suggest the seeds of recovery are sprouting. During the upper turning period, the economy transitions from stability to instability. Economic and financial instabilities have been a cherished topic for both mainstream economists as well as unconventional Marxist philosophers. Since we plan to employ these concepts, we follow Malliaris (2012) to review some definitions and descriptions of financial instability.

WHAT IS FINANCIAL INSTABILITY?

Economic and financial instability do not have exact definitions and are only partially understood. Broadly speaking, economists theorize that economies, with their subsets of the financial sector, are most of the time in a state of equilibrium. When a big shock—such as a war, a natural disaster, a stock market crash, bank runs, currency devaluations and other similar events—takes place, the financial sector and even the economy at large deviate from equilibrium. These deviations are described as instabilities.

There remains the theoretical challenge of integrating the real and financial sectors of the economy with sufficient quantitative details, so that answers can be provided to the following questions: What is financial instability? Under what conditions is the financial sector stable or unstable? What are the causes of financial instability? What can monetary and fiscal policies do, if anything, to stabilize both the financial system and the real economy? What role do asset bubbles and crashes play in causing financial instabilities? What are the relationships between asset bubbles and crashes, booms and busts, exuberance and panic, jubilant animal spirits and depressions, manias and financial crises? Finally, under what conditions do financial crises impact the real economy by reducing GDP and employment?

The theory of general equilibrium, with its prototype of an Arrow-Debreu economy, addresses economic stability as the property of markets. Markets are stable if the economy is well diversified, so no shock can cause large deviations without an eventual return to equilibrium. Real economies are significantly more complex, and if a financial sector is introduced to such economies, then the sources and impact of instabilities amplify significantly. But what is the financial sector of an economy? The financial sector includes the central bank; commercial and investment banks; non-bank financial institutions such as insurance companies; and managed money flowing through financial markets for equity, debt, real estate, commodity, currency, and other derivative instruments traded over the counter or on established exchanges. Perhaps an easier definition is to say the financial sector is the one that allocates financial resources efficiently in the domestic and global economies. Financial sectors may have their roots in a given country, but nowadays extend globally. The concept of a financial sector is dynamic, global, and evolving. As the recent crisis demonstrated, even the best financial experts may not have a comprehensive understanding of its financial and legal intricacies. During the recent financial crisis, a distinction was often made between the banks that had access to liquidity from the central bank and the shadow banks, such as Lehman Brothers, that did not.

In the United States and other advanced economies, the financial sector has total financial assets equivalent to several times the size of their home country's GDP. Adrian and Shin (2009) discuss the current US financial system and its stability, with emphasis on security brokers and dealers. Kaufman (2004) gives a detailed analysis of macroeconomic stability and links it to bank soundness. The Federal Reserve's Flow of Funds accounts describe how the share of assets of commercial banking, measured as a percent of total financial assets in the financial sector, has been declining for several decades, while the share of assets held by other financial institutions and money managers, often described as the shadow banking industry, has been growing.

Let us start with a definition of the stability of the financial sector. Financial stability can broadly be distinguished between "microstability," which involves conditions of individual financial institutions, and "macrostability," which focuses on the efficient functioning of the financial system as a whole. In a more intuitive sense, financial stability means that the financial sector can withstand financial shocks that are large enough to cause economic loss to the real economy. Here, we view macroeconomic financial stability as influenced not only by banks and other financial institutions but also by the volatility of asset prices. For example, when the stock market crashed with prices dropping by 20% on October 19, 1987, the financial sector remained stable. Not one financial institution collapsed. Furthermore, there was no recession in the real economy. Schinasi (2004) discusses the concept of financial stability in detail and proposes the following definition: "A financial system is in a range of stability whenever it is capable of facilitating (rather than impeding) the performance of an economy, and of dissipating financial imbalances that arise endogenously or as a result of significant and unanticipated events" (8).

Mishkin (2007) describes a financial system as stable if it performs the function of efficiently channeling funds to optimal investment opportunities. Friedman and Laibson (1989) focus on the role of stock markets and their extreme movements as part of the financial system allocating scarce capital resources. Suppose that financial stability means that the financial system allocates capital efficiently and the system becomes unstable when it fails to allocate capital resources efficiently. When the system is unstable, two types of interrelated risks emerge. First, the system experiences valuation risk, because the financial instability has increased uncertainty and traders have difficulty correctly measuring fundamental values of assets. Second, there is macroeconomic risk. This means that traders also need to assess the likelihood of a recession as a result of financial disruptions in investment and consumer spending. Thus, financial instability creates uncertainty, asset price volatility, and misallocation of capital—all of which negatively impact the real economy.

Let us proceed to ask what economic policies may contribute to financial stability. A fundamental interplay arises immediately. If an economy is conceptually separated into a real and financial sector—a tradition that goes back to classical economists who viewed money as a veil—the issue of real economic stability becomes relevant. Real economic stability, or just economic stability, means that the economy grows at its potential without inflation. Thus, a real sector that grows with full employment (generating about 250,000 jobs monthly for the United States) and price stability (meaning inflation only between 0% and 2.5%), and a financial sector that allocates capital efficiently—these developments characterize an ideal economic system. The goals of central banks are to ensure both economic and financial stability. Thus, economic and financial stability are mutually interdependent but not equivalent.

One important expectation of monetary policy during the 1970s and 1980s was that price stability would also bring financial stability. When inflation was high during the 1970s, asset prices were distorted. It was debated whether the stock market was a hedge against inflation. Housing prices increased in response to inflation in the late 1970s. The financial sector during this period performed poorly. Monetary policy targeting inflation was believed to lead to financial stability. Taylor (2002) documents the long journey of monetary policy from inflation and financial instability to price stability and the Great Moderation. He discusses how low and stable inflation rates reduce uncertainty and promote sound economic decisions. Price stability removes market distortions in price signals and, by anchoring inflation expectations, reduces risk premia in interest rates, along with the likelihood of misperceptions about future asset returns.

In a seminal paper, Bernanke and Gertler (1999) develop a macroeconomic model and obtain the result that price stability and financial stability are complementary and mutually consistent objectives. Ferguson (2002), Papademos (2006), and Plosser (2008) examine the interplay between price stability and financial stability. Often, an economy simultaneously experiences price and financial stabilities, as occurred during most of the 1990s. However, there have been periods of price inflation and financial stability, as occurred during the 1970s. Between 2000 and 2004, there was price stability with financial instability. Currently, we have price stability, but markets remain financially unstable. Borio and White (2003) tell us that episodes of financial instabilities with serious macroeconomic costs have taken place with greater frequency in the last 30 years than earlier in the midst of price stability, both in developed and emerging markets. In other words, in the presence of price stability, financial markets have recently become more volatile than in the past.

Once inflation was conquered in the early 1980s, the challenge of financial instability arose again. Greenspan (2004, 2005) reflects on this issue of price stability producing a decrease in the volatility of the real sector but, paradoxically, an increase in financial volatility. Rajan (2005) articulates in detail how the financial system has increased risk. Most of the time, central banks pursue their mandated price stability goal; however, during periods of financial crises, central banks give priority to stabilizing the financial sector in order to contain losses to the real sector. Thus, price stability is neither necessary nor sufficient for financial stability.

Borio and White (2003) explore this paradox and argue that, in order to resolve it, one must examine carefully the pro-cyclicality of the financial sector. In an environment of economic growth, with a credible monetary policy that is achieving its primary objective of price stability, the financial sector may expand rapidly and asset prices may increase. Confidence based on sound economic performance tends to drive up both the amount of credit and asset prices. If monetary policy continues to only pursue price stability, the eventual decline in asset prices may destabilize the financial system and the economy.

If a successful monetary policy, such as the one during the Great Moderation, cannot produce long-term financial stability, can financial instability impact monetary policy? Yes. Papademos (2006) argues that a reduction of interest rates, for example, may have weaker effects if the financial system is unstable than under normal conditions, because increasing risk premia may prevent most lending rates from falling, or because of credit rationing arising from a general unwillingness on the part of banks to lend. A striking example of this has been the late 1980s asset price bubble in Japan. Plummeting asset prices and rising nonperforming loans have undermined the solvency position of banks, making them unwilling to lend, or perhaps incapable of lending. The extremely accommodating policy stance, with interest rates close to 0%, did not reopen the bank lending channel. The United States has maintained an essentially zero Fed funds rate and implemented three rounds of aggressive quantitative easing to address its unemployment problem that resulted from the financial crisis. The slow improvement in the job market is evidence that financial instability constrains the efficacy of monetary policy.

Domestic financial stability is also closely interrelated to the global monetary system. Mishkin develops a conceptual framework for global monetary instability and concludes by proposing the following definition: "Financial instability occurs when shocks to the financial system interfere with information flows so that the system can no longer do its job of channeling funds to those countries with productive investment opportunities" (1999, 6).

Rosengren (2011) offers valuable insights into the topic of financial instability. He first declares that the topic is complex and widely acceptable definitions do not currently exist. He explains how the Dodd-Frank Act focuses on financial stability without defining this term. Also, the newly created Financial Stability Oversight Council by the Dodd-Frank Act has not yet proposed a definition of financial stability. Rosengren provides the following definition: "Financial stability reflects the ability of the financial system to consistently supply the credit intermediation and payment services that are needed in the real economy if it is to continue on its growth path" (2011, 2).

Yellen (2014) revisits the topic of financial stability. Central banks are viewed as providers of such financial stability. For the Fed, such a goal must be integrated with the dual mandate of low inflation and maximum employment. What tools are available for the accomplishment of all these goals? Yellen discusses, in detail, how monetary and other policymakers should balance monetary policy with macroprudential approaches, to limit the buildup of systemic risk in an economy and achieve financial stability. It is important to underline, that the European Central Bank has similar views. For example, Vitor Constancio (2015) also proposes macroprudential policies to address financial stability problems.

Beyond the definitions of stability given above, Brock and Malliaris (1989) present a comprehensive exposition of the technical concept of stability and its applications to economics. They define stability as a special property that allows an economic system to return quickly to its original state after an exogenous or endogenous shock. These authors view an economic system as a group of relationships between endogenous variables represented as a vector X, exogenous variables as I, and random shocks as U. Furthermore, one can decompose the vector X into real variables R and financial variables F, so that $X = R + F$. In such a system of real and financial variables, some endogenous to the system while others are exogenous, we begin by identifying one key target variable. Suppose that real GDP is one such key endogenous variable that is used to monitor the stability of the system. Disturbances in such a system may occur because of shocks to X, real or financial, or I, or U. One may wish to characterize the source(s) of instability arising endogenously (drop in productivity, technology), or exogenously (decline in foreign trade or foreign currencies), or from random shocks (terrorist attacks, wars, natural disasters). We may in particular be interested in disturbances in the financial sector F or in any other variable that immediately involves F.

A system $f(X, I, U)$ is stable if shocks to any of the variables R, F, I or U do not translate to deviations from trend GDP. If such shocks cause deviations from trend GDP (say a recession), then we say the system is unstable. In particular the system is financially unstable if a shock in some financial variable F causes a recession, and prevents the economy's GDP from recovering quickly. Mishkin (2007) and Rosengren (2011) focus on financial instability as the case when the financial sector fails to allocate financial resources for the regular operation of the real economy.

It remains a formidable analytical challenge to develop a sufficiently complete macroeconomic model that is capable of addressing factors contributing to macroeconomic instability. Such a model needs to distinguish between endogenously caused instability, due to real or financial factors, and exogenously caused instability, due to random shocks. Asset price bubbles straddle the real and financial sectors with their fundamentals driven by the real sector and the bubble component by the financial sector. If the fundamentals disappoint, the bubbles burst. When the bubble bursts, the financial sector becomes unstable, because of excessive credit and leverage and transmits this instability to the real sector. Acemoglu, Ozdaglar, and Tahbaz-Salehi (2015) develop a unified framework for network interactions and study the role of systemic risk. Haldane (2014) extends these methodological issues even further to consider the global financial system and the systemic risks associated with it.

This brief bibliographical discussion leads to the observation that, when asset price bubbles burst, they often cause financial instability. This instability in turn diminishes the effectiveness of the financial sector to allocate capital efficiently, and it may also reduce the effectiveness of monetary policy. Furthermore, it is not known how long such instability could last; to put it differently, it is unknown how quickly both the financial and real sectors can recover.

METHODOLOGY

As we proceed to analyze the four phases of economic cycles for a variety of economic and financial variables, we distinguish between two broad possibilities. First, if an economy and its financial sector are sufficiently stable to absorb random and significant shocks, then such an economy will exhibit regular cyclical behavior. Second, and more importantly, if the shocks destabilize the financial sector, which in turn destabilizes the real economy, then the four phases of the cyclical behavior get distorted. For example, the expansion phase may exhibit a financial bubble, the recession may be longer and involve a financial crisis, and the lower turning phase may be prolonged and described as a liquidity trap. Mainstream macroeconomics and financial economics is well suited to describe stable economies. The less mainstream ideas of behavioral finance and the Minsky-Kindleberger-Keynes views about financial crises help us understand financial instabilities. When we write Minsky-Kindleberger-Keynes, we denote the special emphasis these economists gave to certain phases of the business cycles. Minsky emphasizes how an economy moves from financial stability to expansive lending, which leads to economic optimism and irrational exuberance with the formation of asset bubbles. Briefly, Minsky claims that financial stability leads to financial instability, which occurs at the upper turning period of the cycle. Kindleberger follows Minsky and discusses how booms develop and how panics and the bursting of asset bubbles follow. Some asset bubbles cause major losses to the real economy as during the Great Crash of 1929, or the recent recession of 2007–2009. Keynes investigates the failure of aggregate demand to generate economic growth during periods of major economic crises. Krugman (2015) briefly talks about the Minsky-Bagehot-Keynes sequence to emphasize the role of central banks as lenders of last resort, during great asset bubble bursts, which freeze the financial system and cause serious economic recessions. Methodologically, we support an integration of orthodox neo-Keynesian macroeconomic analysis with Minsky and Kindleberger.

Both mainstream and less mainstream or neglected methodologies have been employed in numerous narratives of the most recent crises, without clarifications when authors make implicit methodological transitions. To avoid potential confusion, we describe each methodology, briefly, to facilitate our purpose to eclectically rope elements of each in the formation of our four hypotheses.

Prior to the global financial crisis, conventional economics as a discipline was founded on certain well-accepted premises. Chief among them were (and continue to be) rational consumers with explicit utility functions, who choose among various goods with producers who are profit maximizers. Both trade in a price system that correctly forms prices, which act as signals for the optimal allocation of resources and distribution of goods. Such a price system reaches an equilibrium that has the property of being stable. Growth is driven by labor growth and labor productivity that depend upon capital and technology. In such a system, the banking sector and more generally the financial sector facilitate the process of intermediation, by collecting savings from agents that forego today's consumption, and allocating these savings to entrepreneurs for investments. The financial sector and asset prices fully reflect all publically available information, so markets are efficient and prices follow random walks. Agents form rational expectations by correctly assessing all available information and knowing the functioning of the economic system. The role of monetary policy is to make sure prices remain stable and this stability is achieved via a Taylor rule, which determines the Fed funds rate. Haldane (2012) expands this topic and traces its historical foundations.

What does the system described above neglect? It does not allow agents violating rationality, which may in turn, cause the deviation of prices from fundamentals. So asset bubbles are not widely recognized in conventional economics (although there are some minor exceptions). In addition, instabilities are not possible, because the system is self-regulated and prices are flexible. If housing demand collapses, for example, prices automatically drop as low as needed to clear the market. More importantly, this view of the economy does not accommodate the reality of economic crises, since most crises are triggered by instabilities, and the free-market paradigm does not admit instabilities. It was this conventional economics that dominated the Fed's doctrines and policies reported by the *New York Times* on October 23, 2008:

> "I have found a flaw" in free market theory, Greenspan said under intense questioning by Representative Henry Waxman, the Democratic chairman of the Government Oversight Committee of the House of Representatives. "I don't know how significant or permanent it is," Greenspan added. "But I have been very distressed by that fact."

In contrast to conventional economics, behavioral finance considers deviations from rationality. The deviations allowed are not drastic enough to move economic theorizing into the irrational domain of human behavior; rather, behavioral finance recognizes the ontological, economic realities and invokes psychology to explain deviations of prices from fundamentals. Asset price bubbles are viewed by behavioral finance as the consequence of deviations from rationality due to overconfidence by investors, herding, extrapolation from limited samples, and other reasons to be discussed in the next section. Once asset price bubbles are introduced into a modified conventional economic system, asset bubble crashes can be admitted and the possibility of a crisis can be seriously entertained.

Lastly, a Minsky-Kindleberger-Keynes paradigm postulates the fundamental axiom that the capitalist system is inherently unstable. Keynes (1936) connects this instability to investment that is driven by "animal spirits." Koppl (1991) explains this concept in a manner that is truthful to Keynes' conception. Akerlof and Shiller (2009) generalize the idea of animal spirits and give numerous novel illustrations. Minsky attributes the instability of the capitalist system to the financial sector by formulating his famous "financial instability hypothesis," and Kindleberger adopts the Minskyan hypothesis as a theoretical framework to analyze historical economic crises. Therefore it is important to clarify the concept of "animal spirits" and the "financial instability hypothesis."

The concept of animal spirits was introduced in Keynes's book *The General Theory* (1936, ch. 12). In that chapter, Keynes explores the determinants of long-run expectations. These are the expectations that drive economic action, and Keynes identifies animal spirits as their critical determinant. The concept of animal spirits appears only three times in the book, and all three times in the following passages from chapter 12:

> Even apart from the instability due to speculation, there is the instability due to the characteristic of human nature that a large proportion of our positive activities depend on spontaneous optimism rather than on a mathematical expectation, whether moral or hedonistic or economic. *Most, probably, of our decisions to do something positive, the full consequences of which will be drawn out over many days to come, can only be taken as a result of animal spirits—of a spontaneous urge to action rather than inaction, and not as the outcome of a weighted average of quantitative benefits multiplied by quantitative probabilities.* Enterprise only pretends to itself to be mainly actuated by the statements in its own prospectus, however candid and sincere. Only a little more than an expedition to the South Pole, is it based on an exact calculation of benefits to come. *Thus if the animal spirits are dimmed and the spontaneous optimism falters, leaving us to depend on nothing but a mathematical expectation, enterprise will fade and die;*—though fears of loss may have a basis no more reasonable than hopes of profit had before.
>
> It is safe to say that enterprise which depends on hopes stretching into the future benefits the community as a whole. *But individual initiative will only be adequate when reasonable calculation is supplemented and supported by animal spirits, so that the thought of ultimate loss which often overtakes pioneers, as experience undoubtedly tells us and them, is put aside as a healthy man puts aside the expectation of death.* (Keynes 2008 [1936], 144, italics our emphasis)

Several conclusions follow immediately from these passages. First, animal spirits describe the spontaneous urge for action rather than inaction. Put differently, animal spirits are the invisible force in humans that drives thought, feeling, and action. Second, animal spirits describe human emotion that drives optimism. Third, in the face of future long-term uncertainty, careful mathematical calculations become unreliable and thus are not sufficient for action. Action is taken only when probable mathematical expectations are supplemented and supported by animal spirits. Fourth, animal spirits, for Keynes, are both the trigger for action as well as the root of instability. The trigger for action is prompted by mass psychology, described in Keynes's illustration of the beauty contest. Animal spirits are also the root of instability when waves of optimism are replaced suddenly by pessimism.

Minsky (1975, 1986) unwearyingly opined that financial crises have been coupled with capitalism throughout history. He has also argued that Keynes's principal contribution was his hypothesis that capitalism is inherently unstable. Furthermore, such instability originates in the financial sector, due to allocation of capital to investment decisions driven by animal spirits. Minsky (1986) develops these Keynesian ideas into his famous financial instability hypothesis. He argues that in a modern capitalist economy, with expensive capital assets and a complex and sophisticated financial system, actual economic activity is greatly influenced by firms' expectations of future profits and financing decisions by banks and other financial institutions. Minsky proposes a credit cycle model of five stages: displacement, boom, euphoria, profit-taking, and panic. There is an active interplay between the real economy and the financial sector in this process. Minsky (1968) describes how asset managers become optimistic with new technology, such as the Internet, and are willing to finance it. Gradually, this sector grows and an asset boom develops. As the sector attracts new funding, further technologies are developed, and the financial and technological euphoria grows. Certain triggering events, such as disappointing earnings, lead to profit-taking. Further, deterioration in fundamentals translates into a panic. The bursting of an asset bubble leads to financial instability that causes real sector instability. Further detailed analysis of Minsky's ideas is presented in Chapters 3, 4, and 5 in this book.

In spite of Minsky's concerns about the inherent financial instability of capitalism, the Great Moderation doctrine, supported by empirical evidence, led to the conclusion that "this time is different." Reinhart and Rogoff (2009) argue that this assessment of economic conditions is a recurrent theme. They offer comprehensive narratives and analysis of the connections between the financial and real sectors of an economy, how financial crises impact both sectors, and how financial crises appear idiosyncratic. Details may differ, because of the rapidly evolving financial sector, but the essential mechanisms of positive feedback followed by negative feedback persist.

THE RECENT GLOBAL FINANCIAL CRISIS

The financial crisis began as a subprime mortgage lending problem in the summer of 2007 and evolved to become one of the worst recessions since the Great Depression. It quickly impacted the real economy. By the NBER, the economic recession started shortly after the subprime mortgage problems in December 2007 and lasted until June 2009. During this period, more than 15 million workers were permanently displaced from their jobs; the unemployment rate increased from about 4.8% to about 10%; real GDP dropped by about 4% from its previous cyclical peak during the fourth quarter 2007 to the trough of the second quarter of 2009; and the S&P 500 declined from its peak of 1,561 on October 12, 2007, to 676 on March 9, 2009, a drop of 57%. Kolb (2011) gives a clear and comprehensive overview of considerable research conducted during the past five years exploring the causes of the financial crisis.

The likely causes can be categorized in several subgroups, including factors rooted in the microeconomics of housing supply and demand (such as increases in housing prices or bubbles, the formation of expectations of further increases in housing prices, subprime lending, opaque derivative securities, excessive risk taking, and failed risk management strategies), macroeconomics and monetary policy (low interest rates during 2002–04 and the decline in housing prices in late 2006, for example), government deregulation (including the abolition of the Glass-Steagal Act and the absence of regulation for credit derivatives), institutional issues (problems with rating agencies, originate to distribute), global considerations (saving gluts, fixed exchange rates for certain countries such as China), and ethical violations (such as greed and corruption). It is important to observe that this brief list is both incomplete and unsettled.

The intensity, complexity, and length of the crisis justify the multiplicity and interrelatedness of causal factors. These factors are now woven into analytical frameworks and empirical scenarios to facilitate our understanding of why and how it happened, and to help us discover ways to both get out of it and avoid its reoccurrence. In this essay, we refocus the spotlight on the cyclical nature of the business cycle, beginning with the recovery from the previous recession, identifying the formation of a housing bubble as an important driver of the expansion phase of the cycle, then moving to discuss the top turning point and the Great Recession, and concluding with the lower turning point characterized by the liquidity trap phase. We hypothesize the idea of a sequence of asset bubbles that were an integral part of the financial and economic landscape during the last decade, and argue that their investigation can give us valuable clues about both the occurrence of the crisis and its ultimate resolution. Another way to describe the contribution of this paper is to say that the global financial crisis of 2007–2009 has multiple subsets of causes that contribute to an overall complex system.

THE EXPANSION PHASE

As already noted, the most recent cycle, according to the NBER, began in December 2001 and lasted until the end of November 2007. To motivate the discussion of this section, we briefly describe the 2001 recession.

According to the NBER, the 2001 recession began in March 2001 and ended by the end of November in the same year. Compared to historical averages, it was short and shallow. There are numerous detailed analyses about this recession; in this chapter we follow Kliesen (2003) to highlight some important characteristics. To begin with, the recession of 2001 lasted about 8 months in comparison to the average duration of 11 months for all post–WWII recessions. In addition, it was milder, with real GDP growing at about 0.2% during the recession in contrast to an average decline of about 2.6% for all post–WWII recessions. Consumer spending remained above average, but residential construction declined by more than the average of past recessions because conventional mortgage rates had risen from about 6.75% during December 1998 to 8.5% by April 2000. The increase in these long-term rates was impacted by a restrictive monetary policy.

From June 1999 to May 2000, the Federal Open Market Committee (FOMC) had increased Fed funds from about 4.75% to 6.50%. During the recession, the United States suffered from the historic terrorist attack of 9/11 as well as the dramatic declines in equities. The NASDAQ Composite Index, after it had reached a historic peak of about 5,050 in early March 2000, proceeded to decline until it hit about 2,000 in November 2001, when the recession officially ended, but continued to decline until September 30, 2002, when it stood at 1,140, a decline of about 80% from its historic peak. The broader S&P 500 Index peaked at 1,527 in mid-March 2000, declined to about 2,000 at the end of the recession and continued its decline until the end of September 2002 when it closed at about 800, a total decline of about 50%. The most probable trigger of these dramatic declines in equity prices, called the "crash of the tech bubble," was the difficulty to sustain what Chairman Greenspan called "the irrational exuberance" in high-tech hardware and software in 2000 after it became apparent that the exaggerated Y2K fears were unfounded.

To reduce the risks from the bursting of the tech bubble (also called the dot-com bubble), the 2001 recession, and the terrorist attack of 9/11, the FOMC started reducing Fed funds that stood then at 6.50% in January 2001. By December 2001,

Fed funds had dropped to 1.75%, where they remained for most of 2002. They were further dropped to 1.25% during 2003 and then to 1% for about half of 2004 before they began to rise again. This expansionary monetary policy helped the 2001 recession to be shorter and milder. Also, monetary policy remained stimulative, because the recovery was very weak and, perhaps unexpectedly, contributed to the development of the housing bubble.

During the expansion between December 2001 and November 2007, the seeds of the global financial crisis were planted. Yet, Bivens and Irons (2008) give a list of key characteristics of this expansion that offer only limited evidence of what was to follow. In particular, the 2001–07 expansion ranks last in terms of average growth of GDP, investment, employment growth, and employee compensation when compared with the ten expansions since 1949. Only corporate profits were stronger during this expansion when compared to the previous average corporate profits of the last ten expansions. This underperformance becomes a puzzle when we recall that the Bush administration and Congress enacted two major tax cuts in 2001 and 2003, which added over $1 trillion in federal deficit spending. In addition to very stimulative fiscal and monetary policies, during the first years of the expansion and until the Fed proceeded to increase the Fed funds in mid-2004, housing price increases added to household wealth. These wealth increases, record levels of residential investment spending, the ability of households to withdraw equity from their homes for consumption purposes, and the foreign saving glut all contributed to the formation of the housing bubble without accelerating real GDP growth and employment.

What is an asset price bubble? Do bubbles exist in financial markets? Why do they form? Why do they grow? Why do they burst? The term "bubble" was first introduced to describe the famous price run-up and crash of the shares in the South Sea Company in 1720 in England. Since then, numerous financial episodes described as bubbles have occurred and are described in Kindleberger and Aliber (2005).

From the 1960s to the mid-1990s, the market efficiency paradigm of Fama (1970) argued that financial markets reflect all publically available information regarding the fundamental factors that drive asset prices. Using this precise definition of market efficiency, changes in asset prices occur due to changes in information about fundamentals. Rational investors quickly evaluate new information about the fundamentals of an asset, and by taking appropriate positions formulated by the assessment of new fundamentals, market prices are formed. This so-called market efficiency hypothesis, with an exact definition and appropriate empirical testing methods, resulted in a large number of scientific studies during the 1970s and 1980s, to such a degree that market efficiency remains the most contested hypothesis in financial economics. According to this theory, since observed market prices equal fundamental values, asset bubbles cannot exist. Thus, according to the market efficiency hypothesis, asset bubbles cannot exist and, consequently, public policy issues to address such asset bubbles are not pertinent.

In contrast to market efficiency advocates, a group of economists led by Kindleberger (1978) and Minsky (1986) have argued that asset prices could be driven by factors other than fundamentals. In their scenarios, such valuations resulted in asset bubbles. The critical motivation of these authors was to explain the rapid increase of asset prices followed by even faster declines. Such behavior is also described as asset booms and busts. Kindleberger also cites several events such as the boom during the late 1920s that resulted in the Great Crash of October 1929.

Can a phenomenon of asset prices exceeding their fundamentals for several months, perhaps a few years, demonstrate that financial markets are inefficient? Often, after asset prices deviate positively and substantially from fundamentals for a few years, as in 1929, a certain triggering event causes asset prices to decline very rapidly. Thus, if the price of an asset exceeds its fundamentals by a large amount for several months or years, and then price increases reverse quickly, we have what some economists call an asset bubble.

It is worth noting, that the market efficiency hypothesis has difficulty explaining both price increases unjustified by fundamentals as well as sudden reversals, which may also be unjustified by fundamentals. Clearly, this definition lacks precision, since the exact meanings of "fundamentals," "significant amount," "persistence," and "some time" cannot be described with accuracy. If the price of an asset exceeds its fundamentals only by a small amount, the differential may only represent noise instead of a bubble. If the deviation from fundamentals lasts for only a short trading interval, this may represent temporary mispricing.

Currently, an increasing number of financial economists, unconvinced by the theory and empirical evidence of market efficiency, are pursuing the study of financial bubbles. These behavioral, financial economists are attempting to develop theories for several financial anomalies, including asset bubbles. Kindleberger (1978) and Brunnermeier (2008) describe a bubble as an upward price movement over an extended range that suddenly implodes. These authors do not introduce the notion of fundamentals in their definition. They argue that bubbles form because the purchase of an asset is made based not on the rate of return on the investment but in anticipation that the asset can be sold to a "greater fool" at an even higher price.

Not all bubbles are alike; each asset bubble has certain unique characteristics. For example, the Internet bubble of 1994–2000 and the housing bubble of 2002–2007, are not the same. Greenspan summarizes the central features of asset bubbles:

> Bubbles thus appear to primarily reflect exuberance on the part of investors in pricing financial assets. If managers and investors perceived the same degree of risk, and both correctly judged a sustainable rise in profits stemming from new technology, for example, none of a rise in stock prices would reflect a bubble. Bubbles appear to emerge when investors either overestimate the sustainable rise in profits or unrealistically lower the rate of discount they apply to expected profits and dividends. The distinction cannot readily be ascertained from market prices. (2002, 7)

For new innovations, whose future earnings are very uncertain, the pricing of fundamentals can have a particularly large margin of error. Historically, stock bubbles developed and then crashed when new technologies such as railroad, electricity, aviation, automobile, radio, pharmaceutical, Internet, and bio-technology firms were introduced. This uncertainty may also explain the Internet crash that started in early 2000, when the NASDAQ dropped from about 5,000 to 1,140 by mid-2002, a decline of over 75%.

Following Kindleberger, if a bubble develops, because of the high uncertainty surrounding the fundamentals of a new innovation, such as railroad, electricity, or

Internet, these bubbles have very special characteristics, because each innovation differs substantially from previous ones. As already indicated, this implies that each bubble is unique and difficult to discern in its initial development when the uncertainty about the long-run fundamentals has a very wide range of outcomes. If the idea that asset bubbles grow—because of new technological innovations or major policy changes, such as federal housing policies—is acceptable, then the claim that bubbles exist and are frequent makes sense.

Up to this point, we have described conceptual issues about asset bubbles. There is a large and evolving economics literature that addresses these conceptual issues and investigates conditions for the emergence of asset bubbles, reasons for growth, and their eventual bursting. Brunnermeier (2008), Scherbina and Schlusche (2011), and Jones (2015) carefully organize the asset bubble literature and describe rational and behavioral models. Barberis (2013) describes how psychology can help explain bubbles and relates these ideas to the recent global financial crisis.

More specifically, Barberis distinguishes asset price bubbles formed on the basis of investor beliefs from ones formed on investor preferences. Let us first discuss bubbles that are driven by investor beliefs. First, in certain situations like new technological innovations, investors may disagree strongly about the asset's future fundamentals. If in situations of such disagreement, we also add short-sale constraints, the bearish investors become constrained while the bullish are left to drive the price high. Of course, a large pool of bullish investors is needed; such investors buy, because they hope to sell higher to future bullish investors. But, one may ask, where does such bullishness come from? Second, psychology can be used to explain why some investors' beliefs may be very bullish. Suppose that investors carefully research a certain investment, which often leads to overconfidence as investors overestimate the accuracy of their predictions. Furthermore, following Kahneman and Trevsky's (1974, 1992) representative heuristic that claims agents expect small samples to represent well the characteristics of larger population, a relatively small sample of initial successes can easily generate overconfidence, and thus bullishness can be extended into the future. Suppose also that some initial success leads to overconfidence that is extended into the future; if investors materialize certain profits, psychology indicates that investors become less risk averse with their gains.

Behavioral economist Shiller (2002) argues that a key factor influencing the formation of bubbles, and their eventual bursting, is the feedback mechanism. A price increase for an asset leads to investor enthusiasm, which causes increased demand and additional price increases, and so on. The high demand is supported by the public's memory of high past returns, or by optimism that this new asset will generate high future earnings. Different bubbles have different positive feedback mechanisms. But since price increases driven by factors other than the asset's fundamentals cannot be sustained indefinitely, a negative feedback pattern will eventually replace the positive one—that is, the bubble will eventually burst. Usually, the initial price increases are slow; it takes a long time for the bubble to grow. In contrast, bubble crashes take place quite quickly. In this spirit, Akerlof and Shiller (2009) stress the role of Keynes's animal spirits and demonstrate their importance in creating, fueling, and leading to the bursting of bubbles. How can the ideas expressed thus far be formulated into a set of hypotheses describing the expansion from January 2002 to January 2007?

Clearly the most distinctive economic episode of the 2001 expansion was the formation of a housing bubble. We hypothesize that this bubble was fueled by several factors. For example, easy monetary policy, during 2001–2004, may have contributed to the formation of the housing bubble. Recall that we emphasized that the bursting of the dot-com bubble, the major decline in the S&P 500 Index, and the subsequent declines in US wealth; the 9/11 terrorist attack; low inflation; and the subpar economic recovery all made such easy monetary policy suitable for the conditions that prevailed. During the 2001 to the mid-2004 period, the Fed's actions of expansionary monetary policy were in accord with its mandate to pursue maximum employment. Taylor (2007) argues that monetary policy caused the housing bubble. Bernanke (2010) supplies detailed evidence that the housing bubble cannot be attributed to monetary policy. We offer a milder hypothesis that the expansionary monetary policy may have inadvertently contributed to the housing bubble. Hayford and Malliaris (2004, 2005) find similar evidence for the impact of monetary policy during the stock market bubble of 1996 to 2000.

A second factor that may have contributed to the housing bubble is global imbalances. Bernanke (2005, 2007, and 2011) has articulated the role of global imbalances, their impact on long-term interest rates, and their influence on housing prices.

The size and intensity of the housing bubble, as evidenced not only from its sharp increase, but also subsequent decline and stagnation over a period of about five years, calls for both a behavioral finance hypothesis and a broader Keynes-Kindleberger-Minsky hypothesis. The behavioral finance concepts of short-sale constraints, the representative heuristic, and overconfidence are all relevant hypotheses in the formation of the housing bubble. Keynes-Kindleberger-Minsky will go further and hypothesize that the housing bubble was fueled not only by investors driven by behavioral finance arguments but also by the entire financial sector. In particular, Minsky (1986) elaborates on the role of the financial sector in destabilizing the real economy.

A related hypothesis addresses the potential relationship between the NASDAQ, and to a lesser extent the S&P 500 bubbles of 2005–2010, with the housing bubble. After all, it was the crash of the dot-com bubble that partially induced the easy monetary policy of the early 2000s. Is there a connection between the stock market and subsequent housing market bubbles? Jalilvand and Malliaris (2010) explore the possibility of a sequence of bubbles and the issue of the efficient allocation of capital during asset bubbles. In conducting a welfare analysis, consider, for example, the Internet bubble of the late 1990s and the 2000s housing bubble. Again, these bubbles resulted in significant price run ups and subsequent declines in the respective assets (Internet firms and housing), only to be repriced at substantial discounts after the bubbles burst during the financial crisis. Given such volatility, one has to wonder whether capital allocation based on such price bubbles was efficient. The Internet bubble pushed the NASDAQ index to a record level of nearly 5,000 in early 2000, only to have it drop below 1,140 in September 2002. For the housing bubble, the S&P/Case-Shiller National Home Price Index reached a peak of 190 in 2006, only to drop to about 130 in 2008 (see Figure 2.3). Although it is not often considered, these bubbles could have resulted in significant welfare implications. As both bubbles were growing, scarce capital was increasingly allocated to the booming

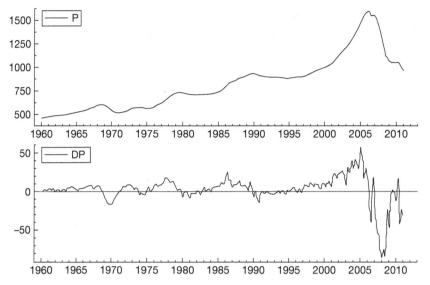

Figure 2.3 US Real House Prices (Deflated by CPI Less Shelter). Seasonally adjusted in upper panel. Lower panel shows first-differences of the same series.
DATA SOURCE: Davis et al. (2008).

sectors. Indeed, Chirinko and Schaller (2012) find evidence that is consistent with a misallocation of capital.

In summary, traditional economic analysis; behavioral finance; a broader Minsky-Kindleberger-Keynes perspective; and government policies for housing, regulation, monetary policies, and global imbalances all together present a more comprehensive perspective of the housing bubble and the otherwise subpar expansion of 2001–2007.

This analysis leads us to realize certain facts that, just a few years ago, at the high period of the market efficiency hypothesis, traditional economists would have expressed serious skepticism over. These are: (1) theoretical models and empirical evidence support the existence of bubbles; (2) asset bubbles are more likely when new technologies, financial innovations, major changes in regulation, and other significant events generate great uncertainty in valuations; (3) bubbles are hard to discern because each bubble appears to have very unique characteristics and conditions for its emergence; and (4) despite the unique characteristics of each bubble, there appears to be a uniform pattern of its evolution.

This evolution is described in some detail by Kindleberger (1978); Minsky (1986); Dudley (2010); and more comprehensively in Evanoff, Kaufman, and Malliaris (2012). The approximate evolution involves several phases. First, certain positive initial triggers emerge, such as new technological or financial innovations, major shifts in social preferences, or unanticipated constructive political and economic changes. Second, asset prices increase in the initial stage slowly; biased beliefs about future profitability and returns are formed with a divergence of opinion between optimists and skeptics. Third, optimists drive prices higher, and market expectations are driven by exuberance; positive feedback drives prices even higher; constraints and risks to short selling cannot moderate price increases. Fourth, the proportion of traders that are optimists increases relative to the pessimists; overconfidence increases; at some point, exuberance and overconfidence are contradicted or challenged by facts; and finally, the proportion of optimists declines sharply and the positive feedback turns negative, causing the bubble to deflate rapidly.

Thus, in the view of a large number of financial economists, bubbles do exist, regardless of how tentative our comprehension of them is. In fact, we argue they need to be further studied so economists get a better understanding of this market phenomenon.

THE UPPER TURNING PERIOD

In the previous section, we described the major economic developments that took place during the economic expansion that the NBER dates between December 2001 and November 2007. We propose that the upper turning period spans from February 2007 to September 2008. Why? First, prior to February 2007, some data had signaled that the expansion was faltering, but there was no solid evidence that it was in serious trouble. For example, by mid-2006, the S&P/Case-Shiller Home Price Index had peaked and started its decline later in that year. These price declines caused the US Home Construction Index to also decline during 2006. Second, 2006 was a challenging year in general for the housing industry, because during that year, the housing market slowed down, home prices fell, construction declined, and an inventory upsurge of unsold homes took place. Third, subprime mortgages that barely existed in 1995 had grown to about 8% of all mortgages in 2004 and up to 20% by 2006. Also, most of these subprime mortgages—90% by 2006—were adjustable rate. These products were riskier and grew because of lower lending standards. By 2006, subprime mortgage delinquencies were growing. Finally, US households had become increasingly overburdened with debt. The debt-to-disposable-income ratio had increased to about 125% by 2006.

These facts contributed to increased uncertainty about the future of the housing bubble. Monetary policy had also become tighter, with Fed funds increasing from about 1% in mid-2004 to 5.25% by mid-2006. However, during 2006, toward the end of the year, there was no clear evidence that the housing boom had come to an unambiguous end. This uncertainty increased during 2007 and reached its highest level in mid-September 2008 when Lehman Brothers failed. Thus, it was between February 2007 and September 2008 that it became highly probable that the expansion was coming to an end and the uncertainty of financial instability had increased. As was reported numerous times, the NBER peak in November 2007 is the approximate midpoint of our turning period.

Let us now consider some of the most relevant events that took place during the February 2007–September 2008 turning period. Broadly speaking, it is during this period that the financial crisis took shape. It was not known then that this crisis would spread to become a global crisis. There were worries about a recession, but no one anticipated its severity.

Some key events that will guide us in formulating our hypotheses include the following: In early April 2007, New Century Financial, which specialized in subprime mortgages, filed for Chapter 11 bankruptcy protection. In June 2007, two of Bear Stearns' hedge funds with large holdings of subprime mortgages experienced large losses and were forced to sell assets affecting other firms such as Merrill Lynch, Goldman Sachs, Citigroup, and J. P. Morgan. In October 2007, Merrill Lynch's chief executive resigned after the bank reported a $7.9 billion exposure to bad debt; it was reported in December 2007 that one million homeowners were facing foreclosures; in March 2008, Bear Stearns was bought by J. P. Morgan. Also in March 2008, the Federal Reserve made $200 billion available to banks and other institutions to try to improve market liquidity. In July 2008, IndyMac became the largest thrift ever to fail in the United States. During September 2008, the crisis escalated: mortgage lenders Fannie Mae and Freddie Mac, accounting for about half of the outstanding mortgages in the United States were rescued by the US government in one of history's largest bailouts; Lehman Brothers filed for bankruptcy; the share price of the Fed's primary money market mutual fund fell below the $1 mark, because $785 million of its $64.8 billion were issued by the bankrupted Lehman Brothers; Bank of America took over Merrill Lynch; Morgan Stanley and Goldman Sachs gave up their status as investment banks and became traditional banks with access to the Fed's discount window. A full "Timeline of Events and Policy Actions" may be found in Federal Reserve Bank of St. Louis web site ttp://timeline.stlouisfed.org/

Next, we proceed to formulate certain hypotheses about the upper turning period.

Price asset bubbles exhibit various patterns: some deflate on their own without any economic or financial consequences to the economy, and others crash with minimal impact on the real economy. For example, the bursting of the dot-com bubble in 2000 had only a limited impact on the economy during the brief 2001 recession. In contrast, some bubbles cause serious problems. Here, we hypothesize that what started as a housing bubble in the late 1990s and accelerated during 2001–2005 because of public policies encouraging home ownership, low interest rates, and the global saving glut progressed into a credit bubble supported by both the banking and shadow banking sectors, financial innovations, and loose financial regulations. The strong interdependence and positive feedback between the housing bubble and the credit bubble, helps explain the intensity of the crisis. It was from January 2007 to September 2008 that the housing bubble was associated with a credit bubble, mostly in the form of mortgage-backed securities.

Traditional economic analysis can easily show that the bursting of the housing bubble had an immediate impact, by causing an increase in housing inventory and quick declines in new home construction, with workers formerly employed in the housing industry becoming unemployed.

Behavioral finance claims that the disutility of losses is more than the utility of equivalent gains. So once the housing bubble could not be supported any longer and housing prices began to drop, prospect theory would argue that the disutility of homeowners from initial losses (beginning in the middle of 2006) caused these homeowners to sell. This was particularly true for households with mortgages bigger than the value of their homes. These households became delinquent in their mortgage payments and subsequently underwent bank foreclosures.

The central episodes of the upper turning period were both financial and economic instability. Our earlier background analysis of instability can be applied at this point. When it became clear in 2007 that the initial declines in housing prices were not temporary but indicative of the housing bubble having burst, the financial system that had supported the housing industry with the expectation of continued increases in prices suddenly froze; it no longer allocated any financial resources to this sector of the economy. Thus, while during periods of stability the financial sector efficiently allocates capital to productive investment opportunities, the financial sector does not allocate any capital during a period of instability. The reason is clear: if the financial sector has allocated capital in housing with inflated prices, price declines decrease the values of the assets held by the financial sector in the form of mortgages, losses are incurred, and—if the declines are large—insolvencies arise. Minsky's financial instability hypothesis is the most elaborate theory that addresses this phase of the crisis. It has remained outside the orthodox market economics paradigm, but the current crisis has brought much attention to his ideas.

Financial instability involves, first, certain events that initiate the crisis, often called triggers. Second, there is a rapid propagation and amplification of the crisis from some financial firms to the entire financial sector and eventually to the real economy. Finally, structural weaknesses in the financial sector that were not apparent during the boom become apparent and complicate the crisis. In addition to these elements of the crisis, the speed and force of responses by the regulating and political authorities become critical, because the expectations of economic agents become fragile and uncertainties are magnified. During such periods of panic, there is a wide range of multiple unstable equilibria.

The most likely triggers of the crisis during the upper turning period were the price declines in the housing market that accelerated during 2007 and the accompanying significant losses on residential subprime mortgages. The pool of these mortgages was about $1 trillion, and the losses were substantial, but in the end, the amplification of the crisis generated significantly bigger losses. Gorton (2008) documents how these initial mortgage losses caused lenders in the commercial paper market to withdraw their funds rather than invest in risky assets. This caused the initial subprime mortgage crisis to spread into various channels of short-term funding for both banks and the shadow banking sector. Cash was hoarded instead of being invested, liquidity dried up, and risk management systems failed, generating further losses and thus amplifying the magnitude of the crisis because of the high levels of leverage. Bernanke (2010) gives a detailed exposition of the process of propagation and amplification.

The hypothesis of financial amplification motivates a corresponding psychological amplification. Barberis (2013) and Krishnamurthy (2010), among others, reason that margin spirals, fire sales cycles, and accumulating losses contribute to significant loss and ambiguity aversion on the part of investors with large positions in risky assets. Behavioral finance has considered these concepts, and applications to the recent crisis can further contribute to our understanding of psychological amplification.

The upper turning period begins with some ambivalence over whether growth will continue or end; as evidence increases that the bubble has no further momentum, it becomes clearer that difficult adjustments lie ahead. Taleb (2013) discusses the two main patterns of transition periods: concave and convex. Naturally, the upper turning period is concave and once it is confirmed at some point past the maximum, investors recognize that the prospects for further gains have evaporated. The concavity property of the upper turning period implies losses and sales of assets, ultimately initiating the recession.

THE GREAT RECESSION OF 2007–2009

As we have already indicated, according to the NBER, the Great Recession began in December 2007 and ended in June 2009. In its September 20, 2010, announcement, the NBER described the downturn as the longest and deepest since the Great Depression. The Great Recession lasted for 18 months, and real GDP decreased by more than all other recessions since WWII. Since we argued that the upper turning period lasted until September 2008, our period of the Great Recession is shorter than NBER's: between October 2008 and June 2009.

In an earlier section, we gave some general characteristics of this Great Recession. Ohanian (2011) gives a detailed analysis and asserts that this recession was much different from others, particularly in terms of its impact on labor markets. The data below indicate that in terms of output, consumption, investment employment, and hours worked, changes from the peak of the cycle were greater for all measures during the 2007–2009 recession than the corresponding measure of the average of all other postwar recessions (see Table 2.1).

Why was the Great Recession of 2007–2009 so severe? Reinhart and Rogoff (2009) address this question by offering a comparative historical analysis that focuses on the aftermath of systemic banking crises. They focus on three dimensions of financial crises: asset market crashes, banking crises, and increases in the real value of government debt. Their evidence is not provided to prove a specific hypothesis; rather, it is presented as empirical evidence supporting the assertion that when recessions are accompanied by financial crises they are more severe. Financial crises are usually associated with banking crises when credit booms become credit busts. This means that banking crises occur when the value of their portfolios of assets and loans decline in value. This may or may not lead to bank runs when depositors who are concerned with the quality of a bank's assets withraw their deposits. Such runs need not occur because of depositors' insurance provided by the FDIC, but loan and asset defaults do in fact occur. For example, investments made in mortgage-backed securities and construction loans to developers lost value because of the housing crisis in the United States, while banks that invested in sovereign debt in certain Eurozone countries also experienced big losses. Such bank losses discourage banks from lending for some time and prolong economic recessions.

Ohanian (2011) considers the hypothesis that the Great Recession was made more severe because of the financial instability and concludes that this hypothesis cannot be supported. However, he finds that the Great Recession was made more severe

Table 2.1. 2007–2009 RECESSION VS. POSTWAR RECESSIONS, UNITED STATES (OHANIAN [2011] PERCENT CHANGE IN PER-CAPITA VALUES).

	Output	Consumption	Investment	Employment	Hours Worked
2007–2009 recession	−7.2	−5.4	−33.5	−6.7	−8.7
Average of other postwar recessions	−4.4	−2.1	−17.8	−3.8	−3.2

because of poor government policies. What were these policies by the government and how successful were they?

Blinder and Zandi (2010) and Auerbach, Gale, and Harris (2010) give a detailed presentation of the various fiscal programs and offer an evaluation of their effectiveness. Here we briefly mention some of the leading fiscal initiatives, including a stimulus package of $152 billion in tax rebates for 2008; tax credits for first-time homebuyers enacted in July 2008 and later extended and expanded in November 2009 and July 2010; the Troubled Asset Relief Program (TARP) enacted under Bush in fall of 2008, allocating $700 billion for the recapitalization of insolvent financial institutions via transfer of funds into banks, purchases of mortgage-backed securities and other private debt from banks, and the nationalization of AIG, the insurance company; the American Recovery and Reinvestment Act of February 2009, which allocated $787 billion for a combination of tax cuts, transfers to individuals and states, and government purchases; and the "cash for clunkers" program in the summer of 2009. These fiscal measures, pooled with aggressive monetary policy, brought the Great Recession to an end. Below, we formulate some key hypotheses for the severity and duration of the Great Recession.

During normal times, housing construction contributes about 5% of employment and output to the real economy. However, during the housing bubble, this sector increased substantially in significance, because of its numerous interrelations, the proliferation of home equity loans, the many financial innovations associated with mortgages, and the impact of these innovations on the growth of the financial industry. Thus the bursting of the housing bubble had a bigger impact than the bursting of the dot-com bubble. Two recent studies by Tcherneva (2012) and Boldrin, Garriga, Peralta-Alva, and Sanchez (2012) explore this issue.

Ohanian (2011) is inclined to attribute the difficulties of the Great Recession to insufficient government policies. Going beyond traditional economics and invoking Keynes's animal spirits, we hypothesize that fiscal policies perform poorly after major housing bubbles burst for two reasons: first, households reduce their spending since they experience substantial loss in their housing equity and thus decrease the magnitude of fiscal multipliers, and second, entrepreneurs simultaneously face increased uncertainty as they anticipate the swelling of future public debt. For fiscal policy to be effective, it needs to both address the short-term weaknesses of the economy and clarify the future reduction in public debt. Only when both issues are addressed is uncertainty reduced and animal spirits turn fear to optimism and inaction to action.

THE LIQUIDITY TRAP: THE LOWER TURNING PERIOD

In its September 20, 2010, announcement, the NBER (2010) Business Cycle Dating Committee reported that it chose June 2009 as the end of the Great Recession. It said it "did not conclude that the economic conditions since that month [had] been favorable or that the economy [had] returned to operating at normal capacity." So even after more than a year had passed since the end of the recession, the economy was growing slowly and unemployment remained above 9% for both 2009 and 2010. This underperformance persisted through 2011 and 2012. These facts lead us to describe the lower turning period as an unusually long period, which began in July 2009 and lasted until November 2010. We considered choosing the lower turning period to be between April 2009 and November 2010, to actually contain the trough of the NBER in June 2009. Doing this would have decreased the duration of the Great Recession to only a few months from October 2008 to March 2009, and we decided against it. Reasons for choosing April 2009, as the beginning of the lower turning period, include the bottoming out of the S&P 500 Index that had reached its lowest point of 683 in early March and started climbing very decisively. There were also numerous articles during March 2009 speculating that equities had reached their bottom. So there was some evidence that equity declines had run their course, but there was no credible evidence that the recovery was going to be strong. The defining characteristic of a lower turning period is the difficulty of rationally calculating future business prospects in view of such uncertainty, as animal spirits continue to be stuck in a state of pessimism.

We described in the previous section that fiscal policy in 2009 aggressively attempted to stimulate the economy. In addition, monetary policy took several forceful steps to reduce the unemployment hovering around 9%. By early 2009, Fed funds were dropped to essentially 0.25% and remained essentially zero during 2009–2015. With short-term rates at zero, the US economy has experienced Keynes's characterization of a "liquidity trap."

What is a liquidity trap? A liquidity trap is defined as an economic condition in which the short-term nominal interest rate is zero, while the real economy operates below capacity with high unemployment and a significant output gap. Keynes (1936) observed this situation of interest rates close to zero during the Great Depression of the 1930s and concluded that monetary policy had become ineffective, because further increases in the money supply had no effect on interest rates that had already reached their lowest bound. Therefore, if monetary policy cannot influence the nominal short-term interest rate any further, it becomes ineffective because it cannot stimulate spending and output any further.

The Keynesian liquidity trap as a theoretical tool was very limited, because it was static and ignored expectations. The monetary policy's ineffectiveness following the liquidity trap condition led Keynes to advocate fiscal policy as an alternative tool to reduce the output gap that prevails during the liquidity trap. But what if, as in today's US economy, fiscal policy becomes constrained because of political considerations? What policy options are available to an economy such as the United States during the current lower turning period?

A modern view of the liquidity trap has emerged from the experience of Japan during the 1990s, and several recent seminal papers and the FOMC published discussions and deliberations during the past few years. The seminal papers include Krugman (1998), Eggertson and Woodford (2003), Werning (2012), and Woodford (2012), among numerous others. These authors argue that if expectations are introduced in a liquidity trap model, such expectations under certain conditions become additional tools of the central bank that may allow monetary policy to become effective. So if a central bank wishes to conduct an effective monetary policy, it must change the agents' expectations about future interest rates when the zero bound will no longer hold. In other words, monetary expansion becomes a tool when the central bank goes beyond the traditional "open market operations" and instead commits to keeping lower future nominal interest rates for a pre-specified period into the future. The application of these tools became known as quantitative easing and was implemented by the Fed in three programs known as Q1, Q2, and Q3.

As previously mentioned, in early 2009, the Fed had lowered Fed funds to essentially zero without being able to accelerate growth and reduce unemployment. During Q1, the Fed purchased large quantities of mortgage-backed securities and bank debt; this lasted from early 2008 to early 2010. Q2 began in mid-2010, when there was evidence that the economic recovery remained weak. During this phase, the Fed purchased $600 billion of long-term Treasury bonds. The Fed's goal was to signal to market participants that it was pursuing expansionary monetary policy even if long-term interest rates were not impacted. Q3 was announced in September 2012 with a new novelty: the Fed switched to buying $40 billion mortgage-backed securities per month with no time limit and no maximum amount specified.

Under these circumstances, what can be hypothesized about the lower turning period, particularly during the first phase of Q1? Neoclassical economics has characterized the 2007–2009 recession as "great" because of the bursting of the housing bubble, the financial crisis that followed because of initial losses in mortgage-backed securities, the spreading of the financial crisis, the substantial losses in wealth, the unusually high level of unemployment that has persisted over five years, and the subpar growth of the economy—all of which have contributed to a very slow recovery. One hypothesis argues that in the case of recessions that result from the bursting of real-estate bubbles, equity crashes, and financial and banking crises, it takes an average of five years for the economy to recover. Others assert that while monetary policy has been aggressively expansionary, fiscal policy has not been sufficient.

From the case of Japan during the 1990s, the United States, England, and the Eurozone during the Great Recession, and various other countries that have experienced asset booms and busts, financial crises, and liquidity traps, what can be hypothesized about asset bubbles and liquidity traps? It is known that not all asset bubble crashes bring about liquidity traps, but some do. If the financial costs of mopping up after the bursting of an asset bubble are substantial with serious difficulties for the financial sector and a recession to the economy leading up in a liquidity trap, is the Fed prepared to consider macroprudential regulation to moderate and, if possible, to contain asset bubbles before they burst? This topic has received much attention. Before the Great Recession, the view that was held was that the central bank should not attempt to control a bubble, because of difficulties to diagnose the bubble. Dudley (2010) acknowledges that bubbles exist, although they are hard to identify, particularly in their early stages of development. Suppose that with some degree of probability a bubble has been identified. The costs versus the benefits of taking action against such a bubble and to limit its growth depend on the available tools and their effectiveness. There is a consensus that using Fed funds is not the appropriate tool; on the other hand, using macroprudential regulation to contain the growth of credit may be a more effective tool. Issing (2009), Jones (2015), and Malliaris (2005, 2012) discuss the prevailing ideas prior to the Great Recession on bubbles and monetary policy, and Jeanne and Korinek (2013) develop an appropriate strategy to deal with a bubble.

What are the current hypotheses proposed by leading scholars and selectively applied by the Fed? First, during a liquidity trap with a short-term nominal interest rate at zero, the real rate of interest is negative and needs to be partially offset by some inflation, say 2% to 3%. This means the central bank needs to avoid deflation at all costs. The experience from Japan tells us that if deflation materializes, it is difficult for the economy to get out of the liquidity trap. Thus, avoiding deflation is the first step. This has been achieved by the Fed thus far, but the Fed has done and continues to do more. It has articulated that, although eventually the economy will return to its potential and Fed funds will increase, it is committed now to keeping the Fed funds at zero until mid-2015. The logic of such a strategy is to ensure that the economy recovers its lost output during the liquidity trap, and consumers and businesses do not postpone their spending, because of the uncertainty surrounding higher nominal interest rates in the future.

What else can be hypothesized beyond orthodox economic theory? Behavioral finance has not proposed a hypothesis about the liquidity trap. Its main contributions lie in asset pricing, risk management, and corporate finance. Both Keynes's and Minsky's ideas may be helpful for formulating a hypothesis that highlights the importance of expectations. Minsky's financial instability hypothesis articulates the interplay between investment and the financial sector and claims, that the financial sector is structurally unstable. Minsky's financial instability may result in a liquidity trap. Both Minsky and Keynes consider monetary policy to be ineffective and instead propose expansive fiscal policy. Currently, fiscal policy is entangled in conflicted political debates. Beyond these debates, it is known that increases in the national debt are not sustainable. As a result, fiscal policy appears severely constrained. Thus, we are left with monetary policy, which is also constrained during a liquidity trap. But as constrained as the central bank may be, it still has tools available to influence expectations. According to Keynes (1936,162), the state of long-term expectations of all economic agents is often steady. People believe that the future will be favorable. Human psychology is largely optimistic about the future. Additionally, this sentiment of hope for the future is stable. The short-term expectations are the ones triggered by the bursting of asset bubbles and financial panics that are volatile and pessimistic. So, we can hypothesize that as the economy slowly recovers and short-term expectations improve, these stable and optimistic long-term expectations exert positive influence on spending and economic growth. It is during the lower turning period that nonlinear returns can be expected because of the convexity property that describes the bottom of the cyclical behavior.

CONCLUSIONS

This chapter argues that it is informative to divide the cyclical behavior of modern mixed capitalist economies into an expansion, upper turning period, recession, and lower turning period. This characterization of the business cycle is more complicated than the one currently followed by the NBER, which considers only the peak and trough of the cycle. However, the complexity of four phases rewards with additional insights. To illustrate the usefulness of this approach, the current global financial crisis is examined by first reviewing the expansion with the development of the housing bubble. Then, the beginning of the crisis is viewed as the upper turning period when the housing bubble burst and financial instability emerged. The initial financial instability evolved into a full crisis during the Great Recession with its burdensome impact on unemployment. Finally, the ending of the crisis during the challenging period of the liquidity trap, as the lower turning period, is also analyzed. Orthodox economic analysis offers valuable insights for both the expansion and recession phases, but can also benefit from behavioral finance and Minsky's analysis. The upper turning period is Minskyan, and the lower turning period is an updated version of the Keynesian-Minskyan liquidity trap. In addition, Taleb's concavity and convexity properties of the upper and lower turning periods offer useful insights that are further discussed in this volume.

NOTES

Earlier drafts were presented at the 11th Biennial Athenian Policy Forum International Conference, July 1–3, 2012, in Chalkidiki, Greece; the 50th Meeting of the Euro Working Group for Financial Modeling, May 3–5, 2012, in Rome, Italy; and the Conference on the Global Financial Crisis: Values, Behavioral Finance, Social Justice and a Robust Society, April 11, 2013, at Loyola University Chicago. The author is thankful to George Demopoulos, Nikos Baltas, Rita D'Ecclesia, Jaap Spronk, Hersh Shefrin, Nassim Nicholas Taleb, Andrew Filardo, Lilian Garcia, Rob Bliss, George Kaufman, Catherine Kyrtsou, Douglas Evanoff and Bala Batavia for valuable discussions on issues of asset bubbles.

REFERENCES

Acemoglu, D., A. Ozdaglar, and A. Tahbaz-Salehi. 2015. "Networks, Shocks, and Systemic Risk." NBER Working Paper No. 20931.

Adrian, T., and H. S. Shin. 2009. "Financial Intermediaries, Financial Stability, and Monetary Policy." In *Maintaining Stability in a Changing Financial System: A Symposium*, 287–334. Kansas City, MO: Federal Reserve Bank of Kansas City.

Akerlof, G. A., and R. J. Shiller. 2009. *Animal Spirits: How Human Psychology Drives the Economy, and Why It Matters for Global Capitalism*. Princeton, NJ: Princeton University Press.

Auerbach, A., W. Gale, and B. Harris. 2010. "Activist Fiscal Policy." *Journal of Economic Perspectives* 24: 141–164.

Barberis, N. 2013. "Psychology and the Financial Crisis." In *Financial Innovation: Too Much or Too Little*, edited by Michael Haliassos, 15–28. Cambridge: MIT Press.

Bernanke, Ben. 2005. "The Global Saving Glut and the U.S. Current Account Deficit." Speech delivered at the Sandridge Lecture, Virginia Association of Economists, Richmond, VA, March 10.

Bernanke, Ben. 2007. "Global Imbalances: Recent Developments and Prospects." Speech delivered at the Bundesbank Lecture, Berlin, Germany, September 11.

Bernanke, Ben. 2010. "Monetary Policy and the Housing Bubble." Speech delivered at the Annual Meeting of the American Economic Association, Atlanta, Georgia, January 3.

Bernanke, Ben. 2011. "Global Imbalances: Links to Economic and Financial Stability." Speech given at the Banque de France Financial Stability Review Launch Event, Paris, February 18.

Bernanke, Ben, and Mark Gertler. 1999. "Monetary Policy and Asset Price Volatility." *Economic Review of the Federal Reserve Bank of Kansas City*, Fourth Quarter, 17–51.

Bivens, J., and J. Irons. 2008. "A Feeble Recovery: The Fundamental Economic Weaknesses of the 2001–07 Expansion." Economic Policy Institute. http://www.epi.org/publication/bp214/htlm.

Blanchard, Olivier. 2015. "Where Danger Lurks." *Finance and Development* 51: 28–31. Extended in "Dark Corners: Reassessing Macroecomincs After the Crisis." Paper presented at the ASSA Meetings in Boston, Massachusetts, January 3–5, 2015.

Blinder A., and M. Zandi. 2010. "How the Great Recession Was Brought to an End." Working paper, Princeton University, Princeton, NJ.

Boldrin, M., C. Garriga, A. Pralta-Alva, and J. Sanchez. 2012. "Reconstructing the Great Recession." Federal Reserve Bank of St. Louis, working paper 2013-006A.

Borio, C., and W. White. 2003. "Whither Monetary and Financial Stability? The Implications of Evolving Policy Regimes." In *Monetary Policy and Uncertainty: Adapting to a Changing Economy*, 131–211. Kansas City, MO: Federal Reserve Bank of Kansas City.

Brock, W. A., and A. G. Malliaris. 1989. *Differential Equations, Stability and Chaos in Dynamic Economics*. Amsterdam: North-Holland.

Brunnermeier, M. K. 2008. "Bubbles." In *The New Palgrave Dictionary of Economics*, edited by Steven N. Durlauf and L. E. Blume. 2nd ed. New York: Palgrave Macmillan.

Chirinko, R., and H. Schaller. 2012. "Do Bubbles Lead to Overinvestment? A Revealed Preference Approach." In *New Perspectives on Asset Price Bubbles*, edited by Douglas Evanoff, G. Kaufman, and A. G. Malliaris, 433–453. New York: Oxford University Press.

Constancio, V. 2015. "Financial Stability Risks, Monetary Policy and the Need for Macro-prudential policy." ECB speech at the Warwick Economics Summit, February 13.

Davis, M., Lehnert, A., and Martin, R. 2008. "The Rent-Price Ratio for the Aggregate Stock of Owner-Occupied Housing." Review of Income and Wealth, 54(2): 279–284. Data located at Land and Property Values in the U.S., Lincoln Institute of Land Policy http://www.lincolninst.edu/resources/.

Dudley, W. 2010. "Asset Bubbles and the Implications for Central Bank Policy." Remarks at The Economic Club of New York, New York City, April 7.

Eggertson, G., and M. Woodford. 2003. "The Zero Bound on Interest Rates and Optimal Monetary Policy." *Brookings Papers on Economic Activity* 1: 212–219.

Evanoff, D., G. Kaufman, and A. G. Malliaris, eds. 2012. *New Perspectives on Asset Price Bubbles*. New York: Oxford University Press.

Fama, E. 1970. "Efficient Capital Markets: A Review of Theory and Empirical Work." *Journal of Finance* 25 (2): 383–417.

Ferguson, R. W. 2002. "Should Financial Stability Be an Explicit Central Bank Objective?" In *Challenges to Central Banking from Globalized Financial Systems: Papers Presented at the Ninth Conference on Central Banking, Washington, D.C., September 16–17, 2002*, edited by Piero C. Ugolini, Andrea Schaechter, and Mark R. Stone, 1–13. Washington, DC: International Monetary Fund.

Friedman, B., and David I. Laibson. 1989. "Economic Implications of Extraordinary Movements in Stock Prices." *Brookings Papers on Economic Activity* 20 (2): 137–190.

Gorton, Gary. 2008. "The Panic of 2007." *Maintaining Stability in a Changing Financial System*. Proceedings of the 2008 Jackson Hole Conference, Federal Reserve Bank of Kansas City.

Greenspan, A. 2002. "Economic Volatility." Speech presented at the Jackson Hole Symposium, August 30.

Greenspan, A. 2004. "Risk and Uncertainty in Monetary Policy." *American Economic Review* 94: 33–40.

Greenspan, A. 2005. "Risk Transfer and Financial Stability." Speech delivered at the Federal Reserve Bank of Chicago's 41st Annual Conference on Bank Structure, Chicago, May 5.

Greenspan, A. 2009. "We Need a Better Cushion Against Risk." *Financial Times*, March 26.

"Greenspan 'Shocked' that Free Markets Are Flawed." 2008. *New York Times*, October 23.

Haberler, G. 1960. *Prosperity and Depression: A Theoretical Analysis of Cyclical Movements.* 4th ed. London: Bradford and Dickens.

Haldane, A. 2012. "Tails of the Unexpected." Presented at The Credit Crisis Five Years On: Unpacking the Crisis conference, University of Edinburg School, June 8–9.

Haldane, A. 2014. "Managing Global Finance as a System." The Maxwell Fry Annual Global Finance Lecture, Birmingham University, October 29.

Hayford, M. D., and A. G. Malliaris. 2004. "Monetary Policy and the U.S. Stock Market." *Economic Inquiry* 42: 387–401.

Hayford, M. D., and A. G. Malliaris. 2005. "How Did the Fed React to the 1990s Stock Market Bubble? Evidence From an Extended Taylor Rule." *European Journal of Operational Research* 163: 20–29.

Issing, O. 2009. "Asset Prices and Monetary Policy." *Cato Journal* 29: 45–51.

Jalilvand, A., and A. G. Malliaris. 2010. "Sequence of Asset Bubbles and the Global Financial Crisis." In *Lessons from the Financial Crisis: Causes, Consequences, and Our Economic Future*, edited by Robert Kolb, 139–145. Hoboken, NJ: John Wiley and Sons.

Jeanne, O., and A. Korinek. 2013. "Macroprudential Regulation versus Mopping Up after the Crash." NBER Working Paper No. 18675.

Jones, Brad. 2015. "Asset Bubbles: Re-thinking Policy for the Age of Asset Management." IMF Working Paper 15/12.

Kahneman, Daniel, and Amos Tversky. 1974. "Judgment under Uncertainty: Heuristics and Biases." *Science* 185 (4157): 1124–1131.

Kahneman, Daniel, and Amos Tversky. 1992. "Advances in Prospect Theory: Cumulative Representation of Uncertainty." *Journal of Risk and Uncertainty* 5 (4): 297–323.

Kaufman, G. 2004. "Macroeconomic Stability, Bank Soundness and Designing Optimum Regulatory Structures." *Multinational Finance* 8: 141–171.

Keynes, John M. 1936. *The General Theory of Employment, Interest and Money.* New York: Harcourt, Brace and World.

Kindleberger, C. P. 1978. *Manias, Panics, and Crashes: A History of Financial Crises.* Hoboken, NJ: John Wiley and Sons.

Kindleberger, C., and R. Aliber. 2005. *Manias, Panics, and Crashes: A History of Financial Crises.* 5th ed. Hoboken, NJ: John Wiley and Sons.

Kliesen, Kevin. 2003. "The 2001 Recession: How Was it Different and What Developments May Have Caused It?" *Federal Reserve Bank of Saint Louis Review* 85: 23–37.

Kolb, R. 2011. *The Financial Crisis of Our Time.* New York: Oxford University Press.

Koppl, R. 2010. "Retrospectives: Animal Spirits." *Journal of Economic Perspectives* 5: 203–210.

Krishnamurthy, A. 2010. "Amplification Mechanisms in Liquidity Crises." *American Economic Journal: Macroeconomics* 2: 1–30.

Krugman, P. 1998. "It's Baaack! Japan's Slump and the Return of the Liquidity Trap." *Brookings Papers on Economic Activity* 2: 137–187.

Krugman, Paul. 2015. "The Case of the Missing Minsky." *New York Times*, June 1. http://krugman.blogs.nytimes.com/2015/06/01/the-case-of-the-missing-minsky/?_r=0.

Malliaris, A. G. 2005. *Economic Uncertainty, Instabilities & Asset Bubbles.* Hackensack, NJ: World Scientific Publishing.

Malliaris, A. G. 2012. "Asset Price Bubbles and Monetary Policy." In *New Perspectives on Asset Price Bubbles*, edited by D. Evanoff, G. Kaufman, and A. G. Malliaris, 407–432. New York: Oxford University Press.

Minsky, H. P. 1968. "Private Sector Asset Management and the Effectiveness of Monetary Policy: Theory and Practice." *Journal of Finance* 24: 223–238.

Minsky, Hyman. 1975. *John Maynard Keynes*. New York: Columbia University Press.

Minsky, Hyman. 1986. *Stabilizing an Unstable Economy*. New Haven, CT: Yale University Press.

Mishkin, F. S. 1999. "Global Financial Instability: Framework, Events, Issues." *Journal of Economic Perspectives* 13: 3–20.

Mishkin, F. S. 2007. "Financial Instability and Monetary Policy." Speech at the Risk USA 2007 Conference, New York, November 5.

National Bureau of Economic Research. 2010. U.S. Business Cycles Expansions and Contractions. http://www.nber.org/cycles.html.

Ohanian, L. 2011. "Accounting for the Great Recession: Why and How Did the 2007–09 Recession Differ from All Others." *Economic Policy Papers*.

Papademos, L. 2006. "Price Stability, Financial Stability and Efficiency and Monetary Policy." Speech at the Third Conference of the Monetary Stability Foundation, "Challenges to the Financial System-Ageing and Low Growth," Frankfurt am Main.

Plosser, C. I. 2008. "Two Pillars of Central Banking: Monetary Policy and Financial Stability." Opening remarks for the Pennsylvania Association of Community Bankers 130th Annual Convention, Federal Reserve Bank of Philadelphia, Waikoloa, HI, April 18.

Rajan, R. G. 2005. "Has Financial Development Made the World Riskier?" In *The Greenspan Era: Lessons for the Future*, 313–369. Kansas City, MO: Federal Bank of Kansas City.

Reinhart, Carmen M., and Kenneth S. Rogoff. 2009. *This Time is Different: Eight Centuries of Financial Folly*. Princeton, NJ: Princeton University Press.

Rosengren, Eric S. 2011. "Defining Financial Stability, and Some Policy Implications of Applying the Definition." Keynote Remarks at the Stanford Finance Forum, Graduate School of Business, Stanford University, June 3.

Scherbina, A., and B. Schlusche. 2011. "Asset Price Bubbles: A Survey." Board of Governors of the Federal Reserve System Working Paper.

Schinasi, Garry J. 2004. "Defining Financial Stability." IMF Working Papers 04/187, International Monetary Fund.

Shiller, R. J. 2002. "Bubbles, Human Judgment, and Expert Opinion." *Financial Analysts Journal* 58: 18–26.

Tcherneva, P. 2012. "Reorienting Fiscal Policy after the Great Recession." Levy Institute of Bard College, Working Paper 719.

Taleb, N. 2013. *Antifragility*. New York: Random House.

Taylor, John B. 2002. "A Half-Century of Changes in Monetary Policy." Conference in Honor of Milton Friedman, University of Chicago. US Department of Treasury Working Paper.

Taylor, John B. 2007. "Housing and Monetary Policy." NBER Working Paper Series 13682.

www.nber.org/papers/w13682.pdf.

Werning, Ivan. 2012. "Managing a Liquidity Trap: Monetary and Fiscal Policy." MIT Working Paper.

Woodford, M. 2012. "Methods of Policy Accommodation at the Interest-Rate Lower Bound." Paper presented at the Jackson Hole Symposium, August 31–September 1.

Yellen, Janet L. 2014. "Monetary Policy and Financial Stability." Presented at the 2014 Michel Camdessus Central Banking Lecture, International Monetary Fund, Washington, DC, July 2.

3

A Minsky Meltdown

Lessons for Central Bankers

JANET YELLEN ■

It's a great pleasure to speak to this distinguished group at a conference named for Hyman P. Minsky.[1] My last talk here took place 13 years ago when I served on the Fed's Board of Governors. My topic then was "The 'New' Science of Credit Risk Management at Financial Institutions." It described innovations that I expected to improve the measurement and management of risk. My talk today is titled "A Minsky Meltdown: Lessons for Central Bankers." I won't dwell on the irony of that. Suffice it to say that, with the financial world in turmoil, Minsky's work has become required reading. It is getting the recognition it richly deserves. The dramatic events of the past year and a half are a classic case of the kind of systemic breakdown that he—and relatively few others—envisioned.

Central to Minsky's view of how financial meltdowns occur, of course, are "asset price bubbles." This evening I will revisit the ongoing debate over whether central banks should act to counter such bubbles and discuss "lessons learned." This issue seems especially compelling now that it's evident that episodes of exuberance, like the ones that led to our bond and house price bubbles, can be time bombs that cause catastrophic damage to the economy when they explode. Indeed, in view of the financial mess we're living through, I found it fascinating to read Minsky again and reexamine my own views about central bank responses to speculative financial booms. My thoughts on this have changed somewhat, as I will explain.[2]

As always, my comments are my own and do not necessarily reflect those of my colleagues in the Federal Reserve System.

MINSKY AND THE CURRENT CRISIS

One of the critical features of Minsky's world view is that borrowers, lenders, and regulators are lulled into complacency as asset prices rise.[3] It was not so long ago—though it seems like a lifetime—that many of us were trying to figure out why investors were demanding so little compensation for risk. For example, long-term interest rates were well below what appeared consistent with the expected future path of short-term rates. This phenomenon, which ended abruptly in mid-2007, was famously characterized by then-Chairman Greenspan as a "conundrum."[4] Credit spreads too were razor thin. But for Minsky, this behavior of interest rates and loan pricing might not have been so puzzling. He might have pointed out that such a sense of safety on the part of investors is characteristic of financial booms. The incaution that reigned by the middle of this decade had been fed by roughly twenty years of the so-called great moderation, when most industrialized economies experienced steady growth and low and stable inflation. Moreover, the world economy had shaken off the effects of the bursting of an earlier asset price bubble—the technology stock boom—with comparatively little damage.

Chairman Bernanke has argued that other factors besides complacency were responsible for low interest rates in this period.[5] A glut of foreign saving mainly generated in developing countries such as China and India fueled demand for dollar-denominated assets. This ample supply of foreign savings combined with a low US personal saving rate, large US government deficits, and high productivity gains to produce a huge current account deficit. As a result, vast quantities of funds began "sloshing around" in our economy seeking investment projects.

Fed monetary policy may also have contributed to the US credit boom and the associated house price bubble by maintaining a highly accommodative stance from 2002 to 2004.[6] This accommodative stance was motivated by what Greenspan called "risk management policy," in which, to reduce the possibility of deflation, the funds rate was held below the level that would otherwise have been chosen to promote a return to full employment.[7] In effect, the Fed took a calculated risk. It took out some insurance to lower the chances of a potentially devastating deflationary episode. The cost of that insurance was an increased possibility of overheating the economy. These policy actions arguably played some role in our house price bubble. But they clearly were not the only factor, since such bubbles appeared in many countries that did not have highly accommodative monetary policies.

As Minsky's financial instability hypothesis suggests, when optimism is high and ample funds are available for investment, investors tend to migrate from the safe hedge end of the Minsky spectrum to the risky speculative and Ponzi end. Indeed, in the current episode, investors tried to raise returns by increasing leverage and sacrificing liquidity through short-term—sometimes overnight—debt financing. Simultaneously, new and fancy methods of financial engineering allowed widespread and complex securitization of many types of assets, most famously in subprime lending. In addition, exotic derivatives, such as credit default swaps, were thought to dilute risk by spreading it widely. These new financial products provided the basis for an illusion of low risk, a misconception that was amplified by the inaccurate analyses of the rating agencies. This created a new wrinkle that even Minsky may not have imagined. Some of the investors who put money into highly risky assets were blithely unaware of how far out on a limb they had gone. Many of those who thought they were in the hedge category were shocked to discover that, in fact, they were speculative or Ponzi units.

At the same time, securitization added distance between borrowers and lenders. As a result, underwriting standards were significantly relaxed. Much of this financing was done in the "shadow banking system," consisting of entities that acted a lot like banks—albeit very highly leveraged and illiquid banks—but were outside the bank regulatory net. Although these developments reached an extreme state in the US subprime mortgage market, risky practices were employed broadly in the US financial system. And this activity extended far beyond our borders as players throughout the global financial system eagerly participated. As banks and their large, nonbank competitors became involved in ever more complicated securitizations, they began to employ sophisticated "new tools" to measure and manage the credit risks flowing from these transactions. But those tools—which I described in my speech 13 years ago—proved insufficient for the task.

This cult of risky behavior was not limited to financial institutions. US households enthusiastically leveraged themselves to the hilt. The personal saving rate, which had been falling for over a decade, hovered only slightly above zero from mid-2005 to mid-2007. A good deal of this leverage came in the form of mortgage debt. The vast use of exotic mortgages—such as subprime, interest-only, low-doc and no-doc, and option-ARMs—offers an example of Minsky's Ponzi finance, in which a loan can only be refinanced if the price of the underlying asset increases. In fact, many subprime loans were explicitly designed to be good for the borrower only if they could be refinanced at a lower rate, a benefit limited to those who established a pattern of regular payments and built reasonable equity in their homes.

In retrospect, it's not surprising that these developments led to unsustainable increases in bond prices and house prices. Once those prices started to go down, we were quickly in the midst of a Minsky meltdown. The financial engineering that was thought to hedge risks probably would have worked beautifully if individual investors had faced shocks that were uncorrelated with those of their counterparties. But declines in bond and house prices hit everyone in the same way, inflicting actual and expected credit losses broadly across the financial system. Moreover, the complexity of securitized credit instruments meant that it was difficult to identify who the actual loan holders might be. Meanwhile, asset write-downs reduced equity cushions of financial firms and increased their leverage just when growing risks made those firms seek less leverage, not more. When they tried to sell assets into illiquid markets, prices fell further, generating yet more selling pressure in a loss spiral that kept intensifying. We experienced a "perfect storm" in financial markets: runs on highly vulnerable and systemically important financial institutions; dysfunction in most securitized credit markets; a reduction in interbank lending; higher interest rates for all but the safest borrowers, matched by near-zero yields on Treasury bills; lower equity values; and a restricted supply of credit from financial institutions.

Once this massive credit crunch hit, it didn't take long before we were in a recession. The recession, in turn, deepened the credit crunch as demand and employment fell, and credit losses of financial institutions surged. Indeed, we have been in the grips of precisely this adverse feedback loop for more than a year. A process of balance sheet deleveraging has spread to nearly every corner of the economy. Consumers are pulling back on purchases, especially on durable goods, to build their savings. Businesses are canceling planned investments and laying off workers to preserve cash. And financial institutions are shrinking assets to bolster capital and improve their chances of weathering the current storm. Once again, Minsky understood this dynamic. He spoke of the paradox of deleveraging, in which precautions that may be smart for individuals and firms—and indeed essential to return the economy to a normal state—nevertheless magnify the distress of the economy as a whole.

The US economy just entered the sixth quarter of recession. Economic activity and employment are contracting sharply, with weakness evident in every major sector aside from the federal government. Financial markets and institutions remain highly stressed, notwithstanding a few welcome signs of stability due mainly to Federal Reserve and federal government credit policies. The negative dynamics between the real and financial sides of the economy have created severe downside risks. While we've seen some tentative signs of improvement in the economic data very recently, it's still impossible to know how deep the contraction will ultimately be.

As I mentioned earlier, the Minsky meltdown is global in nature, reflecting the ever-increasing interconnectedness of financial markets and institutions around the world. The recession is the first during the postwar period to see simultaneous contractions in output in Europe, Japan, and North America. Economic growth in these areas has weakened sharply as the financial pain has spread and the US recession has spilled over to our trading partners. Forecasts for growth in Europe and Japan in 2009 are now even weaker than for the United States. What's more, many developing nations face stark challenges as markets for their products have dried up and capital inflows have abruptly halted, making debt refinancing—if necessary—difficult, if not impossible. The global nature of the downturn raises the odds that the recession will be prolonged, since neither we nor our trade partners can look to a boost from foreign demand.

BUBBLES AND MONETARY POLICY

The severity of these financial and economic problems creates a very strong case for government and central bank action. I'm encouraged that we are seeing an almost unprecedented outpouring of innovative fiscal and monetary policies aimed at resolving the crisis. Of course, fiscal stimulus played a central role in Minsky's policy prescriptions for combating economic cycles. Minsky also emphasized the importance of lender-of-last-resort interventions by the Federal Reserve, and this is a tool we have relied on heavily. I believe that Minsky would also approve of the Fed's current "credit easing" policies. Since the intensification of the financial crisis last fall, the Fed has expanded its balance sheet from around $850 billion to just over $2 trillion and has announced programs that are likely to take it yet higher. In effect, the government is easing the financial fallout resulting from virulent deleveraging throughout the private sector by increasing its own leverage in a partial and temporary offset.[8]

However, as I said at the beginning of my talk, this evening I want to address another question that has been the subject of much debate for many years: Should central banks attempt to deflate asset price bubbles before they get big enough to cause big problems? Until recently, most central bankers would have said no. They would have argued that policy should focus solely on inflation, employment, and output goals—even in the midst of an apparent asset price bubble.[9] That was the view that prevailed during the tech stock bubble and I myself have supported this approach in the past. However, now that we face the tangible and tragic consequences of the bursting of the house price bubble, I think it is time to take another look.

Let me briefly review the arguments for and against policies aimed at counteracting bubbles. The conventional wisdom generally followed by the Fed and central banks in most inflation-targeting countries is that monetary policy should respond to an asset price only to the extent that it will affect the future path of output and inflation, which are the proper concerns of monetary policy.[10] For example, a surging stock market can be expected to lead to stronger demand for goods and services by raising the wealth of households and reducing the cost of capital for businesses. As a result, higher stock prices mean that the stance of monetary policy needs to be tighter, but only enough to offset the macroeconomic consequences on aggregate demand created by a larger stock of wealth. In other words, policy would not respond to the stock market boom itself, but only to the consequences of the boom on the macroeconomy.

However, other observers argue that monetary authorities must consider responding directly to an asset price bubble when one is detected. This is because—as we are witnessing—bursting bubbles can seriously harm economic performance, and monetary policy is hard-pressed to respond effectively after the fact. Therefore, central banks may prefer to try to eliminate, or at least reduce the size of, this threat directly. Under this approach, policymakers would push interest rates higher than would be indicated under conventional policy. The result, of course, would be that output and employment would be reduced in the near-term, which is the price of mitigating the risk of serious financial and economic turmoil later on.

What are the issues that separate the anti-bubble monetary policy activists from the skeptics? First, some of those who oppose such policy question whether bubbles even exist. They maintain that asset prices reflect the collective information and wisdom of traders in organized markets. Trying to deflate an apparent bubble would go against precisely those "experts" who best understand the fundamental factors underlying asset prices. It seems to me though that this argument is particularly difficult to defend in light of the poor decisions and widespread dysfunction we have seen in many markets during the current turmoil.

Second, even if bubbles do occur, it's an open question whether policymakers can identify them in time to act effectively. Bubbles are not easy to detect because estimates of the underlying fundamentals are imprecise. For example, in the case of house prices, it is common to estimate fundamental values by looking at the ratio of house prices to rents, which can be thought of as equivalent to a dividend-price ratio for the stock market.[11] If this ratio rises significantly above its fundamental, or long-run, value, the possibility of a bubble should be considered. Indeed, from 2002 to early 2006, this ratio zoomed to about 90% above its long-run value, far outstripping any previous level. Nonetheless, even when house prices were soaring, some experts doubted that a bubble existed. That said, by 2005, I think most people understood that—at a minimum—there was a substantial risk that houses had become overvalued. Even at that point though, many thought the correction in house prices would be slow, not the rapid adjustment that did occur.[12]

Now, even if we accept that we can identify bubbles as they happen, another question arises: Is the threat so serious that a monetary response is imperative? It would make sense for monetary policymakers to intervene only if the fallout were likely to be quite severe and difficult to deal with after the fact. We know that the effects of booms and busts in asset prices sometimes show themselves with significant lags. In those cases, conventional policy approaches can be effective. For example, fluctuations in equity prices generally affect wealth and consumer demand quite gradually. A central bank may prefer to adjust short-term interest rates after the bubble bursts to counter the depressing effects on demand. The tech stock bubble seems to fit this mold. The price-dividend ratio for these stocks reached dizzying heights and many observers were convinced that a crash was inevitable. But monetary policymakers did not try to stop the relentless climb of tech stock prices, although they raised interest rates toward the end of the period to dampen emerging inflationary pressures. Instead, it was only after tech stocks collapsed that policy eased to offset the negative wealth effect and, as unemployment rose, to help return the economy to full employment. The recession at the beginning of the decade was fairly mild and did not involve pervasive financial market disruptions.

Still, just like infections, some bursting asset price bubbles are more virulent than others. The current recession is a case in point. As house prices have plunged, the turmoil has been transmitted to the economy much more quickly and violently than interest rate policy has been able to offset.

You'll recognize right away that the assets at risk in the tech stock bubble were equities, while the volatile assets in the current crisis involve debt instruments held widely by global financial institutions. It may be that credit booms, such as the one that spurred house price and bond price increases, hold more dangerous systemic risks than other asset bubbles. By their nature, credit booms are especially prone to generating powerful adverse feedback loops between financial markets and real economic activity. It follows then that, if all asset bubbles are not created equal, policymakers could decide to intervene only in those cases that seem especially dangerous.

That brings up a fourth point: even if a dangerous asset price bubble is detected and action to rein it in is warranted, conventional monetary policy may not be the best approach. It's true that moderate increases in the policy interest rate might constrain the bubble and reduce the risk of severe macroeconomic dislocation. In the current episode, higher short-term interest rates probably would have restrained the demand for housing by raising mortgage interest rates, and this might have slowed the pace of house price increases. In addition, as Hyun Song Shin and his coauthors have noted in important work related to Minsky's, tighter monetary policy may be associated with reduced leverage and slower credit growth, especially in securitized markets.[13] Thus, monetary policy that leans against bubble expansion may also enhance financial stability by slowing credit booms and lowering overall leverage.

Nonetheless, these linkages remain controversial and bubbles may not be predictably susceptible to interest rate policy actions. And there's a question of collateral damage. Even if higher interest rates take some air out of a bubble, such a strategy may have an unacceptably depressing effect on the economy as a whole. There is also the harm that can result from "type 2 errors," when policymakers respond to asset price developments that, with the benefit of hindsight, turn out not to have been bubbles at all. For both of these reasons, central bankers may be better off avoiding monetary strategies and instead relying on more targeted and lower-cost alternative approaches to manage bubbles, such as financial regulatory and supervisory tools. I will turn to that topic in just a minute.

In summary, when it comes to using monetary policy to deflate asset bubbles, we must acknowledge the difficulty of identifying bubbles, and uncertainties in the relationship between monetary policy and financial stability. At the same time though, policymakers often must act on the basis of incomplete knowledge. What has become patently obvious is that not dealing with certain kinds of bubbles before they get big can have grave consequences. This lends more weight to arguments in favor of attempting to mitigate bubbles, especially when a credit boom is the driving factor. I would not advocate making it a regular practice to use monetary policy to lean against asset price bubbles. However recent experience has made me more open to action. I can now imagine circumstances that would justify leaning against a bubble with tighter monetary policy. Clearly further research may help clarify these issues.[14]

ANOTHER IMPORTANT TOOL FOR FINANCIAL STABILITY

Regardless of one's views on using monetary policy to reduce bubbles, it seems plain that supervisory and regulatory policies could help prevent the kinds of problems we now face. Indeed, this was one of Minsky's major prescriptions for mitigating financial instability. I am heartened that there is now widespread agreement among policymakers and in Congress on the need to overhaul our supervisory and regulatory system, and broad agreement on the basic elements of reform.[15]

Many of the proposals under discussion are intended to strengthen micro-prudential supervision. Micro-prudential supervision aims to insure that individual financial institutions, including any firm with access to the safety net, but particularly those that are systemically important, are well managed and avoid excessive risk. The current system of supervision is characterized by uneven and fragmented supervision, and it's riddled with gaps that enhance the opportunity for regulatory arbitrage. Such arbitrage was a central component in the excessive risk taking that led to our current problems. It is now widely agreed that such gaps and overlaps must be eliminated, and systemically important institutions—whether banks, insurance firms, investment firms, or hedge funds—should be subject to consolidated supervision by a single agency. Systemic institutions would be defined by key characteristics, such as size, leverage, reliance on short-term funding, importance as sources of credit or liquidity, and interconnectedness in the financial system—not by the kinds of charters they have. Another critical shortcoming of the current system is that it lacks any legal process to enable supervisors of financial conglomerates and nonbanks to wind down the activities of failed firms in an orderly fashion. The need for a resolution framework that would permit such wind-downs of systemically important firms is also widely accepted.

The current crisis has afforded plentiful opportunities for supervisors to reflect on the effectiveness of our current system of micro-prudential supervision. The "lessons learned" will undoubtedly enhance its conduct going forward.[16] But, regardless of how well micro-prudential supervision is executed, on its own it will never be adequate to safeguard the economy from the destructive boom and bust cycles that Minsky considered endemic in capitalistic systems. Analogous to Keynes's paradox of thrift, the assumption that safe institutions automatically result in a safe system reflects a fallacy of composition. Thus, macro-prudential supervision—to protect the system as a whole—is needed to mitigate financial crises.

The roles of micro-and macro-prudential supervision are fundamentally different. In principle, many individual institutions could be managing risk reasonably well, while the system as a whole remained vulnerable due to interconnections among financial institutions that could lead to contagious cycles of loss and illiquidity. For example, it is prudent for institutions to sell risky assets and pay off debt when a decline in asset prices depletes capital. But the simultaneous behavior of many institutions to protect themselves in this way only intensifies the decline in prices. Moreover, when many institutions try to de-lever simultaneously, market liquidity can instantly evaporate. Systemic risk is endogenous to the working of the financial system.

Capital requirements could serve as a key tool of macro-prudential supervision. Most proposals for regulatory reform would impose higher capital requirements on systemically important institutions and also design them to vary in a procyclical manner. In other words, capital requirements would rise in economic upswings, so that institutions would build strength in good times, and they would fall in recessions. This pattern would counteract the natural tendency of leverage to amplify business cycle swings—serving as a kind of "automatic stabilizer" for the financial system. Financial stability might also be enhanced by reforming the accounting rules governing loan loss reserves. A more forward-looking system for reserving against such losses could make regulatory capital less sensitive to economic fluctuations.[17] In addition, most proposals for financial reform emphasize the need for stronger liquidity standards. The funding of long-term assets with short-term, often overnight liabilities, is a source of systemic vulnerability. One interesting recent proposal would disincent overreliance on short-term funding by relating an institution's capital charges to the degree of maturity mismatch between its assets and liabilities.[18] There has been considerable discussion recently of the need for a new macro-prudential or "financial stability" supervisor—whether the Fed or some other agency—with responsibility to monitor, assess, and mitigate systemic risks in the financial system as a whole.

At this stage, the proposed reforms involve broad principles. The translation of those principles into a detailed supervisory program will be challenging, to say the least. But I am hopeful that the lessons we have learned will help us build a more effective system to head off financial crises. If we are successful, then we will have gone a long way toward preventing another Minsky meltdown.

NOTES

1. Presentation to the 18th Annual Hyman P. Minsky Conference on the State of the U.S. and World Economies—"Meeting the Challenges of the Financial Crisis", Organized by the Levy Economics Institute of Bard College, New York City. I would like to thank John Judd and Sam Zuckerman for exceptional assistance in preparing these remarks.
2. I want to give credit to PIMCO's always astute Paul McCulley—who gave last year's keynote address—for leading the Minsky revival and pointing out the relevance of Minsky's work to our current financial troubles.
3. For example, see Hyman P. Minsky, "The Financial Instability Hypothesis," The Jerome Levy Economics Institute of Bard College, Working Paper No. 74, May

1992, http:// papers.ssrn.com/sol3/papers.cfm?abstract_id=161024; and Robert Pollin, "The Relevance of Hyman Minsky," *Challenge*, March/April 1997.

4.   Alan Greenspan, "Federal Reserve Board's Semiannual Monetary Policy Report to the Congress," testimony before the Committee on Banking, Housing, and Urban Affairs, US Senate, February 16, 2005, http://www.federalreserve.gov/Boarddocs/ hh/2005/february/ testimony.htm.

5.   Ben S. Bernanke, "The Global Saving Glut and the U.S. Current Account Deficit," remarks at the Sandridge Lecture, Virginia Association of Economics, Richmond, Virginia, March 10, 2005, http://www.federalreserve.gov/boarddocs/speeches/ 2005/200503102/.

6.   John B. Taylor, "The Financial Crisis and the Policy Responses: An Empirical Analysis of What Went Wrong," NBER Working Paper No. 14631, January 2009, http://www.nber. org/papers/w14631.

7.   Alan Greenspan, "Monetary Policy under Uncertainty," remarks at a symposium sponsored by the Federal Reserve Bank of Kansas City, Jackson Hole, Wyoming, August 29, 2003, http://www.federalreserve.gov/boarddocs/speeches/2003/2003 0829/default.htm.

8.   Paul McCulley has emphasized the importance of such a government role to address what he refers to as the "reverse Minsky journey." See "Saving Capital-istic Banking from Itself," Global Central Bank Focus, PIMCO, February 2009, http://www.pimco.com/LeftNav/ Featured+Market+Commentary/FF/2009/ GCB+February+2009+McCulley+Saving+ Capitalistic+Banking.htm.

9.   Donald L. Kohn, "Monetary Policy and Asset Prices Revisited," speech at the Cato Institute's 26th Annual Monetary Policy Conference, Washington, DC, November 19, 2008, http://www.federalreserve.gov/newsevents/speech/kohn20081119a.htm; Frederick S. Mishkin, "How Should We Respond to Asset Price Bubbles," speech at the Wharton Financial Institutions Center and Oliver Wyman Institute's Annual Financial Risk Roundtable, Philadelphia, Pennsylvania, May 15, 2008, http://www. federalreserve.gov/newsevents/speech/mishkin20080515a.htm.

10.   Glenn D. Rudebusch, "Monetary Policy and Asset Price Bubbles," *FRBSF Economic Letter* 2005–18, August 5, 2005, http://www.frbsf.org/publications/economics/ letter/2005/ el2005-18.html.

11.   Joshua Gallin, "The Long-Run Relationship between House Prices and Rents," Finance and Economics Discussion Series 2004-50, Board of Governors of the Federal Reserve System, Washington, DC (forthcoming in *Real Estate Economics*), http://www.federalreserve.gov/ pubs/feds/2004/200450/200450abs.html.

12.   Kristopher Gerardi, Andreas Lehnert, Shane M. Sherlund, and Paul Willen, "Mak-ing Sense of the Subprime Crisis," Brookings Papers on Economic Activity, Fall 2008, 69–160, http://www.brookings.edu/economics/bpea/~/media/Files/Prog rams/ES/BPEA/2008_fall_bpea_papers/2008_fall_bpea_gerardi_sherlund_leh nert_willen.pdf.

13.   Tobias Adrian and Hyun Song Shin, "Money, Liquidity, and Monetary Policy," *American Economic Review Papers and Proceedings* 99 (2): 600–605.

14.   The following conference volumes provide an introduction and references to the research literature now available: *Asset Price Bubbles: The Implications for Monetary, Regulatory, and International Policies*, ed. William Hunter, George Kaufman, and Michael Pomerleano (Cambridge, MA: MIT Press, 2003); *Asset Prices and Mon-etary Policy*, ed. Anthony Richards and Tim Robinson (Reserve Bank of Australia,

2003), http://www.rba.gov.au/PublicationsAnd Research/Conferences/2003/index.html.

15. See, for example, Timothy Geithner, testimony before the House Financial Services Committee, March 26, 2009, http://www.ustreas.gov/press/releases/tg67.htm; Ben S. Bernanke, "Financial Reform to Address Systemic Risk," speech at the Council on Foreign Relations, March 10, 2009, http://www.federalreserve.gov/news events/speech/bernanke20090310a.htm; Daniel K. Tarullo, "Modernizing Bank Supervision and Regulation," testimony before the Committee on Banking, Housing, and Urban Affairs, US Senate, March 19, 2009 (http://www.federalreserve.gov/newsevents/testimony/tarullo20090319a.htm); Group of Thirty, "Financial Reform: A Framework for Financial Stability," January 2009 (http://www. group30.org/pubs/recommendations.pdf); Markus Brunnermeier, Andrew Crockett, Charles Goodhart, Avinash D. Persaud, and Hyun Shin, "The Fundamental Principles of Financial Regulation," *Geneva Reports on the World Economy* 11, January 2009, http://www.voxeu.org/reports/Geneva11.pdf) "Special Report on Regulatory Reform," Congressional Oversight Panel, January 2009, http://cop.senate.gov/documents/cop-012 909-report-regulatoryreform.pdf.

16. See President's Working Group on Financial Markets, "Policy Statement on Financial Market Developments," March 13, 2008, http://www.treas.gov/press/releases/reports/pwgpolicystatemktturmoil_03122008.pdf; Financial Stability Forum, "Report of the Financial Stability Forum on Enhancing Market and Institutional Resilience," April 7, 2008,http://www.fsforum.org/publications/r_0804.pdf; Senior Supervisors Group, "Observations on Risk Management Practices during the Recent Market Turbulence," March 6, 2008, http://www.newyorkfed.org/newsevents/news/banking/2008/SSG_Risk_Mgt_doc_final.pdf.

17. See Eric S. Rosengren, "Addressing the Credit Crisis and Restructuring the Financial Regulatory System: Lessons from Japan," speech to the Institute of International Bankers Annual Washington Conference, Washington, DC, March 2, 2009, http://www. bos.frb.org/news/speeches/rosengren/2009/030209.htm.

18. Markus Brunnermeier et al., "The Fundamental Principles of Financial Regulation," Geneva Reports on the World Economy (Geneva: International Center for Monetary and Banking Studies, 2009), http://www.princeton.edu/~hsshin/www/Geneva.pdf.

4

Modeling Financial Instability

STEVE KEEN ■

INTRODUCTION

The role of the financial sector in causing the post-2007 economic crisis is not in dispute: disputation instead centers on the causal mechanisms between the financial sector and the physical economy. I follow Fisher (1933), Schumpeter (1934), and Minsky (1980) in assigning key roles to the growth and contraction of aggregate private debt (Keen 1995, 2000), but this perspective is rejected by New Keynesian economists on the a priori basis that private debts are "pure redistributions" that "should have no significant macro-economic effects" (Bernanke 2000, 24), and as a corollary to the oft-repeated truism that "one person's debt is another person's asset" (Krugman 2012c, 43).

My analysis also follows the Post-Keynesian tradition of endogenous money (Moore 1979, 1983) in seeing the banking sector as an essential component of the macroeconomy, yet this is also dismissed by New Keynesian economists on the grounds that banks are merely a specialized form of financial intermediary (Krugman 2012a, 2012b, 2013a; Sumner 2013; Tobin 1963), all of which can be safely ignored in macroeconomic models. When banks are introduced in New Keynesian models, they function not as loan originators but effectively as brokers between savers and borrowers (Eggertsson and Krugman 2012b, 21–22).

In response, authors in the Post-Keynesian and endogenous money traditions express exasperation that New Keynesian authors ignore credit creation and the accounting mechanics of bank lending (Fullwiler 2012, Roche 2013), as laid out in numerous Central Bank publications (Carpenter and Demiralp 2010, ECB 2012, Holmes 1969, Keister and McAndrews 2009).

Given the key public policy role of economics, and the acknowledged failure of neoclassical models in general to anticipate the financial crisis (Bezemer 2009; Blanchard 2009; Blanchard et al. 2010; OECD 2007), the existence within academic economics of two diametrically opposed perspectives which fail to communicate is a disservice to the public.

In this paper I attempt to conclusively determine whether aggregate private debt and banks matter in macroeconomics by putting the two rival models of lending—loanable funds and endogenous money—on a common footing. Using the dynamic open-source monetary modeling program *Minsky*,[1] I first put the New Keynesian model of banking in Eggertsson and Krugman 2012b into a strictly monetary model[2] and I show that, if the structure of lending in this model accurately characterizes actual lending, then the neoclassical perspective that aggregate debt is unimportant,[3] and that banks can safely be ignored in macroeconomics, is correct. I then modify this model to match the Post-Keynesian perspective on the structure of lending, and show that in this structure, changes in the aggregate level of private debt have a direct impact upon aggregate demand, and banks therefore play a crucial role in macroeconomics.

LOANABLE FUNDS VS. ENDOGENOUS MONEY

The neoclassical model of loanable funds and the Post-Keynesian concept of endogenous money are polar opposites in their approach to the nature and significance of banks, debt, and money in macroeconomics. Both models portray the money supply as variable, and hence in one sense endogenous, though by very different mechanisms and to very different degrees (Palley 2013, 411). In the loanable funds tradition, banks function as "mere intermediaries" (Graziani 1989, 8) between savers and borrowers; private debts are "pure redistributions" that "should have no significant macro-economic effects" (Bernanke 2000, 24), and banks, debt, and money can be and are ignored in canonical macroeconomic models (Smets and Wouters 2007, Woodford 2009). In the endogenous money tradition, banks are crucial to macroeconomics because they create money by creating debt (Holmes 1969, Moore 1979), but no consensus has yet emerged on how to represent this phenomenon in Post-Keynesian macroeconomic models (Palley 1991, 2002).

There is little communication between the two approaches, with authors in the loanable funds tradition frequently deriding those in the endogenous money camp (Krugman 2012a, 2012b, 2012e, 2012f), and dismissing the proposition that banks must be included in macroeconomics (Krugman 2012a, 2012b, 2012d; but see Rowe 2013; Sumner 2013).[4] The Bank of England recently emphatically supported the endogenous money perspective (McLeay et al. 2014), but this has not altered the attitude of loanable funds supporters (Krugman 2014).

This dispute can be resolved by an appeal to the Occam's Razor principle that unless a more complex model makes different and better predictions than a less complex one, the simpler should be preferred. Therefore, unless bank lending *necessarily* affects vital macroeconomic aggregates in a significant manner, then even though the "loans create deposits" accounting perspective of endogenous money is technically correct (Carney 2012, ECB 2012, Holmes 1969)—as even Paul Krugman has conceded (Krugman 2013a)[5]—the loanable funds approach is justified, and banks should be excluded from macroeconomics. Conversely, if bank lending necessarily affects macroeconomic aggregates, then banks, debt, and the endogeneity of the money supply are integral to macroeconomics, and models that exclude them are not models of a capitalist economy.

A MONETARY MODEL OF LOANABLE FUNDS

Eggertsson and Krugman note that the vast majority of mainstream economic models ignore debt:

> If there is a single word that appears most frequently in discussions of the economic problems now afflicting both the United States and Europe, that word is surely *debt* ... one might have expected debt to be at the heart of most mainstream macroeconomic models—especially the analysis of monetary and fiscal policy. Perhaps somewhat surprisingly, however, it is quite common to abstract altogether from this feature of the economy. Even economists trying to analyze the problems of monetary and fiscal policy at the zero lower bound—and yes, that includes the present authors (see Krugman 1998, Eggertsson and Woodford 2003)—have often adopted representative agent models in which everyone is alike and the shock that pushes the economy into a situation in which even a zero interest rate is not low enough takes the form of a shift in everyone's preferences. (Eggertsson and Krugman 2012a, 1469–1471)

In order to introduce debt into a New Keynesian two-period model, Eggertsson and Krugman divided agents into two groups who "differ only in their rates of time preference": "patient agents" and "impatient agents," where the latter have a higher rate of time preference than the former, so that "in that case, 'impatient' individuals will borrow from 'patient' individuals." (Eggertsson and Krugman 2012a, 1474). Debt was explicitly modeled throughout this paper,[6] and banking was introduced in the appendix (Eggertsson and Krugman 2012b) as an intermediating function between depositors and borrowers, where borrowing by impatient agents was strictly for investment.[7]

The authors describe their model as a "just the standard New Keynesian model," with one twist: the natural rate of interest, which is normally an exogenous parameter in the *IS* equation, is instead endogenous with borrowers' debt being one of its parameters. Therefore the level of private debt plays a macroeconomic role:

> We need to figure out the evolution of debt of the "borrowers" to figure out the natural rate of interest. In particular we see that if ... the economy is "overleveraged" ... it is easy to get endogenously negative natural rate of interest. (Eggertsson and Krugman 2012b, 24)

The New Keynesian and liquidity trap aspects of this model (see Solow 2003, 2008) are tangential to the topic of this paper, which is a strictly structural one: does bank lending—as opposed to lending by non-bank agents to each other—significantly alter the macrodynamics of the economy? To consider this question, I render the loanable funds aspects of Eggertsson and Krugman 2012b in a strictly monetary form in a *Minsky* model.

Minsky is a system-dynamics program that generates dynamic models of financial flows from double-entry bookkeeping tables (called Godley Tables in the program in honor of Wynne Godley; see Godley 2004, Godley and Lavoie 2007), in which the columns represent bank accounts and the rows are transactions between accounts. The sample model shown in Figure 4.1 generates the dynamic equations shown in Equation (0.1) (more details on *Minsky* are given in the Appendix).

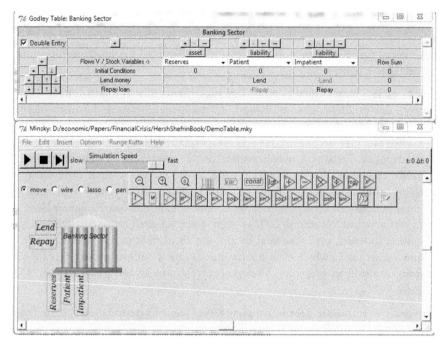

Figure 4.1 Sample Godley Table and Banking Icon in Minsky.

$$\frac{d\text{Reserves}}{dt} = 0$$

$$\frac{d\text{Patient}}{dt} = \text{Repay} - \text{Lend}$$

$$\frac{d\text{Impatient}}{dt} = \text{Lend} - \text{Repay} \qquad (4.1)$$

The loanable funds features of Eggertsson and Krugman (2012b) are:

- that deposits by the "patient agents" enable loans to "impatient agents"; and
- that banks intermediate between saver and borrower and profit by an intermediation fee, but otherwise play no role in lending.

The *Minsky* model shown in Figure 4.2 replicates these features using the bank accounts of four separate entities: the consumption goods sector (with deposit account Dep_{Cons}), which is the lender (Eggertsson and Krugman 2012b); the investment goods sector (with account Dep_{Inv}), which is the borrower; workers (with account *Workers*) who are employed by both the consumption sector and the investment sector;[8] and the banking sector (with the asset account *Reserves* and equity account $Bankers_{NW}$), which intermediates the loans from the consumption sector to the investment sector, and charges a fee for doing so. Each sector maintains a financial table showing the flows into and out of its accounts, and calculates its net worth as a result as the difference between the value of its assets and its liabilities.[9]

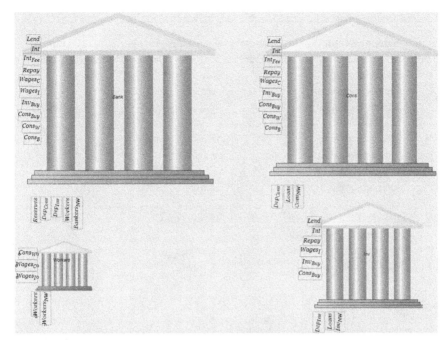

Figure 4.2 Loanable Funds Model—a Four-Account View of Loanable Funds Generated in Minsky.

Table 4.1 shows this financial system from the banking sector's perspective, and Table 4.2 shows it from the perspective of the lender, the consumption sector. Following the conventions in *Minsky*, assets are shown as positive amounts, and liabilities and equity are shown as negatives, while the source of any financial transaction is shown as a positive and its destination as a negative.[10] All entries in the table represent flows, and *Minsky* automatically generates the resulting system of differential equations in LaTeX. The ten flows that define the model are all shown in the banking sector's table, and are respectively:

1. The consumption sector lends to the investment sector via the flow "*Lend*" from the account Dep_{Cons} to the account Dep_{Inv};
2. The investment sector makes interest payments "*Int*" to the consumption sector;
3. The banking sector charges the consumption sector an intermediation fee "Int_{Fee}";
4. The investment sector makes debt repayments to the consumption sector "*Repay*";
5. The consumption sector hires workers via the flow "$Wages_C$";
6. The investment sector hires workers via the flow "$Wages_I$";
7. The investment sector purchases consumption goods "$Cons_I$";
8. The consumption sector purchases investment goods "$Cons_C$";
9. Workers purchase consumer goods "$Cons_W$"; and
10. Bankers purchase consumer goods ("$Cons_B$").

Table 4.1. LOANABLE FUNDS MODEL FROM THE BANKING SECTOR'S PERSPECTIVE.

	Banking Sector	Assets	Liabilities			Equity
Flows	Accounts	Reserves	Dep_{Cons}	Dep_{Inv}	Workers	$Bankers_{NW}$
1	Lending		Lend	-Lend		
2	Interest payments		-Int	Int		
3	Bank intermediation fee		Int_{Fee}			$-Int_{Fee}$
4	Debt repayment		-Repay	Repay		
5	Hire workers (Cons)		$Wages_C$		$-Wages_C$	
6	Hire workers (Inv)			$Wages_I$	$-Wages_I$	
7	Intersectoral purchases by Inv		$-Cons_I$	$Cons_I$		
8	Intersectoral purchases by Cons		$Cons_C$	$-Cons_C$		
9	Workers consumption		$-Cons_W$		$Cons_W$	
10	Bankers consumption		$-Cons_B$			$Cons_B$

Table 4.2. LOANABLE FUNDS MODEL FROM THE CONSUMPTION
SECTOR'S PERSPECTIVE.

	Consumption Sector	Assets		Equity
Flows	Accounts	Dep_{Cons}	Loans	$Cons_{NW}$
1	Lending	-Lend	Lend	
2	Interest payments	Int		-Int
3	Bank Intermediation Fee	$-Int_{Fee}$		Int_{Fee}
4	Debt repayment	Repay	-Repay	
5	Hire workers (Cons)	$-Wages_C$		$Wages_C$
6	Intersectoral purchases by Inv	$Cons_I$		$-Cons_I$
7	Intersectoral purchases by Cons	$-Cons_C$		$Cons_C$
8	Workers consumption	$Cons_W$		$-Cons_W$
9	Bankers consumption	$Cons_B$		$-Cons_B$

Lending from the consumption to the investment sector is recorded in the account *Loans*, which is an asset of the consumption sector as shown in its financial account (see Table 4.2; it also appears as a liability of the investment sector in its table of accounts).[11]

Since (for the sake of simplicity) holdings of cash are ignored in this model, money is the sum of the amounts in the four deposit accounts Dep_{Cons}, Dep_{Inv}, *Workers*, and $Bankers_{NW}$ shown in Table 4.1, while debt is the amount in the account *Loans* shown in Table 4.2. Equation (0.2) shows the equations for the dynamics of money and debt in the model, with the first four equations derived from Table 4.1 showing the dynamics of money in the system while the final equation, derived from Table 4.2, shows the dynamics of debt.

$$\frac{d}{dt}\text{Dep}_{\text{Cons}} = \text{Int} + \text{Repay} + \text{Inv}_{\text{Buy}} + \text{Cons}_W + \text{Cons}_B$$

$$- (\text{Lend} + \text{Int}_{\text{Fee}} + \text{Wages}_C + \text{Cons}_{\text{Buy}})$$

$$\frac{d}{dt}\text{Dep}_{\text{Inv}} = \text{Lend} + \text{Cons}_{\text{Buy}} - (\text{Int} + \text{Repay} + \text{Wages}_I + \text{Inv}_{\text{Buy}})$$

$$\frac{d}{dt}\text{Workers} = \text{Wages}_C + \text{Wages}_I - \text{Cons}_W$$

$$\frac{d}{dt}\text{Bankers}_{\text{NW}} = \text{Int}_{\text{Fee}} - \text{Cons}_B$$

$$\frac{d\text{Loans}}{dt} = \text{Lend} - \text{Repay} \tag{4.2}$$

Defining money M as the sum of the first four accounts, it is obvious that the change in the amount of money is zero:

$$M(t) = \text{Dep}_{\text{Cons}}(t) + \text{Dep}_{\text{Inv}}(t) + \text{Workers}(t) + \text{Bankers}_{\text{NW}}(t)$$

$$\frac{d}{dt}M(t) = 0 \tag{4.3}$$

Therefore the amount of money—which for convenience we can treat as having been created by government fiat, without needing to specify a government sector in the model—remains constant:

$$M(t) = \int_0^t 0 \cdot ds = M(0) \tag{4.4}$$

Without having to define a full economic model, we can now specify aggregate demand AD as being equivalent to the turnover of the money in the economy, using the velocity of money v (see Figure 4.3 and Equation (0.5)).

As is well known, contrary to Milton Friedman's claims (Friedman 1948, 1959, 1969; Friedman and Schwartz 1963), the velocity of money is not a constant: "It is also apparent that money velocities are procyclical and quite volatile" (Kydland and Prescott 1990, 14). However, the identity that $v \equiv Y/M$ can be used in this simple model to map from the money stock to the level of aggregate demand.[12]

Using the subscript LF to indicate that this is aggregate demand in a loanable funds model, we have that aggregate demand at time t is the velocity of money times the stock of money at that time:[13]

$$AD_{LF}(t) = v(t) \cdot M(0) \tag{4.5}$$

Aggregate demand across any defined time period t_2-t_1 will therefore be this instantaneous flow times the time period itself:[14]

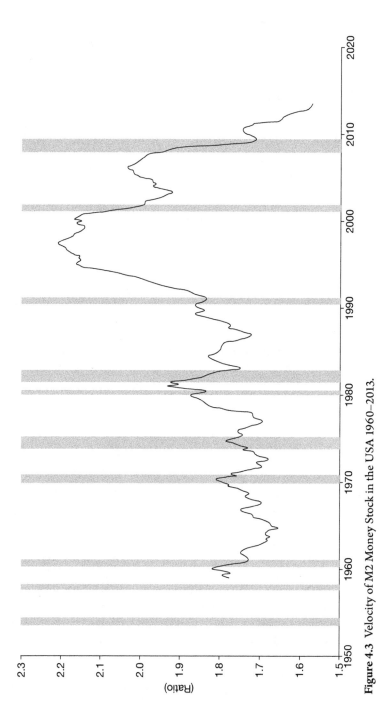

Figure 4.3 Velocity of M2 Money Stock in the USA 1960–2013.

$$AD_{LF}(t_2 - t_1) = v(t) \cdot (t_2 - t_1) \cdot \int_{t_1}^{t_2} 0 \cdot ds$$

$$= v(t) \cdot (t_2 - t_1) \cdot M(t_1)^{15} \qquad (4.6)$$

Finally, using D for brevity in place of *Loans* in Equation (0.7), it is obvious that there is no link between the dynamics of debt and either the stock or the turnover of money, and therefore there is no direct relation between private debt and aggregate demand.[16] The amount of debt can rise or fall substantially over time, without having any effect on the amount of money in circulation, which remains constant:

$$\frac{d}{dt}D(t) = \text{Lend}(t) - \text{Repay}(t) \qquad (4.7)$$

Given the absence of a relationship between lending and the money supply, changes in the amount of debt have only a minor impact on macroeconomic activity, via related changes in the velocity of money.[17]

A MONETARY MODEL OF ENDOGENOUS MONEY

This structural model of loanable funds shown in Figure 4.2 is converted into a model of endogenous money by three simple changes:

- *Loans* are shifted from the assets of the consumption sector to the assets of the banking sector;
- Interest payments are transferred to the equity account of the banking sector, Bankers_{NW}; and
- Since banks are loan originators in this model and receive interest payments, the intermediation fee is deleted.

This revised model is shown in Figure 4.4 and Table 4.3.[18] The changes between the loanable funds model in Table 4.1 and the endogenous money model of Table 4.3 all occur in the first four rows, with the row for an intermediation fee deleted, and locations of the flows *Lend*, *Int*, and *Repay* altered as indicated by the arrows. The two tables are otherwise identical.

The money and debt equations of this model are:

$$\frac{d\text{Dep}_{\text{Cons}}}{dt} = \text{Inv}_{\text{Buy}} + \text{Cons}_W + \text{Cons}_B - (\text{Wages}_C + \text{Cons}_{\text{Buy}})$$

$$\frac{d\text{Dep}_{\text{Inv}}}{dt} = \text{Lend} + \text{Cons}_{\text{Buy}} - (\text{Int} + \text{Repay} + \text{Wages}_I + \text{Inv}_{\text{Buy}})$$

$$\frac{d\text{Workers}}{dt} = \text{Wages}_C + \text{Wages}_I - \text{Cons}_W$$

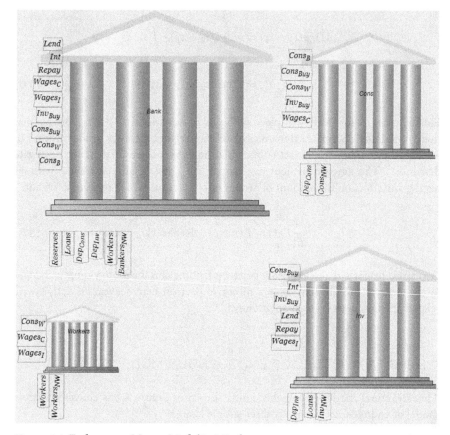

Figure 4.4 Endogenous Money Model in Minsky.

$$\frac{d\text{Bankers}_{\text{NW}}}{dt} = \text{Int} - \text{Cons}_B$$

$$\frac{d\text{Loans}}{dt} = \text{Lend} - \text{Repay} \qquad (4.8)$$

Despite the simplicity of the changes needed to move from loanable funds to endogenous money, the dynamics of money are now profoundly different. The rate of change of money is precisely equal to the rate of change of debt:

$$\frac{d}{dt}M(t) = \text{Lend}(t) - \text{Repay}(t) = \frac{d}{dt}D(t) \qquad (4.9)$$

The stock of money in the economy is therefore the sum of the initial level of money in existence, plus the new money created by the extension of new loans from the banking sector to the investment sector. Assuming for convenience that $D(0) = 0$, this yields:

$$M(t) = \int_0^t \frac{d}{ds}D(s) \cdot ds = M(0) + D(t) \qquad (4.10)$$

Table 4.3. ENDOGENOUS MONEY MODEL FROM THE BANKING SECTOR'S PERSPECTIVE.

	Banking Sector	Assets		Liabilities			Equity
Flows	Accounts	Reserves	Loans	Dep_{Cons}	Dep_{Inv}	Workers	$Bankers_{NW}$
1	Lending		Lend	⇐══	-Lend		
2	Interest payments			Int		⌒	-Int
3	Debt repayment		-Repay	⇐══	Repay		
4	Hire workers (Cons)			$Wages_C$		$-Wages_C$	
5	Hire workers (Inv)				$Wages_I$	$-Wages_I$	
6	Intersectoral purchases by Inv			$-Cons_I$	$Cons_I$		
7	Intersectoral purchases by Cons			$Cons_C$	$-Cons_C$		
8	Workers' consumption			$-Cons_W$		$Cons_W$	
9	Bankers' consumption			$-Cons_B$			$Cons_B$

Using the subscript *EM* to indicate that this is an endogenous money model, aggregate demand is therefore

$$AD_{EM}(t) = v(t) \cdot (M(0) + D(t)) \tag{4.11}$$

Aggregate demand during some given time period t_2-t_1 is therefore a function of the change in debt over that period:

$$AD_{EM(t_2-t_1)} = v(t) \cdot (t_2 - t_1) \cdot \int_{t_1}^{t_2} \frac{d}{ds} D(s) \cdot ds$$

$$= v(t) \cdot (t_2 - t_1) \cdot (M(t_1) + (D(t_2) - D(t_1))) \tag{4.12}$$

We can now compare the symbolic measure of nominal aggregate demand in an endogenous money model with its counterpart in a loanable funds model (the numerical values of velocity, demand and debt will clearly differ substantially, as the simulations in section 7 illustrate) to identify the substantive difference between a loanable funds view of the monetary system and that of endogenous money:

$$AD_{EM(t_2-t_1)} - AD_{LF(t_2-t_1)} = v(t) \cdot (t_2 - t_1) \cdot ((D(t_2) - D(t_1))) \tag{4.13}$$

The loanable funds model thus omits the impact of the change in debt on the level of aggregate demand.

OCCAM'S RAZOR PASSES ENDOGENOUS MONEY AND FAILS LOANABLE FUNDS

If banks make loans to non-banks—as is manifestly the case—and create money in doing so by crediting the deposit accounts of their borrowers—as even the staunch advocate of loanable funds Paul Krugman has conceded—then the loanable funds model is too extreme a simplification of the nature of capitalism. As Einstein put it in relation to physics:

> It can scarcely be denied that the supreme goal of all theory is to make the irreducible basic elements as simple and as few as possible *without having to surrender the adequate representation of a single datum of experience.* (Einstein 1934, 165, emphasis added)

Omitting the capacity of banks to create money, and the impact this has on key macroeconomic aggregates, omits a vital "datum of experience" from macroeconomic models. The capacity of bank lending to alter the level of aggregate demand means that banks, debt, and money must be included in any adequate model of macroeconomics.

In particular, the acknowledgment of the macroeconomic significance of endogenous money requires a dynamic redefinition of aggregate demand and aggregate income to include the change in debt,[19] while remaining consistent with the identity that aggregate expenditure is aggregate income. This formula, derived in Keen (2015), is that aggregate demand and aggregate income are demand and income from the circulation of existing money, plus demand and income from new debt:

$$AD \equiv AY \approx V \cdot M + \frac{d}{dt}D \tag{4.14}$$

This formula corrects a rule of thumb proposition that I have previously asserted, that aggregate demand is the sum of income plus the change in debt (Keen 2014; see also Krugman 2013b),[20] which has been seen to violate the accounting identity that expenditure is income (Fiebiger 2014; Lavoie 2014; but see Rowe 2013).[21]

SIMULATING LOANABLE FUNDS AND ENDOGENOUS MONEY

A simulation of the two models confirms the importance of including the change in debt in aggregate demand. The simple models used here are identical except for the structure of lending, so that the differences in their behavior reflects simply that issue. The models use simple variable time parameters to relate the various monetary flows to each other and the monetary stocks, so that the results do not depend on any behavioral assumptions (see the Appendix for the model equations and default parameter values). The values of two of these parameters—the lending and repayment rates—are varied over the simulations shown in Figure 4.5 and Figure 4.6.

Variations in the lending and repayment rates have a minor effect on income in the loanable funds model (see Figure 4.7) because they impact upon the velocity

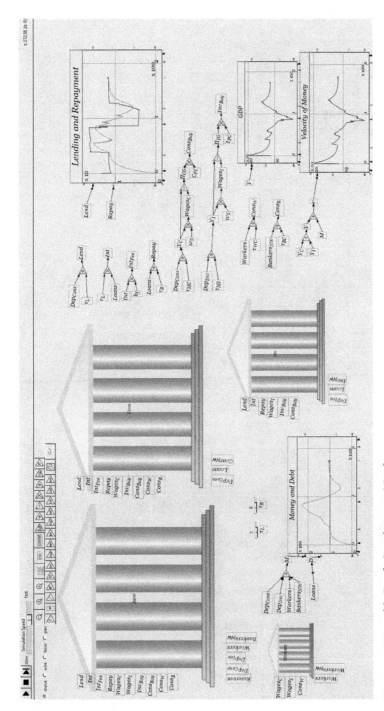

Figure 4.5 Loanable Funds Simulation in Minsky.

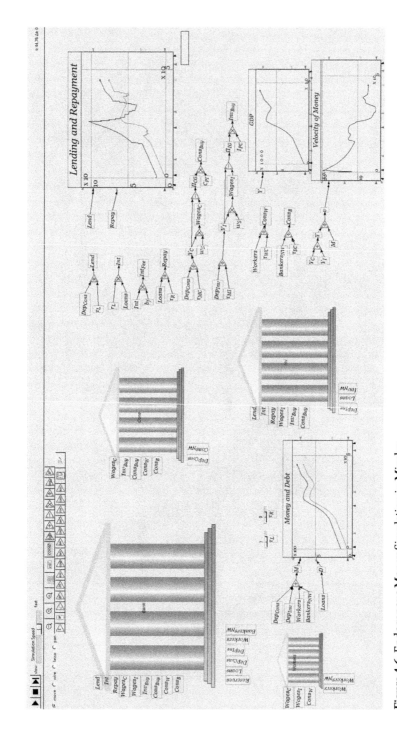

Figure 4.6 Endogenous Money Simulation in Minsky.

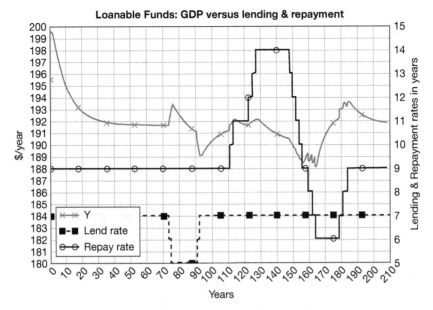

Figure 4.7 GDP as a Function of Lending and Repayment Rates in Loanable Funds.

of circulation of money (see Figure 4.8). However, the level does not rise (or fall) significantly, and there is no trend, since variations in the level of debt have no impact upon the money supply, which remains constant (see Figure 4.9).

In contrast, variations in the lending and repayment rates have a dramatic impact upon GDP in the endogenous money model (see Figure 4.10), because as well as having an impact upon the velocity of money (see Figure 4.11), they alter the rate of creation and destruction of money (see Figure 4.12).

MODELING FINANCIAL INSTABILITY

The preceding proof provides a theoretical justification for the key role given to the level and change in aggregate private debt in Minsky's financial instability hypothesis. Empirical research by Fama and French provides further support, by concluding that the correlations they found (including a 0.79 correlation between aggregate corporate investment and change in long-term corporate debt) "confirm the impression that debt plays a key role in accommodating year-by-year variation in investment" (Fama and French 1999, 1954).[22]

Minsky's succinct summary of his financial instability hypothesis, emphasizes the central role of private debt to his analysis (Minsky 1978; reprinted in Minsky 1982):

> The natural starting place for analyzing the relation between debt and income is to take an economy with a cyclical past that is now doing well. The inherited debt reflects the history of the economy, which includes a period in the not too distant past in which the economy did not do well. Acceptable liability structures are based upon some margin of safety so that expected cash flows, even in periods when the economy is not doing well, will cover contractual debt payments. As the period over which the economy does well lengthens,

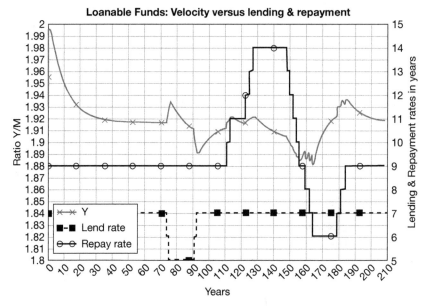

Figure 4.8 Money Velocity as a Function of Lending and Repayment Rates in Loanable Funds.

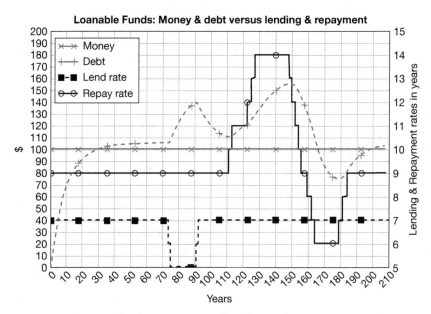

Figure 4.9 Money and Debt as Functions of Lending and Repayment Rates in Loanable Funds.

two things become evident in board rooms. Existing debts are easily validated and units that were heavily in debt prospered; it paid to lever. After the event it becomes apparent that the margins of safety built into debt structures were too great. As a result, over a period in which the economy does well, views about acceptable debt structure change. In the dealmaking that goes on between

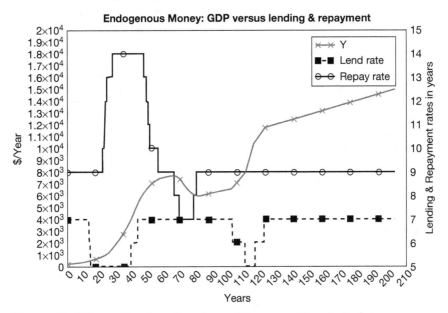

Figure 4.10 GDP as a Function of Lending and Repayment Rates in Endogenous Money.

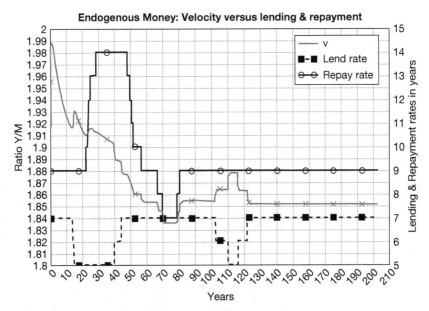

Figure 4.11 Money velocity as a function of Lending and Repayment Rates in Endogenous Money.

banks, investment bankers, and businessmen, the acceptable amount of debt to use in financing various types of activity and positions increases. This increase in the weight of debt financing raises the market price of capital assets and increases investment. As this continues the economy is transformed into a boom economy.

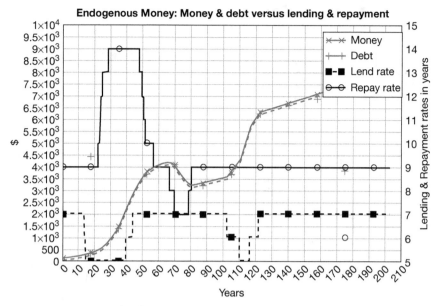

Figure 4.12 Money and Debt as Functions of Lending and Repayment Rates in Endogenous Money.

Stable growth is inconsistent with the manner in which investment is determined in an economy in which debt-financed ownership of capital assets exists, and the extent to which such debt financing can be carried is market determined. It follows that the fundamental instability of a capitalist economy is upward. The tendency to transform doing well into a speculative investment boom is the basic instability in a capitalist economy. (Minsky 1982, 66–67)

I modeled this process by extending Goodwin's cyclical growth model—in which profit-rate-motivated investment and employment-rate-motivated wage demands generated a closed limit cycle in employment and income distribution (Goodwin 1967)—to include debt-financed investment. Goodwin's model reduced to two coupled differential equations in the employment rate (λ) and wages share of output (ω), where $\lambda_{fn}(\lambda)$ is a Phillips-curve relation and $I_{fn}(\pi_r)$ is an investment function depending on the rate of profit ($\pi_r = \Pi/Y$):[23]

$$\frac{d\lambda}{dt} = \lambda \cdot \left(\frac{I_{fn}(\pi_r)}{v} - (\alpha + \beta + \delta) \right)$$

$$\frac{d\omega}{dt} = \omega \cdot (\lambda_{fn}(\lambda) - \alpha) \tag{4.15}$$

I replaced Goodwin's "starkly schematized" (Goodwin 1967, 54) assumption that investment equaled profit at all times with an investment function in which investment exceeded profit at high rates of profit, and was below profit at low rates. An equation to represent debt-financed investment was added—Equation (0.17)—and

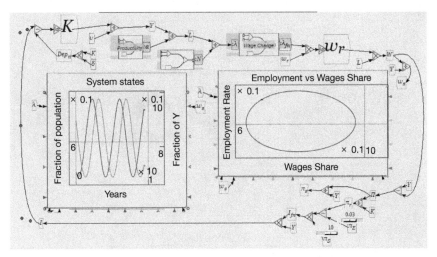

Figure 4.13 Goodwin's Model with Linear Behavioral Functions Simulated in Minsky.

profit was redefined as earnings net of interest payments ($\Pi = Y - W - r \cdot D$):

$$\frac{d}{dt}D = I - \Pi \tag{4.16}$$

This transformed Goodwin's model into a three-state model of Minsky's hypothesis, with the extra equation being the dynamics of the private debt to output ratio $d = D/Y$ (see Keen 2013, 236–38 for the derivation):[24]

$$\frac{d\lambda}{dt} = \lambda \cdot \left(\frac{I_{fn}(\pi)}{v} - (\alpha + \beta + \delta) \right)$$

$$\frac{d\omega}{dt} = \omega \cdot (\lambda_{fn}(\lambda) - \alpha)$$

$$\frac{d}{dt}d = I(\pi) - \pi - d \cdot \left(\frac{I(\pi)}{v} - \delta \right) \tag{4.17}$$

In Keen 1995 and 2000 I used nonlinear functions for both investment determination and wage setting; here I use linear functions to emphasize that both the cyclical behavior of Goodwin's model and the debt-induced breakdown in the Minsky model are endemic rather than products of the assumed functional forms. In the simulations shown in Figure 4.13 and Figure 4.14, the investment and wage change functions are:

$$I_{fn}(\pi_r) = (\pi_r - \pi_E) \times \pi_S$$

$$\lambda_{fn}(\lambda) = \lambda_S \times (\lambda - \lambda_0) \tag{4.18}$$

Figure 4.13 shows the fixed cycle in Goodwin's basic model.

Figure 4.14 shows a typical run of the Minsky model, which has three key characteristics:

- The initial behavior of the model involves a reduction in the volatility of employment and output—effectively a "Great Moderation";

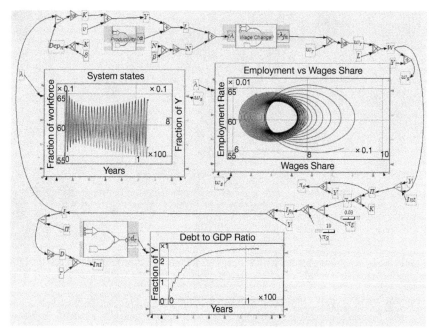

Figure 4.14 Minsky's FIH with Linear Behavioral Functions Simulated in Minsky.

- Workers' share of output has a secular tendency to fall; and
- The initial reduction in employment and output volatility gives way to increasing volatility as the debt to output level rises (with the ultimate outcome of a debt-induced collapse in output and employment).[25]

The fact that this simple model generated outcomes that, in a very stylized way, mirror the empirical record of the recent economic past emphasizes the importance of developing an approach to macroeconomics in which banks and private debt play integral roles. The empirical data, interpreted in the light of the theoretical arguments given here, further emphasizes the importance of paying close policy attention to the hitherto ignored phenomenon of the growth of private debt.

EMPIRICAL DATA

Fortunately, though mainstream economic theory has ignored the role of private debt, statistical agencies have collected the data. Figure 4.15 is an imputed series combining actual Federal Reserve quarterly data on household plus nonfinancial corporate debt since 1952 (and yearly data from 1945 to 1952) with US Census data from 1916 to 1970, and partial Census data on bank loans from 1834 to 1970 (Census 1949; Census 1975).

The causal role of the change in debt in aggregate demand identified in this paper implies that there should be a strong empirical relationship between change in debt and macroeconomic data such as the unemployment rate—in contrast to the loanable-funds-based presumption that "absent implausibly large differences in

Figure 4.15 US Private Debt since 1834.

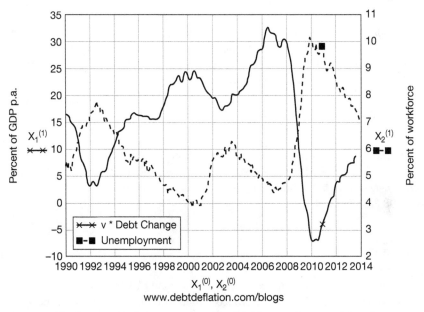

Figure 4.16 Change in Debt Times Velocity and US Unemployment (Correlation −0.92).

marginal spending propensities among the groups … pure redistributions should have no significant macro-economic effects" (Bernanke 2000, 24).[26] This loanable funds presumption is strongly rejected by the data. As Figure 4.16 shows, the correlation of the change in debt times velocity (divided by GDP) with the level of unemployment since 1990 is −0.92.[27]

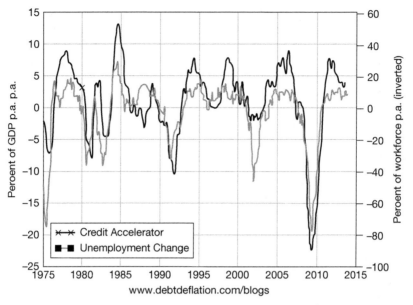

Figure 4.17 Credit Acceleration and Change in Unemployment (Correlation
−0.78).

The first difference of Equation 14 also implies a strong relationship between the
change in the change in debt over two time periods and change in unemployment
over that period. Setting $t_2 - t_1 = t_1 - t_0 = \Delta t$, the change in aggregate demand
between periods $t_2 - t_1$ and $t_1 - t_0$ (normalized by dividing by Y_{t_0}) is:

$$\frac{AD_{t_2-t_1} - AD_{t_1-t_0}}{Y_{t_0}} = \frac{Y_{t_1} - Y_{t_0}}{Y_{t_0}} + v(t) \cdot \Delta t \cdot \frac{D_{t_0} + D_{t_2} - 2 \cdot D_{t_1}}{Y_{t_0}} \qquad (4.19)$$

Setting $\Delta t = 1$, the correlation between equation (0.20), which we term the "credit
accelerator" (see also Biggs and Mayer 2010; Biggs et al. 2010), and the annual
percentage change in the unemployment rate over the period from 1975 until today
is −0.78 (see Figure 4.17).

CONCLUSION

Given that bank lending creates money and repayment of debt destroys it, the change
in debt plays an integral role in macroeconomics by dynamically varying the level of
aggregate demand. The omission of this factor from mainstream economic models
is the reason that these models failed to warn of the dangers of the dramatic buildup
in private debt since WWII—and especially since 1993, when the debt-financed
recovery from the 1990s' recession took the aggregate private debt level past the peak
caused by deflation in the 1930s (see Figure 4.15). It is also the reason why they failed
to anticipate the crisis that began in 2007, and instead predicted that, as the OECD
put it in June 2007, "the current economic situation is in many ways better than what
we have experienced in years . . . Our central forecast remains indeed quite benign"
(OECD 2007). Policymakers relying upon mainstream economists as experts on

the functioning of the economy thus not only received no warning about the worst economic crisis since the Great Depression but were falsely led to expect benign rather than malignant economic conditions.

The erroneous neglect of the dynamics of private debt by the economics profession has therefore resulted in enormous social and economic harm to society. This is the opposite of the intended goal of economic theory and policy. If economic theory and policy are to fulfil their intended role, it is imperative that a reformed macroeconomics be developed in which banks, money, and the dynamics of debt play integral roles.

APPENDIX

Loanable Funds Model

DIFFERENTIAL EQUATIONS FOR MONEY AND DEBT

$$\frac{d\text{Dep}_{\text{Cons}}}{dt} = \text{Int} + \text{Repay} + \text{Inv}_{\text{Buy}} + \text{Cons}_W + \text{Cons}_B$$
$$- (\text{Lend} + \text{Int}_{\text{Fee}} + \text{Wages}_C + \text{Cons}_{\text{Buy}})$$

$$\frac{d\text{Dep}_{\text{Inv}}}{dt} = \text{Lend} + \text{Cons}_{\text{Buy}} - (\text{Int} + \text{Repay} + \text{Wages}_I + \text{Inv}_{\text{Buy}})$$

$$\frac{d\text{Workers}}{dt} = \text{Wages}_C + \text{Wages}_I - \text{Cons}_W$$

$$\frac{d\text{Bankers}_{\text{NW}}}{dt} = \text{Int}_{\text{Fee}} - \text{Cons}_B$$

$$\frac{d\text{Loans}}{dt} = \text{Lend} - \text{Repay}$$

$$\frac{d\text{Reserves}}{dt} = 0 \tag{4.20}$$

OTHER DIFFERENTIAL EQUATIONS

$$\frac{d\text{Cons}_{\text{NW}}}{dt} = \text{Int} + \text{Inv}_{\text{Buy}} + \text{Cons}_W + \text{Cons}_B - (\text{Int}_{\text{Fee}} + \text{Wages}_C + \text{Cons}_{\text{Buy}})$$

$$\frac{d\text{Inv}_{\text{NW}}}{dt} = \text{Cons}_{\text{Buy}} - (\text{Int} + \text{Wages}_I + \text{Inv}_{\text{Buy}})$$

$$\frac{d\text{Workers}_{\text{NW}}}{dt} = \text{Wages}_C + \text{Wages}_I - \text{Cons}_W \tag{4.21}$$

Endogenous Money Model

DIFFERENTIAL EQUATIONS FOR MONEY AND DEBT

$$\frac{d\text{Dep}_{\text{Cons}}}{dt} = \text{Inv}_{\text{Buy}} + \text{Cons}_W + \text{Cons}_B - (\text{Wages}_C + \text{Cons}_{\text{Buy}})$$

$$\frac{d\text{Dep}_{\text{Inv}}}{dt} = \text{Lend} + \text{Cons}_{\text{Buy}} - (\text{Int} + \text{Repay} + \text{Wages}_I + \text{Inv}_{\text{Buy}})$$

$$\frac{d\text{Workers}}{dt} = \text{Wages}_C + \text{Wages}_I - \text{Cons}_W$$

$$\frac{d\text{Bankers}_{\text{NW}}}{dt} = \text{Int} - \text{Cons}_B$$

$$\frac{d\text{Loans}}{dt} = \text{Lend} - \text{Repay}$$

$$\frac{d\text{Reserves}}{dt} = 0 \tag{4.22}$$

OTHER DIFFERENTIAL EQUATIONS

$$\frac{d\text{Cons}_{\text{NW}}}{dt} = \text{Inv}_{\text{Buy}} + \text{Cons}_W + \text{Cons}_B - (\text{Wages}_C + \text{Cons}_{\text{Buy}})$$

$$\frac{d\text{Inv}_{\text{NW}}}{dt} = \text{Cons}_{\text{Buy}} - (\text{Int} + \text{Wages}_I + \text{Inv}_{\text{Buy}})$$

$$\frac{d\text{Workers}_{\text{NW}}}{dt} = \text{Wages}_C + \text{Wages}_I - \text{Cons}_W \tag{4.23}$$

COMMON DEFINITIONS

$$v = \frac{Y}{M}$$

$$\Pi_{\text{CG}} = Y_C - \text{Wages}_C$$

$$\Pi_{\text{IG}} = Y_I - \text{Wages}_I$$

$$Y = Y_C + Y_I$$

$$\text{Wages}_I = Y_I \times w_S$$

$$\text{Wages}_C = Y_C \times w_S$$

$$\text{Repay} = \frac{\text{Loans}}{\tau_R}$$

$$Y_C = \frac{\text{Dep}_{\text{Cons}}}{\tau_{\text{MC}}}$$

$$Y_I = \frac{\text{Dep}_{\text{Inv}}}{\tau_{\text{MI}}}$$

$$M = \text{Dep}_{\text{Cons}} + \text{Dep}_{\text{Inv}} + \text{Workers} + \text{Bankers}_{\text{NW}}$$

$$\text{Inv}_{\text{Buy}} = \Pi_{\text{IG}} \times I_{\text{PC}}$$

$$\text{Int}_{\text{Fee}} = \text{Int} \times b_f$$

$$\text{Int} = r_L \times \text{Loans}$$

$$\text{Lend} = \frac{\text{Dep}_{\text{Cons}}}{\tau_L}$$

$$\text{Cons}_W = \frac{\text{Workers}}{\tau_{\text{WC}}}$$

$$\text{Cons}_{\text{Buy}} = \Pi_{\text{CG}} \times C_{\text{PI}}$$

$$\text{Cons}_B = \frac{\text{Bankers}_{\text{NW}}}{\tau_{\text{BC}}}$$

$$D = \text{Loans} \tag{4.24}$$

COMMON PARAMETERS TO LOANABLE FUNDS AND ENDOGENOUS MONEY MODELS

$$w_S = 0.7$$

$$C_{\text{PI}} = 0.5$$

$$\tau_{\text{WC}} = 0.08$$

$$\tau_R = 9$$

$$\tau_{\text{MI}} = 0.25$$

$$\tau_{\text{MC}} = 0.5$$

$$\tau_L = 7$$

$$\tau_{\text{BC}} = 1$$

$$r_L = 0.04$$

$$b_f = 0.1$$

$$I_{\text{PC}} = 0.1 \tag{4.25}$$

Goodwin model

$$\frac{dK}{dt} = I - K \times \delta$$

$$\frac{dw_r}{dt} = \lambda_{\text{fn}} \times w_r$$

$$\frac{dN}{dt} = N \times \beta$$

$$\frac{da}{dt} = a \times \alpha$$

$$I = I_{\text{fn}} \times Y$$

$$I_{\text{fn}} = (\pi_r - \pi_E) \times \pi_S$$

$$\lambda_{\text{fn}} = \lambda_S \times (\lambda - \lambda_0)$$

$$w_s = \frac{W}{Y}$$

$$\pi_s = \frac{\Pi}{Y}$$

$$\lambda = \frac{L}{N}$$

$$\Pi = Y - W$$

$$W = w_r \times L$$

$$\pi_r = \frac{\Pi}{K}$$

$$Y = \frac{K}{v}$$

$$L = \frac{Y}{a} \tag{4.26}$$

Minsky Model (New and Modified Equations Only)

$$\frac{dD}{dt} = I - \Pi$$

$$\Pi = Y - (W + \text{Int})$$

$$\text{Int} = D \times r \tag{4.27}$$

Common Parameters to Goodwin and Minsky Models

$$\alpha = 0.02$$
$$\beta = 0.025$$
$$\delta = 0.05$$
$$r = 0.05$$
$$v = 3$$
$$\lambda_S = 5$$
$$\lambda_0 = 0.6$$
$$\pi_E = 0.03$$
$$\pi_S = 10$$
$$K(0) = 300$$
$$N(0) = 180$$
$$a(0) = 1$$
$$w_r(0) = 0.9$$
$$D(0) = 0 \tag{4.28}$$

Minsky

Minsky is an addition to the family of system-dynamics programs that began with Jay Forrester's pioneering work on developing a visual metaphor for constructing and simulating dynamic models of complex social and economic processes (Forrester 1968). Forrester's metaphor was the flowchart (see Figure 4.18): a drawing of the relationships in a system became the framework for developing a mathematical model of that system.

The proposed model structure and method of solution retain a one-to-one correspondence between the presumed form of the real economic world and the quantities, coefficients, variables, and decision criteria of the model. Formulation in terms of a "flow diagram" is possible so that a pictorial

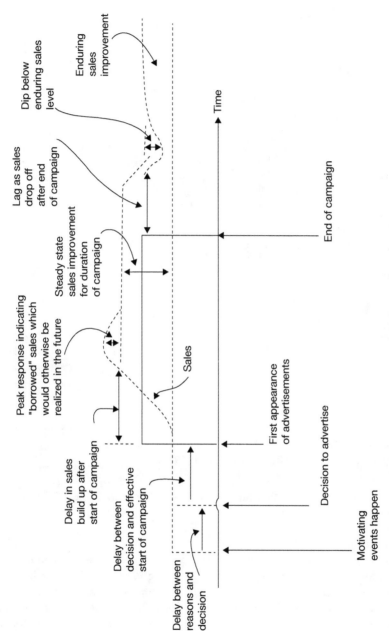

Figure 4.18 The First System-Dynamics Diagram from Forrester 2003 (1956).

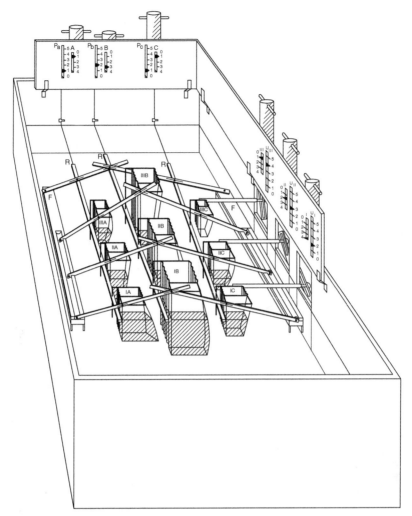

Figure 4.19 Fisher's 1891 Hydraulic Machine for Calculating Walrasian Equilibrium Prices, from Brainard and Scarf (69).

representation of the relationships within the system is available at all times. (Forrester 2003, 344)

There are now at least a dozen programs implementing this modeling philosophy, ranging from the free open-source program Xcos to the $4,000-a-copy commercial program Simulink. This paradigm is now pervasive in engineering, but it failed to take root in economics, despite the fact that Forrester's concept was twice anticipated in economics—firstly by Irving Fisher in 1891 (see Figure 4.19) with a hydraulic model for calculating equilibrium values in a Walrasian model (Brainard and Scarf 2005), and then by the engineer-turned-economist Bill Phillips with genuinely dynamic analog computer systems (Hayes 2011; Leeson 1994a, 1994b, 1995, 2000; Phillips 1950, 1954, 1957) some years before Forrester. However, there was no development in economics comparable to Forrester's innovation (in conjunction with the computer programmers Phyllis Fox and Alexander Pugh—see

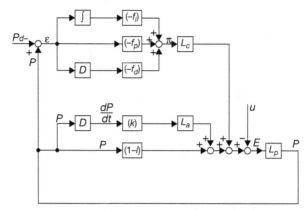

Figure 4.20 Phillips's Schematic Diagram of a Dynamic Multiplier-Accelerator Model, from Phillips (1954, 306).

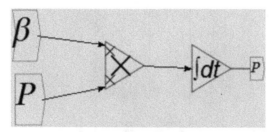

Figure 4.21 A Simple Algebraic Equation in a System-Dynamics Program (Minsky).

Lane 2007) of a digital computer program—DYNAMO—to provide a general purpose foundation for building dynamic models of complex systems.

The core paradigm in system-dynamics programs is the construction of mathematical equations via flowcharts identical in spirit to that developed by Phillips (see Figure 4.20). For example, Figure 4.21 is the system-dynamics equivalent of the differential equation for exponential population growth $\frac{d}{dt}P = \beta \times P$.

Simple expressions like this are just as easily rendered in equations or standard text-oriented computer programs, but the system-dynamics approach makes it easier to comprehend much more complex models—hence its dominance in the engineering field today.

Minsky provides this classic system-dynamics approach, and adds a new method of constructing differential equations to the system-dynamics toolkit that is superior for modeling financial flows: the Godley Table. Based on the accounting concept of double-entry bookkeeping, each column represents the dynamic equation of a given financial account, while each row represents transactions between accounts. This is a more natural way to portray financial transactions which also helps enforce the fundamental rules of accounting—that assets equal liabilities plus equity.

Minsky ensures this in three ways. First, all row operations in a Godley Table must sum to zero—otherwise an error is flagged. Second, the source of any transaction is shown as a positive while the destination (or "sink" in system-dynamics parlance) is shown as a negative.[28] Third, assets are shown as positive while liabilities and equity

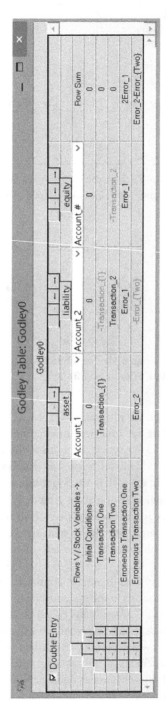

Figure 4.22 A Sample Godley Table.

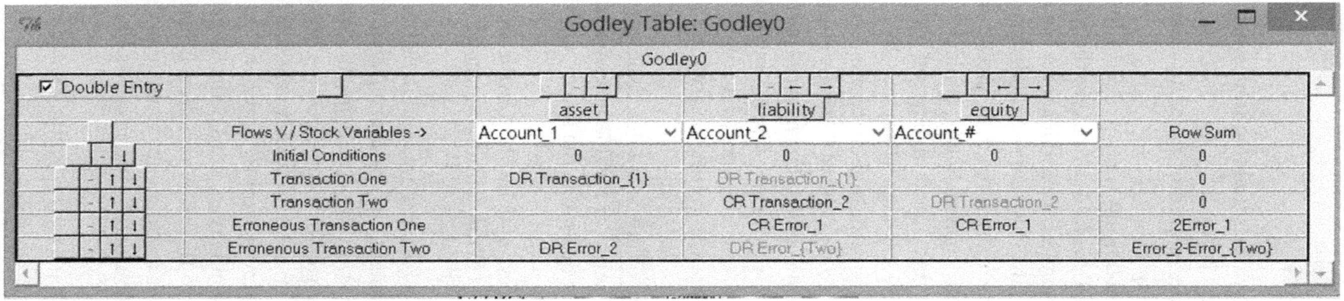

Godley Table: Godley0

Godley0				
	asset	liability	equity	
Flows V / Stock Variables ->	Account_1	Account_2	Account_#	Row Sum
Initial Conditions	0	0	0	0
Transaction One	DR Transaction_{1}	DR Transaction_{1}		0
Transaction Two		CR Transaction_2	DR Transaction_2	0
Erroneous Transaction One		CR Error_1	CR Error_1	2Error_1
Erronenous Transaction Two	DR Error_2	DR Error_{Two}	CR Error_1	Error_2-Error_{Two}

Figure 4.23

are shown as negative. Figure 4.22 illustrates these three conventions—including showing what happens when they are breached.

NOTES

1. Minsky (and the system dynamics tradition from which it emanates) is described more fully in section 5 of the appendix.
2. Consequently all magnitudes in the models in this paper are nominal.
3. Except during a liquidity trap.
4. A typical instance is the following from Krugman in a post entitled "Banking Mysticism": "For in the end, banks don't change the basic notion of interest rates as determined by liquidity preference and loanable funds—yes, both, because the message of IS-LM is that both views, properly understood, are correct. Banks don't create demand out of thin air any more than anyone does by choosing to spend more; and banks are just one channel linking lenders to borrowers. I know I'll get the usual barrage of claims that I don't understand banking; actually, I think I do, and it's the mystics who have it wrong." (Krugman 2012a)
5. "All the points I've been trying to make about the non-specialness of banks are there. In particular, the discussion on pp. 412–413 of why the mechanics of lending don't matter—*yes, commercial banks, unlike other financial intermediaries, can make a loan simply by crediting the borrower with new deposits*, but there's no guarantee that the funds stay there—refutes, in one fell swoop, a lot of the nonsense one hears about how said mechanics of bank lending change everything about the role banks play in the economy.
   Banks are just another kind of financial intermediary, and the size of the banking sector—and hence the quantity of outside money—is determined by the same kinds of considerations that determine the size of, say, the mutual fund industry." (Krugman 2013a, emphasis added)
6. Though not banks or money: initially "borrowing and lending take the form of risk-free bonds denominated in the consumption good" (Eggertsson and Krugman 2012a, 1474).
7. "To motivate borrowing and lending we assume that one of the household types (the borrowers) can investment [*sic*] in capital, while the other type (the saver) can only invest in a one period risk-free bond. In order to have borrowing and lending in steady state we need to ensure that the borrowers cannot self-finance in the long run ... A mathematical [*sic*] equivalent way to accomplishing [*sic*] this is to simply assume the borrower is more "impatient," a short-cut we use here for a better comparison with the other variations of the model in the paper ... The only difference with the model in the main text, then, is that there is a capital income that accrues to the borrower that does not show up in the model without capital." See   http://qje.oxfordjournals.org.ezproxy.uws.edu.au/content/127/3/1469/ suppl/DC1.
8. Employment by the banking sector is ignored since it is inconsequential to the purpose of the paper.
9. Account $Bankers_{NW}$ for the banking sector. Similar measures of net worth are maintained for the other three entities in their respective Godley Tables.
10. *Minsky* can also be set up to use the accounting convention of using DR (debit) and CR (credit).

11.　Table 4.2 also displays the dynamics of the consumption sector's net worth in the column "$Cons_{NW}$."

12.　A full economic model would specify production as well as monetary flows, and derive aggregate demand via expenditure from income, rather than estimate it via a simple identity. However this paper's aims are to (a) identify the crucial differences between loanable funds and endogenous money and (b) show that change in debt plays a crucial role in aggregate demand. The identity approach is adequate for these purposes.

13.　This is an instantaneous measure of aggregate demand for a year, which is the timeframe of these models, in the same sense that a car's velocity at a point in time is its instantaneous "miles per hour."

14.　Where the initial sum of money is $M(t_1)$.

15.　The velocity of money will obviously vary over this time period, so aggregate demand will vary even though the stock of money remains constant—as the simulations later in this chapter indicate.

16.　And via extraordinary events like a liquidity trap, which was the focus of Eggertsson and Krugman's paper but is not considered here.

17.　Any effect will be via the impact of a change in the distribution of money which affect its overall velocity of circulation.

18.　Changes to other tables are derivative of those shown here and are not reproduced for the sake of brevity.

19.　Aggregate supply also needs to be redefined to include asset markets, since a large proportion of borrowed money is used for asset purchases, but this topic is not covered in this paper.

20.　In the post "Secular Stagnation Arithmetic," Krugman made the observation that "underneath the apparent stability of the Great Moderation lurked a rapid rise in debt that is now being unwound . . . Debt was rising by around 2 percent of GDP annually; that's not going to happen in future, which a naïve calculation suggests means a reduction in demand, other things equal, of around 2 percent of GDP." This is similar to my arguments prior to this paper, though as I note in Keen 2014 (and prove here), Krugman's proposition is incompatible with loanable funds.

21.　Nick Rowe verbally derived a similar formula that acknowledged the role of the change in debt in increasing demand, while omitting the impact of the velocity of circulation: "Aggregate actual nominal income equals aggregate expected nominal income plus amount of new money created by the banking system minus increase in the stock of money demanded. Nothing in the above violates any national income accounting identity." http://worthwhile.typepad.com/worthwhile_canadian_initi/2013/08/what-steve-keen-is-maybe-trying-to-say.html. Rowe's statement that the banking sector can create new money indicates that his analysis here went beyond the limitations of the loanable funds model.

22.　Were the loanable funds model empirically valid, this debt-financed investment by the corporate sector would be offset by less income-financed consumption by the household sector. However since the endogenous money model is empirically valid, the increased debt-financed investment by the corporate sector is an important and volatile addition to aggregate demand.

23.　α, β, and δ are respectively the rate of growth of labor productivity, population, and the rate of depreciation

24.　The equations in both models as simulated in *Minsky* are shown in 26–27 in the Appendix.

25.   These cycles are more extreme in magnitude but qualitatively identical to those in
      Keen 1995 and 2000, indicating that the main role of nonlinear behavioral relations
      in complex system models is not to generate cycles themselves but to confine cycles
      to more realistic levels.

26.   There are also strong correlations between change in debt and the level of asset
      prices, since a substantial proportion of borrowing today is for speculative pur-
      chases of existing assets, but this topic will not be considered in this paper.

27.   This correlation is slightly higher than that found for the correlation of the change
      in debt alone as a percentage of GDP with unemployment: −0.923 versus −0.899.
      The correlation of the percentage change in debt with unemployment for this time
      period is ever higher at −0.97.

28.   The accounting convention of DR and CR can also be used. The figure below is
      Figure 4.23 with the option of showing DR and CR selected.

REFERENCES

Bernanke, Ben S. 2000. *Essays on the Great Depression.* Princeton, NJ: Princeton
    University Press.

Bezemer, Dirk J. 2009. "'No One Saw This Coming': Understanding Financial Crisis
    Through Accounting Models." Groningen, The Netherlands: Faculty of Economics
    University of Groningen.

Biggs, Michael, and Thomas Mayer. 2010. "The Output Gap Conundrum." *Intereco-
    nomics/Review of European Economic Policy* 45 (1): 11–16.

Biggs, Michael, Thomas Mayer, and Andreas Pick. 2010. "Credit and Economic Recov-
    ery: Demystifying Phoenix Miracles." SSRN eLibrary.

Blanchard, Olivier. 2009. "The State of Macro." *Annual Review of Economics* 1 (1):
    209–228.

Blanchard, Olivier, Giovanni Dell'Ariccia, and Paolo Mauro. 2010. "Rethinking Macroe-
    conomic Policy." *Journal of Money, Credit, and Banking* 42: 199–215.

Brainard, William C., and Herbert E. Scarf, 2005. "How to Compute Equilibrium Prices
    in 1891." *American Journal of Economics and Sociology* 64: 57–83.

Carney, John. 2012. "What Really Constrains Bank Lending." In *NetNet*, edited by J.
    Carney. New York: CNBC. http://www.cnbc.com/id/46970418.

Carpenter, Seth B., and Selva Demiralp. 2010. "Money, Reserves, and the Transmission
    of Monetary Policy: Does the Money Multiplier Exist?" In *Finance and Economics
    Discussion Series*, 1–58. Washington: Federal Reserve Board.

European Central Bank (ECB). May 2012. "Monetary and Financial Developments." In
    Monthly Bulletin. Brussels: European Central Bank. http://www.ecb.europa.eu/pub/
    pdf/mobu/mb201205en.pdf.

Eggertsson, Gauti B., and Paul Krugman. 2012a. "Debt, Deleveraging, and the Liq-
    uidity Trap: A Fisher-Minsky-Koo Approach." *Quarterly Journal of Economics* 127:
    1469–1513.

Eggertsson, Gauti B., and Paul Krugman. 2012b. Supplementary material to "Debt,
    Deleveraging and the Liquidity Trap." *Quarterly Journal of Economics* 127: Appendix.

Einstein, Albert. 1934. "On the Method of Theoretical Physics." *Philosophy of Science* 1:
    163–169.

Fama, Eugene F., and Kenneth R. French. 1999. "The Corporate Cost of Capital and the Return on Corporate Investment." *Journal of Finance* 54 (6): 1939–1967.

Fiebiger, Brett. 2014. "Bank Credit, Financial Intermediation and the Distribution of National Income All Matter to Macroeconomics." *Review of Keynesian Economics* 2 (3): 292–311.

Fisher, Irving. 1933. "The Debt-Deflation Theory of Great Depressions." *Econometrica* 1 (4): 337–357.

Forrester, Jay W. 1968. "Industrial Dynamics—After the First Decade." *Management Science* 14 (7): 398–415.

Forrester, Jay W. 2003. "Dynamic Models of Economic Systems and Industrial Organizations: Note to the Faculty Research Seminar from Jay W. Forrester." November 5, 1956. *System Dynamics Review* 19 (4): 329–345.

Friedman, Milton. 1948. "A Monetary and Fiscal Framework for Economic Stability." *The American Economic Review* 38 (3): 245–264.

Friedman, Milton. 1959. "The Demand for Money: Some Theoretical and Empirical Results." *The American Economic Review* 49 (2): 525–527.

Friedman, Milton. 1969. "The Optimum Quantity of Money." In *The Optimum Quantity of Money and Other Essays*, 1–50. Chicago: MacMillan.

Friedman, Milton, and Anna Jacobson Schwartz. 1963. *A Monetary History of the United States 1867–1960*. Princeton: Princeton University.

Fullwiler, Scott. 2012. "Krugman's Flashing Neon Sign." In *New Economic Perspectives*, edited by S. Kelton. Kansas City: Stephanie Kelton. http://neweconomicperspectives.org/2012/04/krugmans-flashing-neon-sign.html.

Godley, Wynne. 2004. "Weaving Cloth from Graziani's Thread: Endogenous Money in a Simple (but Complete) Keynesian Model." In *Money, Credit and the Role of the State: Essays in Honour of Augusto Graziani*, edited by R. Arena and N. Salvadori, 127–135. Aldershot: Ashgate.

Godley, Wynne, and Marc Lavoie. 2007. *Monetary Economics: An Integrated Approach to Credit, Money, Income, Production and Wealth*. New York: Palgrave Macmillan.

Goodwin, Richard M. 1967. "A Growth Cycle." In *Socialism, Capitalism and Economic Growth*, edited by C. H. Feinstein, 54–58. Cambridge: Cambridge University.

Graziani, Augusto. 1989. "The Theory of the Monetary Circuit." Thames Papers in *Political Economy*. Spring: 1–26.

Hayes, Brian. 2011. "Economics, Control Theory, and the Phillips Machine." ASSRU—Algorithmic Social Science Research Unit.

Holmes, Alan R. 1969. "Operational Constraints on the Stabilization of Money Supply Growth." In *Controlling Monetary Aggregates*, edited by F. E. Morris, 65–77. Nantucket Island: The Federal Reserve Bank of Boston.

Keen, Steve. 1995. "Finance and Economic Breakdown: Modeling Minsky's 'Financial Instability Hypothesis.'" *Journal of Post Keynesian Economics* 17 (4): 607–635.

Keen, Steve. 2000. "The Nonlinear Economics of Debt Deflation." *In Commerce, Complexity, and Evolution: Topics in Economics, Finance, Marketing, and Management: Proceedings of the Twelfth International Symposium in Economic Theory and Econometrics*, edited by W. A. Barnett, C. Chiarella, S. Keen, R. Marks, and H. Schnabl, 83–110. New York: Cambridge University.

Keen, Steve. 2013. "Predicting the 'Global Financial Crisis': Post-Keynesian Macroeconomics." *Economic Record* 89 (285): 228–254.

Keen, Steve. 2014. "Secular Stagnation and Endogenous Money. *Real World Economics Review* 66: 2–11.

Keen, Steve. 2015. "The Macroeconomics of Endogenous Money: Response to Fiebiger, Palley and Lavoie." *Review of Keynesian Economics* forthcoming 3 (2).

Keister, T., and J. McAndrews. 2009. *Why Are Banks Holding So Many Excess Reserves?* New York: Federal Reserve Bank of New York.

Krugman, Paul. 2012a. "Banking Mysticism." In *The Conscience of a Liberal*. New York: New York Times.

Krugman, Paul. 2012b. "Banking Mysticism, Continued." In *The Conscience of a Liberal*. New York: New York Times.

Krugman, Paul. 2012c. *End this Depression Now!* New York: W. W. Norton.

Krugman, Paul. 2012d. "Minsky and Methodology (Wonkish)." The Conscience of a Liberal. *New York Times*.

Krugman, Paul. 2012e. "Oh My, Steve Keen Edition." The Conscience of a Liberal. *New York Times*.

Krugman, Paul. 2012f. "Things I Should Not Be Wasting Time On." The Conscience of a Liberal. *New York Times*.

Krugman, Paul. 2013a. "Commercial Banks As Creators of 'Money.'" The Conscience of a Liberal. *New York Times*.

Krugman, Paul. 2013b. "Secular Stagnation Arithmetic." The Conscience of a Liberal. *New York Times*.

Krugman, Paul. 2014. "A Monetary Puzzle." The Conscience of a Liberal. *New York Times*.

Kydland, Finn E., and Edward C. Prescott. 1990. "Business Cycles: Real Facts and a Monetary Myth." *Federal Reserve Bank of Minneapolis Quarterly Review* 14 (2): 3–18.

Lane, David C. 2007. The Power of the Bond between Cause and Effect: Jay Wright Forrester and the Field of System Dynamics." *System Dynamics Review* 23: 95–118.

Lavoie, Marc. 2014. "A Comment on 'Endogenous Money and Effective Demand': A Revolution or a Step Backwards?" *Review of Keynesian Economics* 2 (3): 321–332.

Leeson, Robert. 1994a. "Some Misunderstandings Concerning the Contributions Made by A. W. H. Phillips and R. G. Lipsey to the Inflation-Unemployment Literature." *History of Economics Review* 22: 70–82.

Leeson, Robert. 1994b. "A. W. H. Phillips M.B.E. (Military Division)." *Economic Journal* 104 (424): 605–618.

Leeson, Robert. 1995. "A. W. H. Phillips: His Machine and His Curve." *New Zealand Economic Papers* 29 (2): 231–243.

Leeson, Robert. 2000. "A. W. H. Phillips: An Extraordinary Life." In *A. W. H. Phillips: Collected Works in Contemporary Perspective*, edited by R. Leeson, 3–17. Cambridge: Cambridge University Press.

McLeay, Michael, Amar Radia, and Ryland Thomas. 2014. "Money Creation in the Modern Economy." *Bank of England Quarterly Bulletin* Q1: 14–27.

Minsky, Hyman P. 1978. "The Financial Instability Hypothesis: A Restatement." Thames Papers in Political Economy, Autumn.

Minsky, Hyman P. 1980. "Capitalist Financial Processes and the Instability of Capitalism." *Journal of Economic Issues* 14 (2): 505–523.

Minsky, Hyman P. 1982. *Can "It" Happen Again?: Essays on Instability and Finance*. Armonk, NY: M. E. Sharpe.

Moore, Basil J. 1979. "The Endogenous Money Stock." *Journal of Post Keynesian Economics* 2 (1): 49–70.

Moore, Basil J. 1983. "Unpacking the Post Keynesian Black Box: Bank Lending and the Money Supply." *Journal of Post Keynesian Economics* 5 (4): 537–556.

Organization for Economic Cooperation and Development (OECD). 2007. "Achieving Further Rebalancing." In *OECD Economic Outlook*. OECD. http://dx.doi.org/10.1787/eco_outlook-v2007-1-2-en.

Palley, Thomas. 1991. "The Endogenous Money Supply: Consensus and Disagreement." *Journal of Post Keynesian Economics* 13 (3): 397–403.

Palley, Thomas. 2002. "Endogenous Money: What It Is and Why It Matters." *Metroeconomica* 53 (2): 152–180.

Palley, Thomas. 2013. "Horizontalists, Verticalists, and Structuralists: The Theory of Endogenous Money Reassessed." *Review of Keynesian Economics* 1 (4): 406–424.

Phillips, A. W. 1950. "Mechanical Models in Economic Dynamics." *Economica* 17 (67): 283–305.

Phillips, A. W. 1954. "Stabilisation Policy in a Closed Economy." *The Economic Journal* 64 (254): 290–323.

Phillips, A. W. 1957. "Stabilisation Policy and the Time-Forms of Lagged Responses." *The Economic Journal* 67 (266): 265–277.

Roche, Cullen. 2013. "Keep Banks Out of Macro?" In *Pragmatic Capitalism*, edited by C. Roche,. New York: Orcam Financial Group. http://pragcap.com/keep-banks-out-of-macro.

Rowe, Nick. 2013. "What Steve Keen Is Maybe Trying to Say." In *Worthwhile Canadian Initiative*, edited by N. Rowe. http://worthwhile.typepad.com/worthwhile_canadian_initi/2013/08/what-steve-keen-is-maybe-trying-to-say.html.

Schumpeter, Joseph Alois. 1934. *The Theory of Economic Development: An Inquiry into Profits, Capital, Credit, Interest and the Business Cycle*. Cambridge, MA: Harvard University Press.

Smets, Frank, and Rafael Wouters. 2007. "Shocks and Frictions in US Business Cycles: A Bayesian DSGE Approach." *American Economic Review* 97 (3): 586–606.

Solow, Robert M. 2003. "Dumb and Dumber in Macroeconomics." In *Festschrift for Joe Stiglitz*. Columbia University. http://economistsview.typepad.com/economistsview/2009/08/solow-dumb-and-dumber-in-macroeconomics.html.

Solow, Robert M. 2008. "The State of Macroeconomics." *The Journal of Economic Perspectives* 22 (1): 243–246.

Sumner, Scott. 2013. "Keep Banks Out of Macro." In *The Money Illusion*. Bentley: Scott Sumner. http://www.themoneyillusion.com/?p=18953.

Tobin, J. 1963. "Commercial Banks as Creators of 'Money.'" In *Banking and Monetary Studies*, edited by D. Carson, pp. 408–419. Washington, DC: Comptroller of the Currency.

US Census Bureau. 1949.*Historical Statistics of the United States 1789–1945*. Washington, DC: US Census Bureau.

US Census Bureau. 1975. *Historical Statistics of the United States Colonial Times to 1970*. Washington, DC: US Census Bureau. Woodford, Michael. 2009. "Convergence in Macroeconomics: Elements of the New Synthesis." *American Economic Journal: Macroeconomics* 1 (1): 267–279.

5

Assessing the Contribution of Hyman Minsky's Perspective to Our Understanding of Economic Instability

HERSH SHEFRIN ■

INTRODUCTION

There are two psychological dimensions to Hyman Minsky's insightful analysis of financial instability. The first involves the psychological traits of economic agents, in both public and private sectors, which generate the instability characterized by booms and busts (Shefrin and Statman 2013). The second involves the psychological traits of economists, politicians, and members of the media who in the main have resisted Minsky's analysis. The purpose of this chapter is to highlight both dimensions.

The main ingredients of the global financial crisis are delineated in the report of the Financial Crisis Inquiry Commission (FCIC 2011). The mix includes a bubble in housing prices, loose lending practices in the mortgage market, innovation and rapid growth of mortgage-based derivatives, and lax regulation of financial markets. All of these, and more, comprise key elements of Minsky's instability framework. Although the FCIC report makes no explicit mention of Minsky, those who worked on the report were well aware of his work (see Stanton 2012).

This chapter is organized around the main elements in Minsky's dynamic, and juxtaposes direct quotations from Minsky with illustrative excerpts from the FCIC report. The quotations help to make clear the tone and emphasis in his writings. The excerpts help to make clear how relevant is Minsky's framework to understanding the global financial crisis that unfolded more than ten years after his death.[1] In effect, the global financial crisis that erupted in 2008 was a major out-of-sample test for

Minsky's ideas. The juxtaposition also provides an opportunity for readers to judge for themselves a claim often made that Minsky's writings were opaque.

In my view, what lies at the heart of the Minsky dynamic is a concept Minsky called "Ponzi finance." Ponzi finance refers to debt financing for which full repayment only occurs if there is sufficient growth in the price of the assets. Significantly, Ponzi finance is what Minsky believes sustains asset pricing bubbles, up to the point at which they burst. Minsky's discussion does not emphasize the degree to which decisions about Ponzi finance are impacted by different psychological elements. Indeed, one of the purposes of this chapter is to do so, drawing on examples from the financial crisis.

One of the most important psychological elements of Minsky's perspective is the extent to which financial crises are unavoidable. The behavioral decision literature is replete with studies demonstrating the extent to which emotions, heuristics, and biases are hardwired into human cognitive processes. This chapter discusses how this literature adds to Minsky's perspective.

Although Minsky suggests that economic stability is unattainable, he does offer policy recommendations that can help mitigate the extent of instability. In this regard, the Fed has identified the importance of placing financial market regulation on an equal footing to monetary policy as one of the main lessons from the financial crisis. Notably, this was one of Minsky's four major policy recommendations.

Another of Minsky's four policy objectives involved employment policy. Minsky was raised in a socialist, Jewish environment in Chicago, and his perspective reflects his background. He writes: "The humane objective of stabilization policy is to achieve a close approximation to full employment . . . [with] demand for labor being at a floor or minimum wage that does not depend upon long- and short-run profit expectations of business" (1986, 343).

The final issue discussed in the chapter concerns the reaction to Minsky's work, not only during his lifetime, but in the wake of the financial crisis.

The chapter is organized as follows. Section 2 describes eight of the main elements in Minsky's perspective. Section 3 juxtaposes quotations from Minsky (1986) with excerpts from the FCIC report. Section 4 discusses advances in behavioral finance that elucidate the psychological phenomena that are critical to economic instability. Section 5 describes the reaction to Minsky's ideas. Section 6 concludes.

EIGHT ELEMENTS IN MINSKY'S PERSPECTIVE

The global financial crisis drew attention to Minsky's analysis of economic instability, which during his lifetime received limited attention from mainstream economists, policymakers, and members of the media. This section provides a short description of eight key elements which Minsky (1986) highlighted as contributing to instability.

1. **Leverage:** Minsky told us that economists have historically ignored the part of Keynes's theory that relates to the relationship between Wall Street and the overall economy. Minsky's analysis begins with leverage, which he warned

would grow for households, government, nonfinancial firms, and especially financial institutions.

2. **Fringe finance:** Minsky highlighted the role of fringe financial institutions, which in recent years have come to be known as the shadow banking sector. His concern about fringe financial institutions was that their activities lay outside the purview of financial regulators, thereby leading these institutions to take on leverage and risk, with the commercial banks as their lender of last resort.

3. **Ponzi finance:** Lying at the center of Minsky's analysis of what drives a financial crisis is financial innovation involving excessive "Ponzi finance," by which he meant short-term lending by financial institutions against long-term assets, where repayment of the interest as well as the principal on the debt depends heavily on asset price appreciation rather than the generation of cash flows. Just as a Ponzi scheme collapses without sufficient cash inflows from new investors, Ponzi finance collapses without sufficient price appreciation for the asset being financed. Minsky distinguished Ponzi finance from "hedge finance" and "speculative finance." In hedge finance, the maturity of the liability matches the maturity of the asset underlying the debt. In speculative finance, the maturity of the liability is less than the maturity of the asset, the cash flows from the asset are sufficient to cover interest payments, but the debt needs to be rolled over in order for the cash flows from the asset to cover remaining interest and repayment of principal. See the appendix for a graphical explanation of the three types of financing.[2]

4. **Financial innovation and asset values:** Minsky argued that the financial sector uses innovation as a tool to increase leverage and risk. He emphasized that during the evolution of a boom, the shift from hedge finance to speculative and Ponzi finance fuels the creation of price bubbles for particular assets. Moreover, this creates a feedback loop in that these asset bubbles encourage additional reliance on Ponzi finance and short-term lending for the financing of long-term assets. This dynamic exacerbates the bubble during a period of monetary expansion, with the bubble eventually bursting when monetary expansion gives way to monetary contraction. A major danger of Ponzi finance is that the bursting of bubbles leads to defaults and weakness in the balance sheets of lending institutions.

5. **New-era thinking:** Minsky told us that during an economic boom with rising asset values, people concoct new-era explanations, consistent with free-market ideology, to justify the inflated asset prices.

6. **Regulatory failure:** Minsky argued that the financial sector is politically more agile and powerful than the regulators who oversee it, which is why the financial sector ultimately wins the regulatory game. In respect to new-era thinking, he suggests that during booms free-market ideology permeates the mindset of regulators. In this regard, he was very concerned that the Fed has historically over-focused on monetary policy at the expense of overseeing the quality of lending in financial markets. This focus, he suggested, would lead regulators to fail at their task. A particular concern of his was that regulators would fail to monitor the degree of Ponzi finance in the financial system.

7. **Runs on financial institutions and markets:** Economic booms do not last forever, and booms themselves tend to generate increases in interest rates, which eventually bring booms to an end. If leverage and Ponzi finance have been strong during the boom, Minsky tells us that the bust which follows will feature runs on financial institutions and markets for short-term debt such as commercial paper.

8. **Too big to fail:** Large busts threaten the existence of many large financial institutions and other large firms, some of whom require large scale government assistance in order to survive. Moreover, some of those institutions are beneficiaries of this assistance precisely because they are too big to fail. Minsky called this approach "contingency socialism," pointing out that many financial institutions will wind up with weakened balance sheets as a result of the bust.

All eight of the Minsky elements described above were major features of the global financial crisis. Of course, Minsky died more than a decade before the financial crisis, and so he fashioned his ideas on earlier crises such as the credit crunch of 1966, the liquidity squeeze of 1970, the REIT crisis of 1974, the recession of 1975, and the failures of banks such as Franklin National and Penn Square.

The dates of these events are notable. Minsky argued that because of prudent decisions about leverage, risk, and government policy, the fifteen-year period of 1945–1960 was stable. However, he suggested that beginning in 1960, leverage levels and risk began to rise, eventually becoming excessive, so that the economy became more fragile and prone to instability.

Minsky's insights about the causes of the instability that prevailed between 1960 and 1985 were so apparent in the global financial crisis that the latter came to be described as a "Minsky moment." The phrase "Minsky moment" originated with PIMCO economist Paul McCulley in reference to the Asian debt crisis of 1997, and appears in a *Wall Street Journal* quote on the cover of the reprinted edition of Minsky's 1986 book.

In 2007, McCulley (2009) also coined the phrase "shadow banking," which he discusses in connection with Minsky's work. The next section juxtaposes passages from Minsky's book *Stabilizing and Unstable Economy* with excerpts from the report of the FCIC that investigated the causes of the global financial crisis. This juxtaposition allows Minsky to speak for himself and—because his writings occurred two decades before the financial crisis—to demonstrate the extent to which his insights are prophetic. The juxtapositions are organized along the lines of the eight elements described above.

One of the examples Minsky mentions, and which appears in one of the quoted passages, is the 1982 failure of Penn Square Bank, whose history illustrates one of Minsky's key points about financial crises leaving financial institutions with weakened balance sheets. During the late 1970s and early 1980s, Penn Square Bank was a small commercial Oklahoma City bank that invested in high-risk energy loans. Between 1974 and 1982, the price of oil rose dramatically and Penn Square grew rapidly. Indeed, many of Penn Square's deposits came from other banks, which made it systemically important. However, in the early 1980s, a glut of oil led to falling oil prices, which severely reduced the value of Penn Square's assets.

In July 1982, Penn Square Bank failed, and many of its depositors who held high interest-rate, uninsured, jumbo certificates of deposit lost money. Included in this group were Continental Illinois National Bank and Trust Company of Chicago, both of which collapsed after having to write down hundreds of millions in loans that they purchased from Penn Square. Among the other banks who sustained major losses was Seattle First National Bank, which was forced into a merger with Bank of America. Minsky mentions that Bank of America's balance sheet was severely weakened by the acquisition.

One can only speculate what Minsky would have said about more recent events involving Bank of America's financial crisis acquisitions of Countrywide Financial and Merrill Lynch a quarter century after Seattle First. However, there is good reason to think that he would point to the systemic rankings of the Volatility Lab at New York University which, at the end of 2012, ranked Bank of America as the systemically riskiest financial firm in the United States.

In the next section, I assume that readers are generally familiar with the main events associated with the global financial crisis.

MINSKY AND FCIC JUXTAPOSED

The report of the FCIC (2011) provides an excellent analysis of events associated with the financial crisis. The FCIC documents that the global financial crisis that erupted in 2008 featured high leverage across the economy, a large shadow banking system, a boom in housing construction and bubble in housing prices, innovation in mortgage products such as limited documentation loans in the subprime market, adjustable-rate mortgages with low teaser rates and very high subsequent rates, an associated securitization process featuring collateralized debt obligations (CDOs) and credit default swaps (CDSs), deregulation in financial services, two runs on commercial paper, and an eventual deep recession requiring drastic remedial government action in the form of an extremely high deficit and major intervention by the Federal Reserve.

Notably, the FCIC points out that the subprime housing market at the heart of the crisis was relatively small, but its potency stemmed from the manner in which financial institutions took concentrated positions in pools of securitized subprime debt, with little capital coverage. These actions led to the demise of some financial firms and the rescue of other financial firms deemed too big to fail. Government intervention also rescued failing automobile firms, which were deemed either too big or too important to fail.

This section provides a juxtaposition of Minsky (1986) and FCIC excerpts, organized into the eight key elements described in the previous section, to enable readers to see for themselves how prescient were Minsky's insights in respect to the causes and consequences of the financial crisis. For example, the first quotation from Minsky below refers to the ratio of financial net worth to total liabilities for commercial banks and the debt-to-income ratio for households. This is contrasted with statements from the FCIC about leverage in financial institutions and households in the period leading up to the financial crisis. Tables 5.1–5.8 immediately following provide the contrasting juxtapositions.

Table 5.1. LEVERAGE

Minsky	FCIC
Between 1950 and 1960 this ratio trended upward from the neighborhood of 0.074 to 0.086; in the years since 1960 it has declined, falling to 0.056 in 1974 and stabilizing at around 6% in 1978. Thus, the equity protection, even as conventionally measured in commercial banking where assets are not written down to allow for interest rate increases, falls sharply . . . Household liabilities to personal income grew steadily until 1964, at which time a cyclical pattern emerged. (94)	In the years leading up to the crisis, too many financial institutions, as well as too many households, borrowed to the hilt, leaving them vulnerable to financial distress or ruin if the value of their investments declined even modestly. For example, as of 2007, the five major investment banks—Bear Stearns, Goldman Sachs, Lehman Brothers, Merrill Lynch, and Morgan Stanley—were operating with extraordinarily thin capital. By one measure, their leverage ratios were as high as 40 to 1, meaning for every $40 in assets, there was only $1 in capital to cover losses. Less than a 3% drop in asset values could wipe out a firm . . . The kings of leverage were Fannie Mae and Freddie Mac, the two behemoth government-sponsored enterprises (GSEs). For example, by the end of 2000, Fannie's and Freddie's combined leverage ratio, including loans they owned and guaranteed, stood at 75 to 1. But financial firms were not alone in the borrowing spree: from 2001 to 2007, national mortgage debt almost doubled, and the amount of mortgage debt per household rose more than 63% from $91,500 to $149,500, even while wages were essentially stagnant. When the housing downturn hit, heavily indebted financial firms and families alike were walloped. (xix, xx)

Table 5.2. FRINGE FINANCE: THE SHADOW BANKING SYSTEM

Minsky	FCIC
In the early 1960s the mode of behavior of the financial system underwent significant transformation—became more speculative—and this change tended to accelerate the trend toward fragile finance. As a result, the performance of the	In the early part of the 20th century, we erected a series of protections—the Federal Reserve as a lender of last resort, federal deposit insurance, ample regulations—to provide a bulwark against the panics that had regularly

(*Continued*)

Table 5.2. (Continued)

Minsky	FCIC
economy during the first fifteen years of the 1960s is more unstable that it was during the first fifteen years of the postwar era, with a tendency to higher rates of inflation and unemployment. Institutional changes also contribute to the transformation of the financial structure; from 1960 to 1974 fringe banking institutions and practices—such as business lending by finance companies, the issue of commercial paper by corporations, REITs and nonmember commercial banks—have grown relative to other elements of the financial system. As fringe banking institutions have grown, member banks—and especially the large money-market banks—have become their de factor lenders of last resort through relations that are often formalized by lines of credit. (96)	plagued America's banking system in the 19th century. Yet, over the past 30-plus years, we permitted the growth of a shadow banking system—opaque and laden with short-term debt—that rivaled the size of the traditional banking system. Key components of the market—for example, the multitrillion-dollar repo lending market, off-balance- sheet entities, and the use of over-the-counter derivatives—were hidden from view, without the protections we had constructed to prevent financial meltdowns. We had a 21st-century financial system with 19th-century safeguards. (xx)

Table 5.3. PONZI FINANCE: IN CONTRAST TO HEDGE FINANCE AND SPECULATIVE FINANCE

Minsky	FCIC
There are three types of financing of positions in assets that can be identified in the financial structure of our system: hedge, speculative, and Ponzi finance. These financing regimes are characterized by different relations between cash payment commitments on debt and expected cash receipts due to the quasi-rents earned by capital assets or the debtor contractual commitments on owned financial instruments. Hedge-financing instruments and their bankers ... expect the cash flow from operating capital assets (or from owning financial contracts) to be more than sufficient to meet contractual payment commitments now and in the future ...	Subprime mortgages rose from 8% of mortgage originations in 2003 to 20% in 2005. About 70% of subprime borrowers used hybrid adjustable-rate mortgages (ARMs) such as 2/28s and 3/27s—mortgages whose low "teaser" rate lasts for the first two or three years, and then adjusts periodically thereafter. Prime borrowers also used more alternative mortgages. The dollar volume of Alt-A securitization rose almost 350% from 2003 to 2005. In general, these loans made borrowers' monthly mortgage payments on ever more expensive homes affordable—at least initially. Popular Alt-A products included interest-only mortgages and payment-option ARMs.

Table 5.3. (Continued)

Minsky

Speculative-financing units, and their bankers, expect the cash flows to the unit from operating assets (or from owning financial contracts) to be less than the cash payment commitments in some, typically near-term, periods. However, if cash receipts and payments are separated into income and return of principal components (as for example, monthly payments on a fully amortized home mortgage are separated), then the expected income receipts exceed the income (interest) payments on existing commitments in every period . . . Speculative financing involves the rolling over of maturing debt . . .

A Ponzi-financing unit is similar to a speculative financing unit in that, for some near-term periods, the cash payment commitments exceed the expected cash receipts on account of owned assets. However, for at least some near-term periods, the cash payment commitments on income account exceed the expected cash payment receipts on income account . . . so that the face value of the outstanding debt increases; Ponzi units capitalize interest into their liability structure . . .

Debtors and bankers engaged in speculative and Ponzi finance expect payment commitments on debts to be met by refinancing, increasing debts, or running down superfluous stocks of financial assets. (230–232)

The mixture of hedge, speculative, and Ponzi finance in an economy is a major determinant of its stability. The existence of a large component of positions financed in a speculative or a Ponzi manner is necessary for financial instability. (233)

FCIC

Option ARMs let borrowers pick their payment each month, including payments that actually increased the principal—any shortfall on the interest payment was added to the principal, something called negative amortization. If the balance got large enough, the loan would convert to a fixed-rate mortgage, increasing the monthly payment—perhaps dramatically. Option ARMs rose from 2% of mortgages in 2003 to 20% in 2006. 105

The general view . . . was that some of the underlying mortgages "were structured to fail, [but] that all the borrowers would basically be bailed out as long as real estate prices went up. (200)

When the housing and mortgage markets cratered, the lack of transparency, the extraordinary debt loads, the short-term loans, and the risky assets all came home to roost. What resulted was panic. We had reaped what we had sown. (xx)

Minsky

In a system dominated by hedge finance, the pattern of interest rates (short-term rates being significantly lower than long-term rates) are such that profits can be made by intruding speculative arrangements. The intrusion of speculative relations into a system of mainly hedging financing of positions increases the demand for assets and therefore raises asset values—that is, it leads to capital gains. A regime in which capital gains are being earned and are expected is a favorable environment for engaging in speculative and Ponzi finance. Profit opportunities within a robust financial structure make the shift from robustness to fragility an endogenous phenomenon.

In the aftermath of a financial crisis, bankers and businessmen who have been burned shy away from speculative and Ponzi financing. (234)

In a world dominated by hedge finance and in which little value is placed on liquidity because it is so plentiful, the interest rate structure yields profit opportunities in financing positions in capital assets by using short-term liabilities . . . If investment and the government deficit generate ample profits in an economy with a robust financial structure, short-term interest rates on secure investments will be significantly lower than the yield from owning capital.

. . . The existence of a wide spectrum of financial instruments by which bankers can raise money means that bankers are able to finance capital-asset holdings and investment whenever the structure of asset prices and interest rates makes it profitable to do so. (234–235)

FCIC

Between 2003 and 2007, as house prices rose 27% nationally and $4 trillion in mortgage-backed securities were created, Wall Street issued nearly $700 billion in CDOs that included mortgage-backed securities as collateral. (125)

Jamie Dimon, the CEO of JP Morgan, told the Commission [FCIC], "In mortgage underwriting, somehow we just missed, you know, that home prices don't go up forever and that it's not sufficient to have stated income." (111)

Historically, 2/28s or 3/27s, also known as hybrid ARMs, let credit-impaired borrowers repair their credit. During the first two or three years, a lower interest rate meant a manageable payment schedule and enabled borrowers to demonstrate they could make timely payments . . .

But as house prices rose after 2000, the 2/28s and 3/27s acquired a new role: helping to get people into homes or to move up to bigger homes. "As homes got less and less affordable, you would adjust for the affordability in the mortgage because you couldn't really adjust people's income," Andrew Davidson, the president of Andrew

Davidson & Co. and a veteran of the mortgage markets, told the FCIC. Lenders qualified borrowers at low teaser rates, with little thought to what might happen when rates reset. Hybrid ARMs became the workhorses of the subprime securitization market. (105–106)

Option ARMs rose from 2% of mortgages in 2003 to 20% in 2006.

Table 5.4. (*Continued*)

Minsky	FCIC
. . . during good time the interactions between bankers and their borrowing customers increase the weight of assets reflecting speculative and Ponzi finance in the balance sheet of banks. As a result, the financial system evolves from an initial robustness toward fragility, and continuous control and periodic reform . . . are needed to prevent the development of a financially unstable economy. (354) The existence of profit opportunities does not necessarily mean that fragile financing patterns will emerge immediately . . . The ruling borrower's and lender's risk sets limits upon the rapidity with which the opportunities for profits through liability management are exploited . . . Another barrier to the quick exploitation of interest rate differentials in the aftermath of a financial trauma lies in the need to develop institutions that can absorb the preferred liabilities of holders of capital assets and emit instruments that satisfy the need of wealth owners or other financial institutions for liquidity or value assuredness. Bankers—using the term generically to include various financial-market operators—are always seeking to innovate in financial usages. A third barrier to the immediate emergence of fragile financing patterns once profit opportunities from speculative and Ponzi finance exist is the need for assured refinancing by organizations engaging in speculative finance . . . The speed at which financial innovations such as commercial paper occur and spread is a governor that regulates the pace of movement out of hedge and into speculative finance. (234–235)	Simultaneously, underwriting standards for nonprime and prime mortgages weakened. Combined loan-to-value ratios—reflecting first, second, and even third mortgages—rose. Debt-to-income ratios climbed, as did loans made for non-owner occupied properties. Fannie and Freddie continued to purchase subprime and Alt-A mortgage–backed securities from 2005 to 2008 and also bought and securitized greater numbers of riskier mortgages. The results would be disastrous for the companies, their shareholders, and American taxpayers. (125) Fannie Mae and Freddie Mac's market share shrank from 57% of all mortgages purchased in 2003 to 42% in 2004, and down to 37% by 2006. Taking their place were private-label securitizations—meaning those not issued and guaranteed by the GSEs. (105) In the first decade of the 21st century, a previously obscure financial product called the collateralized debt obligation, or CDO, transformed the mortgage market by creating a new source of demand for the lower-rated tranches of mortgage-backed securities. Still, it was not obvious that a pool of mortgage-backed securities rated BBB could be transformed into a new security that is mostly rated triple-A. But math made it so. The securities firms argued—and the rating agencies agreed—that if they pooled many BBB rated mortgage-backed securities, they would create additional diversification benefits.

(*Continued*)

Table 5.4. (Continued)

Minsky	FCIC
	The rating agencies believed that those diversification benefits were significant—that if one security went bad, the second had only a very small chance of going bad at the same time. And as long as losses were limited, only those investors at the bottom would lose money. They would absorb the blow, and the other investors would continue to get paid. (125)
	But when the housing market went south, the models on which CDOs were based proved tragically wrong. The mortgage-backed securities turned out to be highly correlated—meaning they performed similarly. Across the country, in regions where subprime and Alt-A mortgages were heavily concentrated, borrowers would default in large numbers. This was not how it was supposed to work. Losses in one region were supposed to be offset by successful loans in another region.
	The greatest losses would be experienced by big CDO arrangers such as Citigroup, Merrill Lynch, and UBS, and by financial guarantors such as AIG, Ambac, and MBIA. These players had believed their own models and retained exposure to what were understood to be the least risky tranches of the CDOs: those rated triple-A or even "super-senior," which were assumed to be safer than triple-A-rated tranches. (129)

Table 5.5. New Era Thinking: Economic Ideology during a Boom

Minsky	FCIC
As a previous financial crisis recedes in time, it is quite natural for central bankers, government officials, bankers, businessmen, and even economists to believe that a new era has arrived.	In 2005, news reports were beginning to highlight indications that the real estate market was weakening. Home sales began to drop, and Fitch Ratings reported signs that mortgage delinquencies were rising.

Table 5.5. (*Continued*)

Minsky	FCIC
Cassandra-like warnings that nothing basic has changed, that there is a financial-breaking point that will lead to a deep depression, are naturally ignored in these circumstances . . . Endogenous forces make a situation dominated by hedge finance unstable, and endogenous disequilibrating forces will become greater as the weight of speculative and Ponzi finance increases. (237–238)	That year, the hedge fund manager Mark Klipsch of Orix Credit Corp. told participants at the American Securitization Forum, a securities trade group, that investors had become "over optimistic" about the market. "I see a lot of irrationality," he added. He said he was unnerved because people were saying, "It's different this time"—a rationale commonly heard before previous collapses. (p. 18)
As financial and product markets react to profit opportunities in an investment boom, the demand for financing increases interest rates . . . Rising interest rates diminish or eliminate the margins of safety that make the financing of investment possible. This tends to force units to decrease investment or sell out positions. (239)	

Table 5.6. REGULATORY FAILURE: REGULATORS WILL LOSE IN AN UNFAIR GAME

Minsky	FCIC
Conservatives call for the freeing of markets even as their corporate clients lobby for legislation that would institutionalize and legitimize their market power; businessmen and bankers recoil in horror at the prospect of easing entry into their various domains even as technological changes and institutional evolution make the traditional demarcations of types of businesses obsolete. In truth, corporate America pays lip service to free enterprise and extols the tenets of Adam Smith, while striving to sustain and legitimize the very thing that Smith abhorred—state mandated market power. (322)	Where were the regulators? Declining underwriting standards and new mortgage products had been on regulators' radar screens in the years before the crisis, but disagreements among the agencies and their traditional preference for minimal interference delayed action. (171)
	Fed Chairman Greenspan described the argument for deregulation: "Those of us who support market capitalism in its more competitive forms might argue that unfettered markets create a degree of wealth that fosters a more civilized existence. I have always found that insight compelling." (34)
The standard analysis of banking has led to a game that is played by central banks, henceforth to be called the authorities, and profit-seeking banks. In this game, the authorities impose interest rates and reserve regulations and operate in money	Henry Cisneros, a former housing and urban development secretary, expressed a similar view. "OFHEO," Cisneros told the FCIC, "was puny compared to what Fannie Mae and Freddie Mac could muster in their intelligence, their

(*Continued*)

Table 5.6. (Continued)

Minsky

markets to get what they consider to be the right amount of money, and the banks invent and innovate in order to circumvent the authorities. The authorities may constrain the rate of growth of the reserve base, but the banking and financial structure determines the efficacy of reserves.

This is an unfair game. The entrepreneurs of the banking community have much more at stake than the bureaucrats of the central banks. In the postwar period, the initiative has been with the banking community, and the authorities have been "surprised" by changes in the way financial markets operate. The profit-seeking bankers almost always win their game with the authorities, but, in winning, the banking community destabilizes the economy; the true losers are those who are hurt by unemployment and inflation. (279)

Today's standard theory argues that the authorities should focus on the money supply and should operate to achieve a constant rate of growth of this construct … The money supply blinders worn by authorities in effect dismiss the ways in which portfolio transformations occur and how they affect the stability of the economy. The erosion of bank equity bases, the growth of liability management banking, and the greater use of covert liabilities are virtually ignored *until* financial markets tend to break down. At this time, the Federal Reserve's original reason for being comes into play—and the Federal Reserve, acting as lender of last resort, pumps reserves into the banking system and refinances banks in order to prevent a breakdown of the financing system. (280)

FCIC

Ivy League educations, their rocket scientists in their place, their lobbyists, their ability to work the Hill." (322)

Supervisors had, since the 1990s, followed a "risk-focused" approach that relied extensively on banks' own internal risk management systems. "As internal systems improve, the basic thrust of the examination process should shift from largely duplicating many activities already conducted within the bank to providing constructive feedback that the bank can use to enhance further the quality of its risk-management systems," Chairman Greenspan had said in 1999. Across agencies, there was a "historic vision, historic approach, that a lighter hand at regulation was the appropriate way to regulate," Eugene Ludwig, comptroller of the currency from 1993 to 1998, told the FCIC, referring to the Gramm-Leach-Bliley Act in 1999. The New York Fed, in a "lessons-learned" analysis after the crisis, pointed to the mistaken belief that "markets will always self-correct." "A deference to the self-correcting property of markets inhibited supervisors from imposing prescriptive views on banks," the report concluded.

[Richard Spillenkothen was the Fed's director of Banking Supervision and Regulation from 1991 to 2006.] Spillenkothen said that one of the regulators' biggest mistakes was their "acceptance of Basel II premises," which he described as displaying "an excessive faith in internal bank risk models, an infatuation with the specious accuracy of complex quantitative risk measurement techniques, and a willingness (at least in the early days of Basel II) to tolerate a reduction in regulatory capital in return for the prospect of better risk management and greater risk-sensitivity."

Table 5.6. (*Continued*)

Minsky	FCIC

FCIC

But too little was done, and too late,
because of interagency discord, industry
pushback, and a widely held view that
market participants had the situation well
in hand. Fed staff replied that the GSEs
were not large purchasers of private label
securities.

In the spring of 2006, the FOMC would
again discuss risks in the housing and
mortgage markets and express
nervousness about the growing
"ingenuity" of the mortgage sector. One
participant noted that negative
amortization loans had the pernicious
effect of stripping equity and wealth from
homeowners and raised concerns about
nontraditional lending practices that
seemed based on the presumption of
continued increases in home prices.

John Snow, then treasury secretary, told
the FCIC that he called a meeting in late
2004 or early 2005 to urge regulators to
address the proliferation of poor lending
practices. He said he was struck that
regulators tended not to see a problem at
their own institutions. "Nobody had a full
360-degree view. The basic reaction from
financial regulators was, 'Well, there may
be a problem. But it's not in my field of
view,'" Snow told the FCIC. Regulators
responded to Snow's questions by saying,
"Our default rates are very low. Our
institutions are very well capitalized. Our
institutions [have] very low
delinquencies. So we don't see any real big
problem."

In May 2005, the banking agencies did
issue guidance on the risks of home
equity lines of credit and home equity
loans. It cautioned financial institutions
about credit risk management practices,
pointing to interest-only features, low- or
no-documentation loans, high
loan-to-value and debt-to-income ratios,
lower credit scores, greater use of

(*Continued*)

Table 5.6. (*Continued*)

Minsky	FCIC
	automated valuation models, and the increase in transactions generated through a loan broker or other third party. While this guidance identified many of the problematic lending practices engaged in by bank lenders, it was limited to home equity loans. It did not apply to first mortgages.

Once the Fed and other supervisors had identified the mortgage problems, they agreed to express those concerns to the industry in the form of nonbinding guidance.

"There was among the Board of Governors folks, you know, some who felt that if we just put out guidance, the banks would get the message," [Fed governor Susan] Bies said.

Immediately, the industry was up in arms. The American Bankers Association said the guidance "overstate[d] the risk of non-traditional mortgages." They disputed the warning on low-documentation loans, maintaining that "almost any form of documentation can be appropriate." They denied that better disclosures were required to protect borrowers from the risks of nontraditional mortgages, arguing that they were "not aware of any empirical evidence that supports the need for further consumer protection standards."

The need for guidance was controversial within the agencies, too. "We got tremendous pushback from the industry as well as Congress as well as, you know, internally," the Fed's Siddique told the FCIC. "Because it was stifling innovation, potentially, and it was denying the American dream to many people." [Sabeth Siddique was the assistant director for credit risk in the Division of Banking Supervision and Regulation at the Federal Reserve Board.] |

Table 5.6. (Continued)

Minsky	FCIC
	The pressures to weaken and delay the guidance were strong and came from many sources. Opposition by the Office of Thrift Supervision helped delay the mortgage guidance for almost a year. It also appeared some institutions switched regulators in search of more lenient treatment. In December 2006, Countrywide applied to switch regulators from the Fed and OCC to the OTS.
	The OTS approved Countrywide's application for a thrift charter on March 5, 2007. (170–174)

Table 5.7. RUNS ON FINANCIAL INSTITUTIONS AND MARKETS: THE CASE OF COMMERCIAL PAPER

Minsky	FCIC
REITs were the boom financial industry of the early 1970s. These organizations are a creature of the tax laws—if they pay 90% of their earnings in dividends, they do not have to pay a corporate income tax . . . Although a REIT could wholly own and operate real estate, that was a rarity; the REITs that financed construction were heavily indebted . . . As the REIT business exploded in the early 1970s, the industry depended ever more heavily on short-term financing; this made profits and the market value of REITs equity shares vulnerable to runups in interest rates. (68) Accrued income poses a dilemma for REITs. Income is accruing; they need to pay 90% of earnings in dividends to retain their tax advantage, but there is no cash flow. In these circumstances, the REITs have to borrow in order to pay dividends . . . Borrowing in order to pay dividends is one form Ponzi finance . . . takes. The run-up of interest rates, construction	Subprime and Alt-A mortgage–backed securities depended on a complex supply chain, largely funded through short-term lending in the commercial paper and repo market—which would become critical as the financial crisis began to unfold in 2007. These loans were increasingly collateralized not by Treasuries and GSE securities but by highly rated mortgage securities backed by increasingly risky loans. Independent mortgage originators such as Ameriquest and New Century—without access to deposits—typically relied on financing to originate mortgages from warehouse lines of credit extended by banks, from their own commercial paper programs, or from money borrowed in the repo market. (113) Commercial banks used commercial paper, in part, for regulatory arbitrage. When banks kept mortgages on their balance sheets, regulators required them to hold 4% in capital to protect against loss. When banks put mortgages into off-balance-sheet entities such as commercial paper programs, there was no

(Continued)

Table 5.7. (Continued)

Minsky

delays, and excess supply of finished apartments that developed in 1974 so compromised the capital of REITs that they found it difficult to sell commercial paper. REIT commercial paper fell from $4 billion in 1973 to less than $1 billion in 1974. (70)

The only available source of funds to REITs in 1974 was the commercial banks, which in that year increased lending to REITs to $11.5 billion from the $7.0 billion at the end of 1973. Banks were accepting paper from institutions that could no longer sell their paper on the open market. Obviously, at some stage in this process even the bankers must have known they were making loans to organizations whose creditworthiness was suspect. Making loans because of other than profit-making considerations is characteristic of lender-of-last-resort operations . . .

The REIT episode is a classic speculative bubble. But the big crash that usually results did not take place, because institutional lenders refinanced the REITs and because the examining bodies went along with this business judgment . . . As a result of the REIT episode, commercial banks had weakened balance sheets and therefore increased vulnerability to disturbance after future speculative periods. (71)

FCIC

capital charge (in 2004, a small charge was imposed). But to make the deals work for investors, banks had to provide liquidity support to these programs, for which they earned a fee. This liquidity support meant that the bank would purchase, at a previously set price, any commercial paper that investors were unwilling to buy when it came up for renewal. During the financial crisis these promises had to be kept, eventually putting substantial pressure on banks' balance sheets. (114)

In the summer of 2007, as the prices of some highly rated mortgage securities crashed and Bear's hedge funds imploded, broader repercussions from the declining housing market were still not clear. "I don't think [the subprime mess] poses any threat to the overall economy," Treasury Secretary Henry Paulson told Bloomberg on July 26.

Meanwhile, nervous market participants were looking under every rock for any sign of hidden or latent subprime exposure. In late July, they found it in the market for asset-backed commercial paper (ABCP), a crucial, usually boring backwater of the financial sector.

This kind of financing allowed companies to raise money by borrowing against high-quality, short-term assets. By mid-2007, hundreds of billions out of the $1.2 trillion U.S. ABCP market were backed by mortgage-related assets, including some with subprime exposure . . .

When the mortgage securities market dried up and money market mutual funds became skittish about broad categories of ABCP, the banks would be required under these liquidity puts to stand behind the paper and bring the assets onto their balance sheets, transferring losses back

Table 5.7. (*Continued*)

Minsky	FCIC
	into the commercial banking system. In some cases, to protect relationships with investors, banks would support programs they had sponsored even when they had made no prior commitment to do so. (246)
	Soon, panic seized the short-term funding markets—even those that were not exposed to risky mortgages. "There was a recognition, I'd say an acute recognition, that potentially some of the asset-backed commercial paper conduits could have exposure to those areas. As a result, investors in general—without even looking into the underlying assets—decided 'I don't want to be in any asset-backed commercial paper, I don't want to invest in a fund that may have those positions,'" Steven Meier, global cash investment officer at State Street Global Advisors, testified to the FCIC.
	From its peak of $1.2 [trillion] on August 8, the asset-backed commercial paper market would decline by almost $400 billion by the end of 2007. (248)

Table 5.8. Too Big to Fail

Minsky	FCIC
The United States has a type of contingency socialism, in which the liabilities of particular organizations are protected either by overt government intervention or by the grant of monopoly price setting powers.	From 1998 to 2007, the combined assets of the five largest U.S. banks—Bank of America, Citigroup, JP Morgan, Wachovia, and Wells Fargo—more than tripled, from $2.2 trillion to $6.8 trillion. (53)
Financial reform needs to confront the public nature of much that is private. Big or giant corporations carry an implied public guarantee (i.e., contingency liability) on their debts. This introduces a financing bias favoring giant corporations and giant banks, for the implicit public liability leads to preferred market treatment. (354)	During a hearing on the rescue of Continental Illinois, Comptroller of the Currency C. Todd Conover stated that federal regulators would not allow the 11 largest "money center banks" to fail. This was a new regulatory principle, and within moments it had a catchy name.

(*Continued*)

Table 5.8. (*Continued*)

Minsky	FCIC
... Consequently, the already weakened portfolios of some banks are made even weaker when these banks act as proximate lender of last resort to fringe institutions. Furthermore, a succession of episodes in which giant money-market banks bail out fringe banks is likely to result in a cumulative debilitation of the giant banks; Bank of America was not necessarily strengthened when it absorbed Seafirst of Seattle in the aftermath of the Penn Square fiasco of 1982.	Representative Stewart McKinney of Connecticut responded, "We have a new kind of bank. It is called 'too big to fail'—TBTF—and it is a wonderful bank." (37)
The potential for a domino effect, which can cause a serious disruption, is implicit in a hierarchical financial pattern. The introduction of additional layering in finance, together with the invention of new instruments designed to make credit available by tapping pools of liquidity, is evidence, beyond that revealed by the financial data itself, of the increased fragility of the system. (97)	Just as Bernanke thought the spillovers from a housing market crash would be contained, so too policymakers, regulators, and financial executives did not understand how dangerously exposed major firms and markets had become to the potential contagion from these risky financial instruments. As the housing market began to turn, they scrambled to understand the rapid deterioration in the financial system and respond as losses in one part of that system would ricochet to others.
When a Chrysler is bankrupt, the bankruptcy should be handled by a government refinancing corporation, which would take over the business and break it up into parts that can survive in the market and parts that cannot generate profits. (368)	By the end of 2007, most of the subprime lenders had failed or been acquired, including New Century Financial, Ameriquest, and American Home Mortgage. In January 2008, Bank of America announced it would acquire the ailing lender Countrywide. It soon became clear that risk—rather than being diversified across the financial system, as had been thought—was concentrated at the largest financial firms. (22)
	Thain thought that was more than the assembled executives would be willing to finance and, therefore, Thain believed Lehman would fail. If Lehman failed, Thain believed, Merrill would be next. So he had called Ken Lewis, the CEO of Bank of America, and they met later that day at Bank of America's New York corporate apartment. By Sunday, the two agreed that Bank of America would acquire Merrill for $29 per share, payable in Bank of America stock. (335)

Table 5.8. (Continued)

Minsky	FCIC
	In October, Wachovia struck a deal to be acquired by Wells Fargo. Citigroup and Bank of America fought to stay afloat. Before it was over, taxpayers had committed trillions of dollars through more than two dozen extraordinary programs to stabilize the financial system and to prop up the nation's largest financial institutions. (23)
	TARP would wind up costing about $29 billion, mostly owing to the bailout of the automakers General Motors and Chrysler and the mortgage modification program. (400)

PSYCHOLOGY IN MINSKY'S PERSPECTIVE

Nonrational decisions and nonrational market prices are critical ingredients of the Minsky instability dynamic. In this regard, I would also argue that the key forces leading to instability are largely psychological but that Minsky lacked the behavioral vocabulary to identify most of the key psychological phenomena involved.[3] Most importantly, the psychological issues are absolutely central to Minsky's position that financial crises are endemic to capitalism, and therefore unavoidable. I would argue that he is probably correct, and that history—certainly the out-of-sample events that occurred after his death—supports his view.

In this section, I describe five specific psychological phenomena that underlie the types of decisions that Minsky generally identifies as contributing to instability, and illustrate with examples drawn from the recent financial crisis. These phenomena are endemic to human nature, interfere with rational decision making, and are difficult to abate. Their combined problematic aspects and tenacity lie at the heart of why achieving financial stability on a permanent basis is illusory.

Excessive Optimism

In 1986, when Minsky's book on economic instability was published, behavioral economics and behavioral finance were in their infancy. Therefore, it is hardly surprising that specific psychological concepts play little part in his discussion, although he certainly alludes to the role of psychology. In this regard, the term he uses to encapsulate psychological concepts appears to be "euphoria." To see how he uses the term in context, consider the following quotation:

> Success breeds a disregard of the possibility of failure; the absence of serious financial difficulties over a substantial period of time leads to the development of a euphoric economy in which the increasing short-term financing of long positions becomes a normal way of life. (1986, 237)

As neuroscientist and former Goldman Sachs trader John Coates (2012) tells us, euphoria is a state associated with elevated levels of steroid hormones, most notably testosterone. Coates points out that a person in a state of euphoria is typically willing to take on more risk than when not in a euphoric state.

The preceding quotation suggests that Minsky's use of euphoria is closely linked to the notion of excessive optimism in the behavioral approach.[4] Excessive, or unrealistic, optimism involves biased probabilities in which the likelihood attached to favorable events is too high and, correspondingly, the likelihood attached to unfavorable events is too low. Minsky's point about the absence of serious financial difficulties leading to a euphoric economy can be understood as the "hot hand effect" in which an economy which has recently been hot will continue to be hot (see Gilovich, Vallone, and Tversky 1985). Notably, the psychology literature documents the existence of a predisposition toward being excessively optimistic (Weinstein 1980).

Minsky's quotation demonstrates his concern about the dangers of mismatching maturities and financing long-term assets with short-term liabilities. A key aspect of these dangers involves Ponzi finance, whereby full repayment of principal and interest only occurs if there is sufficient price appreciation on the underlying asset, which a bubble threatens. That is why Minsky favors hedge financing, meaning financing in which the underlying cash flows generated by the asset, rather than price appreciation, provide the means of paying promised interest and repaying principal. With this in mind, consider the following quotation from Minsky, which again uses the term euphoria.

> For things to go wrong with a hedge unit, something first had to go wrong someplace else in the economy—unless the hedge characteristics of the initial financing were based upon unrealistic euphoric expectations with respect to costs, markets, and their development over time. (1986, 233)

In this passage, Minsky is effectively stating his view that risks associated with hedge financing tend to be systematic rather than idiosyncratic, unless expectations feature unrealistic optimism.

Foote, Gerardi, and Willen (2012) document excessive optimism about housing prices, describing how many decision makers correctly understood the general consequences attached to a decline in housing prices but failed to appreciate its likelihood or severity.[6]

Excessive optimism was but one of the psychological phenomena that impacted economic decisions in the leadup to the financial crisis. To round out this section, I describe other phenomena that played key roles in the development of the financial crisis. The phenomena in question include overconfidence, aversion to a sure loss, confirmation bias, representativeness (Kahneman 2011), and aspiration-based risk taking (Lopes 1987).

Overconfidence

The primary effect of overconfidence on financial decision tasks is the underestimation of risk (Odean 1998). In this regard, the following excerpts from the FCIC report illustrate important incidents featuring overconfidence:

The CDO machine had become self-fueling. Senior executives—particularly at three of the leading promoters of CDOs, Citigroup, Merrill Lynch, and UBS—apparently did not accept or perhaps even understand the risks inherent in the products they were creating. (188)

The greatest losses would be experienced by big CDO arrangers such as Citigroup, Merrill Lynch, and UBS, and by financial guarantors such as AIG, Ambac, and MBIA. These players had believed their own models and retained exposure to what were understood to be the least risky tranches of the CDOs: those rated triple-A or even "super-senior," which were assumed to be safer than triple-A-rated tranches. (129)

But it would become clear during the crisis that some of the highest leverage was created by companies such as Merrill, Citigroup, and AIG when they retained or purchased the triple-A and super-senior tranches of CDOs with little or no capital backing. (135)

Aspiration-Based Risk Seeking and Aversion to a Sure Loss

Aspiration-based risk taking highlights the role of aspiration levels on risk tolerance, whereby people become willing to take on high risk in an effort to achieve their aspiration levels (Lopes 1987). When the aspiration is to avoid loss, the phenomenon is called "aversion to a sure loss" and features the tendency to be risk seeking in the domain of losses (Kahneman and Tversky 1979). In this respect, consider two examples, one involving Fannie Mae and the other involving Merrill Lynch.

In the passage below, the FCIC describes the framing of the decision task at Fannie Mae as the firm began to lose market share:

In 2005, while Countrywide, Citigroup, Lehman, and many others in the mortgage and CDO businesses were going into overdrive, executives at the two behemoth GSEs, Fannie and Freddie, worried they were being left behind . . .

"The risk in the environment has accelerated dramatically," Thomas Lund, Fannie's head of single-family lending, told fellow senior officers at a strategic planning meeting on June 27, 2005. In a bulleted list, he ticked off changes in the market: the "proliferation of higher risk alternative mortgage products, growing concern about housing bubbles, growing concerns about borrowers taking on increased risks and higher debt, [and] aggressive risk layering."

"We face two stark choices: stay the course [or] meet the market where the market is," Lund said. (178)

Fannie Mae chose to accept the risk of meeting the market where the market was, and subsequently went into receivership after making record losses.

The next passage from the FCIC illustrates how being below aspiration induced high tolerance for risk at Merrill Lynch:

When Dow Kim became co-president of Merrill Lynch's Global Markets and Investment Banking Group in July 2003, he was instructed to boost revenue, especially in businesses in which Merrill lagged behind its competitors. Kim focused on the CDO business; clients saw CDOs as an integral part of their trading strategy, CEO Stanley O'Neal told the FCIC. Kim hired Chris Ricciardi from Credit Suisse, where Ricciardi's group had sold more CDOs than anyone else.

After Ricciardi left, Kim instructed the rest of the team to do "whatever it takes" not just to maintain market share but also to take over the number one ranking, former employees said in a complaint filed against Merrill Lynch. (202)

Confirmation Bias

Confirmation bias is the tendency to overweight information that confirms one's existing view, but to ignore information which disconfirms that view (Wason 1968). The following excerpt illustrates:

> And Merrill continued to push its CDO business despite signals that the market was weakening. As late as the spring of 2006, when AIG stopped insuring even the very safest, super-senior CDO tranches for Merrill and others, it did not reconsider its strategy. (204)

Representativeness

Representativeness bias is the tendency to place excessive emphasis on stereotypes when making judgments (Kahneman 2011). Judgments of objects which rely on representativeness are typically based on the degree to which the object fits a preconceived notion of a stereotype. The following excerpt pertains to the contrast between the stereotypic proportions of subprime mortgages in the CDOs and the CDOs for which AIG was selling protection.

> Told by a consultant, Gary Gorton, that the "multisector" CDOs on which AIG was selling credit default swaps consisted mainly of mortgage-backed securities with less than 10% subprime and Alt-A mortgages, [AIG executive Gene] Park asked Adam Budnick, another AIG employee, for verification. Budnick double checked and returned to say, according to Park, "I can't believe it. You know, it's like 80 or 90%." Reviewing the portfolio—and thinking about a friend who had received 100% financing for his new home after losing his job—Park said, "This is horrendous business. We should get out of it." (200)

Notably, on close inspection, AIG executives learned that the CDOs for which they were selling protection did not fit the stereotypes they had in their minds.

REACTION TO MINSKY'S WORK

Reaction to Minsky's work has been mixed, featuring strong supporters, weak supporters, those who downplay or ignore his work, and contrarians with opposing views. In this section, I provide examples illustrating the diverse spectrum of reaction to Minsky's ideas and suggest some psychological explanations for why Minsky's views failed to gain traction among many academic economists, policymakers, and the media. In this regard, there is no mention of Minsky's name in the FCIC report.[7]

Diverse Perspectives

Promulgators: Economists Wynne Godley, Steve Keen,[8] Mark Lavoie, Jan Kregel, Dimitri Papadimitriou, Charles Whalen, and Randall Wray have been strong promoters of Minsky's perspective. Outside of academia, Paul McCulley has been one of Minsky's strong supporters (see McCulley 2009). The main institutional support for his approach has been Bard College's Levy Institute, which has long been hosting Minsky conferences and is where Minsky ended his career. The Minsky conferences have attracted distinguished speakers such as Joseph Stiglitz, Janet Yellen, Gillian Tett, and Henry Kaufman (who wrote the foreword to the republished version of Minsky's book in 2008).

Academic views, pro and con : During his lifetime, Minsky was an active contributor to academic discourse on financial stability. A good example is his chapter contribution with Summers, Samuelson, Poole, and Volcker (1991), in a volume edited by Martin Feldstein which is based on an NBER conference held in 1989 after the stock market crash of 1987. An interesting contrast in views can be seen in Benston and Kaufman (1995) and Minsky (1995), which appear together in the same journal issue.

Samuelson, in his contribution to the chapter mentioned in the previous paragraph, actually poses the main question under discussion, writing: "Why was the prophet Hyman Minsky for so many decades a voice crying out in the wilderness? 'A qualitative credit crisis is in the intermediate-term cards. Wolf! Wolf!' The answer for his long wait has to be found in the laws of behavior of populist democracy in the 'Age after Keynes.'" By these statements, Samuelson means that U.S. policymakers had learned to react to macroeconomic shocks by using monetary and fiscal policy to limit declines in real output. However, he cautioned that a time would come when doing so would lead to severe inflation.

Cohen (2009) interviewed several academic economists to elicit their views on how the financial crisis has altered their thinking about different schools of thought in economics. Among those she interviewed were James Galbraith at the University of Texas; L. Randall Wray at the University of Missouri; and Philip Reny, economics department chair at the University of Chicago. Galbraith and Wray[9] indicated that the works of Keynes and Minsky were most relevant to understanding events related to the financial crisis. Their view is not universally held, however. In respect to Reny, Cohen writes: "When asked why graduate students don't study Keynes or Minsky, Mr. Reny replied that graduate students work on subjects—like real models of business cycles—that are at the frontier of the field; by contrast Keynes and Minsky are not on the frontier anymore."

Not all current macroeconomists would agree with Reny's perspective. Akerlof and Shiller (2009) discuss behavioral macroeconomic elements in the financial crisis, choosing Keynes's term "animal spirits" as the title of their book. Keynes used the term "animal spirits" to describe decisions to take action that stem from intuition and instinct rather than rational calculation: here "animal spirits" refers to the Latin phrase *spiritus animales*, with *animales* referring to a state of animation or locomotion associated with consciousness (*animus* in Latin). Akerlof and Shiller cite Minsky several times, stating in an endnote to their preface, "Our line of thinking in this book parallels that of Minsky." At the same time, some might regard the degree to which

Akerlof and Shiller invoke Minsky's specific insights as being somewhat on the light side.[10]

Although some academic economists continue to cite his work (e.g., Field 2011), many in both the Keynesian camp and the neoclassical free-market camp either fail to cite him or choose not to emphasize his contributions. Two prominent examples are Reinhart and Rogoff (2009) and Admati and Hellwig (2013), both of which constitute major works analyzing economic instability.

Blinder (2015) provides an insightful review of the 2014 collection *What Have We Learned? Macroeconomic Policy after the Crisis*, which is edited by four very well regarded economists: George Akerlof, Olivier Blanchard, David Romer, and Joseph Stiglitz. While Blinder is generally complimentary about the collection, he points out issues that tend to be downplayed by conventional economists, noting that Minsky was right.

Views of central bankers: In describing Minsky's sixth element, regulatory failure, I quoted a passage from Minsky, which begins: "Conservatives call for the freeing of markets . . ." In this respect, consider two sets of remarks by former Fed chair Alan Greenspan. The first remark comes from a speech Greenspan gave before the crisis, in May 2005, when he stated that "private regulation generally has proved far better at constraining excessive risk-taking than has government regulation" (Lanman and Matthews 2013).

The second set of contrasting remarks comes from Greenspan's Congressional testimony after the crisis broke, in October 2008, when he stated that "an ideology is, is a conceptual framework with the way people deal with reality . . . The question is whether it is accurate or not. And what I'm saying to you is, yes, I found a flaw . . . in the model that I perceived is the critical functioning structure that defines how the world works, so to speak . . . Those of us who have looked to the self-interest of lending institutions to protect shareholder's equity—myself especially—are in a state of shocked disbelief."

The contrast between these two passages is striking, and also consistent with Minsky's perspective. Reflecting back on lessons learned and citing Kahneman's work, Greenspan (2013) writes about the importance of behavioral phenomena (see also PBS 2013). This represents a significant intellectual shift on Greenspan's part. At the same time, Greenspan is unclear about whether, even in hindsight, he would have acted any differently. And he does not cite Minsky.

Academic and central banker Janet Yellen is explicit about Minsky's contributions to understanding the financial crisis and the relevance of these contributions for central bankers (Yellen 2009). At that time, she was president and chief executive officer of the Twelfth District Federal Reserve Bank in San Francisco. In October 2010, she took office as vice chair of the Board of Governors of the Federal Reserve System, and simultaneously began a 14-year term as a member of the board. In February 2014, she succeeded Ben Bernanke as Fed chair.

Although Yellen's article suggests that Minsky's ideas have had some influence at the Fed, *The Economist* (July 7, 2010) suggests that Fed economists have mostly ignored his work. In this respect, *The Economist* article describes only fleeting references to Minsky's work in a staff paper upon which Fed chair Ben Bernanke based one of his speeches.[11] Notably, in that speech, Bernanke did not cite Minsky by name nor did he cite Minsky in a follow-up speech in April 2012. In this regard, the April 2012 speech summarized what Bernanke had previously described as one of the major lessons he learned from the financial crisis, namely the fact that the Fed needed to place regulation on an equal footing to monetary policy. Of course, Minsky had recommended doing so decades earlier; see again his comments about "money supply blinders" in section 3 (failure of financial market regulation).[12]

As with its American central bank counterpart, the Bank of England is aware of Minsky's work, but in its exploration of alternative approaches to regulation appears not to have made explicit use of his ideas. To be sure, the Bank of England focuses on issues related to excessive leverage and risk at the heart of the Basel Accords, but without explicit attention to Ponzi finance in the context of the Minsky dynamic (Haldane and Madouros 2012; Aikman et al. 2013).

The FCIC report: The FCIC report makes no explicit mention of Minsky. Nevertheless, the juxtaposition of Minsky's writings and text from the FCIC report makes clear that Minsky's framework nicely captures the dynamic of the 2008 crisis, as described by the majority members of the FCIC. As noted by Stanton (2012), members of the commission did discuss the relevance of Minsky's work. However, it was not the staff economists but Stanton—an attorney, not an economist—who first raised Minsky's name and asked if he was highly regarded among economists. Notably, it was the non-economists on the staff that looked to Minsky's work for insights but did not have Minsky's writings open in front of them to provide a template for analysis.[13]

Discussion in the media: Discussion of Minsky in the media has been mixed. Articles about Minsky can be found in the *New York Times* by Madrick (2002), Cohen (2009), and Norris (2008, 2009, 2011, 2013a, 2013b); in the *Financial Times* by Wolf (2008); and in the *New Yorker* by John Cassidy (2008). Madrick (2002) appeared well before the onset of the financial crisis. Cassidy (2008) appeared in February, as the crisis was beginning to unfold but months before the Lehman bankruptcy. Wolf (2008) openly endorsed Minsky with an article entitled "What Went Wrong? The Short Answer: Minsky Was Right."

Norris is perhaps the most consistent columnist when it comes to articulating the importance of Minsky's ideas. In particular, Norris (2013b) contains an especially insightful discussion of Bernanke's record as Fed chair and his reluctance to credit Minsky.[14]

At the same time, searches for Minsky's name in the websites for NPR and PBS come back empty. The *Wall Street Journal*, which did use the term "Minsky moment" (Lahart 2007) and is quoted on the jacket cover of the reprint of his book, only mentions Minsky in ten articles between 1987 and 2012. Of these, half occurred before the financial crisis, and only two appeared after the Lehman bankruptcy in September 2008.

In his popular writings, academic Paul Krugman (2009, 2010, 2011, 2012, 2015) offers something of a mixed message in respect to Minsky. On the one hand, Krugman (2011) states: "Hyman Minsky now looms large in many peoples' thinking, my own included, even though he died a very marginal figure." However, Krugman (2012) explains why he himself will "never be a true Minskyite in Keen's sense." Krugman is critical of Keen's model, arguing that the assumptions are unclear and not compelling. To be sure, Minsky did not develop a complete model of his framework, although he did provide a formal framework for some aspects of his approach. Nevertheless, most of Minsky's ideas were expressed qualitatively rather than mathematically. In his academic writings, Krugman does model select features Minsky emphasized, most notably the impact of leverage (see Eggertsson and Krugman 2012).

Krugman (2015) is particularly interesting in that he speaks of three questions associated with the crisis. First is the Minsky question about what makes economies and financial systems vulnerable to crises. Second is the Bagehot question about what causes intermittent financial panic and bank runs. Third is the Keynes question about what factors lead economies to stay depressed in the wake of financial crises. Krugman asserts that progress has been made on the Bagehot question and Keynes question, but not on the Minsky question. In this regard he is critical of traditional macroeconomists for their preference for "mathiness," and for behavioral economists who have not put forward sufficient guidance in respect to asset bubbles, excessive leverage, and the limits of rationality.

It seems to me that Minsky was quite clear about the causes of vulnerability, as encapsulated in the components approach described above. Still, Krugman's message is mixed, and his comments suggest a less than full understanding of Minsky's approach. Krugman fleshes out his Minsky question by asking whether the root cause of vulnerability is associated with deregulation, weak regulation, the failure to remember past crises, or excessively loose policy. Krugman tells us that he has his own views but speaks of an absence of fresh thinking and hard evidence; he says little about Ponzi finance, the asset bubbles fueled by shifts from hedge finance to speculative and Ponzi finance, and all the other issues that Minsky spoke about with passion and force. They still fall on deaf ears, even the ears of those who speak of the "missing Minsky."

Lack of Contagion, Self-Interest, and Confirmation Bias

History suggests that Minsky's ideas are not contagious, plain and simple. The question is why, and one way to address this question is through contagion theory (Lynch 1996). Contagion theory explains how ideas or "memes," such as religious principles, capture "hosts," meaning people who accept the ideas and propagate them. Indeed the concept of religious groups perpetuating their faith traditions through evangelical activities and the raising of offspring has its counterpart among academics economists communicating their ideas through scholarly activities and educating graduate students.[15]

In respect to scholarly activities, think again about the discussion in Cohen (2009), but now through the lens of contagion theory. Cohen's interviews with academic economists tell us that they believe economists are slow to change their views, even in the face of disconfirming evidence.[16] Keep in mind that people who suffer from confirmation bias systematically underweight disconfirming information. In this regard, Cohen points out that at universities such as the University of California at Berkeley, the University of Texas, the University of Chicago, Harvard, Yale, and Stanford, changes in the macroeconomics curriculum in response to the financial crisis have been relatively minor. The adages "Old habits die hard" and "You can't teach an old dog new tricks" appear to apply here.

Cohen quotes Robert Shiller as suggesting that academic economists suffer from "groupthink," which she describes as "the tendency to agree with the consensus." One way to think about groupthink is to view it as collective confirmation bias.

In respect to graduate students, Cohen tells us: "Graduate students who stray too far from the dominant theory and methods seriously reduce their chances of getting an academic job." Anyone familiar with the academic job market knows the importance that dissertation supervisors play in their graduate students finding positions. In other words, self-interest is an issue. Academics represent ideologies and they have intellectual capital to protect.

However, for rookie academics, there is more to self-interest than finding a first position. They need to be productive and publish their research in high-quality journals. Economists tend to build on each other's work. Most economic methodology is quantitative in nature, with economists tending to make heavy use of mathematics in modeling their ideas. Minsky failed to produce enough of a formal framework upon which to build, especially for graduate students studying with him, whose work would need to be accepted in peer-reviewed journals.[17] To an economic theorist, "Minsky is just a story, not a theory."[18]

Schlefer (2013) offers further insight into the question "Why does a model matter?" by telling us that a model explicitly details an economist's thinking, and in so doing enables other economists to use it.[19] In this regard he states: "They cannot so easily clone intuition." Notably, Schlefer's article highlights the work of Wynne Godley, who together with Marc Lavoie (2007) did develop a formal model that shares many of the features emphasized by Minsky. Yet, as Schlefer indicates, the Godley-Lavoie model has gained very little traction among mainstream economists.

The same "traction" comment applies to Keen's work (2012, 2013) which extended Goodwin cycle theory to include capital structure issues emphasized by Minsky. Keen's model is nonlinear, a point to note in light of the position articulated by Olivier Blanchard (2014, 2015), who suggests that macroeconomists have too much relied on linear models. In this regard, Blanchard uses the term "dark corners" to describe parameter configurations in nonlinear models that are associated with instability. Notably, the dynamics that emerge in Keen's model are similar to those that Blanchard indicates are important but not present in linear models; yet, Blanchard appears not to be aware of work, such as Keen's, that models Minsky dynamics.

There is a possibility that even had Minsky produced a formal model, the reaction to his work would have been much the same. Blanchard writes that the late economist Frank Hahn warned him repeatedly about ignoring nonlinear models. See Hahn (1963, 1968, 1970). This raises the question of whether mainstream economists were simply unwilling to accept what Minsky had to say; but if so, why?

Self-interest and confirmation work together. Ideology is important and can trump the search for truth. Academics feel better when their views are vindicated instead of contradicted. As it happens, Minsky was not all that keen on flattering economists of all persuasions. In this regard, he did not consider himself to be either Keynesian or neoclassical. Indeed, he was quite critical of both groups, which given the sociological structure of academic communities and the manner in which academic research is done, might explain why he failed to impact his contemporaries in a major way.[20]

Minsky criticized neoclassical economists using Walrasian equilibrium models for their belief that markets are self-correcting, and he criticized neo-Keynesians for omitting some of Keynes's insights about the contribution of the financial sector to economic instability. Confirmation bias is very strong. Minsky's critique of both neo-Keynesians and neoclassicists is such that members of both major camps would need to accept evidence disconfirming their views.

Those with neoclassical leanings will be reluctant to accept the views of a thinker who advocates active government intervention to mitigate the dynamic underlying economic instability, especially his recommendation for an activist employment policy. Those with Keynesian leanings will be reluctant to accept the views of someone who contends that neo-Keynesians have misunderstood Keynes and developed models that were too accommodating of neoclassical elements.[21] Both camps are prone to reject the idea that economic stability is impossible in a modern capitalist economy, and Minsky chided policymakers and the economists who advise them for suggesting otherwise. Minsky's pill might be hard to swallow for many: confirmation bias will lead many patients to spit out their Minsky pills.

Many policymakers, economists, and media editors would disagree with Minsky's policy recommendations, or what he called reforms. Minsky had strong opinions, although the opinions he held about diagnosing the causes of financial instability were stronger than his opinions about the appropriate remedies.

Minsky's reforms feature four categories: (1) fiscal, (2) employment, (3) industrial, and (4) financial. In respect to fiscal policy, he advocated running a large enough public sector so that fiscal deficits could offset dramatic decreases in aggregate demand in the private sector. At the same time, Minsky cautioned against the public sector becoming too large. He also recommended that corporate income tax be abolished, because he thought that the tax deductibility of interest encourages excessive leverage. In respect to employment policy, he advocated having public employment programs in place to keep employment from plummeting. Minsky's model for employment policy was the collection of programs from the New Deal: Civilian Conservation Corps, National Youth Administration, and Works Progress Administration. In respect to industrial policy, he advocated having measures in place to keep systemically important firms from becoming too large and therefore too big to fail. In respect to financial policy, he advocated the Fed playing a more active role in financing at the discount window, so as to keep tabs on the growth in speculative and Ponzi financing. Of course, Minsky also recommended that the Fed place regulation on the same level as monetary policy, a point discussed above.

At the same time, it is entirely possible that confirmation bias is leading me to make a stronger case for Minsky's perspective than is warranted. I acknowledge this possibility, and would say that even if true, the effort should at least redress some of the existing imbalance. In any case, I leave it for readers to judge the degree to which the argument developed in the chapter is colored by this bias. Indeed, there might be considerable value in examining the various positions on Minsky's work in order to filter out the degree of confirmation bias, and in so doing arrive at a reasonable assessment of his contribution to our understanding of financial instability.

CONCLUSION: SELF-INTEREST COLORED
BY CONFIRMATION BIAS

Minsky did not have a well-developed formal theory or a sophisticated econometric model. However, in my view, he did have a deep insight into the forces that generate economic instability and bring about financial crises, and his insights are yet to be fully exploited.

The global financial crisis provided a dramatic out-of-sample test of Hyman Minsky's ideas, which he developed based on events he observed between 1960 and 1990. The Asian currency crisis of 1997 provided another out-of-sample test. Yet, in spite of their immense value, Minsky's ideas have failed to become mainstream, and his memes have failed to become contagious. The question is why. My short answer is perceived self-interest strongly colored by confirmation bias.

The strong Minsky supporters are vastly outnumbered by those holding other views about the value of his contributions. The positions of those with lukewarm or opposing views might be characterized as follows:[22]

- "Minsky's views are at odds with free-market ideology. Not everyone agrees with the majority portion of the FCIC report: there are two minority sections, contesting the conclusions reached by the majority."
- "Interpreting the financial crisis of 2008–2009 through a Minsky lens is a cherry-picking exercise, the result of hindsight bias, if not confirmation bias."
- "Minsky is just a story, not a model." "Minsky offered no quantitative tools to identify, much less predict, bubbles."

Although there might well be some germ of truth in each of these positions, I would argue that the FCIC analysis and supporting documents on its website provide the most comprehensive characterization we currently have of what drove the financial crisis of 2008–2009. Moreover, although there are some good points in the minority position of the FCIC report, I would argue that the minority position is ideologically driven and suffers from confirmation bias.

In light of the comparison to the majority position in the FCIC analysis, Minsky's ideas, qualitative as they were, strike me as much more insightful than any competing quantitative economic analysis or ideologically based qualitative framework. My recommendation would be that Minsky's critics build on his insights, and develop systematic models, metrics, and terminology that exploit Minsky's insights to limit the extent of financial instability. That would be more constructive than downplaying or ignoring his insights.

Simon (1955) tells us that full optimization is typically unattainable, and that instead we should employ sensible satisficing heuristics that are good enough. Gigerenzer (2008) tells us to develop heuristics that are fast and frugal, meaning heuristics that are easy to implement and rely on small amounts of information. Perhaps what economic policymakers need are fast and frugal Minsky-based heuristics focused on limiting excessive leverage, excessive mismatching of assets and liability maturities, and excessive Ponzi finance.

Haldane and Madouros (2012) focus on fast and frugal microprudential regulatory heuristics for leverage and risk, and this is a good start. Their paper stresses the benefits of using straightforward capital ratios rather than a large collection of highly complex risk-weighted ratios. For that matter, Minsky also relied only on straightforward ratios, for example mentioning minimum equity-to-asset ratios of 5% for financial institutions.[23] This leads me to suggest that regulatory approaches, such as Haldane and Madouros propose, would benefit by controlling the relative sizes of hedge, speculative, and Ponzi finance. I suggest doing so by developing classification algorithms to classify loans and related financial securities.

Minsky told us: "The mixture of hedge, speculative, and Ponzi finance in an economy is a major determinant of its stability. The existence of a large component of positions financed in a speculative or a Ponzi manner is necessary for financial instability" (233).[24] Minsky did not offer quantitative advice on how to accomplish the task. Therefore, the challenge is to find a way to make this advice operational, as opposed to ignoring it.

In theory, classifying loans into three buckets—hedge, speculative, and Ponzi—is straightforward and rests on standard cash budgeting techniques. Traditional free cash flow analysis for project assets involves cash flow from investment and disposal, which can be matched to cash flows from financing. Many capital assets depreciate over time, with expected disposal being less than the required investment. However, the assets underlying Ponzi finance involve the expectation of appreciation, not depreciation, with the appreciation required to cover both a portion of interest and repayment of principal. In practice, the classification task will involve complexity, especially for corporate projects, as debt is typically associated with the corporation as a whole rather than being asset specific (to the asset).[25]

Minsky's concern about excessive Ponzi finance was that it fuels asset pricing bubbles that ultimately result in financial instability. However, Minsky did not suggest that it is easy to identify bubbles ex ante, let alone predict when they will pop in the absence of intervention to pop them. Instead, he offered institutional advice about putting programs in place to detect excessive Ponzi finance, and limiting its use.[26]

Going forward, the question will be how to pursue an agenda that fruitfully applies Minsky's insights. For those insights to be useful, self-interested users will need to see how Minsky's ideas will best serve their own interests. Part of the challenge will be intellectual and the rest will be psychological, as confirmation bias is very strong. In this last regard, we would be well served to remember that it is because of the psychological issues that Minsky emphasized that the economic system is inherently unstable, and that crises are unavoidable. Nevertheless, what we can do is find "humane" ways, to use his term, that mitigate their impact.

*I thank Steve Keen, Floyd Norris, Thomas Stanton, and Meir Statman for comments.

APPENDIX

An easy way to see the difference between hedge, speculative, and Ponzi finance is to consider an example in which the financing structure is fixed, and then to vary the cash flows of the asset being financed. In the example, the interest rate is 10% per year, and a $1000 loan features interest only of $100 per year, with the principal returned when the loan matures after seven years.

Figure 5.1 below illustrates hedge finance, in which the cash flows from the asset being financed are exactly the same as the cash flows associated with the loan. Cash flows and appreciation are depicted by the heights of the vertical bars. In Figure 5.1, the cash flows from the asset are sufficient to cover repayment of principal when the loan matures, and no asset appreciation is required to repay principal in full.

Figure 5.2 illustrates an example of speculative finance, whereby the asset cash flows are sufficient to cover interest payments during the term of the loan. However, the cash flows from the asset at the time the loan matures are insufficient to cover repayment of principal in full. Instead, asset appreciation is required to supplement the actual cash flows in order that the principal be repaid.

Figure 5.3 illustrates the case of Ponzi finance. Here cash flows from the asset are insufficient to cover interest payments as well as repayment of principal. Instead, sufficient appreciation in the value of the asset is required to cover both.

The amount of appreciation depicted in Figure 5.3 will exactly cover required principal and interest over the life of the loan. In Minsky's dynamic, during the bubble phase of a boom, the amount of appreciation might well be more than the

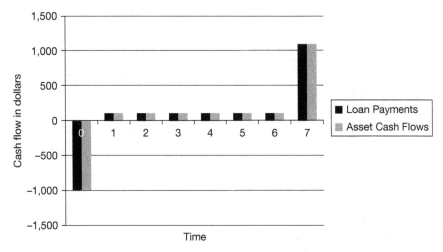

Figure 5.1 Hedge Finance.

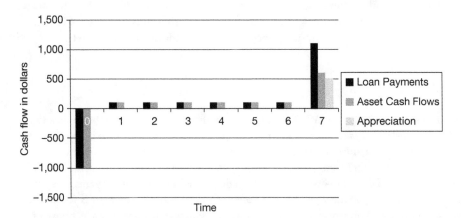

Figure 5.2 Speculative Finance.

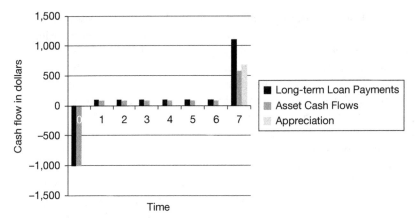

Figure 5.3 Ponzi Finance.

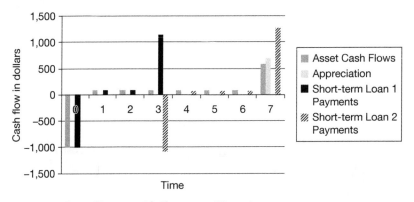

Figure 5.4 Ponzi Finance with Short-term Financing.

minimum required to cover the loan obligations. However, during the later phases of the bubble, the overpricing of the asset will lead expected appreciation to fall below the amount required to cover the terms of the loan. Indeed, expected appreciation might well be negative during the latter stage of a bubble.

Minsky also warned against using short-term financing to fund long-term assets, as doing so entailed interest rate risk (interest rates tend to rise during the latter stages of a boom) and rollover risk (banks stop lending during runs). Figure 5.4 illustrates Ponzi finance with short-term financing being used for longer-term assets.

NOTES

1. Whalen (2007) and Wray (2012) provide important insights on the application of Minsky's ideas to the evolution of the financial crisis that began to unfold in 2007.
2. Minsky's definitions of the different types of financing pertain to corporate finance. For consumer finance, such as mortgages and auto loans, the source of the cash flows is typically consumers' portfolios including their human capital, not necessarily the asset being financed, unless the home is for a rental and the auto is for business purposes. For mortgages that qualify as speculative or Ponzi finance, house price

appreciation is usually needed for the purpose of refinancing, not selling the asset to repay principal or pay interest.

3. During the 1930s, macroeconomists routinely made reference to psychology. Both Fisher (1932) and Keynes (1936) used the term explicitly, usually linked to discussions of excessive optimism and pessimism. These psychological biases are now well studied in the behavioral decision literature, along with many others.

4. The term "irrational exuberance" has come to be understood as extreme excessive optimism about financial markets.

5. In the FCIC excerpt, ARMs are adjustable rate mortgages. A 2/28 ARM has a 30-year maturity featuring a fixed rate for the first 2 years and a floating rate thereafter. A 3/27 ARM features a fixed rate for the first 3 years, and a floating rate thereafter.

6. For example, Table 2 in Foote, Gerardi, and Willen (2012) describes the conditional forecasts from 2005 of losses on subprime investments from Lehman Brothers. The table lists five scenarios, labeled from "aggressive" to "meltdown." A probability of 5% is attached to "meltdown," which is characterized as a 5% decline in house prices for the next three years, and 5% decline thereafter, with cumulative losses of 17.1%. Needless to say, Lehman's "meltdown" scenario was mild compared to the actual decline in house prices.

7. The FCIC report comprises a majority position that is very much in line with Minsky's perspective and a minority position arguing that excessive government intervention in the mortgage market, through Fannie Mae and Freddie Mac, was largely responsible for the financial crisis. Almost surely, the authors of the minority report would reject Minsky's perspective on the root causes of economic instability.

8. See Keen (1995, 2012, 2013). Keen's view is that although systemic elements might be amplified by psychological factors, with the result being euphoric speculation, the accumulation of debt seems almost destined to outpace the growth of output, even with non-euphoric expectations. Keen's model builds on the Goodwin growth model, which features economic cycles. Keen points out that on the systemic front, Minsky's views are very similar to the discussion of "free" cycles in Fisher (1932). Notably, Keen's formal model features a component for aggregate leverage. However, it is a certainty model. Absent from Keen's formal framework are elements associated with risk, hedge, speculative, and Ponzi finance; regulation; financial innovation; asset pricing bubbles; fringe finance; runs on financial institutions; lenders of last resort; and too big to fail. Keen points out that on the systemic front, Minsky's views are very similar to the discussion of "free" cycles in Fisher (1932).

9. Wray, along with Dimitri Papadimitriou, co-wrote a foreword to the 2008 reprinting of Minsky (1986). Wray has been a longtime leader in advancing Minsky's perspective.

10. Apart from a brief mention of Minsky in the preface, Akerlof and Shiller confine the remainder of their comments on Minsky to their book's endnotes, and do not use the term "Ponzi finance." Shiller (2009) states: "Hyman Minsky wrote a 1982 book, 'Can 'It' Happen Again?,' that raised the possibility of a new depression. But the widespread perception then was that the decline was caused by the Federal Reserve, which had clamped down on the money supply to end out-of-control inflation. Depression fear did not take off."

11. The tradition continues. For example, economists at the Fed (e.g., Foote, Gerardi, and Willen 2012) do not cite his work.

12.   In the following sections I discuss the work of economist Steve Keen and a series of articles by *New York Times* columnist Floyd Norris Norris. Norris (2013b) states: "When I talked to Mr. Keen this week, he called my attention to the fact that Mr. Bernanke, in his 2000 book 'Essays on the Great Depression,' briefly mentioned, and dismissed, both Minsky and Charles Kindleberger, author of the classic 'Manias, Panics and Crashes.'"

13.   I thank Tom Stanton very much for an email exchange in which he explained the role that Minsky's work played in the FCIC deliberations. Stanton (2012) devotes an entire chapter to Minsky's ideas.

14.   I do not mean to infer that this is an exhaustive list. Indeed, there are other excellent articles discussing Minksy's insights. I simply want to state my opinion that Minsky's ideas merit much more coverage and attention than they have received.

15.   Some charge that Minsky was less than clear in communicating his views to students. In this regard, see the work of Justin Fox (2009), Minsky's former teaching assistant.

16.   Cohen's focus is the dominant role of neoclassical assumptions among economists. In this regard, she states: "True, some new approaches have been explored in recent years, particularly by behavioral economists who argue that human psychology is a crucial element in economic decision making. But the belief that people make rational economic decisions and the market automatically adjusts to respond to them still prevails." (C1)

17.   To be sure, the models in Keen's work are formal representations of some aspects of Minsky's perspective; however, those models too have failed to generate a contagion. See Krugman's quoted comments above.

18.   I acknowledge Stanford economist Mordecai Kurz for this particular phrase to characterize his view of Minsky's intellectual contributions.

19.   Schlefer attributes this insight to Dirk Bezemer, an academic at Groningen University.

20.   Minsky's views about excessive leverage overlap those of the Austrian school in respect to economic instability. However, Minsky's framework features additional elements such as fringe finance and Ponzi finance.

21.   Some are shifting. See Blinder 2013.

22.   I do not claim that this is an exhaustive list. Confirmation bias will lead those with an Austrian perspective to reject ideas in Minsky's framework that are non-Austrian, those with Marxist leanings to reject ideas in Minsky that are non-Marxist, etc.

23.   See p. 356, where Minsky writes: "A 5 percent asset-equity ratio seems reasonable, especially if capital absorption by covert bank activities is taken into account." In July 2013, the Federal Deposit Insurance Corporation (FDIC) and the Office of the Comptroller of the Currency (OCC) issued a proposal to double minimum capital requirements for large U.S. banks from 3%to between 5 and 6%. By way of contrast, Minsky suggested that the 1950s and early 1960s constituted a period of relative financial stability, which at the time featured a ratio of financial net worth to total liabilities that lay between 7.4 and 8.6%(corresponding respectively to capital to asset ratios of between 7 and 8%). In July 2013, the Basel Committee on Banking Supervision issued a discussion paper about instituting higher capital requirements for the largest global banks. See Gandel (2013). See also Admati and Hellwig (2013), who recommend that for financial firms equity be in the 25–30%range,

and Morgenson (2013), who describes the resistance of the financial sector to the proposal for higher capital requirements.

24. Minsky understood that the relative size of Ponzi finance reflected a balancing issue when he stated: "Federal Reserve policy therefore needs to continuously 'lean against' the use of speculative and Ponzi finance. But Ponzi finance is a usual way of debt-financing investment in process in a capitalist society. Consequently, capitalism without financial practices that lead to instability may be less innovative and expansionary; lessening the possibility of disaster might very well take part of the spark of creativity out of the capitalist system" (364).

25. The discussion in Silver-Greenberg and Corkery (2014) about the market for consumer auto loans suggests the growth of speculative finance and Ponzi finance in this market. On the surface, this type of situation qualifies as something Minsky might well have warned about as a catalyst for financial and economic instability.

26. In June 2013, Kennedy discussed the application of Minsky's ideas to Chinese financial markets based on the analysis of Société Generale SA economist Yao Wei. In July 2013, the*New York Times* reported a surge in financing practices in Chinese markets that correspond strongly to Minsky's cautionary remarks about fringe finance, Ponzi finance, asset bubbles, and regulatory failure. According to Barboza (2013), Chinese financial institutions are engaging in innovations that feature off-balance sheet shadow banking practices intended to evade the oversight of regulators. These innovations provide investors with an opportunity to purchase high-yield, fixed-income short-term debt that is used to fund highly risky long-term real estate projects. A report released in May by JPMorgan Chase stated that at the end of 2012, the size of the shadow banking system had grown to 69% of China's gross domestic product. Barboza indicates that Chinese officials are experiencing difficulty in limiting the growth of shadow banking practices.

REFERENCES

Admati, Anat, and Martin Hellwig. 2013. *The Bankers' New Clothes: What's Wrong with Banking and What to Do about It*. Princeton, NJ: Princeton University Press.

Aikman, David, Mirta Galesic, Gerd Gigerenzer, Sujit Kapadia, Konstantinos Katsikopoulos, Amit Kothiyal, Emma Murphy, and Tobias Neumann. 2014. "Taking Uncertainty Seriously: Simplicity versus Complexity in Financial Regulation." *Financial Stability Paper* No. 28, May.

Akerlof, George, and Robert Shiller. 2009. *Animal Spirits: How Human Psychology Drives the Economy, and Why It Matters for Global Capitalism*. Princeton, NJ: Princeton University Press.

Barboza, David. 2013. "Loan Practices of China's Banks Raising Concern." *New York Times*, July 2, 1.

Benston, George, and George Kaufman. 1995. "Is the Banking and Payments System Fragile?" *Journal of Financial Services Research* 9 (3–4): 197–240.

Bernanke, Ben. 2012. "Some Reflections on the Crisis and the Policy Response." Speech given on April 13 at Princeton Club, New York.

Blanchard, Olivier. 2015. "Dark Corners: Reassessing Macroeconomics after the Crisis." American Economic Association/American Finance Association, January 3.

Blanchard, Olivier. 2014. "Where Danger Lurks." *Finance & Development* 51 (3). http://www.imf.org/external/pubs/ft/fandd/2014/09/blanchard.htm.

Blinder, Alan. 2013. "Financial Collapse: A 10-Step Recovery Plan." *New York Times*, January 20.

Blinder, Alan. 2015. "Can Economists Learn? The Right Lessons from the Financial Crisis." *Foreign Affairs*, March-April. https://www.foreignaffairs.com/reviews/review-essay/2015-02-16/can-economists-learn.

Cassidy, John. 2008. "The Minsky Moment." *New Yorker*, February 8. http://www.newyorker.com/talk/comment/2008/02/04/080204taco_talk_cassidy.

Coates, John. 2012. *The Hour between Dog and Wolf: How Risk Taking Transforms Us, Body, and Mind*. New York: Penguin.

Cohen, Patricia. 2009. "Ivory Tower Unswayed by Crashing Economy." *New York Times*, March 5.

The Economist. 2010. "The Fed Discovers Hyman Minsky," January 7.

Eggertsson, Gauti, and Paul Krugman. 2012. "Debt, Deleveraging, and the Liquidity Trap: A Fisher-Minsky-Koo Approach." *Quarterly Journal of Economics* 127 (3): 1469–1513.

Financial Crisis Inquiry Report. 2011. Washington, DC: US Government Printing Office. http://fcic.law.stanford.edu/.

Foote, Christopher, Kristopher Gerardi, and Paul Willen. 2013. "Why Did So Many People Make So Many ex post Bad Decisions? The Causes of the Foreclosure Crisis." In *Rethinking the Financial Crisis*, edited by Alan Blinder, Andrew Lo, and Robert Solow. New York: Sage Foundation.

Field, Alexander. 2011. *A Great Leap Forward: 1030s Depression and U.S. Economic Growth*. New Haven, CT: Yale University Press.

Fisher, Irving. 1932. *Booms and Depressions: Some First Principles*. New York: Adelphi.

Foote, Christopher, Kristopher Gerardi, and Paul Willen. 2013. "Why Did So Many People Make So Many Ex Post Bad Decisions? The Causes of the Foreclosure Crisis." In*Rethinking the Financial Crisis*, edited by Alan Blinder, Andrew Lo, and Robert Solow. New York: Sage Foundation.

Fox, Justin. 2009. "Hyman Minsky Didn't Have All the Answers." *Time Magazine*, September 15.

Gandel, Stephen. 2013. "Banks May Need to Raise $4.5 billion." *Fortune*, July 2. http://finance.fortune.cnn.com/2013/07/02/fed-capital-rules/.

Gigerenzer, Gerd. 2008. "Why Heuristics Work." *Perspectives on Psychological Science* 3 (1): 20–29.

Gilovich, Thomas, Robert Vallone,and Amos Tversky. 1985. "The Hot Hand in Basketball: On the Misperception of Random Sequences." *Cognitive Psychology* 17: 295–314.

Godley, Wynne, and Marc Lavoie. 2007. *Monetary Economics: An Integrated Approach to Credit, Money, Income, Production and Wealth*. New York: Palgrave MacMillan.

Greenspan, Alan. 2013. *The Map and the Territory: Risk, Human Nature, and the Future of Forecasting: The Age of Turbulence*. New York: Penguin.

Hahn, Frank H. 1963. "On the Disequilibrium Behavior of a Multisectoral Growth Model." *The Economic Journal* 73 (291): 442–457.

Hahn, Frank H. 1968. "On Warranted Growth Paths." *Review of Economic Studies* 35 (162): 175–184.

Hahn, Frank H. 1970. "Some Adjustment Problems." *Econometrica* 38 (1): 1–17.

Haldane, Andrew G., and Vasileios Madouros. 2012. "The Dog and the Frisbee." Speech at a symposium of the Federal Reserve Bank of Kansas City, August 31. http://www.bis.org/review/r120905a.pdf.

Kahneman, Daniel, and Amos Tversky. 1979. "Prospect Theory: An Analysis of Decision Making under Risk." *Econometrica* 5 (2): 263–291.

Kahneman, Daniel. 2011. *Thinking, Fast and Slow*. New York: Farrar, Straus and Giroux.

Keen, Steve. 1995. "Finance and Economic Breakdown: Modeling Minsky's 'Financial Instability Hypothesis.'" *Journal of Post Keynesian Economics* 17 (4): 607–635.

Keen, Steve. 2012. "A Monetary Minsky Model of the Great Moderation and the Great Recession." *Journal of Economic Behavior & Organization* 86: 221–235. http://www.sciencedirect.com/science/article/pii/S0167268111000266.

Keen, Steve. 2013. "Predicting the 'Global Financial Crisis': Post-Keynesian Macroeconomics." *Economic Record* 89: 228–254. http://onlinelibrary.wiley.com/doi/10.1111/1475-4932.12016/abstract.

Kennedy, Simon. 2013. "'Minsky Moment' Alarm Sounded; Economist Concerned Collapse in Asset Values Will Grow into Huge Debt Crisis." *Bloomberg/Vancouver Sun*, June 24.

Krugman, Paul. 2009. "The Night They Reread Minsky." *New York Times Blog*, May 17.

Krugman, Paul. 2010. "Six Doctrines in Search of a Policy Regime." *New York Times Blog*, April 18.

Krugman, Paul. 2011. "Things That Never Happened in the History of Macroeconomics." *New York Times Blog*, December 5.

Krugman, Paul. 2012. "Minsky and Methodology (Wonkish)." *New York Times*, March 27.

Krugman, Paul. 2015. "The Case of the Missing Minsky." *New York Times*, June 1. http://krugman.blogs.nytimes.com/2015/06/01/the-case-of-the-missing-minsky/?_r=0.

Lahart, Justin. 2007. "In Time of Tumult, Obscure Economist Gains Currency—Mr. Minsky Long Argued Markets Were Crisis Prone; His 'Moment' Has Arrived." *Wall Street Journal*, August 18.

Lanman, Scott, and Steve Matthews. 2013. "Greenspan Concedes to 'Flaw' in His Market Ideology." *Bloomberg*, October 23. http://www.bloomberg.com/apps/news?pid=newsarchive&sid=ah5qh9Up4rIg.

Lopes, Lola, 1987. "Between Hope and Fear: The Psychology of Risk." *Advances in Experimental Social Psychology* 20: 255–295.

Lynch, Aaron. 1996. *Thought Contagion: How Belief Spreads through Society*. New York: Basic Books.

Madrick, Jeff. 2002. "Let's Hear from Those Who Feel Government Has a Role in Stabilizing the Economy." *New York Times*, August 8.

McCulley, Paul. 2009. "The Shadow Banking System and Hyman Minsky's Economic Journey." In *Voices of Wisdom: Understanding the Global Financial Crisis*, edited by Laurence B. Siegel. Research Foundation of CFA Institute.

Minsky, Hyman. 1986, repr. 2008. *Stabilizing an Unstable Economy*. New York: McGraw-Hill.

Minsky, Hyman, 1995. "Financial Factors in the Economics of Capitalism." *Journal of Financial Services Research* 9 (3/4): 197–208.

Morgenson, Gretchen. 2013. "Bankers Are Balking at a Proposed Rule on Capital." *New York Times*, July 13. http://www.nytimes.com/2013/07/14/business/bankers-are-balking-at-a-proposed-rule-on-capital.html?partner=rss&emc=rss&_r=0.

Norris, Floyd. 2008. "Determining Who Rides the Lifeboat." *New York Times*, May 2.

Norris, Floyd. 2009. "Financial Giants, Diminished." *New York Times*, December 25.

Norris, Floyd. 2011. "2 Meltdowns with Much in Common." *New York Times*, March 18.

Norris, Floyd. 2013a. "The Physics of Wall Street." *New York Times*, January 6.

Norris, Floyd. 2013b. "The Time Bernanke Got It Wrong." *New York Times*, July 19.

Odean, Terrance. 1998. "Volume, Volatility, Price, and Profit when All Traders Are Above Average." *Journal of Finance* 53 (6): 1887–1934.

PBS, *The Newshour*. 2013. "Greenspan Admits 'Flaw' to Congress, Predicts More Economic Problems." October 23. http://www.pbs.org/newshour/bb/business/july-dec 08/crisishearing_10-23.html.

Reinhart, Carmen, and Kenneth Rogoff, 2009. *This Time Is Different: Eight Centuries of Financial Folly*. Princeton, NJ: Princeton University Press.

Schlefer, Jonathan. 2013. "Embracing Economist Who Modeled the Crisis." *New York Times*, September 11. http://www.nytimes.com/2013/09/11/business/economy/economists-embracing-ideas-of-wynne-godley-late-colleague-who-predicted-recession.html?pagewanted=all.

Shefrin, Hersh. 2009. "How Psychological Pitfalls Generated the Global Financial Crisis." In *Voices of Wisdom: Understanding the Global Financial Crisis*, edited by Laurence B. Siegel. Research Foundation of CFA Institute.

Shefrin, Hersh, and Meir Statman. 2013. "Behavioral Finance in the Financial Crisis: Market Efficiency, Minsky, and Keynes." In*Rethinking the Financial Crisis*, edited by Alan Blinder, Andrew Lo, and Robert Solow. New York: Sage Foundation.

Shiller, Robert. 2009. "Expect the Worst and You May Get It." *New York Times*, February 22.

Silver-Greenberg, Jessica, and Michael Corkery. 2014. "In a Subprime Bubble for Used Cars, Borrowers Pay Sky-High Rates." *New York Times*, July 19. http://dealbook.ny times.com/2014/07/19/in-a-subprime-bubble-for-used-cars-unfit-borrowers-pay-sky-high-rates/?_php=true&_type=blogs&hp&action=click&pgtype=Homepage &version=HpSum&mod.

Simon, Herbert. 1955. "A Behavioral Model of Rational Choice." *Quarterly Journal of Economics* 69: 99–118.

Stanton, Thomas. 2012. *Why Some Firms Thrive While Others Fail: Governance and Management Lessons from the Crisis*. New York: Oxford University Press.

Summers, Lawrence, Hyman Minsky, Paul Samuelson, William Poole, and Paul Volcker. 1991. "Macroeconomic Consequences of Financial Crises." In *The Risk of Economic Crisis*, edited by Martin Feldstein. Chicago: University of Chicago Press, 135–182. http://www.nber.org/books/feld91-2.

Wason, Peter C., 1968. "Reasoning About a Rule." *Quarterly Journal of Experimental Psychology* 20: 273–281.

Weinstein, Neil. 1980. "Unrealistic Optimism about Future Life Events." *Journal of Personality and Social Psychology* 39 (5): 806–820.

Whalen, Charles. 2007. "The U.S. Credit Crunch of 2007." Working paper 92, Levy Economics Institute of Bard College.

Wolf, Martin. 2008. "The End of Lightly Regulated Finance Has Come Closer." *FT.com*, September 16.

Wray, L. Randall. 2012. "Global Financial Crisis: A Minskyan Interpretation of the Causes, the Fed's Bailout, and the Future." Working paper 711, Levy Economics Institute of Bard College.

Yellen, Janet. 2009. "A Minsky Meltdown: Lessons for Central Bankers." *FRBSF Economic Letter*, May.

6

Prelude to the Global Financial Credit Crisis

Growing Turbulence under a Flat Sea

JOHN SILVIA ■

THE THINGS WE TAKE FOR GRANTED — AND THEIR ECONOMIC IMPLICATIONS

During the 30 years preceding the global financial crisis, the US economy drew support from the growing democratization of consumer credit, as well as the broadening out of global capital markets to support US treasury, corporate, and securitized credit. More credit became available to the federal and state governments, corporations, and households along different rankings of the credit quality spectrum than ever before in our economic history. Underlying this credit expansion were the beliefs that growth and home prices were on an upward trend, volatility had died down (the Great Moderation), and inflation would not reassert itself in the near term.[1]

Moreover, in the United States, Europe, and many other nations, there was an assumption that fiscal and monetary policy remained highly effective in achieving stronger economic growth, lower unemployment, and control of inflation. For example, lower interest rates were assumed to reinvigorate housing, while federal spending was expected to have multiplier effects on growth and employment. Yet, the outcomes, as we know, did not generate the expected economic results.

Assumptions on the effectiveness of fiscal and monetary policy actions provided an overconfidence bias on the part of policymakers. Therefore, we witnessed the rise of sovereign debt in both the United States and Europe that outpaced the potential long-run growth rate of the underlying economy. Growth was now unable to generate the revenues to meet future spending commitments, especially on entitlements. When stressed, the assumptions on growth and policy effectiveness were found wanting.

Access to the global credit markets allowed governments to spend on the welfare state beyond what was supportable. Meanwhile, in the private sector, the push to provide a greater rate of homeownership extended the credit qualification beyond the point where homeowners were able to cover their bills under any adverse economic conditions, such as weaker growth, higher unemployment, and rising interest rates. When the economic crunch hit homeowners, delinquencies rose and home prices began their decline. There was a long train of developments that led to the housing crisis, underlined by a philosophy to broaden home ownership that did not include a balanced sense of risk and reward. In early 1994, a system was developed to generate credit scores to predict the payment performance of complex mortgage loans.[2] By 1995, the Department of Housing and Urban Development relaxed the rules on appraisals for Fannie Mae mortgages. In 2001, the Basel Committee on Banking Supervision altered the risk weightings that regulators would apply to mortgage-backed securities. Risk ratings were lowered from 50% to 20% on AAA and AA rated asset-backed securities. Finally, the Federal Reserve kept interest rates below market equilibrium to stimulate the economy. Each of these was a singular small change, but together they significantly altered the risk versus reward balance in lending decisions which, under the assumption of continued, steady economic growth and rising home prices, would have had limited downside risk. But those assumptions on growth, jobs, and home prices were about to be tested—and eventually were found deficient.

Easier standards opened the door for marginal borrowers to access credit and purchase homes; thus began the long slide into the credit market crisis, housing collapse, and Great Recession. As illustrated in Figure 6.1, household debt service ratios rose quickly in the decade prior to the credit crunch as consumers took advantage of the increasing availability of credit. Meanwhile, lenders steadily reduced their spread for loans rates over the cost of funds during the 2002–2006 period (Figure 6.2).

We are witnessing a similar problem today. Student loan debt—pushed by federal policies (again) and taken on by students (previously homeowners) to buy an asset (previously a home) with an expected rate of return on education (previously the house)—is far out of line with a realistic assessment on the return of the investment (education) relative to the cost. This is another failure of public policy to promote activities that do not encourage the taking on of more debt without a realistic assessment of the return on the funds borrowed.

SECULAR SHIFTS MASKED BY SHORT-TERM ECONOMIC PROSPERITY

Since the initiation of countercyclical fiscal and monetary policy beginning in the 1960s, there has been a growing confidence bias in the ability of public policy to solve the economic and credit cycles of the US economy. Beginning in the 1990s, the degree of policy action and the response of the economy have become increasingly disconnected, as increasingly large reductions in interest rates by the Fed have been followed by lower rates of economic and job growth. Underlying these cyclical, but increasingly modest, economic recoveries in jobs and growth since the 1990s have been several secular shifts in the labor and credit markets. Similarly, the European debt problem has stemmed in part from the secular change in trading and production

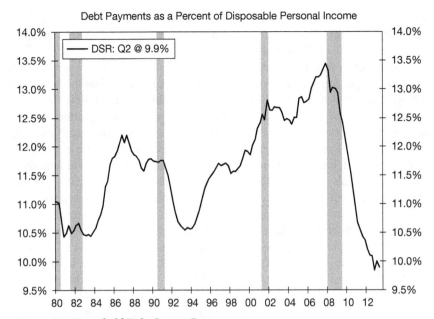

Figure 6.1 Household Debt Service Ratio.

SOURCE: US Department of Commerce and Wells Fargo Securities, LLC.

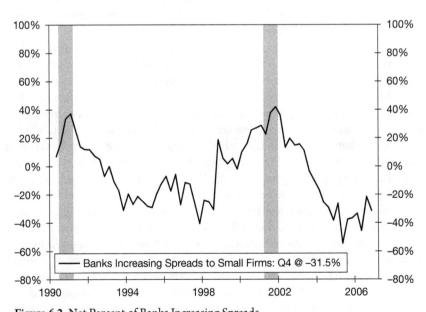

Figure 6.2 Net Percent of Banks Increasing Spreads.

SOURCE: US Department of Commerce and Wells Fargo Securities, LLC.

patterns with Eastern Europe, China, and the rest of the world. This has been compounded by the relentless force of demographics: a smaller working population paying for a growing welfare state.

As illustrated in Figure 6.3, the sovereign debt problem in Europe[3] preceded the Great Recession. The sovereign debt crisis was the outgrowth of southern Europe's demographic imbalance and lack of trade competitiveness prior to the Great Recession. This problem was compounded in the credit markets as regulators failed to allow markets to price sovereign credit differently. As we know now, not all sovereign debt was/is Tier 1 capital and yet regulators gave such debt a zero risk weighting. Spreads narrowed between sovereign debt issuers despite differences in underlying fiscal fundamentals (see Figure 6.4). In the United States, the globalization of trade and production reduced the competitiveness of low- and semi-skilled manufacturing and office workers, while the demographics of an enlarged entitlement state outpaced the growth of the tax base to support that state.[4] Finally, the financial crisis in Europe came after a long period of lost competitiveness in a number of Eurozone countries, including Ireland, Italy, Spain, and Portugal, vis-à-vis Germany (Figure 6.5). This reinforces our view that the financial crisis came at a time when structural forces had altered the playing landscape for workers and nations, and that landscape proved to be a barrier to the effectiveness of traditional policy actions.

Unfortunately, the access to credit by sovereign states in Western Europe and would-be homeowners in the United States continued to rise over the past 20 years while the potential to pay that debt declined. Forecasts of economic renewal based upon models that assumed countercyclical policy would get the economy going again failed to deliver the projected growth following the financial crisis of 2008. The emphasis on cyclical policies could not address the structural realities of the 21st-century economy. These failures were hidden by the apparent, not real, effectiveness of fiscal, regulatory, and monetary policy actions.

The effectiveness of credit and labor markets relies upon the sensitivity of the underlying assumptions of how those markets work. Yet those markets were changing, and so was the effectiveness of those markets to deliver the expected results. With those changes came the failure of home prices and interest rates to reflect the real cost of credit and the real rate of return on housing. As economic growth was less than expected following the crisis, so was the viability of credit, housing, and labor market decisions. To illustrate the change in the underlying forces of the economy and labor markets, Figure 6.6 portrays the growth of manufacturing output in contrast to manufacturing employment. While output gains continued, job opportunities declined. This pattern had gone on for a long time, yet was overlooked when time came to evaluate the effectiveness of output forecasts in delivering job gains.

In this world of economic disequilibrium, we recognize that output, labor, and credit markets are interrelated. Consumption is a function of expected income, credit availability, and wealth. Beginning around 1982, jobs, income, and wealth grew such that households acted upon the perceived prosperity. Gains in expected incomes reflected better job opportunities for many. Labor is a derived demand from expected future output—hire today in anticipation of sales in the future. Meanwhile,

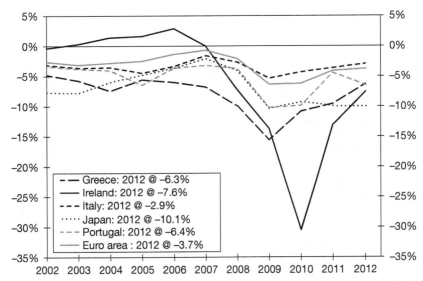

Figure 6.3 General Government Net Lending/Borrowing as a Percent of GDP.

SOURCE: IMF, IHS Global Insight, and Wells Fargo Securities, LLC.

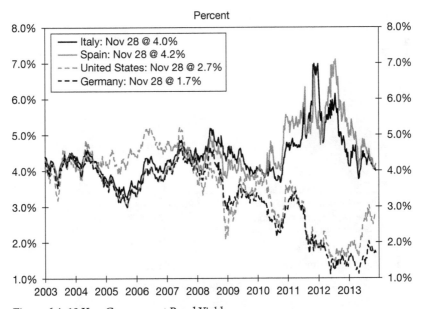

Figure 6.4 10-Year Government Bond Yields.

SOURCE: IMF, IHS Global Insight, and Wells Fargo Securities, LLC.

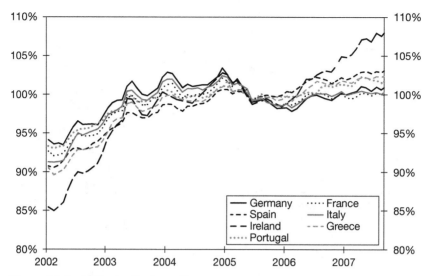

Figure 6.5 Real Effective Exchange Rates.

SOURCE: IHS Global Insight and Wells Fargo Securities, LLC.

Figure 6.6 Production and Jobs in Manufacturing Sector.

SOURCE: US Department of Commerce and Wells Fargo Securities, LLC.

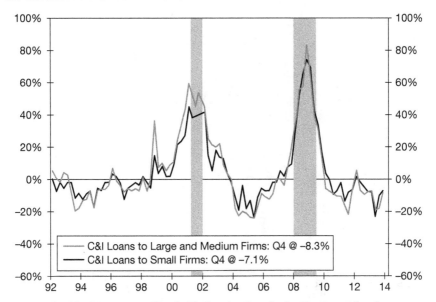

Figure 6.7 Net Percentage of Banks Tightening Standards: Commercial and Industrial Loans.

SOURCE: US Department of Commerce and Wells Fargo Securities, LLC.

employment grew, especially in service and construction, in line with better housing starts and overall economic output. Credit lending for both business and housing reflected the optimism about expected economic growth, reduced risk expectations, and lower interest rates that began in the early 1980s.

However, by the 1990s, the disconnect between greater credit availability and reduced growth prospects set up a collision course for many governments and households. Prior to the financial crisis, there was a growing misallocation of capital and workers. Economic growth potentials were overstated by the extension of credit beyond the point where that credit could be reasonably paid back out of future economic returns. Temporary economic policy stimulus hid the real picture of economic potential. As illustrated in Figure 6.7, prior to the credit shock of 2007–2009, credit terms had been eased so greatly that the problems of delinquencies was already apparent by the Fall of 2006, long before the Lehman moment in September 2008.

Pushing the Credit Envelope

Since the beginning of 2006, we have witnessed a steady decline in the spread of synthetic corporate bonds relative to the cash market (Figure 6.8).[5] This decline reflects a narrower accounting for risk than what may make bank supervisors comfortable. Are synthetic credit spreads too tight? Synthetic credit spreads have been well supported by a strong bid from CDOs (collateralized debt obligations) and other fixed income buyers (correlated equity tranches). This has helped the synthetic basis tighten by 10 basis points over the past several months. However, for most of this year, price movements on credit default swaps (CDS) have been

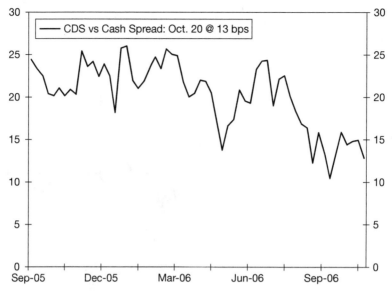

Figure 6.8 cd sig Index less Corporate IG Index: IGCDX less Cash, Basis Points.

SOURCE: Bloomberg LP and Wells Fargo Securities, LLC.

highly correlated with equity prices. The correlation is negative; credit spreads generally tighten as equity prices rise, and vice-versa. The correlation over the past six months has been very strong at -84%. This piece of data suggests that the changes in synthetic credit pricing this year have been largely justified, or alternatively that both synthetic credit spreads as well as equities are both too rich, and therefore vulnerable to corrections. Based on the strength of this relationship, it is prudent that credit investors watch the stock market closely for any signs of a technical reversal to the recent strength.

For another example, we can see in Figure 6.9 that the spread of mortgage-backed securities current coupon yields relative to the cost of funds has narrowed over the last two years prior to the crisis. The declining spread is consistent with the flatter yield curve, which in turn is reflective of the lowered expectations of both growth and inflation and thereby lowered volatility of monetary policy itself. The summer bond rally significantly reduced the book losses in those portfolios, and some banks have taken the opportunity to sell securities and either deleverage or redeploy funds in better yielding assets. Banks have done this in one of two ways: purchasing whole loans and consumer debt, or simply repurchasing their own equity. Like the inverted yield curve, these narrowing spreads also likely reflect large amounts of risk-seeking investors entering these markets, which pushes up demand and could possibly be artificially depressing credit spreads.

By the second quarter of 2006, delinquency rates on adjustable rate mortgages (ARMs) had already risen, suggesting a buildup of the credit problem both nationally and in selected states.[6] Subprime ARM delinquencies had risen significantly more than delinquencies of prime ARMs (Table 6.1). Both the prime and subprime delinquency rates were already significantly higher in 2006 than they were in

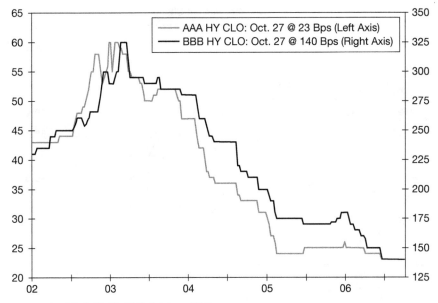

Figure 6.9 High Yield CLO AAA vs. BBB.

SOURCE: Bloomberg LP and Wells Fargo Securities, LLC.

Table 6.1. ARM LOANS PERCENTAGE OF LOANS DELINQUENT, 2ND QUARTER

	Prime Arm		Subprime Arm	
	2005	2006	2005	2006
United States	2.09%	2.58%	10.03%	12.20%
Nevada	1.26%	1.85%	4.91%	7.03%
California	1.32%	1.81%	5.83%	8.18%
District of Columbia	1.48%	1.82%	7.03%	8.84%
Arizona	1.32%	1.40%	5.91%	6.10%
Florida	1.94%	2.44%	8.06%	10.10%

SOURCE: Moody's Economy.com and Wells Fargo Securities, LLC

the prior year. With a further slowing in the economy, we expected the climb in delinquency rates to continue. Historically, delinquency rates tend to lag the pace of growth so that slower economic growth today suggests even higher delinquency rates tomorrow.

HOME PRICES FAIL TO MEET EXPECTATIONS: THE ECONOMIC SHOCK

By 2006, the untenable housing boom came home to roost. The catalyst was the downshift in home price appreciation, illustrated in Figure 6.10. In economics, as in most of life, outcomes reflect disconnect between what we get versus what we expected. For home prices, the disconnect was twofold. First, home prices did not

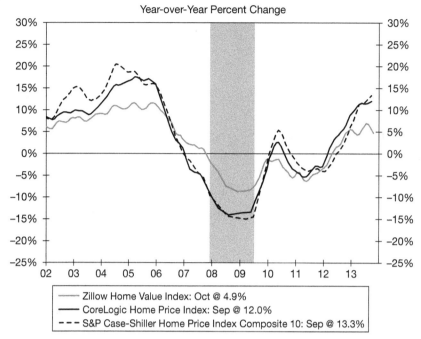

Figure 6.10 Home Prices.

SOURCE: Zillow, Corelogic, S&P Case-Shiller, and Wells Fargo Securities, LLC.

continually rise. Second, the decline in home prices was nationwide—counter to the experience of regional housing busts that altered the expectations of buyers and lenders alike. The drop in home values was compounded further by the upward move in mortgage rates, as teaser rates ended and more market-consistent mortgage rates appeared.

The squeeze on household discretionary income and the turn in home prices led to a decline in credit demand and, in turn, to a decline in construction and labor demand. Meanwhile, credit performance on home loans deteriorated, thereby increasing loan loss reserves and leading to declines in lender profits and capital. For many mortgage brokerage firms there was little depth to their balance sheets, minimal capital and too little liquidity to withstand the downdraft.

FEEDBACK FROM THE CHANGE: CHANGE BEGETS CREDIT REVULSION

Declining home prices and rising delinquencies were the market signals for change. The feedback from this change was a hit to consumer income and therefore overall demand. The loss of aggregate demand in the economy led to a loss in the demand for labor, particularly construction. In addition, demand for housing and related construction and real estate services declined.

Credit is a function of expected economic growth.[7] When households face a binding liquidity constraint through the loss of credit, consumption must match current earnings—not rely upon the future expectation of home price appreciation. This is especially important for middle- and lower-middle-income households, where a decline in credit availability will limit household consumption. Moreover, the increased likelihood of future credit constraints will further lower the consumption of households not currently at their credit constraint limit since such households will fear that credit rollovers will not be available in the future.[8] Finally, the Lehman shock of September 2008 led to the immediate disappearance of liquidity assumptions and the rise of counterparty risk in the marketplace.

FEEDBACK FROM THE CHANGE: IMPACT ON THE LABOR MARKET

For the labor market, the immediate feedback from the credit shock was a downshift in the expectations for growth and therefore a decline in the demand for labor. With growth less than expected, adjustments must be made, and in the short-run the adjustments most often fall upon labor. So began a downshift in labor demand in construction, real estate, and financial services (mortgage lending). As illustrated in Figure 6.11, the employment cycle was extremely severe in the short run relative to earlier recessions; even today, five years later, job gains have not made up the job losses. The cyclical recovery of employment has been hindered by the underlying shift in the risk/return trade-off in credit markets and compounded by the ongoing globalization of production and associated displacement of workers. Moreover, the changes in the service sector continue to reflect the evolution of office technology since the introduction of Microsoft Office 3.0 in 1992.

ECONOMIC GROWTH WITHOUT A LABOR MARKET RECOVERY

More than four years after the Great Recession ended, the unemployment rate remains stubbornly high at more than 7% overall, with some metropolitan areas and states above 9% (Table 6.2). Employment gains reflect a labor market that has added jobs but at an insufficient pace compared to prior economic recoveries (refer back to Figure 6.11) and with significant regional disparities.

These disparities present a significant challenge to decision makers in both the private and public sector. In the private sector, employers must evaluate what the trend is in job and income gains that will support consumer spending and housing starts going forward, since the 2% average economic growth over the past four years is clearly below what many firms and state/local governments expected in this economic recovery. For public sector leaders, the pace of economic growth will determine gains in tax revenue and the ability to close the estimated gap between revenues and spending, especially entitlements, that were promised over the past 30 years. At the US federal level, subpar economic growth will not generate either the expected jobs or the tax revenue anticipated by policymakers. This is especially significant given that Social Security and Medicare are financed based on employment. The sharp rise in unemployment rates in North America (Figure 6.12) is clearly out of character with history.

Meanwhile, significant moves in the unemployment rate are also present in Western Europe (Figure 6.13). For the nations in the Eurozone, the hit to growth has led to large fiscal deficits while also limiting job growth to a pace below what

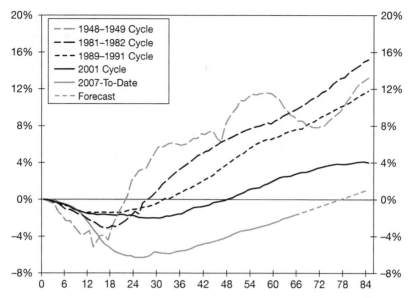

Figure 6.11 US Employment Cycles: Percent Change from Cycle Peak.
SOURCE: US Department of Labor and Wells Fargo Securities, LLC.

Table 6.2. UNEMPLOYMENT RATE BY STATE

	2009	2012
Florida	11.4%	7.9%
Nevada	13.3%	9.8%
California	12.3%	9.8%
Georgia	10.4%	8.7%
Illinois	11.3%	8.6%
Ohio	10.6%	6.7%

SOURCE: US Department of Labor and Wells Fargo Securities, LLC

many policymakers had hoped for with the emergence of the euro. This pattern is compounded by the large fiscal deficits leading to higher market interest rates on sovereign debt and further limiting governments to undertake countercyclical fiscal policy. Further, many commercial banks held sovereign debt in their portfolios, so when interest rates and delinquencies rose on private lending, these institutions faced additional constraints to lending to support economic growth and job gains while the market value of their sovereign debt portfolios declined.

AN ALTERED FRAMEWORK FOR THE LABOR MARKET

Changes in economic expectations and credit availability alter both the supply and demand for labor. The US labor market is not characterized by a dual, parallel market hypothesis but instead is represented by several markets that are distinguished by the character of both demand and supply elements. The demand for labor is limited

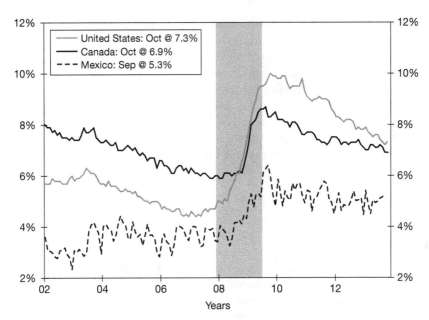

Figure 6.12 Unemployment Rate, Seasonally Adjusted.

SOURCE: US Department of Commerce and Wells Fargo Securities, LLC.

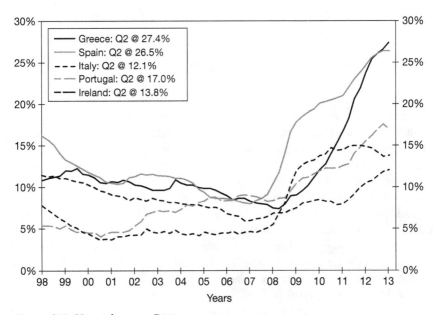

Figure 6.13 Unemployment Rates.

SOURCE: US Department of Commerce and Wells Fargo Securities, LLC.

by the financial quality of firms as well as the availability of credit by lenders as a direct result of the credit crisis that followed from the Great Recession. For many lenders, regulatory actions further limited credit availability by new rules on lending and increased requirements for bank capital.

On the supply side, workers are limited by a new factor—unrealized but significant losses on their personal real estate. This is compounded by the ongoing change in the skills demanded by employers, which no longer match the skills of some workers. Restricted mobility on the part of some workers has become a pervasive national problem in a way it has not before in the United States.[9]

The Reservation Wage Model

In the short run, workers initially seek real wages consistent with the pre-recession period, but these wages are now above the level that equates demand and supply in the post-recession era. This gives rise to the inner dynamic of the labor market we summarize with the concept of a reservation wage. Workers value their time—including leisure time. This trade-off between work and leisure has become increasingly complex because the trade-off is not simply wages for work versus no wages for leisure.

What is the opportunity cost for not working? To the fundamental workings of the labor market we add four recent public policy changes that significantly altered the work/leisure trade-off in this post-Great Recession era.

Movements in aggregate demand lead to changes in the quantity of employment. Yet there is a crucial dynamic between nominal and real wages. Typically, nominal wages move less than inflation, and therefore real wages tend to fall during economic expansions and rise during periods of recession/slowdown as inflation slows. As a result, when aggregate demand shifts occur, the focus by workers on maintaining nominal wages obscures the movement in real wages and results in a real wage that is higher than what is consistent with the supply and demand for labor at a given time. This gives real wages a countercyclical character. Therefore, as workers attempt to retain their nominal wages during periods of economic weakness, the real wage cost of their work rises and contributes to longer-term unemployment. Moreover, wages tend to be associated with certain jobs and not the workers themselves. Therefore, when the wages associated with a job change, often the person associated with the job does not recognize the changes in the short run.

Work/leisure decisions reflect a trade-off for each worker on how to spend their time. The opportunity cost—what a worker gives up by staying at home—is the compensation—wages and benefits for working. However, by choosing not to work, a person does not go without income. What an unemployed person can bring home in income while unemployed is crucial to the dynamic change in the labor market that has become so apparent in the current economic expansion. Finally, we should recognize the growing gap over the years between the cost of labor and the return on labor, as payroll taxes for Social Security and Medicare eat away at the return on labor. This growing compensation gap leads to a dead weight loss in the labor market and thereby a lower wage to workers and lower employment level than would be the case otherwise.[10]

Four policy changes have also altered the opportunity cost of working. First, disability payment eligibility standards have been relaxed over the past 20 years (again, a long-term trend that operated and altered behavior prior to the Great Recession).The rise in disability payments increases the income of those not working and thereby raises the reservation wage for those workers. Autor and Duggan show that the indexation of benefits by the average wage level increased the extent to which disability payments replaced wages for low-wage workers.[11]

Second, unemployment benefits were extended out to as long as 99 weeks, while supplemental nutrition assistance increased. Together these support programs have been relatively more generous during this recovery compared to prior recoveries. This increase in benefits has raised the replacement rate for workers for working—effectively, the ratio of unemployment benefits to previous earnings has risen and there is thus a reduced incentive for the unemployed to seek a new position. Empirical evidence suggests that an increase in the replacement rate through unemployment insurance leads to an increase in the length of unemployment.[12]

Third, the effective tax rate—particularly the steepness of the marginal tax rates for those moving from unemployment to work—has changed over time. Our view is that the move from increasingly generous income supplements to working suggests an increase in the marginal tax rate over time. Therefore, there is a higher hurdle in the decision to move from unemployed to employed which would bias up the unemployment ranks over time. In general, the greater the social safety net, the greater the barrier for any worker moving from unemployed to employed, and therefore a greater reduction in the return to work.

Finally, increases in the minimum wage during 2009 would likely have had two impacts. First, the minimum wage sets a floor on nominal wages, making them inflexible downward and hindering the clearing of the market. This pattern of inflexible downward wages creates additional unemployment in the short run. Over time, workers, especially the young, do not get the work experience which is valuable in seeking employment in the future. This, along with a long-term shift to more education, may be reflected in the decline in labor force participation rates for workers between 16 and 24 years old.

A second impact is that the pre-recession period gave rise to an increasing supply of low- and semi-skilled workers, many of them new immigrants, who had entered the construction, restaurant/leisure, and retail sectors. When the Great Recession hit, the sharp drop in demand for workers in these sectors led to an excess supply of workers.

In contrast, the rise in applied computer technology, communications, and networking has led to excess demand for workers in the science, math, and technology fields such that application backlogs for H-1B work visas for technology professionals continued to build.

As a result, the labor market simultaneously contained an excess supply of low-/semi-skilled labor and a shortage of high-skilled technology, engineering, and math talent. This disparity is readily apparent in Figure 6.14, which presents the disparity of unemployment rates by education during the early years of the economic recovery. Moreover, the persistence of this disparity to the current period bolsters the argument that the labor market reflects distinct submarkets differentiated by skills and geography. The cyclical downturn exposed the structural labor market issues that were the legacy of a misallocation of credit in the pre-recession period.

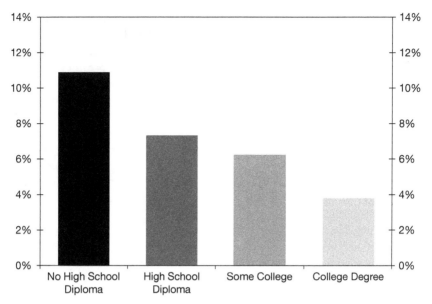

Figure 6.14 Unemployment Rate by Education Level, October 2013.

SOURCE: US Department of Labor and Wells Fargo Securities, LLC.

LEGACY OF A DISPARATE LABOR MARKET AFTER THE CREDIT CRISIS

In a perfectly competitive market in equilibrium, differences between supply and demand for labor would be worked out by adjustments of supply (mobility), demand (increased hiring of flexible talent), and changes in real wages.

However, as we have reviewed above, labor is a derived demand and when the demand for final goods declines dramatically and disproportionately between sectors, labor demand is reduced by unequal amounts in different occupations and locations. Meanwhile, the supply of labor is not mobile by geography due to the home negative-equity problem as well as the differentiated and not easily substitutable skills.

Many measures of the labor market illustrate that this market is quite distinct from the perfect labor market described in the prior section. While the severity of the Great Recession undoubtedly caused cyclical deterioration across the labor market, hints of structural change abound. Moreover, the protracted nature of the labor market creates a risk for typical cyclical changes to become permanent.

DURATION OF UNEMPLOYMENT: NO SIGN OF RECOVERY FOR MANY WORKERS

One signal of the protracted labor market recovery in the current economic expansion is the persistently long length of unemployment. The average duration of unemployment continues to stand near record highs. Such data suggest many workers face long spells of unemployment, and that the headline unemployment rate does not

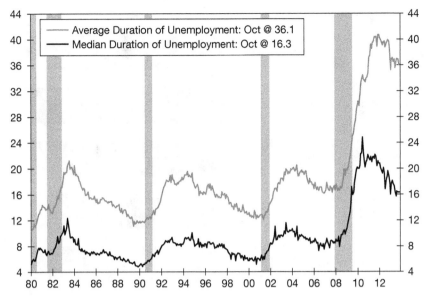

Figure 6.15 Average vs. Median Duration Unemployment, Weeks Unemployed.
SOURCE: US Department of Commerce and Wells Fargo Securities, LLC.

fully capture the severity of the experience for millions of Americans. The median duration of unemployment has come off its post-recession highs, but the discrepancy between the median and average duration—roughly 20 weeks—suggests that a small fraction of workers still face severely long spells of unemployment (Figure 6.15).

For the unemployed, the lack of job opportunities has not only cost workers in terms of lost wages, but also in skills that have atrophied over time. Employers are more apt to hire workers who have been recently employed, as their skills are thought to be more up to date and relevant to the current work environment. Furthermore, as unemployment spells become increasingly long, job search networks also deteriorate for many workers and further constrict the additional avenues of finding employment. As a result, historically, workers with long durations of unemployment are less likely to find employment (Figure 6.16).[13]

Of course, the rise in the unemployment rate only tells part of the story. Labor force participation has declined to its lowest rate in more than a generation (Figure 6.17).[14] The fall is worrisome as less of the population is engaged in the economy and is more reliant on other means of income, such as government transfer payments or support from family and friends. However, the decline in participation since the onset of the recession has not been for a lack of searching. The Bureau of Labor Statistics finds that the average length of time an unemployed worker searched for employment before dropping out of the labor force was 20 weeks in 2010 compared to 8.5 weeks in 2007.[15] Many of these workers would still accept a job were it available, keeping the broadest measure of unemployment, U-6, in double digits.

The Beveridge Curve: Yet to Shift Inward Even as the headline unemployment rate has improved in the typical, albeit slow, cyclical fashion, other indicators on the labor market continue to suggest that today's environment has changed from the past. Job

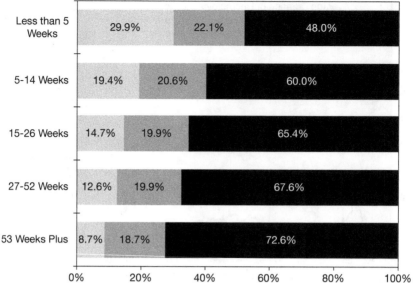

Figure 6.16 Labor Force Flows by Unemployment Duration: 12-Month Moving Average, April 2011.

SOURCE: US Department of Commerce and Wells Fargo Securities, LLC.

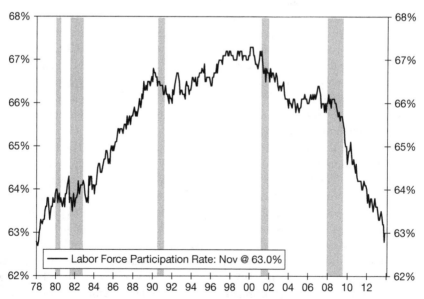

Figure 6.17 Labor Force Participation Rate: 16 Years and Over, Seasonally Adjusted.

SOURCE: US Department of Commerce and Wells Fargo Securities, LLC.

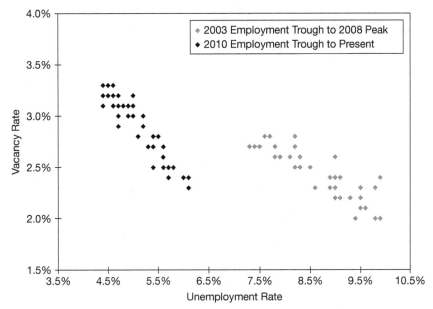

Figure 6.18 Beveridge Curve in Employment Recoveries: Unemployment Rate vs. Vacancy Rate.

SOURCE: US Department of Commerce and Wells Fargo Securities, LLC.

vacancies have become more plentiful as the economy has recovered, evidenced by the vertical axis of Figure 6.18. However, the unemployment rate (horizontal axis) remains high relative to the rate of job openings in the previous cycle and suggests more friction in matching the unemployed with available jobs.

It has been argued that the outward swing in the Beveridge curve is typical during the early stages of a labor market recovery. While some skills mismatch is to be expected as the economy undergoes significant periods of restructuring following a recession, more than four years into this recovery the Beveridge curve remains above its path. The depth of the previous recession posts a challenge to structural frictions beyond the typical pattern. The share of unemployed workers out of a job for more than 27 weeks remains historically high, and the longer these workers are out of a job, the higher the risk that the slow cyclical recovery results in longer-lasting structural mismatch as these workers' skills become increasingly out of date.

A PERMANENT DROP IN THE EMPLOYMENT RATIO?

Another sobering development in this expansion is the widening gap between the unemployment rate and the employment-population ratio (Figure 6.19). In the expansions of the 1990s and the 2000s, the unemployment rate tended to move with the employment-population ratio, as illustrated in the middle chart. However, in the latest expansion, the unemployment rate has dipped—suggesting better economic times—but the employment-population ratio, plotted inversely on the right-hand axis, has not improved. We know that part of the decline in the unemployment rate reflects a decline in the labor force participation rate—especially for young people.

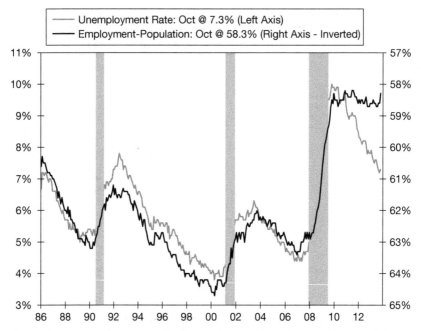

Figure 6.19 Unemployment vs. Employment-Population Ratio: 16 Years and Over, Seasonally Adjusted.

SOURCE: US Department of Commerce and Wells Fargo Securities, LLC.

That said, the lack of improvement in the employment-population ratio suggests a greater challenge to produce growth at a pace similar to earlier expansions given relatively fewer workers.

Moreover, many of those who are working are finding themselves in a less traditional type of job. As illustrated in Figure 6.20, the share of workers in part-time work remains near historic highs. While some workers choose to work part time, a significant change in the labor market this cycle is the historically high share of workers at this advanced stage in the recovery who are employed part time for economic reasons. This measure refers to people who work part time due to an inability to find full-time work or perhaps a seasonal decline in demand. The still-elevated rate suggests continued slack in demand for the goods and services that we produce, but also reluctance for firms to hire the traditional full-time, permanent employee.

This can also be seen in the strength in temporary help employment relative to other hiring in this recovery. Temporary help traditionally has been considered a springboard to stable, permanent, full-time employment, as temporary jobs are perceived to provide workers a means of building their human capital, networking, and gaining better information about permanent job opportunities. Yet, for our purposes, the persistence in the behavior of firms to hire a greater share of temporary help instead of permanent employees this cycle suggests a shift in the way employers manage their workforce. Employers appear to demand more flexibility in the size of their workforce and are less able to commit to the permanent employee position.

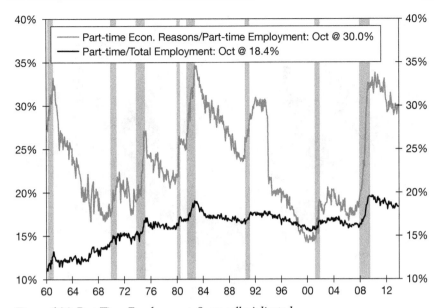

Figure 6.20 Part-Time Employment, Seasonally Adjusted.

SOURCE: US Department of Commerce and Wells Fargo Securities, LLC.

REGIONAL DISPARITIES REFLECT INDUSTRY CONCENTRATIONS

Deterioration in the labor market following the Great Recession has been widespread, with seemingly no type of worker untouched. However, there remains variation in the experiences of workers with different backgrounds and demographic profiles, as well as locations (Figure 6.21). Nationally, just over 3.5% fewer workers are employed than at the start of the recession. In the West that number is around 3% compared to less than 1% in the Northeast.

The varied pace of the labor market recovery across regions reflects the nature of the downturn. The past recession was largely driven by imbalances in the housing market. As a result, areas that saw the most overbuilding saw the largest declines in employment and slowest labor market recoveries. For example, employment in the Mountain region, which includes Arizona and Nevada, remains more than 3% off its peak. In contrast, employment in the neighboring West South Central region, which saw more modest homebuilding activity, has already surpassed its pre-recession employment level. The housing bust took a toll on employment in the Mountain region not only by slashing jobs in the construction industry but also by reducing demand for products and services provided by housing-related industries, such as real estate, finance, and retail. In Figure 6.22, we can identify for some of the hardest hit states the association between negative home equity and high unemployment. In the long run, as these regions work through excess home inventories and see prices stabilize, new construction will become more attractive to builders and incite more homeowners to move as their housing needs change. By state, we identify an association between high levels of unemployment and the prior boom in construction.

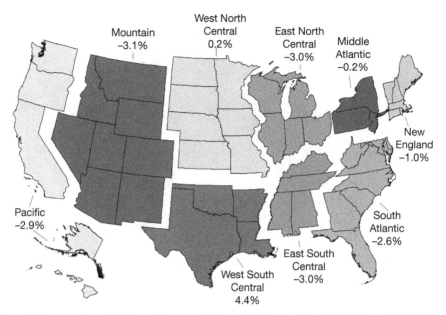

Figure 6.21 Employment Change by Region: Percent Change Since December 2007.
SOURCE: US Department of Labor and Wells Fargo Securities, LLC.

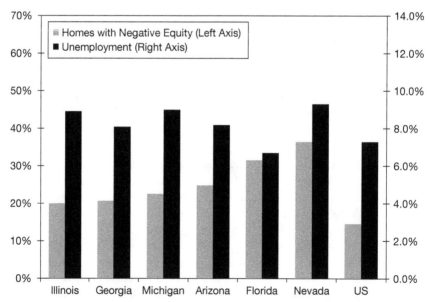

Figure 6.22 Negative Equity and Unemployment: Q2:2013 Negative Equity and
October 2013 Unemployment.

SOURCE: US Department of Labor and Wells Fargo Securities, LLC.

NEW AMERICAN PHENOMENON: CONSTRAINED WORKER MOBILITY

What makes this recovery particularly difficult for the labor market is that workers' mobility—key in reducing regional labor market differences in a large and culturally homogenous market like the United States—has been constrained. While workers could (and did) move to areas recovering more quickly in previous economic cycles, the housing imbalances of this cycle have limited that option for many homeowners. Steep home price declines in some regions of the country have put many homeowners in a negative-equity position. If owners sold their home at current market prices, it would lead to capital losses on home sales.

Furthermore, the opportunities for higher earnings in a new location have typically been a greater factor in labor migration than the desire to simply leave a low-wage, low-growth area. With weak income growth across the country and few areas attractive enough to "pull" workers away from their current locations, regional imbalances have persisted in the current recovery to a greater extent than in prior recoveries.

THE "MANCESSION," THE "MANCOVERY," AND INDUSTRY MIX

Labor market woes brought on by the recession and painfully slow recovery have not been shared evenly across demographic groups, including males and females. Unemployment following the start of the recession rose disproportionately for men, so much so that the recession had been nicknamed a "mancession." Decomposing the headline unemployment rate, the jobless rate for men has been higher than that for women since the onset of the recession. Since the recession began, unemployment has risen markedly for both sexes, but more steeply for males (Figure 6.23). While male unemployment has declined more rapidly than the unemployment rate for females, it has been driven lower by the stark decline in labor force participation, accelerating the long-term decline since the mid-1950s.

What accounts for the variation in unemployment between men and women since the recession? The performance of different industries during the downturn and the share of men and women working in those industries play an important role (Figure 6.24). Predominately male industries such as construction and manufacturing were some of the hardest hit sectors during the recession, as illustrated in Figure 6.25. Conversely, the education and health services industry—where women are more heavily represented—added jobs throughout the recession and recovery.

Thus far, the recovery has been stronger in male-dominated industries such as manufacturing and professional and business services, which has helped bring down the male unemployment rate more quickly. Following the recession, state and local government finances became increasingly strained, leading to cuts in administration and public education—positions that are more likely to be filled by women. Only since early 2013 has state and local government employment started to recover. Still, women are faring better. Education has been a key factor in workers' unemployment experiences, and women are increasingly more likely to hold a college degree than men.

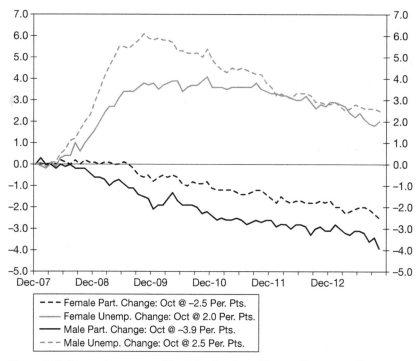

Figure 6.23 Unemployment and Participation Rate Change: Percentage Point Change since December 2007.

SOURCE: US Department of Labor and Wells Fargo Securities, LLC.

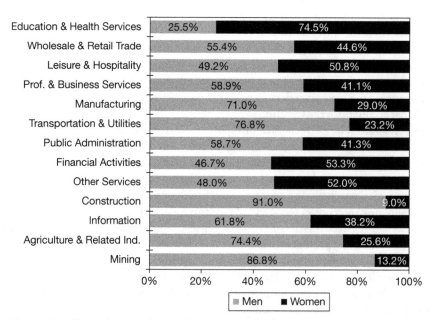

Figure 6.24 Unemployment by Gender: Percent of Industry Unemployment, 2012.

SOURCE: US Department of Commerce and Wells Fargo Securities, LLC.

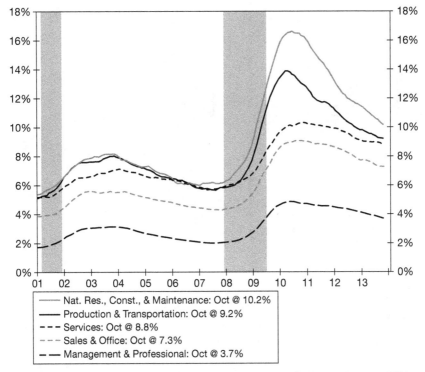

Figure 6.25 Unemployment Rate by Occupation: 12-Month Moving Average, NSA.
SOURCE: US Department of Commerce and Wells Fargo Securities, LLC.

WHERE RACE AND ETHNICITY MATTER

Stark differences are also visible when looking at race and ethnicity. Black jobless-ness, at 16.7%, stands more than seven percentage points above its pre-recession rate and is more than double the unemployment rate for white workers (8%). Furthermore, unemployment for black teenagers is staggeringly high at 47%, making it difficult for this group to gain valuable work experience early in their working years. Unemployment among Hispanics, at 11.3%, falls in between the rate for whites and blacks. However, due to a higher participation rate, Hispanics and whites have roughly equal rates of employment relative to their populations at 59%. Black employment-to-population is notably lower at 51%.

PARTICIPATION RATES: OLDER WORKERS STAY LONGER, YOUNGER WORKERS QUIT?

In an odd twist to the expected pattern of the labor market, the participation rates of older workers have actually risen since 2002, while those of younger workers have declined. Older workers were expected to retire and start second careers. Younger workers were supposedly eager to start their careers. Well, it has not worked out that way. The decline in labor force participation of the young and an increasing participation rate of older workers (Figure 6.26) is pronounced and not likely to be

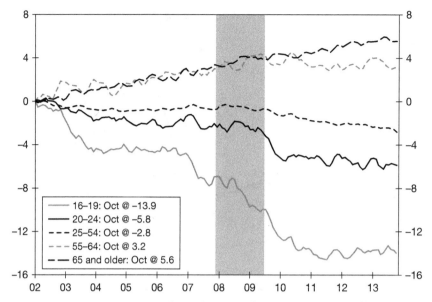

Figure 6.26 Participation Rate Change by Age Cohort, Percentage Point Change since January 2002.

SOURCE: US Department of Labor and Wells Fargo Securities, LLC.

a random event. Labor force participation of the youngest cohorts in the economy has been trending downward over the past decade, but has fallen precipitously following this last recession. Part of the trend can be attributed to a longer-term shift toward higher education, which should help the job prospects of those earning a degree. However, while the number of 16–24 year olds not looking for a job due to schooling increased 60% between 2007 and 2013, discouraged workers in this age group increased by 92%.

UNEQUAL EDUCATION = UNEQUAL RECESSION

Is there a 21st-century job for the 20th-century worker? The severity of the past recession has had broad-based and unequal effects among workers. The rise in unemployment has been highly uneven across subgroups since the start of the recession, with educational attainment the driving factor for stark differences in joblessness. College-educated workers have fared significantly better than their less educated counterparts in the 21st-century job market. Unemployment for college grads has fallen under five percent compared to remaining in the double digits for workers without a high school diploma. This large gap has persisted between the two groups, averaging over 9% between 2009 and 2013. While unemployment has historically been higher for workers with less education, the marked widening between educational groups since the 2007 recession is a departure from the 2001 recession when unemployment rose by a similar magnitude across groups. As employers have had to make tough decisions about firing and hiring since the onset of the recession, their preference for education has been clear. Bachelor's degree

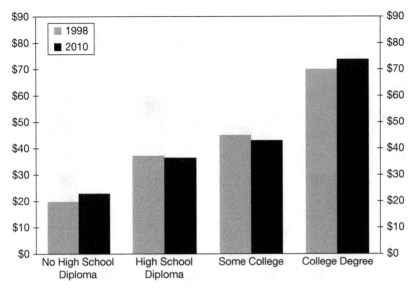

Figure 6.27 Median Income by Education Level, 2010 Dollars Before Taxes, Thousands.

SOURCE: US Department of Labor and Wells Fargo Securities, LLC.

holders in 2013 accounted for 38% of employed workers compared to 34% at the start of the recession. Much of this shift has been driven by the need for well-educated workers in the industries that have been adding jobs during the recovery; about half of the jobs added since employment bottomed have been in the professional and business services and education and health services industries.

DUAL RETURNS TO EDUCATION: HIGHER INCOME AND LOWER UNEMPLOYMENT

Labor market outcomes by education level are evident not only in the unemployment rate but also in earned income. The income of college graduates is more than double the income of workers with only a high school diploma (Figure 6.27). Furthermore, college graduates have seen an increase in real income over the past decade, whereas the income for non-graduates has been flat. Education pays not only in job prospects but in the paycheck of those jobs.

Education, worker mobility, and the financial crisis have played out to produce a much more difficult labor market environment now compared to prior cycles.[16] The benefit of moving in terms of greater income is compared to the cost of the move, including psychic costs such as a loss of friends and community. Traditionally, the cost of moving between jobs is borne in the short run in order to obtain returns over a longer period of time. The longer the time horizon for earnings, the higher the benefit of moving, which has typically benefited young workers.

Three problems arise for many middle-aged, blue-collar and back-office, white-collar workers. First, the decline in home values associated with the financial crisis presents a sunk cost hurdle for these workers. Second, there are significant

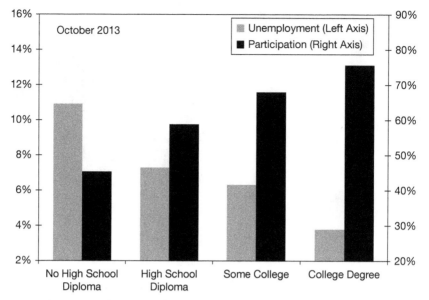

Figure 6.28 Unemployment and Participation by Education Level, Percentage Points.

SOURCE: US Department of Labor and Wells Fargo Securities, LLC.

psychic costs for these middle-aged workers. Finally, job searching at a national level is more difficult for these workers as information about jobs at that level is generally not well known. In contrast, recent college graduates who rely upon the Internet and have less job-specific experienced search the national labor market for jobs. Although many recent college grads are finding the job market less inviting than in other recoveries, their job search experience has been easier than less educated and less mobile middle-aged workers.

HARD REALITIES: FEWER JOBS FOR THE 20TH-CENTURY WORKER IN THE 21ST CENTURY

Fewer job prospects and lower wages for less educated workers in the 21st century has been accompanied by higher rates of unemployment as well as lower rates of participation in the workforce (Figure 6.28). As employers continue to seek workers who are able to add value in a more knowledge-based economy, fewer opportunities will be available for low- and semi-skilled workers—often those without a high school diploma. Younger generations have a higher share of college graduates, but with only around one-third of 25–34 year olds having college degrees, there is still great variation in educational attainment, and this variation is a driving factor for rising income differences.

Two characteristics that distinguish the 21st-century labor market are the character of worker choices and the role of education. The characteristics of choices reflect more than employment or unemployment decisions. In addition, household employment is a conscious decision—especially for the second breadwinner. Therefore, the supply of labor is a function of the wage rate or reservation wage and the trade-off a person is willing to make between household time and money income. We know this because very educated individuals sometimes consciously choose to stay home and take care of the home/children.

A second change has been in the balance between cost and benefit for a college education. College education is both consumption and investment. For a high school graduate, there is a choice between two income streams—the expected earnings with a high school diploma and the expected earnings with a college degree adjusted for the cost of going to college. While the earnings stream from college will, in most cases, exceed the earnings stream for a high school diploma, these earnings should be judged against the costs of the college education. We emphasize here the uncertainty around the expected earnings because we have seen, post-Great Recession, the anecdotal stories of many college graduates whose post-college earnings profiles do not meet the burden of their student loans.[17]

SHOW ME THE MONEY: WAGES AND HOURS

A job can provide many things, like work experience to help build a career or a sense of self-worth. But, importantly to most of us who need to earn a living, it is a source of income. Wages and salaries account for the largest source of income in the United States, making up roughly half of personal income each month. The slow addition of jobs since the recovery began has constrained total income growth, which has taken more than four years to recover following the end of the Great Recession. However, the level of jobs is not the only sign of labor market straits. Growth in average hourly earnings has been extremely weak (Figure 6.29), and the average number of hours worked each week has yet to return to where it was before the downturn (Figure 6.30).

INCOME GROWTH: STILL BELOW PRE-RECESSION PACE

When earnings, hours worked, and the slow pace of job gains are taken together, growth in wages and salaries continues to struggle (Figure 6.31). Moreover, with unemployment still elevated, weak income growth is likely to continue. This is a driving factor limiting the pace of the national recovery and keeping consumer confidence and spending restrained.

A MONETARY POLICY DISCONNECT?

For the Federal Reserve's dual mandate, the pursuit of easier monetary policy, as measured by the federal funds rate, is an assumed channel of policy influence. Yet, Figure 6.32 reminds us that the traditional linkage between policy and unemployment is not what it used to be. In both the prior expansions and recessions, changes in the direction of the Fed funds rate were accompanied by later movements in the unemployment rate. Yet today's historically low target rate and elevated

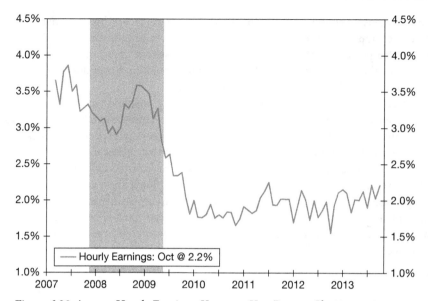

Figure 6.29 Average Hourly Earnings: Year-over-Year Percent Change.

SOURCE: US Department of Commerce and Wells Fargo Securities, LLC.

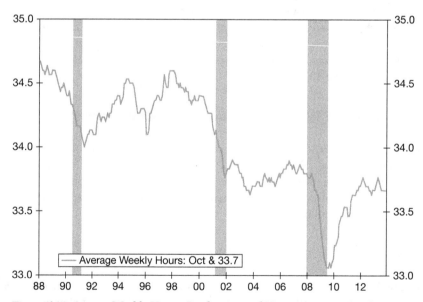

Figure 6.30 Average Weekly Hours: Production and Nonsupervisory Employees; 3-Month Moving Avg.

SOURCE: US Department of Commerce and Wells Fargo Securities, LLC.

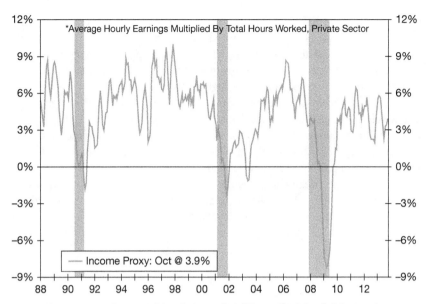

Figure 6.31 Income Proxy: 3-Month Annualized Rate of 3-Month Moving Average.
SOURCE: US Department of Commerce and Wells Fargo Securities, LLC.

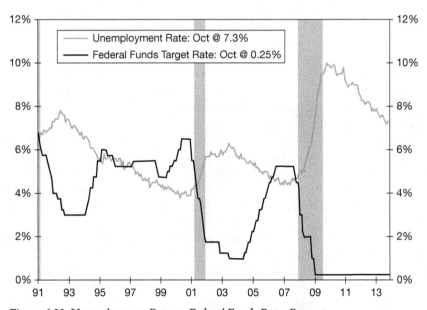

Figure 6.32 Unemployment Rate vs. Federal Funds Rate: Percent.
SOURCE: US Department of Commerce and Wells Fargo Securities, LLC.

unemployment rate illustrates that the traditional response of the unemployment rate to the Fed funds rate has been limited relative to history. Unfortunately, this is one area where the anchoring bias of policymakers, gripped by the past, leads to a focus on the belief that alterations in the federal funds rate would lead to reductions in the structural unemployment issues highlighted in this essay.

Furthermore, recent commentary from Federal Reserve officials suggests that more weight is being placed on the full employment goal than on the inflation goal. Initially, a goal of an unemployment rate of 6.5% was set as a guideline for a shift in monetary policy toward restraint, but when that magic number was hit—and now surpassed—the Fed shifted its commentary toward further progress in its pursuit of greater job gains. Meanwhile, market commentary has given less weight to the 2% inflation goal with a greater weight attached to the likelihood the Fed will allow inflation to drift higher in order to achieve further job gains.

CONCLUSION

The unprecedented expansion of credit in the years leading up to the Great Recession altered the way in which many parts of the economy functioned, including the labor market. With policies pushing homeownership and an expectations bias that home prices would continue to increase, credit flowed easily to borrowers across the credit spectrum. Unfortunately this expansion of credit was not balanced against potential risks, such as rising interest rates and adverse economic conditions. While the adverse effects of rising interest rates came to fruition as early as 2006, strains in the credit sector did not come to a head until late 2008. For many parts of the economy, particularly the labor market, the turmoil was just beginning.

The immediate feedback from the credit shock was a downshift in the expectations for growth and therefore a decline in the demand for labor. By most measures of labor market health, conditions deteriorated to their weakest state in the post-WWII era. The depth of the deterioration, however, varied greatly across subgroups according to gender, education, and age. Disparities across regions were heightened by negative equity, reducing worker mobility.

Underlying the sharp deterioration in the labor market and subsequent slow recovery in the most recent business cycle have been several secular shifts. Included was the globalization of production that reduced the competitiveness of low- and semi-skilled workers and challenged the transmission of monetary policy and countercyclical fiscal stimulus. Moreover, the expansion of credit in previous years overstated the potential rate of growth for the economy.

Amid slower growth and weaker policy transmission, the workout of supply and demand for labor remains protracted. The subtle secular shifts that went unnoticed in good times have now been brought to the forefront. A widening gap between the median and average length of unemployment, a Beveridge curve that has yet to shift in, and a stark drop in labor force participation across the working-age population all suggest a lack of cost adjustment that has kept many workers on the sideline, quite possibly permanently. This has left a significantly lower base to support taxes and entitlement spending, and will alter the rate at which the US economy can ultimately grow.

Finally, as emphasized throughout this essay, beliefs and values provide an underlying stream of patterns of decision making that certainly influenced the extent of the housing boom and the subsequent financial crisis and ongoing adjustments in the real economy, especially the labor market. Economics is a social science; thus it focuses on human behavior and ultimately works within the human character as defined by beliefs and values.

NOTES

1. Ben Bernanke, "The Great Moderation," Remarks by Governor Ben S. Bernanke, Meetings of the Eastern Economic Association, Washington, DC, February 20, 2004.
2. Gretchen Morgenson and Joshua Rosner, *Reckless Endangerment* (New York: Times Books, 2011).
3. For a view on European Central Bank (ECB) intervention to trade sovereign debt and the ECB's contribution to the normal functioning financial markets, see Jean-Claude Trichet, "Lessons to Be Learned from the European Sovereign Debt Crisis," interview with *Liberation, BIS Review* 95, 2010. Interesting to note that Trichet does not consider this a change in policy or its focus on inflation but, from our viewpoint, it certainly reflects a change in the use of alternative policy instruments to achieve alternative policy goals that would not have been considered prior to the financial crisis.
4. John E. Silvia, "Domestic Implications of a Global Labor Market," *Business Economics* 41, no. 3 (July 2006), pp. 23–29.
5. This section and the following were initially presented at the Interagency meetings, "Supervisory Challenges at the Mid-Cycle of the Economic Expansion." Presentation at the Interagency Bank Supervision Conference, November 6, 2006. This reinforces the view that there were in fact market signals that suggested that the allocation and pricing of credit was becoming inconsistent with market fundamentals by mid-2006, long before the Lehman moment in September 2008.
6. This section was taken from the 2006 Interagency presentation.
7. For an analysis of the interrelationship between credit and economic growth, see Ronald I. McKinnon, *Money & Capital in Economic Development* (Washington, DC: The Brookings Institution, 1973).
8. David B. Gross and Nicholas S. Souleles, "Do Liquidity Constraints and Interest Rates Matter for Consumer Behavior? Evidence from Credit Card Data," *Quarterly Journal of Economics* 117 (February 2002): 149–185.
9. Christopher F. Goetz, "Falling Home Prices and Labor Mobility: Evidence from Matched Employer Employee Data," US Census Bureau, August 1, 2013.
10. Ronald G. Ehrenberg and Robert S. Smith, *Modern Labor Economics* (Boston: Addison Wesley, 2003), 79–81.
11. David H. Autor and Mark Duggan, "The Rise in the Disability Rolls and the Decline in Unemployment," *Quarterly Journal of Economics* 118 (2003): 157–206; Mary C. Daly, Brian Lucking, and Jonathan A. Schwabish, "The Future of Social Security Disability Insurance," Federal Reserve Bank of San Francisco Economic Letter, 2013–17, June 24, 2013.

12. James M. Poterba and Lawrence Summers, "Unemployment Benefits and Labor Market Transitions: A Multinominal Logit Model with Errors in Classification," *Review of Economics and Statistics* 77, no. 2 (May 1995): 207–216; Gary Burtless, "Unemployment Insurance and the Labor Supply: A Survey," in *Unemployment Insurance: The Second Half-Century*, edited by W. Lee Hansen and James Byers (Madison: University of Wisconsin Press, 1990).

13. Bureau of Labor Statistics, "How Long before the Unemployed Find Jobs or Quit Looking," Bureau of Labor Statistics, May 2011.

14. For a view that emphasizes the role of demographics in the changing character of labor force participation rates, see James Bullard, "The Rise and Fall of Labor Force Participation in the United States," *Federal Reserve Bank of St. Louis Review,* First Quarter 2014.

15. Ibid.

16. For a deeper discussion on worker mobility, see Ronald G. Ehrenberg and Robert S. Smith, *Modern Labor Economics*, 8th ed. (Boston: Addison-Wesley, 2003), chapter 10: "Worker Mobility."

17. For a review of the student loan problem and educational choices, see John E. Silvia and Sarah Watt, "Student Loans: A Different Financial Market," *Wells Fargo Economics*, February 11, 2013. For a review of the role of uncertainty in the choices for students, see Joseph G. Altonji, "The Demand for and Return to Education When Education Outcomes are Uncertain," *Journal of Labor Economics* 10 (January 1993): 48–83.

7

Mathematical Definition, Mapping, and Detection of (Anti)Fragility

NASSIM NICHOLAS TALEB AND RAPHAEL DOUADY ■

INTRODUCTION

The financial crisis of 2008 was the result of the silent accumulation of tail risks, risks that went chronically undetected by the risk management machinery. We witnessed increases in hidden risks associated with low-probability, large-consequence events across all aspects of economic life, not just in banking. Tail risks could not (and cannot) be reliably priced probabilistically, as uncertainty about key aspects of tail incidences has typically been on the order of, or greater than, understanding of the actuarial price of such risks. Nonlinearity in pricing risk is also exacerbated by an increase in debt, operational leverage and complexity, and the use of complex derivatives. Meanwhile, the opposite effect was seen: a perception of stability of these portfolios. Risks were hiding under the surface.

This paper aims at detecting fragility as tail exposures in place of probabilistic methods of forecasting events. Simply, it relies on acceleration of exposure in the tails, without knowledge of probabilities, and has led to heuristics used by the authors before the crisis to detect fragility in the systems and in various firms, from publicly available information.

WHAT IS FRAGILITY?

The notions of *fragility* and *antifragility* were introduced in Taleb (1997, 2012). In short, *fragility* is related to how a system *suffers* from the variability of its environment beyond a certain preset threshold (when threshold is K, it is called K-fragility), while *antifragility* refers to when it *benefits* from this variability—in a similar way to "vega" of an option or a nonlinear payoff, that is, its sensitivity to volatility or some similar measure of scale of a distribution.

For example, a coffee cup on a table suffers more from large deviations than from the cumulative effect of some shocks—conditional on being unbroken, it has to suffer more from "tail" events than regular ones around the center of the distribution, the "at-the-money" category. This is the case of elements of nature that have survived: conditional on being in existence, the class of events around the mean should matter considerably less than tail events, particularly when the probabilities decline faster than the inverse of the harm, which is the case of all used monomodal probability distributions. Further, what has exposure to tail events suffers from uncertainty; typically, when systems—a building, a bridge, a nuclear plant, an airplane, or a bank balance sheet– are made robust to a certain level of variability and stress but may fail or collapse if this level is exceeded, they are particularly *fragile* to uncertainty about the distribution of the stressor, hence to model error, as this uncertainty increases the probability of dipping below the robustness level, bringing a higher probability of collapse. In the opposite case, the natural selection of an evolutionary process is particularly *antifragile*; indeed, a more volatile environment increases the survival rate of robust species and eliminates those whose superiority over other species is highly dependent on environmental parameters.

Figure 7.1 show the "tail-vega" sensitivity of an object calculated discretely at two different lower absolute mean deviations. We use for the purpose of fragility and antifragility, in place of measures in L^2 such as standard deviations, which restrict the choice of probability distributions, the broader measure of absolute deviation, cut into two parts: lower and upper semi-deviation above the distribution center Ω.

This article aims at providing proper mathematical definitions of fragility, robustness, and antifragility and examining how these apply to different cases.

Intrinsic and Inherited Fragility: Our definition of fragility is twofold. First, of concern is the intrinsic fragility, the shape of the probability distribution of a variable and its sensitivity to s^-, a parameter controlling the left side of its own distribution. But we do not often directly observe the statistical distribution of objects, and, if

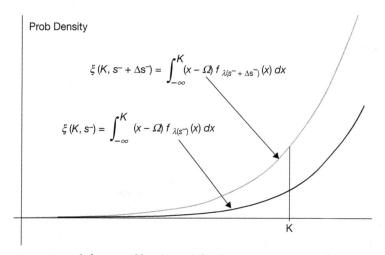

$$\xi(K, s^- + \Delta s^-) = \int_{-\infty}^{K} (x - \Omega) f_{\lambda(s^- + \Delta s^-)}(x)\, dx$$

$$\xi(K, s^-) = \int_{-\infty}^{K} (x - \Omega) f_{\lambda(s^-)}(x)\, dx$$

Figure 7.1 A definition of fragility as left-tail vega sensitivity; the figure shows the effect of the perturbation of the lower semi-deviation s^- on the tail integral ξ of $(x - \Omega)$ below K, with Ω a entering constant. Our detection of fragility does not require the specification off the probability distribution.

we did, it would be difficult to measure their tail-vega sensitivity. Nor do we need to specify such distribution: we can gauge the response of a given object to the volatility of an external stressor that affects it. For instance, an option is usually analyzed with respect to the scale of the distribution of the "underlying" security, not its own; the fragility of a coffee cup is determined as a response to a given source of randomness or stress; that of a house with respect to, among other sources, the distribution of earthquakes. This fragility coming from the effect of the underlying is called inherited fragility. The transfer function, which we present next, allows us to assess the effect, the increase or decrease in fragility, coming from changes in the underlying source of stress.

Transfer Function: A nonlinear exposure to a certain source of randomness maps into tail-vega sensitivity (hence fragility). We prove that

Inherited Fragility ⇔ Concavity in exposure on the left side of the distribution,

and build H, a transfer function giving an exact mapping of tail-vega sensitivity to the second derivative of a function. The transfer function will allow us to probe parts of the distribution and generate a fragility-detection heuristic covering both physical fragility and model error.

FRAGILITY AS SEPARATE RISK FROM PSYCHOLOGICAL PREFERENCES

Avoidance of the Psychological: We start from the definition of fragility as tail-vega sensitivity, and end up with nonlinearity as a necessary attribute of the source of such fragility in the inherited case—a cause of the disease rather than the disease itself. However, there is a long literature by economists and decision scientists embedding risk into psychological preferences—historically, risk has been described as derived from risk aversion as a result of the structure of choices under uncertainty with a concavity of the muddled concept of "utility" of payoff (see Pratt 1964; Arrow 1965; Rothchild and Stiglitz 1970,1971). But this "utility" business never led anywhere except the circularity, expressed by Machina and Rothschild (2008), that "risk is what risk-averters hate." Indeed, limiting risk to aversion to concavity of choices is a quite unhappy result—the utility curve cannot be possibly monotone concave but rather, like everything in nature necessarily bounded on both sides, the left and the right, convex-concave and, as Kahneman and Tversky (1979) have debunked, both path dependent and mixed in its nonlinearity.

Beyond Jensen's Inequality: Furthermore, the economics and decision-theory literature reposes on the effect of Jensen's inequality, an analysis which requires monotone convex or concave transformations—in fact limited to the expectation operator. The world is unfortunately more complicated in its nonlinearities. Thanks to the transfer function we can accommodate situations where the source is not merely convex, but convex-concave and any other form of mixed nonlinearities common in exposures, which includes nonlinear dose-response in biology. For instance, the application of the transfer function to the Kahneman-Tversky value function, convex in the negative domain and concave in the positive one, shows that its decreases fragility in the left tail (hence more robustness) and reduces the effect of the right tail as well (also more robustness), which allows to assert that we are psychologically "more robust" to changes in wealth than implied from the distribution of such wealth, which happens to be extremely fat-tailed.

Accordingly, our approach relies on nonlinearity of exposure as detection of the vega sensitivity, not as a definition of fragility. And nonlinearity in a source of stress is necessarily associated with fragility. Clearly, neither a coffee cup, a house, or a bridge have psychological preferences, subjective utility, etc. Yet they are concave in their reaction to harm: simply, taking z as a stress level and $\Pi(z)$ as the harm function, it suffices to see that, with $n > 1$,

$$\Pi(nz) < n\Pi(z) \text{ for all } 0 < nz < Z^*,$$

where Z^* is the level (not necessarily specified) at which the item is broken. Such inequality leads to $\Pi(z)$ having a negative second derivative at the initial value z.

So if a coffee cup is less harmed by n times a stressor of intensity Z than once a stressor of nZ, then harm (as a negative function) needs to be concave to stressors up to the point of breaking; such stricture is imposed by the structure of survival probabilities and the distribution of harmful events, and has nothing to do with subjective utility or some other figments. If, for a human, jumping one millimeter caused an exact linear fraction of the damage of, say, jumping to the ground from thirty feet, then the person would be already dead from cumulative harm. Actually a simple computation shows that he would have expired within hours from touching objects or pacing in his living room, given the multitude of such stressors and their total effect. The fragility that comes from linearity is immediately visible, so we rule it out because the object would be already broken and the person already dead. The relative frequency of ordinary events compared to extreme events is the determinant. In the financial markets, there are at least ten thousand times more events of 0.1% deviations than events of 10%. There are close to eight thousand micro-earthquakes—that is, those below 2 on the Richter scale—daily on planet earth, about three million a year. These are totally harmless, and, with three million per year, you would need them to be so. But shocks of intensity 6 and higher on the scale make the newspapers. Accordingly, we are necessarily immune to the *cumulative* effect of small deviations, or shocks of very small magnitude, which implies that these affect us disproportionally less (that is, nonlinearly less) than larger ones.

Model error does not necessarily mean preserving. s^-, the lower absolute semi-deviation does not just express changes in overall dispersion in the distribution, such as for instance the "scaling" case, but also changes in the mean, that is, when the upper semi-deviation from Ω to infinity is invariant, or even declines in a compensatory manner to make the overall mean absolute deviation unchanged. This would be the case when we shift the distribution instead of rescaling it. Thus the same vega-sensitivity can also express sensitivity to a stressor (dose increase) in medicine or other fields in its effect on either tail. Thus $s^-(\lambda)$ will allow us to express the sensitivity to the "disorder cluster" (Taleb 2012): (1) uncertainty, (2) variability, (3) imperfect, incomplete knowledge, (4) chance, (5) chaos, (6) volatility, (7) disorder, (8) entropy, (9) time, (10) the unknown, (11) randomness, (12) turmoil, (13) stressor, (14) error, (15) dispersion of outcomes.

DETECTION HEURISTIC

Finally, thanks to the transfer function, this paper proposes a risk heuristic that "works" in detecting fragility even if we use the wrong model/pricing method/ probability distribution. The main idea is that *a wrong ruler will not measure the height of a child, but it can certainly tell us if the child is growing.* Since risks in the tails map to nonlinearities (concavity of exposure), second-order effects reveal fragility, particularly in the tails where they map to large tail exposures, as revealed through perturbation analysis. More generally every nonlinear function will produce some kind of positive or negative exposures to volatility for some parts of the distribution (see Figure 7.2).

Fragility and Model Error: As we saw, this definition of fragility extends to model error, as some models produce negative sensitivity to uncertainty, in addition to effects and biases under variability. So, beyond physical fragility, the same approach measures model fragility, based on the difference between a *point estimate* and stochastic value (i.e., full distribution). Increasing the variability (say, variance) of the estimated value (but not the mean) may lead to a one-sided effect on the model—just as an increase of volatility causes porcelain cups to break. Hence sensitivity to the volatility of such value, the "vega" of the model with respect to such value is no different from the vega of other payoffs. For instance, the misuse of thin-tailed distributions (say Gaussian) appears immediately through perturbation of the standard deviation, no longer used as point estimate, but as a distribution with its own variance. For instance, it can be shown how fat-tailed (e.g., power-law tailed) probability distributions can be expressed by simple nested perturbation and mixing of Gaussian ones. Such a representation pinpoints the fragility of a wrong probability model and its consequences in terms of underestimation of risks, stress tests, and similar matters.

Antifragility: It is not quite the mirror image of fragility, as it implies positive vega above some threshold in the positive tail of the distribution and absence of fragility in the left tail, which leads to a distribution that is skewed right.

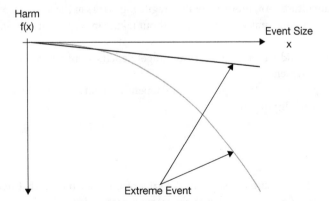

Figure 7.2 Disproportionate effect of tail events on nonlinear exposures, illustrating the necessity of nonlinearity of the harm function and showing how we can extrapolate outside the model to probe unseen fragility.

FRAGILITY AND TRANSFER THEOREMS

The central Table 7.1 introduces the exhaustive map of possible outcomes, with four mutually exclusive categories of payoffs. Our steps in the rest of the paper are as follows:

a. We provide a mathematical definition of fragility, robustness, and antifragility.
b. We present the problem of measuring tail risks and show the presence of severe biases attending the estimation of small probability and its nonlinearity (convexity) to parametric (and other) perturbations.
c. We express the concept of model fragility in terms of left-tail exposure, and show correspondence to the concavity of the payoff from a random variable.
d. Finally, we present our simple heuristic to detect the possibility of both fragility and model error across a broad range of probabilistic estimations.

Conceptually, *fragility* resides in the fact that a small—or at least reasonable—uncertainty on the macro-parameter of a distribution may have dramatic consequences on the result of a given stress test, or on some measure that depends on the left tail of the distribution, such as an out-of-the-money option. This hypersensitivity of what we like to call an out-of-the-money put price" to the macro-parameter, which is *some* measure of the volatility of the distribution of the underlying source of randomness.

Formally, fragility is defined as the sensitivity of the left-tail shortfall (non-conditioned by probability) below a certain threshold K to the overall left semi-deviation of the distribution.

Examples

a. Example: a porcelain coffee cup subjected to random daily stressors from use.
b. Example: tail distribution in the function of the arrival time of an aircraft.
c. Example: hidden risks of famine to a population subjected to monoculture—or, more generally, fragilizing errors in the application of Ricardo's comparative advantage without taking into account second-order effects.
d. Example: hidden tail exposures to budget deficits' nonlinearities to unemployment.
e. Example: hidden tail exposure from dependence on a source of energy, etc. ("squeezability argument").

TAIL-VEGA SENSITIVITY

We construct a measure of "vega" in the tails of the distribution that depends on the variations of s, the semi-deviation below a certain level Ω, chosen in the L^1 norm in order to insure its existence under "fat-tailed" distributions with finite first semi-moment. In fact, s would exist as a measure even in the case of infinite moments to the right side of Ω.

Table 7.1 Introduces the Exhaustive Taxonomy of all Possible Payoffs $y = f(x)$

Type	Condition	Left Tail (loss domain)	Right Tail (gains domain)	Nonlinear Payoff Function $y = f(x)$ "derivative," where x is a random variable	Derivatives Equivalent (Taleb 1997)	Effect of fatailedness of $f(x)$ compared to primitive x
Type 1	Fragile (type 1)	Fat (regular or absorbing barrier)	Fat	Mixed concave left, convex right (fence)	Long up -vega, short down-vega	More fragility if absorbing barrier, neutral otherwise
Type 2	Fragile (type 2)	Fat	Thin	Concave	Short vega	More fragility
Type 3	Robust	Thin	Thin	Mixed convex left, concave right (digital, sigmoid)	Short down-vega, long up-vega	No effect
Type 4	Antifragile	Thin	Fat (thicker than left)	Convex	Long vega	More antifragility

Let X be a random variable, the distribution of which is one among a one-parameter family of pdf $f_\lambda, \lambda \in I \subset \mathbb{R}$. We consider a fixed reference value Ω and, from this reference, the left-semi-absolute deviation:

$$s^-(\lambda) = \int_{-\infty}^{\Omega} (\Omega - x) f_\lambda(x) dx.$$

We assume that $\lambda \to s^-(\lambda)$ is continuous, strictly increasing, and spans the whole range $\mathbb{R}_+ = [0, +\infty)$, so that we may use the left-semi-absolute deviation s^- as a parameter by considering the inverse function $\lambda(s): \mathbb{R}_+ \to I$, defined by $s^-(\lambda(s)) = s$ for $s \in \mathbb{R}_+$.

This condition is satisfied if, for any given $x < \Omega$, the probability is a continuous and increasing function of λ. Indeed, denoting $F_\lambda(x) = \mathrm{Pr}_{f_\lambda}(X < x) = \int_{-\infty}^{x} f_\lambda(t) dt$, an integration by part yields:

$$s^-(\lambda) = \int_{-\infty}^{\Omega} F_\lambda(x) dx.$$

This is the case when λ is a scaling parameter, that is, $X \sim \Omega + \lambda(X_1 - \Omega)$, indeed one has in this case $F_\lambda(x) = F_1(\Omega + \frac{x-\Omega}{\lambda})$, $\frac{\partial F_\lambda}{\partial \lambda}(x) = \frac{\Omega - x}{\lambda} f_\lambda(x)$ and $s^-(\lambda) = \lambda s^-(1)$.

It is also the case when λ is a shifting parameter, i.e. $X \sim X_0 - \lambda$, indeed, in this case $F_\lambda(x) = F_0(x + \lambda)$ and $\frac{\partial s^-}{\partial \lambda} = F_\lambda(\Omega)$.

For $K < \Omega$ and $s \in \mathbb{R}_+$, let:

$$\xi(K, s^-) = \int_{-\infty}^{K} (\Omega - x) f_{\lambda(s^-)}(x) dx.$$

In particular, $\xi(\Omega, s^-) = s^-$. We assume, in a first step, that the function $\xi(K, s^-)$ is differentiable on $(-\infty, \Omega] \times \mathbb{R}_+$. The K-left-tail-vega sensitivity of X at stress level $K < \Omega$ and deviation level $s^- > 0$ for the pdf f_λ is:

$$V(X, f_\lambda, K, s^-) = \frac{\partial \xi}{\partial s^-}(K, s^-) = \left(\int_{-\infty}^{K} (\Omega - x) \frac{\partial f_\lambda}{\partial \lambda}(x) dx \right) \left(\frac{ds^-}{d\lambda} \right)^{-1}.$$

As in the many practical instances where threshold effects are involved, it may occur that ξ does not depend smoothly on s^-. We therefore also define a *finite difference* version of the *vega sensitivity* as follows:

$$V(X, f_\lambda, K, s^-, \Delta s) = \frac{1}{2\Delta s} (\xi(K, s^- + \Delta s) - \xi(K, s^- - \Delta s))$$

$$= \int_{-\infty}^{K} (\Omega - x) \frac{f_{\lambda(s^- + \Delta s)}(x) - f_{\lambda(s^- - \Delta s)}(x)}{2\Delta s} dx.$$

Hence omitting the input Δs implicitly assumes that $\Delta s \to 0$.

Note that $\xi(K, s^-) = -E_{f_\lambda}[X | X < K] \Pr_{f_\lambda}(X < K)$. It can be decomposed into two parts:

$$\xi(K, s^-(\lambda)) = (\Omega - K)F_\lambda(K) + P_\lambda(K)$$

$$P_\lambda(K) = \int_{-\infty}^{K} (K - x)f_\lambda(x)dx,$$

where the first part $(\Omega - K)F_\lambda(K)$ is proportional to the probability of the variable being below the stress level K, and the second part $P_\lambda(K)$ is the expectation of the amount by which X is below K (counting 0 when it is not). Making a parallel with financial options, while $s^-(\lambda)$ is a "put at-the-money," $\xi(K, s^-)$ is the sum of a put struck at K and a digital put also struck at K with amount $\Omega - K$; it can equivalently be seen as a put struck at Ω with a down-and-in European barrier at K.

Letting $\lambda = \lambda(s^-)$ and integrating by part yields

$$\xi(K, s^-(\lambda)) = (\Omega - K)F_\lambda(K) + \int_{-\infty}^{K} F_\lambda(x)dx = \int_{-\infty}^{\Omega} F_\lambda^K(x)dx,$$

where $F_\lambda^K(x) = F_\lambda(\min(x, K)) = \min(F_\lambda(x), F_\lambda(K))$, so that

$$V(X, f_\lambda, K, s^-) = \frac{\partial \xi}{\partial s}(K, s^-) = \frac{\int_{-\infty}^{\Omega} \frac{\partial F_\lambda^K}{\partial \lambda}(x)dx}{\int_{-\infty}^{\Omega} \frac{\partial F_\lambda}{\partial \lambda}(x)dx}.$$

For finite differences,

$$V(X, f_\lambda, K, s^-, \Delta s) = \frac{1}{2\Delta s} \int_{-\infty}^{\Omega} (\Delta F_{\lambda, \Delta s}^K(x))dx,$$

Where λ_s^+ and λ_s^- are such that $s(\lambda_s^+) = s^- + \Delta s$, $s(\lambda_s^-) = s^- - \Delta s$ and $\Delta F_{\lambda, \Delta s}^K(x) = F_{\lambda_s^+}^K(x) - F_{\lambda_s^-}^K(x)$.

MATHEMATICAL EXPRESSION OF FRAGILITY

In essence, fragility is the sensitivity of a given risk measure to an error in the estimation of the (possibly one-sided) deviation parameter of a distribution, especially due to the fact that the risk measure involves parts of the distribution—tails—that are away from the portion used for estimation. The risk measure then assumes certain extrapolation rules that have first-order consequences. These consequences are even more amplified when the risk measure applies to a variable that is derived from that used for estimation, when the relation between the two variables is strongly nonlinear, as is often the case.

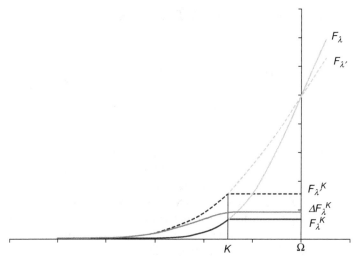

Figure 7.3 The different curves of $F\lambda(K)$ and $F'\lambda(K)$ show the difference in sensitivity to changes at different levels of K.

Definition of Fragility: The *Intrinsic* Case

The local fragility of a random variable X_λ depending on parameter λ, at stress level K and semi-deviation level $s^-(\lambda)$ with pdf f_λ is its K-left-tailed semi-vega sensitivity $V(X, f_\lambda, K, s^-)$.

The finite-difference fragility of X_λ at stress level K and semi-deviation level $s^-(\lambda) \pm \Delta s$ with pdf f_λ is its K-left-tailed finite-difference semi-vega sensitivity $V(X, f_\lambda, K, s^-, \Delta s)$.

In this definition, the *fragility* relies on the unsaid assumptions made when extrapolating the distribution of X_λ from areas used to estimate the semi-absolute deviation $s^-(\lambda)$, around Ω, to areas around K on which the risk measure ξ depends.

Definition of Fragility: The *Inherited* Case

We here consider the particular case where a random variable $Y = \varphi(X)$ depends on another source of risk X, itself subject to a parameter λ. Let us keep the above notations for X, while we denote by g_λ the pdf of Y, $\Omega_Y = \varphi(\Omega)$ and $u^-(\lambda)$ the left-semi-deviation of Y. Given a "strike" level $L = \varphi(K)$, let us define, as in the case of X:

$$\zeta(L, u^-(\lambda)) = \int_{-\infty}^{K} (\Omega_Y - y) g_\lambda(y) dy.$$

The inherited fragility of Y with respect to X at stress level $L = \varphi(K)$ and left-semi-deviation level $s^-(\lambda)$ of X is the partial derivative:

$$V_X(Y, g_\lambda, L, s^-(\lambda)) = \frac{\partial \zeta}{\partial s}(L, u^-(\lambda)) = \left(\int_{-\infty}^{K} (\Omega_Y - y) \frac{\partial g_\lambda}{\partial \lambda}(y) dy \right) \left(\frac{ds^-}{d\lambda} \right)^{-1}$$

Note that the stress level and the pdf are defined for the variable Y, but the parameter which is used for differentiation is the left-semi-absolute deviation of $X, s^-(\lambda)$. Indeed, in this process, one first measures the distribution of X and its left-semi-absolute deviation, then the function φ is applied, using some mathematical model of Y with respect to X and the risk measure ζ is estimated. If an error is made when measuring $s^-(\lambda)$, its impact on the risk measure of Y is amplified by the ratio given by the "inherited fragility."

Once again, one may use finite differences and define the *finite-difference inherited fragility* of Y with respect to X, by replacing, in the above equation, differentiation by finite differences between values λ^+ and λ^-, where $s^-(\lambda^+) = s^- + \Delta s$ and $s^-(\lambda^-) = s^- - \Delta s$.

Implications of a Nonlinear Change of Variable on the Intrinsic Fragility

We here study the case of a random variable $Y = \varphi(X)$, the pdf g_λ of which also depends on parameter λ, related to a variable X by the nonlinear function φ. We are now interested in comparing their *intrinsic fragilities*. We shall say, for instance, that Y is *more fragile* at the stress level L and left-semi-deviation level $u^-(\lambda)$ than the random variable X, at stress level K and left-semi-deviation level $s^-(\lambda)$ if the L-left-tailed semi-vega sensitivity of Y_λ is higher than the K-left-tailed semi-vega sensitivity of X_λ:

$$V(Y, g_\lambda, L, u^-) > V(X, f_\lambda, K, s^-).$$

One may use finite differences to compare the fragility of two random variables: $V(Y, g_\lambda, L, u^-, \Delta u) > V(X, f_\lambda, K, s^-, \Delta s)$. In this case, finite variations must be comparable in size, namely $\Delta u/u^- = \Delta s/s^-$.

Let us assume, to start with, that φ is differentiable, strictly increasing, and scaled so that $\Omega_Y = \varphi(\Omega) = \Omega$. We also assume that, for any given $x < \Omega$, $\frac{\partial F_\lambda}{\partial \lambda}(x) > 0$. In this case, as observed above, $\lambda \to s^-(\lambda)$ is also increasing.

Let us denote $G_\lambda(y) = \Pr_{g_\lambda}(Y < y)$. We have:

$$G_\lambda(\varphi(x)) = \Pr_{g_\lambda}(Y < \varphi(x)) = \Pr_{f_\lambda}(X < x) = F_\lambda(x).$$

Hence, if $\zeta(L, u^-)$ denotes the equivalent of $\xi(K, s^-)$ with variable (Y, g_λ) instead of (X, f_λ), then we have:

$$\zeta(L, u^-(\lambda)) = \int_{-\infty}^{\Omega} G_\lambda^L(y)\,dy = \int_{-\infty}^{\Omega} F_\lambda^K(x) \frac{d\varphi}{dx}(x)\,dx.$$

Because φ is increasing and $\min(\varphi(x), \varphi(K)) = \varphi(\min(x, K))$. In particular

$$u^-(\lambda) = \zeta(\Omega, u^-(\lambda)) = \int_{-\infty}^{\Omega} F_\lambda(x) \frac{d\varphi}{dx}(x)\,dx.$$

The *L*-left-tail-vega sensitivity of *Y* is therefore:

$$V(Y, g_\lambda, L, u^-(\lambda)) = \frac{\int_{-\infty}^{\Omega} \frac{\partial F_\lambda^K}{\partial \lambda}(x) \frac{d\varphi}{dx}(x) dx}{\int_{-\infty}^{\Omega} \frac{\partial F_\lambda}{\partial \lambda}(x) \frac{d\varphi}{dx}(x) dx}.$$

For finite variations:

$V(Y, g_\lambda, L, u^-(\lambda), \Delta u) = \frac{1}{2\Delta u} \int_{-\infty}^{\Omega} \Delta F_{\lambda, \Delta u}^K(x) \frac{d\varphi}{dx}(x) dx$, where $\lambda_{u^-}^+$ and $\lambda_{u^-}^-$ are such that $u(\lambda_{u^-}^+) = u^- + \Delta u$, $u(\lambda_{u^-}^-) = u^- - \Delta u$ and $F_{\lambda, \Delta u}^K(x) = F_{\lambda_{u^-}^+}^K(x) - F_{\lambda_{u^-}^-}^K(x)$.

Next, Theorem 1 proves how a concave transformation $\varphi(x)$ of a random variable *x* produces fragility.

THEOREM 1 (FRAGILITY TRANSFER THEOREM)

Let, with the above notations, $\varphi: \mathbb{R} \to \mathbb{R}$ be a twice differentiable function such that $\varphi(\Omega) = \Omega$ and for any $x < \Omega$, $\frac{d\varphi}{dx}(x) > 0$. The random variable $Y = \varphi(X)$ is more fragile at level $L = \varphi(K)$ and pdf g_λ than X at level K and pdf f_λ if, and only if, one has:

$$\int_{-\infty}^{\Omega} H_\lambda^K(x) \frac{d^2\varphi}{dx^2}(x) dx < 0,$$

where

$$H_\lambda^K(x) = \frac{\partial P_\lambda^K}{\partial \lambda}(x) / \frac{\partial P_\lambda^K}{\partial \lambda}(\Omega) - \frac{\partial P_\lambda}{\partial \lambda}(x) / \frac{\partial P_\lambda}{\partial \lambda}(\Omega)$$

and where $P_\lambda(x) = \int_{-\infty}^{x} F_\lambda(t) dt$ is the price of the "put option" on X_λ with "strike" x and $P_\lambda^K(x) = \int_{-\infty}^{x} F_\lambda^K(t) dt$ is that of a "put option" with "strike" x and "European down-and-in barrier" at K.

H can be seen as a *transfer function*, expressed as the difference between two ratios. For a given level *x* of the random variable on the left-hand side of Ω, the second one is the ratio of the vega of a put struck at *x* normalized by that of a put "at the money" (i.e., struck at Ω), while the first one is the same ratio, but where puts struck at *x* and Ω are "European down-and-in options" with triggering barrier at the level K.

Proof

Let $I_{X_\lambda} = \int_{-\infty}^{\Omega} \frac{\partial F_\lambda}{\partial \lambda}(x) dx$, $I_{X_\lambda}^K = \int_{-\infty}^{\Omega} \frac{\partial F_\lambda^K}{\partial \lambda}(x) dx$, $I_{Y_\lambda} = \int_{-\infty}^{\Omega} \frac{\partial F_\lambda}{\partial \lambda}(x) \frac{d\varphi}{dx}(x) dx$ and $I_{Y_\lambda}^L = \int_{-\infty}^{\Omega} \frac{\partial F_\lambda^K}{\partial \lambda}(x) \frac{d\varphi}{dx}(x) dx$. One has $V(X, f_\lambda, K, s^-(\lambda)) = I_{X_\lambda}^K / I_{X_\lambda}$ and $V(Y, g_\lambda, L, u^-(\lambda)) = I_{Y_\lambda}^L / I_{Y_\lambda}$. Hence:

$$V(Y, g_\lambda, L, u^-(\lambda)) - V(X, f_\lambda, K, s^-(\lambda)) = \frac{I_{Y_\lambda}^L}{I_{Y_\lambda}} - \frac{I_{X_\lambda}^K}{I_{X_\lambda}} = \frac{I_{X_\lambda}^K}{I_{Y_\lambda}} \left(\frac{I_{Y_\lambda}^L}{I_{X_\lambda}^K} - \frac{I_{Y_\lambda}}{I_{X_\lambda}} \right).$$

Therefore, because the four integrals are positive, $V(Y, g_\lambda, L, u^-(\lambda)) - V(X, f_\lambda, K, s^-(\lambda))$ has the same sign as $I_{Y_\lambda}^L / I_{X_\lambda}^K - I_{Y_\lambda}/I_{X_\lambda}$. On the other hand, we have $I_{X_\lambda} = \frac{\partial P_\lambda}{\partial \lambda}(\Omega)$, $I_{X_\lambda}^K = \frac{\partial P_\lambda^K}{\partial \lambda}(\Omega)$ and

$$I_{Y_\lambda} = \int_{-\infty}^{\Omega} \frac{\partial F_\lambda}{\partial \lambda}(x) \frac{d\varphi}{dx}(x)\,dx = \frac{\partial P_\lambda}{\partial \lambda}(\Omega) \frac{d\varphi}{dx}(\Omega) - \int_{-\infty}^{\Omega} \frac{\partial P_\lambda}{\partial \lambda}(x) \frac{d^2\varphi}{dx^2}(x)\,dx$$

$$I_{Y_\lambda}^L = \int_{-\infty}^{\Omega} \frac{\partial F_\lambda^K}{\partial \lambda}(x) \frac{d\varphi}{dx}(x)\,dx = \frac{\partial P_\lambda^K}{\partial \lambda}(\Omega) \frac{d\varphi}{dx}(\Omega) - \int_{-\infty}^{\Omega} \frac{\partial P_\lambda^K}{\partial \lambda}(x) \frac{d^2\varphi}{dx^2}(x)\,dx.$$

An elementary calculation yields:

$$\frac{I_{Y_\lambda}^L}{I_{X_\lambda}^K} - \frac{I_{Y_\lambda}}{I_{X_\lambda}} = -(\frac{\partial P_\lambda^K}{\partial \lambda}(\Omega))^{-1} \int_{-\infty}^{\Omega} \frac{\partial P_\lambda^K}{\partial \lambda}(x) \frac{d^2\varphi}{dx^2}\,dx + (\frac{\partial P_\lambda}{\partial \lambda}(\Omega))^{-1}$$

$$\int_{-\infty}^{\Omega} \frac{\partial P_\lambda}{\partial \lambda}(x) \frac{d^2\varphi}{dx^2}\,dx$$

$$= -\int_{-\infty}^{\Omega} H_\lambda^K(x) \frac{d^2\varphi}{dx^2}\,dx.$$

Let us now examine the properties of the function $\frac{\partial P_\lambda^K}{\partial \lambda}(\Omega) = \frac{\partial P_\lambda}{\partial \lambda}(\Omega)$. For $x \le K$, we have $\frac{\partial P_\lambda^K}{\partial \lambda}(x) = \frac{\partial P_\lambda}{\partial \lambda}(x) > 0$ (the positivity is a consequence of that of $\partial F_\lambda/\partial \lambda$), therefore $H_\lambda^K(x)$ has the same sign as $\frac{\partial P_\lambda}{\partial \lambda}(\Omega) - \frac{\partial P_\lambda^K}{\partial \lambda}(\Omega)$. As this is a strict inequality, it extends to an interval on the right-hand side of K, say $(-\infty, K']$ with $K < K' < \Omega$.

But on the other hand:

$$\frac{\partial P_\lambda}{\partial \lambda}(\Omega) - \frac{\partial P_\lambda^K}{\partial \lambda}(\Omega) = \int_K^{\Omega} \frac{\partial F_\lambda}{\partial \lambda}(x)\,dx - (\Omega - K)\frac{\partial F_\lambda}{\partial \lambda}(K)$$

For K negative enough, $\frac{\partial F_\lambda}{\partial \lambda}(K)$ is smaller than its average value over the interval $[K, \Omega]$, hence $\frac{\partial P_\lambda}{\partial \lambda}(\Omega) - \frac{\partial P_\lambda^K}{\partial \lambda}(\Omega) > 0$.

We have proven the following theorem.

THEOREM 2 (FRAGILITY EXACERBATION THEOREM)

With the above notations, there exists a threshold $\Theta_\lambda < \Omega$ such that, if $K \le \Theta_\lambda$ then $H_\lambda^K(x) > 0$ for $x \in (-\infty, \kappa_\lambda]$ with $K < \kappa_\lambda < \Omega$. As a consequence, if the change of variable φ is concave on $(-\infty, \kappa_\lambda]$ and linear on $[\kappa_\lambda, \Omega]$, then Y is more fragile at $L = \varphi(K)$ than X at K.

One can prove that, for a monomodal distribution, $\Theta_\lambda < \kappa_\lambda < \Omega$ (see discussion below), so whatever the stress level K below the threshold Θ_λ, it suffices that the change of variable φ be concave on the interval $(-\infty, \Theta_\lambda]$ and linear on $[\Theta_\lambda, \Omega]$ for Y to become more fragile at L than X at K. In practice, as long as the change of variable is concave around the stress level K and has limited convexity/concavity away from K, the fragility of Y is greater than that of X.

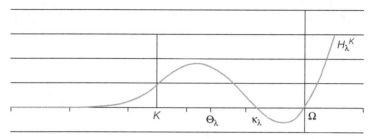

Figure 7.4 The transfer function H for different portions of the distribution: its sign flips in the region slightly below Ω.

Figure 7.4 shows the shape of $H_\lambda^K(x)$ in the case of a Gaussian distribution where λ is a simple scaling parameter (λ is the standard deviation σ) and $\Omega = 0$. We represented $K = -2\lambda$, while in this Gaussian case, $\Theta_\lambda = -1.585\lambda$.

DISCUSSION

Monomodal case

We say that the family of distributions (f_λ) is *left-monomodal* if there exists $\kappa_\lambda < \Omega$ such that $\frac{\partial f_\lambda}{\partial \lambda} \geq 0$ on $(-\infty, \kappa_\lambda]$ and $\frac{\partial f_\lambda}{\partial \lambda} \leq 0$ on $[\mu_\lambda, \Omega]$. In this case, $\frac{\partial P_\lambda}{\partial \lambda}$ is a convex function on the left half-line $(-\infty, \mu_\lambda]$, then concave after the inflexion point μ_λ. For $K \leq \mu_\lambda$, the function $\frac{\partial P_\lambda^K}{\partial \lambda}$ coincides with $\frac{\partial P_\lambda}{\partial \lambda}$ on $(-\infty, K]$, then is a linear extension, following the tangent to the graph of $\frac{\partial P_\lambda}{\partial \lambda}$ in K (see Figure 7.5). The value of $\frac{\partial P_\lambda^K}{\partial \lambda}(\Omega)$ corresponds to the intersection point of this tangent with the vertical axis. It increases with K, from 0 when $K \to -\infty$ to a value above $\frac{\partial P_\lambda}{\partial \lambda}(\Omega)$ when $K = \mu_\lambda$. The threshold Θ_λ corresponds to the unique value of K such that $\frac{\partial P_\lambda^K}{\partial \lambda}(\Omega) = \frac{\partial P_\lambda}{\partial \lambda}(\Omega)$. When $K < \Theta_\lambda$ then $G_\lambda(x) = \frac{\partial P_\lambda}{\partial \lambda}(x)/\frac{\partial P_\lambda}{\partial \lambda}(\Omega)$ and $G_\lambda^K(x) = \frac{\partial P_\lambda^K}{\partial \lambda}(x)/\frac{\partial P_\lambda^K}{\partial \lambda}(\Omega)$ are functions such that $G_\lambda(\Omega) = G_\lambda^K(\Omega) = 1$ and which are proportional for $x \leq K$, the latter being linear on $[K, \Omega]$. On the other hand, if $K < \Theta_\lambda$ then $\frac{\partial P_\lambda^K}{\partial \lambda}(\Omega) < \frac{\partial P_\lambda}{\partial \lambda}(\Omega)$ and $G_\lambda(K) < G_\lambda^K(K)$, which implies that $G_\lambda(x) < G_\lambda^K(x)$ for $x \leq K$. An elementary convexity analysis shows that, in this case, the equation $G_\lambda(x) = G_\lambda^K(x)$ has a unique solution κ_λ with $\mu_\lambda < \kappa_\lambda < \Omega$. The "transfer" function $H_\lambda^K(x)$ is positive for $x < \kappa_\lambda$, in particular when $x \leq \mu_\lambda$ and negative for $\kappa_\lambda < x < \Omega$.

Scaling Parameter

We assume here that λ is a scaling parameter, that is, $X_\lambda = \Omega + \lambda(X_1 - \Omega)$. In this case, as we saw above, we have $f_\lambda(x) = \frac{1}{\lambda}f_1(\Omega + \frac{x-\Omega}{\lambda})$, $F_\lambda(x) = F_1(\Omega + \frac{x-\Omega}{\lambda})$, $P_\lambda(x) = \lambda P_1(\Omega + \frac{x-\Omega}{\lambda})$ and $s^-(\lambda) = \lambda\,s^-(1)$. Hence

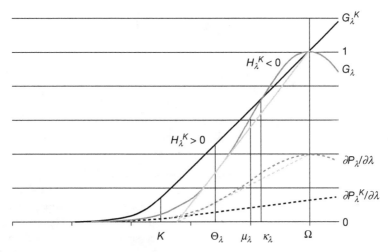

Figure 7.5 The distribution $G\lambda$ and the various derivatives of the unconditional shortfalls

$$\xi(K, s^-(\lambda)) = (\Omega - K)F_1(\Omega + \frac{K - \Omega}{\lambda}) + \lambda P_1(\Omega + \frac{K - \Omega}{\lambda})$$

$$\frac{\partial \xi}{\partial s^-}(K, s^-) = \frac{1}{s^-(1)} \frac{\partial \xi}{\partial \lambda}(K, \lambda) = \frac{1}{s^-(\lambda)}(P_\lambda(K) + (\Omega - K)F_\lambda(K) + (\Omega - K)^2 f_\lambda(K)).$$

When we apply a nonlinear transformation φ, the action of the parameter λ is no longer a scaling: when small negative values of X are multiplied by a scalar λ, so are large negative values of X. The scaling λ applies to small negative values of the transformed variable Y with a coefficient $\frac{d\varphi}{dx}(0)$, but large negative values are subject to a different coefficient $\frac{d\varphi}{dx}(K)$, which can potentially be very different.

Fragility Drift

Fragility is defined at as the sensitivity—that is, the first partial derivative—of the tail estimate ξ with respect to the left semi-deviation s^-. Let us now define the *fragility drift*:

$$V'_K(X, f_\lambda, K, s^-) = \frac{\partial^2 \xi}{\partial K \partial s^-}(K, s^-).$$

In practice, fragility always occurs as the result of *fragility*; indeed, by definition, we know that $\xi(\Omega, s^-) = s^-$, hence $V(X, f_\lambda, \Omega, s^-) = 1$. The *fragility drift* measures the speed at which fragility departs from its original value 1 when K departs from the center Ω.

Second-Order Fragility

The *second-order fragility* is the second-order derivative of the tail estimate ξ with respect to the semi-absolute deviation s^-:

$$V'_{s^-}(X, f_\lambda, K, s^-) = \frac{\partial^2 \xi}{(\partial s^-)^2}(K, s^-).$$

As we shall see later, the *second-order fragility* drives the bias in the estimation of stress tests when the value of s^- is subject to uncertainty, through Jensen inequality.

Definitions of Robustness and Antifragility

Antifragility is not the simple opposite of fragility, as we saw in Table 7.1. Measuring antifragility, on the one hand, consists of the flipside of fragility on the right-hand side, but on the other hand requires a control on the *robustness* of the probability distribution on the left-hand side. From that aspect, unlike fragility, antifragility cannot be summarized in one single figure but necessitates at least two of them.

When a random variable depends on another source of randomness, $Y_\lambda = \varphi(X_\lambda)$, we shall study the antifragility of Y_λ with respect to that of X_λ and to the properties of the function φ.

DEFINITION OF ROBUSTNESS

Let (X_λ) be a one-parameter family of random variables with pdf f_λ. Robustness is an upper control on the *fragility* of X, which resides on the left-hand side of the distribution.

We say that f_λ is b-robust beyond stress level $K < \Omega$ if $V(X_\lambda, f_\lambda, K', s(\lambda)) \le b$ for any $K' \le K$. In other words, the robustness of f_λ on the half-line $(-\infty, K]$ is $R_{(-\infty, K]}(X_\lambda, f_\lambda, K, s^-(\lambda)) = \max_{k' \le K} V(X_\lambda, f_\lambda, K', s^-(\lambda))$, so that b-robustness simply means $R_{(-\infty, K]}(X_\lambda, f_\lambda, K, s^-(\lambda)) \le b$.

We also define *b-robustness over a given interval* $[K_1, K_2]$ by the same inequality being valid for any $K' \in [K_1, K_2]$. In this case we use $R_{[K_1, K_2]}(X_\lambda, f_\lambda, K, s^-(\lambda)) = \max_{K_1 \le K' \le K_2} V(X_\lambda, f_\lambda, K', s^-(\lambda))$.

Note that the *lower* R, the tighter the control and the *more* robust the distribution f_λ.

Once again, the definition of b-robustness can be transposed, using finite differences $V(X_\lambda, f_\lambda, K', s^-(\lambda), \Delta s)$.

In practical situations, setting a material upper bound b to the fragility is particularly important: one need to be able to come with actual estimates of the impact of the error on the estimate of the left-semi-deviation. However, when dealing with certain class of models, such as Gaussian, exponential of stable distributions, we may be lead to consider asymptotic definitions of robustness, related to certain classes.

For instance, for a given decay exponent $a > 0$, assuming that $f_\lambda(x) = O(e^{ax})$ when $x\square - \infty$, the *a*-exponential asymptotic robustness of X_λ below the level K is:

$$R_{\exp}(X_\lambda, f_\lambda, K, s^-(\lambda), a) = \max_{K' \le K}(e^{a(\Omega - K')}V(X_\lambda, f_\lambda, K', s^-(\lambda))).$$

If one of the two quantities $e^{a(\Omega-K')}f_\lambda(K')$ or $e^{a(\Omega-K')}V(X_\lambda,f_\lambda,K',s^-(\lambda))$ is not bounded from above when $K'\,\square - \infty$, then $R_{exp} = +\infty$ and X_λ is considered as not a-exponentially robust.

Similarly, for a given power $\alpha > 0$, and assuming that $f_\lambda(x) = O(x^{-\alpha})$ when $x\,\square - \infty$, the α-power asymptotic robustness of X_λ below the level K is:

$$R_{pow}(X_\lambda,f_\lambda,K,s^-(\lambda),a) = \max_{K'\leq K}((\Omega - K')^{\alpha-2}V(X_\lambda,f_\lambda,K',s^-(\lambda))).$$

If one of the two quantities $(\Omega - K')^{\alpha}f_\lambda(K')$ or $(\Omega - K')^{\alpha-2}V(X_\lambda,f_\lambda K',s^-(\lambda))$ is not bounded from above when $K'\square - \infty$, then $R_{pow} = +\infty$ and X_λ is considered as not α-power robust. Note the exponent $\alpha - 2$ used with the fragility, for homogeneity reasons, such as in the case of stable distributions.

When a random variable $Y_\lambda = \varphi(X_\lambda)$ depends on another source of risk X_λ, we write $Y_\lambda = \varphi(X_\lambda)$.

Definition 2a, left-robustness (monomodal distribution). *A payoff $y = \varphi(x)$ is said (a,b)-robust below $L = \varphi(K)$ for a source of randomness X with pdf f_λ assumed monomodal if, letting g_λ be the pdf of $Y = \varphi(X)$, one has, for any $K' \leq K$ and $L' = \varphi(K')$:*

$$V_X(Y,g_\lambda,L',s^-(\lambda)) \leq aV(X,f_\lambda,K',s^-(\lambda)) + b. \tag{7.1}$$

The quantity b is of order deemed of "negligible utility" (subjectively), that is, does not exceed some tolerance level in relation with the context, while a is a scaling parameter between variables X and Y.

Note that robustness is in effect impervious to changes of probability distributions. Also note that this measure of robustness ignores first-order variations since, owing to their higher frequency, these are detected (and remedied) very early on.

Example of Robustness (Barbells)

1. Trial and error with bounded error and open payoff.
2. For a "barbell portfolio" with allocation to numeraire securities up to 80% of portfolio, no perturbation below K set at 0.8 of valuation will represent any difference in result (i.e., $q = 0$). The same is true for an insured house (assuming the risk of the insurance company is not a source of variation): no perturbation for the value below K, equal to minus the insurance deductible, will result in significant changes.
3. A bet of amount B (limited liability) is robust, as it does not have any sensitivity to perturbations below 0.

DEFINITION OF ANTIFRAGILITY

The second condition of *antifragility* regards the *right-hand side* of the distribution. Let us define the *right-semi-deviation* of X:

$$s^+(\lambda) = \int_{\Omega}^{+\infty} (x - \Omega) f_\lambda(x) dx.$$

And, for $H > L > \Omega$:

$$\xi^+(L, H, s^+(\lambda)) = \int_{L}^{H} (x - \Omega) f_\lambda(x) dx$$

$$W(X, f_\lambda, L, H, s^+) = \frac{\partial \xi^+(L, H, s^+)}{\partial s^+} = \left(\int_{L}^{H} (x - \Omega) \frac{\partial f_\lambda}{\partial \lambda}(x) dx \right)$$

$$\left(\int_{\Omega}^{+\infty} (x - \Omega) \frac{\partial f_\lambda}{\partial \lambda}(x) dx \right)^{-1}.$$

When $Y = \varphi(X)$ is a variable depending on a source of noise X, we define:

$$W_x(Y, g_\lambda, \varphi(L), \varphi(H), s^+) = \left(\int_{\varphi(L)}^{\varphi(H)} (y - \varphi(\Omega)) \frac{\partial g_\lambda}{\partial \lambda}(y) dy \right)$$

$$\left(\int_{\Omega}^{+\infty} (x - \Omega) \frac{\partial f_\lambda}{\partial \lambda}(x) dx \right)^{-1}.$$

Definition 2b, antifragility (monomodal distribution). A payoff $y = \varphi(x)$ is locally antifragile over the range $[L, H]$ if

1. *It is b-robust below Ω for some $b > 0$, and*
2. $W_X(Y, g_\lambda, \varphi(L), \varphi(H), s^+(\lambda)) \geq aW(X, f_\lambda, L, H, s^+(\lambda))$*, where $a = \frac{u^+(\lambda)}{s^+(\lambda)}$.*

The scaling constant a provides homogeneity in the case where the relation between X and y is linear. In particular, nonlinearity in the relation between X and Y impacts robustness.

The second condition can be replaced with finite differences Δu and Δs, as long as $\Delta u / u = \Delta s / s$.

REMARKS

Fragility is K-specific: We are only concerned with adverse events below a certain pre-specified level, the breaking point. Exposures A can be more fragile than exposure B for $K = 0$, and much less fragile if K is, say, 4 mean deviations below 0. We may need to use finite Δs to avoid situations of vega-neutrality coupled with short left tail.

Effect of using the wrong distribution f: Comparing $V(X, f, K, s^-, \Delta s)$ and the alternative distribution $V(X, f^*, K, s^*, \Delta s)$, where f^* is the "true" distribution, the measure of fragility provides an acceptable indication of the sensitivity of a given outcome—such as a risk measure—to model error, provided no "paradoxical effects" perturb the situation. Such paradoxical effects are, for instance, a change in the direction in which certain distribution percentiles react to model parameters, like s^-. It is indeed possible that nonlinearity appears between the core part of the distribution and the tails such that when s^- increases, the left tail starts fattening—giving a large measured fragility—then steps back—implying that the real fragility is lower than the measured one. The opposite may also happen, implying a dangerous underestimate of the fragility. These nonlinear effects can stay under control provided one makes some regularity assumptions on the *actual* distribution, as well as on the measured one. For instance, paradoxical effects are typically avoided under at least one of the following three hypotheses:

a. The class of distributions in which both f and f^* are picked are all monomodal, with monotonous dependence of percentiles with respect to one another.
b. The difference between percentiles of f and f^* has constant sign (i.e., f^* is either *always* wider or *always* narrower than f at any given percentile).
c. For any strike level K (in the range that matters), the fragility measure V monotonously depends on s^- on the whole range where the true value s^* can be expected. This is in particular the case when partial derivatives $\partial^k V/\partial s^k$ all have the same sign at measured s^- up to some order n, at which the partial derivative has that same constant sign over the whole range on which the true value s^* can be expected. This condition can be replaced by an assumption on finite differences approximating the higher-order partial derivatives, where n is large enough so that the interval $[s^- \pm n\Delta s]$ covers the range of possible values of s^*. Indeed, in this case, the finite difference estimate of fragility uses evaluations of ξ at points spanning this interval.

Unconditionality of the shortfall measure ξ: Many, when presenting shortfall, deal with the conditional shortfall $\int_{-\infty}^{K} x f(x)\,dx / \int_{-\infty}^{K} f(x)\,dx$; ; -¶while such measure might be useful in some circumstances, its sensitivity is not indicative of fragility in the sense used in this discussion. The unconditional tail expectation $\xi = \int_{-\infty}^{K} x f(x)\,dx$ is more indicative of exposure to fragility. It is also preferred to the raw probability of falling below K, which is $\int_{-\infty}^{K} f(x)\,dx$, as the latter does not include the consequences. For instance, two such measures, $\int_{-\infty}^{K} f(x)\,dx$ and $\int_{-\infty}^{K} g(x)\,dx$, may be equal over broad values of K, but the expectation $\int_{-\infty}^{K} x f(x)\,dx$ can be much more consequential than $\int_{-\infty}^{K} x g(x)\,dx$ as the cost of the break can be more severe and we are interested in its "vega" equivalent.

Applications to Model Error

In the cases where Y depends on X, among other variables, often x is treated as nonstochastic, and the underestimation of the volatility of x maps immediately into the underestimation of the left tail of Y under two conditions:

a. X is stochastic and its stochastic character is ignored (as if it had zero variance or mean deviation).
b. Y is concave with respect to X in the negative part of the distribution, below Ω.

"Convexity bias" or effect from Jensen's inequality: Further, missing the stochasticity under the two conditions a) and b), in the event of the concavity applying above Ω leads to the negative convexity bias from the lowering effect on the expectation of the dependent variable Y.

CASE 1: APPLICATION TO DEFICITS

Example: A government estimates unemployment for the next three years as averaging 9%; it uses its econometric models to issue a forecast balance B of 200 billion deficit in the local currency. But it misses that unemployment (like almost everything in economics) is a stochastic variable. Employment over three-year periods has fluctuated by 1% on average. We can calculate the effect of the error with the following:

- Unemployment at 8%, Balance $B(8\%) = $ -75 bn (improvement of 125bn)
- Unemployment at 9%, Balance $B(9\%) = $ -200 bn
- Unemployment at 10%, Balance $B(10\%) = $ -550 bn (worsening of 350bn)

The convexity bias from underestimation of the deficit is by -112.5 bn, since $\frac{B(8\%)+B(10\%)}{2} = -312.5$.

Figure 7.6 below shows the probability distribution caused by the missed variable (it is assumed that deficit is Gaussian with a mean deviation of 1%).

Adding model error and metadistributions: Model error should be integrated in the distribution as a stochasticization of parameters. f and g should subsume

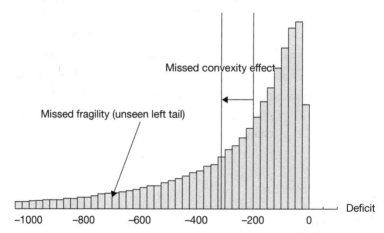

Figure 7.6 Convexity effects allow the detection of both model bias and fragility. Illustration of the example; histogram from Monte Carlo simulation of government deficit as a left-tailed random variable simply as a result of randomizing unemployment of which it is a convex function. The method of point estimate would assume a Dirac stick at -200, thus underestimating both the expected deficit (-312) and the skewness (i.e., fragility) of it.

the distribution of all possible factors affecting the final outcome (including the metadistribution of each). The so-called perturbation is not necessarily a change in the parameter so much as it is a means to verify whether f and g capture the full shape of the final probability distribution.

Any situation with a bounded payoff function that organically truncates the left tail at K will be impervious to all perturbations affecting the probability distribution below K.

For $K = 0$, the measure equates to mean negative semi-deviation (more potent than negative semi-variance or negative semi-standard deviation often used in financial analyses).

MODEL ERROR AND SEMI-BIAS AS NONLINEARITY FROM MISSED STOCHASTICITY OF VARIABLES

Model error often comes from missing the existence of a random variable that is significant in determining the outcome (say option pricing without credit risk). We cannot detect it using the heuristic presented in this paper, but as mentioned earlier, the error goes in the opposite direction as model tends to be richer, not poorer, from overfitting. But we can detect the model error from missing the stochasticity of a variable or underestimating its stochastic character (say option pricing with non-stochastic interest rates or ignoring that the "volatility" σ can vary).

Missing effects: The study of model error is not to question whether a model is precise or not, whether or not it tracks reality; it is to ascertain the first- and second-order effect from missing the variable, ensuring that the errors from the model don't have missing higher-order terms that cause severe unexpected (and unseen) biases in one direction because of convexity or concavity—in other words, whether or not the model error causes a change in z.

Model Bias, Second-Order Effects, and Fragility

Having the right model (which is a very generous assumption), but being uncertain about the parameters will invariably lead to an increase in model error in the presence of convexity and nonlinearities.

As a generalization of the deficit/employment example used in the previous section, say we are using a simple function:

$$f(x\,\alpha), \tag{7.2}$$

where $\overline{\alpha}$ is supposed to be the average expected rate and where we take φ as the distribution of α over its domain $\tilde{A}_\alpha$

$$\alpha = \int_{\tilde{A}_\alpha} \alpha\varphi(\alpha)d\alpha. \tag{7.3}$$

The mere fact that α is uncertain (since it is estimated) might lead to a bias if we perturb from the *outside* (of the integral), that is, stochasticize the parameter deemed fixed. Accordingly, the convexity bias is easily measured as the difference between a) f integrated across values of potential α and b) f estimated for a single value of α deemed to be its average. The convexity bias ω_A becomes

$$\omega_A \equiv \int_{\tilde{A}_x} \int_{\tilde{A}_\alpha} f(x|\alpha) \varphi(\alpha) d\alpha dx - \int_{\tilde{A}_x} f(x|(\int_{\tilde{A}_\alpha} \alpha \varphi(\alpha) d\alpha)dx. \qquad (7.4)$$

And ω_B, the missed fragility, is assessed by comparing the two integrals below K, in order to capture the effect on the left tail:

$$\omega_B(K) \equiv \int_{-\infty}^{K} \int_{\tilde{A}_\alpha} f(x|\alpha) \varphi(\alpha) d\alpha dx - \int_{-\infty}^{K} f(x|(\int_{\tilde{A}_\alpha} \alpha \varphi(\alpha) d\alpha)dx, \qquad (7.5)$$

which can be approximated by an interpolated estimate obtained with two values of α separated from a mid-point by $\Delta\alpha$ a mean deviation of α and estimating

$$\omega_B(K) \equiv \int_{-\infty}^{K} \frac{1}{2}(f(x|\bar{\alpha} + \Delta\alpha) + f(x|\bar{\alpha} - \Delta\alpha))dx - \int_{-\infty}^{K} f(x|\bar{\alpha})dx. \qquad (7.6)$$

We can probe ω_B by point estimates of f at a level of $X \leq K$

$$\omega_B'(X) = \frac{1}{2}(f(X|\bar{\alpha} + \Delta\alpha) + f(X|\bar{\alpha} - \Delta\alpha)) - f(X|\bar{\alpha}) \qquad (7.7)$$

so that

$$\omega_B(K) = \int_{-\infty}^{K} \omega_{\mathbf{B}}'(x)dx,$$

which leads us to the fragility heuristic. In particular, if we assume that $\omega_B'(X)$ has a constant sign for $X \leq K$, then $\omega_B(K)$ has the same sign.

THE FRAGILITY/MODEL ERROR DETECTION HEURISTIC (DETECTING ω_A AND ω_B WHEN COGENT)

Example 1 (detecting tail risk not shown by stress test, $\omega_{\mathbf{B}}$): *The famous firm Dexia went into financial distress a few days after passing a stress test "with flying colors."*

If a bank issues a so-called stress test (something that has never worked in history), of a parameter (say stock market) at -15%. We ask them to recompute at -10% and -20%. Should the exposure show negative asymmetry (worse at -20% than it improves at -10%), we deem that the risk increases in the tails. There are certainly hidden tail exposures and a definite higher probability of blowup in addition to exposure to model error.

Note that it is somewhat more effective to use our measure of shortfall, but the method here is effective enough to show hidden risks, particularly at wider increases (try 25% and 30% and see if exposure shows increase). Most effective would be to use power-law distributions and perturb the tail exponent to see symmetry.

Example 2 (detecting tail risk in overoptimized system, $\omega_{\mathbf{B}}$). *Raise airport traffic 10%, lower 10%, take average expected traveling time from each, and check the asymmetry* *for nonlinearity. If asymmetry is significant, then declare the system as overoptimized. (Both ω_A and ω_B as thus shown)*

Example 3 (detecting error in a probability framework, ω_b). *Change parameter up by a mean deviation; compute left integral below K; lower it by a mean deviation; compute and compare. If there is asymmetry, then the situation is precarious and model error is large to the extent of the asymmetry.*

The same procedure uncovers both fragility and consequence of model error (potential harm from having wrong probability distribution, a thin-tailed rather than a fat-tailed one). For traders (and see Gigerenzer's discussions, Gigerenzer and Brighton 2009, Gigerenzer and Goldstein 1996) playing with second-order effects of simplistic tools can be more effective than more complicated and harder to calibrate methods. See also the intuition of fast and frugal in Derman and Wilmott (2009) and Haug and Taleb (2011).

The Heuristic

Taleb et al. (2012) developed a heuristic in parallel with this paper to apply to stress testing or more generally, valuations.

> *1- First step (first order). Take ψ a valuation. Measure the sensitivity to all parameters p determining V over finite ranges Δp. If materially significant, check if stochasticity of parameter is taken into account by risk assessment. If not, then stop and declare the risk as grossly mismeasured (no need for further risk assessment). (Note that Ricardo's wine-cloth example miserably fails the first step upon stochasticizing either.)*
>
> *2-Second step (second order). For all parameters p compute the second order*

$$H(\Delta p) \equiv \frac{\mu'}{\mu}, \text{where} \mu'(\Delta p) \equiv \frac{1}{2}\left(\bar{f}\left(p + \frac{1}{2}\Delta p\right) + f\left(p - \frac{1}{2}\Delta p\right)\right).$$

> *2-Third step. Note parameters for which H is significantly > or < 1.*

Properties of the Heuristic

> i- **Fragility**: *V' is a more accurate indicator of fragility than V over Δp when p is stochastic or subjected to estimation errors with mean deviation Δp.*
>
> ii- **Model error**: *A model M(p) with parameter p held constant underestimates the fragility of payoff from x under perturbation Δp if H > 1.*
>
> iii- *If H = 1, the exposure to x is robust over Δp and model error over p is inconsequential.*
>
> iv- *If H remains ≥ 1 for larger and larger Δp, then the heuristic is broad (absence of pseudo-convexities)*

We can apply the method to V in Equation 1, as it becomes a perturbation of a perturbation, (in *Dynamic Hedging* "vvol," or "volatility of volatility" or in later lingo vvol), $H = \dfrac{V(x,f,K,\Delta s + \frac{\Delta s}{2}) + V(x,f,K,\Delta s - \frac{\Delta s}{2})}{2V(x,f,K,\Delta s)}$ where K is the fragility

threshold, x is a random variable describing outcomes, Δp is a set perturbation, and f the probability measure used to compute ζ.

Note that for K set at ∞, the heuristic becomes a simple detection of model bias from the effect of Jensen's inequality when stochasticizing a term held to be deterministic, the measure of ω_A.

The heuristic has the ability to "fill in the tail," by extending further down into the probability distribution as Δp increases. It is best to perturb the tail exponent of a power law.

Remarks:

a. Simple heuristics have a robustness (in spite of a possible bias) compared to optimized and calibrated measures. Ironically, it is from the multiplication of convexity biases and the potential errors from missing them that calibrated models that work in-sample underperform heuristics out of sample.
b. It allows detection of the effect of the use of the wrong probability distribution without changing probability distribution (just from the dependence on parameters).
c. It outperforms all other commonly used measures of risk, such as CVaR, "expected shortfall," stress-testing, and similar methods that have been proven to be completely ineffective.
d. It does not require parameterization beyond varying Δp.

COMPARISON OF THE HEURISTIC TO OTHER METHODS

CVaR and VaR: These are totally ineffective; there is no need for further discussion here (or elsewhere), as they have been shown to be so empirically and mathematically. But perturbation can reveal convexities and concavities.

Stress testing: One of the authors has shown where these can be as ineffective owing to risk hiding in the tail below the stress test. See Taleb (2009) on why the level K of the stress test is arbitrary and cannot be appropriately revealed by the past realizations of the random variable. But if stress tests show an increase in risk at lower and lower levels of stress, then the position reveals exposure in the tails.

Note that hidden risks reside in the tails as they are easy to hide there, undetected by conventional methods and tend to hide there.

FURTHER APPLICATIONS

In parallel works, applying the "simple heuristic" allows us to detect the following "hidden short options" problems by merely perturbating a certain parameter p:

a. Size and pseudo-economies of scale
   i. Size and squeezability (nonlinearities of squeezes in costs per unit)

b. Specialization (Ricardo) and variants of globalization

    i. Missing stochasticity of variables (price of wine)
    ii. Specialization and nature

c. Portfolio optimization (Markowitz)
d. Debt
e. Budget deficits: convexity effects explain why uncertainty lengthens, doesn't shorten expected deficits
f. Iatrogenics (medical) or how some treatments are concave to benefits, convex to errors
g. Disturbing natural systems
h. Detects fragility to forecasting errors in projection as these reside in convexity of duration/costs to uncertainty
i. Hidden tail exposure from dependence on a source of energy, etc. ("squeezability argument")
j. Medical applications to assess relative iatrogenics from the nonlinearity in response

ACKNOWLEDGMENTS

Bruno Dupire, Emanuel Derman, Jean-Philippe Bouchaud, Elie Canetti.

JP Morgan, New York, June 16, 2011; CFM, Paris, June 17, 2011; GAIM Conference, Monaco, June 21, 2011; Max Planck Institute, BERLIN, Summer Institute on Bounded Rationality, June 23, 2011; Eighth International Conference on Complex Systems, Boston, July 1, 2011; Columbia University, September 24, 2011.

REFERENCES

Arrow, K. J. 1965. "The Theory of Risk Aversion." In *Aspects of the Theory of Risk Bearing*, edited by Yrjo Jahnssonin Saatio. Reprinted in *Essays in the Theory of Risk Bearing*. 1971. Chicago: Markham. 90–109.

Derman, E., and P. Wilmott. 2009. "The Financial Modelers' Manifesto." SSRN. http://ssrn.com/abstract=1324878.

Gigerenzer, G., and H. Brighton. 2009. "Homo Heuristicus: Why Biased Minds Make Better Inferences." *Topics in Cognitive Science* 1 (1): 107–143.

Gigerenzer, G., and D. G. Goldstein. 1996. "Reasoning the Fast and Frugal Way: Models of Bounded Rationality." *Psychological Review* 103: 650–669.

Kahneman, D., and A. Tversky. 1979. "Prospect Theory: An Analysis of Decision Under Risk." *Econometrica* 46 (2): 171–185.

Jensen, J. L. W. V. 1906. "Sur les fonctions convexes et les inégalités entre les valeurs moyennes." *Acta Mathematica* 30.

Haug, E., and N. N. Taleb. 2011. "Option Traders Use (Very) Sophisticated Heuristics, Never the Black–Scholes–Merton Formula." *Journal of Economic Behavior and Organization* 77 (2): 97–106.

Machina, Mark, and Michael Rothschild. 2008. "Risk." In *The New Palgrave Dictionary of Economics*, 2nd ed., edited by Steven N. Durlauf and Lawrence E. Blume. London: Macmillan.

Makridakis, S., A. Andersen, R. Carbone, R. Fildes, M. Hibon, R. Lewandowski, J. Newton, R. Parzen, and R. Winkler. 1982. "The Accuracy of Extrapolation (Time Series) Methods: Results of a Forecasting Competition." *Journal of Forecasting* 1: 111–153.

Makridakis, S., and M. Hibon. 2000. "The M3-Competition: Results, Conclusions and Implications." *International Journal of Forecasting* 16: 451–476.

Pratt, J. W. 1964. "Risk Aversion in the Small and in the Large." *Econometrica* 32 (January–April): 122–136.

Rothschild, M., and J. E. Stiglitz. 1970. "Increasing Risk: I. A Definition." *Journal of Economic Theory* 2 (3): 225–243.

Rothschild, M., and J. E. Stiglitz. 1971. "Increasing risk II: Its Economic Consequences." *Journal of Economic Theory* 3(1): 66–84.

Taleb, N. N. 1997. *Dynamic Hedging: Managing Vanilla and Exotic Options*. New York: Wiley.

Taleb, N. N. 2009. "Errors, Robustness and the Fourth Quadrant." *International Journal of Forecasting* 25 (4): 744–759.

Taleb, N. N. 2012. *Antifragile*. New York: Random House and Penguin.

Taleb, N. N., Elie Canetti, Elena Loukoianova, Tidiane Kinda, and Christian Schmieder. 2012. "A New Heuristic Measure of Fragility and Tail Risks: Application to Stress Testing." IMF Working Paper.

Van Zwet, W. R. 1964. *Convex Transformations of Random Variables*. Amsterdam: Mathematical Center, 7.

PART THREE

The Global Financial Crisis of 2007–2009 and Psychology

8

The Varieties of Incentive Experience

ROBERT W. KOLB ■

Fear . . . "one tremendous incentive to self-mortification."
—WILLIAM JAMES, *The Varieties of Religious Experience*

The most important development in economics in the last forty years has been the study of incentives to achieve potential mutual gains when the parties have different degrees of knowledge.
—KENNETH J. ARROW, *1972 Nobel Laureate in Economic Sciences*

INTRODUCTION

For some decades now, the idea of incentives has played a key role in economics as well as in public policy analyzes and implementations. Nonetheless, the intellectual range of this absorption with incentives has been quite limited, despite the importance ascribed to it by Kenneth Arrow's quotation. As Arrow implies, the implicit understanding has been that there are gains to be achieved by parties to an agreement, and while Arrow does not specify that the agreement has exactly two parties, the most typical context studied in financial economics, at least, has been the problem of incentive alignment between a principal and the principal's agent. Thus, in their article, "Theory of the Firm: Managerial Behavior, Agency Costs and Ownership Structure," we find Jensen and Meckling (1976) stating: "The *principal* can limit divergences from his interest by establishing appropriate incentives for the agent and by incurring monitoring costs designed to limit the aberrant activities of the agent."

In contrast to this limited conceptualization of incentives as prevailing in an arrangement between two parties, the actual use of the term is much broader. The quotation from James's *The Varieties of Religious Experience* highlights a very different conception of incentive in which an emotion, in this case the emotion of fear, acts as an incentive. This chapter explores some of these broader conceptualizations of incentives and shows how the quintessentially economic understanding of this term constricts our understanding of the full role that incentives play in our discourse and throughout our society.[1]

To do this, the chapter first considers some recent understandings of incentives. Next, I attempt to develop a taxonomy of the very different kinds of incentives that shape all our lives, and illustrate the variety of roles played by incentives in the originate-to-distribute model of mortgage creation, the economic structure that played such a pivotal role in the financial crisis of 2007–2012.

THE RANGE OF INCENTIVES

It is difficult to overstate the impact that Jensen and Meckling's seminal paper has had in economics and finance, and they certainly succeeded in focusing the conceptualization of incentives on the principal-agent relationship. And even within this narrow focus, they helped to make the problem of executive compensation the key exemplar of the principal-agent relationship and a laboratory in which economists have studies the power of incentives.[2] Jensen and Meckling were not, of course, the first to notice the possible misalignment of incentives between principal and agent, and they even quote a famous passage from Adam Smith's *Wealth of Nations* in this connection:

> The directors of such [joint-stock] companies, however, being the managers rather of other people's money than of their own, it cannot well be expected, that they should watch over it with the same anxious vigilance with which the partners in a private copartnery frequently watch over their own. Like the stewards of a rich man, they are apt to consider attention to small matters as not for their master's honour, and very easily give themselves a dispensation from having it. Negligence and profusion, therefore, must always prevail, more or less, in the management of the affairs of such a company.

Also, long after Smith and well before Jensen and Meckling, incentives became important in our understanding of human behavior, particularly economic behavior. Near the beginning of the 20th century, Frederick Taylor described the best system of management being practiced as the management of "initiative and incentive," and it was this system that Taylor sought to replace with his principles of scientific management. According to Taylor's account of the theory then current, to obtain the worker's best effort or the worker's "initiative," the manager must provide the worker with an "incentive."

In the section "The Finest Type of Ordinary Management" Taylor says:

> The writer repeats, therefore, that in order to have any hope of obtaining the initiative of his workmen the manager must give some special incentive to his men beyond that which is given to the average of the trade. This incentive can be given in several different ways, as, for example, the hope of rapid promotion or advancement; higher wages, either in the form of generous piece-work prices or of a premium or bonus of some kind for good and rapid work; shorter hours of labor; better surroundings and working conditions than are ordinarily given, etc., and, above all, this special incentive should be accompanied by

that personal consideration for, and friendly contact with, his workmen which comes only from a genuine and kindly interest in the welfare of those under him. It is only by giving a special inducement or "incentive" of this kind that the employer can hope even approximately to get the "initiative" of his workmen .... Broadly speaking, then, the best type of management in ordinary use may be defined as management in which the workmen give their best initiative and in return receive some special incentive from their employers.

Thus, more than 100 years ago, management thought was using the idea of an incentive as something approximating one of its current meanings, but was applying the term in a broader context than the principal-agent relationship alone.

Even if we restrict our consideration of incentives to the field of economics, the idea of incentives is certainly not constrained to a relationship between two parties. In a different context from the one cited at the beginning of this chapter, Kenneth Arrow discusses incentives when there is really not a second identifiable party. In his paper, "Gifts and Exchanges," Arrow examines Richard Titmuss's famous analysis (1971) of the normative difference between a system in which human blood is sold and an alternative arrangement in which blood is donated as a gift. Examining the question from an economic point of view, Arrow is interested in the incentives facing a commercial blood donor, particularly one who is poor and ill, and he uses the term "incentive" in two contexts. First:

Any-one whose motive for giving is to help others, but who suffers from hepatitis and is aware of the implications of this, will of course refrain from giving. On the other hand, a commercial blood donor, especially one driven by poverty, has every incentive to conceal the truth. (1972, 354)

and second:

It also appears that commercial blood-giving leads to unanticipated risks to the donors, though much less serious than those to the recipients. Commercial blood donors have some incentive to give blood more frequently than is desirable from the point of view of their health. (1972, 355)

In the circumstances Arrow envisages, the prospective commercial blood donor finds himself with incentives, but no second party provides an incentive or induces a behavior. Instead, the donor remains detached from any specific second incentivizing party and merely confronts a social arrangement that rewards (or incentivizes) certain behaviors.[3]

To a considerable degree, the public choice literature is consumed with studying incentives as they affect actors in the political arena. In *The Calculus of Consent: Logical Foundations of Constitutional Democracy*, Buchanan and Tullock repeatedly invoke the word "incentive," particularly in reference to strategic bargaining contexts. One instance will give the general tenor of their usage of the term: "The raison d'être of market exchange is the expectation of mutual gains. Yet, insofar as markets are competitive, little scope for bargaining exists. Individuals have little incentive to invest scarce resources in strategic endeavor" (Buchanan and Tullock 1999). Here, and in other similar contexts, the incentive acts essentially as a prospective reward that might be achieved by strategic maneuver, a reward fully detached from, and certainly not granted by, any second party.

Similarly, in his monograph, "Public Choice: The Origins and Development of a Research Program," Buchanan writes: "At base, the central idea emerges from the natural mind-set of the economist, whose explanation of interaction depends critically on the predictable responses of persons to measurable incentives. If an opportunity that promises to yield value arises, persons will invest time and resources in efforts to capture such value for themselves" (6). Slightly later he says:

> At issue here is the degree to which net wealth, and promised shifts in net wealth, may be used as explanatory incentives for the behavior of persons in public choice roles. Public choice, as an inclusive research program, incorporates the presumption that persons do not readily become economic eunuchs as they shift from market to political participation. The person who responds predictably to ordinary incentives in the marketplace does not fail to respond at all when his role is shifted to collective choice. (9)

In Buchanan's first quotation, he portrays an incentive as merely a goal to be obtained by following some course of action rather than as a reward stipulated by a second party for some performance or achievement. Even more strikingly, Buchanan's second quotation now casts incentives—those same goals that can be obtained by some course of action—as explanatory variables in the public choice research program.

As a final example from the world of economics, consider the recent book by Richard Thaler and Cass Sunstein, *Nudge: Improving Decisions About Health, Wealth, and Happiness*. Thaler and Sunstein recommend a program of "libertarian paternalism" in which policymakers, government agencies, institutions, employers, or even ordinary persons create environments in which other people make decisions. One is a "choice architect" if one "has the responsibility for organizing the context in which people make decisions" (2009, 3). Thaler and Sunstein "argue for self-conscious efforts, by institutions in the private sector and also by government, to steer people's choices in directions that will improve their lives. In our understanding, a policy is 'paternalistic' if it tries to influence choices in a way that will make choosers better off, as judged by themselves" (2009, 5). In other words, we might say that a choice architect is one who gives people a nudge to go in a certain direction, a role for the choice architect that some might compare to that of being a "noodge." Thaler and Sunstein connect their idea of paternalistic nudges to incentives by characterizing some portion of humanity as Econs—those who respond promptly and "correctly" to incentives. Thaler and Sunstein repeatedly characterize incentives as external rewards that can be obtained by a certain course of action, and the choice architect acts to artfully arrange the context of decision making in a way that will lead people to make "better choices" for themselves. Said another way, the choice architect arranges the decision context so that stronger incentives lie with the "better choices."

At this point we come full circle to the world of incentives of 100 years ago. When Taylor advanced his principles of scientific management they were widely seen as oppressive and unethical. As Ruth Grant notes of this era: "'Incentives' came into the language in an atmosphere of heated controversy, moral and political, in American industry. Incentives were offered by people with power to people without it, and everybody knew that" (2202, 120). And Thaler and Sunstein, writing 100 years later, are aware of the same objection to the program they advance: "A general objection to libertarian paternalism, and to certain kinds of nudges, might be that they are insidious—that they empower government to maneuver people in its preferred directions, and at the same time provide officials with excellent tools by which to accomplish that task" (2009, 246). While we may well commend Thaler and Sunstein for recognizing the problematic ethical dimension of the program they favor, their mention highlights the general neglect of the ethics of incentives, a topic to which we now briefly turn.

In a pair of papers, Ruth Grant (2002 and 2006) has done an admirable job of pointing out the history of the idea of incentives and tracing how the use of the word has changed and come to dominate economic and public policy discourse. Her recent book, *Strings Attached: Untangling the Ethics of Incentives*, extends that analysis and then focuses on the ethics of what she calls incentives, "strictly speaking":

> Incentives "strictly speaking" are a particular kind of offer: 1. an extrinsic benefit or a bonus that is neither the natural or automatic consequence of an action nor a deserved reward or compensation; 2. a discrete prompt expected to elicit a particular response; and 3. an offer intentionally designed to alter the status quo by motivating a person to choose differently than he or she would be likely to choose in its absence. (2011, 43)

Of course Grant realizes the much broader scope of the term "incentives" as it is used in our society, even to embrace such procedures as "choice architecture," as advocated by Thaler and Sunstein.

Thus, it is not peculiar to say that "the bonus plan gives the executive the incentive to raise quarterly profits," or that "the presence of the tiger provided a strong incentive to stay out of the cage." And while Grant's analysis of incentives, "strictly speaking," is a quite useful one, it is desirable to realize how extensive and diverse our uses of the idea of incentives really are. To that end, this chapter explores the variety of incentives, "broadly understood," operating in the financial crisis that began in 2007 and focuses particularly on the incentives at play in the originate-to-distribute model of mortgage production that characterized the run-up to the largest financial crisis since the Great Depression.

Before turning to a discussion of the financial crisis, it is necessary to state some of the limitations of this study. The analysis focuses only on what we might regard as positive incentives rather than disincentives. A positive incentive is some additional benefit that might result from pursuing a certain course of action compared to the results expected from the course of action without the impact of incentives. A negative incentive, or disincentive, might be some unfavorable consequence that would result from failing to undertake a specific course of action. Said simply, this chapter considers only carrots, not sticks.

As noted above, Ruth Grant considers the ethics of incentives and contrasts two ways of thinking about incentives. She points out that many who advocate using incentives as elements of public policy emphasize the difference between coercion and incentives. Instead, Grant highlights the obvious use of incentives as an element of control and suggests that we might think of reasons and rational discourse as a way of guiding behavior as opposed to the promise of rewards or incentives as an inducement for people to behave in a certain way.

Once we start to think about incentives primarily as an instrument of control, they cease to appear quite so benign. For example, there is a considerable literature on "coercive offers." While the exact meaning of a coercive offer remains elusive, a coercive offer is essentially some benefit that the recipient of the offer has no choice but to accept, an offer "that one cannot reasonably refuse."[4] Not surprisingly, the plausibility of there being coercive offers depends on one's view of freedom. Those who emphasize the importance of positive rather than negative liberty, to use Isaiah Berlin's distinction, more willingly accept that some offers may be coercive.[5] Alternatively, those who focus on negative freedom tend to deny that any offer of a benefit that improves one's ex ante position can be coercive. For example, libertarians generally deny that there can be coercive offers.[6] This study abstracts from the question of whether there can be coercive offers, and all of the specific examples to be considered seem clearly free of any danger of being regarded as coercive offers.

When we begin to think of incentives as an element of control, it is not difficult to conceive a spectrum of controlling incentives. At the generous end of the spectrum, we could imagine some item of value to be awarded for a specific achievement, with absolutely no ill result from failing to pursue a given course of action. For example, the winning of an Olympic medal might be an incentive for someone, but the failure to obtain a victory and win a medal does not diminish the initial position of the person who aspires to win a medal but fails. But as we imagine a choice architect arranging conditions to give one ever stronger nudges, the ideas of incentives as control and incentives as elements in a coercive offer gain resonance. For the fear is, of course, that very strong arrangements of incentives soon give way to out and out control, as Sarah Conly advocated recently in her new book, *Against Autonomy* (2012). No one study can deal with all of the issues surrounding the concept of incentives, and this study abstracts from the problem of coercive offers and incentives as an element of control. In addition, the incentives on offer in the subprime housing market of the early 2000s were so lucrative that they generated active and even rabid pursuit.

A TAXONOMY OF INCENTIVES

The world of incentives is very broad. At one end of the spectrum we have Grant's incentives construed in a manner that is "strictly speaking"—an intentional offer to a person to elicit a particular behavior. Let us establish the other extreme as a "natural incentive," some physical (nonsocial, nonhuman) state of affairs that gives someone a reason or motive to act one way rather than another. For example, an impending storm provides an incentive to seek shelter, the incentive being the opportunity to remain warm and dry. I believe that all incentives lie along this spectrum and that, further, it is possible to adduce examples of incentives that occupy almost all shades of the spectrum.

Of course, the interesting cases of incentives, especially from the point of view of economics, are those that involve a human factor, and these were certainly the ones in play in the financial crisis. However, no incentive works in a vacuum, and even when a recognizable party offers an incentive, the efficacy of that incentive depends on the surrounding physical and social context.

An ideal taxonomy of incentives provides clear-cut demarcations between different types of incentives and enables anyone to correctly assign a particular incentive example to its rightful slot within the classification system. But the actual deployment of incentives often exemplifies a blend of different pure types of incentives. Further, from an external view of an incentive arrangement it often remains difficult to specify the exact types of incentives at play. As an added complication, incentive arrangements might be intended to elicit one kind of behavior, but the recipient of the incentive might in fact be incentivized to behave in some quite different or even contrary manner. Finally, incentives can be offered or constructed in a manner that is highly ambiguous, such that the provider of an incentive does not fully understand how the incentive will actually operate, and the recipient of the incentive may receive a completely erroneous understanding of the behavior desired by the grantor of the incentive or may act to capture the incentive through behavior that is even detrimental to the incentivizer. All of these dimensions were at play in the originate-to-distribute model of mortgage production, so it provides a laboratory for understanding the varieties of incentive experience.

As Figure 8.1 illustrates, there are ten principal individuals or roles in the originate-to-distribute sequence:

Borrower
Mortgage originator
Mortgage broker
Appraiser
Due-diligence firm
Mortgage servicer
Securitizer
Rating agency
Ultimate investor
Regulatory agencies and officials

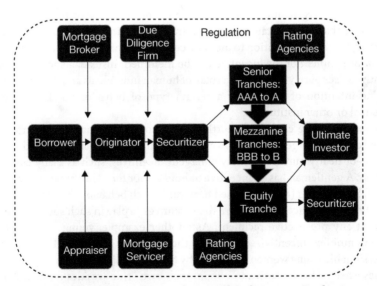

Figure 8.1 The Originate-to-Distribute Model of Mortgage Production.

SOURCE: Robert W. Kolb, *The Financial Crisis of Our Time* (Oxford: Oxford University Press, 2011), 27.

I consider each role in turn, which provides the opportunity to define additional types of incentives and to study the role those incentives played in the behavior of each party. In doing so, I will briefly summarize the key incentives I believe they faced, but I will not defend the impressionistic treatment I offer nor scrupulously list all the incentives that may have been operational. Instead, the goal here is to use the financial crisis to illustrate different types of incentives and to develop a taxonomy of incentives. However, I have addressed the historical nature of these incentives and explained them at some length in other contexts.[7]

The Borrower: During the residential housing boom that characterized the run-up to the financial crisis, many borrowers found themselves with access to easy mortgage credit in amounts and on terms not previously available, with this feast of credit set against seemingly never-ending increases in the price of homes across the United States. Against this background, and sometimes at the prompting of unscrupulous mortgage lending intermediaries, many borrowers took mortgages in amounts and on terms that were unsustainable or sustainable only if housing prices continued their rapid escalation. It is natural to say that the prospects of a high return on a highly leveraged investment with generous financing terms provided the borrower with a strong incentive to buy a home and take a mortgage.

The incentives in this situation were clearly not a matter natural incentives, as homes are bought and mortgages granted only in a well-developed economy. Further, the incentives were not Grant's narrow strictly speaking incentives, as no identifiable party offered the incentive, nor was any incentive offered to a particular individual, at least not according to the way I have characterized the prospective borrower's position. Rather, the borrower's incentives arose from complicated institutional developments that made taking a mortgage to buy a house appear attractive. In an important sense, the prospective borrower faced incentives that were socially emergent.

A socially emergent incentive arises out of the interplay of humans and their institutions that make certain behaviors attractive. But in a purely socially emergent incentive, there is no intention to induce a certain type of behavior and no particular grantor or recipient of the incentive can be identified. Instead, a socially emergent incentive arises purely from the interplay of human individuals and their institutions with no intention of stimulating a certain type of behavior on the part of any individual or other institution.

For reasons to be explained shortly, the borrower's incentives were not purely of the socially emergent type. However, there are some arrangements that create purely—or nearly purely—socially emergent incentives, such as many customs of courtesy. A gentleman has an incentive to hold a door for a lady because the existing social fabric rewards (or at least used to reward) such behaviors. In such a situation, no party offers an incentive, nor are the incentives at play in such social encounters aimed at any prospective recipient. As another example, young men want their own automobiles, incentivized to obtain them, at least in part, by the existence of impressionable young women (or at least by the male belief that such impressionable females exist). This incentive to obtain one's own "ride" resides inherently in the social arrangements that prevail in US society. No party designed or sought to offer such incentives to anyone. Rather, the incentives emerged from the organic development of society.

Some incentives facing the mortgage borrower were also the product of consciously designed social policy, and so not of the socially emergent type. For decades in the United States, all levels of the federal government have advocated and sought to stimulate home ownership. Presidential pronouncements and encouragements going back to the early 20th century, and reinforced by virtually every president of both parties in the ensuing years, eventually found their substantiation in concrete policies designed to incentivize home ownership. For example, the mortgage deductibility of interest has long provided a substantial incentive to own a home. The Community Reinvestment Act of 1977 was designed to attack discriminatory mortgage lending practices and to expand home ownership. This act received new attention and more vigorous enforcement through the National Homeownership Strategy of the Clinton era, which explicitly sought to increase the percentage of Americans living in their own homes. In short, governmental institutions of the United States actively sought to change incentives in the housing market, with the clear intention of changing both the behavior of lending institutions and prospective home-buyer.

Let us call such incentives institutionally constructed incentives. Those who promulgate institutionally constructed incentives are essentially the choice architects that Thaler and Sunstein seem to have most clearly in mind, even though they allow that a single individual can also be a choice architect. An institutionally constructed incentive is one created by some body composed of or embracing many human individuals that formulate conditions or policies that alter the choice environment in which people make decisions. Paradigmatically, governmental agencies perform this function. For example, the income tax code of the United States has hundreds or thousands of provisions designed to alter the behavior of taxpayers. Governments establish tax regimes and grant waivers from taxes to promote some perceived social good and to incentivize certain behaviors while discouraging others. Below the governmental level, almost all organizations establish policies that provide incentives. For example, every firm establishes compensation policies and reward programs explicitly designed to induce certain behaviors, and we will see some of these at play as we consider other actors in the originate-to-distribute model.

These institutionally constructed incentives are unlike the person-to-person or strictly speaking incentives on which Grant concentrates and that seem to be contemplated by the Arrow quotation that begins this chapter. Instead, institutionally constructed incentives generally apply to many people. Because the policies that extend these incentives are general and people are so varied, an institutionally constructed incentive scheme often elicits quite varied responses from diverse individuals. In general, it must be the case that it is easier to construct incentives when the grantor offers an incentive to a particular person who is well known to the grantor.

Institutionally constructed incentives are also the natural habitat of unintended consequences. These broad-scale incentives must be, by their very nature, available to many people at the same time and on the same terms, especially in a democracy. Humans, in their perverse diversity of circumstances, values, and temperament, continue to respond to such incentives in ways never contemplated and often not desired by those who construct them. This aspect of social policy is broader than the question of mere incentives and has been long recognized, well understood, and devastatingly critiqued by Frédéric Bastiat and Robert Merton, and has received withering attention from many who have followed in their footsteps.

In sum, the prospective mortgagor in the financial crisis made decisions about mortgages in an environment greatly altered by the presence of both socially emergent and institutionally constructed incentives. The dominant collective effect of these incentives was to stimulate borrowing, to focus attention and hopes on anticipated gains in housing prices, and to excite the pursuit of houses beyond the reasonable means of many buyers.

The mortgage broker: During the financial crisis, the typical mortgage broker played the role of an intermediary between the prospective mortgagor and the mortgage originator, the financial institution that actually grants mortgage loans. In the ordinary event, the originator compensates a mortgage broker by paying a percentage of the principal amount of the mortgage, with payment occurring when the mortgage closes. What happens to the home owner or the lender after the closing is essentially irrelevant to the mortgage broker.

Under this arrangement, the mortgage broker faced a very clear and simple incentive to get as many deals done at as high a loan value as possible. Given the classification of incentives that we are developing, the mortgage broker's incentives were clearly of the socially emergent variety. No identifiable party constructed the industry in a manner designed to give the mortgage broker the role she came to have, and no party actively constructed the incentives that confronted the mortgage broker, so the incentives were not institutionally constructed, nor were they like Grant's strictly speaking incentives.

In retrospect, the social perversity of these incentives is obvious, and even in *media res* the same should have been obvious to any thoughtful observer—because the structure of these arrangements encouraged the mortgage broker to be indifferent to the welfare of both the home buyer and the lending institutions. Nonetheless, this arrangement persisted, and we will see that other elements of the originate-to-distribute chain exhibit instances of equally perverse incentives.

The mortgage originator: As just described, the mortgage originator is the financial institution that actually lends money to the prospective home owner. A few decades ago, the typical mortgage originator would have been a local savings and loan association (S&L), and the S&L would typically hold the mortgage as an asset on its books for the life of the mortgage. Under this arrangement, the S&L had powerful incentives to grant only reasonable loans and to perform scrupulous due diligence before lending.

In the originate-to-distribute arrangement, the mortgage lender grants a mortgage with the clear intention of selling the mortgage as quickly as possible. This sale generates an immediate profit on the mortgage and frees the principal amount of the mortgage to enable the origination of another mortgage. In the ordinary event, the originator bore financial responsibility for the quality of its mortgages for only 90 days. If the borrower did not default within 90 days after the originator sold the loan, the originator escaped all responsibility for any subsequent loss.

The entire originate-to-distribute model was never designed by any central intelligence. Instead, it was an organic outgrowth that emerged from the interaction of many parties. As such, many of the resulting incentives that characterize the originate-to-distribute model and that led to the financial crisis were of the socially emergent rather than institutionally constructed type. And this seems to be true of the main incentives confronting the mortgage originator. No one intentionally designed a system in which the mortgage originator had clear incentives to grant as many mortgages as possible and sell them off as quickly as possible while avoiding almost all of the financial liability for lending decisions that were injurious to the home buyer and unsupportable from an economic perspective.

The appraiser: During the housing boom in the run-up to the financial crisis, the appraiser who evaluated the collateral of the property that would underlie a prospective mortgage was selected, hired, and paid by the mortgage originator. As a professional, the appraiser has a fiduciary obligation to render an accurate professional judgment of the value of a subject property. However, in an environment in which the originator seeks to initiate a high volume of mortgages and sell them as quickly as possible, the originator requires an appraisal for the mortgage file that will support the lending decision. An appraiser who estimates too low a value merely impedes the process.

In such a circumstance, one might imagine that the originator tells the appraiser what value to report. But such blatant dishonesty is hardly necessary. Any appraiser who wished to be successful in the environment of the real-estate boom quickly came to understand what was expected of her. Those appraisers who too frequently reported bad news in the form of a low appraisal would simply not be selected for further assignments. Instead, the originator would merely shift business to appraisers capable of providing the desired answers.

This situation illustrates a kind of incentive that we have not considered to this point, a cooperative-game incentive. In the situation described, the originator and appraiser have well-aligned incentives that need never be spoken. The originator needs a high appraisal, and the appraiser needs continued employment. The two parties can work together to get the job of floating new mortgages done, and they never need to speak an inappropriate command or explicitly offer an immoral incentive. Rather, in a cooperative-game incentive, two or more parties face incentives in which their interests lead them to cooperate in certain ways.

As described, a cooperative-game incentive is either a socially emergent or institutionally constructed incentive. In the case of the appraiser, both elements are at play. Insofar as it is merely social custom to require an appraisal showing adequate value to support a lending decision, the cooperative-game incentives shared by the originator and appraiser are socially emergent. However, if rules promulgated by the originator's regulators require such an appraisal, then this cooperative-game incentive would be a subclass of an institutionally constructed incentive.

Cooperative-game incentives, generally considered, arise in many contexts. For example, the financial well-being of a husband and wife are closely tied, and this fact gives both spouses a reason to cooperate in managing the household's income and expenditures. But cooperative-game incentives are often perverse or illegitimate. The term "game" highlights those situations in which well-aligned incentives can be socially perverse and lead to immoral conduct. It is often the case that cooperative-game incentives need never be made explicit. Such was the case with the incentives linking appraisers and originators. Instead, both parties understand the incentives they face and understand the incentives of parties participating in their cooperative game. And this mutual comprehension of incentives can lead to cooperation that is perverse and immoral.

In the aftermath of the financial crisis, regulators instituted new rules to govern the appraisal process. Specifically, appraisers are now drawn randomly from a pool and assigned to appraisal requests. This policy should make appraisers' incomes independent of the whims of originators. However, the actual practice under such arrangements is not so benign. The appraiser still often receives a copy of the sales contract showing the contracted price before submitting an appraisal. It has not been unknown for the appraised value to exactly equal the contract price, creating what can be quite a stunning coincidence.[8]

The mortgage servicer: After a mortgage is granted, it must be serviced. The mortgage servicer typically collects the mortgage payments and forwards those receipts to the rightful recipient. In addition, the mortgage servicer also manages the escrow account if there is one, collecting property-tax payments, ensuring that the mortgagor maintains insurance on the property, and so on. As compensation, the servicer receives an annual fee computed as a percentage of the mortgage loan, usually slightly less than 0.5% of the principal of the mortgage loan. As such, the mortgage servicer primarily faces institutionally constructed incentives—those given by the firm that allocates the servicing contract. So the mortgage servicer will generally want to do a sufficiently adequate job to retain the contract, while reducing costs as much as possible. So if we think of the mortgage servicer as merely a role rather than thinking of the particular party that occupies that role, there is little of special interest as far as incentives go.

There is an important complicating factor, however. Often the mortgage servicer is the same financial institution that originated the mortgage, and it has been common for the originator to sell the mortgage, while retaining the servicing rights over the mortgage. This servicing role and the income it represents complicate matters for understanding the mortgage originator's incentives. When the originator contemplates granting a mortgage, we have seen that the plan to sell the mortgage more or less immediately provides a powerful incentive to compromise its demands for financial capacity on the part of the borrower. At the time of origination, the anticipation of a long stream of mortgage servicing income, coupled with the plan to sell the mortgage, can also provide the originator with a socially emergent incentive to grant loans it might deny on economic grounds.

The due-diligence firm: When a prospective purchaser of a pool of mortgages evaluates the value of a the mortgage in the pool, it often hires a due-diligence firm to review the paperwork and to assess the value of the individual mortgages in the pool. Often the purchaser will be an investment bank that plans to securitize the mortgages in the pool. As such, the bank appears to have clear incentives to secure an honest estimate of the value of the mortgages. Even if the bank merely wishes to sell securities based on the cash flows from the mortgages, it surely wishes never to overpay for the mortgages it purchases.

In retrospect, after a high rate of defaults, many due-diligence firms appear to have reported much too favorably on the quality of the mortgages they were analyzing. At first glance, this appears anomalous, as the bank should certainly want to know what the mortgages are really worth. However, it is important to distinguish between the bank as an institution or firm and the employees of the bank who interact with and supervise the due-diligence firm. In other words, investment banks may have their own principal-agent problems with incentive incompatibility.

Consider a bank employee who travels to the site of the originator to evaluate mortgages the originator offers for sale. Employees of the due-diligence firm accompany the representative for the investment bank. In the ordinary event, the bank employee receives compensation based on the volume of mortgages he acquires for the bank. However, if the mortgages are reported to be of low quality, the bank will refuse to buy them or will offer a price that is too low to secure their purchase. Working under time pressure and rewarded for actually buying mortgages, the bank employee on the scene might be tempted to encourage the due-diligence firm to be charitable in its evaluation.

This is another situation in which there need not be an actual solicitation for a party to ignore its duties. Instead, securing the easy review of the mortgages being examined could be accomplished via a cooperative-game incentive. The representative of the investment bank needs to buy the mortgages; the due-diligence firm needs to work cooperatively with the person from the investment bank; the due-diligence firm must expect the bank employee to report to higher management on the performance of the due-diligence firm; and the two parties are quite likely to have to work together in the future. In this context, it is easy to see that the two parties might implicitly reason as follows: We need to work together to get this job done. All the immediate incentives suggest buying mortgages. The investment bank might overpay a bit, but they are going to sell them to someone else right away in any event. And—the clincher—documentation from the due-diligence firm that the mortgages are of high quality will help the investment bank get a good price for the new collateralized mortgage obligations (CMOs) it issues anyway. When we also consider that this line of specious reasoning was taking place in a real-estate boom era, with prices always rising, we can even imagine that someone might think that exaggerating the quality of mortgages would not really hurt anyone anyway.

The securitizer: In the originate-to-distribute model, the key role of the securitizer, which is usually an investment bank, is to first acquire mortgages and collect them into a pool. Based on the cash flows from the pool, the securitizer then creates a package of securities with different instruments having diverse cash flow patterns. To make a profit, the investment bank must construct these securities in such a way that the total flow of payments from the mortgages in the purchased pool are adequate to meet the promised payments of the newly created CMOs. If the investment bank succeeds in doing so, the newly created package of securities will have a greater market value than the mortgage pool that actually throws off the foundational cash flows. This is possible, because some investors may prefer securities with particular characteristics, such as having particular maturities, certain credit quality ratings, and special patterns of cash flows. In short, when the investment bank succeeds, the cash flows thrown off by the mortgages that constitute the pool have an increased value when they are rebundled as new securities.

The securitizer's incentives are fairly clear and belong to the socially emergent type at base: buy mortgages as cheaply as possible; take those purchased cash flows in hand and, based on them, construct the set of securities that the market will value most highly; and then sell the new securities at the highest possible price. Described in this manner, there is little of interest. However, matters become more consequential when we consider a key step in the construction of the new securities—the interaction of the investment bank with credit-rating agencies.

The credit-rating agency: More than 100 years ago, a few businesses were formed that evolved into today's credit-rating agencies. At inception, these were essentially research firms and publishers. In their early days, Moody's and Standard and Poor's researched securities—mostly railroad bonds—formed an opinion of the creditworthiness of those bonds, published their evaluations, and sold those evaluations to the public. Over time, this publishing model became untenable, and credit-rating agencies moved to an issuer-pays business model—today the issuer of a security pays a credit-rating agency a fee for providing a rating of the security.

The industry has an oligopolic structure, with Standard and Poor's, Moody's, and Fitch comprising 90% of the sector. Part of the reason for the oligopoly stems from the designation by the Securities Exchange Commission of particular firms as nationally recognized statistical-rating organizations (NRSROs) and the requirement that new publicly traded securities have a rating from such an organization. This privileged role has long been important, basically providing these agencies with a regulatory license. (This requirement of an NRSRO designation is falling away now in the aftermath of the crisis, but it was fully in place until quite recently.)[9]

Firms issuing securities have always sought better ratings among the handful of NRSROs, but when firms were principally issuing plain vanilla bonds, rating agencies were mostly able to maintain their credibility. The NRSROs played a special role during the financial crisis, however. Unlike a plain vanilla corporate debenture with its quite standard features, the investment bank artfully constructs CMOs from a myriad of possibilities. The securitizer needs to construct securities that will appeal to the tastes of the investor, but also needs to manage their creation in a way that results in the best ratings, all things considered, for the CMOs being constructed. If the securitizer wants to create a security that will receive an AA rating, for example, it wants to do so in a way that minimizes the cost of achieving that rating by putting just enough financial value into the security to obtain the desired rating. Put another way, the securitizer wants to minimally achieve a desired rating and avoid creating an AA rating that is almost an AAA.

Who could possibly know better what it takes to get a particular rating than a credit-rating agency? Perhaps it was a natural outcome of the incentives in this situation, but securitizers began to hire credit-rating agencies as consultants to advise on the construction of the CMOs they were creating. For a handsome consulting fee the credit-rating agency would help firms devise a security that would achieve the desired rating at the lowest possible cost. Then, in their role as a credit-rater, the credit-rating agency would issue a rating that, not surprisingly, matched the target rating that the credit-rating agency and securitizer worked together to create.

This interaction between securitizer and credit-rating agency, conducted against a background requiring that securities receive a rating by an NRSRO, was beset by a variety of diverse and overlapping incentives. Given the regulatory setting and the valorization on NRSROs, securitizers were highly incentivized or even required to secure a rating. This was clearly an institutionally constructed incentive insofar as we choose to regard the impetus as an incentive rather than a strict mandate. There was, however, no requirement for securitizers to secure the consulting services of any credit-rating agency. That so many securitizers found it to their advantage to seek guidance from an agency in constructing their CMOs was a response to a set of socially emergent incentives.

For a credit-rating agency to act both as a consultant in the creation of securities and as a rater of securities involves a clear conflict of interest. An agency could have established a policy of refusing to accept a dual role of consultant and rater. Instead, agencies aggressively responded to the socially emergent incentives to accept the lucrative role of consultant. Rather than thinking of this as a socially emergent incentive, we might initially consider it as a institutionally constructed incentive, because the special role granted to credit-rating agencies was the result of the public policy decision to require new securities to have a rating from an NRSRO. However, the incentive for a securitizer to hire an agency as a consultant was not part of any intended incentive but an unintended consequence of the initial policy, a policy put in place before the widespread practice of securitization. Thus, when an institutionally constructed incentive gives rise to unintended additional or contrary incentives, those are socially emergent incentives. Of course that is almost the kernel of the unintended consequences of governmental action: a policy is established to provide certain institutionally constructed incentives, but the unintended consequence of such a policy is very often the instigation of a host of irrelevant or even contrary socially emergent incentives.

Before NRSROs were designated and ratings by such agencies became required, the rating published by an agency was valuable because of the information it presumably contained, not because it was the requirement of a governmental mandate. As such, a reputation for objectivity and fairness was absolutely essential to the business model of a credit-rating firm. During the CMO boom, credit-rating agencies could more freely engage in the conflicted behavior of acting as a consultant and as a rater for a particular security. After all, a diminution of objectivity and credibility in the rating process matters little if the issuer must purchase a rating in any case. Thus, an unintended consequence of requiring a rating from an NRSRO was to provide an agency with a socially emergent incentive to compromise the value of the ratings they provided by engaging in the obviously conflicted behavior of acting as both consultant and rater.

Even though the issuer of a security had to obtain a rating for the security from at least one of the NRSROs, these rating firms competed to a certain degree. As a result, securitizers shopped for the right NRSROs on the basis of price and, more importantly, malleability. Thus credit-rating agencies and securitizers had an important cooperative-game incentive. They had good reason to work together to create a security designed to achieve a given rating at the lowest possible cost. The agency might have to hold its metaphorical nose when it then granted the desired rating, but, in the spirit of cooperation, the securitizer had an incentive to agree to higher fees to assuage the delicate feelings of the agency. Thus, working together the securitizer and the agency had a cooperative-game incentive to create securities that were financially quite weak for the rating achieved and for the securitizer to lubricate this transaction by agreeing to higher-than-normal fees for the dual services the credit-rating agency provided.

The ultimate investor: At the end of the originate-to-distribute chain of mortgage production stands the ultimate investor—the financial institution that would ultimately buy the newly created CMO and hold it in a portfolio. Of course, the fundamental socially emergent incentive of such an investor was to obtain the highest level of return on the portfolio for bearing a given level of risk.

The charter or long-established operating policies of many financial institutions require them to hold a portfolio of a given credit quality as measured by the ratings of the various securities in the portfolio. In some cases, investors were prohibited from even holding securities with too low a rating. Perhaps not surprisingly, the promised yield on many CMOs was higher than the yield on a plain-vanilla corporate issue with the identical credit rating. Confronted with two AAA-rated securities with different yields, economists immediately presume that the greater yield on one security reflects its higher risk, no matter what the rating indicates. The manager of a typical investment portfolio faces pressure to deliver high yield while honoring the investment policy under which she operates. This provides a socially emergent incentive to the portfolio manager to seek the highest yield for a security with a particular rating. This incentive to "reach for yield" made such portfolio managers the natural customers for, and unwitting victims of, CMOs.

Regulatory agencies and officials: The entire originate-to-distribute chain of mortgage production was subject to close regulatory control by a host of federal regulators and agencies such as the Securities Exchange Commission, Federal Reserve Board, Office of the Comptroller of the Currency, Federal Deposit Insurance Corporation, the Department of Housing and Urban Development, and the Federal Reserve Bank of New York. At least on paper, these regulatory bodies were empowered to fully control all aspects of the industry. The ensuing financial crisis demonstrated that these agencies collectively failed to exercise their powers in a manner that behooved the public, and this was due in no small part to the incentives that regulatory agencies and their employees faced.[10]

The problem of regulatory capture, in which the presumed regulator becomes an advocate for the industry that it should be regulating, has long been familiar, and the unintended consequences of regulation and public policy have long been staples of economic literature, particularly in the field of public choice.[11] The literature on this topic is vast, and the role of regulators in causing the financial crisis is itself so pervasive that it is impossible to treat this topic in a brief compass.[12] However, there are two aspects of national policy that deserve special mention because of their role in providing destructive incentives: the Community Reinvestment Act of 1977 and the National Homeownership Strategy instituted in the 1990s.

The Community Reinvestment Act (CRA) of 1977 was intended to deter the policy of "redlining" in which financial institutions would simply refuse to lend under any terms to certain geographical areas, which were at least metaphorically indicated by a red line drawn on a map to show the excluded territory. The law had limited impact initially but received new enforcement impetus in the 1990s after a report by the Federal Reserve Bank of Boston alleged widespread (at least) de facto discrimination. This report has remained controversial, and its methodology and conclusions have been widely attacked.[13] Similarly, the CRA remains controversial and the understanding of its impact has been quite politicized. For example, Paul Krugman attacked economists at the University of Chicago for alleging that federal action eroded lending discipline in an effort stimulate mortgage lending to low income individuals and to expand home ownership, concluding, "The Community Reinvestment Act of 1977 was irrelevant to the subprime boom, which was overwhelmingly driven by loan originators not subject to the Act."[14]

One of the most recent studies of the CRA poses the key question in its title, "Did the Community Reinvestment Act (CRA) Lead to Risky Lending?," and answers the question in forceful terms: "Yes it did. . . . The effects are strongest during the time period when the market for private securitization was booming [2004–2006.]"[15] Of course, the enduring question of the act's ultimate effects will not be settled here, but it strains credulity to allege that a law that was so vigorously defended and actively enforced had no effect on the expansion of credit and the increase in homeownership that was at the heart of the subprime boom.[16]

Related to the CRA was the National Homeownership Strategy initiated in 1993 and centered in the Department of Housing and Urban Development, which wrote in 1995: "At the request of President Clinton, the US Department of Housing and Urban Development is working with dozens of national leaders in government and the housing industry to implement a National Homeownership Strategy, an unprecedented public-private partnership to increase homeownership to a record-high level over the next six years."[17]

My understanding of the effect of these two efforts is that they did matter to home lending, that they did provide institutionally constructed incentives for financial institutions to reduce their credit requirements, and they did encourage lenders to make home mortgage loans that they otherwise would not have made. In particular, the CRA and the pressures of the National Homeownership Strategy gave institutionally constructed incentives to financial institutions to relax credit standards to minorities. These relaxed standards were then extended to all applicants, as they must have been by law in order to escape charges of discrimination. As a result, financial institutions granted mortgages that they never should have because the borrowers were too financially weak to service the loans. Of course, the laws did not create institutionally constructed incentives to make bad loans, so described. But they did provide socially emergent incentives to make loans that proved to be quite bad.

But there is more to the story than this. Absent the effect of the CRA and the National Homeownership Strategy, some lending institutions were already poised to aggressively relax credit standards and to expand dubious mortgage lending. The potential profits of originating loans and being able to sell off the loans with their attendant risks almost immediately already created socially emergent incentives to make risky loans absent any stimulation from the government. However, the CRA and the National Homeownership Strategy contributed to a strengthening of the already extant incentives for reckless lending.

As a concluding speculation, and one I believe to match reality, it is reasonable also to see the proceedings as an example of cooperative-game incentives between the federal authorities that wished to see expanded lending and financial institutions ready to reap the profits of making more loans. In other words, I argue that the federal agencies urged lenders to relax credit standards while publicly denying any such encouragement. For their part, some financial institutions were all too happy to make bad loans while pretending to uphold rigorous credit standards.

CONCLUSION

This chapter has studied the nature of incentives as they are understood in economics and as they function in our contemporary economy. Incentives dominate our comprehension of the springs of human action, but often we speak of incentives as if there is only one kind and as if the word "incentive" is univocal, when in reality there are many kinds of incentives and the word has many meanings and uses.

The study uses the financial crisis of 2007–2012 as a laboratory for examining the variety of incentives and distinguishes five key types of incentives. First are natural incentives in which purely nonhuman conditions provide incentives to act in certain ways. Second, "strictly speaking" incentives arise when one party makes a specific conditional offer of something of value in order to elicit a particular behavior. Third, socially emergent incentives arise out of the interplay of human elements to create conditions that make certain behaviors attractive, but that do so without anyone intentionally creating those incentives. Fourth, governmental and other human institutions intentionally create institutionally constructed incentives to induce particular behaviors, and these incentives are often accompanied by a host of unintended consequences. That is, the institutionally constructed incentives to do one thing also constitute socially emergent incentives to do other things that are completely unintended. Fifth, and finally, cooperative-game incentives are a type of socially emergent incentive. These incentives encourage two or more parties to pursue a particular course of action while, often, denying that the behavior is related to the incentives that they confront.

Many have regarded the financial crisis as being the product of a "perfect storm" of related causes and events. I believe that a clockwork metaphor is more appropriate. In large part, the financial crisis was the result of many incentives operating together. As we have seen, ten parties in the originate-to-distribute chain had their own particular incentives. These incentives fit together like the springs and wheels of a clock to make a machine of financial destruction. Unlike a clock devised by a human, the clock that drove the financial crisis had no designer but arose organically from a variety of incentives that fit together in the most amazing way and led to an economic ruin that was anticipated by very few.

NOTES

1. Ernst Fehr and Armin Falk criticize the treatment of incentives in economics as having an inappropriate emphasis on monetary incentives and diminishing the importance of the desire to reciprocate, achieve social approval, and secure intrinsic enjoyment for work. By contrast, this chapter focuses on a tendency of economics to emphasize a too narrow conception of incentives.

2. For an explication and critical examination of this literature, see Kolb 2012.

3. In his analysis of the construction of ideal constitutions, Bruno Frey recalls the problem of the crowding-out of civic virtue and in this context mentions the Titmuss argument and speaks of "moral incentives to donate voluntarily." See Frey 1997, 1044.

4. Anderson 2011. See especially section 2.4 on coercive offers. Other key literature on the topic is provided by Stevens 1988 and Lyons 1975.

5. Berlin 1958).
6. See Nozick1974, particularly the discussion that begins on p. 263.
7. See Kolb 2011, 2010a, and 2010b.
8. I base this claim on a small sample drawn from my personal observation. I have seen an appraisal returned with a value exactly equal to a contract price of $710,000 and another appraisal that exactly matched a contract price of $695,800.
9. Frank Partnoy has long studied this issue and has written what we might think of as "Partnoy's complaint" about this industry. See Partnoy 2006, ch. 3, pp. 59–102, and 1999.
10. For an overview of the regulatory incentives that contributed to the financial crisis, see Wallison 2015. Also, Claessens and Kodres address the problem from a perspective that attempts to draw lessons for the futures of regulation.
11. See, for example, Huntington 1952, Laffont and Tirole 1991, and Stigler 1971.
12. For an account of regulation as a prime cause of the financial crisis, see Wallison 2008.
13. Munnell et al. 1992. An early paper that questioned the methodology of the Boston Fed's report is McKinley 1994.
14. Krugman 2010.
15. Agarwal, Benmelech, Bergman, and Seru 2012.
16. Peter Wallison provides an effective summary of the argument for the impact of the CRA in his "Cause and Effect: Government Policies and the Financial Crisis," *Financial Services Outlook*, American Enterprise Institute for Public Policy Research, November 2008. This article contains many references on the topic, as does Agarwal et al., "Did the Community Reinvestment Act (CRA) Lead to Risky Lending?"
17. US Department of Housing and Urban Development 1995.

REFERENCES

Agarwal, Sumit, Efraim Benmelech, Nittai Bergman, and Amit Seru. 2012. "Did the Community Reinvestment Act (CRA) Lead to Risky Lending?" Working paper.

Anderson, Scott. 2011. "Coercion." *The Stanford Encyclopedia of Philosophy*, edited by Edward N. Zalata. Winter edition. Available at http://plato.stanford.edu/archives/win2011/entries/coercion.

Arrow, Kenneth J. 1972. "Gifts and Exchanges." *Philosophy & Public Affairs* 1 (4): 343–362.

Bastiat, Frédéric. 1848. "What Is Seen and Not Seen." Available at http://www.econlib.org/library/Bastiat/basEss1.html#Chapter%201.

Berlin, Isaiah. 1958. "Two Concepts of Liberty." In *Four Essays on Liberty*. Oxford: Oxford University Press.

Buchanan, James M. "Public Choice: The Origins and Development of a Research Program." Available at http://www.gmu.edu/centers/publicchoice/pdf%20links/Booklet.pdf.

Buchanan, James M., and Gordon Tullock. 1999. *The Calculus of Consent: Logical Foundations of Constitutional Democracy.* Indianapolis: Liberty Fund. Available at http://www.econlib.org/library/Buchanan/buchCv3c8.html.

Claessens, Stijn, and Laura Kodres. 2014. "The Regulatory Responses to the Global Financial Crisis: Some Uncomfortable Questions." IMF Working Paper, March. Available at http://www.imf.org/external/pubs/ft/wp/2014/wp1446.pdf.

Conly, Sarah. 2012. *Against Autonomy: Justifying Coercive Paternalism*. Cambridge: Cambridge University Press.

Fehr, Ernst, and Armin Falk. 2002. "Psychological Foundations of Incentives." *European Economic Review* 46: 687–724.

Frey, Bruno S. 1997. "A Constitution for Knaves Crowds Out Civic Virtues." *Economic Journal* 107 (July): 1043–1053.

Grant, Ruth W. 2006. "Ethics and Incentives: A Political Approach." *American Political Science Review* 100 (1): 29–38.

Grant, Ruth W. 2002. "The Ethics of Incentives: Historical Origins and Contemporary Understandings." *Economics and Philosophy* 18: 111–139.

Grant, Ruth W. 2011. *Strings Attached: Untangling the Ethics of Incentives*. Princeton, NJ: Princeton University Press.

Huntington, Samuel P. 1952. "The Marasmus of the ICC: The Commission, the Railroads, and the Public Interest." *Yale Law Journal* 614: 467–509.

James, William. 1902. *The Varieties of Religious Experience: A Study in Human Nature. Being the Clifford Lectures on Natural Religion Delivered at Edinburgh in 1901–1902*. London: Longmans, Green, and Co.

Jensen, Michael C., and William H. Meckling. 1976. "Theory of the Firm: Managerial Behavior, Agency Costs and Ownership Structure." *Journal of Financial Economics* 3 (4): 305–360.

Kolb, Robert W. 2011. *The Financial Crisis of Our Time*. Oxford: Oxford University Press.

Kolb, Robert W. 2010a. "Incentives in the Financial Crisis of Our Time." *The Journal of Economic Asymmetries* 7 (2): 21–55.

Kolb, Robert W. 2010b. "Incentives in the Originate-to-Distribute Model of Mortgage Production." In *Lessons from the Financial Crisis: Causes, Consequences and Our Economic Future*, edited by Robert W. Kolb, 209–216. Hoboken, NJ: John Wiley and Sons.

Kolb, Robert W. 2012. *Too Much Is Not Enough: Incentives in Executive Compensation*. Oxford: Oxford University Press.

Krugman, Paul. 2010. "Things Everyone in Chicago Knows." Krugman.blogs.nytimes.com (blog). June 3.

Laffont, Jean-Jacques, and Jean Tirole. 1991. "The Politics of Government Decision Making: A Theory of Regulatory Capture." *Quarterly Journal of Economics* 106 (4): 1089–1127.

Lyons, Daniel. 1975. "Welcome Threats and Coercive Offers." *Philosophy* 50 (194): 425–436.

McKinley, Vern. 1994. "Community Reinvestment Act: Ensuring Credit Adequacy or Enforcing Credit Allocation?" *Regulation* 17 (4): 25–37.

Merton, Robert K. 1936. "The Unanticipated Consequences of Purposive Social Action." *American Sociological Review* 1 (6): 894–904.

Munnell, Alicia H., Lynn E. Browne, James McEneaney, and Geoffrey M. B. Tootell. 1992. "Mortgage Lending in Boston: Interpreting HMDA Data." Federal Reserve Bank of Boston Working Paper 92–7. Available at www.bos.frb.org/economic/wp/wp 1992/wp92_7.pdf.

Nozick, Robert. 1974. *Anarchy, State, and Utopia*. New York: Basic Books.

Partnoy, Frank. 2006. "How and Why Credit Rating Agencies Are Not Like Other Gatekeepers." In *Financial Gatekeepers: Can They Protect Investors?*, edited by Yasuyuki Fuchita and Robert E. Litan, 59–102. Washington, DC: Brookings Institution.

Partnoy, Frank. 1999. "The Siskel and Ebert of Financial Markets?: Two Thumbs Down for the Credit Rating Agencies." *Washington University Law Quarterly* 77 (3): 619–712.

Smith Adam. *An Inquiry into the Nature and Causes of the Wealth of Nations*, V.1.107.

Stevens, Robert. 1988. "Coercive Offers." *Australian Journal of Philosophy* 66 (1): 83–95.

Stigler, George J. 1971. "The Theory of Economic Regulation." *Bell Journal of Economics and Management Science* 2: 3–21.

Taylor, Frederick Winslow. 1911. *The Principles of Scientific Management*. New York: Harper and Brothers. Available at http://www.gutenberg.org/cache/epub/6435/pg 6435.html.

Thaler, Richard H., and Cass R. Sunstein. 2009. *Nudge: Improving Decisions about Health, Wealth, and Happiness*. New York: Penguin Books.

Titmuss, Richard Morris. 1971. *The Gift Relationship: From Human Blood to Social Policy*. London: Pantheon Books.

US Department of Housing and Urban Development. 1995. "Homeownership and Its Benefits." Urban Policy Brief 2, August.

Wallison, Peter J. 2008. "Cause and Effect: Government Policies and the Financial Crisis." *Financial Services Outlook*. American Enterprise Institute for Public Policy Research, November.

Wallison, Peter J. 2015. *Hidden in Plain Sight: What Really Caused the World's Worst Financial Crisis and Why It Could Happen Again*. New York: Encounter Books.

9

Goals and the Organization of Choice under Risk in Both the Long Run and the Short Run

LOLA LOPES ■

The discipline of experimental psychology was changed profoundly by World War II. A generation of young psychologists became engaged with the war effort, and when they returned to academia, they brought back working knowledge of powerful computational tools for understanding how intelligent systems process information. Ideas from signal detection theory, cybernetics, information theory, image processing, and others provided fertile new ways to think about human information processing. Most importantly, psychologists began to seek out ways to independently confirm the existence and operation of mental processes by finding ways to measure what goes on between stimulus and response and by creating novel and interesting stimuli that would not have been envisioned except for the existence of these new theoretical ideas.

I was lucky to have entered graduate school at the right time and the right place (the early 1970s at the University of California, San Diego) to experience the youth of what was then called the human information processing movement but is now known as cognitive psychology or even, as the focus has moved outside psychology proper, cognitive science. This early cognitive movement provided the basis for how I think about psychology. In short, I try to understand what people do (i.e., their final behaviors) by understanding how they do it. In my particular case, the hows can include a variety of internal processes such as attention, perception, goal seeking, encoding, information integration, comparison, and choice.

Empirically, I focus on choice data supplemented by verbal protocols, but I also have used reaction times and judgments. My primary quantitative tool has been to write and test mathematical models whose internal structure conforms to the psychological mechanisms that I believe underlie people's preferences when they choose among risky options, that is, options whose outcomes are known only in terms of probabilities. These models are tested against arrays of data and evaluated according to their ability to accurately reproduce both the quantitative and qualitative aspects of the arrays.

THE EXCEEDINGLY LONG (AND MOSTLY UNEXAMINED) HISTORY OF THOUGHT ON RISKY CHOICE

I fell into the study of risky choice by accident when I chose to study how people integrate the various pieces of information available in a poker game into a decision about how much to bet against a particular set of opponents while holding a particular hand. Poker players among my readers can rest assured that nothing I studied or discovered will make them better players, but this did get me thinking about current and past academic work on risk taking.

Academic thought on how people choose among risks can be traced back at least to the 17th century. For our purposes today, however, the critical development for risk theory was the idea of expected value first published by Christian Huygens (Daston 1980). This is the idea that, given an uncertain prospect with two or more possible outcomes, the overall value of the prospect is a probability weighted average of its individual possible outcomes.

The expectation principle had immediate useful application to the emerging field of actuarial science, but it seemed to fail when applied to certain extreme examples. The most famous of these is called the St. Petersburg paradox, and it goes like this: A fair coin is tossed until it lands tails, at which point the player is paid 2^n monetary units, say dollars, where n is the toss on which tails occurs. Tails on the first toss pays $2. Tails on the second toss pays $4. Tails on the third toss pays $8, and so forth. The question of interest is how much should a person be willing to pay for a single play of the game? Looked at through the lens of expected value, the answer is simple. The expected value of the game is infinite, and therefore a person should be willing to exchange all he or she has for a single play.

It was obvious to scholars at the time that this was a ridiculous conclusion, and there were several different proposals for how this difficulty with the expected value rule could be bypassed. The most famous of these, suggested by Daniel Bernoulli (1738/1967), continues to provide the structural basis for modern-day theories about valuing risks. Bernoulli's proposal kept the mathematical structure of the expected value rule but replaced the objective value of each outcome by its subjective counterpart or utility. He pointed out that richer men value given increments in wealth less than poorer men, suggesting that the utility of wealth is a negatively accelerated function of actual value. Thus, if people maximize expected utility rather than value, the worth of the game becomes quite small and the paradox disappears.

Since Bernoulli, most researchers on risk have assumed that Bernoulli's idea is essentially right, although the details and rhetoric have changed, and the utility function itself is commonly taken to provide both the cause and the mathematical description of what we call risk aversion, that is, people's typical preference for sure things in favor of actuarially equivalent risks. But strangely, even though Bernoulli's notion of diminishing marginal utility predicts the behavior of risk aversion, there is nothing in his formulation that can be used to define what it means for a gamble to be risky or to relate perceived riskiness to risk aversion.

DISTRIBUTIONAL THINKING: RUIN AND SAFETY-FIRST

Bernoulli's solution for the St. Petersburg paradox underlay my personal rebellion against the expected utility framework. Although I did not doubt that some mild diminishing marginal utility might operate over very large spans of wealth, it seemed evident that this had nothing to do with the perceived low value of the St. Petersburg game. The focus was all wrong. Although the key operation of diminishing marginal utility is to shrink the incremental value of successively larger prizes to virtually nothing, it seemed to me that people evaluating the game focus almost entirely on the small prizes that are most likely to be won.

My first attack on the traditional thinking (Lopes 1981) eschewed diminishing marginal utility altogether and directly questioned the practical value of the game. I imagined an inexhaustibly rich seller, someone like Scrooge McDuck, who was willing to sell the game at the bargain price of $100. Using hundreds of millions of trials in a Monte Carlo simulation, I confirmed the naive intuition that selling the game for $100 would be an almost certain moneymaker for Scrooge and no bargain at all for buyers.

As it turned out, I was not the first to take this approach to analyzing the St. Petersburg game. Some 230 years previously, Buffon (Daston 1980) had simulated the likely outcome of the game by hiring a child to toss a coin 2,000 times. On the basis of his data, Buffon estimated the value of the game to be quite small. More recently, Maurice Allais (1986) used the mathematical theory of ruin to test the importance of the size of the player's fortune in the likely outcome of the game. He found that even if the player can buy the game cheaply, and even if the player has a relatively large fortune, the probability is quite high that the player will be ruined if settlement must be made after every game.

These probability-based solutions differ fundamentally from those that retain the expectation principle in that the locus of their psychological effect involves small payoffs that occur with large probability. They differ also in that no operations are implied that distort or modify given outcomes or probabilities. Instead the focus shifts from Bernoulli's perceptual hypothesis to the computational mechanism that people use to evaluate the likely worth of the game.

Allais's (1952/1979) critique of expected utility did not stop with his analysis of the St. Petersburg game. Instead, he devised new paradoxes that directly attack the principle that the impact of a given outcome in a gamble should be directly proportional to its likelihood of occurring, which is to say that preferences between pairs of gambles should be invariant to linear transformation of their probabilities. If we take a pair of gambles and reduce the probabilities of winning in both by either subtracting a constant or dividing by a constant, the relative attractiveness of the gambles should not change.

Let me illustrate with one of Allais's choice pairs. A subject is offered a choice between Gamble A and Gamble B:

Gamble A	Gamble B
$1 million for sure	.10 to win $5 million
	.89 to win $1 million
	.01 to win nothing

Most subjects choose Gamble A. However, if the same subjects are offered two new gambles,

Gamble C	Gamble D
.11 to win $1 million	.10 to win $5 million
.89 to win nothing	.90 to win nothing

most are likely to go with Gamble D. But the two gamble pairs are linearly related. Gambles C and D are just Gambles A and B with a .89 chance of winning $1 million subtracted from each.

This choice pattern violates the linearity requirement of expected utility, but it is easily understood as demonstrating people's preference for safety. In the choice between Gambles A and B, people pass up a pretty good chance at $5 million to ensure receiving at least $1 million. In this setting, safety comes first. In choosing between Gambles C and D, however, the far likeliest outcome under either scenario is to win nothing, and so people opt to open the possibility of the $5-million outcome.

MODELING DISTRIBUTIONAL THINKING

My empirical research (Lopes 1984, Schneider and Lopes 1986, Lopes and Oden 1999) has not studied paradoxes directly. Instead, I have focused on exploring how people think about gambles or lotteries that have different shapes or distributions. To do this, I created a variety of multi-outcome lotteries that exhibit interesting distributions.

Figure 9.1 illustrates some of the lottery types. Each lottery has 100 prize tickets represented by tally marks. For ease of processing, prize amounts are spaced more or less evenly from high to low. Subjects are told that each lottery has the same total amount of prize money (in other words, the lotteries have equal expected value). The labels that you see—riskless, short shot, and so forth—are just for expository convenience. Subjects were presented with unlabeled lotteries two at a time and were asked to say whether they would prefer the left or the right lottery if they were allowed to draw a ticket from either for free.

In a typical experiment subjects are presented with all possible pairs of lotteries several times each, giving us reliable data about preferences. We also typically select a subset of lottery pairs and ask subjects to tell us the reasons for their choices. These verbal protocols are highly useful for revealing the underlying dimensions and logic of subjects' choices.

For example, here is a subject choosing between the short-shot and the long-shot lotteries. She says: "I choose the [short shot] because too many people got zero in the [long shot]. I would have a good chance of getting $130 in the [short shot] and this is preferable to getting 0–$98 in the [long shot]." Notice that the subject focuses on the low-value end of the distribution and chooses so as to ensure winning something. This is a pattern I have called security-mindedness.

However, when two lotteries are similar at their low ends, some subjects also consider high outcomes. Here is a subject who is normally security-minded nervously choosing the riskier long shot over the bimodal gamble. She says: "Chances of getting zero are greater in the [long shot]. On the other hand, there are better prizes in the

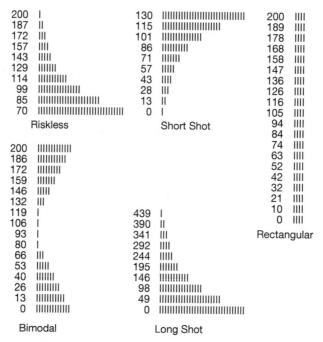

Figure 9.1 Examples of five lottery stimuli. Each tally mark represents 1 (of 100) tickets per lottery. The expected value of each lottery is $100.

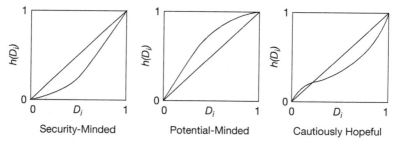

Figure 9.2 Three decumulative weighting functions mapping objective probability (abscissa) against subjective probability (ordinate).

[long shot] once you get a ticket with a prize. In fact, chances of getting a prize of less than 40 or 50 look about the same, and then the [long shot] has better prizes." She then adds: "I'm not sure I'm making a good decision here."

We might say that this subject becomes cautiously hopeful when the safety differences between two gambles are small. Her decision process is lexicographic: If she can make a decision based on safety alone, she chooses the safer lottery. But if the differences seem small, she breaks the tie by bringing in potential. In other words, she is not safety *only*, but truly safety *first*.

Attentional processes like these can be modeled mathematically by what I have called decumulative weighting functions (Lopes 1995). Figure 9.2 shows three such functions. The functions are decumulative rather than cumulative because they measure the probability of achieving an outcome *at least as* large as a focal outcome. For example, 1 refers to the probability of winning *at least* the smallest prize, whereas 0 refers to the probability of winning *more than* the largest prize.

The functions map objective decumulative probabilities on the abscissa against subjective probability weights on the ordinate. The slope of the function gives the amount of attention paid to outcomes at a given point. Steep regions represent strong attention; flat regions represent scant attention. The diagonal line shows the neutral weighting of an expected value maximizer.

The left-most panel represents a security-minded pattern. The function is steep near 1 and shallow near 0 showing that the probabilities of the worst outcomes are weighted more heavily than the probabilities of the best outcomes. The function in the middle represents the opposite pattern, one I call potential-minded. Potential-mindedness is much less common than security- mindedness but no less real (Schneider and Lopes 1986). The right-most function is a hybrid that I call cautiously hopeful. This function is steep for both the lowest and highest outcomes but flat in the middle.

The security-minded and cautiously hopeful patterns are particularly important because the former accounts for classical risk aversion without relying on nonlinear utility, and the latter accounts for the nonlinear shifts of preference that are demonstrated by the Allais paradoxes. I should also note that I do not consider attentional processes in lottery evaluation to reflect errors in assessing probabilities. Instead, they only suppose that people's values for security or potential can be expressed by how much attention is paid to the various regions of the lottery.

GAMBLING WHEN YOU MUST: ASPIRATION AND BOLD PLAY

Although accounting for risk aversion motivated research on risky choice for its first three centuries, recent decades have seen the focus switch to what has been called "risk seeking for losses." For example, in the lotteries just discussed, suppose the various outcomes are defined as losses rather than gains. Subjects are asked which of each pair of lotteries they would choose if they were required to draw a ticket from the lottery and pay the loss out of pocket.

Going back to the choice between the short shot and the long shot, the subject we heard from previously, who chose the short shot because it had the fewest opportunities to win nothing, now chooses the long shot. She says: "I choose the [long shot] because there is more of a chance to lose zero and a good chance of losing less than $130 which would be the likely outcome in the [short shot]."

How shall we explain this switch from risk aversion to risk seeking? One popular account is that subjects have a risk-averse utility function for gains and a risk-seeking utility function for losses, what has been called reflection (Kahneman and Tversky 1979). But this move begs the question. It also makes no sense. Why be risk averse in the benign environment of gains but risk seeking in the much nastier environment of losses?

Fortunately, another explanation is evident in protocols for loss choices. For illustration, here are two subjects, both of whom are reliably security-minded for gains, choosing between the rectangular and short-shot lotteries for losses. The first subject chooses the riskier rectangular lottery, saying: "Another difficult one. I chose the [rectangular] lottery because the odds are equal on each dollar amount, whereas the [short shot] shows the odds in favor of a loss of $70 or more, and very good odds of losing $130. The [rectangular] seems to be a safer risk despite the potential for a higher loss, i.e., $200 max."

The second subject goes the other way and chooses the short shot: "Chances of losing ≤ $100 are about the same for both, but [rectangular] has higher possible loss, so I picked [short shot]. I realize [short shot] gives less chance of a very low loss, which reduces my certainty about choice."

Although both subjects willingly give up the possibility of a large gain in order to avoid winning little or nothing, when confronted with losses they are torn between accepting the almost certain loss of a non-negligible amount on the one hand, and incurring a smaller but still worrisome chance of a really large loss on the other.

People's willingness to accept risk in the service of avoiding devastating loss is called "bold play" and it has been formalized under the rubric of stochastic control (Dubins and Savage 1976). A particularly notable example concerns Frederick Smith, the founder of FedEx. At one point in 1974, the company didn't have enough money to buy the fuel to keep its planes flying. Rather than give up, Smith went to Las Vegas where he gambled his last $5,000 at blackjack, winning enough to keep the company going until other funds could be found. When asked later why he'd been willing to take such a chance, he said: "What difference does it make? Without the funds for the fuel companies, we couldn't have flown anyway" (Hiskey 2011).

The key element in bold play is the operation of a specific aspiration level that lies somewhere above the status quo but typically well below the maximum. For example, Fred Smith needed less than $30,000 to stay in business; he didn't need to break the bank. The bold player, therefore, needn't become risk seeking. He only needs to choose whatever option offers the best probability of achieving the goal.

Our subjects tend to describe themselves as having modest aspiration levels for gains, for example, "winning at least a little something." Modest aspiration levels are completely consistent with security-mindedness, making these two factors hard to tease apart for gains. For losses, however, subjects describe themselves as hoping to lose little or nothing. This goal is inconsistent with security-mindedness and therefore produces the conflicted choices that we have seen previously in protocols.

DEMONSTRATING SECURITY-POTENTIAL AND ASPIRATION LEVEL IN THE LAB

Up to now, I have chosen particular data points to illustrate how subjects think about risky choice, but my experimental approach has been more systematic. In the final part of this paper, I want to show you how the ideas I have sketched here can be brought together quantitatively in a theory I call SP/A theory, SP for security-potential and A for aspiration. SP/A theory can be instantiated in an algebraic model and tested against arrays of choice data generated in the lab. The experimental work and the theoretical development are too complex to be covered here, but they are explained in full in a paper that Gregg Oden and I published in the *Journal of Mathematical Psychology* (Lopes and Oden 1999).

For the present, let me jump in by showing you the stimulus set that we used for this work (Figure 9.3). We began with a set of lotteries similar to those you have

```
$200   IIII                               $200   IIIIIIIIIIIIIIIIIIIII
$165   IIIIIIIII                          $150   IIIIIIIIIIIIIIIIIIIII
$130   IIIIIIIIIIIIIIII                    $100   IIIIIIIIIIIIIIIIIIIII
 $95   IIIIIIIIIIIIIIIIIIIIIII             $50   IIIIIIIIIIIIIIIIIIIII
 $60   IIIIIIIIIIIIIIIIIIIIIIIIIIIIII      $0    IIIIIIIIIIIIIIIIIIIII

          Riskless                                Rectangular

$200   IIII                               $200   IIIIIIIIIIIIIIIIIIIIIIIIIIIII
$150   IIIIIIIIIIIIIIII                    $150   IIIIIIIIIIIIIIII
$100   IIIIIIIIIIIIIIIIIIIIIIIIIIIIIIIIIIIIIIIIII  $100   IIII
 $50   IIIIIIIIIIIIIIII                     $50   IIIIIIIIIIIIIIII
  $0   IIII                                  $0   IIIIIIIIIIIIIIIIIIIIIIIIIIIII

           Peaked                                  Bimodal

$140   IIIIIIIIIIIIIIIIIIIIIIIIIIIIIIIII   $348   IIII
$105   IIIIIIIIIIIIIIIIIIIIIIIII           $261   IIIIIIIII
 $70   IIIIIIIIIIIIIIIII                   $174   IIIIIIIIIIIIIII
 $35   IIIIIIIIII                           $87   IIIIIIIIIIIIIIIIIIIIIII
  $0   IIII                                  $0   IIIIIIIIIIIIIIIIIIIIIIIIIIIIIIIII

         Short Shot                               Long Shot
```

Figure 9.3 Six lotteries in the standard (positive) set.

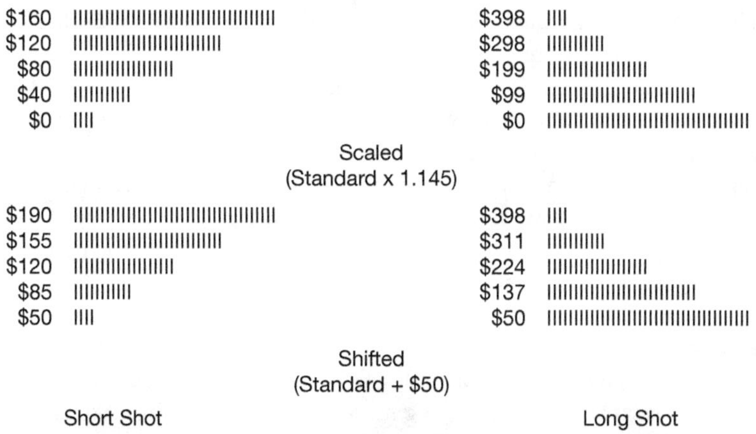

```
$160   IIIIIIIIIIIIIIIIIIIIIIIIIIIIIII    $398   IIII
$120   IIIIIIIIIIIIIIIIIIIIIIIII          $298   IIIIIIIII
 $80   IIIIIIIIIIIIIIIIII                 $199   IIIIIIIIIIIIIIII
 $40   IIIIIIIIII                          $99   IIIIIIIIIIIIIIIIIIIIII
  $0   IIII                                 $0   IIIIIIIIIIIIIIIIIIIIIIIIIIIIIIII

                         Scaled
                    (Standard x 1.145)

$190   IIIIIIIIIIIIIIIIIIIIIIIIIIIIIII    $398   IIII
$155   IIIIIIIIIIIIIIIIIIIIIIIII          $311   IIIIIIIII
$120   IIIIIIIIIIIIIIIIII                 $224   IIIIIIIIIIIIIIII
 $85   IIIIIIIIII                         $137   IIIIIIIIIIIIIIIIIIIIII
 $50   IIII                                $50   IIIIIIIIIIIIIIIIIIIIIIIIIIIIIIII

                         Shifted
                    (Standard + $50)

        Short Shot                                Long Shot
```

Figure 9.4 Examples of short shot and long shot lotteries with scaled transformation (each outcome multiplied by 1.145) and shifted transformation (each outcome with $50 added).

already seen. These are the standard gain lotteries, but we also had standard loss lotteries.

Then we applied a couple of transformations to the stimuli to create four additional sets of lotteries. Figure 9.4 shows the transformed versions of the short-shot and long-shot lotteries. The scaled lotteries have each outcome value multiplied by 1.14 and the shifted lotteries have $50 added to each gain outcome or subtracted from each loss outcome. The scaled lotteries are a control for outcome range and should behave just like the standard lotteries. The shifted lotteries, on the other hand, are theoretically critical because they ensure either an attractive gain or an unpleasant loss. For gains, all lotteries offer a minimum gain of $50 except for the riskless, which

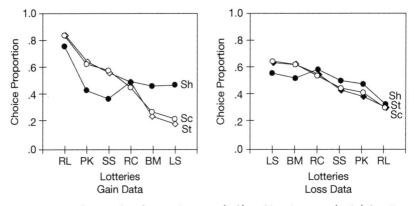

Figure 9.5 Preference data for gain lotteries (left) and loss lotteries (right) for all possible pairs of standard, scaled, and shifted lotteries. Note that preferences for standard and scaled lotteries are identical for both gains and losses. Preferences for shifted lotteries differ because the shift affects the likelihood of achieving the aspiration level.

guarantees $110. For losses, all lotteries entail a minimum loss of $50 except for the riskless, which guarantees a $110 loss.

Each of the standard, scaled, and shifted lotteries was paired with the other lotteries in its set and subjects were asked to choose which lottery of each pair they would prefer if they were allowed (for gains) or forced (for losses) to draw a ticket from the chosen lottery. Altogether, there were 90 possible lottery pairs, 45 for gains and 45 for losses, with two replications per subject per pair.

Figure 9.5 shows the data pooled over subjects, lottery pairs, and replications. The gain data are on the left and the loss data are on the right. Lottery type (standard, scaled, shifted) is the row parameter. Each data point represents the percentage of times the lottery was preferred out of the total times it was available for choice.

The data are listed along the abscissa according to the average preference of subjects for the standard lotteries. First, note that the data for standard and scaled lotteries are virtually identical for both gains and losses. For gains, the preference functions are steeply sloped, dropping more than 60% from the riskless lottery to the long shot. This is consistent with security-mindedness or, if you prefer, with risk aversion.

For losses, however, the functions are reversed in slope and flattened. Preferences are greatest for riskier lotteries such as the long shot and least for safer lotteries such as the riskless, but the difference between high and low is just 35%. Thus, although the signs of the functions are consistent with either potential mindedness or risk seeking, the general flattening of choice proportions suggests a lessening of consistency between subjects or within subjects or both.

The data for the shifted lotteries also differ from their standard and scaled counterparts. For gains, the preference function is convex, being greatest for the riskless and the long shot. We believe this happens because the $50 minimum gain guarantees that the aspiration level will be met, increasing the relative importance of potential via the SP analysis.

For losses, the pattern is concave, with the riskless and long-shot lotteries being least preferred. In SP/A terms, this comes about because the $50 minimum loss

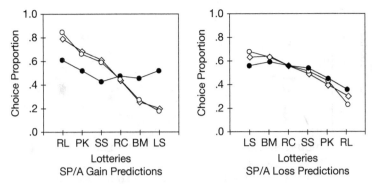

Figure 9.6 Predictions from SP/A theory for the preference data in Figure 9.5 modeled with 6 free parameters and the aspiration level set to > 0 for gains and 0 for losses. SP/A clearly captures the qualitative (shape) aspects of the data arrays.

guarantees that the aspiration cannot be met. Without the possibility of achieving a zero loss, there is less reason to accept the possibility of very high losses. In other words, the importance of security is reasserted.

Admittedly, this is a very complex array of data that may, at first blush, suggest some souped-up form of reflection. But reflection neither predicts nor explains the general flattening of the preference functions for standard and scaled loss lotteries, nor does it predict non-monotonicity in the preference functions for shifted lotteries, nor inversions in the curvature of the shifted preference functions from convex to concave.

SP/A theory, on the other hand, does predict all three phenomena, but showing this requires some model fitting. To do this, Gregg and I had to produce a mathematical model using the basic features that I have described so far. We wrote the simplest version of our model with only six free parameters. Three parameters were used for describing a generalized decumulative weighting function. We didn't use any parameters for aspiration level since we were willing to set the aspiration level for gains to winning more than zero and for losses to losing nothing. But because the SP and A assessments were modeled separately (although not sequentially), we needed one additional parameter to combine the SP and A assessments into a single SP/A value for each lottery, and a final two parameters for describing how the SP/A evaluations of two different gain lotteries or loss lotteries are combined to produce a choice.

You can see how well we did in Figure 9.6. In a nutshell, the predictions of the SP/A model do a good job of capturing the data for both gains and losses. In both panels, the data for the standard and the scaled lotteries are virtually identical, with the slope for the loss data being shallower than the slope for the gain data. For shifted lotteries, we were able to capture both the convexity for gains and the concavity for losses. Overall, the RMSD (root-mean-squared-deviation) between obtained and predicted is 0.0681. This is quite good for fitting 90 data points with six free parameters.

The reason we chose six, by the way, is because we wanted to compare SP/A to cumulative prospect theory (CPT, Tversky and Kahneman 1992), a theory that incorporates decumulative weighting, risk aversion for gains, risk seeking for losses, and a reference point. This required five parameters for CPT itself plus one for fitting the choice rule. Although I cannot go into details here, I can say that the prospect

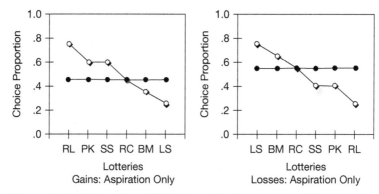

Figure 9.7 Predictions from SP/A theory for the experimental data in Figure 9.5 with 0 free parameters. This replaces decumulative weighting with expected value and sets aspiration level to > 0 for gains and 0 for losses. This highly constrained fit shows the importance of aspiration level in determining the overall shape of the data.

theory fit was less good, RMSD = 0.0810 versus 0.0681 for SP/A, even when the prospect theory parameters were allowed to assume values that are inconsistent with the theory's underlying psychological principles.

Gregg and I also wanted to push the SP/A model to its extremes (see Figure 9.7). In one direction, we eliminated the simplifying assumptions that were necessary to bring the SP/A fit down to six parameters and fit the model with a less constrained (but still respectably few) ten parameters. This reduced the RMSD to 0.0484.

The more interesting extreme, however, pushes the number of parameters as far as possible in the other direction, in other words to zero. The zero-parameter version of SP/A replaces decumulative weighting with expected value. Since the expected value was $100 for all lotteries, this effectively leaves only aspiration level to differentiate among lotteries. That is, the model considers only the probability that the outcome will be greater than zero for gains, and exactly zero for losses.

While the zero parameter fit is visibly crude, you can see that aspiration level by itself does a pretty good job of capturing the gist of the data for all three stimulus types. Quantitatively, the RMSD is 0.1206. This reasonably good approximation on zero parameters is critically important because aspiration level has been mostly ignored in psychological theories of risky choice.

This was not always so. In the early 1980s, John Payne and his colleagues (Payne, Laughhunn, and Crum 1980) did significant work on aspiration level effects in risky choice that has only recently been extended (Payne 2005). Similarly, Sandra Schneider (1992) has examined the conflicts that subjects experience when choosing between losses in the context of framing and suggests how choices among gains and choices among losses can engender different aspiration levels.

CONCLUDING THOUGHTS ON THE IMPORTANCE OF APPLICATION

I started on this line of research hoping to find a closer correspondence between the psychological theory of risky choice and the way that ordinary people experience and talk about risk taking. At the time I started out, most psychologists were devoted to theories derived from expected utility theory (von Neumann and Morgenstern, 1947). The work tended to be highly formal and there was relatively little in the way of new data to test the usefulness of the theory for describing human choice. Indeed, the strongest challenges to the descriptive adequacy of the theory came from people like Maurice Allais (1952/1979) and Daniel Ellsburg (1971), who devised telling counterexamples that struck straight to the heart of the expected utility axioms.

If science worked the way it is supposed to, these counterexamples would have shifted the descriptive focus of psychological research years earlier than they did. But this was not to be for several interesting reasons. One was that the rhetoric of the time tended to vacillate between treating the utility function as a descriptive device based on the psychophysics of value, as it was originally for Bernoulli, to being no more than a convenient notation for summarizing the pattern that we call risk aversion. The fact that diminishing marginal utility has nothing directly to do with riskiness was swept under the rug. Even worse, ideas to the contrary, such as Buffon's focus on probabilities or Allais's focus on security, were treated as manifestations of error and flawed understanding.

Fortunately for me, I discovered that there are many people working in applied fields with concepts that directly relate to human risk taking. For example, one of the most significant ideas that I ran across early on had to do with the comparison of different choice options. Although there had been some work touching on variance and skewness in distributions, this was not of much use for talking about traditional two-outcome gambles. It was only after an economist friend steered me to welfare economics that I discovered that Lorenz curves offered a wonderful way to describe the salient differences between risky distributions. It was Lorenz curves that pushed me into developing my own multi-outcome lotteries and, in a way, moved me toward seeing the need for decumulative weighting by foregrounding the importance of comparisons at the low and high ends of lotteries (Lopes 1984, 1987).

In a similar way, I was lucky to discover how different agricultural economics is from theoretical economics. Learning about subsistence farming and the safety-first principle opened my eyes to alternative ways of formalizing risky choice. Likewise, it was research on stochastic choice and ruin that introduced the notion that maximization of expected utility or expected value could be approached subject to constraints such as meeting an aspiration level. I owe a very great debt to these generous friends from other fields, including Dierdre McCloskey, who were so patient in talking with a psychologist who did not at all share their language. They made a big difference to me.

I am also grateful to more recent friends such as Hersh Shefrin and Meir Statman who have shown me in their own work on behavioral portfolio theory (BPT, Shefrin and Statman 2000) that ideas worked out in the domain of cognitive psychology can be brought back into an applied quantitative context. It feels good to see how threads from my own thinking can be aligned with well-known ideas in finance such as value at risk, and how the two separate criteria of SP/A theory are related to multiple accounts in BPT. I am especially excited to see their interest in the evolutionary implications of different approaches to risk-taking. Interest in the real-world consequences of risk attitudes has been a long time coming.

More than 20 years ago, I moved to Iowa because of my interest in a program on "The Rhetoric of Inquiry" that was founded by Deirdre McCloskey. At one of the seminars, I recall being struck by a notion from a philosopher whose name I cannot now recall. This was the idea that we scholars are engaged in what he called "the conversation of mankind," a conversation that has spanned many centuries. The idea had great force for me personally because I have often imagined myself talking to the distant and the dead, trying to convince them of some point of my own. In time, I lost the sense of a quiet conversation among colleagues and found, instead, that academic life reminded me of how it feels to attend a huge conference and not know a soul. This made it relatively easy for me to move away from research and into other university endeavors.

When Leslie Shaw asked me to participate in this conference, I tried to say no since I knew it would be hard to jump back in after ten years away. But now I am glad that she was persistent since it has shown me that the conversation has continued whether or not I was there. It is not we as people who are the participants in the conversation of mankind, but rather the ideas that we have contributed in our time. These are picked up and used in new formulations much as I picked up and used ideas from Bernoulli and Buffon.

In the long run, this is what is important. All of us have been working on risk within our own disciplinary frameworks and from our own scholarly inclinations. I find it comforting to know that no matter how large the differences can seem between our views, risk itself does not belong to any one discipline. Instead, it is a central and very real aspect of human life, worthy of all our efforts to define it, measure it, control it, and—one would hope—survive and even thrive in the face of it.

REFERENCES

Allais, M. 1952/1979. "The Foundations of a Positive Theory of Choice Involving Risk and a Criticism of the Postulates and Axioms of the American School." In *Expected Utility Hypotheses and the Allais Paradox*, edited by M. Allais and O. Hagen, 27–145. Dordrecht, Holland: Reidel.

Allais, M. 1986. "The General Theory of Random Choices in Relation to the Invariant Cardinal Utility Function and the Specific Probability Function" Working Paper C4475, Centre d'Analyse Economique, Ecole des Mines, Paris.

Bernoulli, D. 1738/1967. *Exposition of a New Theory on the Measurement of Risk.* Translated by L. Sommer. Farnsborough Hants, England: Gregg Press.

Daston, L. J. 1980. "Probabilistic Expectation and Rationality in Classical Probability Theory." *Historia Mathematica* 7: 234–260.

Dubins, L. E., and L. J. Savage. 1976. *Inequalities for Stochastic Processes: How to Gamble If You Must.* 2nd ed. New York: Dover.

Ellsburg, D. 1971. "Risk, Ambiguity, and the Savage Axioms." *Quarterly Journal of Economics* 75: 643–669.

Hiskey, D. 2011. "The Founder of FedEx Once Saved the Company by Taking Its Last $5000 and Turning It into $32,000 by Gambling in Vegas." *Today I Found Out* (blog). June 2. http://www.todayifoundout.com/index.php/2011/06/the-founder-of-fedex -once-saved-the-company-by-taking-its-last-5000-and-turning-it-into-32000-by -gambling-in-vegas/.

Kahneman, D., and A. Tversky. 1979. "Prospect Theory: An Analysis of Decision under Risk." *Econometrica* 47: 263–291.

Lopes, L. L. 1981. "Decision-Making in the Short Run." *Journal of Experimental Psychology: Human Learning and Memory* 7: 377–385.

Lopes, L. L. 1984. "Risk and Distributional Inequality." *Journal of Experimental Psychology: Human Perception and Performance* 10:465–485.

Lopes, L. L. 1987. "Between Hope and Fear: The Psychology of Risk." *Advances in Experimental Social Psychology* 20: 255–295.

Lopes, L. L. 1995. "Algebra and Process in the Modeling of Risky Choice." In *Decision Making from the Perspective of Cognitive Psychology.* Edited by J. R. Busemeyer, R. Hastie, and D. Medin, 177–220. New York: Academic Press.

Lopes, L. L., and G. C. Oden. 1999. "The Role of Aspiration Level in Risky Choice: A Comparison of Cumulative Prospect Theory and SP/A Theory." *Journal of Mathematical Psychology* 43: 286–313.

Payne, J. W. "It Is Whether You Win or Lose: The Importance of the Overall Probabilities of Winning or Losing in Risky Choice." *The Journal of Risk and Uncertainty* 30 (1): 5–19.

Payne, J. W., D. J. Laughhunn, and R. Crum. 1980. "Translation of Gambles and Aspiration Level Effects in Risky Choice Behavior." *Management Science* 26: 1039–1060.

Schneider, S. L. 1992. "Framing and Conflict: Aspiration Level Contingency, the Status Quo, and Current Theories of Risky Choice." *Journal of Experimental Psychology: Learning, Memory, and Cognition* 18 (5): 1040–1057.

Schneider, S. L., and L. L. Lopes. 1986. "Reflection in Preferences under Risk: Who and When May Suggest Why." *Journal of Experimental Psychology: Human Perception and Performance* 12 (4): 535–548.

Shefrin, H., and M. Statman. 2000. "Behavioral Portfolio Theory." *Journal of Financial and Quantitative Analysis* 35 (2): 127–151.

Tversky, A., and D. Kahneman. 1992. "Advances in Prospect Theory: Cumulative Representation of Uncertainty." *Journal of Risk and Uncertainty* 5: 297–323.

von Neumann, J., and O. Morgenstern. 1947. *Theory of Games and Economic Behavior.* 2nd ed. Princeton, NJ: Princeton University Press.

10

The Topology of Greed and Fear

GRACIELA CHICHILNISKY ∎

INTRODUCTION

This article* provides simple axioms that explain our cognitive responses to extremal events and their impact on financial markets. Extreme responses tally with the experimental or empirical observations of Minsky and other pieces in this volume (e.g., Lopes 2016, Shefrin 2016 and Yellen, 2016). The article shows how responses to extreme events arise naturally within a formal axiomatic model of decision processes introduced in 2000 (Chichilnisky 2000, 2009, 2014 and Lauwers, 1993). Extreme responses such as greed and fear arise naturally from the axioms. This helps to explain observed behavior that cannot be explained within the rationality framework provided by expected utility, and helps control negative effects caused by extreme behavior.

The problem with modeling "greed" and "fear" has been that classic theory of choice under uncertainty has no way to formalize these as rational behaviors. As a result, they are considered "irrational phenomena" without explanation. However, the concept of the rationality, as defined by classic axioms of choice under uncertainty, is itself wanting. Allais (1988), Tversky (1995), and Kahneman (1979) have shown that the predictions of standard economic models based on rational behavior conflict with the experimental evidence on how we make decisions.[1] In this article we argue that the problem lies in the standard definition of rationality, which is narrow and exclusively based on testing whether or not we optimize *expected utility*.

Expected utility has known limitations. It underestimates our responses to rare events no matter how catastrophic they may be and disregards the impact of greed and of fear (Chichilnisky 2000). This insensitivity has unintended consequences. It creates an illusion of "irrational behavior," since what we anticipate does not agree with what we observe.

Catastrophes are rare events with major consequences. Examples are asteroids, earthquakes, market crashes, or the 2008 Global Financial Crisis originating from default in mortgages and other asset-backed securities and extending more generally to global financial markets (Chichilnisky 2006, 2009, 2014, Chichilnisky, Heal and Tsomocos 1995).[2]

Although they occur rarely, catastrophes play a special role in our decision processes. Using magnetic resonance, experimental psychologists have observed that our brains react differently to situations involving extreme fear. Certain regions of the brain—for example, the amygdala—often "light up" when a person makes decisions while confronted with events that inspire extreme fear (Le Doux 1996).[3] Neurologists believe that such events alter cognitive processes and the behavior that could be otherwise expected. These observations seem relevant to the issue of rationality in decision making and inspired the results presented in this article.

In financial markets, the impact of fear is well known—as is the impact of greed. Indeed, two other pieces in this volume, Lopes (2014) and Shefrin (2014), directly address a number empirical observations of how greed and fear impact financial choices under uncertainty, in reaction to extreme events in financial markets. These emerge in response to rare events that are negative such as financial catastrophes (Shefrin 2014; e.g., the Global Financial Crisis starting in 2008), and also with positive or aspirational events such as those behind "Ponzi finance," asset bubbles, and "feeding-frenzy" phenomena in capital markets (Shefrin 2014). Both highlight the important role of "goals" and "aspirations" as explained in Lopes (2014) that are not well explained by expected utility or by expected value optimization but are explained by "constraints" that modify expected utility optimization (Lopes 2014). These constraints are a necessary consequence of our axioms, and are discussed below.

This article argues that the insensitivity of expected utility to rare events and the attendant inability to explain responses to events that invoke fear or greed, are the source of many of the experimental paradoxes and failures of rationality that have been found over the years. Theorem 1 traces the problem to a classic axiom of choice under uncertainty that was developed half a century ago in somewhat different forms by von Neumann, Morgenstern, De Groot, Arrow, Hernstein, Milnor, and Villegas, and which provides the foundation of expected utility theory. Arrow calls this axiom monotone continuity (MC)) (Arrow 1971, Chichilnisky 1998).[4] In all cases, the axiom requires that nearby stimuli should lead to nearby responses, which is reasonable enough. However the notion of "nearby" that is used in these classic pieces is not innocent: Theorem 1 establishes that this notion implies a form of *insensitivity to rare events*. Indeed, when introducing the MC axiom, Arrow explains the requirements as follows: "If one action is derived from another by altering the consequences for states of the world on an event which is sufficiently small in this sense, the preference relation of that action with respect to any other given action should be unaltered."[5] Theorem 1 proves that in requiring this axiom, Arrow is requiring that altering arbitrarily the outcomes of two actions on common events of small probabilities, would not alter the ranking; this result holds when utilities are bounded, as in the case in Arrow (1971) and in Chichilnisky (1996b, 2000, 2002).[6] Theorem 1 proves that MC is a form of insensitivity to rare events as is defined in Chichilnisky (1996b, 2000, 2002).[7] Therefore this theorem establishes that expected utility theory is insensitive to rare events due to the underlying axiom MC.[8] The notion of "nearby" implied by these axioms is explained by De Groot as follows:[9] "It distinguishes a probability distribution that is countably additive from one that is only finitely additive."[10] The axioms therefore eliminate purely finitely additive distributions. Indeed, it is now known that countably additive measures give rise to criteria of choice that are insensitive to rare events (Chichilnisky 1996b, 2000, 2002).[11] This in the reason for the paradoxical behavior of expected utility theory, which has been found wanting time and time again since its introduction in the 1950s. Expected utility theory is based on axioms that guarantee insensitivity to rare events. The critical axiom is MC or its relatives.[12] But humans are sensitive to catastrophes, which are rare events. Therefore, expected utility gives rise to a notion of rationality that is somewhat unnatural and contrary to the experimental evidence on how humans behave.

It is important to define rational behavior more broadly, and more in tune with the way humans behave. One solution is to suspend our blind belief on the axiom of MC and its relatives, and require instead *sensitivity to rare events*. This is the approach followed here, which tallies with the experimental evidence presented in other articles in this volume. Theorem 2 requires axioms of choice that include sensitivity to rare events. This is a representation theorem that characterizes all the decision criteria that satisfy the new set of axioms. Based on Chichilnisky (1996b, 2000, 2002), we prove that rational decisions maximize a combination of expected utility with other types of criteria that are sensitive to—indeed, focus on—rare events—which lead to the behavior we identify with greed and fear. Theorem 2 shows that the former are countably additive distributions while the latter are finitely additive ones. Corollary 3 shows that in the absence of rare events, both approaches coincide. Therefore this work provides an extension of classic decision theory. In the face of catastrophes, the new approach suggests new ways of evaluating risks.

As an illustration, consider the rule of thumb "Maximize expected utility while minimizing the worst losses in the event of a catastrophe." This rule is *inconsistent* with expected utility. Therefore any observer that anticipates expected utility optimization will be disappointed, and will believe that there is irrationality at stake. But this is not true. The rule is rational once we take into account rational responses to extreme events (Lopes 2014, Shefrin 2014). It is consistent with what people do on an everyday basis, and also with the experimental evidence on "jump-diffusion processes" and "heavy tails" distributions that are not well explained by standard probability theory.[13] Purely finitely additive measures have also been considered in the work of Brown and Lewis (1981) when studying myopic economic agents, and in Gilles's work on bubbles as equilibrium prices (Gilles 1989). Many examples of these phenomena appear in the articles by Lopes and Shefrin, respectively on distributional thinking, ruin and safety first, as well as in the "Ponzi schemes" behavior that appears in financial institutions that are dominated by greed, as pointed out by Minsky (Shefrin 2014), and discussed below. Here we provide a new rigorous, axiomatic treatment that is analytical and factual.

The key to the new decision criteria that is identified here is to define "nearby" in a way that is sensitive to rare events. This concept of "nearby" is what I call a "topology of greed and fear," can be sharply sensitive to catastrophes even if they are infrequent.[14] A similar topology was used in Debreu's 1953 initial formulation (Debreu 1953) of Adam Smith's invisible hand theorem.[15] The rankings of lotteries that satisfy the new axioms for choice under uncertainty are a mix of "countably additive measures" with "finitely additive measures." This combination has not been used before except in (Chichilnisky 1996a, 1996b, 2000, 2002, Chichilnisky and Shmatov 2005, and Chichilnisky, Kim and Wu 2005). These types of measures could play an important role in explaining how our brains respond to extreme risks. In practical terms this corresponds to Lopes' explanation (Lopes 2014) who observed that cognitive behavior is consistent with expected utility that is "constrained". This observation is inconsistent with classic axioms of choice and the theory of expected utility, but is nevertheless consistent with the axioms presented here.

BACKGROUND AND EXAMPLES

Uncertainty is described by a system that is in one of several states, indexed by the real numbers R with the standard Lebesgue measure μ. In each state in R a utility function $u: R^n \to R$ ranks the outcomes, which are described by vectors in R^n.[16] When the probability associated with each state is given, a description of the utility achieved in each state is called a lottery.[17] In our context a lottery is therefore a function $f: R \to R$, and the space of all lotteries is a function space L that we take to be the space of measurable and essentially bounded functions[18] $L = L_\infty(R)$ with the standard norm $\|f\| = ess\sup_{x \in R} |f(x)|$.

Axioms for choice under uncertainty describe natural and self-evident properties of choice. Continuity is a standard requirement that captures the notion that nearby stimuli give rise to nearby responses. However, as already observed continuity depends on the notion of "closeness" that is used. For example, in Arrow (1971, p. 48), two lotteries[19] are "close" to each other when they have different consequences only in small events, which Arrow defines as follows: "An event that is far out on a *vanishing sequence* is 'small' by any reasonable standards" (1971 p. 48).[20] Our definition of closeness is quite different, and uses a L_∞ sup norm that is based on uniform proximity.[21] Some catastrophic events are small under Arrow's definition but not necessarily under ours, see Example 6 in the Appendix. The core of the matter is that our definition is more sensitive to rare events than Arrow's.

A ranking function $W: L_\infty \to R$ is called insensitive to "rare" events when it neglects "small probability" events; formally, if given two lotteries (f, g), there exists $\epsilon = (f, g) > 0$, such that $W(f) > W(g)$ if and only if $W(f') > W(g')$ for all f', g' satisfying $f' = f$ and $g' = g$ a.e. on $A \subset R$ when $\mu(A^c) < \epsilon$.[22] Similarly, $W: L \to R$ is said to be insensitive to "frequent" events when for every two lotteries f, g there exists such $\delta(f, g) > 0$ that $W(f) > W(g)$ if and only if $W(f') > W(g')$ for all f', g' such that $f' = f$ and $g' = g$ a.e. on $A \subset R: \mu(A^c) > \delta$.

We say that W is sensitive to "rare" events, when W is *not* insensitive to rare events as defined above, and we say that W is sensitive to "frequent" events when W is *not* insensitive to frequent events as defined above. The ranking W is called continuous and linear when it defines a linear function on the utility of lotteries that is continuous with respect to the norm in L_∞. Here are the new axioms introduced in Chichilnisky (2000 and 2002):

> **Axiom 1: The ranking $W: L_\infty \to R$ is linear and continuous on lotteries.**
> **Axiom 2: The ranking $W: L_\infty \to R$ is sensitive to rare events.**
> **Axiom 3: The ranking $W: L_\infty \to R$ is sensitive to frequent events.**

The expected utility of a lottery f is a ranking defined by $W(f) = \int_{x \in R} f(x) d\mu(x)$, where μ is a measure with an integrable density function $\phi(.) \in L_1$[23] so $\mu(A) =$

$\int_A \phi(x)dx$, where dx is the standard Lebesgue measure on R. Expected utility satisfies Axioms 1 and 3, but not Axiom 2:

Example 1: Expected utility is insensitive to rare events.
For a proof see Chichilnisky (1996b, 2000, 2002).

Example 2: Maximization of expected utility or expected value subject to constraints, such as meeting an aspiration level or avoiding a catastrophic outcome. For empirical examples of these criteria, see Lopes (2014). Examples of expected utility subject to constraints are consistent with the new axioms presented above, but are inconsistent with expected utility theory and therefore with the classic axioms of choice under uncertainty that give rise to expected utility.

Example 3: Ponzi schemes that are highlighted in Minsky's work (Shefrin 2014) arise when the value of future utility is discounted with fixed discount factors, since in this case ever increasing borrowing from the future that could cause ruin is an event that is neglected by the "dictatorship of the present" originating from the standards axioms of choice over time (Chichilnisky 1993, 1996).

TWO APPROACHES TO DECISION THEORY

This section compares our approach with the classic theory of choice under uncertainty. Both approaches postulate that nearby stimuli lead to nearby responses or choices. There are, however, different views of what constitutes "nearby." The classic theory considers two lotteries to be close when they differ in events of small measure, while our notion is stricter, requiring that the lotteries be close almost everywhere, which implies sensitivity to rare events (see Example 6 in the Appendix).

The best way to compare the two approaches is to put side by side the decision criteria that each implies. The classic theory of choice under uncertainty, as presented in Arrow (1971) and Hernstein and Milnor (1953) shows that, on the basis of standard axioms of choice, the ranking of lotteries $W(f)$ is an expected utility function.[24]

Our decision criteria are quite different. Expected utility rankings do not satisfy our sensitivity Axiom 2, as shown in Example 1.[25] We need to modify expected utility adding another component called "purely finitely additive" elements of L_∞^*.[26] The latter embody the notion of sensitivity for rare events, and identify the "topology of greed and fear." Purely finitely additive measures are the main difference between our decision criteria and the classic expected utility criterion.

Where exactly does this difference originate? It is possible to trace the difference between the two approaches to a single classic axiom of choice, the axiom of MC stated formally in the Appendix, which contradicts our sensitivity Axiom 2:

Theorem 1: *A ranking of lotteries $W(f): L_\infty \to R$ satisfies the MC axiom if and only if it is insensitive to rare events. Formally MC $\Leftrightarrow \sim$ Axiom 2 above.*
For a proof see Chichilnisky (2009).

The following representation theorem identifies all the decision criteria that satisfy Axioms 1 and 2, and negates MC. Examples are provided in the Appendix.

Theorem 2: *A ranking of lotteries* $W: L_\infty \to R$ *satisfies Axioms 1, 3, and* $\sim$ *MC if and only if there exist two continuous linear functions on* L_∞, ϕ_1 *and* ϕ_2 *and a real number* $\lambda, 0 < \lambda < 1$, such that:

$$W(f) = \lambda \int_{x \in R} f(x)\phi_1(x)dx + (1 - \lambda)\langle f, \phi_2 \rangle, \qquad (10.1)$$

where $\int_R \phi_1(x)dx = 1$, *while* ϕ_2 *is a purely finitely additive measure on* R.[27]

Proof: This follows from Theorem 1 since the set of Axioms 1, 3, and $\sim$MC is equivalent to the set of Axioms 1, 2, and 3, because by Theorem 1 Axiom 2 is equivalent to the negation of MC. Now apply the representation theorem in Chichilnisky (1996b, 2000, 2002), to establish that a ranking that satisfies Axioms 1, 2, and 3 must have the form (10.1).

Observe that the first term in (10.1) is similar to an expected utility, where the density function could be for example $\phi_1(x) = e^{-\delta x}$. Such a density defines a countably additive measure that is absolutely continuous with respect to the Lebesgue measure.[28] The second term of (10.1) is of a different type: $\langle f, \phi_2 \rangle$ represents the action of a measure $\phi_2 \epsilon L_\infty^*$ that differs from the Lebesgue measure as it puts all weight on rare events.

The following rules of thumb provide an intuitive illustration of the decision criteria that satisfy all three axioms in Theorem 2. The actual examples are provided in the Appendix.

Example 2: Choosing a portfolio: Maximize expected utility while seeking to minimize total value losses in the event of a catastrophe.

Example 3 – Network optimization: Maximize expected through-put of electricity while seeking to minimize the probability of a black—out.

Example 4 – Heavy tails: The following function illustrates the singular measure that appears in the second term in (10.1) in a special case, for those lotteries in L_∞ that have limiting values at infinity, $L_\infty' = \{f \epsilon L_\infty : \lim_{x \to \infty}(x) < \infty\}$. Define

$$\Psi(f) = \lim_{x \to \infty} f(x). \qquad (10.2)$$

Ψ is a continuous linear function on L_∞ that is not representable by an L_1 function as in (10.1); it is also insensitive to events that are frequent with respect to the Lebesgue measure because it only takes into consideration limiting behavior, and does not satisfy Axiom 3. This asymptotic behavior tallies with the observation of heavy tails in financial markets (Chichilnisky and Shmatov 2005). Observe that the function Ψ is only defined on a subspace of L_∞; to define a purely finitely additive measure on all of L_∞, one seeks to extend Ψ to all of L_∞. The last section of this article describes what is involved in obtaining such an extension.

If one considers a family of subsets of events containing no rare events—for example, when the Lebesgue measure of all events contemplated is bounded above zero—then the two approaches are identical.

Corollary 3: In samples without rare events, a ranking that satisfies Axioms 1, 2, and 3 is consistent with expected utility theory.

Proof: Observe that Axiom 2 is an empty requirement when there are no rare events, and Axioms 1 and 3 are consistent with expected utility.

THE TOPOLOGY OF FEAR AND THE VALUE OF LIFE

Our new axioms presented above, and Debreu's work (Debreu 1953) use the same notion of continuity or "closeness" of lotteries: proximity of two lotteries requires that the supremum of their distance across all states should be small almost everywhere (a.e.). Distance is therefore measured by extremals. The formal description of this topology is the standard sup norm of L_∞. Since the topology focuses on situations involving extremal events, such as catastrophes, it makes sense to call this the "topology of fear."

Our Axiom 1 requires continuity of the ranking,[29] and it *is* satisfied by expected utility functions. However, our Axiom 2 requires a further condition, that W be sensitive to rare events with major consequences. Expected utility does not satisfy this condition as shown in Theorem 1 above, because expected utility satisfies axiom MC that is equivalent to the negation of Axiom 2. As shown in Theorem 2, the only acceptable rankings W under our new axioms are different from those in De Groot and Villegas; their rankings are expected utilities, or countably additive measures.[30]

One requirement of the classic theory, Axiom MC defined in the Appendix, is key because it creates insensitivity to rare events (Theorem 1). We can illustrate how this works in the following situation that was pointed out by Arrow (1971) about about how people value their lives.

How People Value Their Lives

The following example is from Arrow (1971, pp. 48–49); see also Chichilnisky (1998, pp. 257–258). If a is an action that involves receiving one cent, b is another that involves receiving zero cents, and c is a third action involving receiving one cent and facing a small probability of death, Arrow's MC requires that the third action involving death and one cent should be preferred to the second involving zero cents when the probability of death is small enough. Even Kenneth Arrow says of his requirement, "This may sound outrageous at first blush" (Arrow 1971, p. 48–49). Outrageous or not, we saw in Theorem 1 that MC leads to the neglect of rare events with major consequences, like death.

Theorem 1 shows that our Axiom 2 rules out these examples that Arrow calls "outrageous," because Axiom 2 is the negation of MC. We can also exemplify how our Axiom 2 provides a reasonable resolution to the problem, as follows. Axiom 2 implies that there exist catastrophic outcomes such as the risk of death, so terrible that one is unwilling to face a small probability of death to obtain one cent versus half a cent, no matter how small the probability may be. Indeed, according to our sensitivity Axiom 2, no probability of death is acceptable when one cent and half a cent are involved. However, according to our Axiom 2, in other cases there may be a small enough probability that the lottery involving death may be acceptable. It all depends on what other outcomes are involved. For example, if instead of one cent and half a cent one considers one billion dollars and half a cent—as Arrow suggests in (1971)—under certain conditions we may be willing to take the lottery that involves a small probability of death and one billion dollars over the one that offers half a cent. More to the point, a small probability of death caused by a medicine that can cure an incurable cancer may be preferable to no cure. This seems a reasonable solution to the issue that Arrow raises. Sometimes one is willing to take a risk with a small enough probability of a catastrophe; in other cases one is not. It all depends on what else is involved. This is the content of our Axiom 2.

In any case, absent rare events with major consequences, our Axiom 2 is void of meaning. In this case our theory of choice under uncertainty is consistent with or collapses to the standard expected utility theory. Therefore our work can be viewed as an extension of classic decision theory.

GERARD DEBREU AND THE INVISIBLE HAND

In establishing a mathematical proof of Adam Smith's invisible hand theorem, Gerard Debreu (Debreu 1953) was not explicitly concerned with rare or extremal events. The goal of his article was to show that any Pareto-efficient allocation can be decentralized as the equilibrium of a competitive market. This is the major conclusion from Adam Smith's invisible hand theorem. Yet in his article (Debreu 1953), Debreu proposed that, for markets with infinitely many commodities, such as dynamical models used in finance, a natural space of commodities would be the space of essentially bounded measurable functions L_∞ that we use in this article to describe lotteries. Debreu used the same notion or proximity, or "nearby" lotteries, the sup norm that we use here. Debreu chose this space because it is alone among all infinite dimensional L_p spaces in having a positive quadrant with a non-empty interior. There is a profound mathematical wisdom behind this choice. The property of positive orthants just quoted is crucial to his proof of decentralization by market prices, which relies on Hahn—Banach's separating hyperplane theorem, a theorem that requires the existence of interior or internal points to be valid (see Chichilnisky 1977, Chichilnisky and Kalman 1980).

Debreu's choice of commodity space in (Debreu 1953) leads naturally to Pareto-efficient allocations where prices are in the dual of L_∞, namely in L_∞^* which, as we saw above, contain both standard L_1 functions *and* purely finitely additive measures that are not representable by standard functions (see examples in the Appendix). In the latter case, one may lose the ability of assigning any price to a commodity within a given period of time, or within a given state of uncertainty. A non-zero price can give rise to zero value in each period and each state. Examples of this nature were constructed by Malinvaud (1953) and later on by McFadden (1975) and were extensively discussed in the literature (Radner 1965, Majumdar and Radner 1972, Chichilnisky and Kalman 1980). In 1980, this author and Peter Kalman provided the first necessary and sufficient condition to overcome the problem, a "cone condition" that is necessary and sufficient for the prices that support Pareto-efficient allocations to be always in L_1 (Chichilnisky and Kalman 1980, Chichilnisky 1993). A few years later, this result was followed by a similar uniform properness condition used in Mas Collel (1986). The results in Chichilnisky and Kalman (1980), Chichilnisky (1993), and Mas Collel (1986) modified the original

L_∞ model introduced by Debreu and ensured that all Pareto-efficient allocations would have associated market prices that are well defined in every state and every time period. They resolved the paradoxical behavior of the infinite dimensional model that Debreu had introduced in 1953, by eliminating finitely additive measures.

Debreu's original 1953 formulation was, however, prescient.

Sixty years later, we find that the general L_∞ framework that he proposed in 1953 is consistent with the decision criteria emerging from the new axioms for choice under uncertainty presented here, giving rise to prices in L_∞^* that are partly in L_1 and partly not, as shown in the representation Theorem 2 above. The L_1 part overcomes the concerns expressed above, since it creates non-zero values in each period and in each state. Yet the purely finitely part allows sensitivity to *rare events*. This solution was certainly not contemplated by the literature that followed Debreu's 1953 work, which focused instead on eliminating the purely finitely additive parts. This elimina-tion is not necessary. One can take into account—as shown above—that the criteria may have two different parts, and that one of them (in L_1) suffices to define non-zero prices in all states and periods.

In any case, Gerard Debreu's 1953 theorem on the invisible hand is compatible with the decision criteria postulated in this paper. And while such decision criteria could have seemed paradoxical at the time, it seems now that they may be better suited to explain the experimental evidence and the observations of behavior under uncertainty than expected utility, when catastrophic events are at stake.

THE AXIOM OF CHOICE AND RARE EVENTS

There is yet another interesting mathematical connection with the axioms for choice under uncertainty. The connection is, naturally enough, with the venerable axiom of choice in the foundation of mathematics. The axiom of choice postulates that there exists a universal and consistent fashion to select an element from every set. This section illustrates how it is connected with the axioms of choice under uncertainty that are proposed here.

The best way to describe the situation is by means of an example (see also Yosida and Hewitt 1952, Yosida 1974, and Chichilnisky and Kalman 1980).

REPRESENTING A PURELY FINITELY ADDITIVE MEASURE

Consider the purely finitely measure ρ defined in the Appendix, Example 7: for every Borel measurable set $A \subset R$, $\rho(A) = 1$ whenever $A \supseteq \{r : r > a,\text{for some } a \in R\}$, and $\rho(A) = 0$ otherwise. It is easy to show that ρ is not countably additive, see the Appendix.

Consider a family of countably many disjoint sets $\{V_i\}_{i=0,1,\dots}$ defined as follows

$$\text{for } i = 0, 1, \dots, \quad V_i = (i, i+1) \bigcup (-i-1, -i).$$

Observe that any two sets in this family are disjoint, namely

$$V_i \bigcap V_j = \varnothing \text{ when } i \neq j,$$

and that the union of the entire family covers the real line:

$$\bigcup_{i=0}^{\infty} V_i = \bigcup_{i=0}^{\infty} (i, i+1) \bigcup (-i-1, -i) = R.$$

Since the family $\{V_i\}_{i=0,1,\ldots}$ covers the real line, the measure of its union is one, that is,

$$\rho\left(\bigcup_{i=0}^{\infty} V_i\right) = 1. \tag{10.3}$$

Yet since every set V_i is bounded, each set has ρ—measure zero. If ρ was countably additive we would have

$$\rho\left(\bigcup_{i=0}^{\infty} V_i\right) = \sum_{i=0}^{\infty} V_i = 0, \text{ which contradicts}(10.3)$$

Since the contradiction arises from assuming that ρ is countably additive, ρ must be purely finitely additive, as we wished to prove.

Observe that ρ assigns zero measure to bounded sets, and a positive measure only to unbounded that contain a "*neighborhood of* $\{\infty\}$."[31] We can define an explicit function on L_∞ that represents the action of this purely finitely additive measure ρ if we restrict our attention to the closed subspace L'_∞ of L_∞ consisting of those functions $f(x)$ in L_∞ that have a limit when $x \to \infty$, by the formula

$$\rho(f) = \lim_{x \to \infty} f(x) \tag{10.4}$$

When restricted to functions f in the subspace L'_∞

$$\rho(f) = \int f(x)d\rho(x) = \lim_{x \to \infty} f(x).$$

Observe that one can describe the function ρ as a limit of a sequence of delta functions whose support increases without bound:

$$\rho(f) = \lim_{N \to \infty} \int f(x).\Delta_N = \lim_{N \to \infty} f(N),$$

where $\{N\}_{N=1,2,\ldots}$ is the sequence of natural numbers, and where

Δ_N is a 'delta' measure on R supported on the set $\{N\}$,
defined by $\Delta_N(A) = 1$ when $A \supset (N - \varepsilon, N + \varepsilon)$ for some $\varepsilon > 0,$[32]
and $\Delta_N(A) = 0$ otherwise.

The problem is now to extend the function ρ to a function that is defined on the entire space L_∞. This could be achieved in various ways but, as we will see, each of them requires the axiom of choice.

One can use Hahn-Banach's theorem to extend the function ρ from the closed subspace $L'_\infty \subset L_\infty$ to the entire space L_∞ while preserving its norm.[33] However, it is well known that in its general form, Hahn-Banach's theorem requires the axiom of choice. Alternatively, one can extend the notion of a limit in (10.4) to encompass all functions in L_∞, including those that have no standard limit. This can be achieved by using the notion of convergence along a free ultrafilter arising from compactifying the real line R as in Chichilnisky and Heal (1997). However, the existence of a free ultrafilter requires the axiom of choice.

This illustrates why the attempts to construct purely finitely additive measures that are representable as functions on L_∞ require the axiom of choice. Since our criteria require purely finitely additive measures, this illustrates a connection between the axiom of choice and our axioms for choice under uncertainty. This connection is not entirely surprising since both sets of axioms are about the ability to choose, universally and consistently. What is interesting, however, is that the consideration of rare events that are neglected in standard decision theory conjures up the axiom of choice.

APPENDIX

Arrow's Definition of Monotone Continuity (MC)   •

The following is the definition of continuity used in Arrow (1971, p. 48). A vanishing sequence of sets is one whose intersection is empty. For example, in the case of the real line, the sequence $\{(n, \infty)\}, n = 1, 2, 3 \ldots$ is a vanishing sequence of sets. The following is Arrow's axiom of MC: Given a and b, where $a \succ b$, a consequence c, and a vanishing sequence $\{E^i\}$, suppose the sequences of actions $\{a^i\}, \{b^i\}$ satisfy the conditions that (a^i, s) yield the same consequences as (a, s) for all s in $(E^i)^c$ and the consequence c for all s in E^i, while (b^i, s) yields the same consequences as (b, s) for all s in $(E^i)^c$ and the consequence c for all s in E^i. Then for all i sufficiently large, $a^i \succ b$ and $a \succ b^i$."

Example 5: A ranking that is insensitive to frequent events
Consider $W(f) = \lim \inf_{x \in R}(f(x))$. This ranking is insensitive to frequent events of arbitrarily large Lebesgue measure (see Chichilnisky 2000) and therefore does not satisfy our Axiom 3. In addition, this ranking is not linear.

Example 6: Two approaches to the "closeness" of lotteries,
This example provides two sequence of lotteries that converge to each other according to the notion of closeness defined in Arrow (1971), but not according to our notion of closeness using the sup norm. Our notion of closeness is thus more demanding, implying our requirement of sensitivity to rare events.

Arrow's axiom MC requires that if a lottery is derived from another by *altering its outcomes* on events that are *sufficiently small* (as defined in (Arrow 1971, p. 48), the preference relation of that lottery with respect to any other given lottery should remain unaltered.[34] To define small differences between two lotteries, or equivalently to define closeness, Arrow considers two lotteries (f, g) to be "close" when there is a vanishing sequence $\{E^i\}$, such that f and g differ only in sets of events E^i for large enough i (Arrow 1971, p. 48). This notion of closeness is based on the standard Lebesgue measure. Observe that for any vanishing sequence of events $\{E^i\}$, as i becomes large enough, the Lebesgue measure μ of the set E^i becomes small, formally $\lim_{i\to\infty}\mu(E^i)=0$. Therefore in Arrow's framework, two lotteries that differ in sets of small enough Lebesgue measure are very close to each other. Our framework is different since two lotteries f and g are "close" when they are uniformly close almost everywhere, that is, when $\sup_R |f(t)-g(t)| < \varepsilon$ a.e. for a suitably small $\varepsilon > 0$. The difference between the two concepts of "closeness" becomes sharpest when considering vanishing sequences of sets. In our case, two lotteries that differ in sets of events along a vanishing sequence E^i may never get close to each other. Consider as an example the family $\{E^i\}$ where $E^i = [i,\infty), i = 1,2,\ldots$. This is a vanishing family of events, because $E^i \subset E^{i+1}$ and $\bigcap_{i=1}^{\infty} E^i = \phi$. Consider now the lotteries $f^i(t) = K$ when $t \in E^i$ and $f^i(t) = 0$ otherwise, and $g^i(t) = 2K$ when $t \in E^i$ and $g^i(t) = 0$ otherwise. Then for all i, $\sup_{E^i} |f^i(t)-g^i(t)| = K$. In our topology this implies that f^i and g^i are *not* "close" to each other, as the difference $f^i - g^i$ does not converge to zero. No matter how far along we are along the vanishing sequence E^i the two lotteries f^i, g^i differ by K. Yet since the lotteries f^i, g^i differ from $f \equiv 0$ and $g \equiv 0$ respectively only in the set E^i, and $\{E^i\}$ is a vanishing sequence, for large enough i they are as "close" as desired according to Arrow's (1971) definition. But they are not close according to our notion of closeness, which is more demanding, as we wished to show.

The Dual Space L_{∞}^*

COUNTABLY AND PURELY FINITELY ADDITIVE MEASURES

The space of continuous linear functions on L_{∞} is a well-known space called the "dual" of L_{∞}, and is denoted L_{∞}^*. This dual space has been fully characterized in Yosida and Hewitt (1952) and Yosida (1974). Its elements are defined by integration with respect to measures on R. The dual space L_{∞}^* consists of (i) L_1 functions g that define countably additive measures μ on R by the rule

$$\mu(A) = \int_A g(x)dx,$$

where $\int_R |g(x)|dx < \infty$ and therefore μ is absolutely continuous with respect to the Lebesgue measure, namely, it gives measure zero to any set with Lebesgue measure zero, and (ii) a "non—L_1 part" consisting of purely finitely additive measures ρ that are finitely additive but they are *not* countably additive. A measure η is called finitely additive when for any family of pairwise disjoint measurable sets $\{A_i\}_{i=1,\ldots N}\eta(\bigcup_{i=1}^{N} A_i) = \sum_{i=1}^{N} \eta(A_i)$. The measure η is called countably additive when for any family of pairwise disjoint measurable sets $\{A_i\}_{i=1,\ldots\infty}\eta(\bigcup_{i=1}^{\infty} A_i) = \sum_{i=1}^{\infty} \eta(A_i)$. The countably additive measures are in a one to one correspondence with the elements of the space $L_1(R)$ of integrable functions on R. However, purely finitely additive measures cannot be identified by such functions. Nevertheless, purely finitely additive measures play an important role, since they ensure that the ranking criteria are "sensitive to rare events" (Axiom 2). These measures define continuous linear real valued functions on L_{∞}, thus belonging to the dual space of L_{∞} (Yosida 1974), but cannot be represented by functions in L_1. Observe that a purely finitely additive measure can be absolutely continuous w.r.t. the Lebesgue measure.

Example 7: A purely finitely additive measure that is not countably additive

The following defines a measure that is finitely additive but not countably additive and therefore cannot be represented by an integrable function in L_1: for every Borel set $A \subset R$, define $\rho(A) = 1$ whenever $A\{r : r > a,$ for some $a \in R\}$, and $\rho(A) = 0$ otherwise. ρ is a finitely additive set function but it is not countably additive, since R can be represented as a disjoint union of countably many bounded intervals, $R = \bigcup_{i=1}^{\infty} U_i$ each of which has zero measure $\rho(U_i) = 0$, so the sum of their measures $\sum \rho(U_i) = 0$ is zero, while by definition $\rho(R) = 1$. This measure ρ cannot be represented by an L_1 function.

NOTES

1. These works focus on the predictions of *expected utility* in general terms, and their findings led to the creation of *behavioral economics*.
2. See also Chichilnisky and Gorbachev [2004], [2005]; Chichilnisky [2000], [2002], [1996b]; and Chichilnisky and Heal [1984].
3. Not all rare events invoke fear, but situations involving extreme fear are generally infrequent.
4. Hernstein and Milnor [1953] call his version of this Axiom 2, on p. 293, and De Groot calls it Assumption SP_4 [1970 and 2004], on p. 73.
5. Quoted from Arrow [1971] p. 48, paragraph 2, next to the definition of the "monotone continuity" axiom. The axiom of monotone continuity is the second axiom defined by Arrow for choice under uncertainty; the first axiom is defined on p. 47 of [1971] and is "Ordering: The individual's choice among axioms can be represented by an ordering."
6. Bounded utilities are a standard requirement—they are required by Arrow and many others because they are the only known way to avoid the so-called St. Petersburg paradox that was discovered by Bernoulli, as discussed below in footnote 11. See also [Arrow 1971]. Therefore, in this article, we restrict ourselves to bounded utilities to avoid the St. Petersburg paradox. Arrow attributes the introduction of his monotone continuity axiom to Villegas [1964, p. 1789]. Arrow makes this attribution to Villegas in footnote 2 to page 48 of [Arrow 1971].
7. By analyzing De Groot's Assumption SP_4 that is related to Arrow's monotone continuity, we show the connection with countably additive measures. De Groot writes directly, "A property of this type distinguishes a probability distribution that is countably additive." I have shown separately that countably additive distributions are insensitive to rare events when utilities are bounded, see Chichilnisky [2002] and [2000].
8. Or its equivalents, namely axioms 2 in Hernstein and Milnor [1953], and SP_4 in De Groot [1970 and 2004].
9. Axiom SP_4 is defined on p. 73 of [De Groot 1970 and 2004].
10. De Groot states, when discussing his axiom or assumption SP_4: "A property of this type distinguishes a probability distribution that is countably additive from one that is only finitely additive." Quoted from p. 73, [De Groot 1970 and 2004].

11. This statement was formally established in Chichilnisky [2002], [2000].

12. Its relatives are axioms 2 in Herstein and Milnor [1953] and SP_4 in De Groot [1970 and 2004], and a corresponding axiom in Villegas [1964].

13. In practical terms the criteria we propose can help explain experimental observations that conflict with the standard notions of rationality: see Lopes [2014], Shefrin [2016], and—going back to older ebservations—see the Allais paradox (Chichilnisky [1996b], [2000], [2002]), the equity premium, and the risk-free rate puzzles (Mehra and Prescott [1985], Mehra [2003], Weil [1989], Chichilnisky, Dasol, and Wu, [2005]), and the prevalence of *heavy tails* and jump-diffusion processes in financial markets (Chichilnisky and Shmatov [2005]).

14. This refers to the sup norm in L_∞.

15. Debreu's article was submitted to the National Academy of Sciences by John Von Neumann, but its formulation goes much beyond Von Neumann's own axioms and his own formulation of expected utility.

16. When more is better, the function $u : R^n \to R$ is a monotonically increasing continuous function.

17. The definition of a lottery can take several forms, all leading to similar results. It can be defined by probability distributions given the outcomes in each state, or by outcomes rather than by the utility of these outcomes as we do here. We adopt this definition to simplify the presentation.

18. Boundedness of the utility functions is critical. It is required both for theoretical and empirical reasons, in particular to fit observed behavior, as explained by Arrow [1971], and observed by Bernoulli, who discovered the St. Peterburg's paradox. See also De Groot [1970 and 2004], chapter 7, "Bounded Utility Functions." The space of lotteries used here is the same $L_\infty(R)$ space used in 1953 by Debreu and others to identify commodities in infinitely many states [1953], [Chichilnisky and Kalman 1980]. Choice under uncertainty means the ranking of lotteries. An event E is a set of states. E^c is the set of states of the world not in E. A **monotone decreasing** sequence of events $\{E^i\}_{i=1}^\infty$, is a sequence for which for all $i, E^{i+1} \subset E^i$. If there is no state on the world common to all members of the sequence, $\cap_{i=1}^\infty E^i = \emptyset, \{E^i\}$ is called a vanishing sequence.

19. The equivalent to the notion of "lotteries" in our framework is the notion of "actions" as defined in Arrow [1971].

20. The following is the formal definition of continuity used by Arrow [1971, p. 48]: "Axiom of Monotone Continuity (MC): Given a and b, where $a \succ b$, a consequence c, and a vanishing sequence $\{E^i\}$, suppose the sequences of actions $\{a^i\}, \{b^i\}$ satisfy the conditions that (a^i, s) yield the same consequences as (a, s) for all s in $(E^i)^c$ and the consequence c for all s in E^i, while (b^i, s) yields the same consequences as (b, s) for all s in $(E^i)^c$ and the consequence c for all s in E^i. Then for all i sufficiently large, $a^i \succ b$ and $a^i \succ b^i$."

21. When the set of states R is endowed with a standard Lebesgue measure the notion of smallness according to Arrow's definition implies that a small event has a small Lebesgue measure. In Arrow's definition of closeness, two lotteries are close when they differ in sets of small probability. Infrequent events matter little under his definition. In our case this may not be true in some cases, as seen in the definitions and theorems that follow.

22. A^c denoted the complement of the set A.

23. $L_1(R)$ is the space of all measurable and integrable functions on $R, f \epsilon L_1 \Leftrightarrow \|f\| = \int_R |f(x)| \, dx < \infty$.

24. Expected utility functions are linear functions defined on lotteries and can be identified with countably additive measures. Here the expected utility criterion means that there exists a bounded utility function $u : R \to R$ and a probability density $\delta(t): R \to R$, $\int_R \delta(t)dx = 1$ such that f is preferred over g if and only if $W(f) > W(g)$, where $W(f) = \int_R u(f(t),t)d\delta(t)$. In our framework, the classic axioms imply that the ranking $W(.)$ is a continuous linear function on L_∞ that is defined by a countably additive measure with an integrable density function $\delta(t)$ i.e. δ is in $L_1(R)$.

25. The space L_∞^* is called the "dual space" of L_8, and is known to contain two different types of rankings $W(.)$: (1) integrable functions in $L_1(R)$ that can be represented by countably additive measures on R, and (2) 'purely finitely additive measures' which are not representable by functions in L_1[Chichilnisky 2000] (cf. the Appendix).

26. Indeed, there is an entire subspace of L_∞^* that consists of functions that do not have a representation as L_1 functions in R. This subspace consists of "purely finitely additive measures" that are defined in the Appendix, with examples provided there. Purely finitely additive measures are not representable by countably additive measures, and they cannot be represented as functions in $L_1(R)$.

27. Definitions of "countably additive" and "purely finitely additive" measures are in the Appendix under the heading "the dual space L_∞^*." Observe that phi_2 as defined above cannot be represented by an L_1 function.

28. A measure is called absolutely continuous with respect to the Lebesgue measure when it assigns zero measure to any set of Lebesgue measure zero; otherwise the measure is called singular.

29. With respect to the sup norm.

30. As already pointed out, Arrow [1971, p. 257], introduced the axiom of monotone continuity, attributing it originally to C. Villegas [1964]. It requires that modifying an action in events of small probabilities should lead to similar rankings. At the same time Hernstein and Milnor [1953, p. 293] require a form of continuity in their Axiom 2 that is similar to Arrow's monotone continuity and leads to their continuity theorem on p. 293. The axioms of continuity required by Arrow and by Hernstein and Milnor are quite different from the type of continuity that we require here. See the Appendix, Example 7.

31. By a "neighborhood of 8" we mean the sets of the form.
    $\{x \in R : x > a \text{ for some } a \in R\}$.

32. $(N - \epsilon, N + \epsilon)$ represents an open neihborhood of N.

33. The norm of the function $\lim f(x)$ defined above is one, because by definition $\|\lim(.)\| \sup_{f \in L, \|f\|=1} |\lim f(x)| = 1$.

34. This statement is a direct quote Arrow's own explanation of the axiom of monotone continuity. See [1971, p. 48, para. 2] once one translates the notion of "choosing an action: to the notion of "choosing a lottery."

REFERENCES

Allais, M. 1988. "The General Theory of Random Choices in Relation to the Invariant Cardinality Function and the Specific Probability Function." In *Risk, Decision and Rationality*, edited by B. R. Munier, 233–289. Dordrech, The Netherlands: Reidel.

Arrow, K. 1971. *Essays in the Theory of Risk Bearing*. Amsterdam: North Holland.

Brown, D., and L. Lewis. 1981. "Myopic Economic Agents." *Econometrica* 49 (2): 359–368.

Chichilnisky, G. 1977. "Non Linear Functional Analysis and Optimal Economic Growth." *Journal of Mathematical Analysis and Applications* 61: 504–520.

Chichilnisky, G., and M. Kalman. 1980. "Application of Functional Analysis to Models of Efficient Allocation of Economic Resources." *Journal of Mathematical Analysis and Applications* 30 (1):

Chichilnisky, G. 1993. "The Cone Condition, Properness, and Extremely Desirable Commodities." *Economic Theory* 3: 177–182.

Chichilnisky, G., and G. M. Heal. 1997. "Social Choice with Infinite Populations." *Social Choice and Welfare* 14 (2): 303–319.

Chichilnisky, G. 1996a. "An Axiomatic Approach to Sustainable Development." *Social Choice and Welfare* 13: 321–257.

Chichilnisky, G. 1996b. "Updating Von Neumann Morgenstern Axioms for Choice under Uncertainty." Proceedings of a Conference on Catastrophic Risks, The Fields Institute for Mathematical Sciences, Toronto, Canada.

Chichilnisky, G. 2000. "An Axiomatic Approach to Choice under Uncertainty with Catastrophic Risks." *Resource and Energy Economics*

Chichilnisky, G. 2002. "Catastrophical Risk." *Encyclopedia of Environmetrics*, vol. 1. Chicester: John Wiley and Sons, Ltd.

Chichilnisky, G, and C. Shmatov. 2005. "Risk Measures in Growth and Value Investment," to appear in *Event Risk*. Edited by. Avellaneda. New York: Risk Books and Courant Institute for Mathematical Sciences.

Chichilnisky, G. 1998. *Critical Essays in Mathematical Economics*, Volume III. *The International Library of Critical Writings in Economics* 93. Elgar Reference Collection. Cheltenham, UK, and Northampton, MA.

Chichilnisky, G., and G. M. Heal. 1984. "Competitive Equilibrium in Sobolev Spaces Without Bounds on Short Sales" (with Geoffrey Heal). *Journal of Economic Theory* 59 (2): 364–384.

Chichilnisky, G., G. Heal, and D. Tsomocos. 1995. "Option Values and Endogenous Uncertainty in MBO's ESOP's and Asset Backed Securities." *Economic Letters* 48 (3–4): 379–388.

Chichilnisky, G. 1996. "Financial Innovation in Property Catastrophe Reinsurance: The Convergence of Insurance and Capital Markets." *Risk Financing Newsletter* 13 (2): .

Chichilnisky, G., and O. Gorbachev. 2004. "Volatility in the Knowledge Economy." *Economic Theory* 24 (3): .

Chichilnisky, G., and O. Gorbachev. 2005. "Volatility and Job Creation in the Knowledge Economy." In *Essays in Dynamic General Equilibrium Theory: Festschrift for David Cass*. Edited by A. Citanna, J. Donaldson, H. Polemarchakis, P. Siconolfi, and S. Spear, 45–74. New York: Springer.

Chichilnisky, G. 2006. "General Equilibrium with Endogenous Uncertainty and Default." With Ho-Mou Wu. *Journal of Mathematical Economics* 42: .

Chichilnisky, G. "Catastrophic Risks: The Need for New Tools, Financial Instruments and Institutions," Privatization of Risk—Social Science Research Council. June 2006.

Chichilnisky, G., D. Kim, and Ho-Mou Wu. 2005. "An Axiomatic Approach to Rare Events and Equity Premium." Working Paper, Columbia University, Yale University, and National University of Taiwan.

Chichilnisky in G. 2009. "The Topology of Fear." *Journal of Mathematical Economics*.

Chichilnisky in G. 2014. "The Topology of Change: Foundations of Probability with Black Swans." In *Geometry Mechanics and Dynamics: The Legacy of J. Marsden*. Edited by Darryl D. Holm, Dong Eui Chang, Tudor Ratiu, and George Patrick. Toronto: Fields Institute for Mathematical Sciences, 2014.

Debreu, G. 1953. "Valuation Equilibrium and Pareto Optimum." *Proceedings of the National Academy of Sciences* 40: 588–592.

De Groot, Maurice H. 1970 and 2004. *Optimal Statistical Decisions*. Hoboken, NJ: John Wiley and Sons.

Gilles, C. 1989. "Charges as Equilibrium Prices and Asset Bubles." *Journal of Mathematical Economics* 18.

Heal, G. 2000. *Valuing the Future*. New York: Columbia University Press.

Hernstein, N., and J. Milnor. 1953. "An Axiomatic Approach to Measurable Utility." *Econometrica* 21: 291–297.

Kahneman, M., and A. Tversky. 1979. "Prospect Theory: An Analysis of Decisions under Risk." *Econometrica*.

Lawuers, L. 1993. "Infinite Chichilnisky Rules." *Economic Letters* 4: 349–352.

Le Doux, J. 1996. *The Emotional Brain*. New York: Simon and Schuster.

Lopes, Lola. 2016. "Goals and the Organization of Choice under Risk." this volume.

Machina, M. 1982. "Expected Utility Analysis without the Independent Axiom." *Econometrica* 50: 277–323.

Machina, M. 1989. "Dynamic Consistency and Non-Expected Utility Models of Choice under Uncertainty." *Journal of Economic Literature*, 1622–1688.

Mas Collel, A. 1986. "The Equilibrium Existence Problem in Topological Vector Lattices." *Econometrica* 54, 1039–1053.

Mehra, R. 2003. "The Equity Premium: Why Is It a Puzzle?" *AIMR* 54–69.

Majumdar, M., and R. Radner. 1972. "Shadow Prices for Infinite Growth Paths." In *Techniques of Optimization* Edited by A. V. Balakrishnan. New York: Academic Press.

Malinvaud, E. 1953. "Capital Accumulation and Efficient Allocation of Resources." *Econometrica* 21: 253–276.

McFadden, D. 1975. "An Example of the Non Existence of Malinvaud Prices in a Tight Economy." *Journal of Mathematical Economics* 2: 17–19.

Mehra, R., and E. C. Prescott. 1985. "The Equity Premium: A Puzzle." *Journal of Monetary Economics* 15 (2): 145–161.

Radner, R. 1965. "Maximal Points of Convex Sets." *Proceedings of the 5th Berkeley Symposium on Probability and Statistics*. Berkeley: University of California Press.

Shefrin, Hersh. 2016. "Assesing Hyman Minsky's Insights." this volume.

Tversky, A., and Wakker, P. 1995. "Risk Attitudes and Decision Weights." *Econometrica* 6: 1225–1280.

Villegas, C. 1964. "On Quantitative Probability σ – Algebras." *Annals of Mathematical Statistics* 35: 1789–1800.

Weil, P. 1989. "The Equity Premium Puzzle and the Risk-Free Rate Puzzle." *Journal of Monetary Economics* 24 (3): 401–421.

Yosida, K., and E. Hewitt. 1952. "Finitely Level Independent Measures." *Transactions of the American Mathematical Society* 72: 46–66.

Yosida, K. 1974. *Functional Analysis*. 4th ed. New York and Heidelberg: Springer Verlag.

A Sustainable Understanding of Instability in Minds and Markets

LESLIE SHAW ■

INTRODUCTION

The most complete history of psychological research that was foundational to behavioral economics has been Daniel Kahneman's professional autobiography, *Thinking Fast and Slow* (2011). The book received wide acclaim. If you google the title for reviews of the book you are confronted with at least four full pages of articles to choose from. These include pieces from sophisticated mass media as well as blogs from lesser-known critics and pundits. But for the purpose of discussion in this chapter, one review is especially salient.

The review author is Freeman Dyson, esteemed physics scholar and professor emeritus at Princeton University, where Nobel winner Kahneman also holds emeritus status. Dyson's critique appeared on December 22, 2011, in the *New York Review of Books*, which allows room for more analysis than other publications. Close to 80% of the article praises Kahneman's story, especially as it demonstrates how far our behavior differs from the behavior of the mythical "rational actor" who obeys the rules of classical economics. But then, as we turn the page to approach the last 20% of Dyson's substantive writing, he presents a notion that some would say is stunning. This distinguished scholar of physics suddenly changes the tone of his remarks. Dyson confronts the reader with a curiosity that he says is a notable absence from Kahneman's book. "Notably absent is the name of Sigmund Freud." "In thirty-two pages of endnotes" there is not a single reference to Freud.

Dyson is certainly aware of the degree to which deeper passions inform aspects of Freud's legacy. "Emotions are running high," he says. "Freud is now hated as passionately as he was once loved." "Kahneman evidently shares the prevalent repudiation of Freud." Nevertheless, physicist Dyson remarks that among the many volumes of Freud's productivity were two books: *The Psychopathology of Everyday Life* in 1901 and the *Ego and the Id* in 1923, which "come close to preempting two of the main themes of Kahneman's book." "The psychopathology book describes the many mistakes of judgment and of action that arise from emotional bias operating below the level of consciousness. These "Freudian slips" are examples of availability bias, caused by memories associated with strong emotions." "The *Ego and the Id* describe two levels of the mind that are similar to the System Two and System One of Kahneman; the Ego being usually conscious and rational, the Id usually unconscious and irrational." Dyson proceeds with considerable insight about the passions that are the territory of Freud. He opines that Freud can penetrate deeper than Kahneman because the literature of Freud digs deeper than science into human nature and human destiny. Dyson concludes his review with the observation that William James, another great psychologist of the 19th century, known for his *Varieties of Religious Experience: A Study in Human Nature*, is also ignored by Kahneman. It is physicist Dyson's hope that one day Freud, William James, and Daniel Kahneman will stand as three great explorers of the human psyche because each is enriched by the presence of the others.

To be sure, with the extraordinary recognition today of the discipline that has become "behavioral economics," we overlook a historical truth about the evolutionary relationship of psychology and economics. Many of the insights that are now enriching economics were prefigured in the late 19th and early 20th centuries. These decades were also a period when the border between psychology and economics was not sharply defined. In fact it is possible to discern four basic historical stages in the evolution of the economics/psychology integration, especially with regard to intertemporal choice.[1] In the first stage, time discounting was explained in terms of what psychologists now label "motivational effects"; these refer to emotional and/or hedonic[2] influences on behavior. In the second stage, at the turn of the 20th century, intertemporal choice had become viewed more in cognitive terms—a tradeoff between present and future satisfaction. Discounting was attributed to inadequacies in people's ability to imagine the future.

Remarkably, the third stage entailed an attempt to eliminate psychological content from economics altogether. At the beginning of the 20th century a total distaste for psychology became widespread among economists. They were dismayed over new developments in psychology that did not seem amenable to interpretation as utility maximization. In this regard, utility maximization formally captured economists' operationalization of the classical (Socratic) notion of rationality as choosing an action that leads to the best outcome possible. The "new development" was Freud's theory of unconscious motivation, published in 1900 (*The Interpretation of Dreams*), in which Freud laid the possibility of motivated irrationality on the table. After that event economists sought the complete independence of their profession. The psychological richness that had earlier been included in economics was supplanted by mathematical and graphical analyses intended to render psychology altogether superfluous. Psychological concepts reflecting motivational influences, such as willpower and imagination, gave way to non-evocative terms such as time preferences. These new terms were deliberately agnostic about any potential reality of deep underlying causes in human behavior.[3]

Finally, the fourth stage of the integrative evolution between psychology and economics is the discipline that began in the late 1950s when the research partnership was formed between Daniel Kahneman and the late Amos Tversky. The arrival of computer technology, in the 1960s, made psychological study of judgment and choice more explicit than ever before. Thus the fourth stage has come to maturity with an evolving army of like-minded experimental psychologists. This research army has produced a vast catalog of cognitive heuristics, biases, its own dual systems theory of mental processing, and other contributions to understanding cognitive mechanisms, all of which describe human behavioral contradictions to the classic rationality of economics. To prepare for the focus of discussion in this chapter, a brief summary of the behavioral economics thematic can be seen in Figures 11.1–11.6[4]

SUMMARY OF BEHAVIORAL ECONOMICS: UNDERSTANDING THE MIND AND ITS TWO SYSTEMS

Intuition System 1	Reasoning System 2
• Fast	• Slow
• Automatic execution	• Control process
• Effordess	• Effortful
• Associative	• Rule-governed
• Slow learning	• Slow execution
• Emotional	

Figure 11.1

SUMMARY OF BEHAVIORAL ECONOMICS

• By and large, people run mostly on System 1.
• One function of System 2 is to monitor System 1, but this is very casual.
• Emotional responses of System 1 guide ideas that come to mind; the emotional tail wags the rational dog.
• In System 1 there is a "felt" coherence of connections; in reality, there are certainly connections, but they are not necessarily coherent.
• The associative machinery has incredible richness and subdety; we come up with answers in a "blink."

Figure 11.2

SUMMARY OF BEHAVIORAL ECONOMICS CONTINUED

• Coherence is not possible in a finite human mind; the way we frame information makes a great deal of difference to what people experience.
• In System 1, ideas that are correlated in personal experience facilitate each other.
• For example: Wall Street firms' employees referencing each other versus society because it is "the market"
• Skilled performance migrates slowly, System 2 to System 1.
• Practice is not enough to acquire skill; feedback must be fast; it cannot be ambiguous.

Figure 11.3

SUMMARY OF BEHAVIORAL ECONOMICS CONTINUED

- When we attempt to keep people focused in System 2 "reasoning" effort, this is when human behavior changes in interesting ways.
- For example, people become selfish, angry, not politically correct; in other words, they become anxious and/or depressed.
- Skills are acquired when there are opportunities for feedback and learning within a social network.
- This process is always impaired by complexity.

Figure 11.4

SUMMARY OF BEHAVIORAL ECONOMICS CONTINUED

- People will always substitute something simple when facing complexity; this is easier than dealing with complexity.
- Yet developed skills are necessary for deeper psychological structure that becomes more able to negotiate complexities.
- The rational dog does have a chance to wag the emotional tail.
- It is a rare leader who will allow a team to slow the deliberating process in order to manage the complexities of a situation in an appropriate way.

Figure 11.5

SUMMARY OF BEHAVIORAL ECONOMICS: THE PARADOXICAL REALITY OF HUMAN BEINGS

• Risk Averse	• Risk Seeking
• Fundamental facts about people	• Fundamental facts about people
• Loss Averse	• Illusions of validity about their own skills
• Hate losing more than winning by a ratio of 3 to 1	• Consistently overconfident in their optimistic judgments
• Believe they are risk conservative	• Hence consistently risk-seeking in behavior

Figure 11.6

Will a fifth stage in the integration of psychology and economics begin to evolve in the 21st century? And if so, what might be the innovative directions that will flow into our collective consciousness? The remainder of this chapter establishes the case for incorporating disparate points of view that have long remained theoretically segregated. Part One provides a descriptive history of the philosophical divide that has sustained a polarized relation between academic psychology and psychoanalysis throughout the 20th century and still today. The purpose here is to mitigate the repudiation of either discipline and hope for beginning a conversation between them. An expanded conception of the dual-system point of view, essential to

Kahneman's work, yet a precursor to it, will be included. Part Two advances a recent philosophical argument that directly challenges the validity of rationality as the appropriate foundational construct for a complete understanding of human *being*. Part Three imagines an expanded perspective that includes a psychoanalytic voice for the behavioral economics revolution, and consequently a more sustainable understanding of the endogenous, ubiquitous instability within minds. Along the way we will glimpse a fundamental evolution of Freeman Dyson's physics, which has lurked behind the scenes in the genesis of the psychology-psychoanalysis divide, and how this latent presence may now be one selective factor that can bring us toward more integrative and productive research.

PART ONE: THE PSYCHOLOGY-PSYCHOANALYSIS DIVIDE

In a unique and thorough study of the history of the psychology-psychoanalysis divide, eminent British scholar Stephen Frosh[5] (1989)[6] alerts us that the concept of "mind" has been a complicated one for both psychologists and psychoanalysts. Among psychologists there has been uncertainty about the status of mental phenomena and also of the mind itself as being an object of scientific investigation. This remains true even though the most influential early modern text of psychology defined the discipline as the "science of mental life." That text, by the way, was published in 1890, and the author was William James, the fellow that Freeman Dyson noted as a second great absence in Kahneman's professional autobiography. So we had William James (1890) on "mental life," followed by Freud (1900) during a time when mathematical psychologists/economists behaved as if they were traumatized with the contradictory idea of motivated irrationality.[7] Thereafter, most of the textbook accounts of psychology reformulated the discipline as "the science of behavior." The difference between these two phrases alone symbolized a dichotomy which characterized psychology for the entire 20th century. In the course of its still-brief history, "psychology has been either the science of mind or the science of behavior. It has never been both at one and the same time."

In today's contemporary psychology, it is once again the "science of the mind" tendency that is dominant through the impact of what has come to be known as the cognitive revolution of the past 50 years. This is because advances in computer technology, as mentioned in the Introduction, have made it possible to operationalize mental functions in experimental research. "Computer simulation exhibits a particular view of the mind, a view of mental procedures that can be imitated with computer programs. Essentially the cognitive psychology discipline is a descriptive understanding that answers the question: What does this mental system look like and how does it work? Yet however important this question, it remains a limited one. It describes the syntax of the system, that is to say, the rules by which the system operates. But cognitive psychology makes no comment on semantics, e.g., the *meanings* that the whole human system itself either generates or incorporates."

"Psychoanalytic theory on the other hand has generally been more comfortable with its attitude about mind. Freud's espousal of the notion of the unconscious was intimately connected with his belief in determinism, that is, a belief that psychic events are not random but firmly caused by some underlying principle—hence the concept of an unconscious becomes a necessary one." A continuing predicament in the psychoanalytic approach is that several theoretical derivatives have appeared within the discipline since Freud. These byproducts have constructed differently nuanced images of what might be the structure of mind and therefore the processes that characterize it. A further complication is that psychoanalysis provides no acceptable research to validate clinical superiority for any of the differently nuanced theories. Even more problematic for the overall evolution of psychoanalytic theorizing was the displacement of scientific determinism, generally, which began as early as the 1920s.

Freud had based his original concept of the pleasure principle on the axiom of the conservation of energy, from Newtonian physics. He built his early metapsychology on his own innovative neuron-based unpublished "Project for a Scientific Psychology" (1895). "The language of physiology into which Freud attempted to transcribe the phenomena of psychology was in its turn rather the language of Physics which had been grafted onto the data of Psychology."[8] The early Freud had essentially adopted psychologist Gustav Fechner's theory of stability, which was based on Newton's mechanics and the concept of energy. Fechner had widely disseminated his theory as a factor in all physiological and psychological systems. Freud changed "theory of stability" to "principle of constancy" and built it into his own system. In Freud's first metapsychology, which he elaborated in the *Interpretation of Dreams*, he embedded the Newtonian physics of the day via Fechner's theory. Yet the metapsychology owed nothing at the time to analytic discovery.[9] Then, in the early part of the 20th century, the basic concepts of physics, previously thought to be secure, began to radically change.

In 1926, following Heisenberg's uncertainty principle and Schrodinger's equation in physics, a new system of quantum mechanics was underway. In the Schrodinger equation, quanta particles are treated mathematically like waves. It provides a means for calculating the energy and motion of a particle by using wave mechanics. Subsequent mathematical work interpreted that the waves in Schrodinger's equation were probability waves.[10] As Richard Feynman (1965) put it, "a very important difference between classical and quantum (physics) is that it would be impossible to predict exactly what would happen. We can only predict 'the odds'; only the probability of different events."[11] By the time Freud wrote his *New Introductory Lectures* in 1932, the scientific surety that prevailed everywhere when he wrote the *Interpretation of Dreams* was lost. Yet many of the basic earlier concepts persisted in analytic theorizing. The scientific reality of more probabilistic models of causation, however has been a key factor in behavioral economics' success, throughout the 20th century and today. Even so, probabilistic thinking has largely passed psychoanalysis by, creating confusions and dissension with regard to psychoanalysis's "scientific" status.[12]

Meanwhile, suffice it to say that the mind as visualized by psychologists is constituted by cognitive maps; perceptual, linguistic, and memory processes; and the like. In contrast to this, the "mind" of psychoanalytic researchers contains a collection of ideas, impulses and desires, and internal motivating representations of people. Therefore "when psychologists and psychoanalysts study the mind, they are essentially studying different things. The objective gaze of the psychologist aims to identify the processes that make psychological phenomena possible; the psychoanalyst attempts to make the actions and emotions of the subject intelligible through the provision of a causal explanation that is at the *level of the subject.*" In other words, the explanation is expressive of the intentions and wishes of the person concerned. "The tension between psychology and psychoanalysis is not just one of method. It is a struggle over the position of subjectivity in the scheme of things. It is a struggle about whether the human subject can be explained by processes that describe action, or whether it is necessary to include the structures of meaning and intention that make the direction of the person's enacted behavior intelligible" (Frosh, 1989).

Let us reflect, now, upon the dual-system approach as has become salient in Daniel Kahneman's work. He uses "System 1" and "System 2" as explanatory tools to help his reader understand cognitive heuristics and biases. Notably, Kahneman is not the first, nor does he claim to be the first, psychologist to use a dual-system approach. Variations on primary and secondary thought processes have long been respectable within cognitive psychology.[13] The cognitive dual system parallels the "process-product" differentiation that defines cognitive notions of unconscious. At most, cognitivists employ their dual scheme to describe the difference between thought which is unordered, unmonitored consciousness, irrational, and sometimes creative. This is the historically cognitive view of primary process. The historically cognitive secondary process is logical, well-formed, ordered, and conscious. The value of this scheme, for cognitive psychologists, is that it allows creative and irrational aspects of mental life to be incorporated into the cognitive model. However, because of its refusal of the notion of the dynamic, as in psychodynamic unconscious (which would, by the way, imply the potential of a unified mind), primary processes remain incompletely theorized in the cognitive approach. Again, these processes are described; they are not explained. This makes psychology far less fundamental in its interpretation of primary processes than is psychoanalysis.

"In the psychoanalytic (dual) account, primary processes are the language of the unconscious. They are unfettered expressions of the pleasure principle, that is to say, of the energy of internal pressure or drives as they strive for release, the goal being to return the system to rest by releasing this energy and satisfying drives. Primary processes are carriers of desire—hence the *internal pressure* for expression. They are outside the rules of logic, and they allow for contradictions, associations, and parallel processing that occurs in an unrestricted way. In the psychodynamic view these processes are primary in two senses: they are (1) present in the earliest, primitive patterns of thought that characterize infant life; and (2) the primary processes continue as the sources of the more ordered secondary processes which mark the activities of consciousness. The more ordered psychodynamic secondary processes are what are usually referred to as thoughts (as opposed to fantasies). These secondary processes arise to make ordinary functioning in the social and material world possible. Secondary processes order and integrate the inner chaotic rumblings of the unconscious into a manageable form." See exhibits in Figures 11.7–11.9[14] to review the different interpretations of these dual mind schemes, whether cognitive or psychodynamic; compare and contrast the interpretations that define the very real theoretical struggle between them (Frosh, 1989).

THE PSYCHODYNAMIC DUAL SCHEME

Primary Process	Secondary Process
• Language of the unconscious • Expression of pleasure principle • Carriers of desire • Outside rules of logic possible • Allows for contradiction • Unrestricted parallel processing • Continues as source of secondary process	• Thoughts (as opposed to fantasies) • Arise to make ordinary 'functioning in the sodal and material world • Order and integrate the inner chaotic rumblings of the unconscious into manageable form

Figure 11.7

COMPARE/CONTRAST COGNITIVE VERSUS PSYCHODYNAMIC

System 1	Primary Process
• Fast • Automatic execution • Effortless • Associative • Slow learning • Emotional	• Language of unconscious • *Expression of pleasure principle* • *Carriers of desire* • Outside logic • Allows for contradiction • Unrestricted parallel process • Continues as Source of Secondary Process

Figure 11.8

COMPARE/CONTRAST COGNITIVE VERSUS PSYCHODYNAMIC

System 2	Secondary Process
• Slow • Control process • Effortful • Rule-governed • Slow-execution	• Thoughts as opposed to fantasies • Arises to make ordinary functioning in the social and material world possible • Orders and integrates the chaoic rumblings of the unconscious

Figure 11.9

The work that is done in a psychodynamic dual approach, then, is this:

Unconscious desire generates representations in the form of primary processes which become converted by the ego's defense mechanisms (secondary process) into more manageable states, including more ordered modes of thoughts. Underneath however there always lies the continuing subversive nature of primary activity. Put differently, what psychologists investigate as "cognitive functioning" tends actually to be the products of secondary processing, which is built on the experience of failure and substitution because primary processes themselves are unsustainable in a social world. Cognitive processes are not, therefore, basic ones; they are derivatives of unconscious desire and inner human compromises which are continually produced by the painful realities of life.[15]

In summary, academic psychology has explored mental processes, mapping their relationships and the transformations they impose on behavioral and cognitive information. Psychoanalytic theory, in contrast, focuses on both the conscious and unconscious subjective structure of individuals, the patterns of intention and desire that provide supposed explanation of the direction mental processes may take. Psychology takes as its object of study the already-constructed individual subject and asks: "How do her or his psychological parts work?" Psychoanalytic theory considers what once began as a fragmented neonate and thinks about how this disorganized newborn becomes a complete or whole subject. The organizing metaphor that Stephen Frosh puts forward in his superb analysis is a linguistic one. He shows that academic psychology articulates syntax of human functioning, whereas psychoanalysis is about semantic function. While psychology is describing the grammar of mental life, psychoanalysis is after the content and personal significance of the information itself, the meaning which both generates and is generated by the syntactic transformations. In his comprehensive assessment, Frosh cautions that none of this is to say that the answer is only to add the two disciplines together. Neither one of them is all-insightful. In spite of what was shown about the inclusion of the psychodynamic to the cognitive view of dual systems, psychoanalysis has also been lax in the intellectual progress of its own development. During the past several decades psychoanalysis has failed to adequately recognize the importance of cognitive processes, and this has limited psychoanalytic insight into many aspects of ordinary psychological functioning. There is no question that psychoanalysis has much to learn methodologically and empirically from academic psychology. On the other hand, where individual subjectivity and social relations intersect to produce the social subject—and it was social subjects who caused a financial crisis—"even elegant descriptions of cognitive process cannot develop an understanding of the resonances of subjective experience."

The supposed validity of the cognitive revolution centers on a principled vision of efficiency and rationality. Due to its neglect of subjectivity, psychology fails to theorize change as more than the adoption of different strategies for coping with experience by a central unchanging self. But the psychoanalytic vision is different, and the conceptual significance of its stance is immense. There is no fixed entity, the individual; there is only a subject which becomes fixed through the activities of sociality and desire, a subject which is open to construction and which is no more the starting point of all meanings than it is the end point of all social action. Psychoanalytic theory holds out hope for actual change in the structure of subjectivity as well as in the more superficial operation of ego functions. How odd it seems that cognitive dual-system theories have not even acknowledged an earlier and more dynamic process modeling, one that they might have attempted to negate instead of simply ignore—except that negation would have required acknowledging it (Freud 1925, 235–241). At the conclusion of his exhaustive study, Stephen Frosh asks: "What is it that makes psychology lower its sights renounce its intellectual aspirations, descend to journeyman tabulator of small gains and losses; part functions and miniature processes. What fear is it that prevents psychologists from taking stock of the questions raised by their own personal lives and asking: what has our psychological science to say to this?"(1989, 250–251).

PART TWO: IRRATIONALITY AS A PSYCHO-PHILOSOPHICAL PROBLEM[16]

Jonathan Lear is a philosopher and psychoanalyst at the University of Chicago. He has received considerable and exceptional acclaim in recent years for his innovative work in the philosophical interpretation of psychoanalysis. Lear published an extraordinary essay (1998) in which he reminds us that ever since Socrates there is a presumption of rationality built into the very ideas of agency, action, and mind. Yet we are at an important moment in the history of our life with the concept of mind, because ordinary psychological experience seems to demand room for the idea of an irrational act, even though Socrates claimed that no such space is available. As we go through the basics of Lear's argument, here, the reader may be provoked to ask: "What is wrong with this picture?"[17]

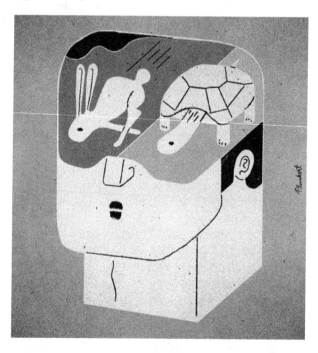

Lear uses the example of akrasia as a more general form of irrationality which he terms "reflexive breakdown," that is, the inability to give a full or coherent account of what one is doing.[18] "Reflexive breakdown is an especially important form of irrationality because humans distinguish themselves from the rest of nature by being self-interpreting animals. Humans are able to think about what they want, to subject their desires and beliefs to self-conscious scrutiny, and to modify them in the light of criticism. Moreover, a person's actions flow through her understandings of what she is doing: her understandings shape and guide her action. Reflexive breakdown is important because it is a disruption of our capacity to be self-interpreting animals. And it represents a kind of irrationality because what we are able to say or think about ourselves is contradicted by what we do."

Lear emphasizes that philosophers since Socrates have tried to make room for the idea of the irrational-mental. And from Lear's perspective the various approaches to the irrational-mental problem can be placed within two essential categories. The first category follows Aristotle, "who accounts for the apparent fact of akrasia while agreeing with Socrates that a pure case of akrasia is impossible. Following this solution, the knowledge of the better alternative is somehow shut down. The akratic, by this picture, is like a drunk, whose judgment momentarily shuts down. At the moment of acting, therefore, the akratic is actually operating from a kind of ignorance." This version of the solution to the akratic problem, as Lear describes, would be reminiscent of the random walk hypothesis of efficient financial market theory. For example, stock prices follow a random walk that would be similar to the path of a drunk walking to some designated destination. The drunk's steps to his goal would be random.

Perhaps more significant is the second category of solutions to the problem of akrasia: to divide the mind into mind-like parts. Within this category of solutions we recognize the dual mind interpretations, psychoanalytic and cognitive, that were compared and contrasted in Part One of this chapter. "Each mind-like part is itself rational, or quasi-rational, and irrationality occurs as a by-product of conflict or interaction between the parts. So each mind-like part satisfies Socratic constraints, though irrationality becomes a possibility for the mind, or agent, as a whole. Irrationality would come about through the conflict between the conscious and unconscious mind." But Jonathan Lear argues that this is not the best way to conceptualize mental functioning or to account for irrationality, though it is important to understand the temptation of the view. According to Lear, the idea that the unconscious is itself a mind-like structure seems not so much an empirical discovery as a conceptual requirement. It flows from taking both seriously and at face value the idea that people have unconscious fears, angers, desires, and beliefs. "With so much rationality seemingly built into the very idea of mind, it's a wonder we can ever take an irrational breath."

The problem with a two-mind account, says Lear, is that while it purportedly makes room for irrationality, just exactly how irrationality could occur remains a mystery. "The two-mind schema is like the solution to a dyadic equation. It tries to solve simultaneously for two apparently conflicting demands which are implicit in the idea of motivated irrationality. However, motivated irrationality *is* a genuinely *psychological* phenomenon. And the two-mind schema leaves unanswered just how the mentality of the cause brings its irrational effect about. It does not adequately illuminate the mentality of an irrational act." To make room for the concept of the irrational, says Lear, we must be able to account for "method-in-madness." We isolate something as an irrational act, as opposed to a meaningless outburst, because we see it or suspect it of having a strange logic of its own. But the two-mind schema, for Lear, does not explain the "cunning (nature) of unreason."

Lear proposes that the problem with the two-mind solution is that as a solution it is not conceptual enough. He believes that we are still not yet sufficiently at home with the concept of mind to understand the place of the irrational mental. One sign of this is that both categorical strategies for answering Socrates—for example, Aristotle's and the two-mind schema—assume that Socrates is basically right: that the concept of mind requires rationality. By contrast, Lear argues that it is intrinsic to the very idea of mind that mind must be sometimes irrational. Rather than see irrationality as coming from the outside, as from an unconscious mind which disrupts a conscious mind, one should see irrational disruptions as themselves an inherent expression of mind. Mind has a tendency to disrupt its own rational functioning. This is not only an empirical discovery about the mind. It also comes to light when we think about what it is to be minded.

Two features express fundamental aspects of mindedness. "First, it is inherent in the very idea of mind that minds are restless. They are not mere algorithm-performing machines, and they do not merely follow out the logical consequences of an agent's beliefs and desires. Rather, it is part of the very idea of mind that mind must be able to make leaps and associations, to bring things together and divide them up in all sorts of strange ways. A mind must have the potential for creativity. This in turn requires that there be certain forms of restlessness embedded in mental activity." Minds must also be embodied. "A mind is a part of a living organism over which the mind has incomplete control, and a mind helps the organism to live in an environment over which the organism has incomplete control. A mind cannot be omnipotent."

Lear maintains that once we can see mind as necessarily embodied and restless, there is much else about it which can come to light. For example, "we can see that the philosophical tradition's approach to irrationality has occurred for the most part at the wrong level. Previous attempts to make room for the irrationality within the concept of mind have failed in roughly the same way that the propositional calculus fails to illuminate the concept of mathematical proof. For previous attempts have it in common that they examine neither the inner structure of the contents of the propositional attitudes nor the various possible mental operations on that inner structure. In akrasia, for example, a reason causes someone to act in a certain way in spite of the fact that there is supposedly a stronger reason within the person to act in some other way. That is, akrasia is displayed as a structure of propositional attitudes leading to an action. But what this structure does not explain is the fact of irrationality itself: in this case, *why the better reason did not engage.*"

It is Lear's view that what Freud actually discovered was mental restlessness. This suggests that "if we are to understand the myriad phenomena of motivated irrationality we have to understand how the mind effects transformations on the inner contents of propositional attitudes and other meaningful bits. Partitioning the mind along the fault lines of reason fails to capture the immanence of human irrationality. And displaying irrational outcomes, like akrasia, as organized structures of propositional attitudes makes it mysterious how the mind is then able, on occasion, to disrupt itself." What Lear wants us to realize is this: "while Socrates may be right that the system of the propositional attitudes and the actions they bring about show the mind to be inherently rational, Freud is right that the disruptions of this system show the mind also to be inherently irrational. Within a single human mind there are heterogeneous forms of mental activity, not all of which are rational."

One other feature of mind, given the nature of its restless embodiment, is that "mind must live with the permanent possibility of falling apart. The human psyche will, as a matter of empirical fact, have a hard time holding itself together because it is a differentiated unity."

Recall from the earlier descriptive history in Part One, that psychoanalysis begins with the idea of the fragmented neonate and asks how this vulnerable disorganization becomes a subject. Lear's argument emphasizes that the human subject is always and is always becoming a differentiated unity.[19] Therefore, in Lear's argument, what is significant about psychoanalysis is that it is the first working out of a truly non-Socratic approach to human irrationality. Rather than starting, as Socrates does, with an argument that mind must be rational, and then wondering how irrationality can be tacked on, psychoanalysis begins with the idea that mind must be sometimes irrational. The possibility of disruption is built into the very idea of mindedness.[20] This becomes especially clear if we think of the mind as a differentiated unity capable of growth. For how could a differentiated unity grow other than by disrupting itself and then, as it were, healing over that disruption?[21] All of this is obscured by any two-mind interpretation by which the unconscious is another mind.[22] Any two-mind approach is the Socratic reading of Freud, and it covers over Freud's most distinctive achievement: a truly non-Socratic answer to Socrates's challenge.

PART THREE: A SUSTAINABLE UNDERSTANDING OF INSTABILITY

The late economist Hyman Minsky, whose work is central to many of the economics chapters in this volume, seems especially prescient in his 1978 review: "The Financial Instability Hypothesis: A Restatement."[23] Minsky writes: "It is trite to acknowledge that the capitalist economies are "not behaving the way they are supposed to." However, most economists—especially the policy advising establishment in the United States—refuse to accept that at least part of the fault lies in the "supposed to." As a result, one source of the troubles of the capitalist economies is that the economic theory that underlies economic policy, which defines the "supposed to," just won't do for these economies at this time." In his assessment Minsky references Kenneth Arrow and Frank H. Hahn, *General Competitive Analysis* (1971) Chapter 14, which is a chapter on the Keynesian model. Minsky makes special effort to cite how Arrow/Hahn begin the Keynesian model discussion with a quotation from W. B. Yeats, "The Second Coming": "Things fall apart, the centre does not hold." Surely this gives us a glimpse that Minsky had some intuitive grasp of the immanence of irrationality, that mind must live with the permanent possibility of falling apart, per Lear in Part Two.

Minsky concludes his "Restatement" appraisal with this:

The financial instability hypothesis (also) suggests that while there are better ways of running our economy than the way it has been run in the recent past, there is no economic organization or magic formula which, once achieved and set in motion, solves the problem of economic policy for all times. Economies evolve, and with the internal evolution of the economic mechanism the apt structure of legislated institutions and policy operations change. There is no way one generation of economists can render their successors obsolete. I am afraid economists can never become mere technicians applying an agreed-upon theory that is fit for all seasons within an institutional structure that does not and need not change. (Minsky 1978)

We know that Minsky left no model of his economic theorizing, and we wonder why. I will offer a simple, hypothetical possibility: Minsky was certain about what he saw as foolish behaviors. Nevertheless, he may have been in over his head, given the tools he had available at the time. Surely we are provoked here to wonder what might have evolved if 21st-century psychoanalytic thinking (e.g., Lear in philosophy) and recent extraordinary productivity in psychoanalytic neuroscience[24] would have been available to engage with Minsky during the years that he was writing. Yet an alternative view is expressed by Hersh Shefrin, mathematical economist and co-editor to this volume. Shefrin has studied Minsky and believes that Minsky was just not good at math. It was something with which Minsky struggled, so Shefrin believes that Minsky consistently avoided working very hard at a model.[25]

Specific modeling that gives needed insight into the cause of bubbles, subsequent crises, and innovative financial management remains a task for economists—especially the behaviorally oriented among them. The remaining purpose in this chapter is to stimulate in the reader the idea that psychoanalytic ideas have something important to offer behavioral economics, if only at the margins of its own empirical progress.

The great body of experimental research that became the behavioral economics revolution was and remains organized around an attempt to subsume human striving under a principle (e.g., the principle of rationality) and then discerning how that principle fails. The volume of doctoral dissertations in behavioral economics and finance over the past three decades or so has organized hypotheses to be tested with some experimental design that "relaxes the assumptions" of classic rationality and then distinguishes results into some defined category of preliminary knowledge.

Suppose, however, that in a quest for a radical evaluation of theoretical possibilities we accept the argument that what we should be seeking is an understanding of the mind's self-disruptiveness, that is to say, its essential endogenous instabilities. Might we accomplish a more innovative research progress without imposing rigid frameworks upon the mind, however *relaxed* that intention has become in recent years?

At the end of his career Freud wrote an essay that attempted to sum up the success and failures of psychoanalysis. In "Analysis Terminable and Interminable" (1937) Freud writes of something that was there at his beginning, in his unpublished paper "The Project" (1895),[26] but was unjustly ignored by him in the subsequent development of his theory. Freud realized that over the decades of his own work he had neglected to attach the same importance to the idea of "quantity" of mental energy (e.g., an internal pressure) as he had attached to the idea of "dynamic." This "quantity" was actually Freud's economic line of approach, and he never used it as he might have. But in 1937, just two years before his death, Freud chose to draw attention to the neglect of his own economic approach.[27] As he points out, "quantities of energy will always be there to overwhelm the mind's defenses, whether those defenses are primitive or sophisticated. Repression is one of the minds most primitive and pervasive defenses against the unwanted and the intolerable;" however, Freud realizes, "repression is of limited value as a defense against quantity."[28]

"Repressions behave like dams against the pressure of water … reinforcements may be set up by fresh traumas, enforced frustrations, or the collateral influence of instincts upon one another. But the result is always the same, and it underlines the irresistible power of the quantitative factor in the causation of illness." Freud amends that one of the aims of analysis is to replace repressions that are insecure by reliable "ego-syntonic controls," but even that does not always achieve a desired aim to its full extent. It is always a question of the quantitative factor, which is so easily overlooked. "If the strength of the instinct is excessive, (even) the mature ego fails in its task, just as the helpless ego failed formerly."[29] Jonathan Lear (2000) emphasizes that from a psychoanalytic point of view, "this is the deepest form of human helplessness: it is helplessness in the face of too much energy. We are vulnerable to repetitions of such helplessness from the beginning to the end of our lives. But this is a peculiar kind of 'repetition' because it is a repetition of something that in itself is without content. It is the breaking through of quantity without quality. It is not a repetition of helplessness, as though helplessness were the content of the experience—as when one feels overwhelmed or anxious. It is just helplessness breaking out again. Whether it becomes a repetition, in the psychoanalytic sense of a repetition compulsion, depends on what happens next. What appear as repetition compulsions are the mind's attempts, at varying levels of failure and success, to inform this breakthrough of quantitative energy with meaning.[30]"

"From the psychoanalytic perspective, there are two distinct senses in which life is too much. First, there is the structural insight that life is consistently lived under conditions of tension. For the mind to discharge all tension is what it would be to die. This was the structural insight in 'Beyond the Pleasure Principle.' Thus it is basically a structural truth that life is too much. Second, because we are always and everywhere living under pressure, we must live with the reality of the possibility of a breakthrough in any psychological structure we have thus far achieved. This is due, in part, to the fact that psychological structure is itself a psychological achievement. Psychological structure is a response to previous deeply human experiences of loss and gain,[31] and as such, that structure is always constitutionally vulnerable. Even a healthy ego is not proof against all possible onslaughts from within or without. There is no such thing as an ego that is invulnerable to trauma. And in actual life, the psychological achievements of maturity do tend to be somewhat fragile. There is always and everywhere the possibility of being overwhelmed."

These last remarks are directly from Freud (1937), though they are as utilized in Lear, 2000. Does anyone reading them, including behavioral economists, not have a glimmer of the relevance of these words for the ubiquitous potential of financial instabilities? And this question has me return to Freeman Dyson, the physicist, and the role that his scientific discipline may have played, as the science of mental life unfolded in the 20th century. To do this I will draw wisdom from yet another psychoanalytic scholar, Ronald Britton, of London.

Freud had built so much of his earlier metapsychology (1895, 1900) on Gustav Fechner's "stability," re-titled as "constancy," that his entire foundation depended on the surety and certainty of Newtonian physics, which prevailed everywhere at the time. Britton records that suddenly, with the very inception of quantum theory, the previous certainty of the Newtonian paradigm was shattered. The unacceptable face of quantum mechanics for some, including Einstein, was the replacement of a deterministic view of matter with one governed by probability. "God does not play dice," Einstein said. If Einstein had trouble transitioning to the new quantum paradigm, can we blame Freud for clinging to his own load-bearing, carefully constructed theoretical substructure?

The psychoanalyst Britton asks: "How much did the destabilization of classical physics penetrate Freud's thinking?" (2011). Britton's clue is that the year 1932 was still early in the life of the new physics, but a well-informed man such as Freud would likely pick up on the disruptive sense of change within science. And so we hear Freud coming to grips with the reality of uncertainty a full four years before his prophetic account of 1937 that was just detailed. In the preface to his "New Introductory Lectures" (1933), Freud was already offering the explicit acceptance that psychoanalysis was not complete or rounded off and "that he would not deny the existence of gaps and uncertainties, nor would he disguise problems." (Britton 2011, 72). Then in 1937, as we saw above, Freud strives to make palatable the uncertain reality of vicissitudes that will forever derive from the endogenous quantities of psychic pressures.

Ronald Britton explains that the quantum formulation that got people philosophically excited at the time it appeared was the fundamental indeterminacy of the position of particles. One could not say that an electron is either here or there—one had to say it is here and there until the moment of measurement, which was called the collapse of the wave packet, that is, the transformation of the probability wave into a point. Britton laments, "All this has produced a world that is calculable but not imaginable"(2011, 70). He continues that the mathematical discoveries of quantum physics also drew attention to the coherence and correspondence theories of truth, which remain prominent today in psychological theorizing. It was presumed that science relied on correspondence and some kind of philosophy relied on the other. Both approaches raise philosophical problems and neither is thought to be altogether satisfactory. Quantum physics relies on neither one nor the other, but both. And, Britton emphasizes that psychoanalysis does also. "A psychoanalyst has to be able to move between the two tests; coherence and correspondence. Either can be misused; the first to indulge the pleasure principle by ignoring external circumstance and the second by dismissing the uncomfortable ideas" (2011, 71).

Britton is a participant in what is, today, the British object relations school of psychoanalytic thought. In other words, this "school" is one of the many derivatives since Freud that was noted in Part 1. But the work of the psychoanalytic Brits in recent years has been innovative and highly regarded. I will appreciably simplify here to say that this British group theoretically describes two major groupings of anxieties and defenses as a conceptual tool. The two groupings have made it easier to examine and think about how mental structures are organized at different levels of human development. Further, the two categorical groupings help conceptualize how mental structures may fluctuate throughout life, depending on how people are able to function, given the vicissitudes of endogenous pressures. This is not about competing mental systems. Rather, these two groupings grasp an internal organized perspective from which someone might view himself and his relationships with the world, throughout different developmental periods in one's life.

To keep this simple for lay understanding, one grouping of anxiety and defense is typical of the vulnerabilities of an earlier disorganized (i.e., "fragmented") infant. This state of mind tends to be characterized by an exclusive concern with one's own interests, by a sense of persecution in the face of pain and emotional distress, and by a focus on self-preservation at all costs. The nature of defense against such fears is a split inner functioning in which people are experienced in very extreme terms, either as unrealistically wonderful (good) or as unrealistically terrible (bad).[32] The second grouping of anxiety and defense is more typical of psychological structure that is achieved via development; hence it is of a form that is an inner integration. What evolves within the person is a somewhat balanced, though ambivalent relationship to the other. Feelings of concern arise, and the capacity to experience remorse for harm done to others by one's own frustrated and angry self begins. Others are experienced as separate whole persons, outside the concerns of one's own immediate personal needs. The rewards of the healthier, more mature psychological structure include feelings of independence and freedom of thought. Yet this integration is not a leap into the light for the lucky. It too can be a period of inner pain because the gains of integration must be earned, not once, but again and again.[33] At the center of this anxiety is the perennially complex problem of the relationship between egoism and altruism.[34]

Recently it has been theorized that there is a dynamic quality between the two basic mental organizations of anxiety and defense.[35] The two basically hold equilibrium with each other, yet neither is forever stabilized.[36] The two fluctuate back and forth, in varying degree, throughout life. These fluctuations may occur in a way that potentially determines a pathological relationship to one's circumstance—however strong the achievement of healthy structure may have seemed under prior circumstances.[37] Basically, the idea is about the reality of variable cycles of alternation between fragmentation and integration in thinking. No one is immune to the possibility of such cycles, with regard to thinking, in an uncertain world.

A counterpart to this in science would be, for example, Kuhn's system of the development of scientific theory as paradigm. Kuhn says that "normal" science begins when a paradigm is established. Discovery, however, creates problems because it reveals anomalies. The anomalies accumulate until the new theories that the anomalies generate provide quantities of pressure that fragment the paradigm. Scholars of the old normal paradigm may experience a fragmenting anxiety within themselves.

The new scientific certainty, by the end of Freud's life, was the probabilistic rather than deterministic nature of the universe. In the meantime behavioral economics has delivered tremendous knowledge with regard to people's choice preferences as they depend on perceptions of probability. Ronald Britton discerns that for some, probability is translated into serene certainty; for others, remote possibility is taken as dreaded certainty. What, if anything, might this imply for innovative research conversations between behavioral economics and a psychoanalytic point of view? —I believe, along with Britton, that just one intriguing question of a common interest is whether or not the concept of probability even exists for some people. If not, such individuals would only be able to entertain either certainty or possibility and any possibility could form the basis for certain hope or certain despair.

Psychoanalyst Britton refers to a statement in the Anglican Church liturgy that expresses this paradox: "in the certain hope of the resurrection." "What is certain hope?" "Is it an oxymoron or does it register a necessary human transformation?" In fact, he says, this side of theology we have to make do with probability and to treat it for all practical purposes as certainty, just as we make do with belief to provide us with the security that knowledge would bring. Otherwise, we could never leave home in a tranquil state of mind.[38]

In order to hold fast to any sense of security while one is lucky enough to be in the less pathological internal organization as a whole subjective self, a belief in probability is necessary. You could call it faith. "Faith in what, you might ask?" Britton suggests "it is faith that an answer exists that will sooner or later be found. In Physics, it is a belief in science; in Psychoanalysis, it is a belief in Psychoanalysis. Fundamentally it is a belief that continued inquiry leads toward it and that things ultimately make sense, though that sense is unknown." It occurs to me here that in economics the belief is still in a rigid principle that is believed to be known, that the aim of life is (still) rationality. Perhaps, then, what economist Minsky was capturing was a pathological aspect of economics own relation to probability. Look back at Minsky's words, here re-quoted: "I am afraid that economists can never become mere technicians applying an agreed-upon theory that is fit for all seasons. " So isn't Minsky telling us why he didn't leave a model? And I suspect that Minsky too would wonder why psychologists remain journeyman tabulators of small gains and losses. What meaning does it give us with regard to an immanence of ourselves falling apart?

A psychoanalytic view would emphasize that there is an important difference between the state of mind where probability offers security and another state of mind where any possibility, however remote, might happen; one that can only be banished by absolute certainty. And I would suggest that this difference has immense importance for how we continue to research the most recent financial crisis, as well as other asset price bubbles, followed by liquidity crises to come. How may financial decision trends become driven by states of mind where possibilities of risk that are *imaginatively perceived* as remote become banished by absolute mental certainty until it is too late. Absolute certainty does not exist in the natural order; it requires a supernatural order and people in that state of mind turn to the supernatural to find it.[39] Is probability-as-security exemplary of a more healthy human developmental state? And remote-possibility-that-must-be banished a cyclical vicissitude into human pathological thinking? According to Britton, experience in psychoanalysis would say "yes." And patients (or people who are not patients) who find their way into an inner pathological organization are characterized by their relationship to probability. Eventually whole societies may find their way into inner pathological (financial) organization. Such a circumstance would likely be typified by increased Ponzi financing as a defense against unwanted inner fragmentation.

I submit that these pathologies happen, in part, because no one wants to deal with an idea of reflexive breakdowns. Breakdowns that are not systematic cannot be easily fixed, even by computers. We never know when and in what form they will happen, just like we never know when there might be a blip in the functioning of the human soul. It is my hope that behavioral economists would open their minds, and hearts, to the idea that the capacity to accept probability as security, and to live by an uncertainty principle, can be enhanced by concepts that derive from *modern* progress in psychoanalytic thinking.

NOTES

1. See Lowenstein 1992.
2. In terms of economic utility, that people maximize pleasure obtained and minimize pain avoided. See Hogarth 2001.
3. In spite of this history, in *Choice Over Time*, it should be pointed out that Lowenstein omits some significant interest in psychoanalysis among economists

and other scholars in England in the 1920s. Frank Ramsey, a student of Keynes at Cambridge, was brilliant in philosophy and mathematics, in addition to economics. He was a close personal friend to the philosopher Wittgenstein. Ramsey suffered from a mild clinical depression throughout his adult life. He chose to undergo psychoanalytic treatment with Theodor Reik, a Freud disciple. Ramsey later joined a group in England that trained to become psychoanalysts. One of the members of Ramsey's psychoanalytic student group was James Strachey, who later edited the *Standard Edition: Complete Works of Freud*. Unfortunately, Ramsey died in 1930, having succumbed to a serious liver disease. This interest in psychoanalysis, within the Cambridge intellectual community, to which Keynes was integral, is briefly mentioned in a lively, well-written history of economics by Boston Globe journalist David Warsh, titled *Knowledge and the Wealth of Nations* (2006). We also know that Keynes read a considerable amount of Freud and was influenced by the basics of Freudian theory (see Skidelsky's biography of Keynes) Further, in Keynes's *General Theory* (1936), he refers to non-economic motives that exist and occur due to "Animal Spirits." In Keynes's context "Animal Spirits" means an endogenous, ever present "mental energy" with its own vicissitudes that are a mobilizing force in human irrationality and decision making. See Akerlof and Shiller 2009.

4. From Shaw 2011.
5. Frosh is professor, Department of Psycho-Social Studies, and pro-vice-master, Birkbeck Institute, University College, University of London.
6. Part One of this chapter utilizes a thorough analysis by Frosh that incorporates varied aspects of academic psychology. I also employ other original sources in this chapter, which are cited, as enhancement to the foundational Frosh interpretation.
7. See H. S. Davenport, "Proposed Modifications in Austrian Theory and Terminology," *Quarterly Journal of Economics* 16: 355–383.
8. Ernest Jones (1957) *The Life and Work of Sigmund Freud*, quoted in R. Britton 2011.
9. Ibid.
10. From "Schrodinger's equation—What is it?" In plus.maths.org, online magazine, August 2012.
11. Feynman 1965; Britton 2011.
12. Erdelyi 1985.
13. Neisser 1967. Also see Hogarth (2001) for use of a tacit and deliberate system; J. Bruner (1986) with logico-scientific and narrative mode; and Freud (1911) "Formulation on the Two Systems of Mental Functioning," which later evolved into "The Ego and the Id" (1923).
14. Charts constructed from Frosh analysis.
15. Frosh 1989.
16. Part Two is my synthesis of Lear's considerable argument which appears in a long essay: "Restlessness, Phantasy and the Concept of Mind." The essay is one among twelve that comprise his book: *Open Minded. Working Out the Logic of the Soul* (1998).
17. Illustration by David Plunkart. It appeared in the *New York Times* review of Kahneman's book, *Thinking Fast and Slow*, on November 25, 2011. The author of the book review is Jim Holt.
18. For the lay reader's understanding, a way to think about reflexive breakdown is "subjective" breakdown.
19. My note: There always remains some semblance of residual fault lines from the fragmented beginning that is always becoming a subject.

20. My note: In the language of economics the possibility of disruption is endogenous to mindedness.

21. My note: Behavioral economics provides tools that seem to correct error; it is silent on the promotion of endogenous, structural human growth.

22. My note: Differentiated unity is more complex and dynamic than dual systems. Further, it should have been noted earlier that the conceptual idea of two-mind systems can become very confusing and detracts from a legitimate pathological phenomenon that is a vertical split in the mind. This is a pathology in which someone lives in two worlds that are experienced as contradictory. Each part of the split exists without any possibility of integration. These people are split into two selves who experience different worlds (e.g., Jekyll and Hyde in classic literature). Recent real-world examples would be Eliot Spitzer and Anthony Weiner. For the definitive description and analysis of this pathology, see Arnold Goldberg's (1999) *Being of Two Minds*.

23. http://digital commons.bard.edu/hm_archive.

24. See R. L. Carhart-Harris and Karl Friston: "The Default-Mode, ego-functions and free-energy: a neurobiological account of Freudian ideas" in BRAIN (2010):133, 1265–1283; Mark Solms, Chair of Neuropsychology at the University of Cape Town; trained Psychoanalyst. He has just finished retranslating all 24 volumes of Freud's psychological writings, a project begun in 1990 and scheduled to be published in late 2016. He has been a prolific scholar on neuroscience and the subjective brain. "What is most significant about the brain, in comparison to other bodily organs, is that it is not just an object but a subject," says Solms. "To truly recognize that has massive implications."

25. Personal communication from Shefrin in which he refers to limited and inadequate math in Minsky's book, *Stabilizing an Unstable Economy* (1986).

26. "The Project" was subsequently published by Strachey in *Complete Works of Freud*.

27. This discussion of Freud's economic approach comes directly from a more recent work by Jonathan Lear (2000) titled *Happiness, Death and the Remainder of Life*. Lear is quoting Freud (1937, 226–230).

28. Ibid.

29. Ibid.

30. Ibid.

31. My note: There is work to be done on this issue that would integrate a psychoanalytic perspective with behavioral economics. There is a need to connect the deeply human loss/gain experience with the journeyman tabulator that was noted by Frosh in Part One. Psychoanalytic neuroscience is making this possible. See *Discover Magazine*, April 2014: "The Second Coming of Sigmund Freud."

32. See Waddell 2002.

33. See Anderson 1997.

34. Waddell 2002.

35. The reader should be taking special note here and reflect upon the difference between conceptual categories of internal structure (e.g., a fragmenting anxiety versus inner integration). These have to do with psychological structure that has a capacity to grow and mature, yet is vulnerable to occasional regressions. Compare/contrast this with the earlier dual mind schemes, whether Kahneman, Bruner, or others. Anxiety/integration deals with the immanence of irrationality, the permanent possibility of falling apart because a center cannot hold. This is about the vicissitudes of subjective psychological structure.

36. See Steiner 1997.
37. Britton 2011.
38. Ibid.
39. Freeman Dyson's other hero of the human psyche, Wm James, wrote about some people's need for the supernatural: *Varieties of Religious Experience* (1902).

REFERENCES

Anderson, Robin. 1997. "The Child in the Adult: The Contribution of Child Analysis to the Psychoanalysis of Adults." In *The Contemporary Kleinians of* London. Edited by Roy Schafer. Madison, CT: International Universities Press.

Britton, Ronald. 2011. "The Pleasure Principle, The Reality Principle and the Uncertainty Principle." In *Bion Today*, edited by Chris Mawson. New York: Routledge.

Bruner, Jerome. 1986. *Actual Minds, Possible Worlds.* Cambridge, MA: Harvard University Press.

Dyson, Freeman. 2011. "Review of Thinking Fast and Slow" in *New York Review of Books*, December 22.

Erdelyi, Matthew. 1985. *Psychoanalysis: Freud's Cognitive Psychology.* New York: W. H. Freeman.

Freud, S. 1911. "Formulations on the Two Systems of Mental Functioning." In *The Standard Edition of the Complete Works of Sigmund Freud.* Edited by James Strachey. London: Hogarth Press.

Freud, S. 1923. "The Ego and the Id." In *The Standard Edition of the Complete Works of Sigmund Freud.* Edited by James Strachey. London: Hogarth Press.

Freud, S. 1925. "On Negation" In *The Standard Edition of the Complete Works of Sigmund Freud.* Edited by James Strachey, London: Hogarth Press.

Freud, S. 1937. "Analysis Terminable and Interminable." In *The Standard Edition of the Complete Works of Sigmund Freud.* Edited by James Strachey. London: Hogarth Press.

Frosh, Stephen. 1989. *Psychoanalysis and Psychology: Minding the Gap.* New York: New York University Press.

Goldberg, Arnold. 1999. *Being of Two Minds: The Vertical Split in Psychoanalysis and Psychotherapy.* Hillsdale, NJ: Analytic Press.

Hogarth, Robin. 2001. *Educating Intuition.* Chicago: University of Chicago Press.

Lear, Jonathan. 1998. "Restlessness, Phantasy and the Concept of Mind." In *Open Minded: Working Out the Concept of the Soul.* Cambridge, MA: Harvard University Press.

Lear, Jonathan. 2000. *Happiness, Death and the Remainder of Life.* Cambridge, MA: Harvard University Press.

Lowenstein, G., and J. Elster, eds. 1992. *Choice over Time.* New York: Russell Sage Foundation.

Minsky, Hyman. 1978. "The Financial Instability Hypothesis: A Restatement." Hyman P. Minksy Archive, Paper 180. http://digitalcommons.bard.edu/hm_archive/180.

Neisser, U. 1967. *Cognitive Psychology.* New York: Appleton-Century-Crofts.

Schafer, Roy, ed. 1997. *The Contemporary Kleinians of London.* Madison, CT: International Universities Press.

Shaw, Leslie. 2011. "A Psychodynamic Voice for the Behavioral Economics Revolution." Unpublished paper presented at Chicago Psychoanalytic Society, November 22, 2011.

Strachey, James. 1958. *The Standard Edition of the Complete Works of Sigmund Freud.* London: Hogarth Press.

Steiner, John. 1997. "Problems of Psychoanalytic Technique: Patient Centered and Analyst Centered Interpretations." In The Contemporary Kleinians of London. Edited by Roy Schafer. Madison, CT: International Universities Press.

Waddell, Margot. 2002. *Inside Lives: Psychoanalysis and the Growth of the Personality.* London: Karnac Books, Ltd.

12

Existence of Monopoly in the Stock Market

A Model of Information-Based Manipulation

VIKTORIA DALKO, LAWRENCE R. KLEIN, S. PRAKASH SETHI, AND MICHAEL H. WANG ∎

INTRODUCTION

Since the founding of organized financial markets, financial crises have occurred regularly (Kinderberger 2000; Reinhart and Rogoff 2009) and have frequently caused economic recessions.[1] After the crises, unemployment increased, income gaps widened, and the population living in poverty increased (Galbraith 1955; Reinhart and Rogoff 2009). This perspective warrants the close examination of the set-up and functioning of the financial markets. The uncovering of underlying trading behavior that can lead to a single security price collapse first, and a market-wide crisis after, is one of the possible approaches to the task. We aim to explore the stock market in this direction. Before our endeavor, we consider how our research is related to two significant theories in modern finance: the efficient market hypothesis (EMH) and the financial instability hypothesis (FIH).

In summarizing the EMH, Fama (1970) stated that in an efficient market, share prices accurately reflect public firms' activities, assuming that all the information is objective and truthful. The subject of his research was the whole market, that is, all investors in aggregate. In his system, market efficiency means that the mean of the return distribution at a future time, $t + 1$, is independent of the information available at the current time, t.[2] There are three levels of efficient markets according to the different types of information built in the price. If the information comprises historical prices only, it leads to a *weak-form* efficient market. If the information includes historical prices and all publicly available information as well, then the efficient market is in a *semi-strong form*. The extreme level is the *strong-form* efficient market where any price-sensitive information, including insider information (called "monopolistic information" by Fama), is added to historical prices and all publicly available information.

Most importantly, Fama (1970, 415–416) states: "At the moment, however, corporate insiders and specialists are the only two groups whose monopolistic access to information has been documented. There is no evidence that deviations from the strong form of the efficient markets model *permeate down* [emphasis added] any further through the investment community." Therefore, Fama proposes the EMH to be a useful description of the stock market because the exceptions that violate the strong form of market efficiency are empirically not important.

However, we found vast empirical research literature that emerged in the last 20 years to document the widespread existence and utilization of monopolistic information in today's financial markets. This empirical literature[3] covers the activities of sell-side equity analysts, business journalists, investment "gurus," and rumormongers—as well as others, including convicted market manipulators.

We found in the same literature that price-sensitive information is frequently *created* for trading purposes. Such information does not have to be objective and true, but its effectiveness is in how much "herding" it can induce. Herding refers to bringing individuals together into a group that moves in the same direction. Therefore, we argue that empirically the markets are not efficient in the strong form, and market manipulation, a violation of the strong form of market efficiency, is a critical and fundamental feature of current financial markets that can lead to financial crisis. It can be the reason why EMH cannot predict bubbles and crashes of either single stocks or an entire market.

Financial history is filled with crises of all types. Minsky (1992) constructed the FIH to understand them. He reasoned that speculative investment bubbles are endogenous to financial markets, and they often lead to financial crises. Kindleberger (2000) coined the terms "mania," "panic," and "crash" as designating the three main stages of a financial crisis. Although they are very descriptive of the phenomena, Kindleberger does not provide a detailed explanation for how mania is initiated in the stock market. Also, his explanation of leveling at high prices is limited to insider selling. However, the FIH does provide a very helpful insight into the systemic nature of financial instability. Our model describes a trading strategy that can cause financial instability, that can generate manias and panics as well as crashes in the stock market. In addition, we take one more step. We also propose policy measures that can help to prevent turning such trading behavior into financial crises. Therefore, our view is that a financial crisis is driven by certain human actions, and once we better understand them, appropriate surveillance and regulatory measures can prevent crisis.

This study focuses on information-based market manipulation[4] by a strategic trader.[5] Hundreds of hand-collected market manipulation cases show that some traders do have the ability to influence a share price and they frequently do so.[6] One important way is that strategic traders generate and publicly disseminate price-sensitive information through credible mass media. Such information can be fully truthful, half truthful, or completely false. The key is that such information induces numerous investors to herd in the direction of its content. The strategic trader (who is the inducer) then trades against the induced investors and often profits from it. Based on these observations, we raise the following research questions:

- What is the source of mania during information-based manipulation?
- What causes return reversal after a good news announcement?
- What is the distribution of gains and losses between the strategic trader and other traders who are induced to trade on the information?
- What potential risks can information-based manipulation bring to the target stock, or even the whole market?

The key findings of the study are that monopoly power in the stock market can be created and exercised through information-based market manipulation by a strategic trader. Successful execution of manipulation can result in substantial profit to the strategic trader but unfair losses to other investors, as well as excess volatility to the manipulated stocks. In addition, we propose that creation and exercise of monopoly power in the stock market is one mechanism that contributes to a widening income gap between market manipulators and the investing public.

The remainder of this study is divided into four parts. The first compares monopoly in the stock market with monopoly in goods and services markets. There is a brief summary of the ample empirical evidence of the existence of stock market manipulation. The next section describes the model of information-based market manipulation. The third section discusses the results of the model and elaborates on the findings. Finally, the last section summarizes our conclusions and offers recommendations for further research.

EXISTENCE OF MONOPOLISTIC TENDENCIES IN THE STOCK MARKET

Monopolies are common in the goods and services markets. Exercise of monopoly power is detrimental both to competition and welfare (measured by the sum of surpluses) and also to fundamental values such as freedom of choice, which is certainly an important characteristic of modern civilization. Competitors, consumers, and suppliers repeatedly call for improved protection of competition. The resulting antitrust laws have been formally enacted since the implementation of the Sherman Act of 1890 (Motta 2004) in several countries, starting with the United States.

We define monopoly power in the stock market as the influence it purposefully exerts on other investors' decisions. This definition is paraphrased from Joseph Nye's definition of soft power in political science (Nye 2008). For the purposes of this study, we discuss only those monopolists who would take advantage of other investors after exerting power on them. The context of this discussion is the secondary stock market as an institution, which from our study perspective, facilitates competition for trading profits.

We call strategic traders those who apply market manipulation techniques. These "inducers" successfully create a perception of reality in the minds of the unsuspecting "induced traders," and consecutively take advantage of them. Both parties are engaged in a series of transactions where one is inducing and the other is being induced.

There are mainly two ways a strategic trader can achieve such a result. One way is through trading activity that results in the creation of a perception about a stock's increased desirability and future higher-than-expected return. The other is through the generation and announcement of explicit news with price-sensitive content. For example, an investment "guru" announces that a particular stock has become a great buy. These two types of market manipulation techniques were called trade-based and information-based manipulation, respectively, by Allen and Gale (1992).[7] The intended result is the same: induced investors will trade according to the design of the manipulator, while the strategic trader will trade against the former. The underlying mechanism is the creation and use of monopoly power by the manipulator.

Comparison between Monopoly Power in the Financial, and the Goods and Services Markets

Even before Fama (1970), there were proponents of the concept that financial markets are truly and perfectly competitive. We found such a view not fitting well with the reality of modern financial markets. Just because there are numerous traders present does not by any means ensure perfect competition where no one participant can influence the price. Once we select specific categories along which we compare monopolistic behavior in goods markets and financial markets, the similarities become more apparent.

We found that the key difference is that the markets of financial assets are fragmented and transient to the extreme, relative to the markets of goods and services. Competition for profit from trading stock X is a different market than the competition for profit from trading stock Y. The competition five minutes earlier is different from that of five minutes later for the same stock X. The markets can be different even for trading the same stock X at the same time if it is traded in two stock exchanges, electronic trading platforms, or even countries.

The extreme fragmentation and transient nature of markets that host the competition for trading profit is probably the most unique characteristic of stock markets relative to goods and services markets. Large profits can be gained in weeks, days, and even minutes in today's markets by trading a single stock using manipulation tactics. Therefore the concept of market power has to be reinterpreted to fit such a transient market.

Next, we compare monopoly power in the stock market and monopoly position in the goods and services markets in more details.

1. Time: In the stock market, length of time regarding monopoly-building is much shorter in general. Becoming a monopoly in the goods market normally takes years. Obtaining monopolistic profit in the stock market can be accomplished in as little as weeks, days, minutes, or even seconds.
2. Simplicity: The effort to become a monopolist in the goods market is multifaceted, and it includes leadership and management; innovation; access to capital, equipment, and real estate; production; marketing; and so on. To form a monopoly in the stock market, it is necessary to have only a large amount of capital, access to credible mass media, a few employees, and in

some cases advanced computer technology. Occasionally, just spreading rumors is sufficient.

3. Investment options: In the products and services market, a firm usually attains monopoly over a few product categories. In the stock market, an investor can gain monopolistic profit from trading any and numerous (linked or unrelated) financial instruments.

4. Two-way profitability: In the goods market, monopolistic profit is generated either by increased prices (if it is a monopolistic seller) or by decreased prices (if it is a monopolistic buyer), but not by price changes of the same product in either direction. In the stock market, depending on the strategy, monopolistic profit can be made from either the rising or falling price of the same stock (as long as short-selling is not banned).

5. Secrecy: In the goods market, monopolistic behavior is naturally exposed because prices have to be public. In the stock market, an investor's stock purchase and sale price, his trading strategies, his involvement with media and particular news releases, etc., are not exposed to other investors. This superior secrecy is crucial to attaining monopoly and generating monopolistic profit.

6. Dynamic and transient: In the goods and services markets, once a monopolistic position is achieved over a particular product category, the monopoly can hardly switch to a different category of products. In the stock market, once monopolistic profit is gained, the investor closes the monopolistic position. The same investor can switch to another stock to establish a new monopolistic position immediately after the previous monopoly. Actually, an investor can change between a monopolistic position and a non-monopolistic position frequently. A monopolist in the goods market can hardly behave this way, because the cost in becoming a monopolist is high and the time it takes is long. In the stock market, monopolistic behavior is always temporary, exhibited only during a specific time period, and not continuously. This creates difficulty for law enforcement, which is basically ex post.

7. Profit dependence on inducement: In the product and service markets, the monopolist defines the selling price of its product. In the stock market, the monopolist achieves a higher selling price than his purchase price either by engaging in trade-based manipulation or information-based manipulation. However, either scenario requires that other investors get induced to buy and bid up the price for the monopolist.

8. Predatory behavior: In the goods market, a monopolistic firm may set a very low temporary price, or "predatory pricing," to drive out competitors. In the stock market, a monopolistic investor can "shake-out" other investors when he acquires the shares that he intends to manipulate. This process essentially results in the exclusion of competition.

9. No liability for the objectivity of touting information: When a monopolistic investor engages in information-based manipulation, he, or those hired by him for that purpose, touts the stock he has accumulated. This way other investors will be induced to buy the same stock and bid up the prices. Then the manipulator will sell the shares to the induced traders. In this sense, touting is similar to marketing in the products and services markets as it aims to induce purchases. However, it is different than marketing, since there is no way to

verify the objectivity of the touting information after buyers act upon it, and there is no legal liability if the content is not truthful.

10. Legal risk: Antitrust laws are enacted in several countries' goods and services markets. However, at the moment, there is still no antitrust law to regulate the stock market. The current main legal risk is a conviction as a market manipulator.

Based on the above comparison, we propose that market manipulation is essentially the creation and exercise of monopoly power in a trading strategy.

Overall, the conclusion is that it is faster, legally less risky, and cheaper to establish monopoly power in the stock market, relative to the markets of goods and services. There is no reason why rational investors would not try to obtain monopolistic profits from designing and practicing such trading strategies. This point is supported by the empirical evidence in securities litigation cases in market manipulation detected in both developed and emerging stock markets, evidence that we briefly summarize in the following section.

Market Manipulation is Widespread, Frequent, and Occasionally Rampant

Klein, Dalko, and Wang (2012) list 394 litigation cases, released by the SEC from 1999 to 2009. Sixty-seven percent, or 264 of the 394 cases, involve information-based manipulation. The authors also collect 18 prosecution cases released by China Securities Regulatory Commission from 2000 to 2006, 13 cases from 1999 through 2007 prosecuted by Hong Kong Securities and Futures Commission, 25 cases filed for prosecution by Japan Securities and Exchange Surveillance Commission between 1998 and 2008,[8] and 28 convicted or settled cases launched by the Securities and Exchange Board of India that span from 1999 through 2005. The recent securities enforcement cases in the above five economies indicate that market manipulation is widespread and frequent.

Occasionally market manipulation becomes so rampant that it results in stock market crisis, particularly when it fails in the final stage to completion. The crisis-causing market manipulations occurred in Latin America, Europe, Asia, and Australia in the last 25 years. These include the Nahas case (1989) in Brazil; the Nomura Securities case (1996) in Australia; the Delta Securities case (1996) in Greece; the Double Play (1998) in Hong Kong; and the Parekh case (2001) in India.[9]

Albeit only hundreds of detected and prosecuted instances are reported in Klein, Dalko, and Wang (2012), given the difficulties of prosecution, these empirical findings reveal that market manipulation remains a widespread, frequent, and occasionally rampant issue facing stock markets in the 21st century. The far-reaching implications of these cases underscore the convicted Canadian stock market manipulator's confession that manipulation of untold numbers of stocks occur every day (Specogna 2003).

Next we build a model of information-based manipulation.

A MODEL OF AN INFORMATION-BASED MANIPULATIVE TRADING STRATEGY

The Set-Up of the Model and Related Literature

We model a trading strategy that benefits from the artificial rise of the stock price in this study.[10]

What are the necessary conditions for the strategic trader to successfully manipulate numerous investors' perception about the stock he is using as a vehicle for gaining monopolistic profit? First, he needs to generate information that is able to arouse numerous investors' interest and create a perception that currently the stock is undervalued; we call this price-sensitive information. The key is its relevance to investors' evaluation of the stock. Second, he has to deliver the information to a large number of investors. In other words, the information needs to gain substantial publicity. Third, the information needs to come from a credible source (e.g., Reuters), a reputable disseminator (e.g., the *Wall Street Journal*), or a trustworthy person (e.g., CEO or investment guru). Otherwise, insufficient investors will be convinced to buy the stock, even when they have received the information. In other words, the information needs to carry high credibility. Three elements—the information's relevance to a target stock, its substantial publicity, and its high credibility—act together to produce the persuasive power of the information for the manipulative trading strategy.[11] Information-based manipulation incurs some cost, such as hiring a stock promoter or employing a sell-side analyst, and requires other resources such as large capital and access to credible information disseminators.

Fundamentally, our paper is related to the abundant literature on information asymmetry. The literature starts with Akerlof (1970), Spence (1973), and Stiglitz (1975). These seminal papers treat information asymmetry as an endowment. Our study goes one step further. The strategic trader has no private information that can be utilized for profit maximization. The strategic trader creates particular asymmetric information; he is not acquiring it, but he generates this information. Then he empowers this newly generated information by attaching publicity and credibility to it before using it in his trading strategy. This is the major difference relative to previous assumptions on information asymmetry in the literature. In fact we are modeling how a strategic trader creates information asymmetry, empowers it, and utilizes the empowered information asymmetry in a trading strategy.

Technically, our paper is closely related to the theoretical literature on market manipulation as trade based (Allen and Gale 1992; Allen and Gordon 1992; Jarrow 1992; Cherian and Jarrow 1995; Avery 1998a, 1998b), information based (Kyle 1985; Vila 1989; Benabou and Laroque 1992; Fishman and Hagerty 1995; John and Narayanan 1997; Huddart, Hughes, and Levine 2001; von Bommel 2003; Chakraborty and Yilmaz 2004; Brunnermeier and Pedersen 2005), or action based (Bagnoli and Lipman 1996). Our distinction from these studies is that we focus on the mechanism that lifts share prices by induced investors, while these researchers assume lifted prices. In addition, we examine the post-distribution price and income distribution, which has rich implications regarding the risks to the target stock and the entire market brought by the trading strategy. Regarding the price impact, our paper is closest to von Bommel (2003) and Brunnermeier and Pederson (2005). The similarity lies in the assertion that the strategic trader profits from other investors' price impact. In our model, the strategic trader may or may not have insider information, which differentiates it from the models in Kyle (1985), Benabou and Laraque (1992), von Bommel (2003), and Brunnermeier and Pederson (2005), in which the strategic trader has insider information (i.e., he knows the true distribution of the future price). In contrast, to fit our model better with the litigation cases reviewed above, we do not assume that the strategic trader knows the true price.

The central assumption in our model, based on empirical evidence, is that the strategic trader is not a price-taker but an indirect price-setter, or a monopolist, which means that he induces other investors to buy up to a specific stock price so he can profitably sell his shares. This assumption prevents us from building a rational expectations model. The essence of our model lies in the notion that the strategic trader deliberately acts to make his planned profit to be realized, while induced investors' expectations on average are unlikely to be realized (Barber and Odean 1999). That is why induced investors herd to sell, even at deep losses, when trends are against their expectations. In fact, there is no mechanism that would make induced investors' expectations realized; hence, we do not model their optimization problem. The strategic trader sets his goal and has the "technology" to target others and induce them to buy until the price reaches the level he planned so he can sell his shares at that price. In other words, he can reduce the uncertainty of his profit to a minimum level. Thus, we build a non-stochastic model in a discrete time, to emphasize this risk minimization feature of the manipulator's trading strategy.

It is a unique feature of our model that generating and disseminating price-moving information, true or false, is costly. Since our model focuses on the price-lifting mechanism, the price change is endogenized through every period once the manipulator has completed accumulation of his shares, while other models have an exogenous price distribution at least in the last period of trade. Our model has the potential to be generalized and extended to include action-based and trade-based trading strategies, primarily through the reinterpretation of the cost of inducement.

Our model contributes to the literature with the following innovations.

First, this chapter focuses on manipulation of perception as a key to information-based manipulation. Perception about the value of the stock is changed by ex-ante generated, empowered, and publicly disseminated asymmetric information. We take a further step from the previous information asymmetry research, where asymmetric information is either ex ante endowment or ex post generation, relative to the contract (Mas-Colell, Whinston, and Green 1995).

Second, we explicitly model inconsistency in the strategic trader's trading activity and his publicly announced information content. This is the crucial part of all manipulative trading strategies. Ways to overcome such inconsistency have important implications for effective securities surveillance and regulatory enforcement.

Third, our model shows that the studied manipulative trading strategy is one of the triggers that can lead to induced investors' information-clustered herding up and sale-initiated herding down, which often results in their trading loss.

Fourth, our model exhibits that such manipulative trading strategies lead to perception reversal first, followed by return reversal. Fifth and very importantly, we illustrate that some information-based manipulative trading strategies may lead to single stock price collapses and widening gap of income inequality.

The Model and Results

We focus on a trading strategy that benefits from artificial price increases, and we build a discrete-time deterministic model. There are three types of market participants: one strategic trader, numerous perception-guided investors,[12] and a market maker. The strategic trader's goal is to influence the view of other traders about the stock, to make it look more valuable in the eyes of other investors than the price currently reflects. Hence, the techniques the strategic trader applies involve information generation, empowerment, and dissemination. The disseminated information is basically an implicit or explicit promise of a certain return on the stock to the investing public. On the other hand, the strategic trader hides the main risk associated with the trade, that is, the planned timing of his sale. For example, the updated analyst research report states that the stock should be traded at 25% higher than its current value in one month but neglects to say that his firm will sell a large number of shares once the stock price increases by 20%. In the following, we refer to such techniques as "information-based manipulation techniques." Notice that we do not assume information discovery, superior analytical techniques applied on private or public information, or endowment of private information. Rather, we assume information generation, empowerment, and dissemination by the strategic trader or a service provider who generates and disseminates information for the strategic trader at a cost. For our modeling purpose, what is important is not whether the trader and the information-based manipulator are the same person; it is that information-based manipulation is frequently effective, albeit costly for the strategic trader.

Our model will address the following questions over *one complete cycle* of trading by all of the investors in the model:

1. Under what conditions can the strategic trader gain from information-based manipulation?
2. Under the above conditions, do the perception-guided investors realize gain or loss?
3. What is the source of thought contagion of the herding of the perception-guided investors?
4. Why do positive returns reverse after the good news announcement?
5. What risks can this type of trading strategy bring to the stock?

We model a complete cycle of an information-based manipulative trading strategy that is under the influence of the strategic trader. No detection of the trading strategy by other investors or regulators is considered. No other information about the target stock is released during the cycle.[13] In this sense, the strategic trader controls the price indirectly, by inducing others to trade according to his design. Hence, price becomes endogenous in the model. There is only one stock traded in the market at volume X and price p. No dividend issue is considered. Since it is one complete trading cycle, the strategic trader starts and ends with no shareholding.

The strategic trader's objective is expected profit maximization subject to his constraints. He plans a target return and incurs expenses to ensure that such target is achieved.[14] We assume that the information-based manipulation technique he employs can be continuously scaled, and the price of deploying such a technique is given exogenously.[15] In addition, we assume that the strategic trader knows the pricing function of the market maker: how the stock price change depends on order flows. The strategic trader faces one type of uncertainty: the number of investors that the information-based manipulation techniques induce to buy the stock. However, the strategic trader has financial and other resources to deliver information-based manipulation techniques repeatedly if necessary to overcome such uncertainty.[16]

We assume that each perception-guided investor submits one buy market order or nothing in response to the good news announcement made by the strategic trader. We assume neither that any of the perception-guided traders will sell at the announcement of the good news nor that there are short-sellers at the good news announcement. This also means that the perception-guided investors do observe the news and do not trade randomly by disregarding the news. After receiving the news, some perception-guided investors change their original perception and assimilate the news. The number of perception-guided investors who submit buy orders depends on the persuasive power of the information. The power of this asymmetric information is composed of the relevance of the information content and the publicity and credibility attached to this information. The perception-guided investors who accept and act upon the announcement are the induced investors. Some induced investors aim to earn a positive return on the stock in a short time. We assume there are some short-term speculators among the induced investors.

The market maker raises the price after observing the order flow of the induced investors. He accepts no net loss over the trading cycle due to his intertemporal budget constraint.

For our model to work, it is critical that the perception-guided investors' collective buy market orders are large enough before the strategic trader places his sell limit order. The justification of this sequencing is that the strategic trader can observe the arrival of buy orders through real-time market data and can purchase and deploy more inducement techniques when necessary so that sufficient buy orders will eventually be placed, according to his needs and accumulated shares. The limit order (minimum) price for selling his shareholding will be set as the same as the target price expected by the strategic trader. It is also the market maker's price after the latter has observed the buy order flow.

Four discrete stages of the trading cycle are detailed below. At the beginning, Time 0, the market maker holds all shares of the stock. The strategic investor has wealth w_0 but no stocks, and none of the perception-guided investors hold any shares either.

Accumulation:[17] The strategic trader purchases (i.e., accumulates) X_1 shares from the market maker at the exogenously given price p_1. The strategic trader minimizes price impact in the accumulation phase so no other investors will be motivated to purchase due to the stock price increase. To lift the share price after accumulation, he purchases Y units of information-based manipulation services at the unit price q, per induced investor. The services are so scaled that Y is also the number of induced investors.[18] He also purchases bonds, at the value of B, which generates one period risk-free rate of return r. So his budget constraint at time one is

$$w_0 = p_1 X_1 + qY + B.$$

Lift: The strategic trader announces potentially price-moving good news through credible media channels to a mass audience (this is the service he paid qY for). At the announcement, in the eyes of perception-guided investors the perceived value of the stock suddenly increases. The current price now looks too low, and optimistic perception about a more valuable future generates herding of induced investors. Each buys one share after they receive the news. Thus, their herding is centered on the news (Agarwal et al. 2011), not that they follow each other, as described by Bikhhchandani, Hirshleifer, and Welch (1992), and Banerjee (1992). The market maker raises the price from p_1 to p_2 at the arrival of Y new buy orders. In other words, the induced investors push the price up as they submit buy market orders to the market maker (Grossman and Miller 1988). That is,

$$p_2 - p_1 = g(Y),$$

where g is the pricing function used by the market maker.

We make a crucial assumption here that, in Period 2, the number of induced investors is exactly equal to the number of shares to be distributed by the strategic trader. In other words, there is exact inducement in Period 2:

$$Y = X_1,$$

and

$$p_2 - p_1 = g(X_1).$$

There is a possibility that more induced investors submit buy orders than X_1, albeit the strategic trader aims at the exact inducement (since inducement is costly). When the over-induced investors enter the market to buy, the strategic trader is already out of the market. So the extra inducement does not enter the strategic trader's optimization problem. Rather, the over-induced investors trade with the market maker, after the strategic investor's distribution is completed.

Distribution: The strategic trader sells his shares X_2 to the induced perception-guided investors at the artificially inflated price p_2 by submitting a series of limit orders after the price jump. He sells all shares he accumulated in Period 1. That is,

$$X_2 = X_1.$$

Overall, taking the above equalities into account, since the strategic trader knows the market maker's pricing function and observes the perception-guided investors' trading behavior; the system can be described by the following problem:

$$\max_{X_1, B}[(p_2 X_1 - p_1 X_1 - q X_1 + rB]$$

s.t.

$$w_0 = p_1 X_1 + q X_1 + B$$

$$p_2 - p_1 = g(X_1).$$

After substitution of the price impact function into the profit function, we obtain:

$$\max_{X_1,B}\{X_1[p_1 + g(X_1)] - X_1(p_1 + q) + rB\}$$

s.t.

$$X_1(p_1 + q) + B = w_0.$$

The Lagrangian is:

$$\mathcal{L}(X_1, B) = \{X_1[p_1 + g(X_1)] - X_1(p_1 + q) + rB - \lambda[X_1(p_1 + q) + B - w_0]\}.$$

The first-order conditions are:

$$\partial\mathcal{L}/\partial X_1 = \{p_1 + g(X_1) + X_1\partial g(X_1)/\partial X_1 - (p_1 + q) - \lambda(p_1 + q)\} = 0$$
$$\partial\mathcal{L}/\partial B = r - \lambda = 0$$
$$\partial\mathcal{L}/\partial\lambda = X_1(p_1 + q) + B - w_0 = 0.$$

Substituting $\lambda = r$ into the first equation, we can obtain the solution X_1^* from the following equation:

$$g(X_1) + X_1\partial g(X_1)/\partial X_1 = q + r(p_1 + q).$$

while solution B^* can be calculated from the budget constraint:

$$X_1(p_1 + q) + B - w_0 = 0.$$

The second-order condition is:

$$2\partial g(X_1)/\partial X_1 + X_1\partial^2 g(X_1)/\partial X_1^2 < 0.$$

We use a popularly proposed price impact function g, a square root function (Gabaix et al. 2006), to find a closed-form solution to the above optimization problem. Subsequently, the first-order condition becomes:

$$X_1^{1/2} + 1/2X_1^{1/2} = q + r(p_1 + q),$$

that is,

$$X_1^* = [2/3(q + r(p_1 + q))]^2.$$

The second-order condition becomes:

$$3/4X_1^{*-1/2} < 0,$$

which cannot hold for any $X_1 > 0$. Thus X_1^* is actually minimizing the profit, since the profit function is convex. The highest profit can be obtained by a corner solution, if there is no investment into bond and as long as the return on bond is sufficiently small. In the case of the square root price impact function, this translates to the condition of

$$r < w_0/(p_1 + q))^{3/2} - q[w_0/(p_1 + q)].$$

Therefore, the solution to the profit-maximization problem, under general conditions regarding the shape of the price impact function g and the return on bond r, is that the strategic trader chooses to spend all of his wealth on the stock and the accompanying inducement techniques. That is, optimally,

$$B^* = 0$$

$$X_1^* = w_0/(p_1 + q).$$

This is the solution to the optimization problem of the strategic trader. He will purchase $X_1^* = w_0/(p_1 + q)$ stock in Period 1 and will sell all of it to the induced investors at price $p_2 = p_1 + g(X_1)$ in Period 2.

No trade (exact inducement) or positive price drift (over-inducement): Once the strategic trader exits the market, there are two scenarios. The first scenario is exact inducement. In this scenario, the number of induced traders exactly matches the number of shares the strategic trader had to sell, so there is no trade in Period 3. The second scenario is over-inducement, under which induced investors spread the news among themselves and other related investors, without the strategic investor incurring additional cost. Since the strategic trader has sold his shares in Period 2, the excess induced traders, z, will purchase the stock from the market maker in Period 3. That will rise the price in Period 3:

$$p_3 = p_2 + g(z).$$

Post-distribution: In this period, some short-term perception-guided investors start to sell their stock, and more and more induced investors follow them. The sales continue until all induced investors have sold their shareholdings back to the market maker at price p_4 that satisfies the zero-profit requirement of the market maker. Thus, the price collapses in Period 4, since the market maker is willing to buy back stocks only at no intertemporal loss. In case of exact inducement:

$$-p_4 X_1 + p_1 X_1 \geq 0.$$

Hence,

$$p_4 \leq p_1 < p_2.$$

This means return reversal after the positive return soon after the good news announcement. We will demonstrate the price behavior with exact inducement in Figure 12.1.

For over-inducement, the market maker's budget constraint is:

$$p_1 X_1 + p_3 z - p_4(X_1 + z) \geq 0.$$

Thus,

$$p_4 \leq (p_1 X_1 + p_3 z)/(X_1 + z).$$

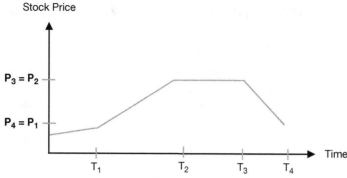

T_0-T_1 Accumulation: strategic trader quietly accumulates X_1.
Announcement of good news at T_1

T_1-T_2 Lift: induced investors push up the price. Strategic trader
distributes his shares to the induced investors at T_2

T_2-T_3 No trade

T_3-T_4 Post-Distribution: induced investors sell X_1 to market maker

Figure 12.1 Price Behavior with Exact Inducement

If $z \leq X_1$, then

$$p_1 < p_4 \leq p_2 < p_3.$$

Figure 12.2 demonstrates the price behavior in this scenario.
If $z > X_1$ and zero-profit condition holds for the market maker, then:

$$p_1 < p_2 < p_4 < p_3.$$

Both lead to return reversal after upward drifting compared to exact inducement.

DISCUSSION OF THE RESULTS

Next, we check how the model answers the five questions raised in Section 2.

Under What Conditions Can the Strategic Trader Profit from Information-Based Manipulation?

We can substitute the amount of buy orders from the induced investors into the market maker's price impact function to find out the price after the inducement:

$$p_2 = p_1 + g[w_0/(p_1 + q)].$$

The price during lifting increases relative to the price during accumulation ($p_2 > p_1$) as long as $g[w_0/(p_1 + q)] > 0$ holds. The condition means that the price impact function needs to be strictly positive if the strategic trader's initial wealth is sufficiently large relative to the stock price and cost of inducement.

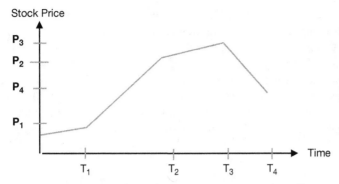

Stock Price

P_3
P_2
P_4
P_1

T_1 T_2 T_3 T_4 Time

T_0–T_1 Accumulation: Strategic trader quietly accumulates X_1.
Announcement of good news at T_1

T_1–T_2 Lift: induced investors push up price. Strategic trader
distributes his shares to them at T_2

T_2–T_3 z additional induced investors create positive drift

T_3–T_4 Post-Distribution: induced investors sell $X_1 + z$ to market
maker

Figure 12.2 Price Behavior with Over-Inducement $(0 < z < X_1)$

The profit/loss of the strategic trader is:

$$\pi = [w_0/(p_1 + q)]\{p_1 + g[w_0/(p_1 + q)] - p_1 - q\}$$
$$= [w_0/(p_1 + q)]\{g[w_0/(p_1 + q)] - q\}.$$

The strategic trader makes profit as long as

$$g[w_0/(p_1 + q)] > q.$$

This condition means that the price impact needs to cover at least the average cost of accumulated shares and inducement when a sufficiently large wealth is deployed by the strategic trader. The opposite is also important; for a too-small wealth, the price impact will not cover the cost of the stock purchasing and the inducement, and an information-based manipulative trading strategy will not be profitable. In summary, under general conditions, the strategic trader's profit is positively correlated in our model with his initial wealth.

Under the Above Conditions, Do the Perception-Guided Investors Realize Gain or Loss?

Do induced investors gain when the strategic trader profits? The total gain of induced investors for exact inducement:

$$\theta = X_1(p_4 - p_2),$$

and for over-inducement:

$$\theta = X_1(p_4 - p_2) + z(p_4 - p_3).$$

For exact inducement, induced investors jointly suffer a loss of $X_1(p_2 - p_4)$. For over-inducement and $z \leq X_1$, induced investors lose in aggregate by $X_1(p_2 - p_4) + z(p_3 - p_4)$. For over-inducement and $z > X_1, \theta < 0$ still holds. Overall, induced investors lose in aggregate in every scenario. A previously unanswered question in investment performance literature is why individual investors consistently lose in the stock market (e.g., Barber and Odean 1999; Barber and Odean 2000; Grinblatt and Keloharju 2000; Choe, Kho, and Stulz 2005; Barber, Lee, Liu, and Odean 2009). Our model provides an insight into why such losses can be systematic.

What Is the Source of Thought Contagion, Leading to the Perception-Guided Investors' Herding?

In our model, herding occurs during both the price-lifting and post-distribution phases. The source of thought contagion (Hirshleifer and Teoh 2009) to the upward herding is the news disseminated to the investing public, not any one of the induced investor's trading activity. This finding corresponds to Agarwal et al. (2011). The downward herding starts with some short-term speculators' sale, similar to the definition by Banerjee (1992) and Bikhchandani, Hirshleifer, and Welch (1992). Theoretically, the source of thought contagion in the latter case is the short-term speculators' sale. In reality, it is the observation of the real-time or delayed trading data circulated on the Internet (e.g., Yahoo! Finance) or TV (e.g., CNBC) or professional services (e.g., Level 2). Overall, the information-based manipulative trading scheme is behind both sources of thought contagion.

Why Do Positive Returns Reverse after the Announcement of Good News?

Our model predicts return reversal. After the strategic trader pulls out of the stock at time 2, the stock price drops below the peak price p_2 (exact inducement) or p_3 (over-inducement). In both cases,

$$p_4 < p_3.$$

The full process of the return reversal is caused by the strategic trader's trading scheme, triggered by some short-term perception-guided investors, exacerbated by the market maker, and precipitated by loss-averse induced investors. It is the credulity or overconfidence of the perception-guided investors in momentum trading that drives them to participate in and precipitate the return reversal. However, the intentional design by the strategic trader (i.e., the inducement based on manipulation of perception and his trading against the induced investors) is the source of the return reversal. This finding sheds a new light on the return reversal literature (e.g., DeBondt and Thaler 1985; Grossman and Miller 1988; Jegadeesh 1990; Lehmann 1990; Campbell, Grossman, and Wang 1993; Jegadeesh and Titman 1995; Barberis, Shleifer, and Vishny 1998; Daniel, Hirshleifer, and Subrahmanyam 1998; Hong and Stein 1999).

What Risks Can This Type of Trading Strategy Create for the Target Stock?

How does the trading volume and price volatility depend on the original wealth of the strategic trader? Since

$$X_1 = w_0/(p_1 + q) > 0,$$

the trading volume X_1 is proportionate to the initial wealth of the strategic trader w_0. In the case of exact inducement, the same volume X_1 is also traded in Period 4; hence, turnover is consistently an increasing function of the initial wealth of the strategic trader. In the case of over-inducement, over time, turnover is positively correlated with the wealth of the strategic trader.

We can also illustrate some characteristics of price volatility. For exact inducement, if the market maker is operating at zero profit, the variance is:

$$\sigma = g(X_1^*)/2.$$

Price volatility is an increasing function of initial wealth of the strategic trader, w_0 for given p_1 and q. For over-inducement and zero profit for the market maker, variance is positively related to the initial wealth.

The above two findings indicate that large manipulative investors may cause large volume and price volatility. These findings correspond to the findings of Aggarwal and Wu (2006) and Allen, Litov, and Mei (2006). Thus, large-scale speculation does have the potential to destabilize prices. In addition, it can create even more serious risks to the stock and, occasionally, the entire market. We illustrate this point next.

Trading schemes based on manipulation of perception make any stock, particularly a relatively illiquid stock, vulnerable to mini-bubbles and even large drops. Occasionally such a scheme shakes the entire market or even the society. The worst case is delisting from the stock exchange and bankruptcy. Enron, WorldCom, and several other companies got delisted partly because of heavy insider trading assisted by previous consecutive earnings manipulation, a repeated perception-manipulation tactic.

We present a numerical example for exact inducement to evidence this analysis. From the simple model above, we can calculate how much minimum wealth deployed in a trading strategy based on manipulation of perception can result in a predefined percentage drop ω in the stock price. We ask the following: What is the minimum wealth w_{0min} so that

$$(p_2 - p_1)/p_1 \geq \omega \text{ (remember that, at most, } p_4 = p_1)$$

or

$$g[w_{0min}/(p_1 + q)] \geq p_1^* \omega?$$

For example, if $\omega = 25\%$, and g is a square root function,

$$w_{0min}/(p_1 + q) \geq p_1^{2*}0.0625,$$

that is,

$$w_{0min} \geq p_1^{2*}0.0625^*(p_1 + q).$$

The minimum wealth w_{0min} that can potentially generate at least a 25% drop of the stock price after distribution is an increasing function of the total cost the strategic investor faces. One consequence, derived from the above analysis, is that the larger the initial wealth (w_{0min}) is, the more severe is the risk to the stock price. That is to say, it is a market-specific characteristic how likely it is that a large shareholding, when used in an information-based manipulative trading strategy, could pose a severe risk to a stock. The trading profit is positively correlated with the strategic trader's initial wealth, and at the same time, the price drop after the completion of the trading strategy is also positively correlated with the strategic trader's wealth. The profitability of the strategic trader and the market risk represent two sides of the same strategy.

In reality, market manipulation is not always successful. The vulnerability of the manipulator is particularly high when he is about to distribute a large shareholding position. One source of the vulnerability comes when other investors, induced or non-induced, sell large volume of the same stock before. The other is when a large short-seller targets the manipulated stock.[19] The third scenario is breaking news—such as the onset of a war, an epidemic, or sovereign default—that prompts panic-selling of the entire market. If any of these scenarios should occur, the manipulator either sells faster than planned or falls into financial distress.

The manipulator's vulnerability can become the vulnerability of the market. The manipulator's response can lead to a large price drop in the stock in a short period of time. The worst scenario arises when a sudden large sale of the manipulated stock causes market-wide panic-selling, which can turn the single stock fall into a market-wide crisis.[20] Notorious stock market crises often result from large manipulators' sudden vulnerability. This point is evidenced by the cases of Naji Nahas (Brooke 1989a and b), Delta Securities (IOSCO 2000), and "Bombay Bull" (Bhaumik 2002).

In sum, the information-based manipulative trading strategy is the creation and exercise of monopoly power. It can reduce uncertainty and generate substantial profit for the manipulator. In addition, it generates artificial price and volume volatility. It causes induced investors to lose on aggregate. Thus it provides one mechanism for the stock market to contribute to the widening income gap. It destabilizes the stock prices, can lead to stock price collapse, and has the potential to generate market-wide panic. Therefore, effective preventive regulatory measures are needed to minimize the consequences brought by the information-based manipulative trading strategy to the stock market and to the society in general.

CONCLUDING REMARKS AND FUTURE RESEARCH

Trading strategies based on information manipulation are frequently encountered in the secondary stock market, as evidenced by millions of episodes in information-based market manipulation, earnings manipulation, insider trading, analyst forecast bias, business news spin, rumors of the last 50 years, and recent securities enforcement cases (Klein, Dalko, and Wang 2012).

This chapter presents our findings that monopoly exists in the stock market; monopoly power is frequently created and exercised in trading, which leads to market manipulation; and occasionally market manipulation can and has caused stock market crises. To formalize the process we build a model of a trading strategy of information-based manipulation. The model shows that information-based manipulation is an effective means for the manipulator to achieve trading profit maximization. The three inseparable components of information-based manipulation are creating information asymmetry by generating potentially price-moving information, empowering it through adding publicity and credibility, and disseminating it to the investing public.

Our model is intentionally technically simple, but it captures many important features of such existing trading strategies and their negative consequences to induced investors, the target stock, and even the entire market. It helps to explain several market phenomena that have puzzled researchers for decades, in a unified framework, such as the consistent trading losses by small investors, return reversal after the announcement of good news, and herding. The model has certain policy implications, since large shareholding is a potential threat to investor protection, market stability, and even systemic stability. It reveals the essential feature of such schemes that the strategic trader sells his stocks—that is, trades against induced investors—after he publicly announces optimistic information about the target stock. It proposes a feasible mechanism for how the functioning of the stock market enables further opening of the income gap.

One issue that the model does not address is that sometimes the post-distribution price declines to below the pre-accumulation price. This is frequently seen in the securities enforcement cases. One possible reason is that the post-distribution price decline causes the non-induced shareholders (long-term investors, perhaps) to sell, often in a panic, to prevent further loss. This would make our numerical example above too conservative. In other words, less initial wealth than what we calculated in the example can cause a price drop of 25%. This is a meaningful future research topic.

Our study contributes to a better understanding of the role that systemically important investors play in the formation and triggering of a financial crisis. The recent fall of Lehman Brothers, Merrill Lynch, Bear Sterns, and other financial institutions precipitated the financial crisis and caused it to evolve into a lasting worldwide crisis in the economic, societal, political, and health areas. This episode warrants more research on how our financial systems are set up, how they operate, in which aspect the markets become vulnerable, and how to detect their critical conditions. As a wider perspective, major economic institutions, particularly financial institutions, need to be comprehensively re-evaluated from the angles of science, health, and civilization.

NOTES

1. The key ideas in this chapter are based on communications with Xin Yan. We thank Günter Strobl and Jeffrey Zhang for their helpful comments. This is a revised and upgraded version of some of the issues presented in our book (Klein, Dalko, and Wang 2012). The introduction and second section are built upon the material published in our book, including the terminology, literature review, and convicted manipulation cases. The rest is new research results.
2. The random walk hypothesis has a stronger assumption that both the mean and the entire return distribution at $t + 1$ is independent of the information at t.

3. See note 1.

4. According to the Securities and Exchange Commission (SEC): "Manipulation is intentional conduct designed to deceive investors by controlling or artificially affecting the market for a security. Manipulation can involve a number of techniques to affect the supply of, or demand for, a stock. They include spreading false or misleading information about a company; improperly limiting the number of publicly-available shares; or rigging quotes, prices or trades to create a false or deceptive picture of the demand for a security. Those who engage in manipulation are subject to various civil and criminal sanctions." See http://www.sec.gov/answers /tmanipul.htm.

5. Stock market manipulation is illegal in the United States. Our study focuses on a trading strategy that may or may not be illegal but has several similarities with market manipulation. This is why we use the terms "manipulator" and "strategic trader" interchangeably, although they are different from a legal perspective.

6. See note 1.

7. The third type of market manipulation is action-based manipulation, according to Allen and Gale (1992).

8. Out of 11,514 public tips about market manipulation, only 25 were found through investigation and filed for prosecution during the 10-year span. The mere 0.2% indicates very low efficiency of prosecution of market manipulation.

9. See note 1.

10. The model is actually useful for exploring how manipulator can gain from falling prices as well; to keep the exposition simple, we concentrate on one direction of manipulation only.

11. Chapter 8 in Klein, Dalko, and Wang (2012) provides detailed analysis of why the three components are inseparable in forming the power of the information that moves stock prices.

12. Perception-guided investors are those who initiate trades after they receive any price-relevant information which includes share price movements, earnings announcements, analyst recommendation revisions, business news stories, and even rumors on the Internet.

13. We have an economy that is, to a certain extent, under the strategic trader's control. That is, before his complete exit from the stock, there is no breaking news such as a war breakout, an earthquake, an epidemic, or any other news about the stock or any rumors related to the stock (e.g., Cutler, Poterba, and Summers 1989; Fair 2002; Klein, Dalko, and Wang 2012).

14. This behavior is similar to that of corporate executives when they decide to launch a new product.

15. One option is that the strategic trader hires a contractor to implement the information-based manipulation method and pays him according to the number of perception-guided investors induced to buy the stock.

16. The Litigation Release No. 20684, issued by the SEC on August 15, 2008, shows that the strategic trader and his stock promoter issued seven press releases in consecutive weeks without any impact. Soon they sent out 2.1 million touting mailers and induced trading volume of more than 1500%. The strategic trader sold all of his 13 million shares later for a profit of $13 million (SEC 2012).

17. A trilogy of accumulation, lift, and distribution well describes market manipulation based on optimistic information (Lang 2004). The objective of the accumulation stage is to purchase a large number of shares at a reasonably low price. At the lift

stage the manipulator seeks to induce a large price impact of other investors by using one or multiple touting tactics. After the accumulation and lift stages have been executed, the remaining stage, distribution, is invoked to obtain the ultimate realized profit.

18. In conventional business in goods and services markets, qY could be called as "consumer acquisition cost."

19. Naturally, the long manipulators try to avoid short-sellers who aim to profit substantially by detecting large positions built by the former. There were several well-known historical cases of cornering short-sellers analyzed recently by Allen, Litov, and Mei (2006).

20. Empirical literature shows that the share price collapses after the completion of the distribution process by the manipulator (Aggraval and Wu 2006; Mei, Wu, and Zhou 2004; and Allen, Litov, and Mei 2006) which is confirmed by the former manipulator (Specogna 2003). This is a natural vulnerability of a manipulated stock. But the consequences of the price collapse of a manipulated stock have similarity to quick dump of a large position by the manipulator. The market suffers no matter if the manipulator's distribution is smooth or rushed by uncertainty.

REFERENCES

Agarwal, Sumit, I-Ming Chiu, Chunlin Liu, and S. Ghon Rhee. 2011. "The Brokerage Firm Effect in Herding: Evidence from Indonesia." *Journal of Financial Research* 34 (3): 461–479.

Aggarwal, Rajesh K., and Guojun Wu. 2006. "Stock Market Manipulation." *Journal of Business* 79 (4): 1915–1953.

Akerlof, George A. 1970. "The Market for 'Lemons': Quality Uncertainty and the Market Mechanism." *Quarterly Journal of Economics* 84 (3): 488–500.

Allen, Franklin, and Douglas Gale. 1992. "Stock-Price Manipulation." *Review of Financial Studies* 5 (3): 503–529.

Allen, Franklin, and Gary Gorton. 1992. "Stock Price Manipulation, Market Microstructure and Asymmetric Information." *European Economic Review* 36: 624–630.

Allen, Franklin, Lubomir Litov, and Jianping Mei. 2006. "Large Investors, Price Manipulation, and Limits to Arbitrage: An Anatomy of Market Corners." *Review of Finance* 10 (4): 645–693.

Avery, Christopher. 1998a. "Manipulation and Herding." Unpublished manuscript, Harvard University.

Avery, Christopher. 1998b. "Manipulative Trading and Herding." Unpublished manuscript, Harvard University.

Bagnoli, Mark, and Barton L. Lipman. 1996. "Stock Price Manipulation through Takeover Bids." *The RAND Journal of Economics* 27 (1): 124–147.

Banerjee, Abhijit V. 1992. "A Simple Model of Herd Behavior." *Quarterly Journal of Economics* 107 (3): 797–817.

Barber, Brad M., and Terrance Odean. 1999. "The Courage of Misguided Convictions." *Financial Analysts Journal* 55 (6): 41–55.

Barber, Brad M., and Terrance Odean. 2000. "Trading is Hazardous to Your Wealth: The Common Stock Investment Performance of Individual Investors." *Journal of Finance* 55 (2): 773–806.

Barber, Brad, Yi-Tsung Lee, Yu-Jane Liu, and Terrance Odean. 2009. "Just How Much Do Investor Lose from Trade?" *Review of Financial Studies* 22 (2): 609–632.

Barberis, Nicholas, Andrei Shleifer, and Robert Vishny. 1998. "A Model of Investor Sentiment." *Journal of Financial Economics* 49 (3): 307–343.

Benabou, Roland J., and Guy Laroque. 1992. "Using Privileged Information to Manipulate Markets: Insiders, Gurus, and Credibility." *Quarterly Journal of Economics* 107 (3): 921–958.

Bhaumik, Subir. 2002. "Broker Held for Calcutta Stock Scam." *BBC*, Tuesday, December 3.

Bikhchandani, Sushil, David Hirshleifer, and Ivo Welch. 1992. "A Theory of Fads, Fashions, Customs and Cultural Change as Informational Cascades." *Journal of Political Economy* 100 (5): 992–1026.

Brooke, James. 1989a. "Check Bounces, and Brazil Shakes." *New York Times*, June 20.

Brooke, James. 1989b. "Brazil Indicts 11 People after Market's Crash." *New York Times*, August 14.

Brunnermeier, Markus K., and Lasse H. Pedersen. 2005. "Predatory Trading." *Journal of Finance* 60 (4): 1825–1863.

Campbell, John Y., Sanford J. Grossman, and Jiang Wang. 1993. "Trading Volume and Serial Correlation in Stock Returns." *Quarterly Journal of Economics* 108 (4): 905–939.

Chakraborty, Archishman, and Bilge Yilmaz. 2004. "Manipulation in Market Order Models." *Journal of Financial Markets*, 7 (2): 187–206.

Cherian, Joseph A., and Robert A. Jarrow. 1995. "Market Manipulation." In *Handbooks in Operations Research and Management Science, Volume 9, Finance*. Edited by R. A. Jarrow, V. Maksimovic, and W. T. Ziemba. Amsterdam: Elsevier.

Cutler, David, James Poterba, and Lawrence Summers. 1989. "What Moves Stock Prices?" *Journal of Portfolio Management* 15 (3): 4–12.

DeBondt, Werner F. M., and Richard H. Thaler. 1985. "Does the Stock Market Overreact?" *Journal of Finance* 40 (3): 793–805.

Fair, Ray C. 2002. "Events That Shook the Market." *Journal of Business* 75 (4): 713–731.

Fama, Eugene F. 1970. "Efficient Capital Markets: A Review of Theory and Empirical Work." *Journal of Finance* 25 (2): 383–417.

Fishman, Michael J., and Kathleen M. Hagerty. 1995. "The Mandatory Disclosure of Trades and Market Liquidity." *Review of Financial Studies* 8 (3): 637–676.

Gabaix, Xavier, Parameswaran Gopikrishnan, Vasiliki Plerou, and H. Eugene Stanley. 2006. "Institutional Investors and Stock market Volatility." *Quarterly Journal of Economics* 121 (2): 461–504.

Galbraith, John K. 1955. *The Great Crash, 1929*. New York: Houghton Mifflin Company.

Grinblatt, Mark, and Matti Keloharju. 2000. "The Investment Behavior and Performance of Various Investor Types: A Study of Finland's Unique Data Set." *Journal of Financial Economics* 55 (1): 43–67.

Grossman, Sanford J., and Merton H. Miller. 1988. "Liquidity and Market Structure." *Journal of Finance* 43 (3): 617–663.

Hirshleifer, David, and Siew Hong Teoh. 2009. "Thought and Behavior Contagion in Capital Markets." In *Handbook of Financial Markets: Dynamics and Evolution*. Edited by Klaus Reiner Schenk-Hoppé and Thorsten Hens, 1–56. Amsterdam: Elsevier/ North-Holland.

Hong, Harrison, and Jeremy C. Stein. 1999. "A Unified Theory of Underreaction, Momentum Trading, and Overreaction in Asset Markets." *Journal of Finance* 54 (6): 2143–2184.

Huddart, Steven, John S. Hughes, and Carolyn B. Levine. 2001. "Public Disclosure and Dissimulation of Insider Trades." *Econometrica* 69 (3): 665–681.

International Organization of Securities Commissions (IOSCO). 2000. "Investigating and Prosecuting Market Manipulation." Technical Committee. Madrid, Spain: IOSCO.

Klein, Lawrence R., Viktoria Dalko, and Michael H. Wang. 2012. *Regulating Competition in Stock Markets: Antitrust Measures to Promote Fairness and Transparency through Investor Protection and Crisis Prevention.* Hoboken, NJ: John Wiley and Sons.

Jarrow, Robert A. 1992. "Market Manipulation, Bubbles, Corners, and Short Squeezes." *Journal of Financial and Quantitative Analysis* 27 (3): 311–336.

Jegadeesh, Narasimhan. 1990. "Evidence of Predictable Behavior of Security Returns." *Journal of Finance* 45 (3): 881–898.

Jegadeesh, Narasimhan, and Sheridan Titman. 1995. "Short-Horizon Return Reversals and the Bid-Ask Spread." *Journal of Financial Intermediation* 4 (2): 116–132.

John, Kose, and Ranga Narayanan. 1997. "Market Manipulation and the Role of Insider Trading Regulations." *Journal of Business* 70 (2): 217–247.

Khwaja, Asim I., and Atif R. Mian. 2005. "Unchecked Intermediaries: Price Manipulation in an Emerging Stock Market." *Journal of Financial Economics* 78 (1): 203–241.

Kyle, Albert S. 1985. "Continuous Auctions and Insider Trading." *Econometrica* 53 (6): 1315–1335.

Lang, Larry H. P. 2004. *Manipulation.* Beijing: Oriental Press. (In Chinese)

Lehmann, Bruce N. 1990. "Fads, Martingales, and Market Efficiency." *Quarterly Journal of Economics* 105 (1): 1–28.

Mas-Colell, Andreu, Michael D. Whinston, and Jerry R. Green. 1995. *Microeconomic Theory.* Oxford: Oxford University Press.

Mei, Jianping, Guojun Wu, and Chunsheng Zhou. 2004. "Behavior-Based Manipulation—Theory and Prosecution Evidence." Unpublished manuscript, New York University.

Minsky, Hyman P. 1992. "The Financial Instability Hypothesis." Working Paper No. 74, The Jerome Levy Economics Institute of Bard College.

Motta, Massimo. 2004. *Competition Policy: Theory and Practice.* New York: Cambridge University Press.

Nye, Joseph. 2008. *Powers to Lead.* New York: Oxford University Press.

Reinhart, Carmen, and Kenneth Rogoff. 2009. *This Time Is Different. Eight Centuries of Financial Folly.* Princeton, NJ: Princeton University Press.

Securities and Exchange Commission. 2012. "Manipulation." http://www.sec.gov/answers/tmanipul.htm.

Specogna, Marino. 2003. *A Convicted Stock Manipulator's Guide to Investing.* Lincoln, NE: iUniverse.

Spence, Michael. 1973. "Job Market Signaling." *Quarterly Journal of Economics* 87 (3): 355–374.

Stiglitz, Joseph E. 1975. "The Theory of Screening, Education and the Distribution of Income." *American Economic Review* 65 (3): 283–300.

Vila, Jean-Luc. 1989. "Simple Games of Market Manipulation." *Economics Letters* 29 (1): 21–26.

Von Bommel, Jos. 2003. "Rumors." *The Journal of Finance* 58 (4): 1499–1519.

13

Crisis of Authority

WERNER DE BONDT ■

Good ideas and trusted leadership are key forces in maintaining order in society and in bringing about institutional change. As a rule, economists focus on material self-interest—for example, the vested interests of teachers or farmers—to the exclusion of other factors. However, people's interests rise above selfishness and, what is more important, commonly include notions about what is moral or fair (Rodrik 2014). As long ago as 1742, David Hume held that "interest itself, and all human affairs, are entirely governed by opinion." Especially in unsettled times, as we live through today, it is not possible either to maintain order or to push society forward without leadership. The world celebrates the great political, social, and cultural entrepreneurs who either saved or revolutionized their respective communities. Leaders need certain qualities. For instance, success often stems from courage and persistence. Pertinently, leaders use ideas to justify their authority and to galvanize or to temper public opinion.

Authority exists whenever a person "voluntarily subordinates himself to the will of another" (Coleman 1980). Authority directs, coordinates, and regulates society. Much of the time, it is remarkably powerful. As a matter of fact, otherwise normal citizens may commit immoral, unthinkable acts under orders from authority (Milgram 1965). Such crimes of obedience are often accompanied by disengagement that lessens feelings of accountability. Detachment slides into indifference (Bandura 1999). People who uncritically obey orders from higher-ups may also see themselves as having no other choice. Or they may respect the perceived legitimacy of the authorities, while conceding that some abuse of trust occurs from time to time.

Put differently, legitimacy accounts for most people's chosen submission to the common will (e.g., decisions made on grounds of efficiency and justice). Legitimacy itself depends on widespread identification with common values. In other words, the legitimacy of authority is negotiated between group members; authority depends on open or implicit consent. Authority is more the power to influence than the power to enforce action. To have authority *over* people does not entail that one has authority *with* people; also, to *possess* authority is less noteworthy than to *be* an expert authority (Beran 1983). Thoughtful individuals feel responsible for what an organization or group does. As a result, when put in the same situation, some members may obey authority while others may not. Constructive obedience, as opposed to uncritical obedience, means that principled people may break the rules and flout illegitimate demands. Ironically, authority derives a central part of its legitimacy from debate and resistance (Harris 1976; Warren 1996; Passini and Morselli 2009).

Expressions of public dissent—such as Occupy Wall Street, rallies against World Trade Organization (WTO) policies, or riots in Athens (Greece) and Ferguson (Missouri)—question the rightfulness of demands formulated by ostensibly legitimate authorities. The protests may be construed as a duty of good citizenship. This is not self-evidently true, but dissent does cast doubt on specific claims of legitimacy. Dissent's usual aim is to undo or to delay decisions. Most people develop a sense of right and wrong as they grow up (Durkheim 1902; Piaget 1932). Still, once disobedience promotes profound social change (as when Nelson Mandela fought apartheid), it may take heroism—beyond moral education—to withstand oppression.

Authority is an asset that is difficult to build and easy to waste. Many careers end in failure. In an uncertain world, some decision fiascos are inevitable. But it is also often the case that the persons in charge do not accomplish much. Hence, there is a periodic need to reaffirm the acceptability of those who are at the top of the pyramid. This is the process of legitimation. It is done in part with committee votes, the advice of outside consultants, board meetings, elections, referendums and so on—all intended to ensure that the governing elite does a fine job, that its efforts are in sync with the organization's mission or with commonly shared values, and that it pays close attention to the public's wishes. A separate method of securing legitimacy is "spin." Sometimes, rhetoric outstrips actual results, or the bar is set low enough that poor results actually look good. Still another practice to sustain legitimacy is procedural justice. Leaders may want to show that they wield power in a fair, neutral, and transparent way. Many people give the fairness of decision processes more weight than the quality of individual decisions (Tyler 2006).

Today's crisis of moral authority is defined by the fact that many people no longer trust that leaders in government and business, even if capable, have people's interests at heart. There is a perception of sleaze and selfishness at the top, of a double standard. It is also thought that those who play by the rules are naive. Hence, people feel less obligated to comply with laws or workplace rules; are less inclined to cooperate, say, with the police (Kirk and Matsuda 2011); and are less willing to invest in the organizations where they are employed or in the communities where they live. (Respect is a two-way street.) The crisis is less acute than it is chronic, but the erosion of consumer, investor, business, and voter confidence—replaced by the anger, anxiety, and disgust that much of the public experiences on a daily basis—is very real in its consequences. Millions of middle-aged workers have left the labor market; small businessmen and investors prefer to hold cash, waiting for economic improvement, rather than to invest; voter turnout is low. Thus, to repeat, a general crisis of authority wears down society's ability to organize and act.

Every chain of command tries to establish, to nurture, and—if necessary—to repair the belief in its legitimacy. Without the approval of its various constituencies, an institution does not have a rightful claim to power and may not be able to reach its end goals. The concept of a "legitimation crisis" is associated with the German sociologist Jürgen Habermas (1973). Theories of authority and legitimacy span many centuries, however. They appear prominently in the works of Plato, Aristotle, Nicolo Machiavelli, Jean-Jacques Rousseau, Max Weber and others (Arendt 1954 and 1956; Wolfe 1977). In a full-scale legitimation crisis, the members of a social system no longer yield to the authority of the leaders. There is a retraction of confidence that may lead to a rebellion that threatens organizational survival, perhaps because rewards are not allocated according to merit or because the common good is not served or because some actions are judged to be morally wrong. Still other causes of crisis are policy incoherence, transparency or accountability deficits, and ineptness.

Today, we live in a world where our leaders and institutions seem unable to address the challenges that we demand them to address. Our future is uncertain. Corruption and broken promises stain many administrative structures. The crisis of confidence is further compounded by global disorder (such as terrorism, war, and environmental degradation) so that even our physical security looks endangered. In a secular society, where institutions are of man's making, our leaders—not God or fate or the laws of history—are kept responsible for the repeated failure to meet expectations.

Evidently, communities benefit if the activities of their members are synchronized. Good social and economic coordination as a rule presupposes proper organization, that is, a certain amount of deliberate planning, role differentiation, and a web of authority relations. No matter whether a society is nominally capitalist or socialist, the complexity of modern life often leads to large-scale administration and bureaucracy (Ellul 1964; Gray 1998; Harcourt 2011). Some individuals will either directly guide the actions taken by other people or delegate that function. However, persons in positions of authority are less likely to be followed if they lack legitimacy.

Legitimacy has various origins. Besides personal charisma and the sanctity of tradition, the main sources are the rationality and legality of action plans (and objective rules and policies) seen to be in the public interest and popularly supported (Weber 1947). Managerial competence, proven by superior performance, strengthens legitimacy. So do honesty and independence from special interests.

Success and integrity are difficult to hold onto in tandem, however. At some point, even the best performers are bound to stumble. In democracies, politicians are by construction "perpetual office seekers . . . always required to court their restless constituents." They "rarely feel they can afford the luxury of telling the whole truth to the people" (Lippmann 1935). The heart of the matter, as explained by Abraham Lincoln, is that "public sentiment is everything. With public sentiment, nothing can fail; without it nothing can succeed" (Basler 1953). That is, confidence is indispensable and legitimacy cannot do without a continual process of legitimation, a never-ending effort by those who are in charge to build and restore trust. Regular, periodic elections are just one manifestation of this need. James Madison said that "the genius of republican liberty" demands that "on one side . . . those entrusted with power . . . should be kept in dependence on the people by the short duration of their appointments" and that "stability, on the contrary, requires that the hands in which power is lodged should continue for a length of time" (Platt 1993). Another derivative of the vital need for legitimacy is the energy spent by leaders in government, business, and finance to manage public relations. The news media play a central role in reporting and interpreting events (Edelman 1998 and 2001).

If the news is bad enough, however, it is hopeless to rewrite history. Since the start of the new millennium, investigative journalism has exposed much dysfunction, ineptitude, cronyism, and injustice. Despite ample spin, there is a growing realization among the general public—and even among old-school commentators like Luigi Zingales (2012)—that many years of failure have not wounded but furthered the wealth and cultural supremacy of the nation's elite. This overt contradiction between success and reward lies behind the skepticism that now prevails with regard to the notion of meritocracy. The standards of responsibility are different for the 1% and the 99%, people believe, and they have branched out in opposite directions just like income and wealth (Wolff 2012; Piketty 2014). That America has lost faith is the end result of (1) acute frustration with economic mismanagement, the bailout of Wall Street, nonstop corporate scandals, political gridlock, and setbacks in war; and (2) the judgment that common people must pick up the tab for all these different forms of "waste, fraud and abuse." The public is angry about past failures, disgruntled with present conditions, and anxious about the future. It feels betrayed. (These sentiments are behind the 2016 presidential campaign of Donald Trump. But the same unease, I hastily add, also afflicts Japan, Britain, and the Eurozone nations.) The disintegration that we are witnessing in market democracies reminds us of the poetic phrase of William Butler Yeats: "Things fall apart; the center cannot hold."

In a nutshell, trust and authority matter—they are vital to society (Fukuyama 1995; Hetherington 1998 and 2006; Phillips 2008; Schneier 2012; Zingales 2012)—and it is essential that they be restored.

Lack of trust has economic consequences. Trust, trustworthiness, and loyalty are key elements of a country's social capital. They complement legal contracts and reduce suspicion, thereby enabling cooperation. Trust, impersonal as well as interpersonal, promotes a peaceful society and a productive economy.

Lack of trust has psychological consequences. It is linked to stress, anxiety, feelings of helplessness (every so often leading to suicide), and anger. Anger is the activation of the body's fight-or-flight response. A related common aftereffect is a tendency to pass blame—not always intentionally—on outsiders such as recent immigrants.

Lack of trust has political, social, and moral consequences. It influences whether citizens are interested in governmental affairs, whether they vote, and whether they voluntarily comply with law. Skepticism with respect to the motives of the world's power elite now seeps into most interpretations of current events. Many people have come to believe that ethics has no place in human affairs and that leaders the world over are untruthful. Cynicism is contagious. When all power is viewed as fraudulent, however, the credibility required to take action is lost. To repeat, good governance necessitates authority. Also, a vicious cycle of management misconduct and low public expectations may take effect, intensifying the spiral of cynicism (Noelle-Neumann 1977; Capella and Jamieson 1997; Bartels 2008).

Among the usual excuses for the current "great unraveling" are technological change and globalization. But, irrespective of whether we live in the "digital age" or "the age of globalization" or whether the heart of the problem is our broken democracy that has transferred power to the 1%, we definitely live in an age of insecurity (Elliott and Atkinson 1998) and anxiety (Tone 2009; Stossel 2013). We must also prepare, it seems, for an age of austerity with considerable social conflict as elected officials, faced with inadequate tax collections and a sea of debt, are forced to make zero-sum choices (Edsall 2012). It all adds up to a renewed political and social debate about the trade-off between efficiency and equality or, stated differently, between prosperity and social justice (Okun 1975; Kuttner 1984).

Alas, there will be no easy return to normalcy—at least as it was previously under-stood. Wishful thinking, avoidance, or outright denial will not save us. Today, people have grave doubts whether economic and technological progress are inevitable and whether market democracies offer the prospect of a better life. This is not new, of course, as anyone knows who has read Tawney (1920 and 1931), Schumpeter (1942), Roepke (1960), Crozier et al. (1975) or Zakaria (2013), not to mention Karl Marx, John Maynard Keynes, Friedrich von Hayek, and Gunnar Myrdal. However, for the last 35 years, we have been told that the "mixed" economy is taking us to a dead end. And, for much of this time, many people were fervently committed to free markets, entrepreneurship, privatization, deregulation, and the impassioned belief that if we kept reforming prosperity would spread. They argued in favor of laissez-faire, and they hoped to downsize the state to a second-order phenomenon, a mere annoyance (Armey and Kibbe 2010). Since 2008, many people judge that this is wrong. The state either allows human beings to flourish or it is an obstacle. But nearly everyone accepts that the state is of first-order importance (Moss 2002). Once more, the quality of our societal institutions—our laws, democracy, government administration, and corporate governance (Acemoğlu and Robinson 2012; Ferguson 2012)—has become the central issue of our time. As it happens, where the state is needed, as in the provision of education and training, it is often performing dismally. But, equally true, a nation's success does not only derive from keeping government out of the way. In general, good institutions may contribute to the nation's well-being, just as bad rules and regulations may impede its success. The central message of this chapter is that no matter what direction future policy and reforms may take, they will require the capacity to decide. That is, they will require authority—competent and credible leadership, presently very much in short supply (Naim 2013).

Hereafter, I first draw a picture of the current economic malaise. Next, I examine the decline in public trust. Finally, I discuss some of the root causes behind the erosion of authority. A brief summary concludes the chapter.

THE AFTERMATH OF 2007–2008

At present, the world's industrialized nations are confronted with a proliferation of unfavorable economic trends: sluggish income growth; high unemployment; rising household, government, and bank debt; and so on. Since the start of the new mil-lennium, the financial excesses of the technology and housing bubbles—followed by big market blowups, bank bailouts, and economic collapse—have caused a great deal of pain.

Figure 13.1 presents indexes of compounded growth in real GDP per capita for nine countries: France (FR), Germany (DE), Ireland (IE), Italy (IT), Japan (JP), Spain (ES), Sweden (SE), the United Kingdom (UK), and the United States (US). The source of the data is *Eurostat*. The indexes are set at 100 on December 31, 1999. Figure 13.1 shows that, among the countries listed, Sweden had the strongest overall growth performance between 2000 and 2013. Germany and Ireland came in second, more or less ex aequo, but their records were very dissimilar. Every year between 1996 and 1999, Ireland's growth rate topped 9%. The strong economic growth continued at a lesser pace—on average, 3.6% per year—through the end of 2007. Next, between 2008 and 2013, Ireland's average annual growth rate was a (negative)

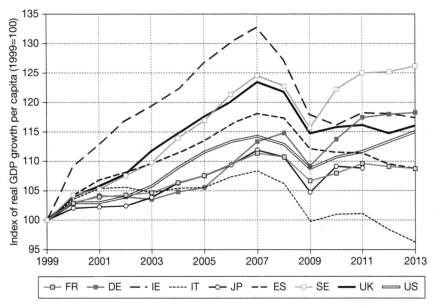

Figure 13.1 Real growth in GDP per capita since 1999 in France, Germany, Ireland, Italy, Japan, Spain, Sweden, UK, and US.

-2% (with a huge drop of -7.3% in 2009). The matching statistics for Germany were 1.6% (2000–2007) and 0.8% (2008–2013). On the whole, the German and US economies went through similar expansion paths but the United States was slower to bounce back after 2009. The UK economy grew faster than Germany until 2007, then shrank further in 2008–2009, and stagnated afterward.

It is remarkable to see how, among the countries examined, the 2011 level of real GDP per capita surpassed the level for 2007 only in Sweden and Germany. The United States exceeded the 2007 number in 2013. No other countries returned to the level of 2007. In Italy, the 2012 level of real GDP per capita fell below what it was at the start of the new millennium. The Italian economy contracted further in 2013.

Current prospects for improvement are poor, in part because the economic mood remains glum. Many advanced economies are in a deep hole and semi-stagnant. Their recovery after the crisis has not been V- but L-shaped. In other words, it looks as if steady growth, at this time halting and uneven, will not return for some time to come.

The Disappearing Middle Class

Ever since the 2008 collapse, there is much nostalgia in the United States for jobs with good wages and benefits, and for the vision of a meritocratic but classless society. Idealism has given way to a pervasive sense of futility and economic insecurity (Madrick 2011; Noah 2012; Smith 2012; De Neve et al. 2014; Broughton 2015). The drop in living standards has hit the middle class disproportionately. The squeeze began already in the 1980s when the link between middle-class income and labor productivity was first broken. On the whole, Americans are overworked and overspent (Currier et al. 2015). Many people feel demoralized. They worry about getting or hanging on to a job, about paying for their children's education, and about funding retirement, in part also because entitlement programs such as social security are put in danger by poor public finances. In a 2015 Gallup poll, 51% of Americans identified themselves as middle or upper-middle class, down from 63% in 2008, and 48% self-identified as working or lower class, up from 35% (Newport 2015).

Workers have paid a terrible price through lost jobs. Since 2007, the US economy has barely recouped the drop-off. The working-age population has continued to grow, though. In many advanced countries unemployment is now dominated by long-term joblessness. A related problem is low and/or stagnant pay. Median US middle-class income decreased by 5% in the last decade, and middle-class wealth fell 28% (Wolff 2012). At the same time, the top 10% ended up with nearly all the income gains since 1998 (Prestowitz 2010; Madrick 2011). From the perspective of inequality, the United States and Britain look like third-world economies (Elliott and Atkinson 2012).

Excessive mortgage and consumer debt is a further problem. Millions of people live in fear of losing their homes. (At the same time, tighter lending standards that came into effect after 2008 are preventing creditworthy borrowers form buying homes, thereby slowing the economic recovery.)

The elderly also struggle to get by. Many retirees grapple with dwindling savings and feel the need to look for part-time employment. Investments in fixed-income instruments earn almost nothing. The zero interest policy in the United States and Europe is destroying those who prefer conservative investing. It forces people who merely want to live off their interest earnings to seek riskier investments. The basic investment flaw, however, is the belief that through their years of employment Americans are able to accumulate enough savings to last a lifetime. That is the premise behind IRAs and 401(k) plans. But, going forward, the concept may not work. Almost all pension plans are grossly underfunded. The massive baby boom population is about to retire with inadequate savings. We are on the precipice of disaster. Personal finance is an oxymoron, says Helaine Olen (2012). The financial challenges that Americans face mainly reflect society's inability to tackle economic insecurity. Yet, the cult of personal finance implies that the middle class has itself to blame. This is false. Indeed, the dilemma of the financial services sector is that an educated customer is a bad, unprofitable customer.

In sum, America is coming apart. Many believe that "the system is rigged." We live in fragmentary social conditions that may produce chaos and disorder—as they do in Greece since the victory of Syriza or even, if everything goes wrong, as they did in Germany between the two world wars (Taylor 2013). US economic mobility has declined over the half century (Murray 2012; Putnam 2015). Americans now enjoy less mobility than their peers in Western Europe and the level of US inequality is comparable to China. Poor families stay trapped. As the affluent transmit their advantages, the life expectancy of middle-aged whites without a high school diploma is dropping (Case and Deaton 2015). More than 50 million people in the United States, including 17 million children, live with food insecurity: "At any given time their families don't know where their next meal is coming from" (see, e.g., the March 1, 2013, interview of Lori Silverbush with Ray Suarez on PBS Newshour). The elite, in contrast, retreats into walled proprietary communities. Neighborliness, the way that citizens routinely help each other in matters great and small, is fading.

A distinctive upper-class culture has emerged. Alongside physical segregation, the result is cognitive stratification.

Nowadays, stock market indexes can rise, corporate profits can skyrocket, and yet many people are unemployed or underemployed. It is often said that US society tolerates inequality in the belief that everyone has a shot at making it into the middle class. This instrumental justification of market democracy appears to be losing its validity.

The New Normal in the Labor Market

Unemployment, it has long been understood, is coupled with poverty in big cities. The view that poverty and joblessness are linked to personal moral shortcomings and race has tended to weaken the support for social programs (Wilson 1997; Gilens 1998). However, globalization and new information technology, both leading causes of the loss of US manufacturing jobs, have put a serious dent in this story. Consider, for example, aircraft manufacturing. Fully 70% of the new Boeing Dreamliner is foreign content. In contrast, the Boeing 727 was originally built with only 2% foreign content (Bartlett and Steele 2012; Tang and Zimmerman 2009).

Elliott and Atkinson (2012) report similar troubles in the UK economy, that is, industrial hollowing out made worse by globalization, followed by slower and more volatile growth, followed by reduced tax receipts and cuts in public spending. The authors chiefly blame trade policy. After all, if, as we are told, "exports help employment," must it not also be true that imports help unemployment?

As manual labor becomes less important, most high earners are well educated and take advantage of machine intelligence. Business increasingly depends on a select few with cognitive skills that complement computers and with personal qualities of character such as diligence and reliability. This has led to a bifurcated job market and wage polarization (Autor 2010; Cowen 2013). The new US jobs are typically service jobs with low pay scales. Another troubling trend is that the shelf life of many skills is short. Hence, the specter of "uselessness" haunts professionals as well as manual workers.

Unsuccessful first-time entrants into the labor force risk becoming unemployable. The career prospects of the young, including college graduates, are mediocre. (Yet student debt is at an all-time high.) People choose between career advancement and family formation. We are moving toward a society that is increasingly childless and single. Skill erosion is a continual threat to older, experienced workers. They are the hardest hit. There is a freelancing explosion among them. Many who are laid off hold out for higher pay and never return to the labor market (see, e.g., The New York Times 1996; Broughton 2015).

Worry and Discontent

As one may expect, the trouble with jobs and the uneven economic performance are reflected in opinion surveys such as those conducted by the Pew Research Center (Kohut 2012). Few people in the advanced economies are "satisfied with the way things are going." Between 2007 and 2012, the fraction of satisfied respondents

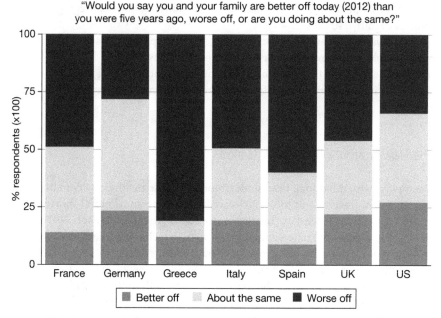

Figure 13.2 Assessment of current economic conditions in Europe and the US.

swung between 22% and 36% in the United States, Britain, and France. On the whole, the public mood worsened. The 2012 economy was described as "somewhat good" or "very good" by 31% of Americans (UK, 15%; France, 19%; Germany, 73%), and majorities in each country, except for Germany, described the economy as "somewhat bad" or "very bad." People with high incomes were often more upbeat, however, and it is also striking that people were more positive about their personal finances.

Today, the worry and discontent continue to be widespread. For example, the banking and sovereign debt crises in the European Union (EU) have mutated into a crisis of confidence in the merits of European integration and the Euro currency. Europeans further agonize about cuts in entitlements and diminished purchasing power. In the nations that border the Mediterranean, these worries have led to anti-German sentiment, partly because of Chancellor Angela Merkel's efforts to rein in government spending. (Merkel's 2012 approval ratings were 80% in Germany, 76% in France, 66% in Britain, and 63% in Spain, but 14% in Greece. Of late, her ratings have taken a big tumble.)

While faith in upward mobility is abysmal the world over (aside from China), the lion's share of Americans and Europeans are of the opinion that they are better off than their parents. Still, people in industrialized nations frequently say that they are worse off than they were five years ago. Figure 13.2 supports this assertion with data assembled in May 2012 by the Pew Global Attitudes Project. It is useful to know that, at the time, dissatisfaction with the "direction of the country" was 65% in Britain, 71% in France, 87% in Italy, 88% in Spain, and 98% in Greece. The recent influx of refugees from the Middle East has only intensified the overall unhappiness of the European public (Christides et al. 2016).

The preceding data stand in contrast with the assessment of economic conditions in the BRIC countries (Brazil, Russia, India, and China) and other emerging markets. In 2012, only 5% of Chinese, 12% of Brazilians, 25% of Indians, and 29% of Russians said that their families were financially worse off than five years earlier. In China and Brazil, majorities thought that their families were better off (Kohut 2012). The sentiment likely reflected real GDP growth between 2007 and 2011: 10.5% per year in China, 4.2% in Brazil, 8.1% in India, and 2.9 % in Russia. More recently, the joyfulness has diminished. People often blame their own governments, but faith in capitalism is also a victim of the slowdown in growth. Fewer survey respondents believe that they are better off in a free-market economy. That attitude is still fairly strong in China (74%) and Brazil (75%) but weaker in Russia (47%) and the Arab countries.

Figure 13.3 employs data published by the Pew Research Center for the People and the Press (August 2014) to put the economic frustrations of the United States public in historical perspective. I plot monthly observations of the fraction of respondents who "all in all" are dissatisfied "with the way things are going today" (99 surveys between January 2000 and August 2014). In addition, I plot monthly observations of the proportion of people who rate current economic conditions as "only fair or poor" (67 surveys between February 2004 and August 2014). When there is more than one survey during a given month, I plot the average for the month. When there is no survey, I use the observation of the last available month to produce extra data points. Figure 13.3 shows individual monthly observations as well as 24-month centered moving averages for both series.

The next two figures are also based on the 2014 Pew Research Center report. Figure 13.4 portrays economic expectations for the next year and shows the percent

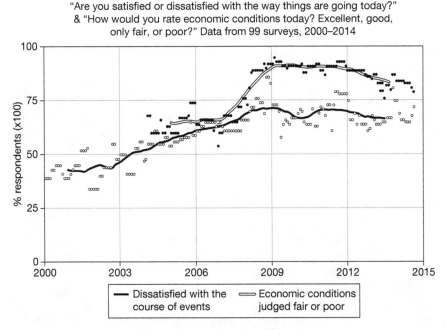

Figure 13.3 Assessment of US current economic conditions.

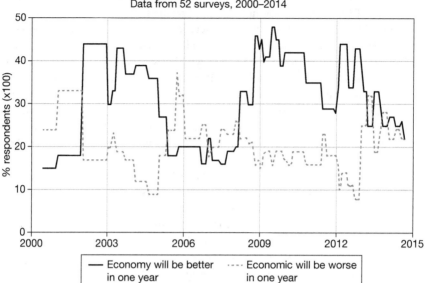

"A year from now, do you expect that economic conditions will be
better than they are at present, or worse, or just about the same?"
Data from 52 surveys, 2000–2014

Figure 13.4 Assessment of US future economic conditions.

of respondents who expect economic conditions to be "better" or "worse" than at present. It is useful to compare Figure 13.4 with Figure 13.3. It is striking that, as discontent grew between 2003 and 2009 by as much as 20%, a plurality of people first projected that US economic conditions would soon improve and, starting around 2005, that the economy would get worse. When the end of the 2008 recession was in sight, the pattern was broken. Still, the fraction of optimists and pessimists became comparable again beginning in 2013.

Equivalently, Figure 13.5 compares present-day assessments of personal finances with future expectations. I use the same methods as before, showing both monthly observations and 24-month moving averages (in this case, based on 52 surveys). Sentiment about personal finances, as measured by the fraction of respondents who judged their situation to be "only fair or poor," deteriorated by about 10 points between Spring 2008 and Summer 2009. Over that same period, forecasts of how personal finances would evolve next became more negative.

PERVASIVE CYNICISM

The anger and anxiety, illustrated by the data and figures presented above, have to be taken seriously. As the American dream has evaporated, so has public trust. Trust requires that government and business are forces for good—that is, committed to a higher purpose and visibly benefiting society. People tend to put faith in people and institutions that reach their objectives with efficiency, transparency, accountability, and fairness, while maintaining decorum. A central reason for the current malaise—fostering stagnation—is that our leaders in government, business,

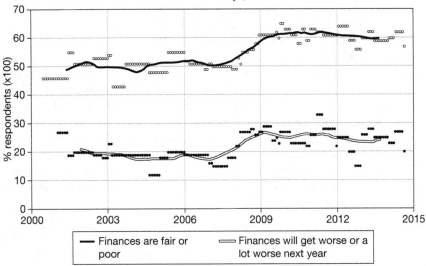

Figure 13.5 Assessment of personal finances.

and finance are no longer trusted. Somehow, the presumption of competence and honesty no longer exists. Above all, the Madoff scandal sowed the seeds of suspicion —whether someone is a con artist, there is no way of knowing, it seems (Henriques 2011). Klaus Schwab, host and founder of the annual World Economic Forum, has said that our leaders are "in danger of completely losing the confidence of future generations" and that "capitalism, in its current [January 2012] form, has no place in the world."

Past literature defines trust in different ways. Some definitions rely on insights from psychology; others, on ideas from economics and sociology. Authentic, willful trust is generated in relationships. It is "a positive affective state based upon confident expectations and a willingness to be vulnerable." (Olsen 2008). Trust "is the very opposite of control . . . its risks and vulnerabilities understood, with distrust held in balance" (Flores and Solomon 1998). A key survey question that has been examined by several US studies and that is part of the *General Social Survey* reads as follows: "Generally speaking, would you say that most people can be trusted or that you can't be too careful in dealing with people?" Low interpersonal trust is related to an individual's lack of economic success, recent trauma (such a divorce), belonging to a discriminated group and living in a racially mixed community (Alesina and La Ferrara 2002).

Trust in people and trust in institutions are analogous but not identical concepts. They are often linked to one another. For example, trust in the US government responds to changes in partisan control of the presidency (Keele 2005). Also, Shaun Bowler and Jeffrey Karp (2004) use US and UK data to show that scandals involving legislators influence their constituents' attitudes toward political institutions. Charles Murray defines social trust as "the generalized expectation that the people around you will do the right thing" (2012, p. 247). Trust is a component of social capital, and social capital plays a role in the creation of human capital. For example, family background helps to predict the likelihood that high school sophomores drop out and do not graduate (Coleman 1988). In the cross section of countries, trust and social capital are related to economic growth (Knack and Keefer 1997). Many measures of social capital started declining in the 1970s, possibly because of rising inequality and ethnic diversity (Putnam 1995 and 2007).

Failure causes distrust. Distrust causes failure. (Or, as Vince Lombardi said, "confidence is contagious and so is lack of confidence.") This vicious circle may be linked to people's loss aversion (that is, their lopsided sensitivity to failure) often becomes a self-fulfilling prophecy (Merton 1948; De Neve et al. 2014). A negative weather forecast does not affect the climate but a business forecast that is unfavorable may well damage the economy. In politics too, credibility builds momentum. Thus, image problems can cause objective failure and become policy problems. In general, trust is fragile but not brittle. Trust and trustworthiness may serve as protective agents. For example, with a high reputation, you get the benefit of the doubt (Yankelovich 2006; Firestein 2009).

To repeat, the economic, social, and political landscape has been changing. Below, I discuss trust primarily as a macro-level phenomenon. I make use of trust and public opinion data put together by numerous organizations such as the Pew Research Center, Edelman, the Gallup News Service, www.realclearpolitics.com, TNS Sofres, and others. My aim is to reveal recent trends in trust in institutions and professions (including government and business leaders), both in the United States and elsewhere. This type of effort does not break new ground. For instance, it is well known that, after being highly trusting of government during the 1950s, the American public became sharply more cynical during the Vietnam era, and that these doubts were followed by an upswing of positive feeling in the Reagan administration (Lane 1965; Miller 1974; Citrin 1974; Yankelovich 1974; Lipset and Schneider 1983 and 1987).

Trust and Distrust: Multicountry Evidence

An important source of data is Edelman's *Trust Barometer*. Edelman is a global public relations firm with over 3,000 employees. Since the year 2000, Edelman has conducted annual surveys of the informed public as well as the general population in as many as 26 countries using either telephone interviews or online questionnaires. The 2008 survey of the informed public involved 4,475 people on 5 continents. The respondents were 25 to 64 years old, were college educated, showed significant interest in news about business and public policy, and had an household income that put them into the top 25% for their age group and country of residence. The profile of the 2008 respondents was typical. However, after 2011, the number of respondents rose beyond 30,000. For a limited number of countries, Edelman has ten or more years of data.

Edelman asks: "How much do you trust government, business, banks, media companies and non-governmental organizations (NGOs) to do what is right?" It also asks: "How much do you trust CEOs and government officials to tell the truth?" Of course, one wonders how the respondents interpret these questions and whether there is meaningful cultural variation in this regard. However, the questions do suggest a contrast between doing well and doing good, in other words, a conflict between self-interest and the public interest. The answers are recorded on a scale between 1 ("do not trust them at all") and 9 ("trust them a great deal"). Below, I report the percent of respondents with scores above 5—the fraction of people who express at least some positive trust (%TRUST). I examine data gathered since 2007 for 17 countries (13 advanced plus the BRIC economies) in 7 regions of the world.

There are lasting differences in overall levels of trust, %TRUST, between countries and regions. For instance, based on 2007–2013 data for government, business, banks, media companies, NGOs, government officials, and CEOs, the average %TRUST was about 55% for Brazil and 70% for China and India. Similar statistics for the G7 or Russia were usually below 50% and they were even below 40% for some European countries that border the Mediterranean.

Figure 13.6 shows national averages for trust in business (over seven years, 2007–2013) and trust in government (over six years, 2008–2013). The data are for an informed public, 35 to 64 years old. In all places except France and China, trust in business (%TRBUS) looked stronger than trust in government (%TRGOV). Relative to %TRGOV, trust in business was strikingly robust in the United States, Japan, Italy, Brazil, and India.

Trust in NGOs and media companies (not displayed in Figure 13.6) was typically high relative to %TRBUS and %TRGOV. In contrast, trust in CEOs and government leaders was weak compared to trust in academic experts. The 2012 medians for 17 countries were, respectively, 39% and 35% (with the statistics for Japan, 22% and 15%, lowest of all).

Figures 13.7 and 13.8 reveal how trust in government and banks has shifted since the start of the economic crisis. For each country and year, I first compute standardized trust scores. (I subtract the mean overall country %TRUST level and

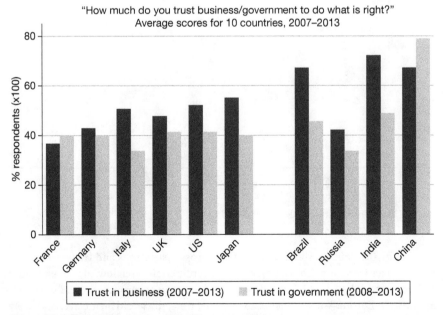

Figure 13.6 Trust in business vs. trust in government.

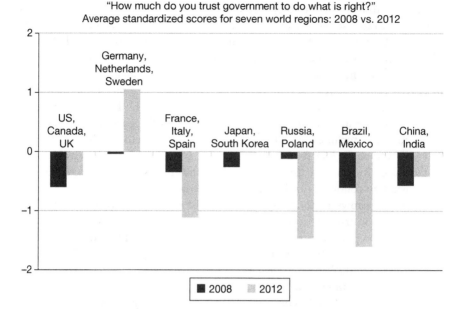

Figure 13.7 How trust in government has changed.

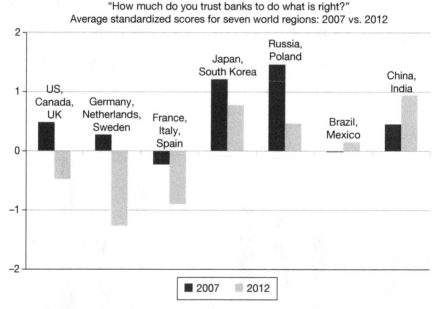

Figure 13.8 How trust in banks has changed.

I divide by the country standard deviation across institutions and leaders.) Next, I find averages by region. To repeat, trust in government is often low. However, Figure 13.7 shows that, between 2008 and 2012, confidence in government actually went up in northern Europe—no doubt because, at that time, the world financial crisis barely touched this corner of the world—and confidence went down in the Mediterranean region (France, Italy, and Spain), Russia and Poland, and Brazil and Mexico. As Figure 13.8 shows, trust in banks broke down nearly everywhere. Insurance, media, and automobile companies suffered similar big declines, at least early in the crisis.

Trust and Distrust in US and UK Public Institutions

Figure 13.9 displays data put together by the Gallup News Service about public trust in major US institutions. Gallup undertook the first survey of this kind in May 1973. With few exceptions, the data were collected annually. The last survey took place in June 2014. In 2014, Gallup conducted telephone interviews of a random sample of US adults 18 years or older. The results were weighted to match the US demographics of age, gender, race, education, region, and other factors. Some interviews were conducted in Spanish. The interviewer read a list of as many as 16 institutions in American society and asked: "Please tell me how much confidence you, yourself, have in each one—a great deal, quite a lot, some, or very little?"

Below, I build separate trend indexes of the percentage of respondents that expressed "a great deal" or "quite a lot" of confidence in six key institutions (banks, big business, churches, newspapers, the US Congress, and the US military). The base value of each individual index in 1985 is set at 100. Next, I divide each index by the average trend index for all six institutions.

The average proportion of respondents who voice confidence (%TRUST2) in key institutions shows no particular trend and only modest fluctuations between 1985 and 2004. For instance, %TRUST2 stood at 47% in 1985 and at 44% in 2004. After that, however, %TRUST2 declined to 36% (2009) and 33% (2014).

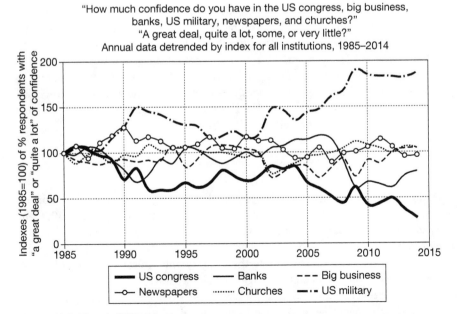

Figure 13.9 Trust in US institutions.

Figure 13.9 allows us to put side by side longer-term fluctuations in public trust of big business, newspapers, and churches, on the one hand, and trust of banks, Congress, and the military, on the other. By and large, relative trust in big business, newspapers, and churches has not changed a great deal. Trust in banks fell precipitously after 2007, however. Trust in the US Congress reached a low point in 2014. Only 7% of Americans said that they had "a great deal" or "quite a lot" of confidence. (This number compares to 42% in 1973, the first year that *Gallup* asked the question, or 39% in 1985.) Americans are most upbeat for the military. Trust in the armed forces appears to have benefited from the first Gulf War, the September 11, 2001 attacks, and later wars. It remained stable after Barack Obama became president. According to the detailed analysis of Stevenson and Wolfers (2011), the Gallup data show that trust in congressmen, bankers, and newspaper journalists is procyclical and related to the nation's unemployment rate. Likewise, Virginia Chanley and her coworkers (2000) conclude that trust in government varies with changing on perceptions of the US economy (as well as public concern about crime and political scandals).

Trust in the US federal government was near a record low in late 2013 (Pew Research Center for the People and the Press, October 2013). Just 19% of the public said that they trust the US government "to do what is right" "just about always or most of the time." (Before 2007, that statistic was usually above 30%.) Also, 85% said that they were angry (30%) or frustrated (55%) with the federal government. (From 1997 to 2013, the anger statistic rose somewhat but it was normally below 20%. It was 8% in 2001, right after the terrorist attack in New York. The frustration statistic is mostly around 50%.) Despite its crushing rejection of the federal government and of members of the US Congress, the public has mostly a favorable opinion of federal government workers. The overall opinion of the US Congress was 73% unfavorable in October 2013, up from 51% in May 2008, 41% in December 1998, and 28% in May 1988.

A parallel analysis for the United Kingdom is possible based on the *British Social Attitudes Survey 2012*, which lists the fraction of people who state that they trust British governments (of any party) "just about always or most of the time," "some of the time," or "almost never." The historical data displayed in Figure 13.10 cover 19 annual surveys between 1986 and 2011. (Some data points are obtained by interpolation.) The fraction of respondents who said that they "almost never" have faith in a UK government swelled from 12% in 1986 to 32% in 2011. The fraction who trust "most of the time" fell from 40% to 22%.

Trust and Distrust in Professions

Figure 13.11 displays Gallup data relating to what the US public thinks of the honesty and ethics of 45 professions. Gallup started this kind of survey in June 1976 and usually implemented it twice a year. The latest data included here were collected in November 2012. The interviewer asked respondents about different career paths: "Please tell me how you would rate the honesty and ethical standards of people in these fields: very high, high, average, low or very low?" Some professionals, like bankers, were included again and again (28 times); others, like grade school teachers (3 times) or auto mechanics (6 times), only sporadically.

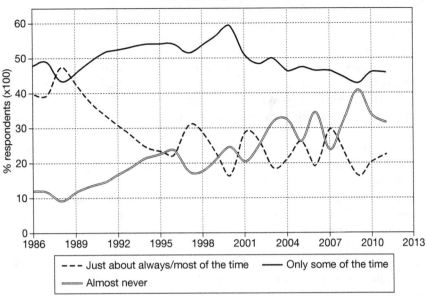

"Do you trust British governments (of any party)?"
Annual data, 1986–2012

--- Just about always/most of the time   — Only some of the time
=== Almost never

Figure 13.10 Trust in the government of the UK.

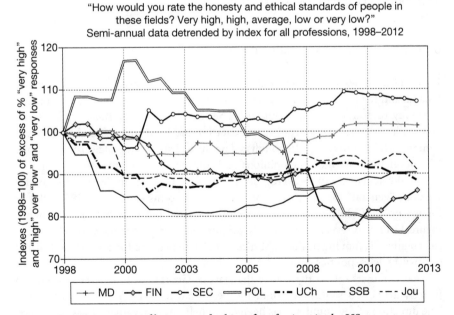

"How would you rate the honesty and ethical standards of people in these fields? Very high, high, average, low or very low?"
Semi-annual data detrended by index for all professions, 1998–2012

—+— MD   —◇— FIN   —o— SEC   === POL   —·— UCh   — SSB   --- Jou

Figure 13.11 Perceptions of honesty and ethics of professions in the US.

To be able to examine unbroken time series, I form seven distinct groups of similar professions: (1) medical (*MD*) (7 career paths); (2) finance and big business (*FIN*) (7); (3) security, engineering, and accounting (*SEC*) (6); (4) politicians, lobbyists, and union leaders (*POL*) (7); (5) teachers and clergy (*UCh*) (6); (6) sales and small business people (*SSB*) (9); and (7) journalists (*Jou*) (3). For example, *MD* consists of chiropractors, medical doctors, dentists, nurses, pharmacists, psychiatrists, and veterinarians. *POL* comprises congressmen, labor union leaders, lobbyists, local politicians, senators, state governors, and state politicians. For the sum total of all professions as well as for each group, I calculate the excess of the percentage of responses that are "high" or "very high" over the percentage of responses that are "low" or "very low," and I multiply these statistics by 100. I also add 100. The observations are semiannual. In the end, I obtain analogous indexes of the honesty and ethics of assorted professions.

There is much persistence in the data. For example, an analysis that starts in 1983 shows that *MD*, *SEC*, and *UCh* all score around 150 and swing between 140 and 160. This means that the proportion of respondents who think highly or very highly of, say, medical professionals usually exceed the proportion who think badly or very badly of them by 50%. On the other hand, *POL* typically scores below 100. The score for *SSB*, also below 100, has improved a great deal since the 1980s, but the score for *Jou* has gone downhill.

Figure 13.11 shows the trust data since the first half of 1998. The seven series are detrended by the index for all 45 professions so that it becomes easier to spot relative changes in perceived trust. Various facts come to light: (1) a considerable fall in the perceived honesty of *SSB*, *UCh*, and *Jou* in the early part of the period (and a modest recovery of *SSB* after 2004, however); (2) the far more dramatic descent of *POL* after 2001; and (3) the collapse of *FIN*, first around 2001 and then again after 2007.

Job Approval Ratings for Government Leaders

Figure 13.12 shows job approval statistics for presidents George W. Bush and Barack Obama and for the US Congress since January 2005. The figure plots the fraction of survey respondents who "approve." The monthly data for Bush are based on 283 Gallup public opinion polls; the data for the US Congress and Obama are computed from 360 and 1,015 polls listed on the website www.realclearpolitics.com. Whenever there are multiple opinions polls during any given month—a common event—I calculate a simple average for the month. The data in Figure 13.12 are for Obama's "general" job approval, not with respect to his economic (495 polls) or foreign policy (235 polls), which are closely related but different measurements. Figure 13.12 also reveals the monthly proportion of respondents who believe that the country "is moving in the right direction." The data are from 1,086 polls listed on www.realclearpolitics.com.

What is remarkable is that, since the start of George W. Bush's second term in January 2005, US sentiment about the performance of government leaders and "the direction of the country" has been overwhelmingly negative. On average, 29% of respondents said that the country was moving in the right direction, and 22% approved the job performance of the US Congress. If we exclude from analysis the six-month honeymoon periods at the start of new presidential terms, there have

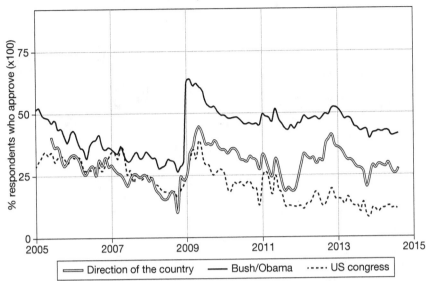

Figure 13.12 Trust in government leaders.

been only eight months since 2005 that presidential job approval topped 50%. Of the eight months, five were in the second half of 2009 (Obama's first year as president) and two were in the fall of 2012, right after Obama was re-elected. The only other month is May 2011, immediately after Osama bin Laden was liquidated. Obama's average economic policy approval was 42% (with disapproval at 53% and 5% neutral). Obama's average foreign policy approval was 46% (with disapproval at 44% and 10% neutral).

Figure 13.13 puts the previous findings in a longer-term perspective. That figure shows monthly job approvals for US presidents from Ronald Reagan to George W. Bush. The data for Reagan and George H. W. Bush are made available by University of North Carolina political scientists Thad Beyle, Richard Niemi, and Lee Sigelman in their *Job Approval Ratings Collection*. The data for President Bill Clinton are based on 217 Gallup polls.

Of the five US presidents since Ronald Reagan, only George H. W. Bush did not get re-elected for a second term. Over his tenure, the fraction of months that President Reagan's approval rating fell below 50% was 37%. For George H. W. Bush, Bill Clinton, and George W. Bush, the corresponding fractions were 36%, 28%, and 56%. (These statistics exclude the six-month honeymoons.) However, for the second term of George W. Bush, and for Obama's first and second terms, the respective percentages are 100%, 81%, and 100%.

All in all, the US data show a long-term trend of mounting disapproval interrupted by brief periods of public support and hopefulness, right after elections. In order to test whether the same pattern is present in other countries, I gathered data for France starting in 1981 with the election of Francois Mitterrand. In the analysis that follows, the last data point is for November 2014. At that time, the approval rating of the current president, Francois Hollande, fell to 13%. This was the lowest score recorded

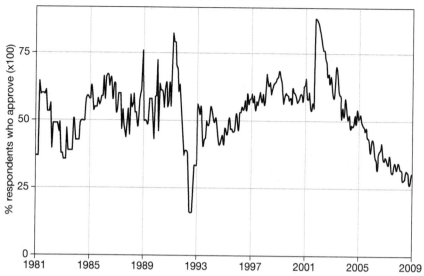

Figure 13.13 Trust in government leaders.

since 1981. The data are produced by TNS Sofres and published by *Le Figaro* maga-zine. They are based on monthly surveys that normally consist of a random sample of 1,000 French citizens, age 18 or older. The sample is stratified by age, gender, profession, and other factors. The respondents are interviewed in person at home.

As in the United States, presidents in France benefit from a honeymoon period at the beginning of a president's new term in office. In France, this period may last up to a year. See Figure 13.14. One difficulty in analyzing the French data is that, starting with the second presidency of Jacques Chirac, the length of the presidential term in France was reduced from seven to five years. So, in order to (1) assess the public's confidence in various presidents (Mitterrand, Chirac, Sarkozy, Hollande) at the same stage in the first or second term of their presidency, and (2) illustrate enduring trends, I plot the trust data by the number of months that have elapsed since the last election (*#months*). Because Hollande was elected in late Spring 2012, the x-axis in Figure 13.14 extends to 36 months but not further. In this manner, Figure 13.14 shows the fraction of respondents who are "very confident" or "confident" that the president of France "is able to solve current problems."

The inference one draws from Figure 13.14 is clear cut. We observe a long-term negative trend in admiration for French presidents. After we control for *#months*, the data for Mitterrand typically plot above the data for Chirac. The data for Chirac plot above the data for Sarkozy and, at the same stage of his presidency, Sarkozy inspired more confidence than Hollande. If we exclude the first six months of a new president's tenure, the average approval rating for Mitterrand I was 49%; Mitterrand II, 46%; Chirac I, 48%; Chirac II, 34%; Sarkozy, 32%; and Hollande, 24%. Correspondingly, the fraction of months that the president of France had an approval rating *below* 50% was for Mitterrand I, 46%; Mitterrand II, 54%; Chirac I, 54%; Chirac II, 89%; and Sarkozy and Hollande, both 100%.

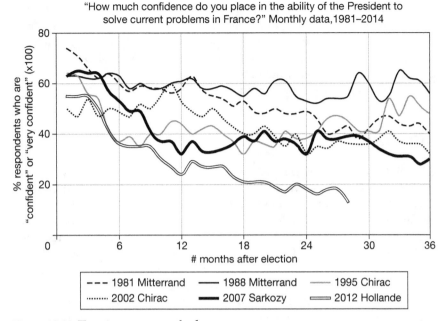

Figure 13.14 Trust in government leaders.

ROOT CAUSES

"Enough is enough." One way to recap the above data and modern-day discontent is to say that in many places history seems to be slipping into reverse, back to the economic, social, and political instability of the first half of the 20th century. In the West, there is much nostalgia for the 1950s and 1960s. (Indeed, in France, the three decades between 1945 and 1974 are remembered as "les trente glorieuses," 30 glorious years.) In the former member states of the Soviet Union, there is newfound respect for what was achieved under communist rule. Lastly, in much of the developing world, Chinese-style authoritarianism (i.e., government with strong central power but limited political freedom) rather than democratic capitalism has become a favorite model for social organization and rapid economic growth.

Niall Ferguson (2012) asks: What has gone wrong? Why are economic liberalism and Western democracy tarnished brands? Prominent among the factors that he considers are the burdens of household, corporate, and financial debt; the need for balance sheet repair (linked to a fall in aggregate demand); and unfunded government liabilities (Medicare, Medicaid, Social Security). Referring to Edmund Burke (1790), Ferguson sees society as a partnership "not only between those who are living, but between those who are living, those who are dead, and those who are to be born." Ferguson further worries about debilitating government red tape and a corrupt, monopolistic elite that uses the state to enrich itself. Bad institutions create bad incentives (see also Acemoğlu and Robinson 2012). "There is government. There is the market. There is the law. And then there is civil society. . . . But the institutions in our times are out of joint," Ferguson says.

How can we interpret the crisis of authority? Is it a failure of the system or is it a failure of people within the system? Or are both failures intertwined so that a crisis of authority is both cause and consequence? This last viewpoint is my preferred interpretation of where society finds itself today. Below, I list and discuss some of the root causes of the crisis of authority. They are technological change; globalization; a long-term decline in social cohesion and civic virtue; disillusionment with big government and democracy; and human irrationality reflected in unfounded fears, status anxiety, and exaggerated expectations.

Technological Change

Capitalism means turmoil. This is conventional wisdom since Western society was first confronted with the wastefulness of the business cycle. Karl Marx and later Joseph Schumpeter (1942) were among the first to explain how competitive markets spur innovation that puts employment at risk. Therefore, vigorous economic growth and social peace must clash. Still, after 1870, with the birth of the large corporation, anarchy started to subside. The great captains of industry built monopolies devised to survive booms and busts. Max Weber associated the emergence of bureaucratic behemoths with rationality and military organization, parallel to how Otto von Bismarck, hoping to pacify German society, erected a megastate and social safety net. Bismarck's prime aim was inclusion, not efficiency. But people could be expected to be loyal to a social system in which everyone had a place, with sufficient built-in stability to allow them to plan for the future and to live the good life. The result was efficiency as well as stability and prosperity, above all during the 30 years after the Second World War.

The 1990s were a turning point, the start of what Peter Drucker (1993) called *post-capitalist society*. The free market remained the chief mechanism of economic coordination, but the decisive resource was *knowledge*, not labor or capital. Specialized knowledge, backed by large-scale data systems, generated a fresh productivity revolution. It also led to outsourcing, a steep decline in manufacturing employment, and the elimination of many mid-level positions (Autor and Dorn 2013). Humans do what cannot be automated. "Manual labor, no matter how cheap," Drucker predicted, would be unable "to compete with knowledge labor, no matter how well paid."

Over the past 30 years, we have dismantled rigid corporate and governmental bureaucracies. There has been a global decline of lifetime employment. This was also foretold by Drucker and others (e.g., Cohen 2003 and 2009). The psychological costs of the new workplace are severe. When firms are re-engineered by outside consultants, employees often have no idea of what will happen to them. Internal labor markets blur the line between colleagues and competitors. Richard Sennett (1998 and 2006) discusses the corrosion of character that follows when there is no place for loyalty, honor, and service. Employees suffer continual worry reinforced by arbitrariness. They seek a steadiness of purpose, but they are treated as disposable. Many individuals feel that their lives are cast adrift. The inability to pursue long-term goals disorients family life. How do you manage life while migrating from job to job and place to place?

Other of Drucker's ideas were anticipated by Lewis Mumford's 1934 study of the history of the machine and by Jacques Ellul (1964). According to Ellul, technology—"the totality of methods rationally arrived at"—is not the servant of man but transforms everything that blocks the internal logic of its further development. The technological order began as a buffer between man and nature. Oddly, the abundance of means is bringing about the disappearance of ends, so that whatever is technically possible is thought to be desirable, and all that does not lend itself to technique gets ignored. Therefore, even as technology widens civilization, it dehumanizes. Ellul believes that technology changes man's thoughts and desires to yield an artificial impression of happiness. This may be why many individuals, often without thinking, are ambivalent about technological "progress" (Arthur 2009). Besides material comfort, technique produces fear. Separated from nature, many people turn to traditional values, fundamentalism, and environmentalism.

Globalization

Drucker (1993) believed that the knowledge society would shape a new world order. Similar ideas have also been put forward and celebrated by William Knoke (1996) and Thomas Friedman (2005). The world is shrinking and the notion of national sovereignty is losing meaning. There are fewer borders for manufactured goods and almost no borders for money, information, pollution, or private terrorist armies. New ideas spread like wildfire. Our society is the most mobile in the history of humanity. Modern transportation offers the means; modern communication, the knowledge.

Free trade is an area where society's long-term interest in economic efficiency clashes with its short-term worry about equity. Governments increasingly look powerless. Globalization curbs the effectiveness of labor law, environmental regulations, and the tax code. The relationship between aggregate demand and employment growth is also breaking down. Policies can stimulate demand, but they cannot redirect supply from offshore outsourcing back to domestic platforms. Evidently, open trade in an era of mobile capital creates pressure to reduce labor costs in expensive countries.

To think that we can reverse globalization seems unrealistic. A huge fraction of the export growth in China comes from Chinese subsidiaries of multinational firms headquartered in the industrialized countries. Yet, regional trading blocs such as the EU do exist while the blossoming of supranational institutions with wide-ranging tax and regulatory powers remains a fantasy. Perhaps the question is not whether to manage global trade but by which criteria to manage it (Goldsmith 1994; Trump 2016). Industrial policy and trade protection can either shelter losers or they can incubate technological breakthroughs. History shows that the state *can* create competitive advantage. Japan, Korea, and China achieved high growth behind high tariff barriers (Rodrik 1998).

A crucial problem with globalism is that people need roots. National character makes us feel at home and placelessness changes relationships. In many parts of the world (e.g., Catalonia, Scotland, Kurdistan, South Sudan), the trend toward globalization is challenged by a new tribalism, a demand for self-rule and/or cultural autonomy. Concurrently, there is much fear of immigration. It has been widely believed that, on balance, the United States benefits from cultural exchange, migration, and the promotion of democratic capitalism. Amy Chua (2003) argues, in contrast, that the export of free-market democracy to developing nations intensifies ethnic resentment. The reason is that capitalism concentrates wealth in the hands of market-dominant but otherwise vulnerable minorities. But the imbalance emboldens democratic majorities to confiscate wealth and, ultimately, this produces instability and anti-Americanism.

Less Social Cohesion and Civic Virtue

One more reason for the public's frustration, no doubt, is rising economic inequality, itself largely the outcome of competing socioeconomic interests and class antagonism. Even before 2008, public trust was low. The facts speak for themselves. Median real household income in the United States has been stagnant for many years. Inequality in income and wealth has soared to what it was before 1914. The US House and Senate appear to be controlled by campaign contributors and celebrity millionaires so that government policy responds more to the interests of the 1% than to the concerns of the 99% (Bartels 2008; Kaiser 2009 and 2013; Smith 2013).

Michael Marmot (2004) and Richard Wilkinson and Kate Pickett (2009) ask whether there are direct links between class disparities, social standing, and anxiety. For instance, they study the rise in anxiety levels among US college students (1952–1993). The level of wealth matters less than inequality, they say. Gross inequality is related to an array of mental and physical ailments, such as drug use, obesity, teenage births, and violence. Social standing is a major cause of ill health. It is not simply a matter of the level of income or wealth. It is the psychological experience of inequality, a lack of control over one's fate and environment. This sense of control declines as one descends the socioeconomic ladder (Ehrenreich 1989; Frank 2007). Nonetheless, some commentators "blame the victims" and point to their "self-destructive moral failures" (French 2016). Andrea Tone (2009) studies the mass consumption of tranquilizers, a billion-dollar business. Thousands of Americans are dependent on them. To some degree, anxiety has become a badge of achievement, an emblem of struggle, with cultural cachet. It is part of the hunger to get ahead.

In contrast, David Rothkopf (2008) and Chrystia Freeland (2012) study "Davos man," that is, the ascent of a global superclass. The interests of the cosmopolitan elite, often tied to international finance, diverge from those of most other citizens but many governments can no longer safeguard the national interest. Borders are irrelevant. Rothkopf provides a portrait and taxonomy of about 6,000 very wealthy people. The superclass is self-serving and entrenched. In the words of Edgar Bronfman, "to turn $100 into $110 is work; to turn $100 million into $110 million is inevitable."

Rothkopf (2012) explores a related theme: large firms have greater power than all but a handful of states. Also, the return on investment from lobbying and kickbacks has become so high that authentic business opportunities may not be worth the effort. Simultaneously, there has been a shift from managerial to shareholder power in large companies. Investors want short-term results. There is a fervent desire to maximize stock prices by any means necessary. For instance, some multinational companies use a "double Irish with a Dutch sandwich" tax avoidance strategy. All this unlocks the door for crony capitalism (Zingales 2012).

The class struggle is to a degree a conflict of ideological visions (Sowell 2002; Haidt 2012). Specifically, Christopher Hayes (2012) suggests that the doctrine of meritocracy lies behind the concurrent increase in inequality and decrease in economic mobility, the so-called Gatsby curve. Meritocracy celebrates ambition, effort, and achievement. In theory, social status rises and falls with accomplishment, a rule that is held to be both morally defensible and efficient—since qualified people end up in positions of responsibility. Indeed, CEOs, top bankers, and hedge fund managers often declare that they have a right to the high pay that they earn. Hence, mostly everyone, liberal or conservative, counts on the good judgment of this natural aristocracy of talent ("the best and the brightest") to preside over the nation.

In actual fact, this socially diverse group is a well-connected power elite (Mills 1956; Lasch 1995; Hedges 2010). To be benevolent, the logic of meritocracy requires that society—through its tax system, its universities, and so on—can bring about genuine equality of opportunity, a level playing field. More realistically, the wealthy elite perpetuates itself. Government leaders, for instance, know how to subvert the democratic process. In business too, not everyone plays by the same rules. Thus, society reproduces past inequalities. For example, 50 years of sweeping reforms in education policy have not improved Britain's social mobility. Indeed, young people who enter the UK labor market today face less auspicious prospects than their parents or grandparents (Goldthorpe 2016).

Jeffrey Sachs (2011) goes even further. A healthy society cannot be organized around "the single-minded pursuit of wealth," he says, and the present-day malaise cannot be separated from a decline in civic virtue. Thus, a moral crisis lies as the root of the economic crisis.

Questionable practices in the drug industry, marketing and finance support Sachs. For instance, over the last decade, Eli Lilly, Sandoz, Bristol-Myers Squibb, Pfizer, and GlaxoSmithKline have all missold pharmaceuticals such as antidepressants. They push doctors to prescribe drugs for uses that are not approved. In addition, their heavy promotion of drugs leads to overuse (Angell 2004). David Boush et al. (2009) survey the psychology of persuasion in marketing. The authors start from the astounding proposition that deception "permeates" the marketplace and that it is "inevitable." Clearly, feeling duped angers consumers and undermines trust, but many firms prey on vulnerable populations such as children and seniors anyhow. Boush et al. discuss how consumers can protect themselves.

In finance, we find the most dramatic evidence of the single-minded pursuit of wealth. Finance appears to generate private rewards disproportionate to its social productivity (Bogle 2005; Phillips 2008; Madrick 2011; Philippon and Reshef 2013; Lazonick 2014) even as, arguably, it spreads opportunity (Rajan and Zingales 2003; Greenwood and Scharfstein 2013). Besides exorbitant pay packages, we observe excessive size, excessive complexity, and excessive risk taking. Because the banks are so extraordinarily big and interconnected, the financial system is nearly unmanageable. The too-big-to-fail approach (TBTF) to bank regulation weakens competition since the presumption of bailout takes away market discipline. TBTF also lowers the borrowing costs of the biggest-banks. (According to Andrew Haldane at the Bank of England, these subsidies amount to several trillions of dollars.)

On top of all this, the risks of complex, often custom-made financial products are inadequately understood. A culture of trust relationships has been displaced by a trading culture. Until a short time ago, lenders were forcefully marketing mortgage loans that were prone to default. (An analysis of *The Plain Dealer*, the largest newspaper in Cleveland, shows that nearly *half* of the subprime loans written in Cleveland in 2005 by five of biggest US subprime lenders resulted in foreclosure.) Yet, at the same time, Wall Street sold these toxic assets to unsuspecting investors.

It was long believed that financial institutions would police their own risks, but in October 2008 Alan Greenspan had to admit that "those of us who have looked to self-interest of lending institutions to protect shareholders' equity (myself especially) are in a state of shocked disbelief" (Andrews 2008). In actual fact, the government-organized industry-wide bailout that followed the banking crisis was tailored to shield politically connected institutions such as Citigroup. In this context, Sheila Bair (2012), chairwoman of the Federal Deposit Insurance Corporation, sharply criticizes other US regulators such as Timothy Geithner, the treasury secretary.

Bureaucratic and Political Malfunctions

Many people nowadays detest big government and democracy. Yet, over the last 100 years, the state became (1) the insurer against the risk of unemployment, bad health, old age, and poverty; (2) the regulator of industry and finance; (3) the provider of utilities, hospitals, schools, and universities; and (4) the protector of social values and civil rights. Throughout the developed world, on both sides of the political spectrum, it became widely accepted that government should manage the macroeconomy; that it is the go-to agent to solve social problems; and that there are almost no limits to what it can tax, spend, or borrow, especially for the purpose of national security.

On the whole, the perception that the megastate has not worked is correct. For instance, the business cycle has not been defeated; the war on poverty has not been won; and international peace is not upon us. (In the Eurozone, many citizens of core countries are losing trust in supranational institutions but retain trust in their national governments. For countries on the periphery, the opposite is true.) Instead, the feeling is that we have a small elite of elected officials and privileged functionaries who enrich themselves by favoring special-interest groups such as teachers, bankers, or the defense industry. (A 2015 Gallup World Poll shows that 38% of Germans, 55% of Japanese, 75% of Americans, and 85% of Spaniards felt government corruption to be widespread). Cash buys influence and influence is cashed out. Personally insulated from the costs of American decline and depending upon funding from large donors, elected officials are the products and the proponents of the status quo. Lou Dobbs (2004) says that the US Congress should oppose "mindless" trade and immigration policies but working people simply "aren't part of the political equation."

Kaiser (2009), Lessig (2011), Carney (2013), Crawford (2013) and Smith (2013) offer surveys and detailed case studies of campaign financing, corporate lobbying and the "legal corruption in politics," for instance, how Jacob Lew became treasury secretary in the Obama administration. As special interests funnel money into politics, trust in government institutions and democracy tumbles. Kaiser (2013) and Salter (2014) try to add some nuance to our understanding of crony capitalism. It is difficult, however, to quantify the costs of subsidies, targeted exemptions and other market distortions that violate the principle of equal treatment.

How do we restore democracy? There is no answer. Many nations drift between elections without resolution of long-term problems, and sensitive decisions are delayed until after elections. Government policy is often directionless. Instead, we get finger-pointing and polarization. Some European governments have suspended basic democratic ground rules to remain capable of acting. Similarly, president Obama relies increasingly on "executive action," with public opinion as the only constraint (Posner and Vermeule 2011).

It does not help democracy when top leaders are remembered for fabrications or lies. For example, in his 2003 State of the Union speech, president George W. Bush said, "The British government has learned that Saddam Hussein recently sought significant quantities of uranium from Africa." This sentence is now known as "the sixteen words." The administration later conceded that evidence in support of the claim was inconclusive and stated, "These sixteen words should never have been included." Another unforgettable line—uttered by president Obama—is, "If you like your health care plan, you'll be able to keep your health care plan." The statement was false, but there are at least 37 instances in which Obama or a top administration official (such as Kathleen Sebelius) referred in this way to health insurance changes under the Affordable Care Act.

Irrational Fears and Expectations

Many stories are dramatized by the 24-hour news cycle, and both politicians and journalists gain from unfounded fears (Glassner 1999). This distorts public opinion. Walter Lippmann's 1922 indictment of democracy is a masterpiece in behavioral science. Among many other ideas, Lippmann introduced mental frames ("the pictures in our head") and the impact of stereotypes on belief formation. Orrin Klapp (1964), Murray Edelman (1998 and 2001), and others explored these concepts further. The political scene is a spectacle, Edelman says. Language forms are central. Invariably, elected officials are smooth with words. Social problems, leaders, and enemies are often constructed to reinforce existing inequalities and the status quo. We do not live in a world of objective facts to which people react logically.

In contrast, Benjamin Page and his co-authors (1992, 1996, 2009) stress the long-term rationality of the voters. Still, they concur that a small number of professional communicators, not representing ordinary citizens, shape public deliberation. Without exposure to alternative ideas, the public is deceived and manipulated. The opinions of the wealthy have a lopsided impact, a point of view also pursued by Larry Bartels. He believes that "economic inequality is, in substantial part, a political phenomenon" (2008, p. 3). The theory is problematic to test and perhaps impossible to falsify. However, it is plausible that, in the area of political communication, the news media succeed in telling readers or viewers "what to think," not merely "what to think about" (Zaller 1996; Glynn et al. 2004). In other words, the influence of the media goes beyond setting the agenda.

Are public opinion polls harmful? Media portrayals of mass collectives seem detrimental to democracy. Citizens interact with a "generalized other," and this causes strong correlations between individual attitudes and perceived popular support. In other words, success succeeds. This is the essence of political momentum. On the other hand, when people think themselves to be in the minority, they may refrain from public expressions of opinion.

Why is trust low and declining? Joseph Cappella and Kathleen Hall Jamieson (1997) argue that voter cynicism is fueled by the manner in which the media covers political issues and events. The press makes it harder for democracy to work. We hear a great deal of talk about the game of politics (e.g., the race for the White House) but less about the substance of the underlying issues. The cynic believes that the political system is corrupt, that politicians want to win rather than govern, and that even selfless actions are calculated attempts to create a false image. Nothing is as it seems. This may start a spiral of cynicism that erodes citizen interest (Noelle-Neumann 1977; Mutz 1998). In agreement with this thesis, exposure to the political humor of *The Daily Show*, a highly rated late-night television program hosted by Jon Stewart, appears to compound sarcasm toward the electoral process and the media (Baumgartner and Morris 2006). Besides, with the rise of political correctness and censorship, there is a tightening of the range of acceptable discourse, furthering skepticism even more (Patten 2016). The problem is global but the industrialized nations seem especially hard hit. In Germany, for example, the concept of "die Lügenpresse" (a favorite term of Joseph Goebbels) is experiencing a revival that produces much soul-searching (Fischer 2016; Di Lorenzo 2016).

In *The Sane Society* (1955), Erich Fromm also deals with the pathology of Western society, the fact that many people are unable to adjust to the modern way of life and show socially patterned symptoms of mental disturbance. That a whole society can be "ill" was already argued by Sigmund Freud in *Civilization and Its Discontents*. Modern life is "in a state of constant and unavoidable disequilibrium," Freud says. Capitalism molds human nature and estranges man from himself. This self-estrangement is alienation. For instance, "consuming is essentially the satisfaction of artificially stimulated fantasies" (Fromm 1955, 122). Also, people feel increasingly insecure even as they are of the opinion that they should not have to take risks. (Note that, while many businessmen speak contemptuously of the welfare state as "killing private initiative," they seek the security of private wealth.) People who are mentally healthy can tolerate the insecurity inherent in human existence without undue fear. However, in modern society, people often feel alone. Alienated persons often become conformists in response (Stossel 2014).

Fundamentally, people seek meaning in their lives, and material success is not enough. Life stops someday. Much anxiety is based on the fact that, no matter how much one prospers, the good life may suddenly end, either because of a random accident or ecological damage or terrorism or for no good reason at all. The media news cycle, with interruptions for "breaking news," greatly contributes to this sentiment. The inventory of things to worry about is huge. Similar ideas are investigated by Wachtel (1989), Myers (2000), Lane (2000) and Schwartz (2004). Since the 1800s, many aspects of Western life have vastly improved. Yet, we have a culture of complaint. According to Easterbrook (2003), the "progress paradox" is: Why the discontent? Why is it that real income has doubled since the 1950s but the fraction of Americans who describe themselves as happy is unaffected? Alain de Botton (2004) and Robert Frank (2007) answer that life satisfaction depends on status. Status is hard to achieve, hard to maintain, and amounts to a gigantic distortion of priorities. Externalities such as traffic congestion are inherent in the process of getting richer. What matters for people to be able to afford "a well-located home in a good neighborhood" is not so much their absolute as their relative income.

Finally, it is essential to consider that the current crisis developed over decades. It is the working out of long-term social and economic trends. Robert Gordon (2016) questions whether past economic growth will persist. The prospects for future long-term US economic growth are bleak, he believes. The United States "faces six headwinds." One of these was the one-time event of women moving into the labor force. This cannot be repeated, and working hours per capita are now declining. Other factors are the poor performance of schools and the cost inflation in higher education; rising inequality; downward pressure on wages brought on by foreign competition; the overhang of past debt; and the efforts to stop global warming, in part a payback for past growth.

CONCLUSION

The world is out of kilter. The world crisis that started in 2007, preceded by a long period of slow economic growth in the industrialized nations, has revealed the fragility of market-based democracies. Their lackluster performance is linked to technological change, the global spread of production, social inequality, and other root causes. Fatefully, the malaise feeds cynicism and anxiety in many parts of the globe. People are in pain, yet also feel powerless. The belief that democratic capitalism is inherently unstable, inefficient, unfair, and corrupt is widespread. This chapter documents the erosion of trust in societal institutions and leaders.

The lack of confidence is not only a psychological burden. Lack of confidence undermines the political and economic leadership that is needed to implement reforms. The fear of stagnation may also become a self-fulfilling prophecy. If Americans and Europeans felt better about the state of the economy, chances are that aggregate demand would rise and society would avoid continuing stagnation.

What can be done to mend voter, consumer, investor, and business confidence if, as Martin Wolf (2014) and others suggest, monetary and fiscal policy are tapped out? After 2007, perhaps the main political response of the so-called establishment has been to leave significant socioeconomic decisions to outside technical experts, above all "independent" central bankers. Needless to say, this is a risky move. Unelected technocrats can be made omnipotent, but they are far from omniscient. What will happen if the imperial central bankers fail?

Another reaction, unintended and largely unforeseen, has been the arrival of charismatic leaders like Marine LePen, Boris Johnson, Bernie Sanders, Donald Trump, Yanis Varoufakis, and Geert Wilders. These new politicians, seen by many as dangerous extremists, present themselves as champions of the forgotten middle class: "They are not afraid to speak boldly, are not compromised by past indecision or straight-out failure, and will not be bought." Substantively, they offer their supporters sweeping changes and a radical way forward (for instance, on international trade and immigration), yet they also promise to restore "the greatness that was lost." What is uncertain is whether these new policies and leaders, if they ever rise to power, can be successful. In contrast, what *is* certain, and what the emergence of Trumpism (Ornstein 2016) seems to bear out, is that Western society—as well as much of the rest of the world—can no longer do without competent, trusted, authoritative leadership.

ACKNOWLEDGMENTS

I am grateful to Ted Azarmi, William Higbee, Monzurul Hoque, Tassos Malliaris, Leslie Shaw, and Hersh Shefrin for encouraging me to write this chapter. Various parts were presented at the Global Finance Conference (Chicago, May 2012), the 50th meeting of the Euro Working Group for Financial Modelling (Rome, May 2012), the European Working Group for Behavioral Finance (London, June 2013), and the University of Heilbronn (Germany). I thank the conference participants, especially Rita D'Ecclesia, William Forbes, Guenter Franke, David Hale, John Holland, Gulnur Muradoglu, and Jaap Spronk. Lastly, I wish to thank Sasirekka Gopalakrishnan for editorial assistance and Richard and Inese Driehaus for generous financial support.

REFERENCES

Acemoğlu, Daron, and James Robinson. 2012. *Why Nations Fail: The Origins of Power, Prosperity, and Poverty.* New York: Crown Publishing Group.

Alesina, Alberto, and Eliana La Ferrara. 2002. "Who Trusts Others?" *Journal of Public Economics* 85: 207–234.

Andrews, Edmund L. 2008. "Greenspan Concedes Error on Regulation." *New York Times,* October 23.

Angell, Marcia. 2004. *The Truth about the Drug Companies: How They Deceive Us and What to Do about It.* New York: Random House.

Arendt, Hannah. 1954. "What Is Authority?" In *Between Past and Future.* Edited by Hannah Arendt. New York: Penguin.

Arendt, Hannah. 1956. "Authority in the Twentieth Century." *Review of Politics* 18 (4): 403–417.

Armey, Richard, and Matt Kibbe. 2010. *Give Us Liberty: A Tea Party Manifesto.* New York: HarperCollins.

Arthur, W. Brian. 2009. *The Nature of Technology. What It Is and How It Evolves.* New York: Free Press.

Autor, David. 2010. "The Polarization of Job Opportunities in the U.S. Labor Market." Working paper jointly released by The Center for American Progress and The Hamilton Project. April.

Autor, David, and David Dorn. 2013. "How Technology Wrecks the Middle Class." *New York Times.* August 24.

Bair, Sheila. 2010. *Bull By The Horns: Fighting to Save Main Street From Wall Street and Wall Street From Itself.* New York: Free Press.

Bandura, A. 1999. "Moral Disengagement in the Perpetration of Inhumanities." *Personality and Social Psychology Review* 3 (3): 193–209.

Bartels, Larry M. 2008. *Unequal Democracy: The Political Economy of the New Gilded Age.* New York: Russell Sage Foundation.

Bartlett, Donald L., and James B. Steele. 2012. *The Betrayal of the American Dream*. New York: Public Affairs.

Basler, Roy P. 1953. *The Collected Works of Abraham Lincoln*. New Brunswick, NJ: Rutgers University Press.

Baumgartner, Jody, and Jonathan S. Morris. 2006. "The *Daily Show* Effect: Candidate Evaluations, Efficacy, and American Youth." *American Politics Research* 34 (3): 341–367.

Beran, Harry. 1983. "What is the Basis of Political Authority?" *The Monist* 66 (4): 487–499.

Beyle, Thad, Richard G. Niemi, and Lee Sigelman. 2002. "Gubernatorial, Senatorial, and State-Level Job Approval Rating: The U.S. Officials Job Approval Ratings Collection." *State Politics and Policy Quarterly* 2: 215–229.

Beyle, Thad, Richard G. Niemi, and Lee Sigelman. 2005. *Job Approval Ratings*. www.unc. edu/~beyle/jars.html.

Bogle, John C. 2005. *The Battle for the Soul of Capitalism*. New Haven, CT: Yale University Press.

Boush, David M., Marian Friestad, and Peter Wright. 2009. *Deception in the Marketplace: The Psychology of Deceptive Persuasion and Consumer Self-Protection*. New York: Routledge.

Bowler, Shaun, and Jeffrey A. Karp. 2004. "Politicians, Scandals, and Trust in Government." *Political Behavior* 26 (3): 271–287.

Broughton, Chad. 2015. *Boom, Bust, Exodus. The Rust Belt, the Maquilas, and A Tale of Two Cities*. New York: Oxford University Press.

Burke, Edmund. 2004 [1790]. *Reflection on the Revolution in France*. Whitefish, MT: Kessinger Publishing.

Capella, Joseph N., and Kathleen Hall Jamieson. 1997. *A Spiral of Cynicism: The Press and the Public Good*. New York: Oxford University Press.

Carney, Tim. 2013. "Jack Lew. From K Street to Wall Street to Treasury." *Washington Examiner*. January 13.

Case, Anne, and Angus Deaton. 2015. "Rising Morbidity and Mortality in Midlife among White Non-Hispanic Americans in the 21st Century." *Proceedings of the National Academy of Sciences* 112 (49): 15078–15083.

Chanley, Virginia, Thomas Rudolph and Wendy Rahn. 2000. "The Origins and Consequences of Public Trust in Government: A Time Series Analysis." *Public Opinion Quarterly* 64 (3): 239–256.

Christides, Giorgos, et al. 2016. "Refugee Crisis Pushes Europe to the Brink." *Spiegel Online*. March 4.

Chua, Amy. 2003. *World on Fire: How Exporting Free Market Democracy Breeds Ethnic Hatred and Global Instability*. New York: Doubleday and Random House.

Citrin, Jack. 1974. "Comment: The Political Relevance of Trust in Government." *American Political Science Review* 68: 973–988.

Cohen, Daniel. 2003. *Our Modern Times: The New Nature of Capitalism in the Information Age*. Cambridge, MA: MIT Press.

Cohen, Daniel. 2009. *Three Lectures on Post-Industrial Society*. Cambridge, MA: MIT Press.

Coleman, James S. 1980. "Authority Systems." *Public Opinion Quarterly* 44 (2): 143–163.

Coleman, James S. 1988. "Social Capital in the Creation of Human Capital." *American Journal of Sociology* 94: S95–S120.

Coleman, James S. 1993. "The Rational Reconstruction of Society." *American Sociological Review* 58: 1–15.

Cowen, Tyler. 2013. *Average Is Over: Powering America beyond the Age of the Great Stagnation*. New York: Penguin Group.

Crawford, Susan. 2013. *Captive Audience: The Telecom Industry and Monopoly Power in the New Gilded Age*. New Haven, CT: Yale University Press.

Crozier, Michel, Samuel P. Huntington, and Joji Watanuki. 1975. *The Crisis of Democracy: Report on the Governability of Democracies to the Trilateral Commission*. New York: New York University Press.

Currier, Erin et al. 2015. "The Precarious State of Family Balance Sheets." Report by The Pew Charitable Trusts.

De Botton, Alain. 2004. *Status Anxiety*. New York: Pantheon Books.

De Neve, Jan-Emmanuel, George W. Ward, Femke De Keulenaer, Bert Van Landeghem, George Kavetsos, and Michael I. Norton. 2014. "Individual Experience of Positive and Negative Growth is Asymmetric: Global Evidence from Subjective Well-Being Data." Working Paper, University College London, September 23.

Di Lorenzo, Giovanni. 2016. "Dresdner Rede: Unser Ruf steht auf dem Spiel." *Zeit Online*. February 29.

Dobbs, Lou. 2004. *Exporting America: Why Corporate Greed Is Shipping American Jobs Overseas*. New York: Warner Business Books.

Drucker, Peter. 1993. *Post-Capitalist Society*. New York: HarperBusiness.

Durkheim, Emile. 1957 [1902]. *Professional Ethics and Civic Morals*. New York: Routledge.

Easterbrook, Gregg. 2003. *The Progress Paradox: How Life Gets Better while People Feel Worse*. New York: Random House.

Edelman, Murray. 1998. *Constructing the Political Spectacle*. Chicago: University of Chicago Press.

Edelman, Murray. 2001. *The Politics of Misinformation*. Cambridge: Cambridge University Press.

Edsall, Thomas B. 2012. *The Age of Austerity: How Scarcity Will Remake American Politics*. New York: Doubleday.

Ehrenreich, Barbara. 1989. *Fear of Falling: The Inner Life of the Middle Class*. New York: HarperCollins.

Elliott, Larry, and Dan Atkinson. 1998. *The Age of Insecurity*. New York: Verso.

Elliott, Larry, and Dan Atkinson. 2012. *Going South: Why Britain Will Have a Third World Economy by 2014*. New York: Palgrave Macmillan.

Ellul, Jacques. 1964 [1954]. *The Technological Society*. New York: Alfred A. Knopf.

Ferguson, Niall. 2012. *The Great Degeneration: How Institutions Decay and Economies Die*. New York: Penguin.

Firestein, Peter. 2009. *Crisis of Character: Building Corporate Reputation in an Age of Skepticism*. New York: Union Square Press.

Fischer, Thomas. 2016. "Die Lügenpresse." *Zeit Online*.February 2.

Flores, Fernando, and Robert C. Solomon. 1998. "Creating Trust." *Business Ethics Quarterly* 8 (2): 205–232.

Frank, Robert H. 2007. *Falling Behind: How Rising Inequality Harms the Middle Class*. Berkeley and Los Angeles: University of California Press.

Freeland, Chrystia. 2012. *Plutocrats: The Rise of the New Global Super-Rich and the Fall of Everyone Else*. New York: Penguin.

French, David. 2016. "Working-Class Whites Have Moral Responsibilities. In Defense of Kevin Williamson." *National Review*. March 14.

Friedman, Thomas L. 2005. *The World is Flat. A Brief History of the Twenty-First Century.* New York: Farrar, Straus and Giroux.

Fromm, Erich. 1955. *The Sane Society*. Robbinsdale, MN: Fawcett Premier Books.

Fukuyama, Francis. 1995. *Trust. The Social Virtues and the Creation of Prosperity*. New York: Free Press.

Galbraith, James K. 2008. *The Predator State: How Conservatives Abandoned the Free Market and Why Liberals Should Too*. New York: Free Press.

Gilens, Martin. 1999. *Why Americans Hate Welfare: Race, Media, and the Politics of Antipoverty Policy*. Chicago: University of Chicago Press.

Glassner, Barry. 1999. *The Culture of Fear: Why American Are Afraid of the Wrong Things*. New York: Basic Books.

Glynn, Carroll J., Susan Herbst, Garrett J. O'Keefe, Robert Y. Shapiro, and Mark Lindeman. 2004. *Public Opinion*. 2nd Edition. New York: Perseus Books.

Goldsmith, James. 1994. *The Trap*. New York: Carroll and Graf Publishers, Inc.

Goldthorpe, John. 2016. "Decades of Investment in Education Have Not Improved Social Mobility." *The Guardian*. March 13.

Gordon, Robert. 2016. *The Rise and Fall of American Growth: The US Standard of Living Since the Civil War*. Princeton: Princeton University Press.

Gray, John. 1998. *False Dawn. The Delusions of Global Capitalism*. New York: New Press.

Greenwood, Robin, and David Scharfstein. 2013. "The Growth of Finance." *Journal of Economic Perspectives* 27 (2): 3-28.

Habermas, Jürgen. 1973. *Legitimation Crisis*. Boston: Beacon Press.

Haidt, Jonathan. 2012. *The Righteous Mind: Why Good People Are Divided by Politics and Religion*. New York: Random House.

Harcourt, Bernard E. 2011. *The Illusion of Free Markets. Punishment and the Myth of Natural Order*. Cambridge, MA: Harvard University Press.

Harris, R. Baine. 1976. *Authority: A Philosophical Analysis*. Tuscaloosa: University of Alabama Press.

Hayes, Cristopher. 2012. *Twilight of the Elites. America after Meritocracy*. New York: Broadway Paperbacks.

Hedges, Chris. 2010. *Death of the Liberal Class*. New York: Nation Books.

Henriques, Diana B. 2011. *The Wizard of Lies: Bernie Madoff and the Death of Trust*. New York: Times Books.

Hetherington, Marc J. 1998. "The Political Relevance of Political Trust." *American Political Science Review* 92 (4): 791–808.

Hetherington, Marc J. 2006. *Why Trust Matters. Declining Political Trust and the Demise of American Liberalism*. Princeton, NJ: Princeton University Press.

Hume, David. 1987 [1742]. "Whether the British Government Inclines More to Absolute Monarchy, or to a Republic." In *Essays, Moral, Political and Literary*. Edited by E. F. Miller. Indianapolis, IN: Liberty Press.

Kaiser, Robert G. 2009. *So Damn Much Money. The Triumph of Lobbying and the Corrosion of American Government*. New York: Alfred A. Knopf.

Kaiser, Robert G. 2013. *Act of Congress. How America's Essential Institution Works, and How It Doesn't*. New York: Alfred A. Knopf.

Keele, Luke. 2005. "The Authorities Really Do Matter: Party Control and Trust in Government." *Journal of Politics* 67 (3): 873–886.

Kirk, David S., and Mauri Matsuda. 2011. "Legal Cynicism, Collective Efficacy, and the Ecology of Arrest." *Criminology* 49 (2): 443–472.

Klapp, Orrin E. 1964. *Symbolic Leaders. Public Dramas and Public Men.* Chicago: Aldine Publishing Company.

Knack, Stephen, and Philip Keefer. 1997. "Does Social Capital Have an Economic Payoff? A Cross-Country Investigation." *Quarterly Journal of Economics* 112: 1251–1288.

Knoke, William. 1996. *Bold New World. The Essential Road Map to the Twenty-First Century.* Bunkyo, Tokyo: Kodansha International.

Kohut, Andrew. 2012. "Pervasive Gloom about the World Economy." Pew Research Center Global Attitudes Project. July 12.

Kuttner, Robert. 1984. *The Economic Illusion: False Choices between Prosperity and Social Justice.* New York: Houghton Mifflin.

Lane, Robert E. 1965. "The Politics of Consensus in an Age of Affluence." *American Political Science Review* 49: 874–895.

Lane, Robert E. 2000. *The Loss of Happiness in Market Democracies.* New Haven, CT: Yale University Press.

Lasch, Christopher. 1995. *The Revolt of the Elites and the Betrayal of Democracy.* New York: Norton.

Lazonick, William. 2014. "Profits without Prosperity: Stock Buybacks Manipulate the Market and Leave Most Americans Worse Off." *Harvard Business Review.* September, 46–55.

Lessig, Lawrence. 2011. *Republic, Lost: How Money Corrupts Congress and a Plan to Stop It.* New York: Hachette Book Group.

Lippmann, Walter. 1922. *Public Opinion.* New York: Macmillan..

Lippmann, Walter. 1935. *Essays in the Public Philosophy.* New York: Little, Brown.

Lipset, Seymour Martin, and William Schneider. 1983. *The Confidence Gap. Business, Labor, and Government in the Public Mind.* Revised Edition. Baltimore: Johns Hopkins University Press.

Lipset, Seymour Martin, and William Schneider. 1983. "The Decline of Confidence in American Institutions." *Political Science Quarterly* 98 (3): 379–402.

Lipset, Seymour Martin, and William Schneider. 1987. "The Confidence Gap during the Reagan Years, 1981–1987." *Political Science Quarterly* 102 (1): 1–23.

Madrick, Jeff. 2011. *The Age of Greed: The Triumph of Finance and the Decline of America, 1970 to the Present.* New York: Alfred A. Knopf.

Marmot, Michael. 2004. *The Status Syndrome: How Social Standing Affects Our Health and Longevity.* New York: Henry Holt.

Merton, Robert K. 1948. "The Self Fulfilling Prophecy." *Antioch Review* 8 (2): Summer.

Miller, Arthur H. 1974. "Political Issues and Trust in Government: 1964–1970." *American Political Science Review* 68: 951–972.

Milgram, Stanley. 1965. "Some Conditions of Obedience and Disobedience to Authority." *Human Relations* 19: 57–76.

Mills, C. Wright. 1956. *The Power Elite.* New York: Oxford University Press.

Moss, David A. 2002. *When All Else Fails: Government as the Ultimate Risk Manager.* Cambridge, MA: Harvard University Press.

Mumford, Lewis. 1934. *Technics and Civilization.* New York: Harcourt, Brace.

Murray, Charles. 2012. *Coming Apart: The State of White America, 1960–2010.* New York: Crown Forum.

Mutz, Diana C. 1998. *Impersonal Influence: How Perceptions of Mass Collectives Affect Political Attitudes.* Cambridge: Cambridge University Press.

Myers, David G. 2000. *The American Paradox: Spiritual Hunger in an Age of Plenty.* New Haven, CT: Yale University Press.

Naím, Moisés. 2013. *The End of Power. From Boardrooms to Battlefields and Churches to States, Why Being in Charge Isn't What It Used to Be.* New York: Basic Books.

Newport, Frank. 2015. "Fewer American Identify as Middle Class in Recent Years." www.gallup.com. April 28.

Noah, Timothy. 2012. *The Great Divergence: America's Growing Inequality Crisis and What We Can Do about It.* New York: Bloomsbury.

Noelle-Neumann, Elisabeth. 1977. "Turbulences in the Climate of Opinion: Methodological Applications of the Spiral of Silence Theory." *Public Opinion Quarterly* 41: 143–158.

Okun, Arthur M. 1975. *Equality and Efficiency: The Big Tradeoff.* Washington, DC: Brookings Institution.

Olen, Helaine. 2012. *Pound Foolish: Exposing the Dark Side of the Personal Finance Industry.* New York: Penguin.

Olsen, Robert. 2008. "Trust as Risk and the Foundation of Investment Value." *Journal of Socio-Economics* 37: 2189–2200.

Ornstein, Norm. 2016. "The Eight Causes of Trumpism." *The Atlantic.* January 4.

Page, Benjamin I., and Robert Y. Shapiro. 1992. *The Rational Public: Fifty Years of Trends in Americans' Policy Preferences.* Chicago: University of Chicago Press.

Page, Benjamin I. 1996. *Who Deliberates? Mass Media in Modern Democracy.* Chicago: University of Chicago Press.

Page, Benjamin I., and Lawrence R. Jacobs. 2009. *Class War? What Americans Really Think About Economic Inequality.* Chicago: University of Chicago Press.

Passini, Stefano, and Davide Morselli. 2009. "Authority Relationships between Obedience and Disobedience." *New Ideas in Psychology* 27: 96–106.

Patten, Chris. 2016. "The Closing of the Academic Mind." *Project Syndicate.* February 22.

Philippon, Thomas, and Ariell Reshef. 2013. "An International Look at the Growth of Modern Finance." *Journal of Economic Perspectives* 27 (2): 73–96.

Phillips, Kevin. 2008. *Bad Money: Reckless Finance, Failed Politics, and the Global Crisis of American Capitalism.* New York: Penguin.

Piaget, Jean. 1932. *The Moral Judgment of the Child.* London: Routledge and Kegan Paul.

Piketty, Thomas. 2014. *Capital in the Twenty-First Century.* Cambridge, MA: Belknap Harvard.

Platt, Suzy. 1993. *Respectfully Quoted: A Dictionary of Quotations.* New York: Barnes and Noble Books.

Posner, Eric A., and Adrian Vermeule. 2010. *The Executive Unbound: After the Madisonian Republic.* New York: Oxford University Press.

Prestowitz, Clyde. 2010. *The Betrayal of American Prosperity.* New York: Free Press.

Putnam, Robert D. 1995. "Bowling Alone: America's Declining Social Capital." *Journal of Democracy* 6 (1): 65–78.

Putnam, Robert D. 2007. "E Pluribus Unum: Diversity and Community in the Twenty-first Century." *Scandinavian Political Studies* 30 (2): 137–174.

Putnam, Robert D. 2015. *Our Kids: The American Dream in Crisis.* New York: Simon and Schuster.

Rajan, Raghuram G., and Luigi Zingales. 2003. *Saving Capitalism from the Capitalists: Unleashing the Power of Financial Markets to Create Wealth and Spread Opportunity.* New York: Crown Business.

Rodrik, Dani. 1998. "Interview: Has Globalization Gone too Far?" *Challenge.* March–April.

Rodrik, Dani. 1998. "Why Do More Open Economies Have Bigger Governments?" *Journal of Political Economy* 106 (5): 997–1032.

Rodrik, Dani. 2014. "When Ideas Trump Interests: Preferences, Worldviews, and Policy Innovations." *Journal of Economic Perspectives* 28 (1): 189–208.

Roepke, Wilhelm. 1960. *A Humane Economy: The Social Framework of the Free Market.* Washington, DC: Henry Regnery.

Rothkopf, David. 2008. *Superclass: The Global Power Elite and the World They Are Making.* New York: Farrar, Straus and Giroux.

Rothkopf, David. 2012. *Power Inc.: The Epic Rivalry between Big Business and Government and the Reckoning That Lies Ahead.* New York: Farrar, Straus and Giroux.

Sachs, Jeffrey D. 2011. *The Price of Civilization: Reawakening American Virtue and Prosperity.* New York: Random House.

Salter, Malcolm S. 2014. "Crony Capitalism, American Style: What Are We Talking about Here?" Edmond J. Safra Working Papers No. 50, Harvard University, October.

Schneier, Bruce. 2012. *Liars and Outliers: Enabling the Trust That Society Needs to Thrive.* New York: Wiley.

Schumpeter, Joseph A. 1942. *Capitalism, Socialism and Democracy.* New York: Harper and Brothers.

Schwartz, Barry. 2004. *The Paradox of Choice: Why More Is Less.* New York: Harper Perennial.

Sennett, Richard. 1998. *The Corrosion of Character. The Personal Consequences of Work in the New Capitalism.* New York: W.W. Norton.

Sennett, Richard. 2006. *The Culture of the New Capitalism.* New Haven, CT: Yale University Press.

Smith, Hedrick. 2013. *Who Stole the American Dream?* New York: Random House.

Sowell, Thomas. 2002. *A Conflict of Visions: Ideological Origins of Political Struggles.* New York: Basic Books.

Stevenson, Betsey, and Justin Wolfers. 2011. "Trust in Public Institutions over the Business Cycle." *American Economic Review* 101 (3): 281–287.

Stossel, Scott. 2014. *My Age of Anxiety: Fear, Hope, Dread and the Search for Peace of Mind.* New York: Alfred A. Knopf.

Tang, Christopher R., and Joshua D. Zimmerman. 2009. "Managing New Product Development and Supply Chain Risks: The Boeing 787 Case." *Supply Chain Forum. An International Journal* 10 (2): 74–86.

Tawney, R. H. 1920. *The Acquisitive Society.* New York: Harcourt, Brace and Howe.

Tawney, R. H. 1931. *Equality.* New York: George Allen and Unwin.

Taylor, Frederick. 2013. *The Downfall of Money. Germany's Hyperinflation and the Destruction of the Middle Class.* New York: Bloombury Press.

The New York Times. 1996. *The Downsizing of America.* New York: Times Books.

Tone, Andrea. 2009. *The Age of Anxiety: A History of America's Turbulent Affair with Tranquilizers.* New York: Basic Books.

Trump, Donald L. 2016. "Disappearing Middle Class Needs Better Deal on Trade." *USA Today.* March 14.

Tyler, Tom R. 2006. "Psychological Perspectives on Legitimacy and Legitimation." *Annual Review of Psychology* 57: 375–400.

Wachtel, Paul L. 1989. *The Poverty of Affluence. A Psychological Portrait of the American Way of Life*. New York: New Society Publishers.

Warren, Mark E. 1996. "Deliberative Democracy and Authority." *American Political Science Review* 90 (1): 46–60.

Weber, Max. 1947. *The Theory of Social and Economic Organization*. New York: Free Press.

Wilkinson, Richard. 2005. *The Impact of Inequality: How to Make Sick Societies Healthier*. New York: New Press.

Wilkinson, Richard, and Kate Pickett. 2009. *The Spirit Level: Why Greater Equality Makes Societies Stronger*. New York: Bloomsbury.

Wilson, William Julius. 1997. *When Work Disappears: The World of the New Urban Poor*. New York: Alfred A. Knopf.

Wolf, Martin. 2014. *The Shifts and the Shocks. What We've Learned and Have Still to Learn from the Financial Crisis*. New York: Penguin.

Wolfe, Alan. 1977. *The Limits of Legitimacy. Political Contradictions of Contemporary Capitalism*. New York: The Free Press.

Wolff, Edward N. 2012. "The Asset Price Meltdown and the Wealth of the Middle Class." Working paper #18559 released by the National Bureau of Economic Research. November.

Yankelovich, Daniel. 1974. "A Crisis of Moral Legitimacy." *Dissent* 21 (4): 526–533.

Yankelovich, Daniel. 2006. *Profit with Honor: The New Stage of Market Capitalism*. New Haven, CT: Yale University Press.

Zakaria, Fareed. 2013. "Can America Be Fixed? The New Crisis of Democracy." *Foreign Affairs*. January–February.

Zaller, John. 1996. "The Myth of Massive Media Impact Revived: New Support for a Discredited Idea." In *Political Persuasion and Attitude Change*. Edited by Diana C. Mutz, Paul M. Sniderman, and Richard A. Brody. Ann Arbor: University of Michigan Press.

Zingales, Luigi. 2012. *A Capitalism for the People: Recapturing the Lost Genius of American Prosperity*. New York: Basic Books.

14

Social Structure, Power, and Financial Fraud

BROOKE HARRINGTON ▪

IBGYBG

In the beginning, there was "après nous le déluge"—a phrase attributed to Madame de Pompadour, mistress of King Louis XV. It signified an elite's "selfish heedlessness" in the face of financial crisis (Sonnenscher 2007, 1). In essence, it was an expression of power: specifically, the power to bankrupt a country without suffering any personal consequences. Madame de Pompadour, who died decades prior to the French Revolution, was correct in her assessment that she and the king would never be affected by the ruinous debt that he had heaped on France. And if others suffered the consequences? Too bad for them.

Over 350 years later, we find the acronym "IBGYBG" in the Congressional testimony of Richard Michalek, former vice president of Moody's Investors Service, a credit rating agency that facilitated the 2008 subprime mortgage crisis and the global financial meltdown that followed (White 2010). In his statement to Congress, Michalek explains that the sources of the crisis included the lack of consequences or accountability for investment bankers who engaged in risky, poorly researched and poorly documented deals; no matter how bad the deal, the banker would always get paid. Michalek describes wrangling with one such banker over following correct procedure for assigning a Moody's rating: the banker told him that the priority should be "get the deal closed, and if there's a problem later on, it was just another case of 'IBGYBG'—'I'll be gone, you'll be gone'" (2010, 5).

The acronym seems to have been popular on Wall Street for some time, a snippet of "bankerspeak" (Dash 2009) familiar to many in the financial industry. Some have suggested that there was a generalized "IBGYBG ethos": a defining feature of 21st-century finance that supplanted any pretense to an ethical foundation the industry once had, developed as a "predictable outcome" of the opportunity structure presented to bankers (Knee 2007). This chapter builds on such observations to argue for a structural view of the sources of the 2008 crisis. This analysis shifts the focus from individual characteristics—such as greed, or lack of ethics—to the structures of incentives, opportunities, and networks underlying financialized capitalism.

To be sure, the historical record going back centuries shows that whenever opportunities for financial speculation have arisen, they have been accompanied by what Fernand Braudel called "a thick scum of fraud and intrigue" (1992, 309). But under financialized capitalism—in which the basis of the world's key political economies has shifted from industry to finance (Krippner 2011)—both the opportunities and rewards for fraud have increased. At the same time, the power of competing institutions, such as states, has decreased. The result is a "criminogenic" environment (Tillman and Indergaard 2007, 482), in which cheating and crises are virtually inevitable.

Moreover, one of the most significant manifestations of power under this economic regime is the ability to reap the benefits of financial speculation without being subject to the same degree of risk and responsibility as others (Sayer 2015). Contemporary financial actors grow in power to the extent that they can capture the advantages of participating in markets (particularly the profits) without subjecting themselves to the disadvantages. For example, knowing that "insurance" is available in the form of bailouts like the Troubled Asset Recovery Program of 2008 creates "moral hazard," undermining the motive to act prudently and avoid reckless risks (Hellman, Murdoch, and Stiglitz 2000). Such configurations of costs and benefits, distorted by the effects of power, create the kind of "not my problem" ethos that inspired Madame de Pompadour's remark about the prospects of financial ruin for France. In brief, IBGYBG is the 21st century's abbreviated, inelegant version of "après nous le déluge."

The remainder of this chapter will explore the social, economic, and political structures that underpinned the global financial crash of 2008. It will also assess the outlook for future crises. The perspective is distinctly sociological, in contrast to the individual-centered analyses of economics and psychology, but the compatibilities among the different levels of analysis will be—it is hoped—clear to the reader. The intended contribution is to shed light on dimensions of the crisis neglected by analyses centered on individual actors.

THE SOCIOLOGICAL PERSPECTIVE ON FRAUD AND FINANCIAL CRISES

A central insight of the sociological perspective is that financial crises keep happening for structural reasons, not moral ones. The crucial distinction is in the level of analysis: sociology puts more emphasis on context than character. This does not imply a view of individuals as helpless pawns with no agency. Rather, a sociological analysis asserts the power of structure—social, economic, and political—in shaping the lines of action that individuals develop (Goffman 1959). Another key sociological insight is that structures tend to reproduce themselves over time, which may partly account for the curious sense of déjà vu that befalls those who study financial history: as Reinhart and Rogoff (2009) have documented exhaustively, the same patterns have repeated themselves over centuries of financial bust and boom.

One reason that crises keep occurring is that their structural sources have remained unchanged in general terms. What John Kenneth Galbraith observed of financial history applies equally well to France in the time of Madame de Pompadour and the United States in the present day:

> The world of finance hails the invention of the wheel over and over again, often in a slightly more unstable version. All financial innovation involves, in one form or another, the creation of debt secured in greater or lesser adequacy by real assets. . . . All crises have involved debt that, in one fashion or another, has become dangerously out of scale in relation to the underlying means of payment. (1993, 19–20)

The debt risk in finance sets the stage for instability and crisis. At the same time, economists argue that eliminating this risk "would mean destroying the existing financial system" (Prates 2013, 7). This analysis explicitly claims that regulatory intervention to prevent excessive leveraging—the assumption of debt disproportionate to assets—is useless. It also rejects the promise of macro-prudential regulation, including the Dodd-Frank Act in the United States (formally titled the Wall Street Reform and Consumer Protection Act of 2010) and the recommendations of Europe's Basel Committee on Banking Supervision (known as Basel III). Both efforts, which were designed to avert breakdowns in the financial system before they occur, have come under fire from economists claiming that the regulations fail to deal with key sources of risk and in many cases create new problems (Greenspan 2011; Hanson, Kashyap, and Stein 2011). This is consistent with findings on the results of regulatory efforts in the wake of previous crises. For example, the Sarbanes-Oxley Act of 2002, created in response to the financial and accounting scandals of the early 20th century, was widely derided as failing to address key systemic problems (Soederberg 2008). The ineffectiveness of these measures in addressing the crisis of 2008 would seem to bear out such judgments. In view of this dismal track record, many see the present crisis-prone financial system as essentially unchanged, ready to implode anew.

Another implication of a structural perspective is that if individuals are behaving badly—for example, committing fraud or taking "selfishly heedless" risks (Sonnenscher 2007, 1)—we should look for the causes, and the possible remedies, in the matrix of opportunities, rewards, and sanctions they face. For example, numerous finance professionals and observers have noted that any account of the recent crisis must acknowledge that there were enormous incentives for exploitative and recklessly risky activity by financial firms and professionals leading up to the 2008 crash; at the same time, there were no meaningful sanctions when those actions led to disaster (Dash 2009; Smith 2012).

Subsequent analyses have confirmed that not only were the firms directly involved in creating the crisis bailed out at taxpayer expense, but executives implicated in the scandal were richly rewarded. For example, a trio of Goldman Sachs traders received huge bonuses for pushing the firm to bet against the mortgage-backed securities they were aggressively selling to clients; when the value of those securities crashed, the firm posted record profits at the clients' expense (Kelly 2007). Boston University economics professor Lawrence Kotlikoff later said of Goldman's failure to disclose this conflict of interest, "This is fraud and should be prosecuted" (Gordon 2009). As this book goes to press, Goldman Sachs has agreed to a $5 billion settlement with the federal government, without admitting guilt–a deal widely derided as a "sham" (Dayen 2016). Furthermore, no individual from Goldman has faced criminal or civil charges in connection with the subprime mortgage crisis. There has been a grand total of one such prosecution stemming from subprime mortgage fraud, and it pointedly avoided implicating any key actors: "The largest man-made economic catastrophe since the Depression resulted in the jailing of a single investment banker—one who . . . was neither a mortgage executive (who created toxic products) nor the C.E.O. of a bank (who peddled them)" (Eisinger 2014, 34).

Just these two structural conditions—the basis of financial innovation and the costs versus benefits of financial fraud—explain a lot about the emergence of crises like the subprime mortgage crash of 2008. Such conditions create a "crimino-genic" (Vaughan 2007; Needleman and Needleman 1979) environment, which may explain why so many finance practitioners and scholars seem to view crises as inevitable (Minsky 1986; Knee 2007). What we have lacked so far is a solid theory to explain why this is so.

As Malliaris, Shaw, and Shefrin observe in the introductory chapter to this volume, "Minsky provided no clear model, either linear or nonlinear, to underlie his contention." While some mathematical modeling has attempted to address this issue (see Keen, this volume), the results often seem more descriptive than predictive and behavioral. A sociological analysis contributes to this gap in knowledge by providing an account of the structures that are likely to produce the forms of cheating and risk taking linked to financial crises. The waves of financial fraud that have hit the markets in the early years of the 21st century even gave rise to a new sociological theory: the "criminogenic markets approach" (Tillman and Indergaard 2007, 482), which examines the ways in which certain institutions, industries, and organizations structurally facilitate or even promote fraud. This involves the "normalization" of fraud as part of firms' standard operating procedures and everyday practices. This routinization and destigmatization became pervasive in accounting and banking during the late 20th century, resulting in the savings and loan crisis and later in the Enron and WorldCom scandals (Tillman and Pontell 1995; Tillman and Indergaard 2005).

STRUCTURE AND MORAL AGENCY

Faced with the prospect of big bonuses when risk taking and fraud turn a profit, and the extreme unlikelihood of facing any penalties if the efforts fail, why would anyone forgo the opportunity to cheat or take reckless risks? The moral arguments against such behavior become increasingly weak as a growing proportion of one's colleagues are seen to engage in it and reap rewards (Paternoster et al. 2013). There is even evidence supporting an imitative model of fraud within the financial industry, suggesting that when individuals or firms appear to prosper through fraudulent practices, competitors follow suit (Schiesel 2002).

Some actors express their agency by self-selecting out of the system. The most vivid recent example of this is the Goldman Sachs director who resigned via a *New York Times* op-ed piece declaring that the firm had become "toxic and destructive" because it was led by "morally bankrupt people" (Smith 2012). For those who remain, it must be with the understanding that ethical considerations are incompatible with personal advancement. This suggests that cheating and fraud are not, as some psychologists suggests, primarily a problem of "self-control" (Gino et al. 2011). Rather, we should be looking at the structure of opportunities, rewards, and sanctions that individuals face.

As the Norwegian social scientist Thorstein Veblen observed of finance over a century ago:

> Freedom from scruple, from sympathy, honesty and regard for life, may, within fairly wide limits, be said to further the success of the individual in the pecuniary culture ... It is only within narrow limits, and then only in a Pickwickian sense, that honesty is the best policy. (2009 [1899], 147)

Veblen alludes here to Charles Dickens's novel *The Pickwick Papers* (2000 [1832]), in which the title character (Mr. Pickwick) and his friend Mr. Bottom exchange insults without really meaning them. The phrase "in a Pickwickian sense" thus means "not to be taken literally." The implication is that ethics in finance are a joke, or—as one observer said in connection with the infamous Enron code of ethics—nothing more than "lip service to traditional pieties" (Arbogast 2008, 244).

Veblen's perspective is not necessarily in conflict with other scholars' claims about the ways that virtue and ethics have actually promoted the growth of capitalism (e.g., McCloskey 2006). But the capitalism to which those other scholars refer includes the historic whole, comprising crafts and industry—making things—as well as trading. The version of capitalism that Veblen had in mind was much closer to what we see now under regimes of financialization, which have come to dominate the global economy. As Krippner (2011) has documented, many leading economies that once were grounded in making and selling things have shifted from creating to distributing wealth. Rather than producing medicines, software, or cars, a financialized economy prioritizes the business of "mov[ing] wealth from one hand to another" (Mukunda 2014). With this structural shift in the basis of national wealth, we have seen a corresponding decline in the role of ethics and values among leading economic actors.

FRAUD AND POWER IN A FINANCIALIZED WORLD

Financialization has been defined as an economic system in which the underlying mechanism of growth is "making money out of money" (Denning 2014). Not only do financial markets come to dominate a nation's economy, but financial actors assume controlling influence over economic policy and outcomes (Palley 2007). Ironically, historical analyses of the phenomenon suggest that it was an adaptive response to mitigate the impact of the recurrent crises in capitalism (Krippner 2005; Arrighi 1994). It now seems, however, that financialization has come to produce new sources of instability.

This is because financialization relies on debt, which—in excessive amounts—is destabilizing (Prates 2013). To give a concrete sense of how "dangerously out of scale" (Galbraith 1993, 20) debt became prior to the crisis, consider that between 1981 and 2008 private sector debt more than doubled (from 123% of GDP to 290%) and leverage (borrowing against assets) more than quintupled, going from 22% of GDP to 117% (Crotty 2009). This was clearly a major threat to economic stability. Some traders and financial firms recognized the dangers years prior to the crash, but—perhaps motivated by the "IBGYBG ethos" (Knee 2007)—neither practitioners nor regulators stepped in to stop it (Morgenson and Story 2009).

Instead, industry insiders exploited this knowledge, cheating their clients out of billions and reaping record profits for themselves (Santoro 2013).

Critical political theorists have described fraud as a critical "form of domination" (Augelli and Murphy 1993, 128). In financialized systems, power manifests as the ability to cheat, flouting both law and moral norms, without negative consequences. This is not the result of aberrant "bad apple" behavior—an explanation which locates agency at the level of individual character. As one recent study of financialization and fraud put it, "it's not about corruption," in the sense of personal moral failure; rather, the problem is systemic distortion of beliefs, opportunities, rewards, and sanctions attached to cheating (Mukunda 2014).

Fraud is the preferred method of domination when the use of force is perceived by actors as too risky or too costly compared to the benefits. As Gramsci observed decades ago, "between consent and force stands corruption/fraud (which is characteristic of situations when it is hard to exercise the hegemonic function...)" (1971, note on pg. 80). The use of fraud to assert power and domination without resort to physical violence (Arrighi 1993) has a long history in the financial realm (Chancellor 2000; Mihm 2007; Harrington 2012; Harrington 2013). Indeed, Veblen called special attention to this feature of financial work more than a century ago. In his analysis, the ability to cheat constitutes a type of core competency in financial practice: "The pecuniary employments give proficiency in the general line of practices comprised under fraud, rather than in those that belong under the more archaic method of forcible seizure" (Veblen 2009 [1899], 151).

Within such a system, individuals have few practical means to effect change, due to the punishments visited upon those who speak out against fraud. In a 2013 report titled *High Retaliation Rate: A Cause for Concern*, the National Business Ethics Survey (NBES) reported that 21% of American workers were punished for reporting fraud in their firms; another 34% of workers said that they witnessed fraud but declined to report it due to fear of reprisals (NBES 2013). Even highly placed finance industry insiders seem to lack the authority to make meaningful change within their organizations: instead, they resign (Smith 2012) or—like the women who blew the whistle on fraud at Enron and WorldCom—must accept being marginalized and ignored until they can get a government agency to take their claims seriously (Pulliam and Solomon 2002).

This suggests a limited role for leadership and governance by individual executives who wish to combat fraud in finance. Furthermore, in an environment in which even highly placed executives may lose their positions as a result of failing to post performance numbers on par with competitors who are cheating (Schiesel 2002), the price of bucking the system is often losing one's power within it. Thus, although there is a robust literature claiming that better leadership can reduce instances of fraud (e.g., Brown, Treviño, and Harrison 2005; Knights and O'Leary 2006; Bragues 2008), the empirical evidence suggests that this scenario is unlikely for structural reasons: namely, the systemic sanctioning of those who refuse to cheat or who act as whistleblowers.

STATE POWER AND FINANCIAL FRAUD

In this context, meaningful change is only possible through institutional support—usually provided by government regulators and prosecutors. In practice, however, this support has been lacking (Galbraith 2004). As one political economist put it shortly after the 2008 crisis occurred, the "deep cause" of the global crash lay in "the flawed institutions and practices of the current financial regime . . . [along] with the era's light government regulation" (Crotty 2009, 564).

This is borne out by the accounts of practitioners on the regulatory side. In a recent speech, a former trial attorney at the SEC used the occasion of his retirement party to lambast the agency for being "tentative and fearful" in the face of Wall Street's power, refusing to use government authority to prosecute the finance industry professionals who created the crisis, despite ample evidence being available to make a case (Kidney 2014). Similar observations have been made about other federal agencies. For example, the Federal Bureau of Investigation actually reduced its personnel assigned to mortgage fraud cases in 2008 (Swedberg 2010), while the Justice Department ignored calls by Congressional representatives to create a financial crimes task force (Lichtblau 2008). In other words, the only entity empowered to impose meaningful sanctions on wrongdoers largely eschewed that role, both in the lead-up to the crisis and in its aftermath (Morgenson and Story 2011).

This is more than passive complicity by the state; some argue that we should regard states as active collaborators in the destruction of their own financial systems (Lewis 2010). This seeming paradox stems from a structure of conflicted interests on the part of those in charge of the government's financial crisis-prevention and mitigation systems. As Useem (1986) showed almost 30 years ago, there are multiple, mutually reinforcing network ties among business and political elites: they often attend the same schools in their youth, see each other socially in adulthood, and recruit each other to join organizations.

The structure of interlocking social and professional networks is particularly powerful in the relationship between finance and government. The problem occurs globally—due in part to the ascendancy of finance as a profession (Fligstein 1990; Zorn 2004)—but was especially pronounced in the political economies most devastated by the 2008 financial crisis: the United Kingdom, Iceland and the United States (Gill 2008; Norman 2011). As one scholar recently described conditions in the United States, "representatives and lobbyists of the financial sector are so entwined with the agencies that are supposed to regulate it that Washingtonians collectively refer to them as 'The Blob'" (Mukunda 2014). These chummy relationships played a role in policymakers' willingness to dismantle the regulatory structure erected after the Great Depression of the 1930s, which "ring-fenced" the risks taken on by the financial services industry—protecting the public, but also limiting the industry's profits (Blundell-Wignall, Atkinson, and Lee 2008; Labaton 2008).

Labor market structures contribute significantly to this problem of conflicted interests. Many have observed what appears to be a "revolving door" between Wall Street and federal regulatory positions (Kidney 2014; Braithwaite 2013). The most famous examples of this are former Treasury secretaries Robert Rubin and Hank Paulson, both of whom held top positions at Goldman Sachs—Rubin as co-chairman of the board of directors, and Paulson as CEO—prior to assuming their roles as regulators (Braithwaite and Makan 2012). Goldman also provided Mark Patterson, a senior banker who became chief of staff to Tim Geithner, who served as Treasury secretary from 2009 to 2013. Geithner, who was known for having "unusually close relationships with executives of Wall Street's giant financial institutions" (Becker and Morgenson 2009, A1), later proposed that those institutions be bailed out at taxpayer expense. This ended up being a windfall for his business allies: "Much of the Troubled Asset Relief Program in effect used taxpayer money to finance bonuses for top bank employees and dividends for shareholders with no positive impact on financial market performance" (Crotty 2009, 578). One of the beneficiaries of the bailout was Robert Rubin, who had joined Citigroup after leaving the Treasury Department; as a major shareholder in the firm, he personally netted $126 million in profits from Geithner's bailout program (Cohan 2012). Following his predecessors through the revolving door, Geithner left Treasury to become president of a private equity firm (December 2013).

This structure of networks, and particularly labor market ties, between finance and government has a name: crony capitalism (Norman 2011, 30). And it is not unique to the crisis of 2008. Rather, it seems to be a red thread linking the entire history of financial disasters. From the 18th century to the present, such crises have seemed to *require* collusion between government agents and financiers to reach full destructive potential (Harrington 2013). In what is widely regarded as the world's first financial crisis—Britain's South Sea Bubble of 1720—the creation of a sham national investment scheme required the cooperation of members of Parliament, the nobility, and business leaders; the historical records indicate that all knowingly participated in defrauding the public to enrich themselves (Reed 1999, Carswell 2002). More recently, the same problems of network structure and conflict of interest observed in the run-up to the subprime mortgage crisis were also noted in Iceland's "incestuous economy" (*Financial Times* 2008); there, national bankruptcy was precipitated by political leaders facilitating—rather than regulating—dangerously risky activity by financiers who were also their friends and sometimes family members (Gill 2008). In view of this history, it would seem that crony capitalism is not an aberration but a recurrent manifestation of power within financial regimes—one unlikely to be addressed effectively by regulation.

INTERNATIONAL CAPITAL FLOWS AND AN INDUSTRY "TOO COMPLEX TO REGULATE"

Another structural condition favoring financial fraud is the increasingly global scope of finance itself. As more and more capital moves across national boundaries, it becomes more difficult for any one state to combat financial fraud. Like collusion among elites, this problem has a long history: it seems to have been born with the advent of international trade. As Braudel writes, "one of the customs agents under Louis XIV wrote to the controller-general of trade, 'Your worship could set an army along the entire coast of Brittany and Normandy but it would never stop fraud'" (1992, 49). The difference now is that the volume of capital is so much greater than ever before, as is the ease with which it can be moved across borders.

The international transmission of capital increased dramatically in the run-up to the financial crisis, peaking at an average of more than 20% of GDP for many countries (James, McLoughlin, and Rankin 2014). Cross-border financial flows increase instability and make crises difficult to contain (Nier, Sedik, and Mondino 2014). To mitigate the risks, what seems to be required is some sort of global coordination in terms of regulation and safety net provisions; suggestions have included the maintenance of fail-safe lending facilities, such as the IMF's 2009 Flexible Credit Line, which was designed to provide emergency liquidity for countries facing financial crises (Turner 2014). However, there appears to be very little public appetite or political will to create new institutions for preventing financial fraud or halting its spread (Rey 2013). And existing institutions have thus far lacked both the capital and political legitimacy to provide effective and enduring solutions (Fernández-Arias and Levy-Yeyati 2010; Moghadam 2011; Sharman 2006).

Even if the political will *were* present to support such institutions, it may be that the system has already become too complex to achieve those aims. Many observers of the 2008 financial crisis noted that Wall Street traders and firms often did not seem to understand the securities they were selling, much less the systemic implications of default (Lewis 2010). Some have branded this the problem of being "too complex to regulate"—a reference to the oft-heard phrase during the post-crisis bailout, "too big to fail" (Orr 2009). Others have gone farther, arguing that "financial institutions and markets are becoming 'too big to understand'—and thus need to be shrunk and simplified" (Tett 2012; Hu 2012). However, political efforts to break up and thus reduce the complexity of large financial institutions have met with ferocious and successful resistance by finance industry leaders and lobbyists (Gandel 2015).

There is a great deal of profit to be made by keeping things complex, both for individual finance professionals and for their firms (Winters 2011). It is even advantageous to some states—particularly tax havens, which sustain themselves economically by exploiting the complexities and gaps in international financial regulation. Tax havens (or "international financial centers," as many prefer to be called) are at the center of interstate competition to attract lucrative finance industry business. They do this by offering an environment of little to no regulation and taxation; in return, the states get jobs for local citizens and revenues in the form of incorporation and transaction fees.

Tax havens made possible both the hedge fund industry and the mortgage-backed securities market (Gordon 2009). While hedge funds can exist anywhere in theory, tax havens have created a particularly attractive business environment, permitting the funds much wider latitude to take financial risks (and therefore to earn higher profits) than do onshore jurisdictions. For example, the laws of tax havens are often written expressly to allow hedge funds to maximize profits by keeping capital requirements lower and permitting the funds to carry more leverage (debt) than would be allowed onshore. The confidentiality offered by tax havens is also appealing to funds, whose formulas for speculation are often closely guarded secrets; unfortunately, this secrecy, and the rarity with which tax havens cooperate in international legal inquiries, also makes it difficult to identify and punish criminal activity connected with financial crises (Harrington 2013).

The combination of high risk and low accountability offered by tax havens has been implicated in financial crises even prior to 2008. The best-known case is that of Long-Term Capital Management (LTCM), whose reckless risk taking was said to have "nearly blown up the world financial system" in 1998 (Jorion 2000, 277). The failure of LTCM, whose funds were maintained in the Cayman Islands, was so threatening to the integrity of the global economy that the US Federal Reserve Bank took the then-unprecedented step of bailing out a failed private enterprise, at a cost of $3.6 billion in public funds. Following the LTCM crisis, however, the hedge fund industry remained largely unregulated and continued to thrive offshore, where it later innovated a new, high-risk financial instrument—the mortgage-backed security—which helped bring down the world economy in 2008.

Cayman also played a key role in that debacle, since its minimalist regulatory framework made it the most attractive jurisdiction for Goldman Sachs and other firms to conduct "secret deals" bypassing US securities and disclosure laws (Gordon 2009). This allowed Goldman to bet against the very investments it was selling its customers, without notifying the customers of the conflict of interest. From Cayman, toxic securities were funneled to investors and institutions worldwide, creating the "channels of contagion" (Crotty 2009, 571) that crashed the financial system (Dodd and Mills 2008, 14).

As these examples suggest, states operating as tax havens provide several crucial components of the legal and political structure that enables financial fraud and financial crises to occur. For one thing, their provision of new legal regimes tailored to the interests of the finance industry multiplies systemic complexity and makes it increasingly difficult to discern legal from illegal activity across jurisdictions. Second, by creating low-to-no-regulation zones, tax havens provide opportunities for dangerous new risks to emerge. Third, tax havens make it easier to hide illegal activity: the conflict of laws among jurisdictions impedes international cooperation and dramatically raises the costs of investigating and prosecuting financial crime (de Willebois et al. 2011). This was crucial to Enron's strategy of fraudulent transactions and tax evasion schemes; the firm used a network of 692 subsidiaries in Cayman, plus another 200 offshore structures, all designed to generate huge paper profits and conceal violations of accounting rules (Batson 2003, Edwards 2005). Finally, by luring so much financial activity away from onshore states, tax havens create a "race to the bottom," undermining efforts to regulate finance in the public interest, to punish fraud, or to prevent future crises from occurring.

CONCLUSION

One indication of the power that has accrued to finance in the social, economic, and political structures is that most of the fundamental instabilities that caused the 2008 crash have never really been addressed (Dayen 2013). As a former investment banker and derivatives trader put it,

> The structures which enabled financial market actors to take excessive risks and the incentives that made it immensely profitable for them to do so are still very much in place. (Kapoor 2010, 6)

In fact, Wall Street has actively and successfully resisted most proposed legal changes that might restrict their ability to take on debt and risk (Mukunda 2014). Far from deterring future frauds, the only impression the crisis seems to have left on the financial industry is the lesson that the cheaters *do* prosper.

As an indication of how little has changed since 2008, eight major investment banks are currently under investigation for defrauding clients between 2009 and 2011—that is, *after* the financial crisis occurred. Not only that, but the fraud consisted of substantially the same activity that created the crisis in the first place: selling junk mortgage bonds while misrepresenting their value and risks (Eaglesham 2014). Even under threat of a collapsing world economic system, these and other financial actors continued to reap significant profits from illegal and unethical activities. And their power continued to grow—enough that they were able not only to secure a massive taxpayer-funded bailout but to resist any meaningful attempts to change their way of doing business. This is a vivid empirical illustration of Arrighi's observation that "corruption and fraud are thus tactical weapons in a rearguard struggle to preserve power" (1993, 149).

This article has offered a sociological analysis to identify some of the key structures that contributed to the 2008 financial crisis and remained in place in its aftermath. Three are particularly significant:

1. *Opportunities and sanctions*
   It continues to be profitable for financial industry insiders to exploit information asymmetries vis-à-vis investors. At the same time, there is a notable lack of punishment for those who are caught (Eisinger 2014, Santoro 2013). But punishment is routinely doled out to whistleblowers who report fraud and ethical violations (NBES 2013).

2. *Conflicts of interest*
   These conflicts are structured by the interlocking social and professional networks underlying the "revolving door" between positions in finance and government (Mukunda 2014). This "crony capitalism" undermines the will and ability of regulators to set limits on the financial industry (Crotty 2009, Harrington 2013).

3. *Legal and financial complexity*
   This includes the creation of financial instruments and institutions that are "too complex to regulate," as well as the emergence of state actors who exploit and increase that complexity for their own economic benefit (Hu 2012, Tett 2012, Winters 2011).

With these structures still in place, the prospect of future financial crises seems immediate and inevitable.

Some see a new subprime meltdown taking shape in the market for securitized student loans, described as bearing an "uncanny resemblance" to the pre-2007 mortgage market (Carrns 2012). Others see a threat from high-speed trading (Baumann 2013). Despite disagreements about its form, there is convergence on the notion that another disaster is on the way. Even the vice chairman of the Federal Reserve Board alluded to this in a recent speech, saying that "the next crisis—and there will be one" will take a new form based on shared underlying causes with past disasters (Fischer 2014). The fatalism of the regulatory authority in the face of recurring fraud-based crises is reminiscent of the observations of one scholar, who concluded of the past 300 years of financial history that "at its core, capitalism was little more than a confidence game" (Mihm 2007, 11).

REFERENCES

Arbogast, Stephen. 2008. *Resisting Corporate Corruption: Lessons in Practical Ethics from the Enron Workplace*. Salem, MA: Scrivener Press.

Arrighi, Giovanni. 1993. "The Three Hegemonies of Historical Capitalism." In *Gramsci, Historical Materialism and International Relations*, edited by Stephen Gill, 148–185. Cambridge, UK: Cambridge University Press.

Arrighi, Giovanni. 1994. *The Long Twentieth Century*. London: Verso. Augelli, Enrico, and Craig Murphy. 1993. "Gramsci and International Relations: A General Perspective and Example from US Policy Toward the Third World." In *Gramsci, Historical Materialism and International Relations*, edited by Stephen Gill, 127–147. Cambridge, UK: Cambridge University Press.

Batson, Neal. 2003. "Second Interim Report of Neal Batson, Court-Appointed Examiner." United States Bankruptcy Court, Southern District of New York. In: re: Chapter 11 Enron Corp., et al., Debtors, Case No. 01-16034 (AJG), Jointly Administered, January 21.

Baumann, Nick. 2013. "Too Fast to Fail: Is High-Speed Trading the Next Wall Street Disaster?" *Mother Jones*, January/February. http://www.motherjones.com/politics/2013/02/high-frequency-trading-danger-risk-wall-street.

Becker, Jo, and Gretchen Morgenson. 2009. "Geithner, Member and Overseer of Finance Club." *New York Times*, April 27, p. A1.

Blundell-Wignall, Adrian, Paul Atkinson, and Se Hoon Lee. 2008. "The Current Financial Crisis: Causes and Policy Issues." *OECD Financial Market Trends*, 1–21. http://www.oecd.org/dataoecd/47/26/41942872.pdf.

Bragues, George. 2008. "The Ancients against the Moderns: Focusing on the Character of Corporate Leaders." *Journal of Business Ethics* 78: 373–387.

Braithwaite, Tom. 2013. "Inside Finance: Jamming Wall St's Revolving Door to Power." *Financial Times*, April 1. http://www.ft.com/intl/cms/s/0/96b66d18-9ad1-11e2-97ad-00144feabdc0.html#axzz3T5GsAt6n.

Braithwaite, Tom, and Ajay Makan. 2012. "US Treasury: Manhattan Transfer." *Financial Times*, February 5. http://www.ft.com/intl/cms/s/0/9c1d6b54-4045-11e1-9bce-00144feab49a.html#axzz3T5GsAt6n.

Braudel, Fernand. 1992. *The Wheels of Commerce (Civilization and Capitalism: 15th–18th Century—Volume 2)*. Berkeley: University of California Press.

Brown, Michael, Linda Treviño, and David Harrison. 2005. "Ethical Leadership: A Social Learning Perspective for Construct Development and Testing." *Organizational Behavior and Human Decision Processes* 97: 117–134.

Carrns, Ann. 2012. "Private Student Loan Gripes Echo Mortgage Complaints." *New York Times*, October 16.

Carswell, John. 2002. *The South Sea Bubble*. Stroud, UK: Sutton Publishing.

Chancellor, Edward. 2000. *Devil Take the Hindmost: A History of Financial Speculation*. New York: Farrar, Strauss, Giroux.

Cohan, William. 2012. "Rethinking Robert Rubin." Bloomberg News Service, September 30. http://www.bloomberg.com/bw/articles/2012-09-19/rethinking-robert-rubin.

Crotty, James. 2009. "Structural Causes of the Global Financial Crisis: A Critical Assessment of the 'New Financial Architecture.'" *Cambridge Journal of Economics* 33: 563–580.

Dash, Eric. 2009. "What's Really Wrong with Wall Street Pay." *New York Times*, September 18.

Dayen, David. 2013. "Banks Are Too Big to Fail Say . . . Conservatives?" *The American Prospect*, March 21. http://prospect.org/article/banks-are-too-big-fail-say-conservatives.

Dayen, David. 2016. "Why the Goldman Sachs Settlement Is a $5 Billion Sham." *The New Republic*, April 13. https://newrepublic.com/article/132628/goldman-sachs-settlement-5-billion-sham.

Denning, Steve. 2014. "Why Financialization Has Run Amok." *Forbes*, June 3. http://www.forbes.com/sites/stevedenning/2014/06/03/why-financialization-has-run-amok/.

de Willebois, Emile, Emily Halter, Robert Harrison, Ji Won Park, and J. C. Sharman. 2011. *The Puppet Masters: How the Corrupt Use Legal Structures to Hide Stolen Assets and What to Do about It.* Washington, DC: World Bank.

Dezember, Ryan. 2013. "Geithner Heads to Private Equity." *Wall Street Journal*, November 16. http://www.wsj.com/articles/SB1000142405270230424390457920032381 3063730.

Dickens, Charles. 2000 [1832]. *The Pickwick Papers.* New York: Penguin.

Dodd, Randall, and Paul Mills. 2008. "Outbreak: U.S. Subprime Contagion." *Finance & Development*, June: 14–18.

Eaglesham, Jean. 2014. "Federal Probe Targets Banks Over Bonds." *Wall Street Journal*, January 7. http://www.wsj.com/articles/SB10001424052702304887104579306941 069018958.

Edwards, Chris. 2005. "Replace the Scandal-Plagued Corporate Income Tax with a Cash-Flow Tax." In *After Enron: Lessons for Public Policy*, edited by William Niskanen, 283–334. Lanham, MD: Rowman and Littlefield.

Eisinger, Jesse. 2014. "Why Only One Top Banker Went to Jail for the Financial Crisis." *New York Times Magazine*, April 30, p. 34.

Fernández-Arias, Eduardo, and Eduardo Levy-Yeyati. 2010. "Global Financial Safety Nets: Where Do We Go from Here?" Inter-American Development Bank Working Paper Series No. 231. http://idbdocs.iadb.org/wsdocs/getdocument.aspx?docnum= 35474343.

Fligstein, Neil. 1990. *The Transformation of Corporate Control.* Cambridge, MA: Harvard University Press.

Financial Times Editorial. 2008. "Icelandic Banks." *Financial Times.* December 14, 14.

Fischer, Stanley. 2014. "Financial Sector Reform: How Far Are We?" Martin Feldstein Lecture, National Bureau of Economic Research. Cambridge, MA, July 10. http://www.federalreserve.gov/newsevents/speech/fischer20140710a.htm.

Galbraith, John Kenneth. 1993. *A Short History of Financial Euphoria.* New York: Penguin.

Galbraith, John Kenneth. 2004. *The Economics of Innocent Fraud.* London: Penguin. Gandel, Stephen. 2014. "Jamie Dimon Calls Regulation Un-American, Once Again." *Fortune*, January 14. http://fortune.com/2015/01/14/jamie-dimon-financial-regulation/.

Gill, A. A. 2008. "Iceland: Frozen Assets." *Sunday Times*, December 14.

Gino, Francesca, Maurice Schweitzer, Nicole Mead, and Dan Ariely. 2011. "Unable to Resist Temptation: How Self-Control Depletion Promotes Unethical Behavior." *Organizational Behavior and Human Decision Processes* 115: 191–203.

Goffman, Erving. 1959. *The Presentation of Self in Everyday Life.* New York: Anchor.

Gordon, Greg. 2009. "How Goldman Secretly Bet on the US Housing Crash." McClatchy News Service, November 1. http://www.mcclatchydc.com/2009/11/01/77791/how-goldman-secretly-bet-on-the.html.

Gramsci, Antonio. 1971. *Selections from the Prison Notebooks of Antonio Gramsci.* New York: International Publishers.

Greenspan, Alan. 2011. "Dodd-Frank Fails to Meet Test of Our Times." *Financial Times*, March 29. http://www.ft.com/intl/cms/s/0/14662fd8-5a28-11e0-86d3-00144feab49 a.html#axzz3TzBKaaNk.

Hanson, Samuel, Anil Kashyap, and Jeremy Stein. 2011. "A Macroprudential Approach to Financial Regulation." *Journal of Economic Perspectives* 25: 3–28.

Harrington, Brooke. 2012. "The Sociology of Financial Fraud." In *The Oxford Handbook of the Sociology of Finance*, edited by Karin Knorr-Cetina and Alex Preda, 393–410. Oxford, UK: Oxford University Press.

Harrington, Brooke. 2013. "States and Financial Crises." In *Introduction to Political Sociology*, edited by Benedikte Brincker, 267–282. Copenhagen: Gyldendal Akademisk.

Hellman, Thomas, Kevin Murdock, and Joseph Stiglitz. 2000. "Liberalization, Moral Hazard in Banking, and Prudential Regulation: Are Capital Requirements Enough?" *The American Economic Review* 90: 147–165.

Hu, Henry. 2012. "Too Complex to Depict? Innovation, 'Pure Information,' and the SEC Disclosure Paradigm." *Texas Law Review* 90: 1601–1715.

James, Elliott, Kate McLoughlin, and Ewan Rankin. 2014. "Cross-Border Capital Flows Since the Global Financial Crisis." *Bulletin of the Reserve Bank of Australia*, June: 65–72.

Jorion, Philippe. 2000. "Risk Management Lessons from Long Term Capital Management." *European Financial Management* 6: 277–300.

Kapoor, Sony. 2010. "Financial Transaction Taxes: Necessary, Feasible and Desirable." Paper presented at the Foundation for European Progressive Studies, March 10. http://europeansforfinancialreform.org/en/system/files/1003_FEPS_FTTpaper_SonyKapoor.pdf.

Kelly, Kate. 2007. "How Goldman Won Big on the Mortgage Meltdown." *Wall Street Journal*, December 14. http://www.wsj.com/articles/SB119759714037228585.

Kidney, James. 2014. "Retirement Remarks." Washington, DC: SEC Union, March 27. http://www.secunion.org/files/RetirementRemarks.pdf.

Knee, Jonathan. 2007. *The Accidental Investment Banker: Inside the Decade that Transformed Wall Street*. New York: Random House.

Knights, David, and Majella O'Leary. 2006. "Leadership, Ethics and Responsibility to the Other." *Journal of Business Ethics* 67: 125–137. Krippner, Greta. 2005. "The Financialization of the American Economy." *Socio-Economic Review* 3: 173–208.

Krippner, Greta. 2011. *Capitalizing on Crisis: The Political Origins of the Rise of Finance*. Cambridge, MA: Harvard University Press.

Labaton, Stephen. 2008. "S.E.C. Concedes Oversight Flaws Fueled Collapse." *New York Times*, September 27, A1.

Lewis, Michael. 2010. *The Big Short: Inside the Doomsday Machine*. New York: Norton.

Lichtblau, Eric. 2008. "Mukasey Declines to Create a US Task Force to Investigate Mortgage Fraud." *New York Times*, June 6. http://www.nytimes.com/2008/06/06/business/06justice.html.

McCloskey, Deirdre. 2006. *The Bourgeois Virtues: Ethics for an Age of Commerce*. Chicago: University of Chicago Press.

Michalek, Richard. 2010. "Statement of Richard Michalek, Former VP/Senior Credit Officer, Moody's Investors Services." Submitted to Permanent Subcommittee on Investigations, United States Senate, hearing on *Wall Street and the Financial Crisis: The Role of Credit Rating Agencies*, April 23. http://www.hsgac.senate.gov/subcommittees/investigations/hearings/wall-street-and-the-financial-crisis-the-role-of-credit-rating-agencies.

Mihm, Stephen. 2007. *A Nation of Counterfeiters: Capitalists, Con Men, and the Making of the United States*. Cambridge, MA: Harvard University Press.

Minsky, Hyman. 1986. *Stabilizing an Unstable Economy*. New Haven, CT: Yale University Press.

Moghadam, Reza. 2011. "Strengthening the International Monetary System: Taking Stock and Looking Ahead." International Monetary Fund Working Paper, March 23. http://www.imf.org/external/np/pp/eng/2011/032311.pdf.

Morgenson, Gretchen, and Louise Story. 2009. "Banks Bundled Bad Debt, Bet against It and Won." *New York Times*, December 24, A1.

Morgenson, Gretchen, and Louise Story. 2011. "In Financial Crisis, No Prosecution of Top Figures." *New York Times*, April 14, A1. Mukunda, Gautam. 2014. "The Price of Wall Street's Power." *Harvard Business Review*, June. https://hbr.org/2014/06/the-price-of-wall-streets-power.

National Business Ethics Survey. 2013. *High Retaliation Rate: A Cause for Concern*. Arlington, VA: Ethics Resource Center.

Needleman, Martin, and Carolyn Needleman. 1979. "Organizational Crime: Two Models of Criminogenesis." *Sociological Quarterly* 20: 517–528.

Nier, Erlend, Tahsin Sedik, and Tomas Mondino. 2014. "Gross Private Capital Flows to Emerging Markets: Can the Global Financial Cycle be Tamed?" IMF Working Paper WP/14/196. http://www.imf.org/external/pubs/ft/wp/2014/wp14196.pdf.

Norman, Jesse. 2011. "The FSA's Report on RBS Doesn't Do Enough to Counter Crony Capitalism." *Guardian*, December 13, p. 30.

Orr, Andrea. 2009. "Too Complex to Regulate?" Economic Policy Institute, June 8. http://www.epi.org/publication/too_complex_to_regulate/.

Palley, Thomas. 2007. "Financialization: What It Is and Why It Matters." Working Paper No. 525, The Levy Economics Institute. Annandale-on-Hudson, NY: Bard College. http://www.econstor.eu/bitstream/10419/31686/1/571722628.pdf.

Paternoster, Ray, Jean Marie McGloin, Holly Nguyen, and Kyle Thomas. 2013. "The Causal Impact of Exposure to Deviant Peers: An Experimental Investigation." *Journal of Research in Crime and Delinquency* 50: 476–503.

Prates, Manuel. 2013. "Why Prudential Regulation Will Fail to Prevent Financial Crises: A Legal Approach." Working Paper 335, Banco Central do Brasil, Brasilia. http://www.bcb.gov.br/pec/wps/ingl/wps335.pdf.

Pulliam, Susan, and Deborah Solomon. 2002. "Uncooking the Books: How Three Unlikely Sleuths Discovered Fraud at WorldCom." *Wall Street Journal*, October 30, A1.

Reed, Christopher. 1999. "The Damn'd South Sea." *Harvard Magazine*, May–June: 36–41.

Reinhart, Carmen, and Kenneth Rogoff. 2009. *This Time Is Different: Eight Centuries of Financial Folly*. Princeton, NJ: Princeton University Press.

Rey, Hélène. 2013. "Dilemma Not Trilemma: The Global Financial Cycle and Monetary Policy Independence." Paper presented at the Jackson Hole Economic Symposium. Jackson Hole, Wyoming, August. http://www.kansascityfed.org/publicat/sympos/2013/2013rey.pdf.

Santoro, Michael. 2013. "Why Haven't the S.E.C.'s Lawyers Held Wall Street Accountable?" *New Yorker*, July 31. http://www.newyorker.com/news/news-desk/why-havent-the-s-e-c-s-lawyers-held-wall-street-accountable.

Sayer, Andrew. 2015. *Why We Can't Afford the Rich*. Bristol, UK: Policy Press.

Schiesel, Seth. 2002. "Trying to Catch WorldCom's Mirage." *New York Times*, June 30, S3, 1.

Sharman, Jason. 2006. *Havens in a Storm: The Struggle for Global Tax Regulation*. Ithaca, NY: Cornell University Press.

Smith, Greg. 2012. "Why I Am Leaving Goldman Sachs." *New York Times*, March 14.

Soederberg, Susanne. 2008. "A Critique of the Diagnosis and Cure for 'Enronitis:' The Sarbanes-Oxley Act and Neoliberal Governance of Corporate America." *Critical Sociology* 34: 657–680.

Sonnenscher, Michael. 2007. *Before the Deluge: Public Debt, Inequality and the Intellectual Origins of the French Revolution*. Princeton, NJ: Princeton University Press.

Swedberg, Richard. 2010. "The Structure of Confidence and the Collapse of Lehman Brothers." *Research in the Sociology of Organizations* 30: 71–114.

Tett, Gillian. 2012. "The Banks That Are Too Complex to Exist." *Financial Times*, June 7. http://www.ft.com/intl/cms/s/0/65281562-b0c1-11e1-a2a6-00144feabdc0.html #axzz3T5GsAt6n.

Tillman, Robert, and Michael Indergaard. 2005. *Pump and Dump: The Rancid Rules of the New Economy*. New Brunswick, NJ: Rutgers University Press.

Tillman, Robert, and Michael Indergaard. 2007. "Corporate Corruption in the New Economy." In *International Handbook of White Collar and Corporate Crime*, edited by Henry Pontell and Gilbert Geis, 474–489. New York: Springer.

Tillman, Robert, and Henry Pontell. 1995. "Organizations and Fraud in the Savings and Loan Industry." *Social Forces* 73: 1439–1463.

Turner, Adair. 2014. "Too Much of the Wrong Sort of Capital Flow." Paper presented at the Conference on Capital Account Management and Macro-Prudential Regulation for Financial Stability and Growth. New Delhi, India: Centre for Advanced Financial Research and Learning, January 13. http://ineteconomics.org/sites/inet.civicactions. net/files/INDIA%20LATEST%20%20-%20Too%20much%20of%20the%20wrong% 20sort%20of%20capital%20flow%20Jan%2013.pdf.

Useem, Michael. 1986. *The Inner Circle: Large Corporations and the Rise of Business Political Activity in the US and UK*. New York: Oxford University Press.

Vaughan, Diane. 2007. "Beyond Macro- and Micro-Levels of Analysis, Organizations and the Cultural Fix." In *International Handbook of White Collar and Corporate Crime*, edited by Henry Pontell and Gilbert Geis, 3–24. New York: Springer.

Veblen, Thorstein. 2009 [1899]. *The Theory of the Leisure Class*. Oxford, UK: Oxford University Press.

White, Lawrence. 2010. "Credit-Rating Agencies and the Financial Crisis: Less Regulation of CRAs is a Better Response." *Journal of International Banking Law and Regulation* 25: 170–179.

Winters, Jeffrey. 2011. *Oligarchy*. New York: Cambridge.

Zorn, Dirk. 2004. "Here a Chief, There a Chief: The Rise of the CFO in the American Firm." *American Sociological Review* 69: 345–364.

PART FOUR

The Global Financial Crisis of 2007–2009 and Values

15

Economics, Self Psychology, and Ethics

Why Modern Economic Persons Cheat and How Self-Psychology Can Provide the Basis for a Trustworthy Economic World

JOHN RIKER ■

Let me summarize the argument I will attempt to make in this chapter:

1. One of the complex of factors bringing about the economic downfall of 2007–2009 was the presence of cheating and playing fast and loose with sound banking practices. Values of personal gain were often put ahead of those of ethics when the two conflicted, leading to both unsound business practices and outright fraud.
2. The loss of trust in the market was not just due to the instability of the market but also a loss of trust in the integrity of some of the key players in the economic world.
3. The violation of ethical and legal principles did not occur by chance, but is a natural tendency of the kind of human being produced by economic society. That is, there is a contradiction at the heart of capitalist market society. It was not the one which Marx saw—an ever-increasing proletariat that would overthrow the bourgeoisie—but one in which the kind of human being who best thrives in a market economy is also someone who is likely to undermine the ethical substructures necessary to maintain the integrity of property and exchange. Understanding the kind of human being which a capitalist market economy tends to produce reveals both why they are inclined to cheat and why morality does not have a strong claim on them.
4. If economic society has a tendency to produce players who are internally pressured to cheat, then it needs to have significant structures of surveillance and regulation, such as those that might be found in the oligopolistic banking sector of Canada—which did not suffer the downturn. While business ethics

      classes might help somewhat, they cannot undo strong personal tendencies to cheat if that is the best way to get ahead.

5. An understanding of the theory of self proposed by psychoanalyst Heinz Kohut allows us to see why modern economic individuals are often narcissistically inclined, as they have suffered injuries to their core selves. Persons with injured selves tend to defend against their inner emptiness by seeking grandiose markers of greatness and will often cheat if those markers are endangered.

6. The long-term solution to the contradiction which destabilizes economic society is the construction of social and economic practices and values which support the generation of self structure in early childhood and sustain it later in adult life. Persons with strong, vitalized selves are not the kind of persons who cheat or who need grandiose markers to shore up an inner sense of worthlessness.

While there are many intersecting causes for the economic collapse of 2007–2009, one I think must be included in our discussion is the significant amount of cheating and playing fast and loose with sound financial practices and principles by major companies, banks, and brokers on Wall Street. If there had been no falsification of books, no hustling connected with subprime mortgages, no insider trading or stock manipulations on Wall Street, or no Ponzi scheming, the collapse might never have occurred and trust in financial institutions and the economic system might not have collapsed. In the end, it is the loss of trust in the economic marketplace that sends it into a tailspin and the restoration of trust that brings it back. What I will show in this chapter is how the modern economic world undermines ethical values and self-structure, producing a narcissistically inclined kind of person who is so prone to cheat that the economic system is constantly in danger of being destabilized. A significant cause of the cheating and desperate search for grandiose markers for oneself is due in large part, I think, to a misguided concept of what it means to be a self and what the proper aims of human life are. I will expose the problems with this conceptualization by confronting it with the notion of self as it been formulated in recent psychoanalytic theory and show that if the economic world adopts concepts, practices, and values to support self structure, a more trustworthy and sustainable economic environment will come into place.[1]

      What psychoanalytic self psychology, a movement initiated by the work of Heinz Kohut in the 1960s and 1970s,[2] discovered is that the key to feeling optimally alive and whole as a person is the development of a psychological set of functions which Kohut termed "the self." Since then the theory that there is an unconscious self that needs to be developed during the first half decade of life and socially sustained thereafter has been richly explored and elaborated, with a great deal of confirmation from infant and child studies.[3] We now understand much more about the social and environmental conditions that are necessary for selves to develop and flourish. What I intend to show is that while economic society creates vastly more opportunities for the possibility of self-actualization than any previous society, it has also generated conceptual and environmental conditions that predispose persons to experience serious traumas to the self, thereby undermining the core psychological configuration needed to feel coherent and vitalized, and predisposing a person to develop narcissistic symptoms. It is this systematic undermining of the self which can explain in part many of the negative features of modern society, such as the burgeoning amount of entitlement behavior, the increasing seriousness of drug, sex, food, and gambling addictions, and, most important for our inquiry, the tendency of modern persons to cheat.

And cheat they do. Americans, both rich and poor, cheat the government out of $250–$500 billion a year on their income taxes, file about $20 billion of fraudulent insurance claims, and lie on 50% of their resumes. The young shamelessly pirate music and movies from the Internet and cheat in their college and high school courses. A number of major companies have published false reports, engaged in Ponzi-type profit schemes, or willfully obscured (lied about) what they were in fact doing. There are countless other ways in which cheating undermines the most important institutions of modern society—there is rampant cheating in medicine, where doctors push drugs for their own profit; in law, where it is common practice for lawyers to pad hours; and in family life, where some estimates say that 50% of spouses cheat on each other. Persons even cheat on themselves, as when they break diets and other important commitments to their health and well-being.[4]

What I will show is that this tendency to cheat is profoundly connected to the concept of what it means to be an economic subject, both because this concept offers no good reason to be moral when morality conflicts with perceived personal interests and because a society that fosters economic individuals tends to undermine internal self structure, making persons desperate for external markers of greatness.

MODERN ECONOMIC SOCIETY

Most societies that have passed beyond hunter-gatherer tribal existence have four fundamental components: stable social relations, political structures of power, religious institutions and practices, and an economic production of material life. While these components usually coexist in some kind of stable but uneasy tension, often one of them will become predominant and define the fundamental values and existential orientations of that society. For instance, ancient Greece and Rome are typically understood as political societies in which hierarchies of power largely determined who one was, what one sought, and how one experienced life. Rome's internecine conflicts to determine who would be emperor ruined the economic system, forced citizens to change religions, and often involved families and friends killing one another. In contrast, Confucian society was fundamentally organized around social relations such that one's life revolved around one's position within the kinship structure and wider social orders. Politics, economics, and religion played secondary roles. Medieval Western society revolved around religious values to the detriment of economic existence and organized political structures, while modern Western society is clearly an economic world in which the bottom line trumps all other values.

Note that in the contemporary world, each of these kinds of societies exists somewhere and a number of the conflicts that seem irresolvable occur because of these different orientations. Putin's Russia is political and when the West replies to its power moves with economic sanctions, they are not as effective as we would hope. The Islamic world seems to be enmeshed in religious struggles, eschewing restraints from economic values and political sanity. Different kinds of worlds respond to values which are predominant in those worlds.

The kind of world I will be concerned with here is Western economic society, a social order that slowly replaced the previous religious society during the 17th–19th centuries. Before the modern economic world came into being, economic exchange was typically overdetermined by values of the other major societal components. If one lived in a village which had a number of kin, then one might have to buy his groceries from cousin Billy, despite the fact that Billy is a drunk and charges more for his second-rate produce than a nonfamily member down the street, a grocer who might also be avoided because he goes to a different church. When economics becomes the predominant value, then the overdetermination ceases and market transactions become governed by the simple principle of getting the best deal for oneself—selling high and buying low. As Deirdre McCloskey, has shown, the rise of economic society has entirely transformed human existence. According to her, the general daily consumption amount for the average human being had not changed since the dawn of time until the 18th century—about $3 a day (expressed in modern-day American prices, corrected for the cost of living), but over the past 200 years it has risen a miraculous 10 times, and up to 45 times in some of the richer first-world countries. The bottom line for everyone has gone up so substantially that even if the greatest benefits have gone to a tiny minority, the great majority of humanity has benefited immensely.

Interestingly, McCloskey attributes the coming into being of the economic world not to any change in economic policies/practices, engineering discoveries, or a shift in material resources, but to a dramatic shift in values. Slowly, it became all right to be interested in material life, all right to make a profit off of fellow human beings, all right to be concerned primarily for one's own well-being. The economic world brings with it a new ontology—a new way of being human—a way of being human in which neither God nor family nor community nor political power is primary; rather, the self-subsistent individual rationally engaging in the market and seeking his own highest well-being is the new paradigm of excellence.

THE ECONOMIC SUBJECT

As McCloskey conclusively demonstrated, it was a change of essential values more than any change in economic or productive practices that brought about the economic revolution of modern life. These values included changes in how persons conceive of what it means to be human and what constitutes a well-lived life. In the previous religious age humans saw themselves as having immortal souls and mortal bodies which could corrupt the immortal soul by dragging it away from spiritual concerns to material/sexual ones. Human life was conceived of as a great cosmic struggle between the forces of darkness/sin and light/salvation, and the battle ground was each individual soul, with God being the omnipresent audience and judge as to which side won. The well-lived life was one which overcame material/sexual desire and achieved a moral goodness that would be rewarded by bliss in an eternal afterlife. Given this conceptualization, persons in general did not concern themselves with economic betterment, for to do so would have been to tilt themselves toward the realm of the material/sinful.

What an enormous, perhaps traumatic, shift it must have been for human beings to declare that experiencing material pleasures in this mortal world is what is most important and the achievement of socioeconomic success through engaging in market activity is a rightful goal of a well-lived life. Why and how this radical change in philosophical anthropology came about is a fascinating question, but one which we cannot treat here. What is most important is that a new kind of human being comes into existence, namely, the economic subject. The rise and flourishing of the economic world is based on the conceptualization of economic subjects—for it is these subjects that are producers and consumers of economic goods—in a way that religious persons could not be, nor the political aristocrats of ancient Greece and Rome, nor the family members of a Confucian society intent on the ritual reproduction of social structures.

The economic subject has the following essential beliefs about life:

1. Each person is an individual subject fundamentally concerned for his own self-interest.
2. Self-interest is primarily thought of in terms of what maximizes pleasure (hence, leaving the individual free to determine what gives pleasure—the freedom of the modern world).
3. The pursuit of pleasure takes place in a highly competitive world in which one can achieve varying degrees of success.
4. The key to competing in the economic world is the development not only of talents and assets that one can trade but also the development of a rational economic point of view in which one can engage in accurate cost-benefit analyses and choose that course of action which best serves one's self-interest.
5. The rational individual who is best able to succeed in this competition is one who is willing to become abstract from all other values and contexts and base decisions solely on an economic calculus. If I live in Colorado Springs but a better position in the socioeconomic world opens in Chicago, then I ought to leave friends, uproot children from their schools, change recreation values from those of the mountains to those of the city, and so on. In short, dependency is likely to obscure rational choices; hence, it is best to be as self-subsistent as possible.
6. In general, the ability to achieve pleasure is based upon having the means to acquire goods and services in the marketplace; hence, as Jeremy Bentham stated, money is typically equated with happiness.
7. For the economic subject, morality is understood as a set of limitations on his pursuit of happiness or, as Kant said, a set of restraints. That is, ethics is not conceived of as a way to self-realization, as the Greek philosophers thought, but as a socially necessary obstacle limiting how one can pursue pleasure. In short, one ought not to achieve success through lying, cheating, murder, etc.

This conceptualization arose from a number of strange bedfellows during the 18th and 19th centuries, not all of which can be mentioned here. First, the rise of democracies put an emphasis on the individual subject who has the freedom to engage in "life, liberty, and pursuit of happiness." Second, there were the great economic theorists, such as Adam Smith, who declared that individuals seeking their advantage would produce the greatest wealth for the whole of a nation.

Third, and closely connected to economists, were the utilitarians—Hume, Bentham, Mill—who proclaimed pleasure to be the fitting and final goal of human life and also asserted that each individual ought to have the most amount of freedom compatible with the freedom of all to seek pleasure. This notion was profoundly substantiated by Darwin's concept of natural selection in which each organism is wired to seek its own advantage in an intensely competitive world. Even the radical individualism of the existentialist thinkers, such as Nietzsche, could be incorporated into this picture. Although the existentialists eschewed pleasure as the end of existence, they did assert the radical primacy of the individual over the collective. And, finally, Freud's psychoanalysis fits perfectly with this conceptualization, as he sees each person as an individual organism that works according to a fundamental pleasure principle.

While there may be many modern persons who still define themselves in a partially religious way or who proclaim the primacy of family, the above conception of what it means to be an economic subject has become predominant and for the most part governs the lives of modern persons and institutions. However, this conceptualization is, I believe, profoundly flawed, for the economic subject will have tendencies to undermine not only the well-being of the market on which he depends but also his ability to achieve a state of well-being.

In another article in this book, Leslie Shaw has carefully revealed why the supposed rationality of the economic subject is mistaken; hence, I will not address this aspect of the economic subject.[5] However, I would like to look at the other major premises: that persons are primarily autonomous organisms who are wired to seek their own self-interest and that self-interest is best identified with the maximization of pleasure. I want to show that this conception is unsound in that it produces a person who has a tendency to cheat and thus undermine the ethical structure which is necessary for the economic marketplace to exist, and that it misunderstands the self in such a way as to generate conditions that actually undermine the self, driving modern persons into an unhappiness which further intensifies their propensities to cheat.

THE ECONOMIC SUBJECT AND ETHICS

As Hegel pointed out, the modern economic world needs its subjects to be moral. Unless exchanges are open and honest, contractual promises binding, and property safe, people will not trust the anonymity of the modern marketplace and will tend to withdraw their investments in it. Since there are bound to be those who will attempt to take advantage of market exchanges by cheating or stealing, modern law enforcement agencies—the police, law courts, and penal system—all had to come into existence in a way that did not exist prior to the economic world coming into being (Unger, Foucault). However, it is not possible for these agencies to monitor anything but exceptions to standard moral practice; if most people were cheating/stealing, then the market would collapse. Economic subjects need to be moral if the economic world is to be sustained.

Further, modernity has articulated exactly the moral systems it needs in order to operate: Kantian deontology and utilitarianism (Poole). Kant's ethic proclaims that persons can seek personal happiness in any way they want so long as they do not break moral laws, such as those forbidding cheating, lying, or stealing. To affirm an immoral act is to enter into a self-contradiction, for if everyone cheated when they felt like it, there would be no such thing as legitimate exchange; if everyone lied, there would be no possibility of communication; and if everyone stole, there would be no such thing as property. As John Rawls put it, modern persons are free to pursue happiness in any way they want, but they must play fair—must follow rules which are good for the welfare of all. The utilitarians, on the other hand, were much more concerned about the production of human welfare and held that morally right acts were those which promoted "the greatest happiness for the greatest number." It was not enough not to break moral laws, one had to be concerned about promoting human flourishing. Since engaging as a productive member of the economic order is in general the best way to produce a general welfare, all one really needs to do in order to act in a utilitarian way is to be productive and engage in market exchanges. Also, since any competitive system must by necessity produce losers, the call to promote general welfare includes being concerned about those less fortunate.

While philosophers can still find problems with these systems of ethics and can especially point out how they can conflict, for the most part these two systems have become so predominant that we are held accountable for abiding by their values. We are to play fair, be productive, and be concerned for the less fortunate; when we are not, we receive disapprobation either in the form of moral censure or legal penalty. If everyone acted morally, we would not need to pour the enormous amount of resources which we do into the penal system. We might not have a deficit if no one cheated on their taxes; we might not have had the housing bubble burst had bankers and brokers been playing fair and following sound banking rules; we might not have even had the 1929 stock market crash if the Florida real estate scandal of a few years earlier had not happened and begun to destabilize the market.

The question which then appears before us is why, if the market needs its subjects to be moral and socializes them to be moral, there are so many instances of cheating and stealing. Thorsten Veblen would answer that we are comparative creatures and being wealthy is not enough—we want to be wealthier than the guy next door. Hence, there is intense pressure to succeed more than anyone else and this pressure leads to cheating. Thomas Callahan would add that the competition in contemporary society is so stiff and the payoffs at the top are so great everyone feels pressure to get ahead, and cheating is one of the ways to do so. Neither of these accounts, however, can explain why morality, which typically has held unethical behavior in check, has less of a hold on contemporary humans. Also, both need a deeper psychology to explain why so many successful competitors exhibit such debilitating symptoms as drivenness, addiction to a substance or activity, entitlement behaviors, overeating and overindulging in other ways, and lack of a sense of well-being despite their successes.

First, let us address the question of why moral reasons do not seem to be compelling for those economic subjects who decide that cheating is better than playing by the rules. Part of the answer lies in the failure of contemporary economic culture to provide an adequate answer to the question "why be moral?" when being moral appears to conflict with one's perceived personal interests. In the previous religious era, there was an excellent reason always to be moral: God had perfect surveillance of everything one did and was willing to mete out appropriate penalties in this life or later for those who strayed. But to be a modern economic person is to forgo having religious reasons for one's decisions.

Imagine a person, who has absorbed the modern concept of what it means to be human, faced with a choice in which it appears that it is clearly in his interest to cheat and there is a high probability of never getting caught. Perhaps it is a college student, who if he cheats (50% of all college students do cheat), will get an A in organic chemistry, a grade that will propel him into medical school. Yet if he takes the test on his actual knowledge and mental dexterity (he got drunk last night and is quite hungover), he will fail and his dream of being a physician will crash. He realizes that the exam proctor is distracted by an intense cell phone messaging dialogue (which our student has cleverly arranged) and will almost certainly not notice his cheating. Why should he be moral? Economic society has good reasons for raising moral persons, but it also must produce self-interested persons whose primary task is to calculate what action will optimize pleasures over a lifetime. Most of the time the two perspectives coexist nicely, but there are crucial times when they conflict, and when they do, modern economic society offers no good reasons—other than the fear of being caught—for being moral.

The great moralists of modernity, Kant and Mill, fail to offer us good reasons for following their moral systems when being moral conflicts with perceived self-interest. Kant said that the benefit for being moral was that we experience dignity. However, dignity is a value and as such must compete against other values, and this competition takes place in the arena of what grants the most happiness or pleasure. One can indeed get pleasure by feeling that one has not been self-serving and risen above egoistic desires; however, this satisfaction must compete against all the pleasures one might get from cheating or stealing. What might a trader say after reaping a hundred million dollars on insider information? "Moral dignity?—personally, I like the dignity that comes from wealth and all the fabulous pleasures it buys and all the accolades it receives." That is, dignity does not trump other values, and if the payoff from cheating is great, dignity is going to lose out in the hedonistic calculus.

John Stuart Mill wrote that we will want to be moral because we are a social species that cares for its fellow human beings. Even if this is true (and I think it is), he also said that persons are wired to seek their own pleasures. So why should I choose to optimize the pleasure of others when such an action conflicts with the optimization of my own pleasure? Again, no adequate answer is forthcoming. In short, one of the reasons why a modern person cheats is that there is no good reason not to when one's perceived self-interest conflicts with social interest and getting caught is unlikely.

The emphasis on economic value over social and religious values, plus the failure of modern society to offer compelling reasons for being good, might seem to be enough to explain the plague of cheating which has overtaken the modern world; however, I think that there is a more profound reason for the cheating and also for many of the other personal ills of modern society—the addictions, entitlements, rage, tsunami of failed love relations, obesity, obsessions with grandiosity and being the best—and it has to do with how economic society undermines self-structure, causing persons to suffer narcissistic symptoms and a desperate need to fill up an emptiness at the core of the psyche. To understand this phenomenon we need to address the question of what it means to have a self.

SELF-PSYCHOLOGY

Many psychoanalysts think that the most important development in their field since Freud has been the development of a psychology of the self that began in the last third of the 20th century and is continuing. While others, such as D. W. Winnicott, had a notion of the self as a psychological configuration separate from the ego before him, it is Heinz Kohut who is usually recognized as the founder of self-psychology, for he developed a theory which explains what a self is, how it develops, how it can be injured, and how it can be restored. The crucial difference between Freud and Kohut can be put into a nutshell. For Freud, the primary task for psychological life is to manage the libidinal and aggressive drives in a society that does not allow free expression of them (especially the incestuous oedipal configurations of libido), while for Kohut the indispensable task is to develop and sustain a self as the core psychological configuration. Like Freud, Kohut thought that humans began life in a state of narcissistic libido, but unlike Freud, who claimed that we must transform narcissistic libido into object libido, Kohut thought that narcissism did not need to be relinquished but must develop from infantile forms to more mature forms of self-love. The key to this development was the transformation of early grandiose narcissism into a self that was permeated with strong self-esteem, structured around personal ideals, and motivated by ambitions—organized energy for shining forth through accomplishments in the world.

Here is a thumbnail sketch of Kohut's theory for how the self develops. Each person begins life in a state of narcissistic splendor—what Freud called "his majesty, the baby." From what we can tell from infant research and persons who have pathologically retained their sense of infantile narcissism, babies feel themselves to be perfect, omnipotent, and grandiose, with a strong tendency to want to exhibit their greatness. They demand to be center stage and seem to care not a hair about others; others are there to serve them. In functional households, everyone is fine with this scenario. To its parents the baby is the greatest thing, and they want to tend to its every need. This makes the baby feel omnipotent—all it needs is to have a wish, gesticulate, and—*voila*—the wish is fulfilled.

Sooner or later, however, the parents will fail to be responsive in a somewhat traumatic way and the baby experiences intense anxiety as it realizes its complete helplessness. Its fundamental psychological tool for dealing with this trauma is to project its perfection into its caretakers, making them (in the baby's mind) a god and goddess who are all-powerful. These perfect beings have as their fundamental concern the baby's well-being; therefore, the child has not given up (as it had to in the face of reality) its perfection but endowed his caretakers with it. Henceforth, the child will view the parents in an idealized light and will lean on their strength and calmness in moments of fragmentation and helplessness (which happen multiple times a day) in order to soothe the inner tension. If the parents perform this task with minor, nontraumatic failures, the child between the ages of four and six will slowly reintegrate its sense of perfection in the terms of nascent ideals, ideals which will form an essential sector of the self. In short, the child has gone from "I am perfect" to "You are perfect and I am part of you" to "I have ideals which are perfect and which, if I can realize them, will make me feel great." What ideals do for us is give life meaning plus strength and calmness to persist through troubles. They also motivate us to develop beyond ourselves; that is, they make the self dynamic.

However, ideals are only part of the self. The other major sector of the self which must develop is what Kohut terms the "pole of ambitions"—organized energy for productivity in the world. We don't just want our ideals to shine; we want to shine and be recognized as great in ourselves. This pole is a transformation of that side of early narcissism which feels itself to be omnipotent and grandiose and which seeks to exhibit its greatness in the world. To assert itself in the world, the self needs to be grounded in a positive self-esteem, and this esteem develops only if others empathically respond to the child. For Kohut, empathy is not only how we know what a child is feeling, but is also a confirmation to the child that she is both important and connected to others. Empathy is the food which more than anything else builds the bones of a strong self, for it is the fundamental way in which self-esteem is generated and sustained. Self-esteem has the property of always being vulnerable to failures, slights, and nonrecognition, and thus we need lifelong empathic responses from others to sustain this side of the self.

The process of building this ambitious, productive, and vitalized side of the self needs one other ingredient, namely, frustration. That is, the child must be nontraumatically challenged to come out of her omnipotent grandiosity into a modulated and realistic sense of what actual power and possibilities are available to her. For instance, before toilet training, children feel themselves to be so great that they can eliminate their wastes wherever and whenever they feel like it, for others will take care of the mess; after toilet training they are responsible for knowing when their bodies need to eliminate, getting to a toilet on time, and cleaning themselves. If this difficult and frustrating process goes well, they will transform from "I am great because I am" to "I am great because of what I accomplish." This kind of "optimal frustration" happening over and over again in childhood builds up a tolerance for frustration, a love of accomplishment, and an ability to be sustained by the recognition that comes with accomplishment. If this side of development goes well, the child will develop a pole of ambitions by the age of six and will love challenges, crave accomplishments, and be sustained by the sense of worth they give. However, this path through challenging events is dangerous and pitfalls are everywhere, for failure is often shamed or successes go unrecognized—in both cases, self-esteem plummets.

We must add one other factor to complete the notion of the self, namely, that the ideals and ambitions must be adjusted to the idiosyncratic talents and propensities of the person. If they are not, then there is the feeling that our selves are too much the outcome of having values imposed upon us from the outside and we will develop what Winnicott calls a false self. Our ideals and ambitions must relate to our particularity, not to some generalized code of what is valuable.

Finally, we can see how and why others are crucial to the development and sustenance of the self, for they play self functions when the self is unable to. When the child is unable to soothe itself, the calm, idealized caretaker must play this function; when self-esteem plummets due to failures or slights, the empathic mirroring of others helps restore it. Whenever someone is performing a self function for another, they become what Kohut calls "selfobjects." Kohut claims that we all need selfobjects throughout our lives, because the self is the most vulnerable of our psychological configurations and can always get disturbed, knocked off balance, or traumatized. In a famous statement, Kohut said that others are as necessary for psychological life as oxygen is for biological life. Others can be literally part of one's self.

Thus, for Kohut, the self is an amalgam of ideals, ambitions, and personal traits whose health can be monitored along four registers: coherence—fragmentation, vitality—depletion, harmony (of the sectors of the self)—disharmony, and the degree to which one belongs to a sustaining matrix of persons willing to be selfobjects when one needs them. Persons with strong selves feel coherent, vitalized, harmonious, and firmly supported by others. They do not have warring inner parts; they do have a strong set of ideals that give life meaning; an organized reservoir of energy with which to bring the ideals to fruition in a way in which they, too, shine forth; and a matrix of friends who can offer support. When a person's self is engaged in activities in which ideals and ambitions are being realized through the use of the person's favored traits or talents, the person feels intensely that she is being herself, fills with a joyful exuberance, and senses that life is profoundly meaningful.

It is crucial to note that the self is only one of a number of psychological centers of motivation. The psyche is also motivated by basic needs/drives, ingressed social codes and values (what Freud called the superego), and by a conscious ego whose fundamental task is to negotiate with reality and which seeks power and control in order to accomplish its mission. The richest and most fulfilling organization of the psyche is when an educated, disciplined ego aligns with the self to help realize its ideals and ambitions in reality. The ego also has the task of maintaining psychic order. If the self has been traumatized (neglected, abused, severely misunderstood, etc.) and harbors so much pain and rage that it threatens the ability of the ego to have an organized consciousness, the ego will do what it can to defend against the traumatized self, including repressing it. If the ego loses connection with the self, then it will typically take as its function the satisfaction of desires which derive from a biological base or from social pressures. It will fundamentally work on the pleasure principle and appear to be very much like a model economic subject.

However, to live with an injured, repressed, or ignored self has profound consequences: for such the psyche must now symptomize. The major symptom that appears with the loss of the self is an inner emptiness—a black hole at the core of psychic life that threatens to suck everything into its sense of despair. To make sure this dark chasm doesn't surface, persons will manically attempt to stay busy. Sometimes this takes the form of addictions—to drugs, sex, gambling, eating, busyness itself—anything that might fill one with excitement rather than deadness. There is a driven quality to life, a ceaseless attempt to run away from the quicksand at the core of the psyche. One of the primary symptoms of a depleted, injured, or neglected self is the attempt to substitute external grandiosity for an internal sense of worth—attempting to make oneself feel great by owning a great car or mansion or trophy spouse. A second common consequence of having a traumatized self is a regression to earlier, more infantile, forms of narcissism. This appears to be the cause of much of the entitlement demands that so sour modern social life. People expect rewards even though they have not earned them or to get their way regardless of others. They push ahead of you in lines, tailgate and honk for you to get out of their way on the roads, take up way too much space in conversations, and are envious of anyone who takes center stage instead of them. Because they feel themselves to be innately superior (as a defense against inner worthlessness), they also can easily think that they are above the rules. The rules are for lesser people, not me!

Third, persons with injured selves tend to harbor vast amount of narcissistic rage, a kind of anger that seems never to diminish and which often comes out at inappropriate persons or institutions which have somehow become associated with the narcissistic injury to the self. How much of the road rage, work rage, and general violence that is so prevalent in American society comes from persons with injured selves it is hard to say, but I cannot think of anyone with an intact and flourishing self engaging in this kind of behavior.

Hence, one can easily see why someone with an injured self is likely to be driven to cheat or steal, especially in situations in which his fragile self is threatened by the loss of esteem, status, or wealth. The emptiness must be overcome with high amounts of success, stimulants, grandiose property, and so on, and the narcissistic entitlement lowers concerns about the rules or laws. It is also true that while in this semi-omnipotent state the narcissistic cheater is likely to underestimate his chances of getting caught. Thus if we can show that the contemporary economic world systematically destabilizes self structure, we have another reason for why this world is producing cheaters who undermine its viability.

In sum, self-psychology puts forth a new understanding of human nature that differs significantly from that of the economic subject. It has the following three crucial principles:

1. The self is the most important of all psychological configurations such that if it is well developed and active, then a person feels vitalized, joyful, and whole; but if it is injured or neglected, there will be a sense of depletion, a rise of infantile grandiosity, and the harboring of narcissistic rage. While a person can and does experience pleasure by satisfying desires that arise in other sectors of the psyche, a deep sense of well-being and happiness can come only from having a coherent, vitalized self engaged in activities and relationships in which it is realizing its ownmost values. Pleasure is not the end; self-realization is. Indeed, the pursuit of easy pleasures often distract us from the difficult work of self-realization.

2. The self is not a given in life but the outcome of a complex developmental sequence which is highly dependent upon the optimal responsiveness and empathy of others. Even if a coherent self comes into being in mid-childhood, it remains vulnerable to injury throughout life and constantly needs the empathic responsiveness of others to restore it to wholeness. That is, the self is not an autonomous, self-contained structure, but one which is necessarily relational and dependent on others for a lifetime.

3. Self psychology provides us with good reasons for being ethical. If we need others to sustain our selves, then, in adult life, we must be willing to be reciprocal. It is not hard to show that in order to engage in reciprocity one needs to develop empathic responsiveness, a sense of fairness, and those character traits Aristotle calls the moral virtues—traits which allow one to moderate the power of the passions and act thoughtfully. These traits include justice, courage, temperance, and generosity. In short, to be the kind of person best able to sustain oneself, one must be able to be a selfobject for others, and this requires one to become a just, generous, courageous, temperate, and empathic person—that is, a moral person. Ethics is not a restraint on a person's endeavors, but the best way for him to realize himself.[6]

SELF-PSYCHOLOGY AND THE ECONOMIC WORLD

If the most important task in psychological life is the development and sustenance of a self, then, certainly, the most important task for society—after it has secured the mechanisms for economic and political survival—is to establish social practices and values which aid the development and sustenance of the self. In evaluating the success of any society in relation to this task, we must examine the extent to which that society allows caregivers to give full attentiveness to children in the first half decade of life, how much it encourages or obstructs the formation of selfobject matrixes in adult life, and how many differentiated roles it offers for the expression of idiosyncratic, particularized selves. Previous societies in which almost the entirety of the population was typically involved in small farm production probably did well with the presence of caretakers in early life and the formation of kinship or friendship groups in later life. But they were miserable in offering varied and adventurous possibilities for self-realization.

In contrast, contemporary economic society offers more variegated possibilities than any previous society for adventurous, lifelong ways to realize the self in its multiple professions, extraordinary leisure activities, and open personal relations. These opportunities provide not only avenues for self-expression but also the needed recognition for one's grandiosity to be satisfied in mature ways that can keep developing over a lifetime. Economic society is also encouraging of self-development to the extent to which it favors differentiation and individuation of persons rather than a strong conformity to a set of standardized codes. In providing such extensive opportunities for differentiated self-expression, no other kind of society in the history of humankind has been so supportive of the development of selves as contemporary economic society. This opening up of possibilities for self-expression—freedom—is so important that even if contemporary economic society fails the self miserably in the other ways, it has made such an incredible advancement in this area as to never be abandoned for other less free systems.

On the other hand, its current practices and values are such that it fails the self wretchedly in the other important sectors: allowing and aiding caretakers to provide the necessary selfobject supplies for young children and fostering selfobject matrixes in adulthood. As any parent of a young child knows, raising a child to have a coherent, positive sense of self requires an enormous commitment of time, energy, and care. The number and frequency of instances in which young children need empathic mirroring, calm idealized presences to soothe them when they fall apart, and gentle frustrations so that they can grow simply consumes one. Indeed, the task is so difficult that the only ones who can typically be counted on to do it are either the biological parents of the child or those so desirous of having a child that they are willing to adopt. In short, the basic unit of care for an infant or young child is the family, and it is here where contemporary economic society fails selves the most, as it tends to destabilize and deplete family life, making the possibility of full attentive care for the first half decade of a child's life almost impossible.

There are a number of elements which have contributed to generating this negative condition for children. First, the mobility demanded by economic society has significantly reduced the possibility of having an extended family (grandparents, aunts, uncles, etc.) participate in the difficult chores of child-rearing. Second, and most important, it is quite common for both parents to have to work, in part because two incomes are necessary to sustain material adequacy for many households, but mainly because having a position within the socioeconomic world is necessary for one to have an identity—to be "someone." It used to be that being "a mother" was a recognized and honored identity, but since there was neither a salary nor economic status attached to it, being a mother ceased to provide the all-important source of recognition that persons need to flourish. To be fair, the pressure to be more than a homemaker does not come only from economic society but also from individuals who feel that the workplace is simply a more exciting and fulfilling site to actualize the self than is the home. Third, when caretakers do come home from work, they are often exhausted and tense from the hassles of the day and unable to be the source of selfobject supplies either for one another or for their children. It is not unusual for caretakers to soothe themselves with an alcoholic elixir, making them less able to be fully responsive to the selfobject needs of their children, who all too often disappear into their rooms to electronically network with other desperate children in other homes. Finally, there is the problem of divorce. With so much mobility in the world and so much time taken up with work, one cannot count on friends the way one used to, and so pressure is put on partners to supply almost all of the selfobject needs for one another. There are bound to be traumatic failures to give such supplies and if the partners' selves are not strong, there is a tendency to fall apart with the absence of support. The other is harshly blamed for being inadequate, hostilities ensue, the enraged partners split, and the household is ripped apart—along with the safety, security, and loving care that is the crucial environment for children's selves to develop.

Even as early as 1977, Kohut saw the depletion of the modern household as the great problem of our age.

> The psychological danger that puts the psychological survival of modern Western world in the greatest jeopardy is changing. . . . The environment which used to be experienced as threateningly close, is now experienced more and more as threateningly distant; where children were formerly *over*stimulated by the emotional (including the erotic) life of their parents, they are now often *under*stimulated; where formerly the child's eroticism aimed at pleasure gain and led to internal conflict because of parental prohibitions and the rivalries of the oedipal constellation, many children now seek the effect of erotic stimulation in order to relieve loneliness, in order to fill an emotional void. (p. 277)

In short, if intensive care, empathy, and presence of calm, strong caretakers is needed in order for selves to come into existence, the contemporary Western household is incredibly impoverished. What are desperate, empty persons with strong cognitive egos but weakened, incomplete selves going to be when they grow up? Certainly a leading possibility is that they will crave the excitement of being a high roller, playing fast and loose with established practices and the law, thinking that one is cleverer than the dolts who might investigate, and intensely needing to be super-grand in order to fill the void where the self should be. Put simply, the modern world is likely to produce executives who are cheaters.

There is another way in which contemporary economic society fails to sustain whatever self-structure there might be in adults. Before the last quarter of the 20th century, it was not uncommon for friendships to develop within the workplace;

indeed, for many the workplace came to provide the supportive social connections that the village used to. Two prongs of modern society intersected to significantly diminish the availability of selfobject supplies for adults in the workplace. First, the increasing demand that all decisions about personnel be made on the strict basis of objectively certified competence and objective economic factors rather than "old-boy networks" or friendships significantly increased the insecurity and competitiveness with one's fellow workers. Second, when women entered the professional workforce in large numbers, there was a tendency of men to sexualize the workplace in an egregious and unjust way. This sexualization had to be eliminated, but with its elimination a certain amount of normal human warmth, care, and concern also left the workplace. In short, the workplace is less a realm of friendship and camaraderie than it used to be, and as such become an institution less able to give selfobject supplies to adults.

If the workplace can no longer offer much by the way of friendship, where do adults get their selfobject needs met? The answer must be the home, but we have already found that the home has all too often ceased to be the place of love, comfort, and cherishing, but an empty nest in which angry narcissists keep asking, "What have you done for me, lately?" Adults are often left as desperate for selfobject supplies as their children.

As devastating as the above critique is for the development and sustenance of the self in contemporary economic society, the absence of coherent self-structure is hardly noticed because the paradigm for being a successful human being is to be an autonomous, ego-dominated, rationally calculating player in the socioeconomic world. The ideal is "to be an individual" not "to have a self." The self and its needs for love, responsiveness, ideals, and meaningfulness often get in the way of being a model economic individual competitively establishing his greatness in the world. Thus the needs of the self are often stifled.

However, as we have discovered, an injured or neglected self does not just disappear, but produces symptoms in a person, including a sense of drivenness, of never being nourished by successes, of forever needing excitement and ever greater narcissistic markers, and a tendency to be so needy and demanding in relationships that they are very difficult to sustain. In sum, while the contemporary economic world provides more avenues for self-actualization than any previous culture, it undermines the possibility of persons developing and sustaining selves due to its radical destabilization of family life and its cold objective workplace standards.

CONCLUSIONS AND RECOMMENDATIONS

While economic society has proven to be without parallel in the production of goods and services, it has done this by generating a concept of the person as an independent economic subject seeking pleasure through market exchanges rather than as someone with a vulnerable self that needs the empathic responses from others and seeks avenues of self-realization rather than pleasure. The downside of being a purely economic subject is that persons will tend to lack selves, become narcissists, and be tempted to be cheaters. Cheaters, in turn, undermine the necessary conditions of trust needed for the economic system of investment and exchange to flourish. Would the economic downturns of 2007–2009 have occurred if the major players in stocks and real estate had been straight shooters? Can catastrophic downturns be partially prevented by having ethical persons with intact selves everywhere in the system? It is the view of this author that such is the case and that it is crucial for economic society to cease valuing its economic version of individuality and accommodate some of its practices and values to the most important of all psychological tasks—the production of persons with coherent vitalized selves.

How does contemporary economic society need to change in order to accommodate the discoveries of self-psychology? First, and most obviously, it needs to make sure that children ages 0–5 have access to consistent, secure selfobject supplies. I am not a sociologist and don't claim to know how best to do this. My supposition is that this will involve a number of intersecting changes: longer maternal and paternal leaves; the development of a cadre of persons trained in early child-rearing development and certified in empathy, patience, and other crucial qualities who will be able to care for young children while the primary caretakers cannot be home; and daycare centers with workers trained in self-psychological theory and techniques of empathic responsiveness. I do not think that economic society can or will relinquish its demand to have all or most adults participate in its statuses, recognitions, and monetary rewards, and it is very difficult for young persons who have spent their early decades being educated to participate in this world to drop out of it for half a decade. Hence, a large part of the answer must be to have a large cadre of persons with exceptional empathic responsiveness, trained self psychologically in early childhood development, and remunerated well for addressing themselves to this vital need of society. It is doubtful that most young parents can pay for such services and so they will have to be subsidized by governmental agencies. Will it be worth it? Absolutely, since people with coherent selves will not be attracted to criminality or cheating, the amount of public monies spent on the legal system ought to decrease remarkably. Also, people with strong selves will not be as likely to engage in addictive drug behavior or overeating; hence, the savings in the health sector ought to be enormous.

Second, because it represents the principle of justice in the workplace, I do not want the merit criterion to cease reigning as the highest value for determining who gets what rewards. Somehow, more friendliness, empathy, and care needs to come back into the workplace such that it can once again be a place not just of accomplishment but of nurturance. Most of life's other sectors involves a complex balancing of values—social, political, religious, economic, and psychological—and while the productivity of the workplace might have increased marginally with the excision of all other than economic values, a number of companies and institutions have revealed how a balanced set of values, especially values that prioritize the well-being of the workers, help their companies flourish.

The changes I am advocating in how we conceive of ourselves and in our social and economic practices are difficult and likely to take a long time to take hold. In the meantime, I think we need to recognize the incredible pressures on economically constructed persons to cheat, and, given this reality, we need to develop even finer methods of surveillance and regulation. While I intensely dislike a culture of policing, I think it is a necessary outcome of the way the economic world is creating the subjects that inhabit it. Until we decide to create human beings with more secure self-structure, the need for intensive policing will remain.

In sum, I think that cheating and the desperate quest for grandiosity among major players in the economic sector played a substantial role in the economic downturn of 2007–2009. I have tried to demonstrate that one of the causes of the downturn is modernity's profound misconception of the self as an independent individual whose fundamental aim in life is the optimization of satisfactions brought about by successfully engaging the market economy. This conceptualization gives a person no adequate grounds for being moral and also undermines practices and institutions which are requisite for the development of the self. If the modern world can balance its economic values with values which promote the development and flourishing of people's selves, then I think that not only will the world be a happier place but it will likely have more robust economics.

NOTES

1. I have written at length on this issue in *Why It Is Good to Be Good: Ethics, Kohut's Self Psychology, and Modern Society* (Lanham, MD: Jason Aronson, 2010).
2. Kohut's first statement of his psychology of the self was in his article "Forms and Transformations of Narcissism." (Pp. 61–87 in *Essential Papers on Narcissism*. Edited by Andrew Morrison. New York: New York University Press, 1986). He then elaborated it in three books: *The Analysis of the Self* (New York: International Universities Press, 1971), *Restoration of the Self* (New York: International Universities Press, 1977), and *How Does Analysis Cure* (Chicago: University of Chicago Press, 1984).
3. In particular see the work of Daniel Stern and Beatrice Beebe.
4. See David Callahan's *The Cheating Culture* (New York: Harcourt, 2004) for a full account of cheating in America.
5. See Chapter 11 in this volume, "The Global Financial Crisis: Economics, Psychology, and Values."
6. See chapter 5 of my *Why It Is Good to Be Good* for a full statement of this point.
7. See chapter 5 of my *Why It Is Good to Be Good* for a full statement of this point.

REFERENCES

Callahan, David. 2004. *The Cheating Culture*. New York: Harcourt.

Foucault, Michel. 1979. *Discipline and Punish*, translated by A. Sheridan. New York: Penguin.

Hegel, G. W. F. 1991. *Elements of the Philosophy of Right*, translated by H. B. Nisbit. Cambridge: Cambridge University Press.

Kant, Immanuel. 1964. *Foundations of the Metaphysics of Morals*, translated by Lewis White Beck. Indianapolis, IN: Bobbs-Merrill.

Kohut, Heinz. 1977. *The Restoration of the Self*. New York: International Universities Press.

McCloskey, Deirdre. 2010. *Bourgeois Dignity*. Chicago. University of Chicago Press.

Mill, John Stuart. 1957. *Utilitarianism*. New York: MacMillan.

Poole, Ross. 1991. *Morality and Modernity*. New York: Routledge.

Rawls, John. 1971. *A Theory of Justice*. Cambridge, MA: Harvard University Press.

Riker, John. 2010. *Why It Is Good to Be Good: Ethics, Kohut's Self Psychology, and Modern Society*. Lanham, MD: Jason Aronson.

Unger, Roberto. 1976. *Law in Modern Society*. New York: The Free Press.

Veblen, Thorsten. 1958. *The Portable Veblen*, edited by Max Lerner. New York: Viking.

16

Financial Professionals in the Market for Status

MEIR STATMAN ∎

Financial professionals are prominent among the top 1% by income, but not by status or trust. The 2013 Edelman Trust Barometer reveals that the financial services industry is least trusted "to do what is right." A 2013 CFA/Edelman report explained why: "Hit by the shock of the 2008 financial crisis and ongoing scandals around money laundering, rogue trading, rate manipulation, and insider trading, the industry lost the faith of its key constituents—the clients, investing public, and other participants that help it function on a day-to-day basis."

The gap between income and status is a measure of the gap separating the "deserving rich" from the "undeserving rich." Physicians are also prominent among the top 1%. Yet the gap between their standing by income and by status is narrow relative to the gulf among financial professionals. Indeed, the Occupy Wall Street movement that ignited the 1% debate positioned itself squarely against financial professionals.

STATUS

"Status refers to one's standing in a social hierarchy as determined by respect, deference, and social influence," wrote Ridgeway and Walker (1995, 281). We can think of the status market as one where each of us, rich or poor, powerful or powerless, holds status tokens we can bestow on those who earn our respect and claw back from those who lose it.

Status symbols that yield status tokens vary across countries and their cultures. The InterNations website (2015) notes that status symbols among Chinese business people include fancy cars and properties abroad.[1] Rich young men in the Persian Gulf earn status tokens by owning lions, cheetahs, and other big cats. Fancy cars do not yield many status tokens in the Japanese business world, but a window-facing desk with a nice view does.

Status symbols also vary within countries. Ustuner and Holt (2010) found that perfect command of English along with college education in the West ranks high among cosmopolitan upper-middle-class secular women in Turkey. Less-educated upper-middle-class women signal their status through expensive goods deemed prestigious by upper-class Turks and enjoy public displays of deference by salespeople in luxury stores.

UNDERSTANDING THE MARKET FOR STATUS AND MODIFYING IT

The price of status tokens reflects a country's culture. The Power Distance Index is a cultural dimension by Hofstede reflecting expectations about the distribution of power among people in a country. People in countries where power distance is high consent to an unequal power distribution, and the poor and powerless in such countries also consent to bestow status tokens at low prices on the rich and powerful. Malaysia is first in power distance among 88 countries. Brazil stands at the 6th place, Russia at the 8th, and China at the 14th. Austria is last in power distance, standing at the 88th place, Switzerland at the 80th, and the United States at the 71st. Winterich and Zhang (2015) found that philanthropy is common in countries where power distance is low, and Statman (2015) found that preference for income equality is low in countries where power distance is high. Philanthropy yields many status tokens in countries where power distance is low, but it yields few in countries where power distance is high.

Financial professionals who engage in philanthropy, donating millions to universities or hospitals, acquire status tokens as their names are chiseled into stone above the entrance to buildings. Conversely, claw-backs of status tokens from financial professionals accompany bailouts of financial institutions and practices that place the interests of financial professionals ahead of their clients.

Not all financial professionals understand the market for status. Leon Cooperman, founder of the Omega Advisors hedge fund, was angry when President Obama urged America's "millionaires and billionaires" to pay their fair share. Cooperman said that he would be willing to pay higher taxes, "if treated with respect." Taxes, however, do not buy status token—the IRS would not chisel Cooperman's name into stone above the entrance to its building even if he were to pay billions in taxes.

Talent, entrepreneurship, and hard work can yield both income and status tokens, but the quantity of status tokens bestowed is proportional to the benefits provided to the general public. "Yes, the wealthy can be deserving," wrote Gregory Mankiw (2014), noting an actor, an author, an entrepreneur, as well as financial professionals. Robert Downey Jr. was paid $50 million for his role in *The Avenger*. "When I talk to people about it," wrote Mankiw, "most are not appalled by his income." Downey earned some status tokens in addition to the $50 million, as the movie brought pleasure to viewers, but he did not earn many status tokens, as other movies are ready substitutes. The same is true for author E. L. James, who earned $95 million in royalties from *Fifty Shades of Grey*. Steve Jobs earned many status tokens along with billions in income because we would have waited longer for the benefits of equivalents of iPod, iPhone, and iPad had he not introduced them.

Mankiw argued that financial professionals deserve status tokens along with their income, as there is no doubt that [the financial] sector plays a crucial economic role. Those who work in banking, venture capital and other financial firms are in charge of allocating the economy's investment resources. They decide, in a decentralized and competitive way, which companies and industries will shrink and which will grow. It makes sense that a nation would allocate many of its most talented and thus highly compensated individuals to the task.[2]

Mankiw might persuade financial professionals that they are receiving too few status tokens along with their incomes for their resource allocating services, but he is not likely to persuade many outside their cocoon. As Statman (2004, 2013) wrote, many financial professionals live as if in a cocoon, viewing salaries and bonuses in the millions as ordinary and fair and expecting status tokens on top of them. Financial professionals often maintain the naïve belief that everyone agrees with them. They do not. Outcomes in the market for status involve the general public, and the views of many in the general public are very different from the views of financial professionals.

Financial professionals face both internal and external obstacles in relating to the public's culture and rules of fairness. The internal obstacle is in adherence to a self-serving libertarian notion of fairness, where the right to freedom from coercion is paramount and the right to equal power is overlooked or dismissed. The external obstacle is the difficulty in explaining the benefits of financial professionals' work in "allocating the economy's investment resources," whereas it is easy to explain the benefits of the work of physicians, engineers, or plumbers.

Attempts to modify the market for status and influence the price of status tokens are common. Status is relative and some try to block others striving to acquire status tokens that might eclipse their own. Adam (2006) wrote that "old money" in New York tried to block acquisition of status tokens by "new money." Struggles between new and old money in New York were so deep that they resulted in the construction of two different spheres of philanthropic engagement: the old elites established the Metropolitan Museum of Art and the new elites established the American Museum of Natural History. The Metropolitan Opera House, financed exclusively by new money, marked the transition of power from the old to the new elites.

More recent attempts take the form of names by which to call the 1%. Tom Perkins (2014), a wealthy venture capitalist, wrote in a letter to the *Wall Street Journal*: "From the Occupy movement to the demonization of the rich embedded in virtually every word of our local newspaper ... I perceive a rising tide of hatred of the successful one percent."[3] Sam Zell, a wealthy real estate investor, called them the hard-working 1% in a Bloomberg Television interview.[4] He argued that the 1% should be granted higher status because "the 1% work harder, the 1% are much bigger factors in all forms of our society." Other names offered by those who attempt to lower the price of status tokens include "job creators," "risk takers," and "deserving rich." Names offered by those who attempt to raise the price of status tokens include "fat cats," "exploiters," and "undeserving rich."

CULTURE WARS

Perkins's and Zell's words hint at a broader struggle that Arthur C. Brooks (2010) president of the American Enterprise Institute, described as a "culture war." This is a war between competing visions of culture and rules of fairness reflected in disagreements about the proper strengths of safety nets, levels of income redistribution, and grants of status. "These visions are not reconcilable," wrote Brooks. "We must choose."

"In one," wrote Brooks, "America will continue to be an exceptional nation organized around the principles of free enterprise—limited government, a reliance on entrepreneurship and rewards determined by market forces. In the other, America will move toward European-style statism grounded in expanding bureaucracies, a managed economy and large-scale income redistribution."

Brooks emphasized differences between the culture and rules of fairness in the United States and those in Europe and highlighted their effects on generating income and redistributing it. These differences are also at the center of an analysis by Alesina and Angeletos (2005) who observed that income redistribution in the United States is relatively meager, whereas it is relatively generous in continental Western Europe. They attributed the difference, at least in part, to different cultures, adhering to different rules of fairness and different perceptions of the sources of income inequality. Americans lean toward the belief that income and wealth come mostly from hard work, whereas Europeans lean toward the belief that income and wealth come mostly from luck. They noted that the World Value Survey found that 71% of Americans believe that the poor could become rich if they just tried hard enough, whereas only 40% of Europeans share that belief.

Alesina and Angeletos argued that the American and European systems of beliefs and redistribution policies can exist side by side. On one side of the Atlantic, the prevalent American belief that income and wealth come mostly from hard work promotes policies of low taxes and meager redistribution. Consequently, Americans, knowing that they will not be supported by the rich, work hard and accumulate more wealth than they otherwise would. This perpetuates the belief that income and wealth come mostly from hard work. On the other side of the Atlantic, the prevalent European belief that income and wealth come mostly from luck promotes policies of high taxes and generous redistribution. Consequently, Europeans, knowing that they will be supported by the rich, do not work as hard and accumulate less wealth. This perpetuates the belief that income and wealth come mostly from luck.

Yet the picture painted by Alesina and Angeletos exaggerates the distinction between American and European cultures. In truth, some Americans attribute income and wealth mostly to hard work while others attribute it mostly to luck, even if a higher proportion of Americans than Europeans attribute income and wealth to hard work rather than luck. Moreover, the financial crisis has shifted many Americans away from the belief that income and wealth come mostly from hard work, evidenced by the Occupy Wall Street movement and counterattempts to reinforce the belief that income and wealth come mostly from hard work. Sam Zell said that Americans "should not talk about envy of the 1-percent, they should talk about emulating the 1-percent."[5]

We see Americans' differing views and preferences in Stokes's (2014) description of a Pew Research Center survey. Almost half of Americans regard the gap between the rich and the poor as a very big problem for the country. Almost one-third regard the gap as a moderately big problem, while one-fifth regard it as a small problem or no problem at all. Differing views and preferences reflect ideological divides. Fully 59% of Democrats view inequality as a major national economic challenge, as do 49% of independents. But only 19% of Republicans agree. Among Republicans, 39% say that the gap between rich and poor exists because "some people work harder than others," but only 17% of Democrats agree. Among Democrats, 17% say that the gap is due to "how much workers are paid," but only 7% of Republicans agree. Differing views about the causes of inequality lead to different preferences for redistribution and safety nets. Among Democrats, 71% prefer "high taxes to fund programs for the poor," but only 17% of Republicans agree. Among Republicans, 71% prefer "low taxes to encourage investment and growth," but only 19% of Democrats agree.

Freedom from coercion is one of seven fairness rights discussed by Shefrin and Statman (1992, 1993), and equal power is another. The fairness right of freedom from coercion entitles people to choose to enter or refrain from entering contracts. By that fairness right, contracts are fair when people enter into them voluntarily, and transactions are fair if people engage in them voluntarily. The fairness right of freedom from coercion underlies much of advocacy for free markets and libertarian policies.

The fairness right of equal power entitles people to equal power in negotiations leading to contracts or transactions and equal power in making subsequent changes in contracts or transactions. The right to equal power underlies advocacy of strong safety nets, income redistribution, and minimum wages.

Beliefs about the sources of income and wealth—hard work or luck—interact with the preference for fairness rules—freedom from coercion or equal power. The fairness right of freedom from coercion is compatible with a belief that the entirety of income and wealth comes from hard work and none comes from luck. The fairness right of equal power, however, is compatible with that belief that some of high income and wealth comes from good luck and some of low income and wealth comes from bad luck, justifying actions that equalize power by distributing the fruits of good luck among those with bad luck.

THE BENEFITS AND COSTS OF THE WORK OF FINANCIAL PROFESSIONALS

Financial professionals provide many benefits to the public, some of which can be easily grasped and acknowledged. Bankers provide mortgage loans that let people buy houses without paying full prices in cash. Bankers also provide credit cards that facilitate purchases by allowing payments in installments. Money managers in mutual fund companies, private equity firms, and hedge funds convert people's savings into diversified investment portfolios that help people reach financial goals such as retirement income, education, or bequests.

Still, it is not easy to explain to the general public the benefits of the very large financial services industry and the high incomes of some financial professionals. Telling the public that financial professionals are worthy of their high incomes because they are in "charge of allocating the economy's investment resources" is much too abstract to be persuasive, even if true.

Moreover, many doubt that the financial services industry provides benefits to the general public that are commensurate with its size and the resources it consumes. "Why did we get the bloated finance industry of today instead of the lean and efficient Wal-Mart?" asked Philippon (2012, 235). "Why is the non-financial sector transferring so much income to the financial sector?" One simple answer, he wrote, is that technological improvements in finance have mostly been used to increase trading. Yet Philippon found no evidence that increased trading brought social benefits. Securities prices are no more informative today than in earlier days when the volume of trading was much lower, and securities provide no better risk sharing today than in earlier days.

Greenwood and Sharfstein's (2013) assessment of the social benefits of the finance industry is not as harsh as Philippon's, but it is hardly all sanguine. They wrote, first, that a large part of the growth of finance is in asset management, which provides social benefits in increased diversification and household participation in the stock market and in making it easier for young companies to raise funds. Some amount of active asset management is necessary for informational efficiency and adequate monitoring but asset management is very costly, and there are many reasons to believe that there is too much of it.

Second, Greenwood and Sharfstein noted the benefits of changes that facilitated the expansion of household credit, mainly in residential mortgage credit. Yet they added that there are a number of societal costs from such an expansion, including instability from excessive household leverage.

Costs imposed by financial professionals need to be subtracted from whatever benefits they provide to the general public. Costs include not only salaries and bonuses paid to financial professionals but also costly legal and illegal behavior such as money laundering, rate manipulation, and insider trading.

Credit cards are one example, described by Shefrin and Statman (2009), of the behavior of financial professionals eventually leading to backlash in the form of the Credit Card Accountability, Responsibility and Disclosure Act of 2009 (CARD). The act favors cardholders over credit card companies, restricting fees charged by credit card companies and limiting their ability to increase the interest rates they charge.

Financial professionals advocating lax regulation of credit cards emphasize the fairness right of freedom from coercion, noting that credit card companies do not coerce anyone to hold their cards. All the terms of the cards, including the criteria determining penalties and interest rate increases, are noted in pages that accompany cards, even if in small print and words that only lawyers can comprehend. Those advocating restrictive regulation of credit cards note that credit card companies violate the rights to equal power since poor cardholders have little power when unemployed or facing onerous medical bills.

President Obama, who signed the bill, recalled stories he heard during the presidential campaign from people "choking backs tears" as they recounted credit card predicaments caused by unforeseen medical bills or mortgage payments. Obama accused credit card companies of writing contracts "designed not to inform but to confuse." Noting that one provision of the law requires credit card companies to inform customers in advance of changes in payment due dates, he added his personal experience as a cardholder: "This always used to bug me."[6]

CONCLUSION

In 2010, Arthur C. Brooks was alarmed by the protests of Occupy Wall Street and the demand for strong safety nets, describing them as "European-style statism." By 2014, however, he seems to have changed his mind, apparently after meeting poor people who fell through a frayed safety net. He titled his 2014 article "Be Open Handed toward Your Brothers," drawing from Deuteronomy 15:11: "There will always be poor people in the land. Therefore I command you to be open-handed toward your brothers and toward the poor and needy in your land." And he drew from Proverbs 14:21 at the end of his article, "He that despiseth his neighbor, sinneth: but he that hath mercy on the poor, happy is he."

"To deny that some Americans are genuinely needy requires willful blindness," wrote Brooks, and America cannot solve the problems of poverty by private charity. "Consider the present total that Americans give annually to human-service organizations that assist the vulnerable. It comes to about $40 billion, according to Giving USA. Now suppose that we could spread that sum across the 48 million Americans receiving food assistance, with zero overhead and complete effectiveness. It would come to just $847 per person per year."

Contributions to human-service organizations that assist the vulnerable are one way for financial professionals to increase their status. They can add to their status by understanding the market for status before attempting to modify it, persuading the general public that their work provides benefits, adding to these benefits, and removing costs.

NOTES

1. http://www.internations.org/magazine/status-symbols-around-the-world-17426.
2. http://www.nytimes.com/2014/02/16/business/yes-the-wealthy-can-be-deserving.html?partner=rss&emc=rss&_r=0.
3. http://www.huffingtonpost.com/2014/02/05/sam-zell-1-percent_n_4733196.html.
4. http://www.bloomberg.com/news/videos/b/75f58b37-90f1-42f0-86c1-014aeb39a3e9.
5. http://www.bloomberg.com/news/videos/b/75f58b37-90f1-42f0-86c1-014aeb39a3e9.
6. http://www.whitehouse.gov/videos/2009/May/20090522_Credit_Card_Reform.mp4.

REFERENCES

Adam, Thomas. 2006. "Buying Respectability. Philanthropy and Cultural Dominance in 19th-Century Boston." *Traverse*, 29–46.

Alesina, Alberto, and George-Marios Angeletos. 2005. "Fairness and Redistribution." *American Economic Review* 95 (4): 960–980.

Brooks, Arthur. 2010. "America's New Culture War: Free Enterprise vs. Government Control," *Washington Post*, May 23, http://www.washingtonpost.com/wpdyn/content/article/2010/05/21/AR2010052101854.html.

Brooks, Arthur. 2014. "'Be Open-Handed Toward Your Brothers' A conservative social-justice agenda," *Commentary*, February 2014. https://www.commentarymagazine.com/articles/be-open-handed-toward-your-brothers-1/.

Greenwood, Robin, and David Scharfstein, 2013. "The Growth of Finance." *The Journal of Economic Perspectives* 27 (2): 3–28.

Philippon, Thomas. 2012. "Finance Versus Wal-Mart: Why Are Financial Services So Expensive." In *Rethinking Finance: New Perspectives on the Crisis*, edited by Inin Blinder, Alan, Andrew Lo, and Robert Solow. New York: Russell Sage.

Ridgeway, Cecilia L., and Henri A. Walker. 1995. "Status Structures." In *Sociological Perspectives on Social Psychology*, edited by K. Cook, G. Fine, and J. House. Upper Saddle River, NJ: Pearson Education.

Shefrin, Hersh, and Meir Statman. 1992. *Ethics, Fairness, Efficiency, and Financial Markets.* Charlottesville, VA: CFA Institute Publications.

Shefrin, Hersh, and Meir Statman. 1993. "Ethics, Fairness and Efficiency in Financial Markets." *Financial Analysts Journal*, November/December, 21–29.

Shefrin, Hersh, and Meir Statman. 2009. "Striking Regulatory Irons While Hot." *Journal of Investment Management* 7 (4): 29–42.

Statman, Meir. 2004. "Fairness Outside the Cocoon." *Financial Analysts Journal* 60 (6): 34–37.

Statman, Meir. 2013. "Finance Professionals in the Financial Crisis: Values, Fairness, and Culture." *Journal of Investment Management* 11 (4): 12–21.

Statman, Meir. 2015. "Culture in the Preference for Income Equality and Safety Nets. *Journal of Behavioral Finance*, forthcoming.

Stokes, Bruce. 2014. "Debate over Inequality Highlights Sharp Partisan Divisions on the Issue." Pew Research Center, October 20, 2014.

Ustuner,Tuba, and Douglas B. Holt. 2010. "Toward a Theory of Status Consumption in Less Industrialized Countries." *Journal of Consumer Research* 37 (1): 37–56.

Winterich, Karen Page, and Yinlong Zhang. 2014. "Accepting Inequality Deters Responsibility: How Power Distance Decreases Charitable Behavior." *Journal of Consumer Research*, August.

17

Why Risk Management Failed

Ethical and Behavioral Aspects

JOHN BOATRIGHT ■

INTRODUCTION

Although the recent financial crisis was exceedingly complex, the basic outlines are familiar from past episodes in which the bursting of an asset price bubble led to strains in the banking system.[1] As the book *This Time is Different: Eight Centuries of Financial Folly* (Rogoff and Reinhart 2009) amply demonstrates, financial crises are remarkably similar, especially in the belief that high asset prices are justified "this time" by some new factor. However, this time was different in one way: it was the first major financial crisis in which risk management played a prominent role. Modern risk management, which employs highly sophisticated mathematical measures and models, is a development of the past few decades. And in its first major test, risk management failed—demonstrably and spectacularly.

A complete explanation for the failure of risk management in the recent crisis would be impossible within a short space and would involve some highly technical matters (for one account, see Hubbard 2009). The focus of this chapter is on the more limited task of addressing this failure with a view to its ethical and behavioral aspects. Even this more limited scope is an immense undertaking, especially in view of the explosion in the nascent field of behavioral ethics (see Trevino, Weaver, and Reynolds 2006), which overlaps to a great extent with behavioral economics and behavioral finance. A full ethical and behavioral explanation of how risk management failed in the recent crisis would touch on virtually all the discoveries that have been made about the psychology of ethical behavior. The discussion offered here is, of necessity, brief and partial.

RISK MANAGEMENT IN THE CRISIS

Managing the uncertainties of life has always been a human concern, which led in ancient times to occult means of appeasing the gods, whose will determined people's fate. In his book *Against the Gods: The Remarkable Story of Risk*, Peter Bernstein (1996a) dates the development of risk management to the Renaissance with the discovery of the mathematics of probability. Subsequently, this mathematical approach to risk was employed by the modern banking and insurance industries, as well as by government. (Bernstein notes that the word "statistics" has "state" at its root because of the early use of data in governing.)

However, risk management in its current form began around 1970 with theoretical advances in finance, which laid the basis for highly sophisticated mathematical measures and models. Modern mathematically based risk management has been a decided boon for mankind. However, critical questions can be raised about it, because, as Bernstein cautions, risk management could become "a new kind of religion, a creed that is just as implacable, confining, and arbitrary as the old" (Bernstein 1996b, 47). In his view, an overreliance on numbers may lead to errors as serious as those committed by priests of old who depended on omens and offerings. As Niall Ferguson (2008) has quipped, "those whom the gods want to destroy they first teach math."

Risk management played a role in the recent financial crisis, first, by facilitating the construction of new financial instruments, including the kind of derivatives that Warren Buffett (2002) described as "financial weapons of mass destruction." In particular, risk management tools facilitated the structuring of collateralized debt obligations (CDOs), which are securities that bundle together large numbers of loans and divide them into tranches with different risk levels and rates of return. These securities would be impossible to construct without mathematical models to determine the risks and hence the appropriate prices for individual tranches. The rating agencies relied on the same or similar models to rate these new securities, often awarding the highest score to securities that later became virtually worthless.

More mathematical models were needed for the construction of other exotic financial instruments, such as synthetic CDOs and credit default swaps (CDSs). (Synthetic CDOs are second- and third-order derivatives based on CDOs or various indices, and CDSs are essentially insurance policies on debt instruments that can be purchased by any investor, even those who do not hold the loans or securities being insured.) Not only did the major banks issue CDOs, CDSs, and other securities, collecting hefty fees for doing so, but they also held many of them for their own account and used credit default swaps issued by other firms to insure their positions. The crisis occurred when some securities held by banks declined in value and the banks could not borrow against them because of this decline and—more crucially—because of uncertainty about their value. A source of risk that had not been considered was a loss of liquidity, which is to say that the securities suddenly had no buyers.

A second use of risk management occurred when banks assessed the risk of their portfolios, which included large volumes of CDOs and similar securities. Although they assumed very substantial risks by leveraging their capital—in some instances more than 30 to 1—the banks were able to do this with great confidence because they had measured their risks very precisely by newly developed model-based techniques. In particular, value at risk (VaR) became a widely adopted tool for determining the risks posed by a bank's portfolio. VaR gave users a great sense of confidence that their firm's risks were being managed prudently—mistakenly, as it turned out.

CRITICISM OF RISK MANAGEMENT

Modern risk management has been criticized on many different grounds. The most common criticism is that the models used in managing risk failed in the crisis due to a deadly combination of inadequate data, limited variables, and mistaken assumptions (Cassidy 2010, Stulz 2008). In some cases, the fault lay with the models themselves, while other failures resulted from the misuse of otherwise good models. An aim of much risk management is to predict low-probability, high-impact events, and some question not only the possibility but even the meaningfulness of attempting to do so (Rebonato 2007, Taleb 2007). This is especially true for "unknown unknowns," which may have never occurred or perhaps even been conceived. Such events, which are unpredictable in principle, cannot be captured in models but may be the risks most in need of management.

Another kind of criticism is that models themselves may affect the events being predicted, with the result that models often fail in crises because they lead everyone to act in the same way (Daníelsson 2002). A forecast of rain, for example, may lead people to carry an umbrella, but doing so has no effect on the weather, unlike predictions about markets, which may affect how people trade. A broader critique is that the human behavior which is being predicted is nondeterministic and hence incapable of being modeled. Even when behavior is regular enough to be modeled, it can change in response to events, so that models lose their predictive power (Pollock 2008).

Further criticism has been directed at specific measures, especially the concept of VaR, which is a dollar figure of the amount that can be lost within a certain period of time with a certain degree of probability (Leippold 2004, Nocera 2009). One problem with this measure is that the amount that can be lost in the margin of error is unlimited. In addition, it, too, can fail in a crisis when herd behavior occurs. For this reason, VaR has been compared to an airbag that always works except in crashes (Einhorn and Brown 2008). The widely accepted assumption that correlations among defaults could be determined from current rather than historical data has also been challenged, and even described as "the formula that killed Wall Street" (Salmon 2009, see also Jones 2009 and Li 2000).

These main criticisms of risk management do not obviously involve ethics except insofar as the management of risk was done carelessly or, even worse, maliciously. Certainly, the great harm that the crisis inflicted on the whole of society is lamentable, but like the injury from a defective product, it is morally wrong only if there was some intent to harm or, at least, culpable negligence. Although no one may have intended to wreak the damage that ensued, many people were aware that some borrowers would lose their homes and perhaps life savings and that great losses would be inflicted on countless investors worldwide from risky mortgage-backed securities.

The oft-expressed attitude "I'll be gone; you'll be gone" (enshrined in the cynical acronym IBGYBG) casts doubts on the moral character of many individuals engaged in the mortgage lending and securitization processes. And the instances in which investment banks bet against the very mortgage-backed securities that they sold to investors are ethically suspect, despite the defense that the banks were dealing with "sophisticated investors," who knew what they were doing and wanted the risk exposure (Storey 2010). The ethical fault, if any, in such instances lies in a confusion of roles: Were the banks serving as trusted advisers with a fiduciary duty to protect the interests of clients, or were they merely counterparties who could rightly exploit any misjudgment by others during market transactions?

Finding ethical fault in the financial crisis is made more difficult by unclear lines between deliberate wrongdoing or culpable negligence and colossal misjudgment that in retrospect might even be called gross stupidity. One caution comes from what has come to be known as Hanlon's razor: "Never attribute to malice that which can be adequately explained by stupidity!" A revision of this counsel is: "Never attribute to malice or stupidity that which can be explained by moderately rational individuals following incentives in a complex system of interactions" (Hubbard 2009, 55). This explanation seems to fit much of the behavior in the recent financial crisis.

Much of the criticism of risk management, for both its technical shortcomings and possible unethical misuse, considers specific applications of risk management measures and models or focuses on risk management as an instrument or tool. In order to explore the ethical and behavioral aspects of risk management, it is essential to consider two matters: first, the ways in which risk management affects and is affected by the people who use it and, second, the consequences for risk management when it is implemented in organizations, including its utilization for regulatory purposes. With regard to the first matter, modern risk management is more than a technical analysis of the probability of certain events occurring; it is a critical part of a comprehensive approach to decision making that has immense implications for individual conduct and organizational functioning. The second matter reflects the point that when risk management is implemented in organizations, it must be made to accord with organizational modes of operation and organizational rationality.

THE USE OF RISK MANAGEMENT

As with many innovations, the value of risk management depends crucially on how it is used. Its use, in this case, is not merely a matter of the ends to which it is a means, but also the manner of its use—which is to say how *wisely* risk management is used. Wisdom is the holy grail of decision making, of course—all decision makers should be wise—but this admonition is of little guidance without an understanding of what constitutes wisdom in risk management. How, specifically, was risk management not used wisely in the recent financial crisis?

To begin, too many parties—investment banks, investors worldwide, and individual homeowners, to name the main culprits—took too many risks. A common impression is that these risks were not carefully assessed, but quite the opposite was the case: the banks, in particular, used very sophisticated risk management systems to calibrate precisely the risks in the securities they issued and those they kept in their own portfolios. The fact that monumental mistakes were made does not detract from the immense risk management effort that took place. Indeed, it might be argued that too much risk management—or perhaps the wrong kind and too much reliance on it—was at the heart of the crisis.

One source of mistakes was certainly a false sense of confidence that the risks were understood and under control. This resulted not only from the sophistication of the risk management measures and models being used, but also from some of the biases and heuristics which affect all decision making and form the basis of behavioral economics and behavior finance. For starters, the results obtained from risk management tools fit easily into the confirmation bias, which makes people receptive to confirming evidence and resistant to anything contrary, and it also leads them to seek out only the former. Every model, for example, is created to answer some specific question, and so only the questions asked will receive an answer from a model.

The availability heuristic inclines people to rely more heavily on the evidence that is already present, and the ubiquity of risk management models ensures that a certain kind of evidence is most readily available. The causation bias, which results from a belief that the causes of events are known and operating, increases confidence in the results of risk management efforts. Risk management assures us not only that events are predictable but also that they have been correctly predicted, and this assurance reinforces an illusion of control. In addition, the framing effect ensures that when decisions are framed in terms of the risks as presented by risk management models, these framed factors will dominate one's thinking, to the exclusion of other factors. Finally, the financial reward of taking certain risks is a powerful incentive to believe that these risks have been shown by risk management models to be the prudent ones to take.

Not only does risk management increase the confidence with which risks are taken—perhaps leading to more risk being assumed than is realized—but it also leads to the taking of greater risks knowingly. One reason for this outcome, aside from greater confidence that risk is being well managed, is that risk management provides a valuable commodity, namely plausible deniability. Risk management allows a failed decision maker to shift the blame to others who were responsible for projections that proved to be faulty. The decision maker can say, "My risk management people told me this was safe!" The confidence that blame can be shifted in the event of failure thus encourages more risk taking. This blame-shifting is all the more effective when the decision maker is far removed from the risk management experts who are generating the results, which is often the case. In general, the higher the level of decision making about risks, the more the decision maker can benefit from plausible deniability.

A more subtle factor encouraging risk taking is that the existence of risk management results supporting a course of action with high potential rewards makes it difficult for a decision maker to support any alternative that offers a lesser return. Not only is the burden of proof on such a decision maker to show why the higher-potential action should not be taken, but any defense is likely to be less technically based and hence less persuasive. Raghuram Rajan (2010, 144) has observed, "Not taking risks one doesn't understand is often the best form of risk management." However, any decision maker who follows this advice is admitting a failure to understand something (which is very difficult for a "Master of the Universe" to do), and the reason being given ("I don't understand this") is rather "soft" when compared with the "hard" results of risk management. (If only our lack of understanding could be quantified!)

Yet another source of mistakes is using risk management to focus on specific risks that have already been assumed rather than to determine what future risks to assume. Once a decision has been made to invest heavily in CDOs, for example, then risk management tools can enable a firm to manage the risks of *that* portfolio. But is such a heavy investment a sound decision in the first place? Put another way, risk management can be used in the realm of formulating strategy or implementing it, and all too often only the latter is made the focus of a firm's efforts. The same point applies to the use of risk management to raise questions. Rather than using risk management to question a firm's overall strategy, where the serious problems may lie, it is too often used merely to justify specific tactical, implementation decisions, such as which securities to buy or sell in a portfolio.

Joe Nocera (2009) tells the story of how Goldman Sachs bankers decided to rein in their risks after they sought to discover the cause of declining results from their profit and loss models, which were still satisfactory but worrisome. Many firms might have used similar results to confirm the soundness of their current strategy, but the bankers at Goldman were worried and sought the cause of the decline. Their investigation led to a major strategic decision to "get closer to home" by sharply reducing their exposure to the housing market. Thus, Goldman Sachs avoided some losses by asking questions that competitors overlooked. In other words, the successful use of risk management depends on how its measures and models are interpreted and what action is taken in response.

Regardless of whether risk management is used to formulate or implement strategy, decisions must be made about *how* risk is managed. Typically, risk management systems identify the risks being taken and measure the amount of risk that they entail, but this information gives little guidance for actually managing the risks, except insofar as the cost-effectiveness of each means can be determined. The usual response is to achieve the desired overall level of risk at the lowest cost. However, this approach assumes that the goal is to identify all risks and to find means for addressing each one—because this is what risk management systems are capable of doing.

A serious problem with this approach is that the focus is on the risks themselves, which are typically low-probability, high-impact events. Not only are these events large in number, but the most likely dangers are ones that may not be anticipated or even conceived. Attempting to develop a comprehensive plan to address all of these risks is unnecessarily costly and likely to fail. In addition, the kind of low-probability, high-impact events that risk management systems address may not pose the greatest danger to a firm. Large losses can occur from events with many different probability distributions. As one nameless risk manager confessed, "We had not fully appreciated that 20% of a very large number can inflict far greater losses than 80% of a small number" (Anonymous 2008).

An alternative to this approach—of finding the most cost-effective means to reach a desired level of risk—is to focus not on specific risks but on general preparedness. This point is well expressed by Taleb, Goldstein, and Spitznagel:

> Instead of trying to anticipate low-probability, high-impact events, we should reduce our vulnerability to them. Risk management, we believe, should be about lessening the impact of what we don't understand—not a futile attempt to develop sophisticated techniques and stories that perpetuate our illusions of being able to understand and predict the social and economic environment. (2009, 79)

They add that it is more effective to focus on consequences, on the possible impact of extreme events of any kind, rather than on the likelihood of certain specific events. This advice may be succinctly expressed as, "Prepare, don't plan!"

A final source of mistakes in the use of risk management is an exclusive reliance on it as a substitute for individual judgment. Mathematical measures and models are useful tools, but they cannot wholly replace human judgment and must be used always in conjunction with it. This is the theme of a recent book by Amar Bhidé (2010a). In *A Call for Judgment: Sensible Finance for a Dynamic Economy*, Bhidé argues that in modern finance, the use of mathematically based models has created a new form of centralized decision making that largely replaces an older decentralized system in which the judgments of numerous individuals are aggregated to produce sound, informed decisions. In this shift from decentralized to centralized decision making, not only is the information which individuals provide in a market lost, but such information is no longer even relevant. Centralized decision making requires a different kind of information that can be processed in mathematical models.

An example of this point is the development of automated mortgage-loan processing, which has the great advantage that approvals of loan applications can now be obtained in minutes instead of days, and at much lower cost. This process, however, makes little use of the judgment of the creditworthiness of a borrower by a traditional loan officer, who often has a great deal of firsthand information about the specific case—or else can acquire this information readily. The creditworthiness of the borrower becomes largely irrelevant in automated loan processing, since the algorithm for the process requires mainly data about default rates in the aggregate rather than the probability of default by any particular borrower. In this way, the decision-making process has not only become centralized but also relies on different kinds of information.

Bhidé argues for a "sensible balance" between individual judgment in a decentralized system of decision making and mathematical models in a collective mode, and this happy medium also requires judgment. So the primacy of human judgment is essential. He concludes, "Yet if we are to preserve the primacy of human judgment, we must learn to harness and control these models, not submit to them" (Bhidé 2010b). This is akin to Bernstein's warning against making risk management a new kind of religion (1996b, 47).

THE MANAGERIALIZATION OF RISK

Modern risk management cannot be understood apart from its implementation in organizations. Not only do the ways in which organizations implement risk management deeply affect its functioning, but this implementation itself has created the field of risk management. By definition, risk management *is* what organizations do to deal with the inevitable uncertainty they face. This point is expressed in the title of Michael Power's (2007) book, which describes risk management as *organized uncertainty*. In Power's view, the kind of risk that has been traditionally handled by banks, insurance companies, and other risk specialists in technical ways was addressed in the 1990s by management control systems that were adopted by firms in all industries.

An account of the impact of risk management on organizations may be left to Power's book; the focus here is on how organizations impact the practice of risk management. Organizations have certain modes of operation which employ practices, routines, policies, and the like; they take particular structural forms, most of which are hierarchical and bureaucratic; and they make decisions in processes that exhibit certain kinds of organizational rationality. Because these features powerfully shape anything within their reach, organizations constitute a procrustean bed in which to lay risk management. Risk management is thus just one example of the ubiquitous phenomenon, noted by Taleb (2010), of forcing reality to fit into preconceived forms.

In Greek mythology, Procrustes was a bandit who stretched his victims' limbs or cut them off in order to fit their bodies into a bed of fixed length. A procrustean bed has thus become a metaphor for fitting anything into some arbitrary standard or form. In fitting risk management into organizations, certain adjustments occur—some of which are inevitable, while others involve deliberate choices.

First, risks that bear most heavily on a manager's own standing in an organization are more likely to receive attention. Any manager seeks, above all, to be rewarded for success and to avoid blame for failure. Between low-probability, high-impact events and high-probability, low-impact events, the latter have first priority, because they are evident to all, and a failure to address them will be noticed—even if they do not come to pass. Highly improbable events, by contrast, pose less of a threat to a manager, not only because they are, by definition, less likely to occur ("That's never going to happen!") but also because the failure to plan for them is more excusable ("Who could have seen that coming?").

In addition, the choice among risks is influenced by the availability of an effective means of protection. Little credit is given to a manager whose valiant attempts to avoid a loss from a known risk prove futile, no matter how careful the planning. So risks that can be managed effectively—and with confidence in the outcome—are more attractive to a manager. Some risks are intrinsically more manageable than others, but the availability of effective, assured means may also be due to past experience. Thus, a risk that was previously encountered and effectively addressed is more likely to receive the attention of a manager than an uncommon event with no ready remedy.

Second, organizational factors have important consequences for how risk is actually managed. Not only can some risks be managed more effectively than others, but, more importantly, some means of management are more suited for an organization. In managing risk, an organization must consider its resources and capabilities, its modes of decision making and operation, its objectives and incentives, and all the constraints placed on it. In short, an organization must ask about any given risk, "What actions can we take that will effectively address this risk given who we are, what we have, and how we act?"

In organizations, responsibility for all matters, including risk, must be assigned to particular office holders, who have various capabilities. This assignment of responsibility affects both the conduct of risk management and its quality. In the past two decades, responsibility has been pushed up in organizations to higher levels, including the C-level officers and even a new role of chief risk officer. Although such high-level attention to risk has some definite benefits, it also creates a distance between ultimate decision makers at the top and the technical experts in risk at lower levels. The effect is also to remove some responsibility for managing risk from other members of an organization, such as traders and portfolio managers.

All of these factors result in a focus in organized risk management on common, well-known mishaps and malfunctions, and not on the kind of truly damaging rare events with which risk management perhaps ought to be concerned. The danger, therefore, is a kind of "displacement" in which firms focus on what can be managed in an organization rather than on the real sources of risk, which may, in truth, be unmanageable. Thus, Power (2004, 30–31) writes, "The burden of managing unknowable risks . . . is replaced by an easier task which can be successfully reported to seniors. . . . Killer events and sources of fear become translated into routines, regulations and data collection processes."

SOCIAL IMPACTS OF RISK MANAGEMENT

From an ethical point of view, a crucial characteristic of modern risk management is the way in which multiple risks that affect everyone in society are made the province of corporate decision making and subjected to the conditions of decision making in such narrowly economic enterprises. In modern risk management, firms assume the task of identifying risks, deciding on their treatment, and—perhaps most important—choosing an overall level of risk. In taking on this responsibility, firms make decisions which have wide-ranging impacts on many groups in society.

First, in carrying out this task of managing societal risk, a business firm implements risk management with a view solely to maximizing the firm's value for shareholders. Specifically, a firm identifies only those risks that create a potential loss for the firm itself and ignores any impacts that are borne solely or predominantly by other parties. For example, in the recent financial crisis, the risks of loans, including subprime mortgages and the CDOs that were securitized from them, were of little concern to banks once these risks were transferred to other parties. The main managed risks were confined to the banks' own portfolios; any losses that might result from these "toxic assets" were someone else's problem.

Second, business firms practicing risk management choose the means they prefer to handle the risk. There are basically five means for managing risk: avoid the risk, reduce the risk, transfer the risk, hedge it, or accept it. And within each of these means, many methods exist; reduction of risk, for example, can be done in many ways. Typically, firms will select the combination of means and methods which achieves the desired level of risk at the lowest cost. However, each possible response will have different impacts on different groups, and each group may have a different preference for the overall level of risk.

For example, a firm that avoids certain risks might deny benefits that people would otherwise enjoy, as when the uncertainties of flood damage lead insurance companies to cease issuing such policies, thereby forcing homeowners to assume that risk on their own—or else transfer it to government. A company that reduces the risk of workplace injury by making safety improvements does so in a way that benefits workers, but if it chooses instead to transfer that risk by purchasing an insurance policy, then the benefit to workers is changed in ways they might not prefer. They have traded ex ante safety on the job for ex post compensation in the event of an accident, which may not be their preference, or in their best interests.

The transfer of risk, which often occurs without much awareness or consideration, is a major development in recent history. In *The Great Risk Shift*, Jacob Hacker (2008) documents how corporations and governments are shedding many of their traditional responsibilities and putting a greater burden on ordinary people in such areas as employment, health care, education, and retirement, with a resulting erosion of economic security. This shifting of risk has been driven not only by corporate profit seeking but also by an ideology of personal freedom and responsibility that would reduce the role of government in people's lives. An additional factor is a decline in large corporations as a source of support and a corresponding increase in the importance of financial markets (Davis 2009). This massive transfer of risk, whether good or bad, is certainly a fit subject for ethical examination.

A third area in which risk management has wide social impacts lies in the determination of an acceptable level of risk. In managing risk, a firm identifies its own appetite or tolerance for risk and acts accordingly. Because shareholders generally prefer a higher level of risk than other groups do, risk management systems which increase the overall level of risk create tensions between shareholders and other groups over their risk preferences. Moreover, conflicts may be created not only over the level of risk but also over the types of risks that each group is willing to bear. Groups with equal risk tolerances may still differ over which risks they prefer to bear.

Fourth, risk management may create a false sense of confidence that leads all groups to assume too much risk. The existence of apparently sophisticated risk management systems may create an illusion that all the risks are understood and under control, so that even a high level of risk is deemed acceptable. As Taleb (2007) has observed, the greater danger comes not from a high level of known risks but from the unknown risk of low-probability but high-impact events, which are by their nature unpredictable—and hence unmanageable. So risk management systems may themselves be a source of risk by creating a false sense of confidence that blinds managers and the public to the hazards that they actually face.

THE PURPOSE(S) OF RISK MANAGEMENT

Although business firms may implement risk management systems to maximize firm value or shareholder wealth, specific decisions must still be made about how to achieve this general objective. Some of these specific decisions are indirect but necessary means for achieving the ultimate objective, but others are misdirected reasons for adopting risk management systems, which may undermine firm value. In particular, risk management may be employed by managers in ways that advance their own interests over those of shareholders and subtly shift the purpose of the risk management system to other, less legitimate objectives. The possible misuses of risk management considered here are the additional purposes of increasing individual compensation, meeting challenges to corporate legitimacy, and complying with regulatory requirements.

First, the ideal of using risk management with competence and commitment to increase firm value was subverted in the recent financial crisis by managers who used it as a smokescreen to obscure their pursuit of trading profits that gained them high compensation. Not only can the best risk management systems be gamed through clever manipulation to generate greater, but perhaps unsustainable, profits, but poorly designed or improperly implemented systems conduce more readily to the same end.

When the Senior Supervisors Group of the Securities and Exchange Commission. compared the use of risk management by firms that won and those that lost in the recent financial crisis, striking differences were evident. They found that the losers were firms which had a hierarchical rather than a cooperative organizational structure, did not promptly share information across the firm and engage in probing discussions, were determined to expand their exposure to CDOs and similar products, relied on credit ratings rather than developing their own in-house expertise, did not charge business lines for the riskiness of the capital allocated to them, used a limited number of models, and did not adequately stress test their models under varied assumptions (Senior Supervisors Group 2008). The differences between these winning and losing groups did not lie in the existence of risk management systems but in the varying quality of their design and operation.

Some of these differences between winners and losers simply reflect poor risk management practices, but they are also indicative of risk management systems that were not aimed at truly managing risks but served rather as a cover for reckless risk taking. The loser firms were also ones in which risk managers were often regarded as hindrances or obstacles to profitable trading, so that their counsel was ignored or minimized. In such firms, risk departments were assigned a low status, staffed with less-than-competent people, and deprived of significant resources. Firms which are serious about using risk management in the intended way must take care to correct these numerous deficiencies, which result not from defects in risk management systems but from a lack of commitment to them.

Second, risk management systems are often adopted in order to meet societal demands for legitimacy, especially with regard to the responsible management of risk. Of course, corporations should manage risks responsibility, and doing so contributes toward maximizing firm value to the extent that this is impacted by society's expectations. However, risk, especially from low-probability, high-impact events, is very difficult, if not impossible, to manage, but the legitimacy of business may depend on maintaining a convenient fiction of competent control. Thus, Mary Douglas and Aaron Wildavsky ask, "Can we know the risk we face, now or in the future? No, we cannot: but yes, we must act as if we do" (1982, 1). The result, in Michael Power's view, is risk management systems which deceive the public by erecting a "managerial smokescreen" to maintain "myths of control and manageability" (Power 2004, 10).

This deception is all the more serious if it forestalls the search for available but more difficult means of protection. Used in this way, risk management is not about actually managing risk but managing people's *perceptions* of risk. And the solution for many sources of risk may be fundamental, systemic change that may be ignored in the focus on risk management. For example, the fragility of the banking system might require extensive structural reforms that address the problem of too-big-to-fail or too-interconnected-to-fail, but a focus merely on better management of the risk in the banks' own portfolios is apt to divert attention away from substantive, effective change.

Third, to the two charges that risk management is a smokescreen to hide risky trading and to maintain a myth of managerial control can be added a third: that it is a smokescreen that preserves the illusion of regulatory compliance. Rajan observes, "In many of the firms that got into trouble, risk management was used primarily for regulatory compliance rather than as an instrument of management control" (2010, 140). Although the management of risk is an aim of much regulation, the regulation in question is *of* business *by* government *for* some social good. The use of risk management *by* corporations *to* enhance firm value is a different end that may conflict with that of government regulation, no matter how worthy the latter.

Consequently, trouble is a likely outcome when firms employ risk management for purposes of regulatory compliance.

However, risk management and regulation are deeply entangled. In Power's account, risk management developed in organizations as a transformation of the internal control function. He writes, "The private world of organizational internal control systems has been turned inside out, made public, codified and standardized and repackaged as risk management" (Power 2004, 27–28). Moreover, risk management is part of a system of regulation that Ayers and Braithwaite (1992) call "enforced self-regulation," which has been a main thrust of the government's approach to business regulation. This approach involves a shift from ex post enforcement of regulations by means of sanctions to ex ante prevention and self-discovery by means of internal compliance systems (Ayer and Braithwaite 1992, 38). Finally, risk management has been employed in the Basel II and Basel III Accords in the mechanisms for setting bank capital reserve requirements by adopting a risk-based rather than a rule-based approach. Since the amount of capital a bank may be required to hold is now based on the amount of risk assumed and the quality of its risk control systems, banks have been forced to focus on risk management as a regulatory concern.

Regardless of whether enforced self-regulation and the Basel risk-based approach to capital requirements constitute good government regulation, their impact on the practice of risk management is open to question. Aside from distracting managers from the use of risk management to increase firm value by introducing the additional objective of regulatory compliance, these developments may also degrade the quality of risk management systems. Like any regulation, risk management can be gamed. In banking, this may take the form of traders seeking investments in which the risk is not readily detected by risk models. In particular, regulation by VaR measures is vulnerable to trading that exploits the risk in the uncharted territory beyond the margin of probability. When trades are closely regulated by risk management systems, traders have the opportunity to take the greatest risk permitted by the regulations rather than being guided their own judgment of appropriate risk.

The gaming of risk-based regulation is merely one instance in which the regulation affects human behavior. Any form of risk management, when used for regulatory purposes, is vulnerable for this reason. Jón Daníelsson (2002) expresses this point by noting that a corollary to Goodhart's Law ("Any statistical relationship will break down when used for policy purposes") is, "A risk model breaks down when used for regulatory purposes." Thus, models that work well for the management of risk may fail when used in regulation because of the effect that models have on the behavior being modeled. In addition, Daníelsson, Jorgensen, and de Vries argue that the use of risk management for regulation leads banks to adopt lower quality risk management systems than they otherwise would. The result, they claim, is that "inappropriately chosen regulation may, perversely, induce banks to put less effort into risk management" (2002, 1423).

CONCLUSION

Modern risk management, with its rich array of sophisticated mathematical measures and models, is a cardinal achievement of the past two decades. The ability of finance and, indeed, all business to enrich our lives has expanded greatly due to this remarkable development. However, risk management also has its weaknesses, which were all too evident in the recent financial crisis. Although it was only one of many causes of this crisis, the failure of risk management must cause considerable soul-searching among its practitioners and ultimate users. Much of this soul-searching has been of a technical nature, conducted by those most deeply involved in the field. The ethical and behavioral aspects of the failure of risk management have been comparatively neglected, and yet this perspective provides a valuable addition to the ongoing investigation of the crisis.

Ultimately, risk management is a tool, and its contribution to human welfare depends critically on how it is used. Since risk management is employed by human decision makers, it is vulnerable to all the biases that psychological research has discovered in cognitive processes and to the creation of a dangerous false sense of confidence that risks are well managed. Some features of organizational decision making also lead to errors, such as using risk management merely for implementing strategy and not for developing it as well, failing to draw the right conclusions or develop an effective response, and substituting mechanical models for sound judgment.

The organizational setting for the implementation of risk management systems also has far-reaching consequences. Managerial incentives may lead to a focus on risks that can be easily and effectively managed, which are often well-known, common risks rather than the low-probability, high-impact events that may pose the greatest danger. In addition, risk management by organizations has profound impacts on society, especially in the identification of the risks to be managed, the means chosen to manage these risks, the determination of an acceptable level of risk, and the creation of a possibly false sense of confidence that risks are being well managed.

Finally, risk management may be criticized for acting as a smokescreen to obscure reckless risk taking in the pursuit of profit, to maintain a convenient myth of managerial control, and to demonstrate mere regulatory compliance rather than real risk management. None of these ethical and behavioral aspects are fatal to the enterprise of modern risk management, but they indicate concerns that need to be addressed in order to realize the full promise of this remarkable development.

NOTES

1.   Some material in this chapter is taken from Boatright 2010, 2011a, and 2011b.

REFERENCES

Anonymous. 2008. "Confessions of a Risk Manager: A Personal View of the Crisis." *Economist*, August 7.
Ayers, Ian, and John Braithwaite. 1992. *Responsive Regulation: Transcending the Deregulation Debate*. New York: Oxford University Press.
Bernstein, Peter L. 1996a. *Against the Gods: The Remarkable Story of Risk*. New York: Wiley.

Bernstein, Peter L. 1996b. "The New Religion of Risk Management." *Harvard Business Review* 74: 47–51.

Bhidé, Amar. 2010a. *A Call for Judgment: Sensible Finance for a Dynamic Economy*. New York: Oxford University Press.

Bhidé, Amar. 2010b. "The Judgment Deficit." *Harvard Business Review*. September: 44–53.

Boatright, John R. 2010. *The Ethics of Risk Management in the Information Age*. Waltham, MA: Bentley University Center for Business Ethics.

Boatright, John R. 2011a. "The Ethics of Risk Management: A Post-Crisis Perspective." *Ethics and Values for the 21st Century*. Madrid: BBVA.

Boatright, John R. 2011b. "Risk Management and the Responsible Corporation: How Sweeping the Invisible Hand?" *Business and Society Review* 116: 145–170.

Buffett, Warren. 2002. *Berkshire Hathaway Annual Report*.

Cassidy, John. 2010. "What's Wrong with Risk Models?" *New Yorker* Blog, April 27.

Daníelsson, Jón. 2002. "The Emperor Has No Clothes: Limits to Risk Modelling." *Journal of Banking and Finance* 26: 1273–1296.

Daníelsson, Jón, Bjørn N. Jorgensen, and Casper G. de Vries. 2002. "Incentives for Effective Risk Management." *Journal of Banking and Finance* 26: 1407–1425.

Davis, Gerald F. 2009. *Managed by the Markets: How Finance Re-Shaped America*. New York: Oxford University Press.

Douglas, Mary, and Aaron Wildavsky. 1982. *Risk and Culture: An Essay on the Selection of Technological and Environmental Dangers*. Berkeley: University of California Press.

Einhorn, David, and Aaron Brown. 2008. "Private Profits and Socialized Risk." *Global Association of Risk Professionals*, June–July, 10–26.

Ferguson, Niall. 2008. "Wall Street Lays Another Egg." *Vanity Fair*, December.

Hacker, Jacob S. 2008. *The Great Risk Shift: The New Economic Insecurity and the Decline of the American Dream*. New York: Oxford University Press.

Hubbard, Douglas W. 2009. *The Failure of Risk Management: Why It's Broken and How to Fix It*. New York: Wiley.

Jones, Sam. 2009. "The Formula that Felled Wall St." *FT Magazine*, April 24.

Leippold, Markus. 2004. "Don't Rely on VaR." *Euromoney* 35: 46–49.

Li, David X. 2000. "On Default Correlation: A Copula Function Approach." *Journal of Fixed Income* 9: 43–54.

Nocera, Joe. 2009. "Risk Management: What Led to the Financial Meltdown." *New York Times*, January 4.

Pollock, Alex J. 2008. "The Human Foundations of Financial Risk." American Enterprise Institute for Public Policy Research, May.

Power, Michael. 2004. *The Risk Management of Everything: Rethinking the Politics of Uncertainty*. London: Demos.

Power, Michael. 2007. *Organized Uncertainty*. Oxford: Oxford University Press.

Rajan, Raghuram G. 2010. *Fault Lines: How Hidden Fractures Still Threaten the World Economy*. Princeton, NJ: Princeton University Press.

Rebonato, Ricardo. 2007. *The Plight of the Fortune Tellers: Why We Need to Manage Finance Risk Differently*. Princeton, NJ: Princeton University Press.

Rogoff, Kenneth, and Carmen M. Reinhart. 2009. *This Time is Different: Eight Centuries of Financial Folly*. Princeton, NJ: Princeton University Press.

Salmon, Felix. 2009. "Recipe for Disaster: The Formula that Killed Wall Street." *Wired Magazine*, February 23.

Senior Supervisors Group. 2008. *Observations on Risk Management Practices during the Recent Market Turbulence.* Washington, DC: Securities and Exchange Commission.

Storey, Louise. 2010. "Panel's Blunt Questions Put Goldman on Defensive." *New York Times,* April 27.

Stulz, René M. 2008. "Risk Management Failures: What Are They and When Do They Happen." *Journal of Applied Corporate Finance* 20: 58–67.

Taleb, Nassim. 2007. *The Black Swan: The Impact of the Highly Improbable.* New York: Random House.

Taleb, Nassim N. 2010. *The Bed of Procrustes: Philosophical and Practical Aphorisms.* New York: Random House.

Taleb, Nassim N., Daniel Goldstein, and Mark W. Spitznagel. 2009. "The Six Mistakes Executives Make in Risk Management." *Harvard Business Review,* October: 78–81.

Trevino, Linda, Gary R. Weaver, and Scott J. Reynolds. 2006. "Behavioral Ethics in Organizations: A Review." *Journal of Management* 32: 951–990.

18

The Global Financial Crisis and Social Justice

The Crisis Seen through the Lens of Catholic Social Doctrine

PAUL FITZGERALD, SJ ∎

In a *New York Times* article in March 2013,[1] a front-page story chronicled a pattern of abuses by brokers at LPL Financial, the fourth largest brokerage firm in the nation. The article noted that "state and federal authorities censured the company and its brokers with unusual frequency. LPL brokers have been penalized for selling complex investments to unsophisticated investors, for speculative trading in customer accounts, and, in a few cases, for outright stealing from clients." The *New York Times* story also noted that regulatory actions were taken by the Financial Industry Regulatory Authority against Wells Fargo, Bank of America/Merrill Lynch, Morgan Stanley Smith Barney, and Edward Jones during the same period of time—just not as often. Several years after the global financial crisis hit, this story illustrates that some of the same unethical commercial practices that had led to the crisis continue to plague the financial services industry. The victims of these unethical acts included retirees who lost significant portions of their retirement savings and had to return to work. One ought to feel not only outrage at the callousness of the censured brokers but also a justifiable concern that, even as the US economy is only slowly returning to a healthier posture, we continue to see widespread examples of exactly the sort of behavior that drove us to the brink of collapse.

One wonders whether our society as a whole has lost a general sense of ethics and justice. In a word, too many professionals have lost an interior sense of "true north," and their moral compass is hopelessly untrustworthy. If this is so, then our commonweal is in grave danger. Through work and thrift, ordinary people want to be able to build up savings, purchase homes, pay for their children's education, and have enough money in their senior years for a comfortable retirement. In a free and just society with an honest marketplace, people should be able to depend upon the honesty and the ethics of the professionals who would do business with them as they seek to realize their financial plans. Alas, the financial crisis and its aftermath have revealed that the marketplace is far too frequently dishonest and that the professionals who work in it are far too often untrue to the ethical ideals of their chosen professions.

Under the rubric of Catholic social doctrine, the Catholic Church has reflected on the ethics of the modern marketplace, on the legitimate human desire to own property and to accumulate wealth, and on the ethical responsibilities of contemporary business professionals. Catholic scholars have anchored this reflection in the long tradition of Catholic teachings on personal virtue and social morality, based in turn on Sacred Scripture and religious practice. In this chapter, after reviewing the relevant theological principles to be found in Catholic social doctrine, we will then note the moral failures of individual human beings and groups of people that contributed to the crisis. We will conclude by identifying the moral virtues that business people should adopt to complement new legal structures that, in tandem, could lessen both the frequency and the severity of future financial crises.

In the Judeo-Christian tradition, these moral norms and ethical practices are ultimately based on a set of spiritual intuitions and faith statements. Religions and philosophical traditions grapple with the problem of unethical behavior (often under the rubric of personal sin) and the social consequences (social or structural sin) that such behavior causes using a variety of concepts and images, and here we will confine our inquiry to the Roman Catholic tradition, leaving to other scholars the task of inquiring into the other world religions and ethical traditions. One could contend that these religious insights, whether perceptions of personal integrity, inalienable human dignity, or the common good, are ultimately based on an intuitive insight into God and the very nature of reality. If this is true, then the norms and ethical practices detailed in this chapter would in fact have universal applicability.[2] Indeed, given the ever-greater complexity and interconnectedness of the world economy, universal solutions are desperately needed, for only an attentiveness to universal principles and improved practices on a global scale will afford humankind a global economy that serves the best interests of all.

SCRIPTURAL FOUNDATIONS OF CATHOLIC SOCIAL DOCTRINE

Sacred Scripture and two millennia of subsequent tradition inform modern Catholic philosophical and theological approaches to personal and social ethics. The Hebrew Scriptures present a long historical development of legal prescriptions to regulate economic activity as an integral aspect of the religious maturation of the Chosen People. When Abraham purchased the Machpelah cave (Genesis 23), he insisted that Ephron name and accept a price for the complete transfer of the cave, exemplifying the ancient notion that a transaction has to satisfy the heart of the seller as well as that of the buyer. In other words, both parties treat each other with integrity, and both are able to achieve the end that they truly sought. The Jubilee laws found in Leviticus (e.g., 25:13ff) intended a structure of social stability wherein ancestral land owned by extended families could never be finally transferred from a seller to a buyer who was not a kinsman but only leased for a period of time before it would revert to the seller or his descendants, in effect guaranteeing that families would not become impoverished over time, even if a family suffered some temporary misfortune. As well, the Jubilee laws intended that land would remain distributed throughout society, guaranteeing social stability and precluding the formation of a landless proletariat. In addition to such legal texts, Hebrew Scriptures also contain prophetic texts that refresh religious memory, teach moral reasoning, and lay out ethical standards. In the fifth chapter of Isaiah, the author laments the ethical misbehavior of the people that has earned them God's wrath in the form of invading foreign armies. Isaiah condemns, for example, the actions of wealthy land-grabbers who are dispossessing the peasantry in order to form large estates: "Woe! Those who join house to house, who connect field with field, until no space remains, and you alone dwell in the midst of the land!"

Both the law and the prophets were based upon a founding historical memory (the Exodus) and a founding theological construct (the creation stories in Genesis).[3] The Exodus story is one of deliverance from appalling social hardship under an unjust political and economic order (slavery in Egypt) and the creation of an identity as a people related to God and to each other in a covenant that was at once social, economic, political, and religious. The Decalogue is the first legal expression and codification of a set of vertical and horizontal relationships, answering the questions, "What does it mean to love God?"—first three commandments—and "What does it mean to love one's neighbor?"—the latter seven commandments. The institutionalization of a charism (divinely revealed law translated into human laws) is the subtext of the history of ancient Israel, a story that is retold and relived by every generation, for the identity of the people is carried by memory of their ancestors' experiences and also relies upon the ongoing religious experience of the abiding presence of God, standing in covenantal relationship with the people and calling them to holiness. The Chosen People are also always a people under the judgment of God, who calls them to a high standard of righteousness. Personal sins and failures can and do have social consequences, and yet God is merciful when the people repent and reform their lives and their social structures to be more just and merciful.

A second strand of religious discourse arose from, and contributed to the further redaction of, the creation stories, which lay out in narrative form a theological claim that founds a universal morality—albeit one whose universal applicability makes it an ideal toward which to strive rather than a minimum standard of accepted and institutionalized practice. The two creation narratives posit that the first human persons, and by extension, all human persons, are created in the image and likeness of God and therefore have inalienable worth and dignity. The Priestly creation story of Genesis 1:1–24a and the Yahwist creation story of Genesis 2:4b–24, while different in source and narrative structure, are complementary and completing: men and women are equal; men and women are complementary; humanity is meant to have a harmonious relationship with the rest of creation (stewardship); humanity is meant to have an intimate relationship with God. In the story's telling, the divine intention was thwarted by sinful human rebellion, and paradise is lost, yet in the theological reasoning that undergirds the story, God remains present to an always fallen humanity and, through the law and the prophets, continues to offer invitations to form more perfect relationships as salvation history unfolds. The theological insights contained in the Exodus and creation stories form the ethical horizon toward which Hebrew society strove, the standards against which its laws were fashioned and refashioned, and the ideals by which Israel would judge itself and its neighbors. Like any social system, that of ancient Israel was prone to legalism and corruption, but the prophetic voice provided a perennial corrective to these dangers by reminding Israel of her vocation to personal holiness and social righteousness as God's Chosen People. As such, the Israelites were to embrace justice and mercy, and they were to be especially attentive to the situation of the weakest members of their society, for the nation would be judged by God according to treatment of the widow, the orphan, or the foreigner sojourning among the people (Jeremiah 7:6, Zechariah 7:10, etc.).

Christian Scriptures recapitulate these themes as they tell the story of the life, death, and resurrection of Jesus of Nazareth, and the beginnings of the Christian communities that sprang up across the Roman Empire in the decades that followed. When asked by a scribe which is the first of all the commandments, Jesus sums up the law and the prophets with a two-staged moral teaching: "You shall love the Lord your God with all your heart, with all your soul, with all your mind, and with all your strength ... You shall love your neighbor as yourself" (Mark 12:28ff). In Matthew (7:12), this teaching takes the form of, "Do to others whatever you would have them do to you. This is the law and the prophets." It sets the minimum standard of just behavior. Jesus also sketches out a higher standard of supererogatory behavior: "Love your enemies; pray for your persecutors" (Matthew 5:44). In this, Jesus would crown justice with mercy, asking his followers to imitate him in all aspects of their lives. This sets the horizon of perfection toward which Christians were to strive and by which they should judge their own religious communities and the larger societies in which these early Christian communities subsisted. Subsequent legal development would continue to elaborate the requirements of justice and charity in these two relationships. Throughout the fifth chapter of Matthew's Gospel, one finds Jesus's restatement of the heart of the law for the Christian community going forward. There would be no antithesis between law and grace but rather the endless task of reconciling justice and mercy in all aspects of life and community. In the post-apostolic era, during the persecutions, Christians judged the Roman Empire to be sinfully corrupt to the core, yet they had to participate in the economy of the empire even while abstaining from participation in the civil religion of the state.[4] With the conversion of Constantine and the legalization of Christianity, Christians were challenged to recast their thinking about the state, and with the collapse of the Western empire, ecclesial authorities in many instances became secular rulers as well.[5] Over time, within a great diversity of socioeconomic contexts, with many stumbles along the way, the Christian Churches elaborated social critiques and models of personal virtue that sought to name both the minimum standards of justice and ethical behavior on the one hand, and the maximal ideals of charity and mercy on the other.[6]

HISTORICAL FOUNDATIONS OF CATHOLIC SOCIAL DOCTRINE

Modern Church teaching on social justice can be traced to Pope Leo XIII's *Rerum Novarum* (1891), in English, *On the Condition of the Working Classes*. This encyclical letter was addressed to all the bishops of the world in communion with Rome, but it was intended for an even wider audience. As a public act of teaching—though not at the level of dogma and not with a claim of infallibility—the text was a revolutionary document that ended a century of papal disengagement from political and social issues in Europe that had arisen after a string of perceived political losses by the Church from the French Revolution through the Risorgimento in Italy. Pope Leo's immediate predecessors had been content to condemn the social and economic changes engendered by the political and industrial revolutions that had swept away the old order.[7] Vincent Joachim Pecci, the future Pope Leo, moved beyond the merely negative stance of his predecessors to one of active engagement with the flow of social, economic, and political change, in part because of his direct experience of the effects of changing social conditions on the members of the poorer classes. He had served as papal nuncio (ambassador) in Brussels before being consecrated archbishop of Perugia. In both assignments, he witnessed firsthand the blessings and the curses of urbanization and industrialization as experienced by the workers and their families who were migrating from the countryside into the expanding cities with their mills, transportation systems, and construction projects.

This encyclical (i.e., general) letter begins with a litany of woes that have befallen humankind in the new economy. Leo bemoans the outbreak of class conflicts, caused by "the abounding wealth among a very small number and destitution among the masses" (1), the great majority of whom "live undeservedly in miserable and wretched conditions" (5). Leo feared that the greed of the wealthy and the envy of the poor would provide political agitators with the opportunity to foment a second wave of revolutions that would put an end to private property and give rise to an all-powerful state (7). Leo opposed calls from socialists to abolish private property, a proposal that he saw as counterproductive for the working class and as a violation of the natural right of all persons to own private property. Instead, the pope argued that a worker who freely chose to put his labor into a larger productive process had a right to a decent wage and full control over that wage so that he might provide for the immediate needs of his family and, if he were thrifty, convert his savings at some point into productive land or machinery to further his economic progress. The Church had long held that control over one's private property is a natural right that ought to be protected by the state. The Church made a distinction, however, between personal private property—one's immediate possessions, one's home, one's savings—as compared to private property that took the form of a large farm, a mine, or a manufacturing plant. If an owner possessed something so large as to need the cooperation of other workers for it to be fruitful, then the personal dignity of each collaborator and the common good of all who cooperate in the project must be respected. Leo described the relationship between owner and laborer in terms of corporatism, a social organizational principle wherein diverse parts all served harmoniously for the good of the whole: "For just as in the human body the different members harmonize with one another, whence arises that disposition of parts and proportion in the human figure rightly called symmetry, so likewise nature has commanded in the case of the State that the two classes mentioned (labor and capital) should agree to work harmoniously and should form equally balanced counterparts to each other" (28). The pope then proceeded to list the mutually beneficial rights and duties of workers and owners that allow all to be productive in ways that are respectful of each other's inalienable dignity. Workers have the duty to work diligently at the tasks that they have agreed to perform, and they must also respect and protect the property and the person of their employers. In return, workers have the right to fair and just compensation; they have the right to safe and humane working conditions; they have the right to be free from the sin of usury.

Owners have corresponding duties toward their workers in all of these aspects, and they have the right, after the just compensation of their workers, to the profits that the market affords them. Throughout the encyclical, and in the subsequent encyclical letters and conciliar documents that built on Leo's teachings, owners and workers are not simply exhorted to be kind to each other; rather, people are called upon to be just to each other, and this justice is in turn based upon a spirit of love which undergirds and motivates all just action in society.[8] Leo's social ideal was certainly inspired by a nostalgia for the feudal corporatism of the Middle Ages, when social classes lived in mutually responsible social structures—at least if the laws and customs were obeyed—that constructed interlocking relationships with mutually advantageous rights and duties. While he may have yearned for a return to an agrarian social order, Leo knew that a new economic and social order had come, and so he felt duty-bound to try to steer that new order in as just and as humane a direction as possible.

In the ensuing 12 decades, Leo's teachings were expanded upon and adapted to the evolving global economy by several popes and by the College of Bishops gathered at the Second Vatican Council.[9] The basic tenets of Catholic social doctrine build upon the two theological notions mentioned at the outset: just social relationships and personal virtue, both of which are in turn based upon theological articulations of core beliefs.[10] It is important to note that this genre of Church teaching operates at three levels of normativity simultaneously: fundamental norms, middle-level axioms, and concrete applications to specific situations in the form of a prudential judgment. Fundamental norms are offered for reasoned consideration and faithful contemplation; these norms are general expressions of divinely revealed truth, accepted by faith (for example, that all human persons have inalienable worth and dignity). Such norms cannot be proven empirically; indeed, the history of humanity is replete with examples of affronts to human dignity and with the denial of human worth. Fundamental moral norms articulate that horizon of ultimate meaning toward which human beings and communities ought to strive. Such norms are expressed in very general terms that then need to be applied in particular historical and social contexts, resulting in middle-level axioms (for example, in a wage-based economy, respect for human dignity finds expression in a living wage and safe working conditions). And finally, at a third level of narrowing specificity, a prudential judgment must be made in a particular case (for example, the actual amount of money such a living wage would be in a particular city at a given time). Prudential judgments are always provisional, tentative, and open to vigorous debate. While reasonable persons of good will can differ as to the terms of the prudential judgment, there ought to be relatively easy agreement about the truth of the fundamental norm, and consensus as to the middle-level axiom ought not to be too difficult to arrive at, if all parties see it as a necessary consequence and application of a fundamental norm. As we now turn our attention to the global financial crisis, it will become apparent that many actors did in fact fail to act in accordance with fundamental norms and derived axioms.

THE RUN-UP TO THE GLOBAL FINANCIAL CRISIS

As noted above, the Catholic view of the economic order is that workers should be paid a living wage such that, through work and thrift, they can afford decent housing for themselves and their family, and, if they are fortunate, accumulate some working capital to invest. For those workers in present-day America who decide to buy a home, they should be treated with respect by the realtors and bankers who interact with them in their purchase. For those persons who would deposit their savings in banks or buy investment securities, they too should be treated with respect, as ends in themselves, receiving honest advice about the value, the potential gains, and the real risks of the investments in which they are entrusting their savings. The dream of home ownership gained great resonance in the United States during the 20th century and took on an especially strong allure following the Second World War, when unprecedented numbers of working class families, thanks to the GI Bill, were able to purchase homes with affordable mortgages. In addition to single-family homes in the new suburban developments, ownership of condominiums in urban settings also gained in popularity, often serving as both a physical shelter and a relatively sure means of safeguarding a family's savings qua capital. In the years leading up to the current crisis, an acceleration of housing prices gave rise to the false notion that housing was an excellent investment with high returns and little risk, given the seemingly insatiable demand for homes.

During the housing bubble in the late 1990s and early 2000s, did realtors and bank loan officers choose to sell homes to people at relatively high prices, prices reflective of values that were likely to tumble in the near future? Were houses sold to buyers at prices that were more than they could likely afford, given their incomes? Were mortgages drawn up for these buyers that were at a heightened risk of default? Was the likelihood of such default obvious to reasonable, educated professionals? Were those risky mortgages then commercialized and resold by professionals in the finance industry to investors who were misled as to the risks and the likely future value of these investment securities? Did some bankers then bet against the customers to whom they had just sold these investments? Did this become a generalized practice throughout the banking industry in more than one country? Each of these questions, and many related ones, have a variety of answers, depending on the discipline of the one posing them. Here we seek to frame the financial crisis within a moral crisis, as defined by Catholic social doctrine.

It seems that individual actors did not respect the fundamental dignity of the persons with whom they entered into business relationships, nor were they attentive to the damage that their individual actions would have on the common good. From the vantage of Catholic social doctrine, the brokers did not treat their customers as ends in themselves (and seek to provide them with suitable and affordable housing) but rather as a means to an end (increased earnings for the brokers, their firms, and their stockholders). "Caveat emptor" is neither an expression of justice nor of love. Buyers count on the advice of professionals (realtors, bankers, brokers) in the process of making a major financial decision (to buy a house or to invest money). It seems that there arose a generalized practice of greed and deception, expressed as a willingness to take advantage of customers who did not have the appropriate information or the methodological skill to make a wise decision. Beyond the harm caused to individual investors, there is also the harm that was caused to the global financial system. The cumulative effect of so many bad actions was to damage the trust and confidence upon which markets depend. Each unethical act was both a sin against the individual buyer/investor and a sin against the common good. How did such widespread misbehavior arise?

In November of 2012, the Pontifical Council for Justice and Peace published a thoughtful reflection entitled "Vocation of the Business Leader"[11] partially in response to the global financial crisis and partially as an elaboration of the moral and ethical principles laid out in Pope Benedict XVI's 2009 encyclical letter, *Caritas in Veritate*. The authors begin by naming several obstacles that hamper business professionals in living a life of integrity. Chief among these obstacles is what they term a "divided life," one in which "the split between the faith that many profess and their daily lives" leads to, among other ills, "the abuse of economic power in order to make even greater economic gains." Professionals "who do not see themselves serving others and God in their working lives will fill the void of purpose with a less worthy substitute" (10). Such fragmentation can lead in turn to idolatry qua misplaced devotion, "an all-too-common occupational hazard of business life that threatens both individuals and organizations" (11) where, for example, the maximization of profit becomes the sole criterion for action and utilitarian reasoning becomes dominant. "Business leaders may be tempted, whether from self-centeredness, pride, greed or anxiety, to reduce the purpose of business solely to maximizing profit, to growing market share, or to any other solely economic good. In this way, the good that a market economy may do, for individuals and for society, can be diminished or distorted"(12). In the run-up to the bursting of the housing bubble, it does indeed seem that many bankers and brokers acted in ways that did in fact diminish and distort the market economy with very bad global consequences.

TOWARD AN ETHIC OF VIRTUOUS BUSINESS LEADERSHIP

The authors of the reflection then go on to name three broad business objectives and elaborate six supportive ethical principles that would serve to renew business culture and put it on a sustainable track. Together, they show how respect for human dignity and care for the common good can be harmonized with the practical purposes of business activity. Each of the six deserves careful consideration here.

The first business objective is "meeting the needs of the world through the creation and development of goods and services" (50). This should be done in accord with two principles: businesses contribute to the common good by producing goods that are truly good and services that truly serve. In the case of the financial sector, this would entail the creation of investment securities that represent real value and reasonable, transparent risk. And it would involve investment brokers and real estate agents providing good service that is a professional expression of their respect for the inalienable dignity and worth of their clients and customers. The second and corresponding principle is that businesses ought to be in solidarity with the poor by being alert for opportunities to serve deprived and marginalized populations and individual persons in need. The Catholic notion of the preferential option for the poor is based on the belief in the inalienable worth and dignity of every human person and the consequential observation that those who are marginalized in society need special attention because they are likely least able to help themselves and most in need of help. Their simple being-in-need creates a moral responsibility for any person in a position to help them. Vulnerable people ought not to be taken advantage of but rather shown special care and concern. They should not be enticed into buying homes that they cannot afford nor taking on debt that could push them into foreclosure and the loss of their savings. Unethical banking practices that led to the global financial crisis have produced secondary effects that have hurt the poor who did not participate in the housing bubble directly. The great recession and its aftermath pushed up unemployment most severely for that section of the workforce that is least skilled. Deprived of tax revenues, cities and states have cut back on services for the poor. And personal stress engendered by economic troubles places great strains on marriages and family ties as well, such that innocent children are caused harm by the unethical business practices that led to the financial crisis. In ancient Israel, a society was judged to be holy or not based on how they treated the weakest and most vulnerable members of society: the widow, the orphan, and the foreigner. If one contemplates the worldwide effects of the financial crisis, then even more so does this standard appear to have been grossly violated.

The second business objective is "organizing good and productive work." This should be done in such a way that businesses make a contribution to the community by fostering the special dignity of human work. Catholic teaching on work in the corpus of Pope Leo XIII and his immediate successors dealt mostly with unacceptable working conditions and was concerned for the health and safety of workers based on the absolute call to recognize and respect the inherent dignity of workers as human persons, as ends in themselves and not means to an end (e.g., maximized profit). In more recent decades, especially in the writing of Pope John Paul II, Catholic reflections on work have come to focus on it as a positive contribution both to the development of the individual person and to the common good. Human work is viewed theologically as cooperation with God in the ongoing dynamic of creation. In his encyclical celebrating the 100th anniversary of the publication of *Rerum Novarum*, Saint John Paul taught that the purpose of business "is not simply to make a profit, but is to be found in its very existence as a *community of persons* who in various ways are endeavoring to satisfy their basic needs, and who form a particular group at the service of the whole of society."[12] Business firms are communities of persons in which each worker develops his or her talents and abilities at the service of the mission of the enterprise. It is the responsibility of the managers and leaders of, for example, real estate firms, banking institutions, and investment brokerages to create and foster an ethical climate within their organizations so that their workers are encouraged and required to be persons of integrity who always act ethically in the performance of their professional duties. And since "ought implies can," managers must create and foster the conditions for the possibility of the ethical integrity of all of their workers. The collective goals of each firm should be clearly and intentionally just, respecting the dignity of all and seeking the good of all. Beyond mere compliance with regulatory statutes, ethical business practices intend the good of all parties involved in every business transaction (more on this in the following). The second principle that seeks to shape the culture of firms calls on business leaders to embrace subsidiarity so as to provide opportunities for employees to exercise appropriate authority as they contribute to the mission of the organization. The principle of subsidiarity, first enunciated by Pope Pius XI, posits that "a community of a higher order should not interfere in the internal life of a community of a lower order, depriving the latter of its functions, but rather should support it in case of need and help to co-ordinate its activity with the activities of the rest of society, always with a view to the common good."[13] Applied to the companies that contributed to the crisis, subsidiarity stipulates that officers with higher levels of oversight, responsibility, and authority should assist persons, offices, and agencies at lower levels to take up problems and find just solutions in matters that most directly concern them. This principle seeks to avoid undue centralization and to permit the growth of mediating structures in larger organizations. In this way, every worker is empowered, informed, and obliged to engage in the work of the enterprise as a partner in a mission that is worthy of the efforts of all, each bringing all of her or his freedom, moral sense, and intelligence to every project and procedure.

The third business objective is to create sustainable wealth and distribute it justly. In this third instance, the authors embed two moral principles in the objective itself, something they did not do in the first two objectives, yet something they stress throughout the reflection as necessary if business activity is to serve the common good. Businesses should exercise stewardship over the resources—whether capital, human, or environmental—that they have received. In Catholic social doctrine, the notion stewardship has a rich tradition. Certainly, it continues to reflect the Leonine notion of responsible ownership of both personal and productive private property. This would apply to the owners, but by extension also to the managers, of banks and real estate agencies. They have a duty to be good stewards, that is, ethical leaders who create and sustain a corporate culture based on sound moral principles and ethical conduct. Good stewardship would also be measured over time and not just in a single snapshot. Indeed, short-term measurements of success in the forms of quarterly earnings reports may well be a hindrance to good stewardship, for business leaders are tempted to sacrifice long-term, sustainable business practices for short-term gains.

In the buying and selling of real estate, the notion of stewardship also applies to the customer, for it denotes a responsibility on the part of the buyer to make wise and informed choices about taking on debt in order to purchase a home for oneself or one's family. Of course, the ability to make wise choices depends upon the integrity of the professionals who act as the agent of the buyer or who act as the agent of the seller. Stewardship calls for creativity and productivity, and the goal of good stewardship is the creation of wealth and well-being. In businesses, one measure of effective stewardship is profit, but it is not the sole measure. Good stewardship would also be seen in the respectful treatment of every stakeholder. The authors flesh out this latter point in the second ethical principle in support of good stewardship, namely, that businesses ought to be just in their treatment of all stakeholders: employees, customers, investors, suppliers, and the community. This is an interesting application of the Catholic notion of economic justice. The Church has broadened its concept of justice to include the notion that all persons have a right to a share in this earth's goods.[14] Not that the goods of the earth should be distributed equally to everyone but rather that there should be a just distribution, one that takes into account the dignity of all persons. In the case of the leaders of the business organizations we are studying, this notion would oblige them to seek the good of all of their employees in a holistic way, as we have described. It would also oblige business leaders to seek the holistic good of their customers, the rampant violation of which seems to be at the root of the current global financial crisis. It would further oblige business leaders to be proactively attentive to economic and social consequences of their actions on people not directly involved in their transactions but who are affected by the ripples that spread out into the local, regional, and international economic environments in which their businesses operate.

The Church teaches this last moral imperative under the rubric of global solidarity.[15] Beginning with the encyclicals of Pope John XXIII, especially his groundbreaking 1963 encyclical *Pacem in Terris*, a regard for the rights and the lives of all humankind has become a centerpiece for all subsequent theological reflections. Every person who can work and who wants to work should be given the opportunity to work as an expression of solidarity with all other persons. The global nature of the economy is simply a fact. Catholic thinkers have since emphasized the urgency of keeping in mind the new global dimension of most every issue, and this is especially true in economic matters.

A GLOBAL SOLUTION

In this chapter, we have applied principles from Catholic social doctrine to the sources of the global financial crisis and its aftermath. We have suggested a set of ethical principles for business leaders that would radically reduce the frequency and the severity of such crises going forward. These suggested ethical practices would also reduce the hardship suffered by many individual people who otherwise would be the victims of unscrupulous vendors. And we have also suggested that this ethical renewal of business culture must intend the good of persons not only directly involved in individual transactions but also of all persons on the entire planet. This would require a globalization of respect for the dignity and worth of all persons.

Catholic thinkers understand that perfect charity is not likely before the Parousia, and so the Church also proposes a globalization of justice. Saint John XXIII noted the growing interconnectedness of the one human community and bemoaned the lack of political institutions at the global level that would seek to insure the "objective needs of the universal common good."[16] He hoped that one day "a true world political authority" (12) would be created. Benedict XVI's Pontifical Council for Justice and Peace, building on the Pope's encyclical letter *Caritas in Veritate*, carried out a study in 2011 on the causes and consequences of the great recession.[17] Catholic social doctrine has always seen a positive role for civil authority in the regulation of commerce and industry. Respecting the principle of subsidiarity, which would limit and focus the role of higher authority as one that should assure that justice is done by helping and empowering more local authority and providing the means necessary for the accomplishment of justice at the local level, Catholic thought in this regard nevertheless sees the necessity of a world authority to oversee the global banking system and related industries. A supranational institution, gaining legitimate authority through the consultation and consent of sovereign nations to establish and charge such an agency, would work to guarantee "a free, stable world economic and financial system at the service of the real economy" (3.2). It should be structured such that it has adequate, effective mechanisms equal to its mission and the expectations placed on it, especially those in regards to effective monetary and financial systems that are global in reach and/or consequence. One cannot refrain from noting that, should such a global banking authority be established, one of its first tasks might be to suggest a restructuring of the Institute for Religious Works (the Vatican Bank), which has of late been unable to satisfy EU officials in Brussels and agencies that oversee banks that use the Euro.

In November of 2013, Pope Francis affirmed the need for political leaders to oversee a "rigorous change of approach" to assure the reform of financial institutions along the lines of a Catholic approach to ethics. "I urge them to face this challenge with determination and an eye to the future, while not ignoring, of course, the specifics of each case. Money must serve, not rule ... I exhort you to generous solidarity and to the return of economics and finance to an ethical approach which favors human beings."[18] With this exhortation in mind, in addition to better government oversight, it is clear that the professions themselves need to engage in the sort of rigorous ongoing formation of their practitioners. Annual formation for the renewal of the licenses of realtors, mortgage officers, and investment counselors should include not only exercises to assure compliance with legal standards but also opportunities for professionals to reflect upon the highest ethical principles of their chosen vocations. Indeed, legal standards always represent the minimum acceptable level of professional behavior. Ethics, according to Socrates, is "no small matter but how we ought to live," and is therefore far more than compliance with rules.

CONCLUSION

While changes to laws and regulations will certainly be necessary to lessen the frequency and the severity of future financial crises, better laws and better law enforcement—whether on a national or an international level—will never by themselves be able to perfect the ethical practices of individual actors, small firms, or global corporations. Even the creation of a global financial authority with broad oversight and regulatory power, while necessary, will not by itself assure an increase of virtuous behavior. Human reason alone, unaided by a well-formed conscience and by a commonly held system of ethical ideals, will simply find ingenious ways around new regulations for any person who lacks a commitment to virtuous behavior. Only a collective commitment to, and widespread adoption of, known and respected moral principles and their enactment as routine ethical practices will contribute to broad improvements in the world economy. All legitimate human work is an expression of our calling to be instruments of the good, working for the increase of justice and the increase in virtue, whether we name this the reign of God or the good society. In either case, such a life project requires a fusion of justice and love, of reason and faith.

NOTES

1. Nathaniel Popper, "A Financial Firm in Rural U.S. Often Tangles with Regulators," *New York Times*, late edition, vol. CLXII, No. 6083, March 22, 2013.
2. John Rawls's early work on the search for an "overlapping consensus" among the world religions on matters of social justice is rich and suggestive in this regard. See his *A Theory of Justice* (Cambridge, MA: Harvard University Press, 1971).
3. For a thorough study of the Exodus story as a social template, see Michael Walzer's *Exodus and Revolution* (New York: Basic Books, 1985). For a more general overview

of the Old Testament, see John David Pleins's excellent work, *Social Visions of the Hebrew Bible* (Westminster, UK: John Knox, 2000).

4. Saint Cyprian, bishop of Carthage from 249 until his martyrdom in 258, held the typically ambiguous view of the Roman Empire that was common among Christians living under capriciously hostile emperors. The moral weaknesses of Roman civilization were patent (hypocritical rulers, instead of providing security for their subjects, promote insecurity, smiling as they punish, flattering to fool, exalting in order to destroy—*Quod idola* 7), yet at his trial, as recorded in the *Acta*, Cyprian confessed to have prayed daily for the emperor. Cyprian was convinced that earthquakes, floods, and droughts were sure evidence that the world had grown old and the end was near, yet he urged Christians to pray constantly for an end to plagues, droughts, and wars, and for the peace and the salvation of the pagans (*ad Demetr.* 20). See, for example, J. Patout Burns Jr., *Cyprian the Bishop* (New York: Routledge, 2002).

5. Bishops and abbots as landlords during the medieval period blurred a distinction that the Church wanted to defend, even as it possessed land as a necessary means of income. Pope Gelasius I (492–496), in a letter to Emperor Anastasius, distinguished between two types of authority (two swords) by which society is ruled, the spiritual and the secular. They are quite distinct, with the former, exercised by the priests, being weightier and holding sway over the latter, which is held be secular rulers. This vision of the collaboration of altar and throne, with the former having precedence, was the Church's default position through the investiture controversies and up to the revolutionary era.

6. The classic overview of the first 19 centuries of this tradition is that of Ernst Troeltsch, *Die Soziallehren der christlichen Kirchen und Gruppen* (1911). The best synthesis in English remains H. Richard Niehbuhr's, *Christ and Culture* (1951).

7. Pope Gregory XVI opposed all forms of liberalism and modernism and condemned, for example, the construction of railroads, calling them "chemins d'enfer" because of the social disruption he felt they caused. His successor, Pope Pius IX, summed up the Catholic anti-modernist position in his *Syllabus of Errors* (1864). For a helpful collection of, and commentary on, the essential documents of this development, see David O'Brien and Thomas Shannon's *Catholic Social Thought: The Documentary Heritage* (Maryknoll, NY: Orbis Books, 2010).

8. For a lengthier discussion of *Rerum Novarum*, see Stephen Pope's eponymous article in the *New Dictionary of Catholic Social Thought*, edited by Judith Dwyer (Collegeville, PA: Liturgical Press, 1994).

9. While many allocutions and addresses have recapitulated and advanced this line of thought, the major works are generally thought to be the following: Pope Pius XI's *Quadragesimo Anno*; Pope John XXIII's *Mater et Magistra* and *Pacem in Terris*; the Second Vatican Council's *Dignitatis Humanae* and *Gaudium et Spes*; Pope Paul VI's *Populorum Progressio* and *Octagesima Adveniens*; Pope John Paul II's *Centesimus Annus, Laborem Exercens*, and *Sollicitudo Rei Socialis*, Pope Benedict XVI's *Caritas in Veritate* and *Deus caritas est*, and Pope Francis's *Lumen Fidei* and *Evangelii Gaudium* (see especially numbers 57 and 58 on financial systems).

10. There is ample literature on this topic. See, for example, Michael J. Schultheis, Edward P. Berri, and Peter J. Henriot, *Catholic Social Teaching: Our Best Kept Secret*, 3rd rev. ed. (Maryknoll, NY: Orbis Books, 1992).

11. http://www.stthomas.edu/cathstudies/cst/VocationBusinessLead/VocationTurk sonRemar/VocationBk3rdEdition.pdf.

12. John Paul II, *Centesimus Annus*, 35.

13. *Catechism of the Catholic Church for the United States of America* ©1997, United States Catholic Conference, 48 §4; cf. Pius XI, *Quadragesimo Anno* I, 184–186.

14. John Paul II, *Laborem Exercens*, 14.

15. Saint Cyprian imported the term from Roman legal theory into Catholic theology in *de Unitate*, 5. It is a formal legal principle of solidarity, more specifically of common legal ownership of an indivisible object, a clubhouse, or a boat or some other entity that can have multiple owners and yet cannot be divided. "*Episcopatus unus est cujus a singularis in solidum pars tenetur*" can be understood to mean that the episcopacy (i.e., the college of bishops) is one unity which each [bishop] for his part possesses entirely in its wholeness.

16. *Pacem in Terris*, 11.

17. Pontifical Council for Justice and Peace, "Towards Reforming the International Financial and Monetary Systems in the Context of Global Public Authority," Rome October 24, 2011. http://www.vatican.va/roman_curia/pontifical_councils/just peace/documents/rc_pc_justpeace_doc_20111024_nota_en.html.

18. Pope Francis, *Evangelii Gaudium*, 58.

19

Three Ethical Dimensions of the Financial Crisis

ANTONIO ARGANDONA ■

Crisis means that certain postulates are exhausted and that certain ways of coping with life are no longer relevant to emerging issues. In my view, the crisis makes man tremble deeper when that obsolescence affects the idea of progress.

(POLO 1991, 25)

THE FINANCIAL CRISIS

In the summer of 2007,[1] financial markets were shaken by the first episodes of what would become a deep financial crisis.[2] Some financial institutions in the United States experienced an increase in mortgage loan defaults, especially in the so-called subprime segment. The fact that ownership of those loans had been transferred to other investors, or used as collateral for other assets (securitization), generated considerable suspicion about the true value of these assets and the level of risk involved, which, coupled with a lack of transparency, also raised doubts about the solvency of the institutions that owned them, as well as many other institutions connected as counterparties to these operations. The international financial system was very quickly affected by a serious crisis, which was first a liquidity crisis, as investors stopped lending to almost all entities, and then a solvency crisis. Moreover, the problem quickly spread to other markets and countries through contagion.

From the beginning, central banks provided large amounts of liquidity to the banks, but this could not solve the main problem, which was the loss of confidence in the soundness of the institutions involved. Governments therefore adopted extraordinary measures for recapitalization and cleaning up the banks' balance sheets. The situation seemed contained until, in September 2008, the bankruptcy of the investment bank Lehman Brothers put the global financial system on the brink of a widespread collapse, caused by investors' panic. The governments' actions allowed them to overcome this critical phase of the crisis, which had resulted in a deep recession.

To address the problems of the banking system and to overcome the recession, governments introduced generous programs of fiscal stimulus. These led to large public deficit which, combined with the high level of debt that some countries had already accumulated, generated a crisis of sovereign debt, led by Greece but followed closely by other countries, mainly in Europe.

All this revealed the interconnection between various crises and their remote origins (Gross 2007; Hoffman et al. 2007; Kindleberger 1978). For years, the overly lax monetary policy of the US Federal Reserve had been creating a housing bubble in the United States (Bhattacharya and Yu 2008). The overvaluation of assets, high debt, and a feeling of euphoria gave rise to the first crisis, which began, as already noted, when the growth of housing prices stopped, slowing demand and causing many customers to default. This crisis was also reproduced, in various ways in other European countries, as a result of the similarly lax policy of the European Central Bank.

The second crisis arose from the bursting of the bubble and its effects on the balance sheets of financial institutions: loss of assets value, increase in bad debts, funding difficulties, and lack of capital. This crisis occurred not only in countries where a bubble had formed, such as the United States, Britain, Spain, and Iceland, but also in others, such as Germany and Belgium, whose banks had invested in "toxic" assets. It was also compounded in some cases by a currency crisis, when the domestic currency depreciated, abruptly increasing the debt levels of households, firms, and financial institutions, as happened in Iceland.

In some countries, the third crisis was one of sovereign debt and was caused by the high liabilities incurred by governments through their fiscal stimulus measures and the support to troubled banks. The possibility of default by some governments created a new wave of mistrust, raising the risk premium and forcing those governments to carry out tough fiscal consolidation plans, which aggravated the recession and the difficulties of their banks.

The preceding paragraphs provide a brief history of the recent financial crisis.[3] Like all complex phenomena, this crisis had economic, psychological, social, political, and ethical causes: they are interdependent. Some analysts blame governments and central banks for their lax monetary policy in the years before 2007, as well as the regulators and controllers of the financial system, ratings agencies, managers of financial institutions, mortgage sellers, home buyers, developers and builders, and so on.

It has often been argued that this is an ethical crisis,[4] because moral errors may explain why economic and political failures can lead to situations of crisis. To explain this, we will develop our analysis on three levels. The first concerns the moral failings of individuals, manifested in inappropriate behaviors that can lead to a crisis. The second is the organizational level: the strategies and cultures of the nonfinancial companies, banks, investment funds, rating agencies, central banks, regulators and supervisors, and governments show the existence of ethical lapses at an organizational level. The third level is that of social and theoretical ethics and finance, where failures have hampered the mechanisms of correction or aggravated the moral consequences of individual or organizational decisions.

The next section of this chapter discusses a repertoire of morally wrong or questionable behaviors arising during the recent crisis. In attempting to introduce these behaviors into the operation of financial organizations, we wonder to what extent the ethical crisis was also—perhaps above all—a crisis of management or governance of these entities. This will take us to an analysis of the concept of ethics that emerges in these explanations and which will shed light on the nature of the deeper social problems that have arisen in the crisis. The article ends with conclusions, where some ideas to avoid these problems in the future are presented.

PERSONAL ETHICS

In this section, we review some of the behaviors that refer in one way or another to the actions that have resulted in crisis (Argandoña 2009, 2010a, b, c; Graafland and van de Ven 2011; Hawtrey and Johnson 2009). It is not, of course, an exhaustive analysis, but only a quick inventory showing that the moral dimension has indeed been present in the crisis.[5]

It has been said, over and over again, that the cause of the crisis was greed, defined as a selfish and excessive desire for more of something (money) than is needed. A distinction should be made between this vice and legitimate economic rationality, which takes advantage of opportunities, such as buying when prices are low and selling when high, or going into debt when interest rates are low (Miller 2009).[6]

The list of trampled virtues also includes temperance, specifically the ability to restrain the desire for success, wealth, or social recognition, which thus become obstacles to proper professional conduct, and, on the side of vices, cowardice, complicity and lack of strength. For example, some managers, despite realizing what was happening, evaded some difficult decisions that might have jeopardized their career or their remuneration. There were also attitudes of pride, arrogance, and hubris among financiers, but also among economists, regulators, and governments—all convinced that their knowledge and skills were superior, that they had no reason to submit to the supervision of others, or that they were above the law. In short, they placed a high value on honor, glory, wealth, fame, and everything else that could have been achieved through professional excellence, but also through lies, and showed that they were more willing to lie than to restrain their desires or reorient their values (Torres 2009).

And all this led to situations of injustice (Hawtrey and Johnson 2009), specifically commutative justice (Pieper 1966): withholding due information, misleading advertising, multiplication of unnecessary operations (churning) to generate higher commissions, manipulation of stock recommendations, and so on. Consideration of the responsibility for one's actions in the common good was also omitted, as in, for example, moral hazard problems, when financial institutions take advantage of the limitation of their risks, thanks to the legal provision of limited liability or the existence of public guarantees that limited their losses (Sinn 2008).

Prudence or practical rationality is the main virtue of the banker (Termes 1995), but it is difficult to exercise in an environment of high growth, low interest rates, and extraordinary opportunities for profit, leading to higher leverage and a reduction in the perception of risk. All of these constitute the perfect environment for poor management. There are many manifestations of such recklessness. Complacency, for example, often takes place in upturns (Lo 2008),[7] and herd behavior, which can be rational, but can also increase volatility that spreads to other markets, leading to panic, another herd behavior.

This brief summary of immoral behavior shows, as we said before, that the crisis has an ethical dimension. However, these vices are always present in one way or another in all human activity. And a cause that is present whether the effect occurs or not cannot be a satisfactory explanation.[8] Put another way, if many agents have been motivated by greed in many places and for centuries, why did the crisis occur here and now, and not at other times and other places?

One answer to this question might be that these behaviors are widespread and have exceeded a certain threshold above which we cannot guarantee the stability of the results. We have no conclusive empirical evidence on this, although some social, legal, and institutional changes can be identified that accentuated the roles of greed and other vices. For example, the economic conditions for the formation of a bubble can generate abnormally high earnings expectations. There may have been also situations of "induced greed" by encouraging and rewarding those who succeed in their greedy behavior and making it harder to behave otherwise: "greed is good."[9] A particular case of this "moral contagion" could be the institutionalization of these actions, for example, in the practices of firms, regulators, and financial intermediaries.

On the other hand, society has long developed protective mechanisms, not against immoral behavior itself but against its consequences, ranging from law, courts, and fines to the social rejection of offenders. It is possible that these social mechanisms have relaxed in recent years,[10] and this brings us to the next level of ethics.

THE ETHICS OF ORGANIZATIONS

The crisis we are looking at is often presented as a crisis of leadership or governance in organizations as varied as commercial and investment banks, hedge funds, monolines, rating agencies, supervisory bodies, central banks, and governments.[11] For example, there have been cases of bad governance and lack of professional competence on the part of directors, senior managers, and analysts in organizations of all kinds. Often, the role of analysis and valuation of assets, and even buying or selling decisions, was entrusted to inexperienced young professionals, who used sophisticated models based on overly simplistic assumptions, but nobody dared to criticize them because nobody had any better models and also because they provided high profits to their employers.[12] Furthermore, superiors didn't know what their subordinates were doing, nor did they understand the models they were using, nor did they exercise adequate oversight. In other words, there was a lack of "an understanding of the mechanisms of structured products combined with the economic knowledge to put them in context and the management skills to run the organizations that marketed them" (Kay 2009a).[13]

These failures were manifested mainly in risk analysis and management, leading to "key personnel in virtually all major financial institutions... taking excessive risks" (Crotty and Epstein 2009, 4; cf. Hawtrey and Johnson 2009). There were many reasons for this. The financial institutions, for example, had established rigorous mechanisms to identify and monitor these risks, but these were based on overly optimistic assumptions, built on the hypothesis that catastrophic events or "black swans" (Taleb 2007) were highly unlikely and therefore could be omitted. The mechanisms for covering the risks of the portfolios were based on evidence of recent decades, which were particularly stable in many of these markets, and also assumed that the risks of various assets were largely independent of each other—an assumption that was clearly proven false. These assumptions created the illusion that risk had been eliminated from the portfolio of the institutions by the credit default swaps, without allowing for the fact that this risk was reintroduced in other ways. They had created public agencies for supervision and control, but each was acting locally, meaning that no one was supervising systemic risk. In addition, they had eliminated or mitigated various mechanisms and institutions established to monitor its effects.[14]

It has often been argued that the crisis was due to the creation of perverse incentives in the management of financial and non-financial institutions. Incentives, financial or otherwise, are intended to promote certain behaviors that are expected to lead to desired results, but they can also cause unwanted effects, perhaps because they are poorly designed ("the folly of rewarding for A when hoping for B"[15]): perhaps the managers are remunerated by the share prices in the short term rather than the achievement of sustainable value in the long term, or the system of incentives may be manipulated by those who will benefit from them, or they assume that agents are only motivated by economic interests which crowds out non-material motivations.[16]

It is likely that many of the inappropriate behaviors in the recent crisis had been related to the existence of perverse incentives. For example, the attempt to align the interests of managers and analysts with those of shareholders has led to compensation systems that emphasize short-term results, which may have led to undesirable behaviors such as excessive risk taking and manipulation of financial results or the stock price.[17] In any case, the design and implementation of these remuneration systems was also reckless and a sign of bad governance, precisely because those undesirable results were not anticipated.

A particular case of perverse incentives would be the conflicts of interest that have arisen, for example, in the rating agencies, whose income depended in large measure on the valuation of their clients' assets. Of course, there were other problems, such as the inadequacy of the agencies' models, the lack of a sufficiently long and varied history to incorporate in the parameters of those models, and the fact that their best analysts ended up being hired by their clients, which accentuated the conflicts of interest.

In the crisis, there were also cases of "regulatory arbitrage," which moves operations to countries with lax controls or changes the nature of operations to circumvent the regulations. Lack of transparency (opacity of operations and concealment of information from customers, regulators, and even shareholders) was another characteristic of many of the behaviors that led to the crisis.

The regulation and control mechanisms also failed: the abolition of the US Glass-Steagall law which separated the commercial banking and investment banking businesses; public incentives for subprime mortgage lending, by companies under the patronage of the state, such as Fannie Mae and Freddie Mac in the United States; resistance to regulation of some financial derivatives; and so on. And these are not just technical problems, because these mechanisms are created and managed by people and therefore are also decisions with an ethical dimension.

THE SOCIAL DIMENSION OF ETHICS

Earlier we mentioned ethical lapses by persons and organizations who succumbed to the temptation of very favorable financing conditions or to the opportunity to earn high profits by means less honest, and this is already one explanation for why this is a moral crisis. But we have also noted that social conditions were created that probably encouraged—or at least did not stop—these behaviors, and impeded the functioning of legal, institutional, and social mechanisms which, in other circumstances, would have slowed the effects of those behaviors. What we offer here is not a complete analysis but rather some suggestions that try to explain why this is an ethical crisis, and why ethical behaviors are needed to avoid its recurrence.

Some experts (economists, but also moralists) deny that ethics play a role in the current crisis. According to the anthropological model that inspired neoclassical economics, the agents' decisions are based on preferences which economics takes as data (Aranzadi 2006). Everything that makes a rational agent in this model is ethically neutral (Miller 2009); ethics and economics are disconnected realities (the "separation thesis," Harris and Freeman 2008). Ethics deals with values that are subjective and which cannot be assessed objectively, while economics deals with facts (J. N. Keynes 1890; Robbins 1935). The rational agent, who maximizes his utility subject to the usual restrictions, is not undertaking ethically relevant actions: economics is an amoral exercise. Or, to put it another way: if the market takes care of the self-regulating economic relations, individual actions, which ethics regulates, are not important; whatever their conduct, the market will find a social optimum (Zamagni 2009).

If this is so, the crisis was caused by the fortuitous confluence of events such as a credit expansion sustained for too long; some financial innovations; and an array of failures in the mechanisms of monitoring, prevention, and control that had been created.[18] In any case, the people to "blame," if anyone, will be the consumers, entrepreneurs, analysts, and executives of financial institutions which did not act rationally (and this is not easy to identify because, a priori, their behavior could agree with economic rationality, even though the results were disastrous); the governments, which altered the incentives and constraints of private agents, pursuing unsustainable policies (e.g., giving poor people access to housing, or the suppression of certain financial regulations); and the supervisors and regulators, who did not do their jobs.

In some sense, this moved the problem to the realm of politics. But the meaning and moral assessment of politics has also changed, at least in Western societies.[19] Throughout modern times, these societies have set up political projects oriented toward rational and universal purposes: freedom, equality, development, welfare. But now many of those political goals have been met, and there remain fewer collective tasks to perform. "The rationalization of the means has replaced the ideal of rational ends . . . The result is, to a large extent, fragmentation: there are no common goods, the pursuit of social goals is a thing of the past, inequality invites creativity and competition" (Flamarique 2010, 107). It was this same creativity and competition that gave rise to many of the financial innovations that later led to the crisis.

More important is the change in attitudes. Citizens of many rich countries tend to attribute to abstract actors (the government, the market, the system) the guarantee of their economic and social rights (employment, pension, health, safety, etc.), and give up an important part of their autonomy in these areas in exchange for a hopeful security in their living standards. This implies that the economic world would be, again, only a technical world, which works with its own rules and which has no reason to be guided by ethics. What we hope of this world is the materialization of a perfect productive, organizational, and regulatory structure "which makes its citizens' honesty superfluous" (Pérez-Soba 2011, 6).

At least until the outbreak of the crisis, "in political life, boredom is detected in the same way in which the procedures of election, representation and distribution of welfare operate smoothly, but also within immovable limits. Public attention has turned to other things. It is not that expectations were not met: in essence, citizens are comfortable with the institutional regime. It is rather that the expectations are now individual, not universal" (Flamarique 2010, 107). The citizens became individualistic, to an extent that has probably not occurred in the past, and so is their ethics: they no longer have to deal with major social challenges, except perhaps for humanitarian actions. "The dream of a definitely just future society has died; the time of revolutions has passed, but the number and intensity of our desires have increased ... While the idea of equality and social rationality rules the imagination that sustains our system and political culture, popular culture invites private codes, individual criteria" (Flamarique 2010, 108). It is the time of an increasingly individualistic collection of "new rights."

And, at the same time, emotions become the space in which the citizen can be "himself," which means giving priority to the moment, the fleeting, and the fashionable.[20] Ethics becomes "emotivist" (MacIntyre 1981, Taylor 1989); what is "authentic" becomes "moral"; the emotional response wins over judgment and reflection, and it settles all responsibilities. The citizens are willing to admit that we are all responsible for everything (Jonas 1984), but this may be just a subterfuge to deny the sense of personal responsibility: responsibility is transferred to the collective and, ultimately, to the state.[21] The private life, presumably guided by sentiment, authenticity, and experiences, is divorced from public ethics.

But even the meaning of public ethics itself is changing because the private rights, which citizens claim as necessary and inalienable for their self-realization, cease to be based on more or less objective ideals about what is good; driven by feelings, these private rights are relative and changing, and they only hold insofar as the law supports them. In public discourse, ethical values become blurred: they are reduced to the private sphere, to the point of considering that democracy requires moral relativism, and that the existence of solid values must be rejected as fundamentalism.

At the same time, in a multicultural society, one must accept the plurality of values and therefore cultural—and moral—relativism. However, a system of ethics based on changing and relative values ends up being judged only on its results. This, in politics, has two consequences. In the first place, it leads to disenchantment: giving voice to all just leads to a cacophony and the feeling that the private demands of each are not met. Without the support of ethics, politics becomes volatile and ambiguous.

Second, the traditional means of political or social representation (trade unions, parties) give way to new social movements. These movements are occasional (citizens join only for the defense of personal interests that they value), but with claims to generality (all interests, however particular, become a social interest, and acquire the supposed right to enter the moral agenda of society). And they are also subject to media and commercial manipulation.

If this description of our societies is true, then many citizens, politicians, and experts will agree that the cause of the crisis was that "someone" (politicians, bankers, regulators) did not fulfill some "technical" duties that became "moral" duties when they were understood as the obligation to generate the outcomes of welfare, safety, growth, and so on that the citizens demanded.[22] And this could explain citizens' bewilderment about the current crisis: the rise and duration of unemployment, job insecurity, doubts about the sustainability of the welfare state, unequal distribution of income and wealth, and widespread uncertainty show, in this interpretation of what has happened, that the market and the state have not fulfilled their part in the social contract between the public (economic prosperity, welfare state, security) and the private (our autonomous personal life). But the crisis cannot be attributed any more to external events, but to the behaviors of the very citizens who complain against the crisis, but which are responsible of problems such as the demographic crisis, the breakup of the homogeneity of cultural models, and even climate change. And the problem is not transient, despite the promises of governments, central banks, and economists that the next package of measures will be effective.

Everything suggests that the economic system, supposedly self-sufficient and self-regulating, is neither. The intended solution seems to be more regulation: the state must intervene to limit abuses that can occur in the functioning of the market (Polo 1993), and this intervention must be undertaken not only as a technical duty but also a moral obligation. But it does not seem that the insistence in the same measures can produce radically different results.

It seems, therefore, that we should turn our attention to ethics. But there are many ethical theories: what are those that can solve our problems? Not, of course, the private ethics in force, which, as we said before, is relativistic, individualistic, emotivistic, and also "socially utilitarian," because the citizen

> accepts a new method of "assessing" human actions based on two radically different criteria, which can only be lived to the extent that they remain in two completely different levels. He accepts the utilitarian system of social valuation that seeks to maximize the results according to objective measures that permit the comparison of interests [the economic and social goals: welfare, growth, security, etc.] ... Moreover, the inner world of private emotions identified as "feeling good," which happens to occupy the entire field of consciousness." (Pérez-Soba 2011, 7–8)

In the end, moral contents are transferred to the law, which then becomes a source of morality. In an individualistic society, in which common goods are not feasible, the majority rule becomes "the" moral criterion. This leaves the individual faced with a previously unknown freedom of choice, but plunged into uncertainty, which is then discharged into the law. What the law allows is good, what it prohibits is bad, and if this is displeasing, the individual can demand the recognition of the right to disagree, which can lead to the exception becoming a new standard. The state eventually takes previously private behaviors and makes them obligatory moral standards. "Hyper-judicialized societies, like the present one, favor the assumption of decreed obligations (as well as the claim of rights) but not of a responsible actions towards the future. Responsibility is a term that always appears whenever injury or damage occur; these are, in every case, anonymous, legal, and institutional responsibilities, with respect to the past, and for this there is the state, insurance, etc." (Flamarique 2010, 110).

Polo (1996b) outlines some of the consequences of applying purely technical solutions to human (i.e., ethical) problems: 1) segmentation, the result of a lack of a comprehensive overview, which results from the specialization and one-sidedness of the "experts": the proposed economic solutions to the crisis are not operational because they omit other dimensions (political, sociological, psychological, and ethical); 2) perverse effects, which can occur in other areas: we are not able to organize the means without causing dangerous side effects, because we have no unconditional principles from which we can deploy practical action, and because we cannot guarantee the consistency of our uncoordinated projects (the explosion of systemic risk in the crisis may be an example of this); 3) anomie, the state of discouragement of those who have no guidelines for action, but only stimuli (for example, markets become dependent on the actions of central banks); and 4) social entropy: institutions lose their function.

Can there be an objective ethics, capable of validating public and private behavior in the financial world? If what we have said so far is at least an approximate description of our moral environment, then the answer is no. The proposed solutions to the crisis overlook its ethical dimension and seek only technical solutions, such as reform of regulatory and supervisory frameworks or quantitative easing, which are based, in any case, on results-oriented consequentialist ethics or on results-oriented public ethics, which just add a spurious moral dimension to public decisions.

In summary, we believe that the failures in the conduct of financial institutions, regulatory bodies, and governments which the crisis has highlighted were not isolated events but rather point to flaws in the anthropological and ethical models that have governed the conduct not only of those agents, but much of our society, at least in developed countries. That is to say, models built from incomplete or erroneous assumptions led to wrong managerial approaches in incentive, monitoring, reporting, and accounting systems; in the selection, training, and compensation of human capital; and in the very culture of the organizations.[23] And with these wrong approaches, one could only reasonably expect the proliferation of misguided behaviors such as greed, recklessness, pride, fraud, and dishonesty, as well as stronger business objectives, control systems, cultures, systems of incentives, and rules of conduct.

CONCLUSION

We wondered whether it is possible, in the financial world, to conceive of objective ethics that would be able to validate the public and private behavior. By observing our advanced societies, we reached a negative conclusion, but that was too hasty. This is not the right place to develop how an ethical conception should be, in order to correct the problems created by the crisis and to prevent their recurrence, but we can at least make some suggestions.

There should not be a different ethic for the economy, for politics, and for individuals; ethical schizophrenia leads to inconsistency and, concretely, to the systemic crisis of the person (that person who is utilitarian in social life and emotivist in private life, who demands external results as a moral requirement, but does not accept personal responsibility for their achievement), organizations, and society as a whole. The economic system, in particular, is not self-regulating: the stability of the market requires a legal and regulatory system, but this is not enough. The existence of traffic rules and physical barriers does not guarantee safe and smooth driving on the highways; if drivers break the rules at a cost to others, or if those who make and change the rules do so for objectives other than the welfare of citizens.

The reader will certainly object that there already exist ethical rules in our societies, and that, nevertheless, they were not been able to avert the crisis. But this has probably been because not all ethics are equally effective. Ethics must be based on the actions of rational people in a social setting (Abbà 1992; Argandoña 2011; Den Uyl 2009). This excludes, first, utilitarian ethics, focused on obtaining results, which forgets that the most important result is people learning; second, individualistic ethics, which does not sufficiently take into account that the person is social and grows in his relationships with others and learns from them and with them; and, third, ethics that focus only on actions as separate units, and which do not account for character, the development of virtues.

Paraphrasing economics, we can say that ethics is the equilibrium condition of individuals, organizations, and societies. This equilibrium is dynamic, because whenever an action takes place the agent undergoes a change and produces changes in others, so that what is now an equilibrium may cease to be tomorrow. Therefore, an ethics understood as a set of external rules (laws, social norms, or corporate codes) rather than an ethics centered on the acting person may not be good guide to action. This does not mean that norms do not have an important role: we definitely need an ethic of virtues (that explains how the agent improves or worsens in his actions, and how he develops or hinders the ability to behave ethically in the future), goods (which is what the agent should achieve), and norms (which should be observed to not deteriorate as a person and to improve as one) (Polo 1996a).

All this leads to two further conclusions. First, ethics cannot be separated from economics. There are no economic decisions and ethical decisions: there are decisions that are, at the same time, economic, ethical, and political. Economics deals with means, but not means for given goals, because ethics governs the goals; the separation between economics and ethics is one of the ultimate causes of the crisis. And second, for the same reason, politics should be tightly linked with ethics—again, the omission of this relationship has a lot to do with the current crisis.[24]

Purely economic interpretations of the crisis are not necessarily wrong, but they are incomplete because they omit at least some important consequences of the decisions of the decision maker on himself (because he learns to act either well or poorly), on others (who also learn), and on the organization (in which moral or immoral cultures are created, and in which trust is promoted or destroyed). Ethics must add to the economy a richer conception of the person and, therefore, explanations not necessarily different but more complete, in which one can better outline the consequences of decisions, not only in economic terms. And this will serve to better identify problems, to better understand the nature of the failures that have occurred, and to offer better solutions. But these solutions will not be developed by the moralist alone, but by the economist, taking into account the criteria of ethics.

Ethics has three dimensions: personal, organizational, and social. The solution to the problems created by the crisis demands an ethical response at these three levels. People should be ethical (and, of course, efficient), organizations must allow the agents to act in accordance with ethics (and efficiency), and society should promote individuals who act ethically. And this has a theoretical aspect (what is ethics and how does it relate to economics and politics) and a practical one (how to spread behaviors and how to create the conditions wherein policy and institutional constraints can block unethical actions). The three dimensions are all needed.

"While the music plays, you have to dance," said Charles ("Chuck") Prince, CEO of Citigroup, in the *Financial Times* in July 2007. He added: "We're still dancing." This phrase summarizes the situation for many financial institutions in recent years: a riotous dance, from which, like the game of musical chairs, no one could withdraw. "These words are now the epitaph of the global credit boom."[25]

NOTES

1. This chapter is a document of the "la Caixa" Chair of Corporate Social Responsibility and Corporate Governance, IESE Business School, University of Navarra.

2. A financial crisis is a situation in which there are big changes in the value of financial institutions' assets, their access to financing, or the confidence of its customers, to the extent that the sustainability of the financial system is in danger. See Abberger and Nierhaus (2008), Claessens et al., (2009), Mendoza and Terrones (2014).

3. There are many excellent analyses of this crisis, for example, Baily et al. (2008), Blundell-Wignall et al. (2008), Bordo (2009), Brunnermeier (2009), Diamond and Rajan (2009), Eichengreen (2008), Gross (2009), Hellwig (2008), Kane (2009), Morris (2008), Pezzuto (2013), Taylor (2009a, b), and Tett (2009).

4. After all the episodes of boom, euphoria, and subsequent financial crisis, widespread ethical failures have been reported. See, for example, Bogle (2006) and Kindleberger (1978).

5. Based on interviews with managers before the crisis, Coleman and Pinder (2010) identified several attitudes leading to foresee the moral problems of the crisis, like a preference for the short term, the transient bias ("this time it's different"), the inability to cope with new risks, and the reluctance to hedge those risks.

6. On the extent of greed and avarice in the business world, see Handy (2002), MacIntyre (1995), and Solomon (1992).

7. A typical case is to consider that rare events are, in fact, impossible (Taleb 2007).

8. Miller (2009) concluded that this was not an ethical crisis, because the behaviors listed in the text were the rational response of economic agents to changes in their environment that they did not cause. This theory is correct, in the sense that we cannot judge moral behavior without taking into account the agents' incentives, knowledge, and circumstances, but it is incorrect as far as it suggests that economic actions are not ethical but purely technical (i.e., that the "rational" response of the agents cannot be subject to moral evaluation).

9. The famous phrase of Gordon Gekko, the protagonist of the movie *Wall Street* (1987).

10. The high yield of greed and low social protection have led to a proliferation of fraud, scams, and hoaxes, which did not cause the crisis, but are some of its most striking symptoms. The frauds of Bernard Madoff and the like also highlight other moral weaknesses: pride (the desire to feel privileged as part of an elite group of investors), recklessness (trust in the qualities of an expert, not subjected to verification), and some obfuscation (the "desire" to believe that it is possible to have abnormally high returns over long periods of time).

11. On the supervisory institutions' share of the blame, see Levine (2010).

12. The question of economists' and financial theorists' responsibility deserves careful examination. See Acemoglu (2010) and Caballero (2010).

13. The complexity of certain financial instruments need not be morally problematic if decision makers know the nature of the challenges that this complexity can create, and they act accordingly, for example, providing customers with all the necessary information.

14. Due to, among other reasons, political pressure from the regulated entities themselves, for example, concerning over-the-counter operations (Kane 2009).

15. That is the suggestive title of the article by Kerr (1975). See also Rosanas (2006).

16. Some examples of perverse incentives in the current crisis: 1) The compensation of mortgage brokers in the United States was based on the volume of loans, not on their expected solvency; this fosters the reckless granting of credit and even the falsification of information in applications. 2) The banks that granted the mortgages quickly securitized them and took them off their balance sheets, thus reducing the need to monitor their customers' conditions and follow the loan repayments, at least in part. 3) Some debtors bought their houses with the intention of soon defaulting on payments and re-mortgaging when house prices rose. 4) Financial institutions often incurred problems of "moral hazard," leading to overly risky operations, with explicit or implicit government guarantee of its liabilities. 5) The investment banks, which had been unlimited liability companies (private partnerships), became limited liability (public corporations), thereby reducing their liability for losses, which encouraged higher-risk strategies. 6) The growth of directors and managers' compensation, often based on stock options, led them to seek short-term profitability, even through accounting fraud or manipulation. See Kane (2009).

17. The high salaries of executives and financial analysts have often been presented as the main cause of the crisis, but instead they appear to have been an effect of the speculative bubble: money goes to whatever is fashionable, and in recent years this meant real estate and financial assets. And where money goes, prices increase, and this generates extra profits or rents that the various actors involved try to capture. Managers have a comparative advantage when it comes to knowing what those profits are, where they are generated and how to capture them, and the same applies to analysts and other experts, whose contribution is necessary for the creation of these rents.

18. "The reasonable explanation for a crisis of this magnitude... is that a combination of a number of complex and highly interrelated factors have strongly contributed to this global financial turmoil. The factors are related to economic elements, to the corporate governance of banks and financial institutions, to the US government's

monetary policy, to the lack of rigorous supervisory controls in the banking industry and financial markets, to the high leverage credit culture of people in the United States and United Kingdom, to the banking management culture and philosophy, to the role played by the rating agencies" (Pezzuto 2008, 6–7).

19. This point has been developed by Flamarique (2009, 2010).

20. "There is a gap between what is done, which belongs to the realm of the 'outside,' and the 'inside' world of feelings, centered in a weak sense of intimacy. Sentimental man 'locks' himself in a way to his 'feelings' ... quite separate from social relationships" (Pérez-Soba 2011, 7).

21. When trust disappears, the solution is not sought in virtuous life or in human relationships, but in the law and institutions. In a financial world where relationships multiply and become depersonalized, trust is placed in the law (I trust my bank because the law requires him to act according to some agreed standards), institutions (e.g., the deposit guarantee fund), and the self-interest of financial institutions ("The first and most effective line of defense against fraud and insolvency is counterparties' surveillance. For example, JPMorgan thoroughly scrutinizes the balance sheet of Merrill Lynch before it lends. It does not look to the Securities and Exchange Commission to verify Merrill's solvency": Greenspan 2007, quoted by Kay 2009b). But all this collapsed. The law by itself cannot build trust: indeed, if the law is effective, then trust is not needed, but if it ceases to be effective, what can we trust in? (Rosanas and Velilla 2003). Nor can we rely on the banks' capacity for self-regulation, because they have other objectives (profitability) more important than control of their debtors.

22. This has led, it seems, to a crisis of legitimacy of the system (Habbu 2011).

23. See the excellent explanation in Sahlman (2010).

24. The consideration of economics as a science of a more complete human action is opening its way with difficulty among the economists. This also affects finance, which shares with economics the problems of epistemological autonomy and the extension of the neoclassical paradigm to other areas of human life, giving rise to the so called "financialization" of the society (Dembinski 2009).

25. Mackenzie 2009.

REFERENCES

Abbà, G. 1992. *Felicidad, vida buena y virtud*. Barcelona: Ediciones Internacionales Universitarias.

Abberger, K., and W. Nierhaus. 2008. "How to Define a Recession?" *CESifo Forum* 4: 74–76.

Acemoglu, D. 2010. "The Crisis of 2008: Structural Lessons for and from Economics." In *Globalization and Growth. Implications for a Post-Crisis World*, edited by M. Spence and D. Leipziger, 37–45. Washington, DC: International Bank of Reconstruction and Development.

Aranzadi, J. 2006. *Liberalism against Liberalism. Theoretical Analysis of the Works of Ludwig von Mises and Gary Becker*. London: Routledge.

Argandoña, A. 2009. "Crisi financera: a la recerca de criteris ètics." In *La situació econòmica global. A la recerca d'uns criteris ètics*, 77–96. Barcelona: Facultat de Teologia de Catalunya.

Argandoña, A. 2010a. "La dimensión ética de la crisis financiera." In *La crisis de 2008. De la economía a la política y más allá*, edited by A. Costas, 183–198. Almería: Fundación Cajamar.

Argandoña, A. 2010b. "Más allá de la eficiencia: Lecciones éticas de la crisis para la cultura empresarial." In *Hacia una nueva ética económica global. Innovación vs. statu quo*, edited by T. Jiménez Araya, 203–226. Barcelona: Huygens Editorial.

Argandoña, A. 2010c. "¿Puede la responsabilidad social corporativa ayudar a entender la crisis financiera?." In *Ética y Responsabilidad ante la Crisis*, edited by M.A. Arráez and P. Francés, 51–83. Granada: Ediciones Sider.

Argandoña, A. 2011. "Las virtudes en una teoría de la acción humana." In *La persona al centro del Magistero sociale della Chiesa*, edited by P. Requena and M. Schlag, 49–71. Roma: Edusc.

Baily, M. N., R. E. Litan, and M. S. Johnson. 2008. "The Origins of the Financial Crisis," Washington, DC: Brookings Institution, Fixing Finance Series Paper 3.

Bhattacharya, U., and X. Yu. 2008. "The Causes and Consequences of Recent Financial Market Bubbles: An Introduction," *The Review of Financial Studies* 21 (1): 3–10.

Blundell-Wignall, A., P. Atkinson, and S. Hoon Lee. 2008. "The Current Financial Crisis: Causes and Policy Issues." *Financial Market Trends*. Paris: OECD.

Bogle, J. 2006. "The Depth and Breadth of the Financial Scandals." *Challenge* 49: 23–32.

Bordo, M. D. 2009. "An Historical Perspective on the Crisis." In *Towards a New Framework for Financial Stability*, edited by D. Mayes, R. Pringle, and M. Taylor. London: Central Banking Publications.

Brunnermeier, M. K. 2009. "Deciphering the Liquidity and Credit Crunch 2007–08," *Journal of Economic Perspectives* 23 (1): 77–100.

Caballero, R. J. 2010. "Macroeconomics after the Crisis: Time to Deal with the Pretense-of -Knowledge Syndrome." *Journal of Economic Perspectives* 24 (4): 85–102.

Claessens, S., M. Ayhan Kose, and M. E. Terrones. 2009. "What Happens during Recessions, Crunches and Busts?" *Economic Policy* 60: 653–700.

Coleman, L., and S. Pinder. 2010. "What *Were* They Thinking? Reports from Interviews with Senior Finance Executives in the Lead-Up to the GFC." *Applied Financial Economics* 20 (1-2): 7–14.

Crotty, J., and G. Epstein. 2009. "Regulating the U.S. Financial System to Avoid Another Meltdown." *Economic and Political Weekly* 44 (13): 87-93.

Dembinski, P. H. 2009. *Finance: Servant or Deceiver? Financialization at the Crossroad*. New York, NY: Palgrave Macmillan.

Den Uyl, D. J. 2009. "Homo moralis." *Review of Austrian Economics* 22 (4): 349–385.

Diamond, D. W., and R. Rajan. 2009. "The Credit Crisis: Conjectures about Causes and Remedies." *American Economic Review* 99 (2): 606–610.

Eichengreen, B. 2008. "Origins and Responses to the Current Crisis." *CESifo Forum* 4: 6–11.

Flamarique, L. 2009. "Emociones *versus* normas. El confinamiento psicológico de la experiencia social." *Pensamiento y Cultura* 12 (2): 321–339.

Flamarique, L. 2010. "En 1989 terminó la era de las revoluciones y de las utopías socialistas, y nació una nueva cultura política." *Nuestro Tiempo* 660: 104–110.

Graafland, J. J. and B. W. van de Ven. 2011. "The Credit Crisis and the Moral Responsibility of Professionals in Finance." *Journal of Business Ethics* 103 (4): 605–619.

Greenspan, A. 2007. *The Age of Turbulence: Adventures in a New World*. New York, NY: Penguin.

Gross, D. 2007. *Pop! Why Bubbles Are Great for the Economy*. New York, NY: Harper-Collins.

Gross, D. 2009. *Dumb Money: How Our Greatest Financial Minds Bankrupted the Nation*. New York, NY: Free Press.

Habbu, A. 2011. "The Neoliberal Legitimation Crisis of 2008." *Carceral Notebooks*, Paper No. 2.

Handy, C. 2002. "What Is a Business For?" *Harvard Business Review*, December, 49–55.

Harris, J. D. and R. E. Freeman. 2008. "The Impossibility of the Separation Thesis." *Business Ethics Quarterly* 18 (4): 541–548.

Hawtrey, K., and R. Johnson. 2009. "On the Atrophy of Moral Reasoning in the Global Financial Crisis." *Journal of Religion and Business Ethics* 1 (2): 1–23.

Hellwig, M. 2008. "The Causes of the Financial Crisis." *CESifo Forum* 4: 12–21.

Hoffman, P. T., G. Postel-Vinay, and J. L. Rosenthal. 2007. *Sustaining Large Losses*. Cambridge, MA: Harvard University Press.

Jonas, H. 1984. *The Imperative of Responsibility: In Search of Ethics for the Technological Age*. Chicago: University of Chicago Press.

Kane, E. J. 2009. "Ethical Failures in Regulating and Supervising the Pursuit of Safety Net Subsidies." *European Business Organization Law Review* 10 (2): 185–211.

Kay, J. 2009a. "Greenspan Could Have Found a Cure at the Pharmacy." *Financial Times*, February 25.

Kay, J. 2009b. "Introduce Professional Standards for Senior Bankers." *Financial Times*, February 18.

Kerr, S. 1975. "On the Folly of Rewarding A while Hoping for B." *Academy of Management Journal* 18 (4): 769–783.

Keynes, J. N. 1890. *The Scope and Method of Political Economy*. London: Macmillan.

Kindleberger, C. P. 1978. *Manias, Panics and Crashes: A History of Financial Crises*. New York, NY: John Wiley and Sons.

Levine, R. 2010. "An Autopsy of the U.S. Financial System." *Journal of Financial Economic Policy*, 2 (3): 196–213.

Lo, A. W. 2008. "Hedge Funds, Systemic Risk, and the Financial Crisis of 2007–2008." Washington, DC: US House of Representatives Committee on Oversight and Government Reform, November 13.

MacIntyre, A. 1981. *After Virtue. A Study of Moral Theory*. Notre Dame, IN: Notre Dame University Press.

MacIntyre, A. 1995. *Marxism and Christianity*. London: Duckworth.

Mackenzie, M. 2009. "Cautionary Tale from Citi for New Giants of Finance." *Financial Times*, January 17.

Mendoza, E., and M. E. Terrones. 2014. "An Anatomy of Credit Booms: Evidence from Macro Aggregates and Micro Data." In *Capital Mobility and Monetary Policy*, edited by M. Fuentes and C. Reinhart. Santiago: Central Bank of Chile.

Miller, R. T. 2009. "Morals in a Market Bubble." *University of Dayton Law Review* 35 (1): 113–137.

Morris, C. R. 2008. *The Trillion Dollar Meltdown. Easy Money, High Rollers, and the Great Credit Crash*. London: Public Affairs.

Pérez-Soba, J. J. 2011. "La renovación moral en la vida económica." In the Symposium on Social Doctrine of the Church. Madrid: Fundación Pablo VI, June.

Pezzuto, I. 2008. "Miraculous Financial Engineering or Toxic Finance? The Genesis of the U.S. Subprime Mortgage Loans Crisis and its Consequences on the Global

Financial Markets and the Real Economy." Swiss Management Center Working Paper No. 12/2008.

Pezzuto, I. 2013. *Predictable and Avoidable. Repairing Economic Dislocation and Preventing the Recurrence of Crisis.* Farnham: Gower.

Pieper, J. 1966. *The Four Cardinal Virtues: Prudence, Justice, Fortitude, Temperance.* Notre Dame, IN: University of Notre Dame Press.

Polo, L. 1991. *Quién es el hombre. Un espíritu en el mundo.* Madrid: Rialp.

Polo, L. 1993. "La ética y las virtudes del empresario. Entrevista a Leonardo Polo." *Atlántida* 14: 80–92.

Polo, L. 1996a. *Ética. Hacia una versión moderna de los temas clásicos.* Madrid: Unión Editorial.

Polo, L. 1996b. *Sobre la existencia cristiana.* Pamplona: Eunsa.

Robbins, L. 1935. *An Essay on the Nature and Significance of Economic Science.* London: Macmillan.

Rosanas, J. M. 2006. "Indicadores de gestión, incentivos, motivación y ética en el control de gestión." Barcelona: IESE Business School, *Occasional Paper*, OP 06/11.

Rosanas, J. M. and M. Velilla. 2003. "Loyalty and Trust as the Ethical Bases of Organizations." *Journal of Business Ethics* 44: 49–59.

Sahlman, W. A. 2010. "Management and the Financial Crisis (We Have Met the Enemy and He Is Us . . .)." *Economics, Management, and Financial Markets* 5 (4): 11–53.

Sinn, H. W. 2008. "The End of the Wheeling and Dealing." *CESifo Forum* 4: 3–5.

Solomon, B. 1992. *Ethics and Excellence. Cooperation and Integrity in Business.* New York, NY: Oxford University Press.

Taleb, N. N. 2007. *The Black Swan: The Impact of the Highly Improbable.* New York, NY: Random House.

Taylor, Ch. 1989. *Sources of the Self. The Making of the Modern Identity.* Cambridge: Cambridge University Press.

Taylor, J. B. 2009a. "Economic Policy and Financial Crisis. An Empirical Analysis of What Went Wrong." *Critical Review: A Journal of Politics and Society* 21 (2–3): 341–364.

Taylor, J. B. 2009b. *Getting Off Track. How Government Actions and Interventions Caused, Prolonged, and Worsened the Financial Crisis.* Stanford, CA: Hoover Institution Press.

Termes, R. 1995. "Ethics in Financial Institutions." In *The Ethical Dimension of Financial Institutions and Markets*, edited by A. Argandoña, 118–135. Berlin: Springer Verlag.

Tett, G. 2009. *Fool's Gold. How Unrestrained Greed Corrupted a Dream, Shattered Global Markets and Unleashed a Catastrophe.* London: Little, Brown.

Torres, M. 2009. "Getting Business off Steroids." In *Doing Well and Good: The Human Face of New Capitalism*, edited by J. Friedland, 3–30. Charlotte, NC: Information Age Publishing.

Zamagni, S. 2009. "The Lesson and Warning of a Crisis Foretold: A Political Economy Approach." *International Review of Economics* 56 (3): 315–334.

20

The Moral Benefits of Financial Crises

A Virtue Ethics Perspective

JOHN DOBSON ■

The road to virtue and that to fortune ... are, happily, in most cases very nearly the same.

—ADAM SMITH, *Theory of Moral Sentiments*

INTRODUCTION

An advantage of writing this article in the summer of 2013, and not earlier, is that it is now possible to view the recent global financial crisis (referred to hereafter as simply "the crisis") in a historical context. With stock market indexes returning to their pre-crisis record highs, and banks in several cases recording record profits, it is now safe to declare the crisis officially over (Subramanian 2013). Of course, aftershocks are still being felt, notably in the weaker economies of southern Europe. Also, some casualties of the crisis are probably gone forever, such as the generous provision of subprime mortgages and the widespread acceptance of triple-A ratings on synthetic collateralized debt obligations (Pettis 2013).

Overall, the crisis that began in such dramatic fashion in 2007 can now be seen as one of numerous such crises that have punctuated the history of financial markets and, indeed, of capitalism in general; periodic economic crises are characteristic of all capitalist systems (Ho 2009). Since the Civil War, for example, the US economy has experienced an economic crisis of one sort or another roughly every decade (Bloom 2011). As 20th-century economist Hyman Minsky famously observed, "it is not possible to design a crisis-proof financial system" (in Pettis 2013,8). These crises—albeit all superficially similar in terms of a dramatic decline in the value of financial assets and a corresponding slow-down in aggregate economic activity—have each been unique in certain characteristics, which usually reflect the prevailing influences on the economy at the time. The recent crisis has been characterized by its global nature, reflecting the oft-observed convergence of the major world economies (Subramanian 2013). It is also labeled as a "financial" crisis, reflecting the increasing role that financial institutions play in global economic activity (Khurana and Nohria 2008). A great deal has already been written about the causes and implications of the crisis and, indeed, of economic crises in general, and no doubt a great deal more has yet to be written. This volume, which analyzes the crisis from the perspective of psychology and values, is a reflection of this ongoing interest. This chapter can be categorized as analyzing ethical implications of the crisis. However, I do so strictly through the lens of virtue ethics theory. Why virtue ethics? What additional light, moral or otherwise, can this context shed on the causes and implications of this crisis, or indeed crises in general?

First, recent developments in virtue ethics provide a comprehensive moral construct of the modern corporation, what might be called a "theory of the firm" (Moore and Beadle 2006, Jensen 2001, Coase 1937). Unlike the familiar theory of the firm developed in neoclassical economics, however, this virtue-ethics based theory places morality—or more specifically, moral worth—at the heart of the nature of the firm. Virtue ethicists often refer to this theory as the virtue-practice-institution model, which hereafter I will abbreviate as the VPI model (Moore 2002).

The VPI model envisages all business organizations (abbreviated hereafter as "firms")—whether banks, hedge funds, manufacturers, or healthcare providers—as pursuing two distinct types of goods: external goods (roughly the goods of effectiveness) and internal goods (roughly the goods of excellence). The VPI model is also both descriptive and prescriptive. Firms are, and should be, economic and moral communities in which human flourishing is achieved through the pursuit of external and internal goods. Thus, the VPI model provides a comprehensive view of what the modern firm is and what it should be. This view is inclusive of both the moral worth of the modern firm and its economic worth. (I use the phrase "modern firm" here in line with Roberts [2004], to denote contemporary business organizations operating in global capital markets.)

The prescriptive aspect of the VPI model is not in dispute; all virtue ethicists agree that this is how firms should ideally be (Keat 2008; Moore 2002; MacIntyre 1994). The dispute arises when one turns to the descriptive accuracy of the VPI model. Does this theory depict a feasible reality for modern firms? Here there are two distinct schools of thought. One argues that firms, such as the VPI model describes, may have existed in the past—and may still exist in remote enclaves of the global economy—but that the advance of global capitalism is eviscerating the VPI model as a realistic description of the modern firm. In essence, global capitalism is, according to this school, fundamentally antithetical to the VPI model. As such, global capitalism is—at least from the perspective of virtue ethics—fundamentally immoral and incapable of nurturing human flourishing. The most prominent, though by no means the only, advocate of this school is Alasdair MacIntyre, and so for simplicity I will refer to this school hereafter as the "MacIntyre view." The broad implication of the MacIntyre view is that modern firms, and perhaps particularly financial institutions, cannot be expected to serve societal interests; they must be, at a minimum, tightly supervised and regulated and, ideally, deconstructed into smaller communal enterprises.

But there is an alternative view on the actual viability of the VPI model. This school counters MacIntye by arguing that global capitalism, in the guise of the modern firm, *can* embrace the VPI model. Thus, there is no *fundamental* antipathy between global capitalism and the attainment of human flourishing. This school does not hold that all firms currently manifest the characteristics of the VPI model, but it does hold that some firms do and that they thrive by doing so. Rather than reversing the march of globalization, therefore, this school argues merely for some "fine-tuning." Two adherents to this general view of the viability of the VPI model are Geoff Moore and Russell Keat, and so hereafter for simplicity I will refer to this as the "Moore-Keat view."

Returning to the recent global financial crisis, what are its implications for the VPI model? Specifically, which school of thought does the crisis tend to support? From the perspective of virtue ethics, should the crisis be viewed as stark evidence of the modern firm's inability to generate internal and external goods and, consequently, as evidence of the modern firm's moral impotence? Or is this a too simplistic reading of the implications of the crisis and indeed of economic crises in general?

Here I argue in support of the latter interpretation. I defend the Moore-Keat view and extend it to focus explicitly on the implications of economic crises for the modern firm. I argue that such crises actually assist firms in maintaining the fine balance between the pursuit of external and internal goods, between the goods of effectiveness and the goods of excellence. Furthermore, in the context of banks and other financial institutions, given the esoteric nature of much of their activities, the role of financial crises to maintain the practice-institution balance and reign in "rogue" practices is particularly important.

THE GLOBAL FINANCIAL CRISIS

The opening chapter of this collection provides a detailed overview of the global financial crisis, so I will just supply a cursory review. In particular, I would like to demonstrate how ethics of one sort or other is frequently placed center stage both as a cause and a potential remedy of the financial crises. Indeed, the recent crisis is often invoked as a morality tale in which the vices of greed and avarice corrupted the virtues of modesty and restraint. The implication is thus frequently taken that the financial crisis revealed the "true colors" of financial professionals as dangerously undisciplined—hence the calls for, and imposition of, regulations to rein in these moral excesses (MacIntyre 2013; Bloom 2011). An alternative view is that the crisis was not primarily one of ethics but rather one of economics or politics, or some combination of the two. Supporters of this view frequently point to the relatively rapid recovery once certain economic and regulatory interventions were undertaken. Thus, according to this view, the history of the past five years (2008–2013) actually reflects financial markets that are fundamentally morally sound (Ho 2009).

This ongoing debate over the causes and implications of the crisis is comprehensively and succinctly reflected in Robert Bloom's overview of the findings of the Financial Crisis Inquiry Commission, established by Congress in 2009. Bloom begins with a concise one-sentence summary of the crisis:

The financial crisis can be distilled into the following scenario: Unsound loans were made and then securitized into investments that were improperly rated by the credit rating agencies. Thereafter, these investments "backed" by troubled mortgages were sold to the public. (2011, 6)

Bloom goes on to list eight factors that were identified by the commission as primary causes of the crisis:

1. Enterprise risk management
2. Moral hazard
3. Deregulation
4. Fair valuation
5. Capital maintenance
6. Variable interest entities
7. Credit rating agencies
8. Ethics

He acknowledges that the commission found all these factors played a significant role, but, interestingly in the current context, he notes that of all these factors, "ethics" was viewed as primary: "Reading between the lines in the report, it appears to the author that the following factors [listed above] were underlying causes of the crisis: *above all ethics*" (2011,8, my emphasis).

However, the role of ethics in the crisis and the implications for ethics education to avoid future crises are complex. Some observers have argued that management needs to become a profession:

The financial crisis has raised fundamental issues about corporate regulation, governance and business culture. Our first priority must be to get the financial system moving again. But, longer term, it is essential to restore legitimacy to and trust in the profession and practice of management. (Khurana and Nohria 2008, 1)

Other observers push for educational reform. For example, Giacalone and Wargo argue in their article, "The Roots of the Global Financial Crisis Are in our Business Schools," that the solution lies in more ethics education: "Our studied conviction is that great business leaders must have *character* rather than just *charisma*" (2009, 166). The idea of character formation is something I will return to, but suffice it to note here that the implications of this turn to business ethics education are far from straightforward. For example, Beverungen, Dunne, and Hoedemaekers, in their article "The Financialisation of Business Ethics," argue that the field of business ethics has already been "corrupted" by the globalization of market values. If finance turned to ethics for guidance, therefore, it would merely be turning to a mirror reflection of its own fundamental values. There is no longer any view or perspective from "outside" the values of the market:

We have argued in this paper that neither of these responses (professionalisation of the institution and ethicalisation of the curriculum) directly tackle and confront the fundamental conditions that have allowed the financial crisis to take place. ... The university is presently too deeply entwined with finance to be able to meaningfully deliver upon the promise of business ethics. (2013, 114)

In the above two articles, we can see the essence of the conflict that I analyze here. Although neither article explicitly addresses virtue ethics, both deal with notions of virtue and moral character. Giacalone and Wargo essentially support the Moore-Keat view: the financial crisis revealed moral problems in financial markets that are fixable within the current capitalist structure. Indeed, they conclude with a discussion of character as "foundational to leadership that creates long-term success in organizations. . . . Business schools can go a long way, in our opinion, in inculcating the habit of using these virtues [of character] in making business decisions" (2009, 166).

Contrarily, Beverungen et al.'s essential argument about "financialization" reflects the MacIntyre view. The system itself is in essence corrupt, and any solution will necessitate a fundamental recalibration system-wide:

> It is the very pervasiveness of financialization, across our everyday lives, and across the academy and its curricula, which we have provisionally set out to challenge in the name of business ethics. A challenge to the financial crisis, in the name of business ethics, cannot but consider the ways in which finance conditions [academic] study as a challenging but necessary point of departure. (2013, 114)

In short, the prevailing view of ethics in the financial crisis is negative: a lack of ethics on the part of practitioners caused or at least exacerbated the crisis. In what follows I do not dispute this "conventional wisdom." Rather, I deconstruct it by revealing two distinct value systems at work in the firm: the values of the institution and the values of the practice. Rather than a single moral universe, therefore, the firm actually comprises two universes. To better reveal and analyze these two universes, I now turn to a morally encompassing model of the firm.

THE VPI MODEL

The VPI model is a theory of the firm that encompasses both material and moral dimensions. The material dimension is that supplied by conventional economic theory. The firm is an institution that pursues economic rents. The VPI model broadens this institutional pursuit by using the concept of "external goods." MacIntyre defines external goods as follows:

> It is characteristic of what I have called external goods that when achieved they are always some individual's property or possession. Moreover characteristically they are such that the more someone has of them, the less there is for other people. . . . External goods are therefore characteristically objects of competition in which there must be losers as well as winners. (1985, 190–191)

Economic wealth, prestige, and power are frequently cited as examples of external goods, and these goods are supplied by the institutional foundation of the firm. In the traditional neoclassical theory of the firm, the firm-as-institution, when operating "efficiently," provides a hierarchical structure that minimizes transaction costs and so provides these goods more abundantly than a simple market exchange: the firm is a transaction-cost minimizer (Coase 1937). How efficiently a given firm performs this function bears on the worth of the firm. The VPI model recognizes this material characteristic of the firm as an institution producing external goods and regards it as an essential function. But the VPI model also recognizes an additional dimension of the firm as equally essential; this is the moral dimension as characterized by the firm-as-institution's ability to create and nurture *practices*. As with institutions, practices generate goods, but these goods are termed "internal" goods, in contrast to the "external" goods of institutions. Internal goods are pursued by individuals who perceive themselves as part of a practice. Practices are housed within institutions but are distinguishable from institutions by their acquisition of internal goods over external goods. MacIntyre defines a practice as

> any coherent and complex form of socially established cooperative human activity through which goods internal to that form of activity are realized in the course of trying to achieve those standards of excellence which are appropriate to, and partially definitive of, that form of activity, with the result that human powers to achieve excellence, and human conceptions of the ends and goods involved, are systematically extended. (1985, 187)

In light of this definition we can isolate three central features of practices:

1. Practices establish their own standards of excellence and, indeed, are partly defined by those standards.
2. Practices are teleological, that is, goal directed. Each practice establishes a set of "goods" or ends that is internal or specific to it, and is inextricably connected to engaging in the practice itself. In other words, to be engaging in the practice is to be pursuing these internal goods.
3. Practices are organic. In the course of engaging in the practice, people change it, systematically extending both their own powers to achieve its goods and their conception of what its goods are.

Unlike external goods, which are varied, internal goods are unique to a particular activity. They are the goods of excellence within that activity. They are typically not easy to quantify or define because they are the goods that both define and redefine the practice through time. They extend beyond the collective ego of practitioners; their pursuit necessitates a certain disinterestedness on the part of those engaged in the practice. Internal goods are in essence goods "for their own sake," and they are characterized by their physical intangibility. They are intrinsic satisfactions derived from some activity, and they are traditionally related to the satisfactions derived from productive crafts. Klein, for example, notes,

> the ideal of craftsmanship is to create that which has quality or excellence; personal satisfaction, pride in accomplishment, and a sense of dignity derived from the consequent self-development are the motivations. (1988, 55).

Following the craft analogy, MacIntyre emphasizes the communal nature of internal goods:

> The aim internal to such productive crafts, when they are in good order, is never only to catch fish, or to produce beef or milk, or to build houses. It is to do so in a manner consonant with the excellences of the craft, so that not only is there a good product, but the craftsperson is perfected through and in her or his activity. (1994, 284)

Chytry draws a distinction between the craftwork and the commodity: "What immediately distinguishes the craftwork from the commodity is the former's embeddedness not so much in profit or value-creation motivations as in what used to be celebrated as a 'calling' (*Beruf*) or vocation" (Chytry 2007, 42). This notion of a calling or vocation recognizes the moral dimension of internal goods. Kekes defines internal goods as "satisfactions involved in being and acting according to our conceptions of good lives. ... internal goods are satisfactions involved in the successful exercise of some of our dispositions in the context of a way of life to which we have committed ourselves" (1988, 656). In a similar vein, MacIntyre relates internal goods to the concept of a practice: "Internal goods are indeed the outcome of competition to excel, but it is characteristic of them that their achievement is a good for the whole community who participate in the practice" (1985, 190–191). Thus internal goods, as the motivational force within practices, possess three distinct features:

1. Internal goods are unique to a particular activity. For example, in the context of chess, MacIntyre talks of "those goods specific to chess ... the achievement of a certain highly particular kind of analytical skill, strategic imagination and competitive intensity" (1985, 188). Similarly, Keat notes that "the internal goods of different practices are qualitatively distinct from, and not substitutable for, one another" (2008, 245).
2. Internal goods are not of finite supply. Thus, my achievement of any given internal good of, say, "strategic imagination" in no way inhibits your achievement of similar goods.
3. They are intangible in the sense that they do not readily lend themselves to quantification or enumeration. This may explain why they have been largely ignored by corporate incentive structures.

Within the VPI model, the moral (and economic) health of the firm over time requires a balanced application of virtues. In essence, virtues are desirable character traits exhibited by individuals engaged in sustaining institutions and practices. Many lists of virtues have been supplied, but for our purposes it will suffice to note that some virtues tend to adhere more to institutions and correspondingly to the achievement of external goods, and some more to practices and correspondingly to the achievement of internal goods. Thus, the virtues associated with the above notions of craftwork and following a "calling" will tend to adhere more to practices, for example, perseverance, loyalty, or artistic integrity.

Conversely, virtues such as fairness and trustworthiness will tend to be highly prized in institutions. Hirsch, for example, lists five key institutional virtues: "truth, trust, acceptance, restraint, and obligation" (1978, 141). These are institutional virtues in the sense that they support the practice of maintaining the institution; thus, as with all virtues these facilitate the pursuit of internal goods. But these "institutional virtues" also facilitate the pursuit of external goods. For example, Maitland observes: "Virtues like trustworthiness and fair-dealing may be a source of significant economic benefits to those who possess them" (1997, 25). Of course, all these virtues could be beneficial within institutions and practices; the issue is balance. A healthy firm is one that achieves a balance of these virtues, facilitating the successful pursuit of both internal and external goods through time. This balance invokes additional virtues, such as courage, to resist the temptation to sacrifice internal goods for external goods and vice versa, and discernment, to discern where the ever-evolving frontiers of the practice and the institution lie.

Clearly, in the context of the modern firm, to achieve this balanced application of virtue is a significant challenge. But the normative thrust of the VPI model is that to facilitate human flourishing and so to be morally justified, the modern firm must meet this challenge. I turn now to an evaluation of the two opposing views regarding the feasibility for modern firms of meeting this challenge. Can modern firms, operating in contemporary global capital markets, nurture the virtues of both practices and institutions?

THE MACINTYRE VIEW

The MacIntyre view is that contemporary global capitalism creates firms in which the institutional dimension corrupts and destroys the associated practices. Modern capitalism privileges the pursuit and attainment of external goods to such an extent that internal goods—the goods that can only be pursued through practices—are eviscerated. Thus, the modern firm, in MacIntyre's view, is an "institution" only: the ubiquitous drive for economic efficiency has eclipsed any historical notion of moral excellence.

> Managers themselves, and most writers about management, conceive of them-selves as morally neutral characters whose skills enable them to devise the most efficient means of achieving whatever end is proposed. Whether a given manager is effective or not is on the dominant view, a quite different question from the morality of the ends which his effectiveness serves or fails to serve. (1985, 74)

The proof of this for MacIntyre is that, in contemporary discourse on business, "efficiency" is no longer even recognized as one value among alternatives but rather as the value sine qua non. Conversely, moral excellence is no longer even recognized as an institutional value, and as MacIntyre points out:

> No practices can survive for any length of time unsustained by institutions . . . the tradition of the virtues is at variance with central features of the modern economic order and more especially its individualism, its acquisitiveness, and its elevation of the values of the market to a central social place. (1985, 194 and 254)

Within the MacIntrye view, therefore, the global financial crisis was merely a reflection of the moral vacuity of contemporary globalization. As such, we should expect such excesses of speculation and abuse of trust to continue with increasing rapidity and intensity. The global financial crisis is simply the new normal. It is the inevitable surfacing of a morally bankrupt economic order, characterized by financial institutions populated with traders and others who are entirely devoid of any ability for sound moral judgment. It is a reflection of a system in which virtues, practices, and internal goods are entirely unintelligible constructs: "The practice of the virtues . . . is something difficult to reconcile with functioning well in the present economic order" (2008, 4). To introduce any genuine notion of ethics into business would require a complete from-the-ground-up reconstructing of contemporary corporate culture. In short, from the perspective of the MacIntyre view, the prognosis for global capitalism is dire indeed, and the global financial crisis should be viewed as lending support to this prognosis.

THE MOORE-KEAT VIEW

Fortunately, for those who wish to view financial crises in a more positive light, the MacIntyre view is not the only one. Within virtue ethics there is another view of contemporary business organizations vis-à-vis their moral worth. Many authors have contributed to this alternative view; two who have perhaps articulated it most clearly, at least in the current context, are Geoff Moore and Russell Keat. So for simplicity—but with due deference to other contributors—I name it here the Moore-Keat view.

To begin, both MacIntyre and Moore-Keat agree that—contrary to conventional wisdom among neoclassical economists—market economies are not ethically neutral. Thus, markets are not merely conduits of ethical preferences held in the broader society. Markets themselves possess an implicit moral agenda. Thus, for example, Keat agrees with MacIntyre that "any defence of markets must be (at least partly) an ethical one" (Keat 2008, 251). The divergence between MacIntyre and Moore-Keat arises in identifying the precise nature of this moral agenda. As we have seen, under the MacIntyre view, this influence is corrupting: the institutions of contemporary capitalism, with their pre-occupation with external goods, necessarily crowd out the internal goods of practices. As such, the global financial crisis was a case of capitalism showing its true colors, and it should thus be viewed as a harbinger of worse to come. For MacIntyre, therefore, the future indeed looks bleak, as the institutions of modern capitalism continue their global moral contagion of the last remaining vestiges of practice-based communities.

Within the Moore-Keat view, however, the future need not be so bleak. This optimism rests on two basic premises. First, there are "varieties of capitalism" (Keat 2008, 250) some of which nurture virtue. Second, this nurturing arises from a clearer understanding of the relationship between institutions and practices.

Keat's varieties of capitalism lie on a spectrum between "so-called 'impatient capital' ... generally regarded as a hallmark of Anglo-American economies, by contrast with the 'patient capital' of coordinated market economies" (2008, 250). Keat invokes the contemporary German economy as an exemplar of the latter, in which "industry-wide associations play a central role in promoting cooperation in research and development, and in apprenticeship-based forms of training" (2008, 250). In this regard, Keat faults MacIntyre for focusing exclusively on the "impatient" end of the capitalist spectrum. As evidence of this, Keat cites MacIntyre's famous "fishing crew" comparison, in which the capitalist fishing crew perishes as a result of overfishing engendered by the impatient hunt for short-term profit with no regard for long-term sustainability. Keat counters by observing that some capitalist fishing crews would indeed recognize a longer-term view and so would nurture resources. Not all capitalists are "impatient." Thus the Moore-Keat view begins by recognizing that there are nuances and variations in the contemporary organizational form. Although we often broadly label our system as capitalist, or free market, the actual manifestations of this system at the micro level vary significantly both cross-sectionally and over time. In short, malleability is a defining characteristic of contemporary capitalism. The MacIntyre view largely ignores this, viewing, the modern firm and the modern economy as a one-size-fits-all intellectual structure.

Turning now to the Moore-Keat view's second premise, namely of a more sympathetic relationship between external and internal goods, Keat begins with a clear definition of the contemporary market economy:

> The market might be understood as a complex social institution which includes the contractual exchange of goods for money, private property rights, competition between firms aiming to maximize profits, the use of prices as signals, and so on—all of which are in various ways backed by the powers of the state; and it might then be argued that this institution operates in such a way that "producers" can only succeed in acquiring external goods if they do so in ways that enable "consumers" to acquire what *they* regard as "good." (2008, 248)

Within such market systems Keat sees institutions as playing a more inclusive role in the nurturing of practices. Unlike the MacIntyre view, in which institutions do little more than supply material support for practices, the Moore-Keat view sees institutions as providing an essential moral grounding for practices: "One of the reasons why practices need institutions is that they cannot rely wholly on the virtues, or on other forms of moral constraint not backed by sanctions. . . . one of the essential functions of external goods is to provide sanctions when the virtues fail"(247). So for example Mercedes-Benz Corporation, as institution, will ensure that some young apprentice engineer does not become so obsessed with the intricacies of fuel injection systems that she loses sight of the ultimate goal, namely the instrumental role of fuel injection systems in the broader practice of producing an excellent automobile.

Also, Moore and Keat counter MacIntyre in the latter's separation of the goods of effectiveness from the goods of excellence. For example, Keat recognizes that commodities, such as automobiles, may be goods of effectiveness and that the wages earned and profits made by the producers of said automobiles are external goods. However, Keat also recognizes that these external goods, far from just having the potential to corrupt practices, are actually essential to the attainment of certain internal goods:

> The fact that neo-classical economists talk *merely* about "preferences" does not entail that people's *actual* "preferences" are merely that. . . . although the acquisition of consumer "goods" takes place through exchange*within* the market (or economic) domain, the realization of their value typically takes place in *non*-market (non-economic) domains. . . . So these "commodities," and the money one uses to buy them, provide one with access to the internal goods of practices and their enjoyment. (2008, 248–249)

So, continuing with our example, the production of the automobile provides external goods of money, status, power, and so on. But it also provides internal goods associated with the practice of maintaining the automobile-manufacturing institution. Also, the consumption of the automobile, albeit superficially an external-good market transaction, also facilitates the pursuit of internal goods—such as the goods associated with auto maintenance—and the sustenance of practices such as membership in an owners' touring club and the like.

Specifically, the Moore-Keat view does not rule out the potential for modern firms to create and nurture practices. This view recognizes the undeniable institutional power of these organizations as engines of cash flow but acknowledges that, if correctly structured, these engines can also drive the formation of practices. As such, modern firms are not inherently and irremediably alien to virtue. True, institutions may corrupt practices if the former become too powerful; but there is also a strong symbiotic relation between institutions and practices. Indeed, as discussed, the maintaining and enhancing of the institution can, in and of itself, be viewed as a practice of first importance (Moore and Beadle 2006).

Thus, although Moore and Keat agree that practices require institutions and, consequently, internal goods require external goods, they additionally emphasize that institutions require practices. More specifically, to flourish long-term as producers of economic external goods, institutions need to be linked to non-economic internal-good-pursuing practices. In short, the corporate institutions of modern capitalism cannot survive and flourish without the existence of practices. Sadly, neoclassical economics has largely ignored the practice side of the market equation, and we are undoubtedly indebted to Moore, Keat, and MacIntyre for redressing this omission. Keat argues, therefore, for a more far-reaching invocation of the market-based economy:

> We can conceive of "instituting markets" in large-scale societies as a (possible) collective, ethically-based decision about how to secure the institutional conditions for certain kinds of goods, a decision that would be accompanied by recognizing the need also to secure and protect the existence of *other* domains in which very different kinds of goods are likewise made available to all members of the political community. (2008, 254)

Along similar lines, Moore emphasizes the essential synergy between these two corporate moral universes of external and internal goods:

> The corporation must continually be aware that it is founded on and has as its most important function the sustenance of the practice. This is simply because, without the practice, the institution dies. Thus a retailing organization that is so focused on external goods, such as profit and shareholder value, that it fails to nurture the practice it sustains—the specific business practice of retailing—will eventually find itself without the skills and resources it requires to sustain the practice. It will, in effect, kill itself from the inside. (2002, 28)

In a later article, Moore re-emphasizes this point: "All business activities, irrespective of their form of institutionalization, must contain the vestiges of a practice and the virtues to some degree" (2005, 679). He also revisits an observation first made by MacIntyre concerning the umbilical link between institutions and practices, noting that, as mentioned earlier, purely sustaining the institution can itself be regarded as an important practice: "In other words, those who have, in one sense, outgrown the practice and now represent the institution that houses it also have the same opportunity to exercise the virtues in the making and sustaining of the institution" (2005, 663). Finally, by developing the notion of corporate "character," Moore counters

MacIntyre's argument that managers of institutions become "compartmentalized" into an exclusive focus on external goods and thus limit their exercise of the virtues:

> The corporation of virtuous character, then, will in general require *systems and processes* that ensure the corporation is not "compartmentalised" from other institutions in society but sees itself as one part of a larger whole. Equally, the corporation of virtuous character will need to possess and exercise the virtues of temperance, to withstand the inherent tendency to focus on external goods, and justice in order to weigh its own advantage with that of the wider community. It is also, and most notably, the corporate virtue of temperance that will encourage a *supportive culture.* (2005, 671)

In summary, the Moore-Keat view clearly sets out the argument in favor of the VPI model as not just an ideal but a feasible reality within the milieu of contemporary capitalism. Unlike MacIntyre, they believe that practices not only can survive but indeed must survive if firms are not to "kill themselves from the inside." This symbiotic balance between the institution and the accompanying practices—between the pursuit of internal and external goods—is clearly a finely balance one. Both the MacIntyre and the Moore-Keat views place much emphasis on the potentially corrupting power of institutions—and their concomitant pursuit of external goods—to "swamp" the practices they support. Moore, for example, as the above quotations illustrate, accepts that only "vestiges" of practices might survive in many firms. However, I argue in the next section that in sustaining the internal-good–external-good balance envisaged by the VPI model, the threat works both ways. In fact, the threat is as great if not greater when practices within a given firm can corrupt its institutional foundation. Practices can and do corrupt institutions. The corruption wreaked by practices is more subtle, given the subtle nature of internal goods. But in many ways the corrupting power of practices is more insidious and more threatening to the surrounding economy and society. This is where the disciplinary power of periodic financial crises becomes not only important, but quite possibly essential.

THE ROLE OF FINANCIAL CRISES

In this section I support and extend the Moore-Keat view by examining the implications of financial crises for the VPI model. Recall that the empirical viability of the VPI model requires that, for any given firm, a symbiotic relation between practices and the underlying institution endures through time. Institutions and practices are defined by the pursuit of external and internal goods respectively. The successful pursuit of these goods entails in turn the cultivation of virtues, that is, desirable character traits among all actors (whom we might call stakeholders) who interact to a greater or lesser degree with this nebulous and porous construct—this "legal fiction which serves as a nexus of contracts" (Jensen and Meckling 1976, 241)—called the firm. Note that the successful pursuit of external goods also requires the exercise of virtue because the maintenance of the institution is a practice. MacIntyre observes:

> The making and sustaining of forms of human community—and therefore of institutions—itself has all the characteristics of a practice; and moreover of a

practice which stands in a peculiarly close relationship to the exercise of the virtues ... the ability of a practice to retain its integrity will depend on the way in which the virtues can be and are exercised in sustaining the institutional forms which are the social bearers of the practice. (1985, 194–195)

Given that the survival of the institution is necessary for the survival of any practice, these institutional virtues could be called "primary virtues." In addition there are those virtues that adhere more directly to practices that, though still supported by the institution, are not directly focused on maintaining the institution. These could be termed "secondary virtues." Correspondingly, we can term the practices associated with these virtues as "primary practices" and "secondary practices."

A reasonable question to ask at this stage is why firms would support secondary practices given that, by definition, these practices are not directly concerned with sustaining the institution? The answer is that secondary practices have the potential to provide the dynamic internal goods that sustain the firm through time. Within capitalism, especially contemporary global capitalism, firms must—to use the familiar shark metaphor—keep swimming. Or, as Moore colorfully puts it in the earlier quote, a firm that fails to maintain secondary practices will "kill itself from the inside." Thus both primary and secondary practices are necessary if the firm is to contribute to human flourishing and, indeed, survive long term. As Pettis notes, in the context of banking, "long-term wealth creation accrues most to societies in which the financial system most willingly funds risk-taking entrepreneurs [i.e., secondary practices]" (2013, 8).

Actors in the firm may be involved in both primary and secondary practices to greater or lesser degrees. Senior management will understandably tend to be more directly concerned with the primary virtues. Moore and Beadle observe:

Senior managers—those who have, in one sense, outgrown the [secondary] practice and now represent the institution that houses it—also have the same opportunity to exercise the [primary] virtues in the making and sustaining of the institution. (2006, 373)

Senior management can thus be seen as the "guardians of the flame" in nurturing the primary virtues necessary for the institution to thrive. They also act as gatekeepers in discerning the worth of secondary practices. This is no simple task given that secondary practices are by nature entrepreneurial and experimentally innovative. These secondary practices may foster virtues that are different from—and to some extent—threaten the primary virtues. Actors within the firm cannot exercise all virtues evenly. Thus, to some extent, there will be competition for allegiance between primary and secondary virtues. MacIntyre also observes: "Conceptual conflict is endemic in our situation [of choosing between virtues]. Each of us therefore has to choose with whom we wish to be morally bound and by what ends, rules, and virtues we wish to be guided. ... I must choose between alternative forms of social and moral practice" (1979, 268).

External goods such as power and status, which are typically associated with institutions, would play a role in practices. Social virtues typically associated with practices, such as temperance, courage, and justice, will also be applicable in pursuit of external goods in institutions. Indeed, even the market-based institutions involve much nonmarket social interaction and hierarchy. As Karen Ho observes in her extensive ethnographic study of Wall Street:

Recent anthropological and sociological works ... [demonstrate] that economic practices take place in complex webs of social relations, which change in form and degree over time. Just as "nonmarket" gift exchanges are characterized by a high degree of formal calculation, market economies are more fully embedded in social networks that Polanyi's strict separation allows. ... The "actual practice[s] of economies' defy top-down notions of market: high finance is largely concerned with personalities, private perks and little interest groups, prestige, imagination, almost anything but what might be called a market. (Ho 2009, 32)

Thus, the modern firm is best characterized as a cauldron of market, social, and hierarchical relations. Individuals within a firm continually interact within both institution-like structures and practice-like structures, perhaps even simultaneously. So the notion of a clean separation between the pursuit of external goods versus internal goods and between activity within practices versus within institutions, though intellectually convenient, is illusory.

For firms that survived the financial crisis, we can now see a distinct moral benefit. The financial rigors induced by the crisis forced institutions to examine the moral grounding of the various practices within their purview. All practices, by definition, were pursuing excellence through the applications of certain virtues, but perhaps not all practices were serving the broad moral and economic mandate of the institution. Within the VPI model, therefore, the financial crisis provided a type of moral cleansing. Moore makes a similar observation:

There may, for example, be times when the practice becomes so introverted and self-satisfied that it no longer sets out to achieve "those standards of excellence that are appropriate to, and partially definitive of, that form of activity" ... An important role of those who represent the corporation [i.e., institution], therefore, is to act when they observe excellence not being pursued and to remind those engaged in the practice of their responsibility. This may well be more observable by those who represent the corporation for they will see, in the performance indicators used to measure the achievement of external goods, the failure of the practice to meet "best practice" elsewhere. (2002, 29)

Similarly, as noted in the previous section, Keat recognizes institutions as providing an essential moral grounding for practices: "One of the reasons why practices need institutions is that they cannot rely wholly on the virtues, or on other forms of moral constraint not backed by sanctions. ... One of the essential functions of external goods is to provide sanctions when the virtues fail" (247).

Thus, institutions act as filtering or censuring mechanisms for the limitless array of potential practices and their concomitant internal goods. Institutions provide a "marketplace of morality" (Dunfee 1998), which ensures the nurturing of practices that serve the common good. The power of institutions to censure practices comes from the former's production of wealth and power. Competitive capital markets ensure that power is disseminated broadly through the public ownership of corporations. Of course, we know corporate democracy is far from perfect, but its institutions are clearly more broadly democratic than its practices. As MacIntyre notes, practices are by nature exclusionary and undemocratic in that they represent "a particular type of moral community, one from which fundamental dissent has to be excluded" (1982, 59–60).

To illustrate, let's return to the example of an automobile manufacturer. Cars are clearly commodities, and in the design, production, and sale of cars, many institutional virtues will be applied. But in the design, production, and sale of cars, there are also clearly desirable practices associated with the craft of engineering and manufacture and also with the pure aesthetic of concept and design. A successful car company entails art, craft, and manufacture. These activities are not entirely independent. However, certain virtues will tend to be more prominent—or some aspect of the virtue applied more directly—in practices, and institutional divisions will be linked more directly to one or other activity. So virtues associated with aesthetic appreciation, creativity, and perseverance will be prized in certain activities, while virtues associated with social interaction, justice, and kindness will be more prized in other activities. This is not to say any of these virtues are mutually exclusive to the art, craft, or manufacture of automobiles. However, the emphasis of particular virtues will clearly vary, and if the pursuit of one particular virtue or group of virtues were to become dominant, this development could threaten the fine balance between the maintenance of practices and institutions that forms the foundation of the VPI model. How is this balance to be maintained?

Note that with the VPI model, as with virtue ethics theory in general, there is no absolute set of cardinal virtues or criteria from which to weigh and judge the relative merits of all the virtues at play with our automobile company, whether they be virtues of artistic appreciation, justice, or diligence. Each virtue or group of virtues must be continually weighed and judged from the perspective of other virtues and groups of virtues. This is where financial crises play a critical role.

Financial crises reassert the value of those virtues associated with the firm-as-institution. Thus, such crises force the various practices that the institution supports to be evaluated from the perspective of institutional virtues. For example, our automobile firm may comprise a secondary practice centered round the aesthetic appreciation of various tail-light designs. The virtues of aesthetic appreciation and contemplation may be fully vindicated from within this practice or similar practices, but their "true" significance within the broad spectrum of practice-based and institutional virtues may become apparent only with the renewed scrutiny precipitated by a financial crisis.

In the current context, this scrutiny is not primarily economic. This tail-light design practice may be relatively costless in economic terms. However, if its virtues of aesthetic appreciation and contemplation were to become too highly prized, that could corrupt other practice-based and institutional virtues, thereby destabilizing the fine practice-institution balance that defines the firm.

FINANCIAL CRISES AS ARBITERS BETWEEN PRIMARY AND SECONDARY VIRTUES

When will institutions be most effective at disciplining practices? Institutions will be most effective in this regard when their very survival is threatened—when external goods become hardest to attain, which occurs during financial crises. As discussed, practices provide the dynamic innovative spark for institutions, but spurious practices can equally drain corporate resources and distort institutional virtues. During prosperous economic times, institutions may be willing and able to support a broad array of secondary practices, many of which provide little if any institutional benefit. But during financial crises, this generous state of affairs will dramatically alter. Institutions will be forced to evaluate secondary practices from the perspective of institutional virtues.

This evaluation is not simply an economic filtering of practices. For sure, the economic pressures of a financial crisis will induce managers of institutions to evaluate the extent to which a given practice provides economic benefit. But in addition, and most importantly here, a crisis will induce institutions to evaluate practices from the perspective of institutional virtues. What are institutional virtues?

Many lists of desirable character traits have been supplied in the virtue ethics literature, and some have already been mentioned in this chapter. Often, virtues are differentiated into those that concern primarily care of the self, such as courage and temperance, and those that concern more one's interaction with others, such as generosity and honesty (Kupperman 2009). Most writers on virtue ethics tend to focus on virtues in respect to furthering the ends of practices and resisting the power of institutions. For example, MacIntyre argues that "without justice, courage and truthfulness, practices could not resist the corrupting power of institutions" (1985, 194).

But in addition to those virtues that tend to aid the pursuit of internal goods, there are also those that tend to aid the pursuit of external goods. Institutional virtues are those that aid in the pursuit of external goods and, to a greater or lesser degree, aid the institution in resisting the corrupting powers of practices. As previously mentioned, these market or institutional virtues can be broadly defined as the primary" virtues. They may not, in many instances, be that different from the virtues associated with practices. For example, the virtues of honesty and diligence could be seen as beneficial in the sustenance of institutions and practices. However, the emphasis of the institutional virtues will be more mundane and more universal, reflecting the worldliness and universality of external goods such as wealth and status. These external goods and the associated virtues may not be sufficient to morally justify the VPI model, but they are necessary. Thus, any practice-based virtues that corrupt these institutional virtues are a threat to the entire VPI construct of the firm as a moral entity.

As noted above, within the VPI model, and indeed within virtue ethics theory in general, there is no absolute criterion of moral worth. As such, both practices and institutions can only evaluate their moral worth from the perspective of other practices and institutions that comprise the firm. The economic effects of a financial crisis, therefore, may encourage the firm to evaluate practices from the perspective of the virtues of the institution. In essence, the economic crisis reasserts the moral power of the institution within the practice-institution balance that defines the VPI model. Somewhat paradoxically, therefore, the economic woes of the institution—precipitated by the financial crisis—may actually enhance the moral power of the institution to discipline practices. The crisis can serve to redress an imbalance between the moral power of the institution and that of the practice.

Thus, the recent global financial crisis, by enforcing institutional discipline, induced business organizations to evaluate their multifarious activities, not just economically but also morally. Given their disciplinary effects, periodic financial crises may—given certain conditions—actually be morally beneficial and desirable (Dobson 2014).

IMPLICATIONS FOR FINANCIAL INSTITUTIONS

The sheer size and profitability of financial institutions, not to mention their dramatic growth in recent years, also bears witness to their success as institutions, a success that presumably entails the exercise of primary virtues. Also, despite the excesses that undoubtedly occurred in the use of financial innovations, such as credit default swaps and collateralized debt obligations, these innovations were indeed "innovations" with clear external good benefits in the form of value creation and risk allocation. These innovative activities that characterize financial institutions would also entail the exercise of secondary virtues. The literature on practices typically refers to traditional activities such as farming or fishing, but I see no reason why the activities undertaken by financial institutions—many of which have thrived for centuries—would not also qualify as practices. As Knorr and Bruegger observe in their extensive study of "The Virtual Societies of Financial Markets," much financial innovation involves communal pursuit—albeit not always face to face—with clear standards of excellence and ample evidence of internal goods in the form of "strategic imagination" and "competitive intensity." They observe the following structural characteristics of financial markets:

> The reciprocal interlocking of time dimensions among actors ... conversation structures ... for global transaction and relatedness, the structural use of interaction devices, bodily anchoring, and the grounding of activities in a commerce of knowledge. (Knorr and Bruegger 2002, 944)

Within these diverse and global financial markets, Knorr and Bruegger also observe the exercise of basic primary virtues of trust, obligation, and fairness:

> [Financial traders] manage and sustain a global order—through a variety of means ... which include overtly stating that one is noting someone's misbehavior or asserting the breakoff of the business relationship. ... This deployment occurs in a domain where legal sanctions are almost entirely unavailable and would be considered inefficient by participants. (939)

Indeed, the retrenchment induced by financial crises may be particularly pronounced in financial institutions given the rapid level of innovation. Many secondary practices may not pass muster once their associated secondary virtues are evaluated from the perspective of the primary virtues of the institution. Of course, not every "rogue" practice is identified internally before it harms the institution both morally and financially, but financial crises may assist in bringing these rogues to light before the vicious nature of their practice reaps irremediable harm. The prescriptive implication here is that senior managers of financial institutions should ensure that the secondary virtues of the multifarious and innovative practices are evaluated in terms of the primary virtues of the supportive institution. But managers must not panic during financial crises and retrench too far; secondary practices must still be respected. As Pettis notes:

> The system that delivered the subprime crisis also funded the computing and internet revolutions. The Belgian historian Raymond de Roover once explained that, in the 19th century, "reckless banking, while causing many losses to creditors, speeded up the economic development of the United

States, while sound banking may have retarded the economic development of Canada." (2013, 8)

Thus, as with the *economic* activities of financial institutions, we can characterize their *moral* activities as being "leveraged up" by the esoteric and innovative nature of the business. The secondary practices of financial institutions will tend to be even more secondary than the surrounding economy; think, for example, of the dramatic growth in size and complexity of financial derivatives. As such, their evaluation by the primary practices that directly sustain an institution need to be correspondingly nuanced. Implementing primary virtue structures such as virtue ethics theory-based notions of corporate character (Moore 2006) or professionalism (Kuhman and Nohria 2008) may be particularly wise in financial institutions. Such measures will also ameliorate the disruptive financial-crisis-induced culling of rogue secondary practices. The challenge for senior managers of financial institutions, therefore, is to heed the warnings of a financial crisis vis-à-vis rogue practices. But, in addition, managers must remember that such secondary practices are the lifeblood of a financial institution and indeed of a dynamic economy as a whole.

THE EXAMPLE OF GOLDMAN SACHS

A clear example of this challenge, and of the disciplinary effect of a financial crisis, was supplied recently by Goldman Sachs. In May 2010, as a direct reaction to the financial crisis, chairman and CEO Lloyd Blankfein established the Business Standards Committee (BSC): "the most extensive review of the firm's business standards and practices in the firm's 144 year history" (2013, 3). The committee examined Goldman's diverse activities through six working groups, each with a particular area of focus: client relationships and responsibilities, conflicts of interest, structured products, transparency and disclosure, committee governance, and training and professional development.

In addition to the more prosaic activity of Goldman's self-examination as an institution, several aspects of these working groups' activities can be seen as heightening the evaluation of primary and secondary practices. For example, in the case of *Structured Products* (e.g., the mortgage-backed derivatives I identified earlier as particularly esoteric and thus susceptible to rogue practices), the BSC group "examined how to improve the process for identifying structured products that should be subject to heightened review" (2013, 2). In the case of training and professional development, the respective BSC group "examined how to ensure that our training and professional development ... enhanced our culture" (2013, 2). The use of the word "culture" here, in the context of training and professional development, once again opens up the possibility of evaluating virtues within practices: the very essence of "professionalism" in virtue ethics.

Notions of professionalism are often linked, in virtue ethics, with the idea of pursuing some higher calling: "Good professional roles must be part of a good profession, and a good profession ... is one that involves a commitment to a key human good, a good which plays a crucial role in enabling us to live a humanly flourishing life" (Oakley and Cocking 2001, 74). Typical lists of professional virtues might include "fortitude, temperance, justice, and prudence" (Moore 2005, 676), or "honesty, fairness, trustworthiness, toughness, loyalty, honor, empathy, [and] self-control" (Blackburn and McGhee 2004, 110–111).

It is the successful pursuit and nurturing of these virtues or character traits that define the professional in virtue ethics. So, for example, as Edward Hartman notes, "a group of investment bankers who enjoy working in an atmosphere of trust and cooperation to create a financial instrument that is far riskier than it appears to potential customers is not acting virtuously, whatever internal goods characterize their praxis" (2011, 5). Hartman captures the essence of what I label here as the "rogue practice." Professional judgment and discernment require a broader, all-encompassing appraisal. The mere adherence to some standard of conduct is not sufficient: "There are several negative aspects of using a professional code or standards approach to regulate behavior in business. ... Codes typically have a low degree of precision ... [and] do not provide ironclad guarantees of clarity and transparency" (Blackburn and McGhee 2004, 97–98). This observation is also made by the authors of the BSC report. In addition to the predictable strengthening of Goldman's "Code of Business Conduct and Ethics" (2013, 4), the report recognizes that "while formal processes and rules are very important, they alone cannot substitute for sound judgment and experience" (2013, 5).

Thus the crisis-induced need to rein in rogue practices is readily apparent in the BSC's focus on "heightened review" and "enhanced culture." The overall results of all six working groups' deliberations—over an eight-month period—resulted in the publication of the *Business Standards Committee Impact Report* in January of 2011. The report begins as follows:

> Nearly five years since the onset of the financial crisis, the public continues to ask if anything has changed at large financial institutions to strengthen business standards and practices. Certainly, the financial system is safer and more resilient. ... But, amid these changes, many in the public worry about whether financial institutions have reviewed and made improvements in how they conduct themselves, communicate and manage their responsibilities to their clients and fulfill their obligations to the health of the financial system. (2013,1)

Thus many of the activities of Goldman's BSC can be seen within the broader context of the VPI model as a crisis-induced vetting of secondary practices. Two central characteristics of the ongoing institutional challenge of sustaining healthy practices are reflected in the report, namely, the necessity of the moral evaluation of virtues embedded within practices to *transcend rules*, and the continual evolution of virtues and practices *over time*. In the spirit of the VPI's concept of primary and secondary practices, the report recognizes that "many aspects of our business standards and culture are not easily measured or quantified" (2013, 21). The report also recognizes that "the work underlying the BSC is part of a much larger, ongoing commitment by the firm to be self-aware, to be open to change and to learn the right lessons from recent experiences. Going forward, we know we will inevitably make mistakes, but we commit to learn from them" (2013, 5). So, as with modern firms in general, a financial institution such as Goldman Sachs can be characterized in the VPI schema. Again, senior management can be viewed as the guardians of the flame in terms of maintaining the institution, and as the gatekeepers in terms of vetting secondary practices. This vetting is abetted by crisis-induced activities such as Goldman's self-examination through the BSC report.

CONCLUSION

The recent financial crisis is typically viewed as morally problematic. Indeed, from the perspective of conventional business ethics, financial crises in general are viewed as evidence of moral failure either at the individual level or at the level of capitalism in general—hence the calls for more regulation, more ethics education, or even the overthrow of capitalism itself.

In this chapter, I cast financial crises in a different moral light. I invoke the concept of the business organization as derived from recent developments in virtue ethics theory. Within this theory, morally justifiable business organizations are viewed as combinations of institutions and practices. Both institutions and practices pursue their own distinct kind of moral good by cultivating a distinct balance of virtues. This practice-institution balance requires vigilance by members of business organizations. Too exclusive a focus on cultivating the virtues associated with either practices or institutions could threaten this balance.

I focus here on the potential of practices to corrupt institutions. I argue that financial crises actually serve the morally beneficial role of tempering the corruptive power of practices. Financial crises do this by focusing attention on the value, to the organization as a whole, of those virtues associated primarily with institutions. In short, by placing economic pressure on the institution, crises force institutions to evaluate practices in terms of the institutional virtues. Crises in essence reassert the power of institutional virtues as foundational to the organization's moral worth.

REFERENCES

Beverungen, Armin, Stephen Dunne, and Casper Hoedemaekers. 2013. "The Financial-isation of Business Ethics." *Business Ethics: A European Review* 22 (1): 102–117.

Blackburn, Margaret, and Peter McGhee. 2004. "Talking Virtue: Professionalism in Business and Virtue Ethics." *Global Virtue Ethics Review* 5 (4): 90–122.

Bloom, Robert. 2011. "The Financial Crisis Inquiry Report: Analysis and Commentary." *The CPA Journal.* May: 6–9.

Coase, Robert H. 1937. "The Nature of the Firm." *Economica.* New Series 4: 386–405.

Chytry, Josef. 2007. "Organizational Aesthetics: The Artful Firm and the Aesthetic Moment in Contemporary Business and Management Theory." Working paper, University of California, Berkeley.

Dare, T. 1998. "Virtue Ethics and Legal Ethics." *Victoria University of Wellington Law Review* 28 (1): 18.

Dobson, John. 2014. "Against MacIntyre: The Corrupting Power of Practices." In *Handbook of Virtue Ethics in Business and Management,* edited by Alejo José G. Sison, 128. New York: Springer.

Dunfee, Thomas W. 1998. "The Marketplace of Morality: First Steps Toward a Theory of Moral Choice." *Business Ethics Quarterly* 8 (1): 127–145.

Giacalone, Robert A., and Donald T. Wargo. 2009. "The Roots of the Global Financial Crisis are in Our Business Schools." *Journal of Business Ethics Education* 6: 147–168.

Goldman Sachs. 2013. "Business Standards Committee Impact Report." http://www.goldmansachs.com/a/pgs/bsc/files/GS-BSC-Impact-Report-May-2013-II.pdf.

Graafland. 2009. "Do Markets Crowd Out the Virtues?" *Journal of Business Ethics* 91: 1–19.

Hartman, Edwin M. 2011. "Virtue, Profit, and the Separation Thesis: An Aristotelian View." *Journal of Business Ethics* 99: 5–17.

Hirsch, Fred. 1978. *Social Limits to Growth.* Cambridge, MA: Harvard University Press.

Ho, Karen. 2009. *Liquidated.* Durham NC: Duke University Press.

Jensen, Michael C. 2001. "Value Maximization, Stakeholder Theory, and the Corporate Objective Function." *Social Science Research Network Electronic Paper Collection.*

Jensen, Michael C., and William M. Meckling. 1976. "Theory of the Firm: Managerial Behavior, Agency Costs and Ownership Structure." *Journal of Financial Economics* III: 305–360.

Keat, Russell. 2007. "Ethics, Markets and MacIntyre." Paper for the conference on Alasdair MacIntyre's Revolutionary Aristotelianism, HRSJ Research Institute, London Metropolitan University, June 29–July 1.

Keat, Russell. 2008. "Ethics, Markets, and MacIntyre." *Analysis and Kritic* 30: 243–257.

Kekes, John. 1988. "What Makes Lives Good?" *Philosophy and Phenomenological Research* 48 (4): 655–668.

Khurana, Rakesh, and Nitin Nohria. 2008. "Management Needs to Become a Profession." *Financial Times*, October 20, 12.

Klein, Sherwin. 1988. "Is a Moral Organization Possible?" *Business and Professional Ethics Journal* 7 (1): 55.

Klein, Sherwin. 1998. "Don Quixote and the Problem of Idealism and Realism in Business Ethics." *Business Ethics Quarterly* 8 (1): 43–63.

Knorr, Karin, and Urs Bruegger. 2002. "Global Microstructures: The Virtual Societies of Financial Markets." *American Journal of Sociology* 107 (4): 905–950.

Kupperman, Joel J. 2009. "Virtue in Virtue Ethics." *The Journal of Ethics* 13 (3): 243–255.

MacIntyre, Alasdair. 1977. "Utilitarianism and Cost-Benefit Analysis: An Essay on the Relevance of Moral Philosophy to Bureaucratic Theory." In *Values in the Electric Power Industry*, edited by K. Sayre, 1–15. Notre Dame: University of Notre Dame Press.

MacIntyre, Alasdair. 1979. "Corporate Modernity and Moral Judgment: Are They Mutually Exclusive?" In *Ethics and Problems of the 21st Century*, edited by Kenneth E. Goodpaster and K. M. Sayer, 268. Notre Dame: University of Notre Dame Press.

MacIntyre, Alasdair. 1982. "Why Are the Problems of Business Ethics Insoluble." In *Moral Responsibility and the Professions*, edited by Bernard Baumrin and Benjamin Friedman, 59–60. New York: Haven Publishing.

MacIntyre, Alasdair. 1985. *After Virtue.* 2nd ed. Notre Dame: University of Notre Dame Press.

MacIntyre, Alasdair. 1994. "A Partial Response to My Critics." In *After MacIntyre: Critical Perspectives on the Work of Alasdair MacIntyre*, edited by John Horton and Susan Mendus. 284. Notre Dame: University of Notre Dame Press.

MacIntyre, Alasdair. 1999a. *Dependant Rational Animals.* Illinois: Open Court Publishing.

MacIntyre, Alasdair. 1999b. "Social Structures and Their Threat to Moral Agency." *Philosophy* 74 (289): 311–329.

MacIntyre, Alasdair. 2008. "How Aristotelianism Can Become Revolutionary." *Philosophy of Management* 7 (1): 3–7.

Maitland, Ian. 1997. "The Market as School of the Virtues." *Business Ethics Quarterly* 7 (1): 17–31.

Moore, Geoff. 2002. "On the Implications of the Practice-Institution Distinction: MacIntyre and the Application of Modern Virtue Ethics to Business." *Business Ethics Quarterly* 12 (1): 19–32.

Moore, Geoff. 2005. "Corporate Character: Modern Virtue Ethics and the Virtuous Corporation." *Business Ethics Quarterly* 15 (4): 659–685.

Moore, Geoff. 2007. "Re-imagining the Morality of Management: A Modern Virtue-Ethics Approach." Proceedings of *Alasdair MacIntyre's Revolutionary Aristotelianism*, June 29–July 1. Moore, Geoff, and Ron Beadle. 2006. "In Search of Organizational Virtue in Business." *Organization Studies* 23 (3): 369–389.

Oakley, J., and D. Cocking. 2001. *Virtue Ethics and Professional Roles.* Cambridge: Cambridge University Press.

Pettis, Michael. 2013. "Why the World Needs Reckless Bankers." *Financial Times*, March 26, 8.

Roberts, John. 2004. *The Modern Firm: Organizational Design for Performance and Growth.* Oxford: Oxford University Press.

Smith, Adam. 1937. *Wealth of Nations.* New York: Modern Library. (Originally published in 1776)

Smith, Adam. 1937. *The Theory of Moral Sentiments.* New York: Modern Library. (Originally published in 1759)

Subramanian, Arvind. 2013. "This Is a Golden Age of Global Growth." *Financial Times*, April 8, 9.

PART FIVE

Epilogue

21

Lessons for Future Financial Stability

A Virtue Ethics Perspective

A. G. MALLIARIS, LESLIE SHAW, AND HERSH SHEFRIN ■

I am turned into a sort of machine for observing facts and grinding out conclusions.

—CHARLES DARWIN

The great enemy of truth is very often not the lie—deliberate, contrived and dishonest—but the myth—persistent, persuasive and unrealistic. Too often we hold fast to the clichés of our forebears. We subject all facts to a prefabricated set of interpretations. We enjoy the comfort of opinion without the discomfort of thought.

—JOHN F. KENNEDY

INTRODUCTION

This book is unique because it examines the financial crisis variously through three different lenses—economic, psychological, and philosophical (social values). In this respect, what sets our volume apart is our discussion of considerations that have been overlooked in the debates about the crisis, and how a narrow framing of issues has impacted the social discourse about financial instability. The act of overlooking corresponds to the behavioral pitfall of confirmation bias. In this regard the neglected work of Hyman Minsky provides us with connective tissue linking economic, psychological, and social values. In both the introduction and in several chapters, methodological arguments are presented in favor of such a multidisciplinary approach.

In this last chapter we hope to demonstrate that having chosen multiple perspectives of an already complex topic, our final product brings otherwise disparate elements toward a comprehensive whole. Collectively, the span of contributions in our volume, and the connections among them, provide a fresh perspective on past intellectual contributions together with new insights about how to address the multifaceted issues associated with financial fragility and economic instability.

The 20th-century economist Hyman Minsky offered us the financial instability hypothesis, which had considerable prescience about the underlying drivers of financial instability. Although the global financial crisis came as what had previously been perceived, subjectively, as an unanticipated low probability event, the subsequent surprise brought with it an inherent trauma. But the crisis would not have surprised Minsky. Throughout his career Minsky forcefully argued that Keynes's emphasis on the agency of psychological sentiment within business cycles had been ignored for too long. For example, moods such as pessimism, euphoria, or eventual panic were endogenous psychological states that varied over time with differing perceptions of uncertainty. The intensity of these varying psychological states contributed to the depths of recessions that resulted. While the crisis has led some who ignored Minsky's warnings to revisit his views, we believe that the number of mainstream thinkers who embrace Minsky's perspective remains far too few.

Our volume not only highlights Minsky's perspective but also explores a latent fundamental rationale as to why mainstream thinkers have had difficulty embracing Minsky. We attempt a radical reconsideration of combined factors that contributed to the crisis. We elect to connect market financial instability to the endogenous psychological instability that is inherent in human beings. In turn we associate this psychological instability with the social values fostered and championed by a society. We first review the historical context of economics and psychology in order to construct an intellectual space that will enable readers to assimilate a contemporary understanding of endogenous instability.

ECONOMICS AND PSYCHOLOGY: HISTORY AS PROLOGUE

The academic disciplines of economics and psychology have had a long and varied relationship. Many of the insights that enrich economics today were prefigured as early as the late 18th, the 19th, and early 20th centuries. During these periods, the boundary between psychology and economics was not as sharply defined as it is today.

We believe it is useful here to expand some descriptive breadth and depth to the historical economics-psychology relationship. We hope that an enhancement of this history will provide clues to macroeconomic failures in dealing with Olivier Blanchard's "dark corners" during the history of economics, and to why a process of macroeconomic regression remained sustained for more than a century.

The first stage of the economics-psychology dalliance began when Adam Smith drew on his considerable education in classic literature. It was in Smith's treatise *The Theory of Moral Sentiments* (1759) that he introduced a two-system model for making moral choices. Smith suggested that a man's "passion" drives his instincts to act, while his "impartial spectator" provides moral oversight. And while some economists might wish to claim that Adam Smith introduced a System 1, System 2 approach to reasoning, now famous in Daniel Kahneman's *Thinking: Fast and Slow*, Smith does not have such original ownership. Distinctions have been proposed between two systems of reasoning for centuries—at least since Plato's "oligarchical psyche," which delineates two psychic parts: a ruling part and a ruled. Since then, by whatever name throughout the centuries, the metaphorical System 1 has always been basically associative, while System 2—whatever it be named—has always been the basically rule based. Most importantly, the rule-based system can suppress the associative, but it can never completely inhibit it.

Nevertheless, with the advent of Smith's writings, first in *Moral Sentiments*, and then in *Wealth of Nations*, the first stage of economics-psychology was begun. In subsequent years, the concept of time discounting was explained in terms of what psychologists now label "motivational effects"; these refer to emotional and/or hedonic influences on behavior. During the second stage, near the end of the 19th century, intertemporal choice came to be viewed more in cognitive terms, as a tradeoff between present and future satisfaction.

Remarkably, a third stage in this history then unfolded, with economists seeking to eliminate formal psychological concepts completely from their frameworks. In this respect, many economists were dismayed over new developments in psychology that were not amenable to interpretation as utility maximization. The new development that caused such antagonism from economists was Freud's theory of unconscious motivation, published in 1900 as *The Interpretation of Dreams*. In this book Freud put forth the possibility of a "motivated irrationality," which contrasts with the classical philosophical view of Socrates. The economics profession refused to engage with the idea that people are, at their core, irrational.

Despite early 20th-century economists having marked out a stance that excluded the central issues being emphasized by psychologists such as Freud, many economists nevertheless did include important psychological features in their work. Notable in this regard was Irving Fisher (1930), who emphasized the importance of what he believed to be psychological weaknesses such as imperfect self-control and imperfect foresight. Particularly, he proposed a discounting model to describe choices involving a tradeoff between present and future satisfaction.

In an interesting twist, the framework that Fisher had used to capture psychological features, such as imperfect self-control and imperfect foresight, was reinterpreted as a model of rational choice. Or to put it in somewhat starker terms, despite rejecting Freud's notion of motivated irrationality, economists nevertheless reinterpreted some irrational behaviors as being rational. Economists were willing to model imperfect behavior, as long as that behavior was consistent with an optimization process.

John Maynard Keynes, arguably the most influential macroeconomist of the first half of the 20th century, explicitly acknowledged the role of psychology in his writings. His best known work, *The General Theory of Employment, Interest, and Money*, was published in 1936 and made many references to the same concepts that are prevalent in modern-day behavioral economics.

Keynes emphasized that economic agents are vulnerable to the influences of "optimism" and "confidence." He argued that financial market equilibria reflect "sentiment." He dismissed the idea that financial managers make capital budgeting decisions by using net present-value methodology based on discounted expected cash flows. In this regard, he argued that present-value methodology involves complexities which managers are ill equipped to handle. Indeed, throughout his career, Keynes's work stressed the concept of uncertainty over risk, meaning that when people make decisions, most do so without having precise probabilities in mind. In today's behavioral terminology of System 1 (intuition) and System 2 (deliberate thought), we might say that Keynes was arguing that the managerial System 2 is inadequate to the overall governance task, and that people therefore rely, often unknowingly, on System 1.

As it happens, Keynes had read a considerable amount of Freud, despite the economics profession's longstanding rejection of Freud's pioneering ideas on individual psychology. There is no evidence that Keynes and Freud ever met, although Keynes was very active in the late 1920s and early 1930s with the Bloomsbury Group. This was an influential group of English writers, intellectuals, philosophers, and artists, many of whom lived in the district of West London known as Bloomsbury. Among them were Virginia Woolf, EM Forster, Lytton Strachey, and others. Psychoanalysis was included in the intellectual discussions of the time. Virginia Woolf and her husband had founded Hogarth Press in 1917, which later published the English translations of Freud. James Strachey, brother to Lytton, was executive editor of the translations. Further, by the time Keynes published his *General Theory* (1936), he differed from classical economics by stressing the crucial role of a phenomenon that for Keynes was like an entrepreneurial psychology within market institutions. He conceived of it with the term of animating or "animal spirits." And his use of the term had a resemblance to the notion of the Freudian unconscious.

Economist Roger Koppl (1991) believes that Keynes borrowed the term "animal spirits" from Descartes's "Passions of the Soul" (1649) in which Descartes's theory of the pineal gland explained how people can act contrary to their own best judgment. In 1936, Keynes chose to explain "animal spirits" as a spontaneous urge to action. He believed that because of "animal spirits" it was wrong for classical economics to treat markets as self-correcting. Nobel laureate economists George Akerlof and Robert Shiller (2009) chose *Animal Spirits* for the title of a recent book in which they clarified the original use of the term. They write that in its ancient and medieval Latin form "spiritus animalis," the word *animal* means "of the mind" or "animating." Akerlof and Shiller emphasize that Keynes's use of "animal spirits" refers to a basic mental energy, a non-economic motive that is an endogenous life force. These two authors believe that Keynes's animal spirits are "*the keynote* to a different view of the economy," a view "that explains the underlying instabilities of capitalism" (Akerlof and Shiller 2009).

In addition to his animal spirits, Keynes had also continued to introduce new, important, and more typical psychological concepts throughout his work. These included the propensity to consume, the marginal efficiency of capital, the motives for the demand of money, and the "beauty-contest" paradigm of financial market equilibrium. Unfortunately however, following the publication of *The General Theory*, Keynes's followers rooted out almost all of the animal spirits, the non-economic motives and irrational behaviors that were the heart of Keynes's explanation for the Great Depression. Keynes's professional followers left just enough animal spirits to yield a least-common-denominator theory that minimized the intellectual distance between *The General Theory* and the fundamental classical economics of the day. Economists returned to a classical view where people act only for economic motives and they act only rationally. Consider the words of Hyman Minsky (1982), quoted by Akerlof and Shiller: "The reconstructed Keynesian theory was reduced to 'banality' in that it 'does not allow for disruptive internal dynamic processes.'" One almost senses an economics déjà vu with these classical economists. The earlier, more rigid view rejected Keynes's animal spirits, after 1936, in the same way they had rejected the motivated irrationality of Freud, after 1900. And Keynes's "animal spirits" were basically inferring a non-economic motivation that would have been perceived, at the time, as a motivated irrationality. Today's behavioral economists should view the eventual rejection of animal spirits as a regression to the mean in the productive work of classical economics at the time. Economists returned to their comfort level, circa 1900. Contemporary psychoanalytic thinkers would say that the economists' regression to their own mean, after 1936, was also uncanny (Freud 1919). Something that was intellectually unsettling to the economics profession had once again come in to a theoretical light, and it was eerily disturbing to them. They ignored its consideration, in the same way they had in 1900. Lone publications discussing the relevance of experiments to finance appeared intermittently, such as Burrell (1951) and Markowitz (1952), but gained no traction at the time. However, Markowitz's contribution did exert a major influence on Kahneman and Tversky's development of prospect theory, discussed below.

The fourth stage of the integrative evolution between psychology and economics did not commence until the 1960s as psychologists began to investigate how people make choices involving risk. The names of Daniel Kahneman and the late Amos Tversky are the best known of this group, though there were many contributors. It was the arrival of computer technology at this time that made the study of judgment and choice more exacting than it had previously been. An evolving army of experimental psychologists produced a vast catalogue of cognitive heuristics and biases, along with its own dual systems theory of mental processing, which Daniel Kahneman articulated so well. Perhaps the most significant feature of this literature is that it demonstrated that human economic behavior could not be described in terms of an optimization framework. Therefore, human imperfections could not be accommodated within the rational paradigm, as had earlier been theorized with Irving Fisher's framework.

During the 1970s, a small group of economists began to reintroduce academic psychology into formal economic frameworks. Hersh Shefrin and Richard Thaler did so in their "economic theory of self-control," which proposed a formal two-system model of intertemporal choice. Amazingly, in 1972, psychologist Paul Slovic, one of the foremost contributors to the heuristics and biases approach, wrote a prescient article in the *Journal of Finance*. Slovic recognized the implications which the emerging literature on heuristics and biases would have for finance. Economists were slow to develop the trend that Slovic identified. However, they eventually did so, with behavioral finance coming into existence as a subfield during the 1980s.

The first behavioral finance session took place at the American Finance Association in 1984, and was organized by Hersh Shefrin and Meir Statman. At this time, in addition to the established heuristics and biases literature, behavioral research emphasized the application of Kahneman and Tversky's prospect theory (1979), with "loss-aversion" as one of its core concepts.

In his book, *Thinking Fast and Slow* (2011), Kahneman says that prospect theory was "the most significant work" that the Kahneman and Tverky team ever did. They modified expected utility theory using an approach from a field of psychology called psychophysics. The approach had been founded and named by a German psychologist and mystic, Gustav Fechner (1801–1887). According to Kahneman, Fechner was obsessed with the relation of mind and matter. On one side there is a physical quantity that can vary, such as energy of light or frequency of tone. On the other side there is a subjective experience of brightness, pitch, or value. Mysteriously, variations of the physical quantity cause variations in the "intensity" or quality of subjective experience. Fechner's project was to find the psychophysical laws that relate the subjective quantity in the observer's mind to the objective quantity in the physical world. Kahneman and Tversky applied variations in quantities of money and studied subjective reactions to gains and losses.

It was likely a consequence of prospect theory, in part as the 1980s unfolded, that many researchers began to have growing concerns that deviations from a presumed standard principle of rationality should not be the only phenomenon requiring explanation. New approaches began to be considered in behavioral decision making (see Beach and Mitchell 1987, Lopes 1987, Hastie 1991, and Tetlock 1991).

At the turn of the 21st century, behavioral psychologists associated with the heuristics and biases approach were moving to incorporate studies that involved the role of emotion (see Lopes, this volume). This was a research advance beyond the sole reliance on cognitive processes. Therefore, it became natural for economists to follow suit. Behavioral economists also began to rely on insights from psychologists such as Gerd Gigerenzer who emphasize fast and frugal heuristics, an approach related to but distinct from the heuristics and biases approach. This "fast" approach was popularized in Malcom Gladwell's book *Blink: The Power of Thinking Without Thinking* (2005). In addition, behavioral economists have taken their own approach to how issues of cheating and trust impact economic phenomena (Ariely 2012).

In spite of this extraordinary progress and innovative integration of cognitive psychology with economics, it remains rare, at best, more than 100 years since Freud, for economists of any stripe to cite the formally rejected psychodynamic psychology that began with Freud and caused the palpable split between the disciplines. Yet recently there have been indirect allusions, such as Akerlof and Shiller's book *Animal Spirits* (2009), described above. A subsequent book by Akerlof and Rachel Kranton titled *Identity Economics* (2010) has moved in the direction of intimating a more recent genre of psychodynamic understanding. Psychodynamic theorizing specifically focused on identity of "the self" includes theoretical concepts that have evolved with breadth and depth since Freud. Such concepts are among the many advances that have happened since Freud and they have productively moved beyond him. Although Akerlof and Kranton write as economists and employ economic methods, they attempt to utilize subjective experience of self and the role of self in making one's own choices for economic well-being. Even more important is that this work offers a link between the endogenous lens of self-subjectivity and the potential construction of that internal subjective self via its interaction with an outside social process. John Riker, in this volume, makes superb use of contemporary psychodynamic self-psychology. He shows its potential value for policy construction to contradict problems of human vulnerabilities that result in a destabilized economy.

A third contemporary allusion to psychoanalytic thinking and financial economics comes from the research team of Richard Taffler (2008), a finance professor at Warwick Business School, and David Tuckett, psychoanalytic researcher at University College London (2011) They essentially draw on one of several British views of object relations and theorize about investments and the professional money management world as dealing with "phantastic" objects. Taffler and Tuckett report findings from in-depth interviews with 50 fund managers around the world. These researchers see conventional risk models as providing pseudo defenses against uncertainty. Among their arguments is that the research tool of statistical regressions on historical data relationships can lull individuals into believing they know more about the future than is possible. This over-optimism regarding the future or overconfidence about ability to control for uncertainty facilitates fund managers in psychic splitting, enabling them to focus on potential gains since they feel as if they have already managed risks. This interpretation of unconscious processing is consistent with Kahneman and Lovallo's (1993) finding that the mere investigation of uncertainty can lead to an illusion of control and an under-appreciation of risk.

At a broad level, over time, any academic knowledge moves forward by means of the adversarial technique. Different schools of thought develop, often in opposition, and the members of those schools engage each other in confrontations that can be long lasting. Among psychologists, one school of thought promoted the idea that behavior was cognitively driven, with emotions essentially being a side show. This persuasion has tended to deal with "beliefs." An opposing group argued that emotions were the main drivers of behavior. The psychodynamic nomenclature within this view has been about wishes and desires. Even among psychologists studying bounded rationality exclusively, one group argued that heuristics were to be viewed as deviations from rational behavior, while another group argued that heuristics are ecologically rational responses to underlying decision environments (Gigerenzer et al. 1991).

Given that psychologists do not agree among themselves, it should come as no surprise that the relationship between psychology and economics has exhibited so much flux. Moreover, academics are human and subject to the same biases that they study in others. Confirmation bias and availability bias are strong. Academics belonging to a particular school of thought are reluctant to accept evidence that runs counter to the ideas they represent. They are also prone to excessive reliance on recent literature because it is readily available. In this respect, the concept of "hidden factors," which is the main theme of this volume, has its roots in the psychology under discussion.

Consider, as example, the writings of Clark Glymour (1991). Glymour is emeritus professor of philosophy at Carnegie Mellon University, and also senior research scientist at the Florida Institute for Human and Machine Cognition. He has written extensively on Freud, and he makes the argument that many basic ideas of contemporary cognitive science actually emerged in the late 19th century, in what is very close to their present form. The 19th-century work came from a special coterie of prominent neuropsychologists and neurophysiologists: Hermann von Helmholtz, Theodor Meynert, Ernest Brucke, and others, one of whom was Freud. At the time Freud was in fact a spokesman for this movement. Yet Freud's earliest and most significant work, *The Project for a Scientific Psychology* (1895), was not published until years after his death. Consequently, the work has remained unread by most academic psychologists, or anyone else.

Glymour reasons that Freud's *Project* is his clearest and bravest attempt at a physiology of the mind. The most striking difference between the *Project* and contemporary cognitive science is that today we possess the computer and the computational pictures of how the mind works that the computer has provoked. In the same manner as many contemporary cognitivists, Freud held the brain to be a machine, although he did not use that word. Freud's model was a collection of neurons joined together at synapses like the vertices of a graph. He held the computations of the system to be governed by quasi-thermodynamic principles and in particular by the principle that the system seeks the lowest energy state and that learning takes place by facilitation.

The nervous system in Freud's *Project* is roughly this: The nerve cells are connected at synaptic junctions; they pass something among them which changes their physical energy state. Denote this "something" as "Q" for quantity. There are two ways in which Q might increase in the nervous system: through stimuli from the external world, and through "internal stimuli" from the cells of the body, which is to say through the internal chemical mechanisms of the instincts. The amount of this quantity in the nervous system is not constant but can be increased or decreased by both internal and external causes. As Freud conceives the system it behaves like any other physical system; it tends to the lowest possible energy states, and the state transitions have a psychological correlate. Increase in energy or Q is painful; decrease is pleasurable. The organism is so structured that it reacts automatically to avoid the increase of Q from external stimuli by automatic motions, or reflexes. But reflex motions cannot avoid Q from sources that are internal to the person. To shut off internal sources requires rather definite physical situations, and the motion of the organism must therefore be directed toward realizing them. The hungry baby, for example, must find the mother's breast. A kind of computational process in which energy is stored in nerve cells temporarily carries out such motions. That store of energy constitutes thought and desire and planning, and the nervous system tolerates it only because it leads, in the long run, to lower internal excitation than would otherwise occur (Glymour 1991).

Philosopher and Freud scholar Jonathan Lear (2000) enhances our understanding. The singular function of the various neural networks that comprise the mental mechanism is to discharge or diffuse stimuli. Each "neurone" is capable of receiving and storing energy, though the basic tendency is toward discharge. One set of neural networks allows for free flow of energy through the system. This accounts for loose associations of ideas, found in dreams or symptoms. The energy in this system is fairly "mobile," and its flow through neuronal pathways tends to dominate the system. A second, more complex network accounts for the tighter, more reality-based conscious thinking. For this reality-based thinking to succeed, it is necessary that it further contain the free flow of energy. The mind does this by forming complex connections among neurones which not only connect ideas in complicated connections but also, from an economic point of view, tend to diffuse energy across the system. The energy becomes bound in the system. Thus thinking directed toward reality-based action—real-life satisfaction of needs and desires—can occur. At this level of generality the difference between mind functioning at the level of pleasure principle and level of reality principle is minimal. In both cases mind is working toward discharge of energy, though more circuitously at the level of reality principle (Lear 2000).

This "pleasure principle" regarding energy is Freud's computational model, and it is fundamentally an economic viewpoint. It is all about the movement of capital; with capital, in this case, being internal quantities of energy. We emphasize here that the model is clearly one of optimization, albeit flow-of-energy internal optimization. Freud was interested in the mind's optimal stability as a coordinated response of the mind, to any situation that would tend to disturb its normal condition. It was the nature of mind to process or metabolize stimulation from the outside or from the internal chemical mechanisms of the subjective world and essentially to maintain an overall endogenous stability (Lear 2000).

The reality of the *Project* and its pleasure principle existed in 1895. Freud wanted to invent a "science of the mind," but the Victorian tools of the time were not up to the task. He had to abandon the *Project* because it was too bold for 1895. And though the *Project* was not found until the 1950s, then posthumously published, it remains one of Freud's most significant works. It is of interest then to learn that Freud had used the equivalent theoretical approach to his pleasure principle that Kahneman and Tversky used, 94 years later, as an origin of their thinking for prospect theory. Freud's pleasure principle drew from the same psychophysical work of Gustav Fechner, as Kahneman (2011) describes. These different psychological thinkers, 94 years apart, were each relating sensation to the logarithm of intensity (Stigler 1999). But Freud was interested in internal biological stimuli whereas Fechner had considered only independent variables of intensity that were exogenous to the person.

Jonathan Lear emphasizes that early Freud variously treated an emotion as quantity, discharge, or subjective experience of discharge of energy.

> His early theory of emotions does not allow Freud to conceive of emotions as providing a framework through which the world is viewed. Nor can he conceive emotions, at that early time, as constituted by beliefs, attitudes, justifications, and motivations that help to orient the person to the world. Yet within his medical practice Freud is constantly relying on these same features of emotions to make his diagnoses of patients; however, he omits these very same features from his theory of the emotions. Why?
>
> The value of treating an emotion as being a quantity of energy, the discharge of that quantity, or subjective appreciation of that discharge is that it holds open the possibility of explaining mental life in quantitative terms. And a quantitative treatment conforms to Freud's scientific image of himself. The quantitative treatment allows him to believe he is providing a third-person mechanistic explanation of the phenomena of emotion. The cost of a quantitative treatment, though, is that it prevents Freud from seeing that what is at issue is an emotional (subjective) orientation to the world. (Lear 1990)

It is not until the end of World War I that Freud begins to realize that with the pleasure principle he is self-consciously in over his head. He knows he is in the midst of profound issues. What brings him here is the traumatic neuroses of the war, today's PTSD. These awful traumatic dreams are astonishing for Freud. He cannot account for them in terms of the pleasure principle. The trauma of the traumatic was now a trauma for psychoanalysis. Prior to 1920, Freud had seen that the ability to sustain a certain level of anxiety was not so much a feeling as a psychological capacity to be in a state of readiness in living. The ability to be reflective about the space of anxiety that exists within living is an individual psychological achievement. But "fright" is when the world itself or subjective experience becomes so overwhelming that we are flooded with the stimulation to the point that something breaks. If you do not have a fuse or a circuit breaker the system blows. The capacity to make meaning becomes temporarily disrupted. This is because the bound or inhibited psychic energy that is used by secondary process to establish meaning has been completely overwhelmed (Lear 2000).

It is with this apprehension of meaning regarding inordinate or excessive subjective experience that we return to our discussion of Hyman Minsky and the contributions of this volume.

HYMAN MINSKY AND FUNDAMENTAL ISSUES

The extreme trauma of the financial crisis is, of course, the nature of a tail event. Our volume contains three interconnected chapters dedicated to tail events. The first, by Nassim Taleb and Raphael Douady, not only warns of black swan events, but also asks us to consider what makes some systems fragile and other systems anti-fragile. The second, by Lola Lopes, develops an approach to the psychology of risk that emphasizes the importance of how we view tail events emotionally, of which Taleb's black swans are special cases. The emotions upon which Lopes focuses are fear, hope, and the anxiety attached to the risk of failing to achieve aspirations. While fear leads people to overemphasize left-tail events, hope and aspiration can offset this emphasis by shifting attention to right-tail events. The third chapter, by Graciela Chichilnisky, develops an axiomatic framework and associated theorems that formalize how these emotions can be incorporated into a value function.

Minsky's ideas provide the connective tissue for our volume. The chapter contributions by all three editors address his work. The chapter by Janet Yellen, now chair of the Federal Reserve System, describes the lessons Minsky offers for central bankers. The chapter by Steve Keen provides a formal nonlinear model emphasizing the implications of excessive leverage, one of Minsky's main concerns. Keen's model demonstrates that excessive leverage can lead an economy to experience tranquility for long periods, but then suddenly become unstable. This chapter addresses the frequent criticism of Minsky for not providing a credible mathematical model that captured his ideas. Moreover, as we noted in the Introduction, Olivier Blanchard at the IMF emphasizes that for too long, mainstream macroeconomists relied on linear models, which predisposed them to ignore the "dark corners" in the parameter space of nonlinear models that are associated with instability. Keen's model is an example of a nonlinear framework, which mainstream macroeconomists long overlooked.

The central questions addressed in this volume pertain to what was missed and what we need to learn from the global financial crisis of 2007–2009. By all accounts, the trigger event that converted a serious downturn into full-blown instability and crisis was the Lehman Brothers bankruptcy on September 15, 2008. As a consequence, financial markets froze in the sense that market liquidity was significantly reduced, buyers were not willing to buy unless prices were drastically reduced, and sellers who were forced to sell at very low fire-sale prices encountered serious losses.

All these rapidly evolving market developments led to a severe impairment of financial intermediation. Succinctly stated, financial panics create such intense uncertainty that distinct financial products and services cannot be traded. This market failure in the financial sector rapidly infects the real economy, because business lending for new investments is drastically reduced and unemployment consequently increases. It is an intensity of uncertainty such that the system just breaks. Wells Fargo economist John Silvia reflects in this volume on a pre-crisis overconfidence bias in the ability of fiscal and monetary policy to restore economic growth. He shows the subsequent risk aversion in the labor market that remains stalled at the time of this writing.

We have already stated that Minsky (1982) essentially believed that financial intermediation became impaired because the New Classical critics of Keynes, that emerged in the 1970s, did "not allow for disruptive internal dynamic processes." And recently, George Akerlof (2007) in "The Missing Motivation in Macroeconomics" writes a thorough analysis of the New Classical fundamentalism and its constructed methodology. The New Classical approach undermined Keynesian conclusions about the behavior of the economy and the impact of stabilization as an economic policy. Akerlof analyzes how the new research program had not been sufficiently attentive to the role of human intent in choices. The new anti-Keynes program also failed to appreciate the extent to which Keynesian views were reflective of reality because these views had been based, additionally, on experience and observation. The issue of how impairment of intermediation generated panic is where psychology and psychoanalysis are important and why the contribution of each is a purpose of this volume, such that capable intermediation can potentially restrict panic.

Four additional papers from psychology offer unique contributions that relate to behavior as basically derived from structural systems within financial markets. These include Kolb on the myriad varieties of incentive experience that are opaque to any risk measurement. Dalko et al. look at information-based manipulation in the stock market, its potential for systemic risk that could threaten the entire market. Harrington is interested in the structures of incentives, sanctions, and networks within a global financialized economy. She shows how structure more than individual ethical lapse is an important reason why opportunities and rewards for financial fraud have increased. And Werner De Bondt decries the absence of structural integrity anywhere within the global financial system.

Finally the scholars who write in this book about values all agree that at its roots, the crisis is an ethical crisis. These include studies about psychology and ethics: Boatright on the failure of risk management, Riker on self-psychology, and Statman on the internal and external obstacles of finance professionals in relating to culture and rules of fairness that are held by the general public. John Dobson analyzes the moral implications of financial crises via the external goods of the firm as institution and the internal goods of the firm as a collection-of-practices. Argandona agrees with De Bondt on a crisis of leadership, but he reviews ethical and anthropological assumptions that, in his analysis, have failed the economic and social model of financial institutions. Finally, Paul Fitzgerald reflects on moral failures of individuals through the lens of the Catholic social doctrine.

The centrality of our insights emerges from a detailed analysis of Minsky's financial instability hypothesis. Minsky contradicts the traditional economic paradigm of macroeconomic stability that is achieved via monetary and fiscal policies and driven by the rationality of economic agents and the efficiency of the markets. Minsky advocates instead that financial instability is the foremost characteristic of a capitalist market economy. Recall again that Akerlof and Shiller believe that Keynes's animal spirits "are the keynote to a view of the economy that explains the underlying instabilities of capitalism." We transition to our conclusion with this clearly expressed social apprehension about the dark side of market capitalism from philosopher and psychologist Stephen Frosh:

It is a social order premised on individualism. The society that works in this way hides its power by holding out the promise of individual autonomy to subjects; but behind this lurks an uncanny sensation that something is being denied. Despite appearances, each subject knows that it is not really whole, that this seeming-self of identity is a cover for a disturbing dis-integrative pulsation. This produces a paranoid sensation, which it might be argued is one of the characteristics of the triumph of capitalism; arising from the sense of being promised something that is always about to be taken away. (Frosh 2010)

MAIN CONCLUSIONS

What modern economists historically overlooked in the perspectives of Keynes and Minsky is their emphasis on the importance of nonrational behavior. At the same time, academic psychologists neglected a contribution from Freud that was significant for cognitive psychology and prefigures the recent development of neuro-economics. Freud's work attended to people's ability to metabolize stimuli that was internal to them, not just external. Conceptually, Keynes's animal spirits feature a strong internal component. For example, aspirations, a topic discussed by several authors in this volume, have a significant component that is internal to the person.

Economists and academic psychologists have made great strides in advancing knowledge over the past century. At the same time, academic discourse tends to be deep but narrow, a consequence of the need to specialize in order to produce groundbreaking work. This narrow focus comes at a cost, namely, the overlooking of important ideas. In combination with susceptibility to confirmation bias, economists, and psychologists have overlooked critical insights articulated by Minsky, Keynes, and Freud, all of which left them unprepared to understand, appreciate, and anticipate the events of the global financial crisis.

As was discussed earlier in this chapter, Freud was the leading psychologist during the first half of the 20th century, and there is a connectivity chain from Freud to the Bloomsbury Group, a multidisciplinary intellectual community if ever there was one, to Keynes, whose *General Theory* is replete with references to psychology. In this regard, the emphasis Keynes places on the influence of psychology on economics is not on therapeutic issues for which Freud's reputation is mostly associated, but on Freud's more fundamental ideas about how people make judgments and choices. Of course, it was the manner in which psychology influences how people make *economic* judgments and choices that most interested Keynes, and Minsky built on Keynes's perspective about the role of emotions and biases in driving economic booms and busts, as well as the values issues associated with unemployment and income disparities.

Although it was Freud's ideas about judgment and choice, rather than therapy, which were at the heart of the thought chain just described, Minsky certainly recommended specific public policy reforms. In making his recommendations, he accepted that free societies cannot prevent people from becoming euphoric during booms, and that as a result, financial fragility and economic instability can only be mitigated, not avoided. That said, his recommendations concerning fiscal policy, central bank regulation of speculative and Ponzi finance activity, government employment programs, and policies for dealing with firms that have become too big to fail can be characterized as therapeutic, if not psychoanalytic.

Thus, three main conclusions emerge from the consideration of the financial crisis as a major catastrophe that was produced by systemic instabilities in financial markets related to the minds of economic agents and their values.

First, for the foreseeable future it appears that the probability of eliminating financial crises is very low. Minsky certainly held that view, and the large variety and frequency of financial crises documented by Reinhart and Rogoff support his view. Before the crisis, most of the world ignored what Minsky said. In the wake of the financial crisis, he has gotten more attention, but the whole world has hardly beaten a path to his door. Even many of those who claim to support his views are Minsky-*lite*. This is evidence about the gulf between awareness and behavioral change that is pertinent to the main issue we are tackling.

Second, logically and mathematically, the region of stability in large-scale models is often narrow. There are many dark corners. Given individual and group psychology and society's values, self-regulation in markets will not alone produce the desired stability. Thus, some regulation is needed, not to prevent instability, which might well be impossible, but to limit its cost when instability erupts. Successful regulation must be considered across several systems: financial, economic, psychological, and philosophical. We mention these since they are the ones we have studied.

Should economists take animal spirits seriously? "Yes" is the third conclusion of the analysis in this book. Notably, it would not mean giving up on economic theory. Behavioral economists, after all, have been getting at the reality of animal spirits with a broadening of research in recent years. The acceptance of our spirits should mean finding limits to the application of standard rational choice models, as refined in neoclassical economics, after 1936. Minsky wanted us to better cope with euphoria during good times and its inevitable evaporation during a bust. And though this book does not propose a perfect solution, we encourage a new multiple system or large-scale system of interdisciplinary approach. As psychologists claim, the gift of a crisis is similar to the gift of grief. After personal pain, economic loss, and slippage in societal values, a new appreciation of incompleteness emerges that will hopefully bring us to new possibilities.

REFERENCES

Akerlof, G. 2007. "The Missing Motivation in Macroeconomics." *American Economic Review* 97: 5–36.

Akerlof, G., and R. Kranton. 2010. *Identity Economics: How Our Identities Shape Our Work, Wages and Well-Being*. Princeton, NJ: Princeton University Press.

Akerlof, G., and R. Shiller. 2009. *Animal Spirits: How Human Psychology Drives the Economy and Why It Matters for Global Capitalism*. Princeton, NJ: Princeton University Press.

Ariely, D. 2012. *The Honest Truth about Dishonesty*. New York: Harper.

Beach, L. R., and T. R. Mitchell. 1987. "Image Theory: Principles, Plans and Goals in Decision Making." *Acta Psychologica* 66: 201–220.

Burrell, O.K., 1951. "Possibility of an Experimental Approach to Investment Studies." *Journal of Finance* 6:2, 211–19.

Descartes, Rene. 1989 [1649]. *Passions of the Soul.* Cambridge, MA: Hackett.

Fisher, Irving. 1930. *The Theory of Interest.* London: Macmillan.

Freud, S. 1958 [1895]. *The Project for a Scientific Psychology.* Freud Standard Edition. London: Hogarth Press.

Freud, S. 1958 [1900]. *Interpretation of Dreams.* Freud Standard Edition. London: Hogarth Press.

Freud, S. 1958 [1919]. *The Uncanny.* Freud Standard Edition. London: Hogarth Press.

Frosh, Stephen. 2010. *Psychoanalysis Outside the Clinic: Interventions in Psychosocial Studies.* Basingstoke, Hampshire: Palgrave Macmillan.

Gigerenzer, G., U. Hoffrage, and H. Kleinbolting. 1991. "'Probabilistic Mental Models' A Brunswickian Theory of Confidence." *Psychological Review* 98: 506–528.

Gladwell, M. 2005. *Blink: The Power of Thinking Without Thinking.* New York: Little, Brown

Glymour, C. 1991. "Freud's Androids." In *The Cambridge Companion to Freud,* edited by Neu Jerome. Cambridge: Cambridge University Press.

Hastie, Reid. 1991. "A Review from a High Place: The Field of Judgment and Decision Making as Revealed in its Current Textbooks." *Psychological Science* 2: 135–138.

Kahneman, D. 2011. *Thinking: Fast and Slow.* New York: Farrar, Straus, Giroux.

Kahneman, D., and D. Lovallo. 1993. "Timid Choices and Bold Forecasts: A Cognitive Perspective on Risk Taking." *Management Science* 39 (1): 17–31.

Kahneman, D., and A. Tversky. 1979. "Prospect Theory: An Analysis of Decision Under Risk." *Econometrica* 47 (2): 263–292.

Keynes, John M. 1936. *General Theory of Employment, Interest and Money.* London: Palgrave Macmillan.

Koppl, Roger. 1991. "Retrospectives: Animal Spirits." *Journal of Economic Perspectives* 5 (3): 203–210.

Lear, Jonathan. 1990. *Love and Its Place in Nature: A Philosophical Interpretation of Freudian Psychoanalysis.* New Haven, CT: Yale University Press.

Lear, Jonathan. 2000. *Happiness, Death and the Remainder of Life.*Cambridge, MA: Harvard University Press.

Lopes, L. L. 1987. "Between Hope and Fear: The Psychology of Risk." *Advances in Experimental Social Psychology* 20: 255–295.

Markowitz, H., 1952. "The Utility of Wealth," *Journal of Political Economy,* 60, 151–158.

Minsky, Hyman. 1982. *Can It Happen Again? Essays on Instability and Finance.* Armonk, NY: M. E. Sharpe.

Shefrin, H., and R. Thaler. 1981. "Economic Theory of Self Control." *Journal of Political Economy* 89 (2): 396–402.

Slovic, Paul. 1972. "Psychological Study of Human Judgment: Implications for Investment Decision Making." *Journal of Finance* 27 (4): 779–799.

Smith, Adam. 1759. *The Theory of Moral Sentiments.* London: A. Millar,.

Smith Adam. 1776. *The Wealth of Nations.* London: Methuen and Company.

Stigler, Stephen. 1999. *Statistics on the Table: The History of Statistical Concepts and Methods.* Cambridge, MA: Harvard University Press.

Taffler, Richard. 2008. "Phantastic Objects and the Financial Markets Sense of Reality." *International Journal of Psychoanalysis* 89 (2): 384–412.

Tetlock, P. E. 1991. "An Alternative Metaphor in the Study of Judgment and Choice: People as Politicians." *Journal of Theory and Psychology* 1: 451–475.

Tuckett, David. 2011. *Minding the Markets: An Emotional Finance View of Financial Instability.* London: Palgrave.

CPSIA information can be obtained
at www.ICGtesting.com
Printed in the USA
BVHW042034241120
594037BV00007B/14/J